Islamic Contract Law

Islamic Contract Law

ILIAS BANTEKAS
JONATHAN G. ERCANBRACK
UMAR A. OSENI
IKRAM ULLAH

OXFORD
UNIVERSITY PRESS

OXFORD
UNIVERSITY PRESS

Great Clarendon Street, Oxford, OX2 6DP,
United Kingdom

Oxford University Press is a department of the University of Oxford.
It furthers the University's objective of excellence in research, scholarship,
and education by publishing worldwide. Oxford is a registered trade mark of
Oxford University Press in the UK and in certain other countries

Published in the United States of America by Oxford University Press
198 Madison Avenue, New York, NY 10016, United States of America

British Library Cataloguing in Publication Data

Data available

Library of Congress Control Number: 2023930621

ISBN 978–0–19–289379–6

DOI: 10.1093/law/9780192893796.001.0001

Printed and bound by
CPI Group (UK) Ltd, Croydon, CR0 4YY

Contents

Table of Cases xix
List of Abbreviations xxi

Introduction 1

1. General Principles and Sources of Islamic Contract Law: A General Theory? 5
Umar A. Oseni
1. Introduction 1.01
2. A General Theory of Contract? 1.07
2.1 Conceptual Theory of Contractual Obligation 1.09
2.2 Is There a Theory of Contract in Islamic Law? 1.14
2.3 Express and Implied Contract 1.19
3. The Debate on Form and Substance 1.21
4. Sources of Islamic Contract Law 1.31
4.1 The Primary Sources 1.33
4.2 The Secondary Sources: A Select List? 1.38
4.2.1 *'Ijmā'* 1.40
4.2.2 *Qiyās* 1.43
4.2.3 *Istiḥsān* 1.47
4.2.4 *'Urf* 1.52
4.3 Positive Law: A Tertiary Source? 1.54
5. An Overview of the Essential Elements of a Valid Contract 1.55
5.1 Form of Contract (*ṣigha*) 1.57
5.2 Parties (*'āqidān*) 1.59
5.3 Subject Matter of Contract (*ma'qud 'alaihi*) 1.60

2. Offer and Acceptance 29
Ilias Bantekas
1. Introduction 2.01
2. Types of *Ījāb* and *Qabūl* 2.02
2.1 Express *Ījāb* and *Qabūl* 2.04
2.1.1 The Concept of *Ījāb* and *Qabūl* 2.05
2.1.2 Form of *Ījāb* and *Qabūl* 2.06
2.1.2.1 *Ṣīgha* by disabled persons and *ṣīgha* in sign language and *kināya* 2.09
2.1.3 Characteristics of *ṣīgha* 2.11
2.1.3.1 Conformity of *Qabūl* with *Ījāb* 2.12
2.1.3.2 Conditional offer 2.13
2.1.3.3 Counter-offer 2.14
2.1.3.4 Fresh offer 2.15
2.1.3.5 *Ṣafaqa wāḥida* and *ṣafaqa mutafarraqa* 2.16
2.1.4 Words to be Used for a Contract 2.20

2.2 *Ījāb* and *Qabūl* through Conduct and *Mu'āṭāt* 2.22
2.2.1 *Mu'āṭāt* 2.24
2.2.1.1 Permissibility of *mu'āṭāt* 2.26
2.3 Mutual Assent (*tarāḍī*) and Intention to Contract 2.32
2.3.1 Intention to Contract 2.33
2.3.2 Consent of the Coerced Party 2.34
2.3.3 Consent of *Hāzil* 2.35
2.3.4 Consent of Intoxicated Person 2.36
2.4 Communication of *Ījāb* and *Qabūl* 2.37
2.4.1 *Ījāb* and *Qabūl* from and to the Concerned Parties 2.38
2.4.2 Modes of Communication of *Ījāb* and *Qabūl* 2.39
2.4.2.1 Instantaneous method 2.40
2.4.2.1.1 Email, SMS, WhatsApp, and other forms of electronic communication 2.41
2.4.2.2 Postal communication 2.42
2.5 When a Contract is Completed with the *Ījāb* and *Qabūl* 2.43
2.5.1 Direct Communication 2.43
2.5.2 Postal Communication 2.44
2.6 Session and its Expiration 2.46
2.6.1 *Khiyār* Relating to the *Majlis* 2.48
2.6.1.1 The basic concept of *khiyār* 2.49
2.6.1.2 Justification 2.51
2.6.1.3 Termination of *khiyār al qabūl* and *khiyār al majlis* 2.53
2.6.1.4 Contracting out of *khiyār al majlis* 2.54
2.7 The Contract with *Khiyār al majlis* 2.56
2.7.1 Termination of Offer 2.57
2.7.1.1 Rejection 2.58
2.7.1.2 Revocation of Offer 2.59
2.7.1.3 When the offer can be revoked 2.61
2.7.1.4 Communication of the revocation 2.63
2.7.2 Change of Subject Matter 2.64
2.7.3 Death of Party, Lapse of Time, and Non-Fulfilment of Condition Precedent 2.65

3. Legal Capacity (*Ahliyya*) 49
Jonathan G. Ercanbrack
1. Introduction 3.01
1.1 Definitions 3.04
1.1.1 The Concept of *Al-Dhimma* (Human Accountability to God) 3.05
1.2 *Anwā' al-Ahliyya* (Forms of Legal Capacity) 3.09
1.3 Legal Bases or Foundations (*Nuṣūṣ Shari'iyyah*) 3.10
1.3.1 *Ahliyya Al-Wujūb* and *Ahliyya Al-Adā'* 3.13
1.4 Impediments to Legal Capacity (*'Awāriḍ Al-Ahliyya*) 3.16
1.4.1 Definitions 3.16
1.4.2 Types of Attributes 3.18
1.5 *Ḥajr* (Interdiction) 3.22
1.6 Capacity of the Minor (*Ṣabī*) 3.23
1.6.1 The Non-discerning Child 3.24
1.6.2 The Liability of the Discerning Child 3.27

1.7 The Age of Majority 3.34
1.7.1 The Signs of Puberty 3.35
1.7.2 Puberty and the Capacity for Performance 3.39
1.8 Insanity (*Junūn*) or Mental Incompetence 3.43
1.8.1 Definitions 3.43
1.8.2 Interdiction (*Ḥajr*) of the Insane (Mental Incompetence) 3.45
1.8.2.1 Distinctions between types of insanity and legal effects 3.47
1.8.2.2 Legal bases of interdiction 3.48
1.9 Imbecility (*Al-Maʿtūh*) 3.55
1.9.1 Definitions 3.55
1.9.2 Interdiction of the Imbecile 3.56
1.10 Prodigality (*Safah*) 3.58
1.10.1 Definitions 3.58
1.10.1.1 The legal bases 3.63
1.10.2 Interdiction of the Prodigal (*Safīh*) 3.65
1.10.3 The Effects of Prodigality on Contract 3.70
1.10.3.1 The legal capacity of the prodigal (*Safīh*) 3.72
1.11 Terminal Illness 3.79
1.11.1 Definitions 3.79
1.11.2 Interdiction of the Terminally Ill Individual 3.80
1.11.2.1 The rights of heirs 3.82
1.11.2.2 Debts of the terminally ill 3.83
1.12 Women's Legal Capacity 3.86
1.13 Women's Testimony (*Shahādah*) 3.101
1.13.1 Types of Evidence 3.102
1.13.2 The Number of Witnesses 3.103
1.13.3 The Requirements of Testimony 3.104
1.13.4 Conclusions 3.106

4. The Role of Intent (*Niyya*) 85
Jonathan G. Ercanbrack
1. Introduction 4.01
1.1 The Role of Intent in the *Fiqh* of Worship (*Al-ʿIbādāt*) 4.08
1.1.1 *Niyya* in Ritual Actions and Speech 4.11
1.2 Intent in Contract Law 4.16
1.2.1 The Schools' (*Madhāhib*) Approaches to Intent in Contract 4.17
1.2.2 The Oral Nature of Contract Law 4.19
1.3 The Role of Intent in Contractual Formation 4.22
1.3.1 The Definition of Contract 4.25
1.3.2 Party Autonomy in Contract 4.26
1.3.3 Revocable and Irrevocable Contracts 4.28
1.3.4 Contemporary Jurists' Views of Intent 4.31
1.4 Verbal Utterances in the Formation of Contract 4.35
1.4.1 Apparent or Hidden Intent 4.35
1.4.2 Explicit or Allusive Speech 4.36
1.4.3 The Use of Verbal Tenses in the Formation of Contract 4.40
1.4.4 The Hanafis' Categorization of Speech Acts 4.42
1.4.5 The Malikis' Approach to Language 4.45
1.4.6 Signs, Customs, and Silence in Contractual Formation 4.47

1.5 Complex Actions and Intent 4.50
1.5.1 The Schools' (*Madhāhib*) Approaches to Complex Intentions 4.53
1.5.1.1 The lawfulness of the *bay' al-'īna* (legal ruse) 4.55
1.5.2 The Hanafis' and Shafi'is' Formalistic Approach to Contractual Interpretation 4.57
1.5.3 The Malikis' and Hanbalis' Subjectivist Approach to Contractual Interpretation 4.61

5. *Maḥal Al 'aqd* 107
Ilias Bantekas
1. Introduction 5.01
2. Legality of Subject Matter and Underlying Cause 5.06
2.1 Permissible Subject Matters 5.10
2.1.1 When a Permissible Subject Matter Becomes Impermissible 5.15
2.2 Impermissible Subject Matters 5.17
2.2.1 Permitting Impermissible Subject Matters 5.20
2.2.1.1 Benefit 5.21
2.2.1.2 Necessity 5.22
2.2.1.3 Mixing of wine or other impurities with a pure subject matter 5.24
3. Existence of Subject Matter 5.25
4. Certainty of Delivery of Subject Matter 5.29
4.1 Hurdles to the Delivery of the Subject Matter 5.30
4.1.1 *Shar'ī* Capacity to Deliver 5.31
4.1.2 *Ḥissī* Capacity to Deliver 5.33
5. The Subject Matter Should Be Owned by the Seller 5.37
5.1 Sale of Permissible Things 5.38
5.1.1 Pasture 5.39
5.1.2 Water 5.40
5.1.3 Other Subject Matters 5.41
5.2 Perfect and Imperfect Title 5.42
5.2.1 Absence of Title 5.43
5.2.2 Sale by a *Wakīl* 5.44
5.2.3 Encumbrance on the Title of the Owner 5.45
5.2.4 Jointly Owned Property 5.46
5.3 Establishment of Ownership 5.47
6. Subject Matter Should Be in the Custody/Possession of the Seller 5.48
6.1 Transfer of Possession 5.55
6.2 *Al Takhliya* 5.56
6.3 Possession of Immovable Property 5.57
6.4 Possession of Movable Property 5.60
7. The Subject Matter Should Be *Ma'lūm* 5.65
7.1 Extent of Knowledge of Subject Matter 5.66
7.2 Acquiring Knowledge of the Subject Matter 5.67
7.2.1 Knowledge through Inspection or Examination 5.68
7.2.2 Knowledge by Description 5.69
7.2.2.1 Occasions when sale by description takes place 5.70
7.2.2.2 Description of packaged goods 5.71
7.2.3 Need for Specification 5.72
7.2.4 Immovable Property 5.74

6. The Main Prohibited Elements in Contract 135
Umar A. Oseni
1. Introduction 6.01
2. The Theory of Prohibition in Contractual Dealings 6.05
3. *Ribā* and *Gharar*: A Practical Approach 6.15
3.1 *Ribā* 6.16
3.1.1 Two Broad Classifications of *Ribā* 6.20
3.1.2 Is There Any Difference between Profit and Interest? 6.23
3.1.3 Loan Moratorium: Between Interest and Profit Rates 6.26
3.1.4 Interest and Late Payment Compensation 6.30
3.1.5 Waiver of Interest Clause 6.36
3.2 *Gharar* 6.38
3.2.1 The Legal Basis for the Prohibition of *Gharar* 6.39
3.2.2 Classification of *Gharar* 6.40
3.2.3 *Gharar* Red Flags in Contracts 6.42
3.2.4 Prohibition of *Gharar* in Civil Codes 6.46
4. Other Prohibited Elements in Contract 6.48
4.1 Impermissible Subject Matter 6.49
4.2 *Maysir* (Game of Chance) and *Qimār* (Gambling) 6.50
4.3 Fraud, Deception, and Misrepresentation 6.55
4.3.1 Nature and Meaning 6.56
4.3.2 Elements 6.60
4.3.3 Effects on Contract 6.64
4.4 Coercion 6.66
4.5 Hoarding, Illegal Profiteering, and Price Fixing 6.72
4.5.1 Permissible Price Control: Exception to the General Rule? 6.76
4.5.2 Effect of Profiteering on Contracts 6.77
4.5.3 Has Islam Stipulated a Profit Limit? 6.79
4.6 Usurpation (*Ghasb*) 6.81
4.6.1 Prohibition of *Ghasb* 6.82
4.6.2 What Happens to the Usurped Property? 6.85
4.6.3 Effect on Contract 6.91
5. Flipping the Coin: The Positive Dimension 6.94

7. Invalid Contracts 171
Ilias Bantekas
1. Introduction 7.01
2. Valid Contracts 7.02
2.1 Conditions for a Valid Contract 7.04
2.1.1 Conditions for the Formation of a Valid Contract 7.05
2.1.1.1 Offer and acceptance 7.06
2.1.1.2 Capacity of the parties 7.09
2.1.1.3 Subject matter 7.10
2.1.2 Conditions for *Nifādh* of a Contract 7.11
2.1.3 Conditions for *Ṣiḥa* of a Contract 7.12
2.1.4 Conditions for *Luzūm* of a Contract 7.13
2.1.5 Conditions for External Attributes of a Contract 7.14
2.1.5.1 *Gharar* 7.15
2.1.5.2 *Ribā* 7.16
2.2 Types of Valid Contract 7.18

2.2.1 The *Lāzim* Contract 7.20
2.2.2 The *Ja'iz* or *Ghayr Lāzim* Contract 7.21
2.2.3 *Mawqūf* 7.22
2.2.3.1 Causes of suspension 7.23
3. *Fāsid* Contracts 7.34
3.1 Causes for *Fāsid* Contracts 7.35
3.2 The Effects of a *Fāsid* Contract and its Revocation 7.37
3.3 Instances of *Fāsid* Contracts 7.38
3.3.1 *Bay' al-majhūl* 7.38
3.3.2 *Bay'al- īnā* 7.39
3.3.3 Two Sales in One and Conditions in Sale 7.40
3.3.4 Sale with Defective Conditions 7.44
3.3.5 *Bay' al-wafā* 7.45
4. Invalid Contracts 7.46
4.1 Causes of Invalidity 7.47
4.1.1 Causes Associated with the Capacity of the Parties 7.47
4.1.2 Causes Associated with the Subject Matter 7.48
4.1.3 Illegality of the Object of the Contract 7.49
4.2 Effect of an Invalid Contract 7.50
4.3 Instances of Invalid Contracts 7.51
4.3.1 Sale of Liabilities, Including Debts 7.52
4.3.2 Sale of Impure Objects 7.56
5. Types of *Shurūṭ* (Conditions) 7.57
5.1 Valid Conditions 7.62
5.1.1 Conditions Which Are in Conformity with the Contract 7.63
5.1.2 Conditions Which Emphasize the Objectives of the Contract 7.64
5.1.3 Conditions Validated by the *Shar'* 7.65
5.1.4 Conditions Based on *'Urf* 7.66
5.2 *Fāsid* Conditions 7.68
5.3 *Bāṭil* Conditions 7.69

8. Contractual Terms: The Rights of Option (*Khiyārāt*) and Conditions (*Shurūṭ*) 191
Jonathan G. Ercanbrack
1. Introduction 8.01
2. The Typologies of the Rights of Option 8.06
3. The Default Condition: *Khiyār Al-Sharṭ* 8.09
3.1 Duration of the Option 8.11
3.2 Extinguishing the Option 8.13
3.3 Loss or Damage to the Object of Sale 8.14
4. Other Option Types 8.21
4.1 *Khiyār Al-Majlis* 8.22
4.2 *Khiyār Al-Waṣf* 8.23
4.3 *Khiyār Al-Naqd* 8.25
4.4 *Khiyār Al- Ta'yīn* 8.26
4.4.1 Necessary Conditions for Validity 8.28
4.5 *Khiyār Al-Ru'ya* 8.29
4.6 *Khiyār Al-'Ayb* 8.31
4.6.1 Buyer's Choices when Object of Sale is Defective 8.32
4.6.2 Diminution in Value 8.34

4.6.3 Caveat Emptor? 8.35
4.6.4 Liability 8.37
4.6.5 Proofs 8.38
4.6.6 The *Shafi's'* Options 8.40
4.6.7 The Hanbalis' Options 8.41
5. Conditional Stipulations (pl. *Shurūṭ*; sing. *Sharṭ*) 8.42
5.1 The Role of Party Autonomy 8.42
5.1.1 The Schools' Policies Toward Freedom of Contract 8.43
6. The *Hanafis'* and *Shafi'is'* Approach to Conditions (*Shurūṭ*) 8.50
6.1 Types of Conditions 8.51
6.1.1 Customary Conditions 8.53
7. The *Hanbalis'* and *Malikis'* Approach to Conditions (*Shurūṭ*) 8.55
7.1 The Juristic Foundation 8.56
7.1.1 Permissible Terms 8.57
7.1.2 The Hanbalis' Freedom to Contract 8.60

9. Bilateral Contracts 213
Umar A. Oseni
1. Introduction 9.01
2. Classification of Bilateral Contracts 9.06
3. A General Contract of Sale 9.08
3.1 Elements 9.09
3.2 Classification 9.11
3.2.1 Classification on the Basis of the Subject Matter of Contract 9.12
3.2.2 Classification on the Basis of Price Stipulation 9.16
4. Usufruct-Based Contracts 9.22
4.1 Lease Contract 9.22
4.2 Lending for Gratuitous Use 9.33
5. Partnership Contracts 9.37
6. Security or Guarantee Contracts 9.56
7. Other Ancillary Contracts of Service and Supply 9.62
8. Types of Contracts of Sale and Applicable Legal Principles 9.66
9. Prohibited Contracts of Sale 9.76
9.1 Reasons for Prohibition 9.79
9.2 Types of Prohibited Sales 9.82

10. Equity-Based Partnership Contracts 241
Ikram Ullah
1. Introduction 10.01
2. Co-ownership (*Sharikat al-amlāk*) 10.03
2.1 Types of Co-ownership 10.04
2.2 Rights of Co-owners 10.05
3. *Sharikat al-ʿaqd* (Partnership) 10.08
3.1 Types of *Sharikat al-ʿaqd* 10.10
3.2 Formation of a *Sharikat al-ʿaqd* 10.12
3.3 Entitlement to Profit 10.14
3.4 Legal Nature of Partnership 10.15
3.5 *Sharikat al-amwāl* 10.16
3.5.1 Conditions for *Sharikat al-amwāl* 10.17
3.5.1.1 Presence of capital 10.18

3.5.1.2 Mixing of capital 10.19
3.5.1.3 Form of capital to establish a partnership 10.21
3.5.2 Kinds of *Sharikat al-amwāl* 10.23
3.5.2.1 *'Inān sharikat al amwāl* 10.24
3.5.2.1.1 Formation of *'inān* partnerships 10.25
3.5.2.1.2 Types of *sharikat al-'inān* 10.26
3.5.2.1.2.1 General *'inān* 10.27
3.5.2.1.3 Basics of the *'inān* partnership 10.28
3.5.2.1.3.1 Agency between partners 10.29
3.5.2.1.3.2 Equality in contribution of capital and distribution of profits 10.31
3.5.2.1.3.3 Rights of partners in an *'inān* partnership 10.34
3.5.2.1.4 Dissolution of the *'inān* partnership 10.40
3.5.2.2 *Mufāwaḍa sharikat al-amwāl* 10.45
3.5.2.2.1 Legitimacy of *mufāwaḍa* 10.46
3.5.2.2.2 Formation of the *mufāwaḍa* partnership 10.47
3.5.2.2.3 Conditions of a *mufāwaḍa* partnership 10.48
3.5.2.2.4 Rights and duties of partners in *mufāwaḍa* partnerships 10.53
3.5.2.2.5 Dissolution of *sharikat al-mufāwaḍa* 10.56
3.6 *Sharikat al-abdān* 10.57
3.6.1 *Inan sharikat al-abdān* and its Conditions 10.58
3.6.1.1 Nature of the subject matter 10.59
3.6.1.2 Similarity of profession 10.61
3.6.1.3 Acceptance of work and liability thereof 10.62
3.6.1.4 Distribution of profit 10.64
3.6.2 *Mufāwaḍa Sharikat al-abdān* 10.65
3.7 *Sharikat al-wujūh* 10.66
3.7.1 *Inan Sharikat al-wujūh* 10.67
3.7.2 *Mufāwaḍa Sharikat al-wujūh* 10.69
4. *Muḍāraba* 10.70
4.1 Justification of *Muḍāraba* 10.71
4.2 Elements of *Muḍāraba* 10.74
4.3 Relation between the Parties 10.75
4.4 Conditions of *Muḍāraba* 10.76
4.4.1 Capacity of Parties for *Muḍāraba* Agreement 10.77
4.4.2 Capital of *Muḍāraba* 10.78
4.4.3 Profit-Sharing in *Muḍāraba* 10.79
4.4.4 Types of *Muḍāraba* 10.81
4.4.4.1 Permissible acts for the *muḍārib* under absolute *muḍāraba* 10.82
4.4.5 Dissolution of the *Muḍāraba* 10.83
4.4.5.1 Unilateral termination 10.84
4.4.5.2 By expiry of a fixed time 10.85
4.4.5.3 By death or insanity of the partners 10.86
4.4.5.4 By violation of agreement or directions of the *rab al-māl* 10.87
4.4.5.5 By destruction of capital 10.88
5. Financing through *Sharika* and *Muḍāraba* 10.89
5.1 Diminishing *Mushāraka* 10.90

11. Ancillary Contracts 267
Ikram Ullah
1. Introduction 11.01
2. *Wakāla* (Agency) 11.02
2.1 Essential Elements of *Wakāla* 11.03
2.1.1 Parties to the *Wakāla* Contract 11.04
2.1.1.1 Principal 11.05
2.1.1.2 Agent 11.06
2.1.2 *Ṣīgha* 11.07
2.1.2.1 Offer 11.08
2.1.2.2 Acceptance 11.09
2.2 When Agency Takes Effect 11.10
2.3 Object of Agency 11.11
2.4 Things Allowed to Be Delegated in an Agency 11.12
2.4.1 Contracts 11.13
2.4.2 Pecuniary Acts of Worship 11.14
2.5 Matters Which an Agent Cannot Undertake on Behalf of the Principal 11.15
2.5.1 Testimony, Oaths, and Vows 11.16
2.5.2 Sinful Actions and Crimes 11.17
2.5.3 Bodily Acts of Worship 11.18
2.6 Matters Delegated upon which Jurists Disagree 11.19
2.6.1 *Ḥajj* and *'Umra* 11.19
2.6.2 Woman Marrying through an Agent 11.20
2.7 Legal Effects of Agency 11.21
2.7.1 Agency in Sale 11.22
2.7.1.1 Absolute power or with no express limitation on the power of an agent 11.23
2.7.1.2 Agent with qualified power to sell property 11.25
2.7.2 Agency to Purchase a Property 11.27
2.7.3 Agency in Litigation 11.28
2.8 Agency with Consideration 11.30
2.9 Termination of Agency 11.33
2.9.1 Dismissal or Resignation 11.33
2.9.2 Death 11.34
3. *Juʿāla* 11.35
3.1 Elements of *Juʿāla* 11.36
3.1.1 *Ṣīgha* 11.37
3.1.2 Parties to the Contract of *Juʿāla* 11.38
3.1.3 Subject Matter of *Juʿāla* 11.39
3.1.3.1 Consideration in *Juʿāla* 11.42
3.2 Effects of *Juʿāla* 11.43
3.3 Termination of *Juʿāla* Contract 11.45
3.4 Difference between *Juʿāla* and *Ijāra* 11.46
3.5 Contemporary Applications of the *Juʿāla* Contract 11.47
4. *Ijāra* 11.48
4.1 Nature of the *Ijāra* Contract 11.50
4.2 Elements of *Ijāra* 11.51
4.2.1 *Ṣīgha* 11.52
4.2.2 Parties to the Contract 11.53

4.2.3 Object of the Contract 11.54
4.3 Effect of *Ijāra* 11.55
4.4 Obligations of the Lessor 11.56
4.4.1 Surrender of Possession of the Leased Property 11.56
4.4.2 Guaranteeing the Usurped Property from Usurpation 11.57
4.5 Obligations of the Lessee 11.58
4.6 Termination of *Ijāra* 11.59
4.7 Application of *Ijāra* by Islamic Banks 11.61
4.8 The Application of *Ijāra* in Personal Financing 11.62
5. *Salam* 11.63
5.1 Essential Elements of *Salam* 11.64
5.1.1 *Ṣīgha* 11.65
5.1.2 Parties to the Contract of *Salam* 11.66
5.1.3 Object of *Salam* 11.67
5.1.3.1 Conditions applicable to both commodity and consideration 11.67
5.1.3.2 Requirements of *salam* payment (*Ra's Māl al-Salam*) 11.68
5.2 Requirements or Conditions of the Commodity 11.69
5.3 Ownership of the Exchanged Commodities 11.74
5.4 Delivery of the Subject Matter (Commodity of *Salam*) 11.75
5.5 Seller's Inability to Make the Delivery 11.76
5.6 Security as to the Obligation in *Salam* 11.77
5.7 Modern Applications of the *Salam* Contract 11.78
6. *Istiṣnā*ʿ 11.83
6.1 Defining the Rule of *Istiṣnā*ʿ 11.84
6.2 Essential Elements of *Istiṣnā*ʿ 11.85
6.2.1 *Ṣīgha* of *Istiṣnā*ʿ 11.86
6.2.2 Parties to the Contract of *Istiṣnā*ʿ 11.87
6.2.3 Object of *Istiṣnā*ʿ 11.88
6.3 Effect of *Istiṣnā*ʿ 11.89
6.4 Types of *Istiṣnā*ʿ 11.90
6.4.1 Traditional or Normal *Istiṣnā*ʿ 11.90
6.4.2 Parallel or Investment *Istiṣnā*ʿ 11.91
6.5 Difference between *Istiṣnā*ʿ and *Salam* 11.93
6.6 Difference between *Istiṣnā*ʿ and *Ijāra* 11.94
6.7 Termination of *Istiṣnā*ʿ 11.95
7. *Ṣarf* 11.96
7.1 Legality of *Ṣarf* 11.97
7.2 Conditions for the Validity of *Ṣarf* 11.98
7.3 Legal Effects of *Ṣarf* 11.99

12. Unilateral Contracts 301
Ilias Bantekas
1. Introduction 12.01
2. *Wa'ad* (Binding Promise) 12.04
2.1 Permissibility of *Wa'ad* 12.05
2.2 Lawfulness of Actions Invoking Promises 12.06
2.3 Is a Promise Binding on the Promisor? 12.08
2.3.1 Non-obligatory Nature of the Promise 12.10
2.3.2 Binding Nature of the Promise 12.12
2.3.3 Promise Becomes Binding Only if There is a Condition Precedent 12.15

2.3.4 Promise Becoming Binding When Linked with a Cause and the Promisee's Reliance on Promise 12.17
2.4 Conditions Applicable to the Binding Promise 12.19
2.5 Revocation of Promise 12.20
3. Gift (*Hiba*) 12.21
3.1 Nature and Validity of Gift 12.21
3.2 How the Gift is Different from Other Transactions 12.23
3.3 Requirements of a Valid Gift 12.24
3.3.1 Offer and Acceptance 12.25
3.3.2 Parties 12.27
3.3.3 Subject Matter 12.28
3.3.4 Possession (*Hauzi*) in a Gift 12.29
3.4 Witnessing a Gift 12.32
3.5 Gift by a Father to his Children 12.33
3.6 Revocation of the Gift 12.34
4. Loan (*Qarḍ*) 12.37
4.1 Concept of *Qarḍ* 12.37
4.2 Legal Nature of *Qarḍ* 12.38
4.3 Essential Elements of Loan and their Requirements 12.39
4.3.1 Offer and Acceptance 12.40
4.3.2 Contracting Parties 12.42
4.4 Can the *Bait al-Māl* (Public Treasury) Take a Loan? 12.43
4.5 Subject Matter of Loan 12.45
4.5.1 Fungible 12.46
4.5.2 Real Property 12.48
4.5.3 The Requirement of Being 'Known' 12.49
4.6 Types of Loans 12.50
4.7 Interest in Loan 12.51
4.8 Termination of a Loan 12.52
5. Will (*Waṣiyya*) 12.53
5.1 Meaning and Nature of Will 12.53
5.2 Conditions of a Valid Will 12.54
5.2.1 Parties 12.54
5.2.2 Quantum of Will 12.55
5.3 Conditional Will 12.56
5.4 Revocation of the Will 12.57
5.5 Invalid Wills 12.59
6. Endowment (*Waqf*) 12.61
6.1 Meaning and Nature of *Waqf* 12.61
6.2 Creation of a *Waqf* 12.62
6.3 Conditions for a Valid *Waqf* 12.63
6.3.1 *Waqf* Associated with Conditions 12.63
6.3.2 Conditions for the Subject Matter 12.64
6.3.2.1 Nature of subject matter 12.65
6.3.2.2 Delivery 12.67
6.3.3 Capacity and Authority of the Parties 12.69
6.3.3.1 *Wāqif* 12.69
6.3.3.2 Beneficiary 12.70
6.4 Life of *Waqf* 12.72
6.5 Purpose of *Waqf* 12.73
6.6 Administration of *Waqf* Property 12.74

6.7 Things Associated with the *Waqf* Property 12.75
6.8 Types of *Waqf* 12.76
6.9 Termination of the *Waqf* 12.77

13. Contracts and Third Parties 329
Umar A. Oseni
1. Introduction 13.01
2. Privity of Contract 13.05
3. Some Contracts with Third-Party Rights 13.15
3.1 Guarantees in Contracts (*Kafāla*) 13.15
3.2 *Wakāla* and Third-Party Rights 13.25
3.3 Third-Party Rights in Contract of Debt Assignment (*Ḥawāla*) 13.34
3.3.1 Definition 13.35
3.3.2 Legality 13.38
3.3.3 Types 13.39
3.3.4 Elements and Conditions for its Validity 13.41
3.3.5 Legal Consequences 13.44
4. Third-Party Rights in Contract of Pre-emption (*Shufʿa*) 13.45
4.1 Definition 13.46
4.2 Legal Validity 13.49
4.3 Elements and Parties to Pre-emption 13.53
4.4 Conditions for the Validity of Pre-emption 13.62
4.5 Some Specific Rules Conferring Third-Party Pre-emption Rights 13.64

14. Performance, Termination, and Rescission of Contracts 349
Ikram Ullah
1. Introduction 14.01
2. Performance 14.02
2.1 When a Contract is Deemed as Having Been Performed 14.03
2.2 Which Party Must Perform First 14.05
2.3 Performance of Contract Involving Debt or *Dayn* 14.07
2.3.1 Delivery of Debt 14.08
2.3.2 Alternatives to the Payment of Debt 14.10
2.3.3 Failure to Deliver Debt 14.11
2.4 Delivery of *ʿayn* (Specific Property) 14.14
2.5 Breach (Non-performance) of Contract 14.16
3. Termination of Contracts (*Inhā al-ʿAqd*) 14.21
3.1 Unilateral Termination 14.26
3.2 Negotiated Termination (*Iqāla*) 14.30
3.2.1 The Requirements of *Iqāla* 14.31
3.2.2 The Effect of *Iqāla* 14.32
3.2.2.1 *Iqāla* with less or more than the original price 14.35
3.2.2.2 Right of pre-emption (*Shufa*) over the subject matter of *Iqāla* 14.36
3.2.2.3 *Iqāla* of agents 14.37
3.2.2.4 Subject matter of *Iqāla* 14.38
3.2.3 Effect of Irregular Stipulations on *Iqāla* 14.39
3.2.4 *Iqālat al-Iqāla* (Reversal of *Iqāla*) 14.40
3.2.5 Invalidator of *Iqāla* 14.41
3.3 *Force Majeure* and Impossibility of Performance 14.43
3.3.1 Damage to the Subject Matter of the Contract 14.44

3.3.1.1 Executed contracts 14.45
3.3.1.2 Executory contracts 14.46
3.3.1.2.1 Lease 14.47
3.3.1.2.2 Partnership 14.48
3.3.1.2.3 Agency 14.49
3.3.2 Death of One or Both Parties to a Binding Contract 14.50
3.3.3 Annulment of Non-binding Contracts because of Death 14.51
4. Rescission of Contract (*Faskh*) 14.53
4.1 Modes of Rescission of Contract 14.54
4.1.1 Rescission by Court Judgment 14.55
4.1.2 Rescission Due to Lawful Justification 14.56
4.1.3 Rescission Due to Bankruptcy and Insolvency 14.58
4.1.4 Rescission by Exercising the Right of Option (*Khiyār*) 14.59
4.1.4.1 Purpose of *khiyār* 14.60
4.1.5 Types of *Khiyār* 14.61
4.1.5.1 *Khiyār al- Sharṭ* 14.62
4.1.5.1.1 Legality of *khiyār al-sharṭ* 14.63
4.1.5.1.2 Creation of *khiyār al-sharṭ* 14.64
4.1.5.1.3 Requirements of *khiyār al-sharṭ* 14.66
4.1.5.1.3.1 The creation of *khiyār al-sharṭ* 14.67
4.1.5.1.3.2 The period for exercising *khiyār al-sharṭ* 14.68
4.1.5.2 *Khiyār al-'Ayb* (option of rescinding a defective commodity) 14.70
4.1.5.2.1 Contracts on which *khiyār al-'ayb* can be applied 14.72
4.1.5.2.2 When *khiyār al-'ayb* may be exercised 14.73
4.1.5.2.3 Nature of contract with *khiyār al-'ayb* 14.75
4.2 Rescission of Irregular Contracts (*'Aqd Fāsid*) 14.77
4.3 Effects of Rescission 14.78

15. Damages and Other Remedies 373
1. Introduction 15.01
2. *Khiyārāt* (Options) 15.02
2.1 *Khiyār al-ru'yā* 15.03
2.1.1 Legality and the Nature of *Khiyār al-ru'yā* 15.03
2.1.2 Time when *Khiyār* is Established 15.06
2.1.3 Conditions for the Establishment of *Khiyār al-ru'yā* 15.07
2.1.4 How to Conduct the Inspection 15.09
2.1.4.1 When the *mabī'* is a single object 15.10
2.1.4.2 Where subject matter comprises more than one object 15.11
2.1.4.3 When the *mabī'* is a collection of dissimilar objects 15.12
2.1.5 Elimination of *Khiyār al-ru'yā* 15.13
2.1.6 Termination of the Contract 15.17
2.1.7 Inheritance of *Khiyār al-ru'yā* 15.18
2.1.8 Time Available to Exercise *Khiyār al-ru'yā* 15.19
2.2 *Khiyār al 'ayb* 15.20
2.2.1 Establishment of *Khiyār al 'ayb* 15.21
2.2.2 Justification for the *Khiyār al 'ayb* 15.22
2.2.3 *Ḥukm* of *bay'* 15.23
2.2.4 Time to Return the Subject by Exercising *Khiyār al 'ayb* 15.24
2.2.5 Conditions for *'Ayb* Establishing *Khiyār al 'ayb* 15.25

2.2.6 Proving *'Ayb* 15.26
2.2.7 Return of Subject Matter after *Faskh* of the Contract 15.27
2.2.7.1 Increment in the subject matter to be returned 15.28
2.2.8 Factors Eliminating *Khiyār al 'ayb* and Rendering the Contract *Lāzim* 15.29
2.2.8.1 *Nuqṣān* before transfer of possession to the buyer 15.33
2.2.8.2 *Nuqṣān* after transfer of possession to the buyer 15.34
2.3 *Khiyār al tadlīs* 15.35
2.3.1 Prohibition of Sale of Defective Objects 15.37
2.3.2 *'Ayb in Khiyār al-tadlīs* 15.38
2.3.3 Period for *Khiyār al-tadlīs* 15.39
2.3.4 Payment of Compensation in Case of Return of the Subject Matter 15.40
2.4 *Khiyār al ta'yīn* 15.41
2.4.1 Conditions for *Khiyār al-ta'yīn* 15.42
2.4.2 *Ḥukm* of *Bay* 15.43
2.4.3 Circumstances Rendering *Khiyār al-ta'yīn bāṭil* and *Bay' Lāzim* 15.44
2.4.3.1 *Ikhtiyārī* 15.45
2.4.3.2 *Ḍarūrī* 15.46
3. Compensation 15.47
3.1 Possession 15.48
3.2 Destruction or Damage (*Itlāf*) 15.49
3.3 Contract 15.50
3.3.1 Types of Contracts Involving *Ḍamān* 15.54
3.3.2 Nature and Amount of Compensation 15.55
3.3.3 Transformation of *Ma'qūd a'laih* from *Amāna* to *Damān* 15.56
3.4 Difference between *Ḍamān* Arising from Contract, Possession, or *Itlāf* 15.57
3.4.1 Capacity 15.58
3.4.2 Nature of Compensation 15.59
3.4.3 Who Can Be Sued 15.60
3.4.4 *Ijāza* (Approval or Ratification) 15.61
3.4.5 Time for the Entitlement of *Damān* 15.62
3.5 Specific Performance 15.63

16. The Application of Islamic Contract Law in Muslim-Majority Jurisdictions 395
Jonathan G. Ercanbrack
1. Introduction 16.01
2. Background of the Egyptian Civil Code 16.05
3. The *Sanhūrī* Connection: The Civil Codes of Other Arab States 16.13
4. The Law of Obligations and the Sharī'ah 16.18
5. The UAE Civil Code and *Ribā* 16.25
6. UAE Legislation and the Courts' Interpretation of Sharī'ah-Related Provisions 16.35
7. The Egyptian Civil Code and the Regulation of Interest 16.46
8. The UAE Commercial Transactions Law (Commercial Code) 16.55
8.1 The Rate of Interest 16.55
8.2 Delay Interest 16.59
8.3 Financing Charges 16.66
9. Which Code Governs the Transaction? 16.71

Index 421

Table of Cases

ENGLAND

Dana Gas PJSC v. *Dana Gas Sukuk Ltd* [2017] EWHC 2340 (Comm) 16.79–16.81
Dana Gas PJSC v. Dana Gas Sukuk Ltd and others [2018] EWHC 277 (Comm) 1.03
Golden Belt 1 Sukuk Co BSC(c) v BNP Paribas FCOF II UB Securities LLC v BNP Paribas [2017] EWHC 3182 (Comm) 5.01
Holland v Hodgson (1872) LR 7 CP 328 . . . . 6.87
Lloyds Bank Ltd. v. Bundy [1974] EWCA 8 . . . . 6.58
Riyad Bank v Ahli United Bank (UK) Plc [2005] EWHC 279 (Comm) 5.06
Shetty v Al Rushaid Petroleum Investment Co [2013] All ER (D) 86 . . . . 6.38

MALAYSIA

Arab-Malaysian Finance Bhd v Taman Ihsan Jaya Sdn Bhd & Ors [2008] 5 MLJ 631 . . . . 1.28
Bank Islam Malaysia Bhd v. Adnan Bin Omar Civil Suit No. S3-22-101-91 (Unreported) 1.54
Bank Kerjasama Rakyat Malaysia Bhd v. EMCEEE Corporation Sdh Bhd [2003] 1 CLJ 625 . . . . 1.54
Mohd Alias Ibrahim v. RHB Bank Berhad & Anor [2011] 4 CLJ 654 . . . . 1.54
Pan Northern Air Services Sdn Bhd v Maybank Islamic Bhd and another appeal [2021] 3 MLJ 408 . . . . 6.33
Woo Yew v Yonq Yang Hoo [1978] 1 LNS 240 FC 1.28

NIGERIA

Adamu v Ibrahim, (2016) Pt 1 SQLR 143 . . . . 12.26–12.27
Adamu and Three Others v NDA (2014) Pt 2 SQLR 101 . . . . 12.29
Buriye v Kurama (2015) 3 Pt 1 SQLR 105 . . . . 12.32
Muhammadu v Secretary and Another v Adamu (2013) 1 Pt 3 SQLR 44 . . . . 12.33
Usman v Kareem (2013) 1 Pt 1 SQLR 91 . . . . 12.33
Zarami and Another v Maina Kafa (2015) 3 Pt 1 SQLR 143 . . . . 12.35

PAKISTAN

Supreme Court Judgment 1999 [on riba] 6.22

UAE

Civ. Appeal No. 5 (Dubai, 21 November 1979) 16.42
Federal Supreme Court No. 294/12 dated 28 May 1991 . . . . 16.74
Federal Supreme Court No. 290/17 dated 28 November 1995 . . . . 16.73
Dubai Cassation Court No. 352/1994 dated 22 April 1995 . . . . 16.67
Federal Supreme Court No. 287/18 dated 31 March 1996 . . . . 16.73
Federal Supreme Court No. 371/18 dated 30 June 1998 . . . . 16.69
Federal Supreme Court, No. 245/20 (7 May 2000) 16.59
Federal Supreme Court No. 220/21 dated 31 December 2001 . . . . 16.64
Federal Supreme Court No. 435 and 516/21 dated 12 June 2001 . . . . 16.63
Federal Supreme Court No. 417/21 dated 20 June 2001 . . . . 16.63
Federal Supreme Court No. 371/21 dated 24 June 2001 . . . . 16.63, 16.69

Federal Supreme Court No. 332/21 dated 25 September 2001 .... 16.69
Dubai Cassation No. 349/2002 dated 29 December 2002 .... 16.74
Dubai Cassation Court Judgment No. 125/2007 .... 1.29
Federal Supreme Court No. 85/2009 dated 18 November 2009 .... 16.44

USA

Marquette Nat. Bank of Minneapolis v. First of Omaha Service Corp 439 U.S. 299 .... 6.22

List of Abbreviations

AAOIFI	Accounting and Auditing Organization for Islamic Financial Institutions
AD	anno domini
AH or (H)	anno hegirae or Hijra year
All ER	*All England Reports*
Am J Comp L	*American Journal of Comparative Law*
Arab LQ	*Arab Law Quarterly*
Art.	article
BAFT	Bankers Association for Finance & Trade
BBA	*bai' bithman ajil*
BNM	Bank Negara Malaysia
CE	common era
CF	cost and freight
Ch	Chancery
CIF	cost, insurance and freight
Clevel State L Rev	*Cleveland State Law Review*
CLJ	*Current Law Journal*
Colum J Transnatl L	*Columbia Journal of Transnational Law*
CP	Common Pleas
edn	edition
eds	editors
EWCA	England and Wales Court of Appeals
EWHC	England and Wales High Court
FOB	free on board
Fordham LR	*Fordham Law Review*
Harv L Rev	*Harvard Law Review*
IIFM	International Islamic Financial Markets
I.L.& S	*Islamic Law & Society*
Ind J Glob L Stud	*Indiana Journal of Global Legal Studies*
ISDA	International Swaps and Derivatives Association
LIBOR	London Interbank Offered Rate
LNS	Legal Network Series
LQR	*Law Quarterly Review*
LR	*Law Reports* (England)
MENA	Middle East and North Africa
MLJ	*Malay Law Journal*
NC L Rev	*North Carolina Law Review*
n.d.	no date
n.p.	no publisher
No.	Number
OJLS	*Oxford Journal of Legal Studies*

Ors	Others
OUP	Oxford University Press
Pt	Part
RM	Ringgit Malaysia (currency)
R.S.C.	Revised Statutes of Canada
SAC	Shariah Advisory Council
SOFR	Secured Overnight Funding Rate
SQLR	*Supreme Court Quarterly Law Reports* (Nigeria)
trans	translation
Vol.	volume
UAE	United Arab Emirates
UKSC	United Kingdom Supreme Court
UNCITRAL	UN Commission on International Trade Law
U.S.	*US Supreme Court* [Reports]

Introduction

It is well known that contracts were largely peripheral to the economy of England prior to the nineteenth century and the same is true of most European nations before the effective abolition of feudalism. In the Islamic world, contracts were central not only to the economy of the fledgling community but also for the preservation of its social fabric. Indeed, unlike the feudal systems of Europe whose economy was predicated on the fruits of land tenure, the Arab world was chiefly built around trade and commerce, both internal and external. Unlike other monotheistic faiths, Islam's Prophet was a successful trader in his own right as were his rightfully guided Companions and, subsequently, leading Islamic jurists. It is no wonder therefore that an entrepreneurial spirit came to infuse the regulation of contracts. Such regulation, however, was not aimed solely at profit maximization, but rather sought to ensure social well-being, fairness, and social justice. The core of these principles was enunciated by the Prophet and later elaborated by *fiqh* scholars. Much like English contract law, which is chiefly predicated on the common law with only a handful of statutes, so too only the key notions of Islamic contract law are found in the two primary sources of Islam, namely, the Qur'ān and the *sunnah* (the actions and sayings of Prophet Mohammed and his Companions). The bulk of the jurisprudence and practice of contract law in Islam is derived from the writings of renowned jurists as these have existed through the centuries, as well as more recently. This has allowed the law to develop in a dynamic fashion, which also encompasses the diversity of opinion on several issues among the four major schools of Islam. One cannot fully appreciate Islamic contract law without distinguishing the diverse reasoning of jurists belonging to the four schools (and the diversity inside the schools themselves) and, eventually, how each school has influenced the laws of nation states in which it became entrenched. As a result, the subject matter of this book should not be conceived as monolithic and immutable. It is very much a dynamic and pluralistic law, and its intended audience should not feel constrained to apply it in its broader contemporary context.

This book is aimed particularly at the non-Arabic legal audience, for which Islamic contract law may seem an exotic remnant of past times. This is hardly the case. In the last two decades the global volume of Islamic finance has increased spectacularly, even among non-Muslim users. Although Islamic finance instruments are structured according to Islamic contractual rules and principles, they are most frequently governed by the laws of secular legal systems. The result is an insufficient understanding of the contractual principles underlying such instruments. The courts, arbitral tribunals, and non-expert lawyers dealing with these instruments in major jurisdictions, such as London, Paris, and New York, rely on expert opinions in order to assess their conformity with Islamic contract law. The absence of a comprehensive and accessible treatise setting out both the foundations as well as the nuts and bolts of this system of law prompted the writing of this book. Western contract lawyers may be surprised to discover the existence of numerous and very elaborate works on Islamic contracts, each with its own followers, both in theory and practice. However, this extensive body of knowledge had not until now been made accessible in the English language to the non-Arabic speaking professional legal audience. This book does not attempt to emulate these treatises. Instead, the authors were of the opinion from the very outset that the regulation of contracts in the Islamic legal tradition was invisible in the West and, in many cases, it has even been dismissed as a coherent and structured legal discipline altogether. Given the wealth of resources from which the authors could draw their material and the limited amount of space that modern textbooks allow for, several important decisions were warranted. First, in order to resonate with our intended audience, the chapters were structured in a manner reflecting secular (Western) contract law textbooks. As the reader will come to appreciate, this was not altogether an insurmountable task since Islamic and Western contract laws share far more commonalities than differences. Secondly, as already explained, the most prominently used sources of Islamic contract law are secondary in nature. We have chosen to rely on those scholars whose writings have made an impact in academia, the courts, and state institutions, even though Islamic contract law as such is not the dominant feature of the civil laws of most Muslim-majority states. Finally, the authors felt that because of the practical nature of this book for its intended audience, there was little need to explain why or how one scholar is more significant or influential than another. Such a task would have required an altogether different effort. Instead, we take it for granted that the scholars cited in these pages have penned some of the classic works of Islamic contract law, even if they themselves never claimed to make such neat distinctions within the broader disciplines of Islamic studies and Islamic law.

This book would not have been possible without the publisher's belief not only that there was a gap the market, but also that it was worth writing. We would like to thank our original commissioning editors Eleanor Capel-Smith and Rachel Mullaly for their unwavering support and committing us to draconian deadlines that we seldom kept. We would like to extend our gratitude to Eleanor's successor, Alex Johnson and, at the very end, Eleanor Hanger, who ensured that the manuscript went successfully to print. A number of institutions and individuals were instrumental in supporting us both personally as well as collectively. Ilias Bantekas would like to thank Qatar Foundation for its institutional and financial support, as well as Umar Alkali, Mohamed Shetina, and Sidra Zulfaqar for their wonderful research assistance. Jonathan G. Ercanbrack would also like to thank Nikola Dukas Sardelis and Ali Ali for their excellent research support. Similarly, Umar A. Oseni would like to thank Afif Shatir Ahmad Shukri for helping to format the final drafts of his chapters. Equally many thanks to Professor Syed Nazim for bringing the authors together and providing spiritual inspiration for the subject matter of this book.

Ilias Bantekas wrote Chapters 2, 5, 7, and 12. Jonathan G. Ercanbrack wrote Chapters 3, 4, 8, and 16. Umar A. Oseni wrote Chapters 1, 6, 9, and 13. Ikram Ullah wrote Chapters 10, 11, 14, and 15. The work is current up to 1 August 2022. The authors welcome comments and suggestions.

1

General Principles and Sources of Islamic Contract Law

A General Theory?

1. Introduction

The modern world is witnessing a turning point in the continuous interaction, which is sometimes interpreted as tension, between major world legal systems, with specific reference to Islamic law. Even though there are many areas of similarities amongst major world legal systems, with varying degrees of historical influence on each other's development, it behoves experts in these legal systems to seek an in-depth understanding of other legal systems with a view to understanding their theoretical bases as well as key areas that could influence legal transplants in the modern world. **1.01**

The influence of Islamic law, being one of the world's major legal systems, is being felt in major transactions at both the corporate level as well as at the sovereign and multilateral levels. This has again brought to the fore the relevance of Islamic law in contractual matters within the general ambit of modern legal systems.[1] At the domestic level, the legal systems of most countries in the Middle East and North Africa (MENA) have elements of Islamic law in their civil codes, which generally include commercial law. This is due to major legal reforms carried out during the twentieth century which still have a major impact on most MENA states.[2] **1.02**

While the sweeping reforms toward the end of the first half of the twentieth century crept into the laws of several Arab countries, the emergence of Islamic contracts in different forms, particularly fuelled by the increasing prominence of the Islamic financial services industry, has further presented a situation where English law could be viewed from the Islamic contract perspective, or the prevailing civil codes in the MENA states are assessed through the lens of English law.[3] **1.03**

[1] P. Nicholas Kourides, 'The Influence of Islamic Law on Contemporary Middle Eastern Legal Systems: The Formation and Binding Force of Contracts' (1970) 9 Columbia Journal of Transnational Law 384.

[2] The Sanhuri Codes introduced sweeping reforms in the MENA states. The chief architect of Egypt's Civil Code enacted in 1948 was Abd al-Razzaq al-Sanhuri. The original code is a mix of Islamic legal principles as well as customary legal principles based on the prevailing socio-political and legal climates of Egypt at that time. See Nabil Saleh, 'Civil Codes of Arab Countries: The Sanhuri Codes' (1993) 8(2) Arab Law Quarterly 161–67.

[3] *Dana Gas PJSC v Dana Gas Sukuk Ltd and others* [2018] EWHC 277 (Comm) was an eye-opener for practitioners on both sides of the divide: English-trained lawyers on one side and Islamic law experts on the other. The case presented a clear example of conflict of laws and the need to introduce clarity on fundamental principles underlying Islamic contract law, particularly for practitioners drafting major financial agreements. In this case,

1.04 In order to ensure clarity on the core principles of Islamic contract law, which will invariably provide a guide to practitioners, this chapter introduces the general principles and sources of Islamic contract law. It also provides a general theory of contract while discussing the dichotomy between form and substance which has triggered the unending debate that touches on the spirit of a transaction based on Islamic law.[4] The debate on form and substance in Islamic contract law is not a recent phenomenon, as it appeared in the debate among the early Muslim jurists, but different terminologies have been used in the past.[5]

1.05 With the increasing integration of world trade across different jurisdictions, there is a great deal of interaction between the Muslim world and Western countries, particularly with regard to trade. These trade relationships are underpinned by contractual agreements. As witnessed over the past few decades, such trade relationships have spiralled into significant financial transactions through the issuance of Islamic bonds (*ṣukūk*) and other similar transactions. With the world turning into a global village, it is projected that such transactions will increase substantially in the coming years,[6] and in order to ensure that disputes do not balloon significantly as a result of increased cross-continental trade, a proper understanding of not only the English law but also the Islamic law of contract is required.

1.06 Consideration of the theory of contract is relevant in the modern structuring of Islamic products, whether financial products or halal goods.[7] Therefore, in modern legal documentation used in contracts, it is essential to examine how individuals and corporate entities construct and develop such agreements. Beyond simply analysing the contractual relationship and the intention to create legal relations among contracting parties, one might wonder how parties with conflicting interests would structure their contracts. This is more relevant today where a conflict of laws often emerges not just after the execution of the contract but even at the time of drafting the contracts. While the motivation to enter into some contracts is often premised on incentives, performance of contractual obligations is strictly regulated by the law, hence the need to identify

there were conflicting decisions by both the English court in England and a Sharjah court in the United Arab Emirates on similar legal issues.

[4] See for example Bill Maurer, 'Form versus Substance: AAOIFI Projects and Islamic Fundamentals in the Case of Sukuk' (2010) 1(1) Journal of Islamic Accounting and Business Research 32–41.

[5] See for instance Al-Shatibi, al-Muwāfaqat (Dar Ibn Affan, 1997) Vol. 3, p. 107; Ibn Taymiyyah, Bayān al-Dalīl 'alā buṭlān al-Taḥlīl (al-Maktab al-Islami, 1998) p. 159; Ibn al-Qayyim, I'lām al-Muwaqi'īn 'an Rabb al-'Ālamīn (Dar al-Ḥadīth, 2004) Vol. 3, p. 189.

[6] Noor Mohammed, 'Principles of Islamic Contract Law' (1988) 6(1) Journal of Law and Religion 115–30, p. 117.

[7] The process of financial engineering has taken on a different dimension with the mandatory Sharī'ah requirements in structuring Islamic finance products. Complex financial instruments have been developed through shrewd structuring efforts. Nevertheless, no matter how complex an Islamic finance product is, the underlying structure must fulfil fundamental principles of Islamic contract law. See generally Kabir Hassan, Rasem N. Kayed, and Umar A. Oseni, Introduction to Islamic Banking & Finance: Principles and Practice (Pearson Education, 2013).

several permutations underpinning classical principles of Islamic contract law and their modern relevance in structuring English-style legal documentation.

2. A General Theory of Contract?

In classical Islamic jurisprudence, the word *ʿaqd* is generally used to denote an agreement between two parties to a transaction where one party makes the offer and the other provides the acceptance.[8] Beyond a two-party transaction, the word *ʿaqd* has also been used for unilateral dispositions where there is only one offer and there is no requirement for acceptance.[9] Further analysis of juristic manuals reveals that the term *ʿaqd* has been used for some general juristic dispositions such as marriage and manumission of debts. In addressing some eschatological issues and determining one's obligations towards God, the word *ʿaqd* has also been used to emphasize the covenant between God and mankind. So, in addition to interpersonal relationships among people, the word has been used to denote commercial obligations among parties who conclude a contract. **1.07**

Etymologically, the word *ʿaqd* (pl. *ʿuqūd*) is derived from a verb *a-q-d* which literally means 'to tie' or 'to contract', 'to fasten with a knot', 'to put together'.[10] In *Lisān ʿArab*, *ʿaqd* is defined through a description of the word in certain contexts such as: *ʿaqd al-ʿahd* (covenant contract) and *ʿaqd al-yamīn* (oath agreement).[11] From the legal perspective, *ʿaqd* means a contract that comprises an agreement between two parties in a legally acceptable form with the intention to effect a binding legal relationship.[12] Muslim jurists have defined *ʿaqd* as 'a legally valid combination between an offer and acceptance in such a manner that its effect leaves its consequential mark on its subject matter'.[13] It has also been described as the agreement between two willing parties to establish **1.08**

[8] Al-Ghazaāli, Abu Hamid, al-Wasīt Fi al-Madhāhib (Dar al-Salam, 1997) Vol. 3, pp. 5–8; al-Sarkhasi, Abu Bakr Muhammad, al-Mabsūṭ (Dar al-Maʿrifah, 1993) Vol. 12, pp. 108–09.

[9] Al-Zuhaili, Wahbah, al-Fiqh al-Islami Wa Adillatuhu (Dar al-Fikr, n.d.) Vol. 4, p. 2925.

[10] Hans Wehr, A Dictionary of Modern Written Arabic, ed. J. Milton Cowan (Spoken Language Services, 1976) p. 627.

[11] Ibn Manzur, Muhammad bin Mukarram, Lisān ʿArab (Dar Sadir, 1414 AH) Vol. 3, pp. 296–97.

[12] The word *ʿaqd* has been defined in the Civil Codes of various MENA countries. For instance, Article 125 of The Civil Code of the United Arab Emirates provides the following definition: 'A contract is the coming together of an offer made by one of the contracting parties with the acceptance of the other, together with the agreement of then both in such a manner as to determine the effect thereof on the subject matter of the contract, and from which results an obligation upon each of them with regard to that which each is bound to do for the other' (see the Civil Code of UAE as amended by Federal Law No. 1 of 1987). Similarly, Article 64 of the Qatari Civil Code defines *ʿaqd* as follows: 'A contract shall be concluded by the mere confluence of offer and acceptance if the object of and reason of the contract are legally acceptable without prejudice to any special formalities the law may require for the conclusion of certain contracts' (see Law No. (22) of 2004 Promulgating the Civil Code). Also, the Egyptian Civil Code defines *ʿaqd* as follows: 'A contract is created, subject to any other special formalities that may be required by law for its conclusion, from the moment the two parties have exchanged two concordant intentions' (promulgated by Law No. 131 of 1948, in force since 15 October 1949). Similarly, but using a different approach, section 12 of the Bahraini Contract Law defines contracts as follows: 'All agreements are contracts if they are made by free consent of parties, competent to contract, for a lawful consideration and with lawful object, and are not hereby declared to be void' (see the Contract Law 1969, Ramadan 1389/November 1969).

[13] Al-Zarqa, Mustafa Ahmad, al-Madkhal al-fiqhi al-ʾam (Dar al-Qalam, 2004) Vol. 1, pp. 382–83 (hereafter Al-Zarqa, *al-Madkhal*).

a right, effectively transfer it, or even terminate it.[14] These definitions emphasize the basic elements of a contract, which include offer and acceptance, meeting of minds or consent, subject matter of the contract or object, and the consideration, with the effect of creating a binding legal relationship with associated consequences.

2.1 Conceptual Theory of Contractual Obligation

1.09 Muslim jurists have examined the general theory of contractual obligation from the perspective of sanctity of contract as enshrined in the Qur'ān: 'O you who have believed! Fulfil your undertakings.'[15] The word used to describe the sanctity of contract in this verse is the plural form of contract in Islamic law, *'uqūd*. This general application of the principle of sanctity of contract is a rule of general application which is not only limited to commercial transactions. Other references to different forms of contracts such as covenant (*'ahd*) were used in the theological sense to refer to agreements between mankind and God Almighty.

1.10 Another related term used in the Qur'ān is *mīthāq*, which could also mean a covenant, compact, pledge, or treaty.[16] Both *'ahd* and *mīthāq* could be used interchangeably; while the former appears twenty-nine times, with its verbal form appearing nine times in the Qur'ān, the latter is used twenty-five times.[17] In relation to contractual obligations, the word *mīthāq* often implies reciprocity between two parties, which could be considered from the perspective of the performance of contractual obligations by parties to a contract.[18]

1.11 Another commonly used term in contractual obligation is *wa'd*, which simply means a unilateral promise.[19] This concept of promise has been further developed in Islamic jurisprudence as an underlying principle for non-commutative or gratuitous contracts (*'uqūd al-tabarr'u*) where its derivative *muwā'ada* (bilateral promise) has emerged. Muslim jurists have distinguished between a contract and a bilateral promise; while the former is binding, the latter is not. If *muwā'ada* is considered binding on the parties, then there would not be any difference between it and a contract.[20] Due to the slim difference between a contract and *muwā'ada*, it is important to consider how Muslim jurists have defined *muwā'ada*. This would provide some insights on the differences

[14] Al-Sabuni, Abd Al-Rahman, Al-Madkhal Lidirasat Al-Fiqh Al-Islami (Al-Matba'ah Al-Jadidah, 1978) Vol. 2, p. 116.

[15] Qur'ān 5:1.

[16] The word '*mīthāq*' appears numerous times in Al-Qur'ān. For example, in Qur'ān 13:20, Allah states that one of the qualities which will lead mankind to the most coveted Paradise includes fulfilling the covenant of Allah and not breaking the trust.

[17] Joseph E.B. Lumbard, 'Covenant and Covenants in the Qur'ān' (2015) 17(2) Journal of Qur'ānic Studies 1–23, p. 3.

[18] Ibid, p. 4.

[19] Malik bin Anas, al-Mudawanah al-Kubra (Dar al-Kutub al-'Ilmiyyah, 1994) Vol. 3, p. 270.

[20] Nazih Kamal Hammad, 'al-Wafā' bi al-Wa'd fi al-Fiqh al-Islamī', Majallah al-Majma' al-Fiqh al-Islami, Session 5, Vol. 2, p. 831.

between a contract and *muwāʿada*. According to Ibn Rushd, *muwāʿada* is when two parties make promises to each other (on an issue) in a mutual manner that can only occur between two persons.[21] A contemporary Muslim jurist defines *muwāʿada* as a declaration made by two persons with a mutual intention to enter into a future contract with the required legal consequences.[22] This definition introduces the future dimension into the discourse and connects *muwāʿada* to contracts.

In essence, going by the definition, one could consider *muwāʿada* as a future contract or future mutual undertaking. However, it is possible to engage in *muwāʿada* for purposes other than those of a contract. Nazih Hammad had argued that none of the early Muslim jurists considered that *muwāʿada* could be binding on either or even both parties. However, he discussed the possibility of both parties in *muwāʿada* agreeing that the future contract would be binding on them. In such a situation, the *muwāʿada* automatically turns into a contract and all applicable rulings relating to a contract will apply.[23] He premised this conclusion on the legal maxim that states: 'In contracts, effect is given to meaning and intention, and not to words and forms' (*ḥal al-ibrah fi al-ʿuqūd bi al-maqāṣid wa al-maʿāni aw bi al-al-fāẓ wa al-mabāni*).[24] **1.12**

Regardless of whatever term was used by early scholars to denote a contract-like arrangement, the Islamic rules of contract were derived from original sources of Islamic law which were applicable to issues that transcend mere commercial transactions. In fact, there was no clear definition of contract during the early days, but, based on in-depth study of Muslim jurists and their extrapolation from primary sources, scholars later provided some definitions or descriptions of what could be regarded as a contract under the law. It is pertinent to note that the early references to contract-like issues did not provide for specific issues such as the fundamental elements of contract. However, subsequent centuries after the advent of Islam saw gradual development in Islamic jurisprudence which led to the discussion on issues relating to contract and specific matters based on the developments witnessed in cross-boundary trade.[25] These developments in the theory of contract were reflected in most of the treaties of Islamic jurisprudence, particularly those relating to commercial law or *fiqh al-muʿāmalāt*.[26] In some cases, dedicated chapters were written on contract law in books on Islamic jurisprudence generally.[27] **1.13**

[21] Ibn Rushd, Muhammad Ibn Ahmad, al-Muqaddimat al-Mumahhidat (Dar al-Gharb al-Islami, 1988) Vol. 3, p. 267.
[22] Nazih Kamal (n 20)Vol. 2, p. 730.
[23] Ibid, Vol. 2, p. 831.
[24] Zain al-Abidin Ibn Nujaym, Al-Ashbah wa al-Nazā'ir 'ala Madhhab Abi Hanifah al-Nu'mān (Dar al-Kutub al-Ilmiyyah, 1993) p. 207. On this legal maxim, Ibn Qayyim al-Jawziyyah emphasized thus: 'Should the law take into account only the manifest meaning of expressions and contracts even when the purposes and intents appear to be otherwise? Or do aims and intents have an effect which requires paying attention to them and taking them into consideration? The evidence of the sources of law and its rules concur that intentions in a contract determine whether the contract is legal or illegal.' See Ibn al-Qayyim al-Jawziyyah, I'lām al-Muwaqqi'īn an Rabb al-'Ālamīn (Al-Muniriya Press) Vol. 3, pp. 96–98 (hereafter Ibn al-Qayyim, *I'lām al-Muwaqqi'īn*).
[25] Mohd Daud Bakar and Engku Rabiah, Essential Readings in Islamic Finance (CERT Publications, 2008) p. 48.
[26] Mohamed H. Reda, Islamic Commercial Law: Contemporariness, Normativeness and Competence (Brill/Nijhoff, 2018) Vol. 12, p. 13.
[27] Ibid.

2.2 Is There a Theory of Contract in Islamic Law?

1.14 A fundamental issue to explore is whether there was a general theory of contract formulated by early Muslim jurists. In other words, beyond the general theory of Islamic jurisprudence which gave birth to Islamic commercial law principles, it remains doubtful whether there was a general theory of contract upon which Islamic contract law was predicated. Under the common law, contract law was developed from three unique theories: formalistic, interpretative, and normative.[28] However, it appears that the theory of Islamic contract law was not specifically developed by early Muslim jurists in classical Islamic law.

1.15 Similar to other areas of Islamic law, fundamental principles of Islamic jurisprudence were developed as interpretative techniques rather than theoretical abstractions. As such, the early Muslim jurists did not attempt to define the term 'contract' and failed to provide any underlying theory to support Islamic contract law. From the perspective of general principles, one would therefore argue that the underlying theory of Islamic contract law is based on the need for people to fulfil their obligations.[29] Although such a theory results from moral persuasion, Muslim jurists later adopted the textual evidence to support the binding nature of contractual obligations.

1.16 It is important to clarify that there is a difference between moral injunctions and legally binding principles. However, some Muslim jurists have argued that the line dividing moral injunctions from legally binding principles is sometimes blurred. In some cases, commands and prohibitions in the Qur'ān and Sunnah occur in different forms. A legally binding injunction will usually be accompanied by an imperative mood or simple past tense in the language used. In some other cases, moral condemnation could form the basis of a prohibition in a contract. In addition, commands and prohibitions could be in the form of a reference to the consequences of a specific form of conduct.

1.17 From the above variety of forms of commands and prohibitions, the language used in the Qur'ān and Sunnah is quite different from modern positive legislation. The former seeks to appeal to people's conscience first as this reflects the normative character of divine injunctions in Islam. Such an appeal comprises some measured persuasion, strong warning, or even a reference to potential benefit or harm that may result from any omission or commission. In some other cases, the element of reward and punishment is linked to eschatological recompense.[30] Conversely, due to the influence of the positivist school of jurisprudence as theorized by Jeremy Bentham and John Austin,[31] modern statutory laws do not contain elements of persuasion and appeal; the laws are considered as commands of a higher authority or sovereign and are binding on

[28] Melvin Eisenberg, Theories of Contract Law In Foundational Principles of Contract Law (Oxford University Press, 2018).

[29] This is based on Qur'ān 5:1, 4:33, and 16:91.

[30] Mohammad Hashim Kamali, Principles of Islamic Jurisprudence (Islamic Texts Society, 1991).

[31] See John Austin, The Province of Jurisprudence Determined (Cambridge University Press, 1955).

subjects.[32] Understanding this fundamental theoretical basis of the nature of Islamic law and modern positive law will provide a good basis to comprehend the nature of Islamic contract law.

As an alternative theoretical framework, Muslim jurists had to develop what Hussein Hassan referred to as 'a law of contracts', which provided individual contracts with their own unique rules.[33] This led to the categorization of various contracts into different classes of nominate agreements (*'uqūd mu'ayyana*) on one hand and innominate contracts on the other (*ghayr al-mu'ayyana*).[34] This unique categorization ushered in the birth of 'a law of contracts'.[35] As a result, some modern scholars opined that Islamic law has a general theory of contract.[36] Even though some other scholars disagree,[37] it can however be argued that a combination of four unique principles—the original basis of permissibility in Islamic commercial law, prohibited elements in Islamic law such as *ribā* and *gharar*, the requirement for Muslims to fulfil their contractual obligations, and the prohibition on consuming others' property—could be considered as the basis of a general theory of contract in Islamic law. Nevertheless, one would still admit that classical jurists never attempted to formulate a theory of contract as such. **1.18**

2.3 Express and Implied Contract

Since the advent of Islam, Islamic law recognizes both an express contract, whether documented or not, and an implied contract through a generally acceptable customary practice or conduct. Under the common law, contract by conduct is also recognized. Therefore, in Islamic law, an offer or even its acceptance could be made orally, in writing, or by conduct. The only condition required to have a valid contract whether explicit or implied is the legal capacity of the parties; in order words, the parties must **1.19**

[32] H.L.A. Hart, 'Positivism and the Separation of Law and Morals' (1958) 71 Harvard Law Review 593, pp. 601–02.

[33] Hussein Hassan, 'Contracts in Islamic Law: The Principles of Commutative Justice and Liberality' (2002) 13(3) Journal of Islamic Studies 257–97, p. 258.

[34] See a comprehensive discussion on nominate and innominate contracts in Al-Mumini, Ahmad Muhammad, Fiqh al-'uqud al-musammah wa ghayr al-musammah bayna al-Shariah wa al-Qanun (Dar Majdalawi lil-Nashr wa al-Tawzi', 2013).

[35] Nominate contracts are unique agreements that have standardized contractual terms and conditions with a particular name in Islamic law which effectively distinguishes them from other forms of contracts. These include *'aqd al-bay'* (sale contract), *hiba* (gift deed), *sharika* (partnership), *'ijāra* (lease contract), *muqāwala* (a contract to make a thing or perform a task), and *wakāla* (agency contract). While this list is not exhaustive, the idea of nominate contracts is the treatment jurists have accorded to them through separate treatment in the treaties of Islamic jurisprudence. On the other hand, innominate contracts are agreements that are neither classified under any specific heading nor given specific treatment by jurists. The only thing required for innominate contracts as provided by the law is the express agreement of the parties. Most of the innominate contracts are often used as ancillary or auxiliary contracts while structuring new Islamic contracts. Examples of innominate contracts include *'istiṣnā'a* contract (commissioned manufacturing contract), *bay' al-wafa* (redemption sale), and *bay' al-istijrār* (supply sale contract). See Abd al-Razzaq al-Sanhuri, al-Wasiṭ fi sharḥ al-qānūn al-madani (Dar al-Nahdha al-'Arabiyya, 1952) Vol. 4, pt. 1, p. 1.

[36] Coulson and Schacht consider Islamic law as a law of contracts. See Noel J. Coulson, Commercial Law in the Gulf States: The Islamic Legal Tradition (Graham & Trotman, 1984) pp. 17, 23–31. Also see Joseph Schacht, Introduction to Islamic Law (Oxford University Press, 1964) p. 144.

[37] Hassan (n 33) p. 258.

have the requisite legal capacity to enter into the contract.[38] This reflects the principle of freedom of contract which emphasizes party autonomy and the need for the consent of parties to any contract to ensure its validity.

1.20 The relevance of this classification is seen in modern contracts involving electronic transactions. Electronic contracts are considered valid in the laws of most jurisdictions throughout the world.[39] With the continuous proliferation of e-commerce transactions and the massive volume of such transactions taking place every second, offers and acceptances are being made all the time via electronic means and millions of contracts are being concluded. Modern Muslim jurists have also validated such electronic contracts on the basis of the general principle of permissibility in Islamic law. In the absence of a clear-cut prohibition in the primary sources of Islamic law, the rule in Islamic commercial law remains that of permissibility.[40] Such contracts could also be validated based on public interest (*maṣlaḥa*), as e-commerce is of immense public interest and provides unprecedented convenience for parties concluding contracts remotely.[41] The electronic platform is merely a means to an end. Therefore, the rules of Islamic contract law, as described in subsequent chapters of this book, apply to e-commerce contracts even though the form of contract may not expressly fulfil the requirements of the traditional contracts known in Islamic jurisprudence.

3. The Debate on Form and Substance

1.21 A major issue which requires further discussion is the continuing debate between form and substance in Islamic contract law. This debate has continued for centuries and, up to the present day, scholars have attempted to formulate a consistent theory to structure modern contracts while complying with Islamic law principles. This issue has been further exacerbated with the increasing disputes over terms and conditions in Islamic financial contracts coming before the English courts. Legal enforceability of some Islamic contracts has been called into question; hence, this requires some analysis to identify the need for a consistent framework in Islamic contract law.

1.22 The debate on form and substance was addressed by early Muslim jurists in their treatises using different terminologies. The most important term used by classical scholars is *hila* or legal ruse.[42] However, the debate in the modern sense has significant implications for the nature of modern Islamic contracts used in the Islamic financial

[38] Abdur Rahman I Doi, Shariah: The Islamic Law (Ta Ha Publishers, 1984).
[39] See the UNCITRAL Model Law on Electronic Commerce with Guide to Enactment 1996 with additional Art. 5*bis* as adopted in 1998.
[40] Ibn Taimyya's *Fatawi* (Legal Decisions) compiled by Ibn Qassem Abdulrahman (Al-Risalah, 1997) Vol. 29, p. 226.
[41] Al-Sanad Muhammad, al-Ahkam al-Faqhiya lel Ta'amolat al-Electroniyya (Dar al-Warraq Publisher, 2004) p. 167.
[42] Ibn Taymiyyah (n 5) 159; Ibn al-Qayyim, I'lam al-Muwaqqi'in (n 24) Vol. 3, p. 240.

services industry.[43] There has been continuous criticism of the forms of contracts used in Islamic financial transactions today.[44] Most of the contracts are being referred to as mere replication of conventional financial contracts without the fundamental substance of Islamic law. There is also an alternative argument that, even if modern Islamic contract law complies with principles of Islamic law, most contracts do not meet the substance and spirit of the law where the economic substance of the transaction should have been emphasized.[45]

In discussing the debate on form and substance, the first thing to establish is that the basic requirements of a contract in Islamic law, which are reflected in the essential elements for its validity, discussed in Section 5 of this chapter, should be present. This refers to the form (*ṣigha*) of the contract itself. The economic substance, the nature of what the parties intend, and the implications of the contract are reflected in the substance of the contract. In essence, both form and substance are essential for the validity of a contract in Islamic law and, in interpreting the implications of a contract, any competent court should ordinarily look into both the form and the substance of such a contract. Despite the apparently clear picture of both form and substance painted here in theory, the difficulty is always seen in the practical application of these principles. **1.23**

From the practical perspective, an example of the debate on form and substance is seen in the contract of lease (*ʾijāra*), with particular reference to a lease contract that provides for a lease that ends with ownership (*ʾijāra muntahiya bi al-tamlīk*).[46] In this contractual arrangement, there are two phases; first, the lessor leases a particular property to the lessee for a specified period of time during which the latter pays agreed rent to the former; and secondly, at the end of the agreed lease period, the legal ownership of the asset is automatically vested in the lessee. Within the contractual arrangement, there is an ancillary contract in the form of *waʿd* (promise) from the lessor to transfer the ownership of the underlying property to the lessee at the end of the lease period and, concurrently, there is a promise from the lessee to acquire the property at the end of the lease period based on the terms of the agreement. Transfer of ownership can be achieved through various options such as a sale contract using a symbolic token price, sale at a predetermined market price, through a deed of gift, or through the rental paid over the lease period. **1.24**

In practical reality, depending on the type of this lease-to-own contract agreed upon by the parties, the contractual arrangement may involve two separate contracts: the lease contract and the sale contract (*ʿaqd al-bayʿ*). This gives an indication of the form **1.25**

[43] Mohamed Hamour, Mohmmad Hassan Shakil, Ishaq Mustapha Akilanso, and Mashiyat Tasnia, 'Contemporary Issues of Form and Substance: An Islamic Law Perspective' (2019) 11(1) International Journal of Islamic Finance 124–36.

[44] Zubair Hasan, 'Risk Sharing Versus Risk Transfer in Islamic Finance: A Critical Appraisal' (2015) 7(1) International Journal of Islamic Finance 7–26; Muhammad Hanif, 'Economic Substance or Legal Form: An Evaluation of Islamic Finance Practice' (2016) 9(2) International Journal of Islamic and Middle Eastern Finance and Management 277–95.

[45] Hanif (n 44).

[46] This form of contract is similar to a hire purchase agreement under the English common law.

of the contract, and if such a transaction has to be recorded in the financial statements, it will be recognized as two separate contracts. In fact, the whole chain of transactions and underlying promises constitute only one single contract, a rent-to-own contract. This reflects the approach which prefers form over substance, as the emphasis is on the forms of contracts involved rather than the economic substance. On the other hand, if the principle of substance over form is applied, the chain of transactions can be collapsed into one single transaction, but this will be similar to the conventional hire purchase contract.

1.26 As emphasized by Muslim jurists, both form and substance are important in Islamic contract law. For the form of the contract, ideally, two contracts should not be combined (*ijtimaʿ al-ʿuqūd*) into one,[47] as Prophet Muhammad forbids (combining) a sale and a loan, thus two sales in a single sale (*bayʿatain fi bayʿ*).[48] However, there are exceptions to this general principle and the case of *ʾijāra muntahiya bi al-tamlīk* is such an exception since it involves a lease and a sale. This position is in agreement with the opinion of Ibn al-Qayyim who said: 'It is permissible in principle to form up (two) contracts and conditions, except for what has been prohibited in Islamic law.'[49] This argument of whether or not combining two contracts is allowed focuses more on the form rather than the substance of the contract.

1.27 The approach generally adopted by modern scholars is reflected in some legal maxims: 'Matters are determined according to the intentions (behind them)';[50] 'In contracts, effect is given to intentions and meanings and not words and forms.'[51] Ibn Qayyim also emphasized the need to focus on the substance of a contract rather than the form while ascertaining the intention of the parties: 'You should never neglect the intention of the speaker and his motives; if you do, you would harm him, and you would harm the Sharīʿah by attributing to it something that does not befit it. A sound-minded jurist would ask, "What did you intend?" and a shallow-minded jurist would ask, "What did you say?" '[52] In interpreting Islamic contracts, there are instances where there could be a clear conflict between the form and substance. In such a situation, preference is often given to the substance.[53]

[47] It is reported that the Prophet forbade (combining) selling and lending (contracts). Malik said: 'The explanation of what that meant is that one man says to another, "I will take your goods for such-and-such if you lend me such-and-such." If they agree to a transaction in this manner, it is not permitted. If the one who stipulates the loan abandons his stipulation, then the sale is permitted.' See Ibn Anas Malik, Muwatta, ed. Mahammad Fuad Abdul Baqi (Dar Ihya al—Turath al-Arabi, n.d.) Vol. 5, p. 657.

[48] Al-Sarakhsi, Shams al-Din, al-Mabsut (al-Saʿada Press, 1324 AH) Vol. 13, pp. 15–18.

[49] Ibn al-Qayyim, *I'lam al-Muwaqqi'in* (n 24) Vol. 3, p. 354.

[50] Al-Zarqa', Ahmad, Sharh al-Qawa`id al-Fiqhiyyah (Dar al-Qalam, 1989) p. 47.

[51] Ali Ahmad al-Nadwi, Jamharah al-Qawa`id al-Fiqhiyyah fi al-Mu`amalat al-Maliyyah (Sharikat al-Rajhi al—Masrafiyyah li al-Istithmar, 2000) Vol. 1, p. 550.

[52] Ibn al-Qayyim, Iʿlām al-Muwaqqiʿīn (n 24) Vol. 3, p. 53.

[53] Consistent with the preference for substance over form, the Sharīʿah Advisory Committee of Bank Negara Malaysia resolved: 'In principle, "substance" and "form" are equally important and highly taken into consideration by the Shariah. In this regard, the Shariah emphasises that "substance" and "form" must be consistent and shall not contradict one another. In the event of inconsistency between "substance" and "form" due to certain factors, the Shariah places greater importance on "substance" rather than "form".' See Bank Negara Malaysia, Shariah Resolutions in Islamic Finance (Bank Negra Malaysia, 2010) p. 192.

It is pertinent to note that the practice in common law jurisdictions with significant interest in Islamic finance contracts, such as Malaysia, has been to adopt a similar approach even for common law contracts. For instance, in *Arab-Malaysian Finance Bhd v Taman Ihsan Jaya Sdn Bhd and others (Koperasi Seri Kota Bukit Cheraka Bhd, third party)*[54]—a case involving a deferred payment contract otherwise known as *al-bayʿ bithman ājil* (BBA), the court emphasized the principle thus: 'It has been said with obvious justification, that what matters in discerning the true nature of contracts and transactions is the substance and not the words and structure.'[55] This approach seems to be consistent with the apex court's approach in Malaysia in an English law-styled contract where it emphasized: **1.28**

> In our view, the correct approach would be to look at the substance, not just the label which had been attached to the letter. The law will always look beyond the terminology of the document to the actual facts of the situation, and it is no longer a question of words but substance.[56]

A similar decision was handed down by the Dubai Cassation Court in its judgment No. 125 of 2007, where the court opined: **1.29**

> According to the tradition of this court, and to the provisions of articles 258, 265(2) of the Civil Transactions Act, the contract's aim is defined by the true intentions and meanings [of the parties] and not the wording or the syntax. If there is a room for construing the contract, then the mutual intention of the contracting parties shall be considered without stopping at the literal meaning of the contractual wording.[57]

The above opinions do not mean that the form of the contract should not be analysed as well but there is always the need to look beyond the form by also considering the economic substance of the agreement. This balanced position, where both the form and substance are important while preference is given to substance in the event of inconsistencies in a contract, should be adopted as an interpretative technique for Islamic contracts. **1.30**

4. Sources of Islamic Contract Law

As discussed above, the theory of contract in Islamic law is predicated on the primary sources of Islamic law which are often supplemented by the secondary sources. While the fine details of the principles and conditions underpinning contract law were developed over time after the demise of Prophet Muhammad, such principles developed by **1.31**

[54] [2008] 5 MLJ 631.

[55] Ibid, p. 645.

[56] See *Woo Yew v Yonq Yang Hoo* [1978] 1 LNS 240 FC.

[57] Abobakr Dafalla, 'The Interpretation of Contracts under the UAE Civil Code' (Al Tamimi & Company, 2014). See <https://www.lexology.com/library/detail.aspx?g=556a220d-7266-418a-9b92-0dd4f0409b1d> accessed 5 January 2022.

Muslim jurists are based on general rules in the Qur'ān and Sunnah.[58] This is part of the general nature of legislation and rulings in Islamic jurisprudence, where substantial flexibility is adopted in issues relating to Islamic commercial law in order to allow the general principles to always remain valid.[59] This evergreen feature is the hallmark of the primary sources of Islamic law which allows the adaptation of principles according to times and climes within a certain contextual framework.

1.32 Nevertheless, it is pertinent to note that there are numerous secondary sources. For the purpose of this chapter, the most relevant secondary sources have been selected for discussion. In addition to the primary sources and secondary sources, one could also consider the relevance of positive laws which do not derogate from the rules and principles established in the primary and secondary sources of Islamic law. Though this third category of sources could be classified broadly under *ʿurf*, as described below, it might be more appropriate to give it its own unique treatment as a tertiary source of Islamic contract law, particularly in the modern sense.

4.1 The Primary Sources

1.33 The primary sources of Islamic law are basically the Qur'ān and Sunnah, where the former is considered the word of Allah and the latter comprises prophetic precedents which, in most cases, provide clarity or practical application of the general rules in the former. The Qur'ān and Sunnah are generally considered complementary sources in Islamic jurisprudence.[60] During the time of Prophet Muhammad, all the legal rulings (*aḥkām*) applicable to all matters were derived from the Qur'ān, while the Prophet explained such matters in his unique ways to guide his Companions and future generations of Muslims.[61] Therefore, issues relating to fundamentals of faith, family relations, criminal law, and commercial law matters, including contracts, were derived from both the Qur'ān and Sunnah at that time and were presented in ways and manners that would make them relevant for future generations.[62]

1.34 As discussed earlier, much textual evidence in the Qur'ān emphasizes the sanctity of contract, whether in commercial transactions or otherwise. The foremost verse often quoted is: 'O you who have believed! Fulfil your undertakings.'[63] In their interpretation

[58] Al-Shatibi (n 5) Vol. 4, p. 143.

[59] The primary sources, particularly the Qur'ān, contains general principles, rules, and divine guidance on both legal and theological issues while presenting a number of historical events that serve as guidance to current and future generations. According to Muslim jurists, the Qur'ān contains general principles or *ru'ūs al-aḥkām* which provide room for further elaboration in the Sunnah. This further requires qualified Muslim jurists to undertake analogical deductions on new issues (*nawāzil*); hence the often-quoted verse in Qur'ān 6:38: 'We have neglected nothing in the Book.' As a result, over many centuries, Muslim jurists developed and continue to develop Islamic contract law principles depending on the needs of the time. An example of this is the rulings applicable to electronic contracts; these are considered new but subject to general rules of Islamic contract law.

[60] Al-Shatibi (n 5) Vol. 4, p. 143.

[61] Ibid, Vol. 4, p. 184.

[62] Ibid, Vol. 4, p. 183.

[63] Qur'ān 5:1.

of this verse, Ibn 'Abbas, Mujahid, and other leading Companions interpreted fulfilling *'uqūd* (sing. *'aqd*) as fulfilling the terms of treaties. In order to further buttress this point, Ibn Jarir emphasized that there is a consensus among the Companions on this interpretation. During the time of the Prophet, treaties were made in writing with proper clauses on each issue agreed upon.[64] Numerous peace treaties were concluded during the time of the Prophet,[65] and this direct command to fulfil such obligations reinforces the sanctity of contractual obligations in Islamic law. Other scholars have provided alternative interpretations of this verse where *'uqūd* is interpreted as covenants between mankind and God; hence, mankind is expected to fulfil such covenants by obeying the commands of God.[66]

From the commercial perspective, there is a reference to consent or meeting of minds in commercial dealings where the Qur'ān emphasizes: 'O you who have believed, do not consume one another's wealth unjustly but only [in lawful] business by mutual consent.'[67] The element of mutual consent here implies some sort of oral or written agreement between the parties to engage in a trade activity or commercial transaction. Mutual consent is better expressed through documentation for future reference. In commercial transactions there is often the need to buy commodities on credit which requires some form of documentation once agreed by the parties. In order to forestall future disputes, such transactions are required to be duly documented, as further elaborated in the longest verse of the Qur'ān (*aya al-dayn*): **1.35**

> O you who have believed, when you contract a debt for a specified term, write it down. And let a scribe write [it] between you in justice. Let no scribe refuse to write as Allah has taught him. So let him write and let the one who has the obligation [i.e., the debtor] dictate. And let him fear Allah, his Lord, and not leave anything out of it.[68]

In the Sunnah, numerous prophetic precedents provide a good basis for contracts in Islamic law. Most collections of *ḥadīth* have dedicated some chapters to *kitāb al-buyū'u*, which is loosely translated as Islamic commercial law. Therefore, specific transactions—which could be interpreted to mean contract in this sense—have been explained in the *ḥadīth*. While some of those transactions have been declared forbidden, some others have been approved by the Prophet. In a *ḥadīth* relating to the conditions one should stipulate in a contract, the Prophet said: 'How can men stipulate conditions that are not in the Book of Allah [Qur'ān]? All conditions that are not in the Book of Allah are **1.36**

[64] *Ḥadīth* Nos 2731–2732. See Al-Bukhari, Al-Jāmi' al-Saḥiḥ (Al-Matba'ah al-Salafiyyah, 1980) Vol. 2, pp. 279–84 (hereafter Al-Bukhari, *Al-Jāmi' al-Saḥiḥ*).

[65] The peace treaties concluded by the Prophet in the form of documented agreements include: The Treaty of Madinah, the Treaty of Hudaibiyyah, and the Treaty of Najran. See generally Ibn Hisham, al-Sirah an-Nabawiya, ed. Umar Abd Salam Tadmor (Dar al-Kitab al-Arabi, 1996) and Ibn Ishaq, al-Sirah an-Nabawiyah, ed. Ahmad Farid al-Mazidi (Dar al-Kutub al-`Ilmiyah, 2004).

[66] This other view is further buttressed by another verse of the Qur'ān (Qur'ān 2:27) which states: 'Those who break the covenant of Allah after contracting it and sever that which Allah has ordered to be joined and cause corruption on earth; it is those who are the losers.'

[67] Qur'ān 4:29.

[68] Qur'ān 2:282.

invalid, be it a hundred conditions. Allah's Book is more trustworthy, and His conditions are more worthy to obey.'[69] The essence of this *ḥadīth* is that party autonomy is paramount in contract law. Freedom of contract should be respected at all times except in situations where parties stipulate conditions that are expressly prohibited in the eyes of the law.[70]

1.37 In a *ḥadīth* narrated by Kathir bin 'Amr bin 'Awf Al-Muzani, the Prophet said: 'Reconciliation is allowed among the Muslims, except for reconciliation that makes the lawful unlawful, or the unlawful lawful. *And the Muslims will be held to their conditions, except the conditions that make the lawful unlawful, or the unlawful lawful*'[71] (emphasis added). This *ḥadīth* provides a clear-cut direction on how terms and conditions of contracts should be drafted to ensure compliance with fundamental rules of Islamic law. It also emphasizes the need to comply with one's contractual stipulations and ensure performance of one's obligations insofar as such conditions are lawful.[72] Just as in English common law, parties are not allowed to perform an illegal contract. In a similar vein, a contract made for an illegal purpose will be void *ab initio*. In addition, another related *ḥadīth* condemns deliberate breach of contract or promises made therein as such an attitude is considered hypocritical: 'Whenever he makes a promise, he always breaks it . . . and whenever he makes a covenant, he proves treacherous.'[73] This further reinforces the emphasis on the need to fulfil contractual obligations as a dispute avoidance strategy among contracting parties.

4.2 The Secondary Sources: A Select List?

1.38 In Islamic jurisprudence, there are numerous secondary sources which complement, and comprehensively expand upon, the primary sources.[74] These sources were based on issues on which the Companions of the Prophet had a unanimous opinion, and other sources developed by Muslim jurists which are often used as interpretative techniques when deducing the rule applicable to novel issues.[75] The secondary sources took their origins from the primary sources and they cannot in any way derogate from the general or the specific rules and principles established in the primary sources.

1.39 As in other areas of Islamic jurisprudence, contract law also takes its origins from secondary sources such as *ijmāʿ* (*consensus omnium* among the Companions), *qiyās*

[69] *Ḥadīth* No. 2155, see Al-Bukhari, Al-Jami' al-Sahih (n 64) Vol. 2, p. 103. Also see Ahmad ibn Hanbal, Al-Musnad (Dar ihya' Turath Al-'Arabi, 1993) Vol. 7, pp. 119–20.

[70] Al-Zabidi, al-Tajrid al-Sarih li Aḥadīth al-Jami al-Sahih (Bulaq, 1287 AH) Vol. 1, p. 147.

[71] Al-Tirmidhi, Imãm Hãfiz Abü Isa Mohammad, English translation of Jami'Al-Tirmidhi, trans. Abu Khaliyl (Darussalam, 2007) Vol. 3, p. 142, *Ḥadīth* No. 1352.

[72] Ibn Qudamah, al-Mughni (Maktabat al-Qahirah al-Tab'ah, 1968) Vol. 5, p. 397 (hereafter Ibn Qudamah, *al-Mughni*).

[73] Muhammad Ismā'īl Bukhari, The Translation of the Meanings of sahih Al-Bukhari, trans. M. Muhsin Khan (Dar al-Salam, 1997) Vol. 1, *Ḥadīth* Nos 33 and 34.

[74] Abd al-Wahhab Khallaf, 'Ilm Usul al-Fiqh (Dar al-Qalam, 1986) p. 21.

[75] Ibid, p. 22.

(analogical deduction), *sharḥ man qablana* (revealed laws preceding the Sharīʿah of Islam), *qawl al-ṣaḥabi* (ruling of a Companion of the Prophet), *istiḥsān* (equitable ruling), *maṣlaḥa mursala* (public interest consideration), *ʿurf* (custom), *istisḥāb* (presumption of continuity), and *ṣadd al-dharāʾi* (blocking the means). From this long list of secondary sources, the following four have been identified for further elaboration: *ijmāʿ*, *qiyās*, *ʾistiḥsān*, and *ʿurf*.

4.2.1 *ʿIjmāʿ*

The consensus of opinion of the Companions of Prophet Muhammad on issues is considered a secondary source of Islamic contract law.[76] While premised on rational proof, *ijmāʿ* is a binding proof if it is the result of a universal consensus among the Companions. After the death of Prophet Muhammad, any universal agreement of the Muslim jurists among the Muslim community in a certain period upon a specific rule of Islamic law is also considered *ijmāʿ*.[77] For any *ijmāʿ* to be valid as a rule of Islamic contract law, it must fulfil the following conditions: first, such unanimous agreement must occur among qualified Muslim jurists (*mujtahid*) who can conduct independent legal reasoning or *ijtihād* to arrive at an Islamic ruling; secondly, such agreement must be unanimous without any room for divergence of opinion; thirdly, the qualified jurists must come from the Muslim community with wide recognition among the people; fourthly, the agreement among the qualified Muslim jurists must occur after the demise of Prophet Muhammad; fifthly, such agreement on a ruling must come from among qualified Muslim jurists of a particular era even though future jurists of subsequent eras may have a different opinion; sixthly, the agreement must occur on a rule of Islamic law which has not been expressly covered in the primary sources; and, seventhly, the qualified Muslim jurists should have relied on a clear evidence (*sanad*) for arriving at their unanimous agreement.[78] **1.40**

For *ijmāʿ* to be valid, it must have supporting evidence from the primary sources of Islamic law. An example of *ijmāʿ* that is based on the Qurʾān which has some implications on the marriage contract in Islamic law is the prohibition of a marriage contract with one's grandmother or granddaughter. Even though there is no clear prohibition on concluding a marriage contract with one's grandmother or granddaughter, Muslim jurists unanimously agree that such a contract should be proscribed on the basis of Qurʾān 4:23: 'Prohibited to you (for marriage) are your mothers, daughters'. Therefore, the prohibition in the verse has been interpreted unanimously by Muslim scholars to consider **1.41**

[76] The basis of *ijmāʿ* is contained in Qurʾān 4:59 which states: 'O you who have believed, obey Allah and obey the Messenger and those in authority among you. And if you disagree over anything, refer it to Allah and the Messenger, if you should believe in Allah and the Last Day. That is the best [way] and best in result.' The phrase 'those in authority among you'—or *uli al-amr*—has been interpreted to mean Muslim scholars of any particular time or place. Therefore, in the case of a unanimous agreement among them, such Islamic law rule will be regarded as *ijmāʿ* and will have the force of law.

[77] Al-Amidi, Sayf al-Din, al-Ihkam fi Usul al-Ahkam (Dar al-Samiʾi, 2003) Vol. 1, p. 262.

[78] Al-Zarkashi, Muhammad ibn Bahadur, Al-Bahr al-Muhit fi Usul al-Fiqh (Dar al-Kutubi, 1994) Vol. 6, pp. 410–16.

'mother' as a generic term that implies an origin which could extend up to one's grandmother. On the other hand, the word 'daughter' represents a branch and should be extended to one's granddaughter and so on.

1.42 Sunnah can also form the basis of *ijmāʿ*. For example, inheritance in Islamic contract law is a unilateral contract which does not require acceptance as it operates automatically by operation of law in transferring assets from a deceased Muslim to his or her legal heirs.[79] After the demise of the Prophet, a grandmother approached the then Caliph Abu Bakr and asked him about her entitlement to inheritance. He replied: 'There is nothing for you in the Book of Allah and there is nothing for you in the Sunnah of the Messenger of Allah. So, return until I ask the people (about it).' So the Caliph asked the people and Al-Mughirah bin Shu'bah said: 'I was present when the Messenger of Allah gave her (case of a grandmother) a sixth.' So the Caliph said: 'Was anyone else with you?' Muhammad bin Maslamah stood to say the same as Al-Mughirah bin Shu'bah had said. So Abu Bakr implemented that for her. Then the other grandmother came to 'Umar bin Al-Khattab to ask him about her inheritance. He said: 'There is nothing in the Book of Allah for you, but there is that sixth. So if the two of you are together then it is for both of you, and whichever of you remains), then it is for her.'[80]

4.2.2 *Qiyās*

1.43 When new issues emerge, which is a common occurrence in the modern financial system where structured products are being engineered, one could always draw some parallels between specific conduct or practices regulated in the primary sources and the new issue. Once this is established, scholars will draw inferences from the old case and apply the same ruling to the new case. Such a thought process is what is known as analogical deduction or *qiyās*.[81] In Islamic jurisprudence, *qiyās* is defined as the thought process of extending a Sharīʿah rule from an original case (*'aṣl*) to a new case (*far'*) where it is established that the new case has the same effective cause (*ʿilla*) as the old case.[82] In this regard, the ruling in the old case is applied to the new case which was not hitherto regulated by the law since both cases have a common effective cause. The result of the well-guided thought process is a ruling (*ḥukm*) which is applied to the new case.

1.44 In Islamic contract law, *qiyās* has been applied to different aspects to arrive at new rulings on issues that were not previously regulated by law. From the perspective of a civil contract, only the Hanafi school of jurisprudence allows a mature woman to conclude a marriage contract without the need for a guardian. The basis of this ruling is the inference made from the analogy to a ruling in the Qur'ān which permits both males and females with requisite legal capacity to conclude a business transaction.[83] In other words,

[79] Ibid.
[80] Abu 'Isa al-Tirmdhi, Sunan al-Tirmdhi (Mustafa al-Babi al-Halabi, 1975) p. 210; Abu Daud, Sunan Abu Daud (al Maktabah al-'Asriyyah) p. 2894; and *Ḥadīth* No. 2724, see Ibn Majah, Sunan Ibn Majah (Dar al-Risalah al-'Alamiyyah, 2009) Vol. 4, pp. 26–27. Imam al-Tirmidhi evaluated this *ḥadīth* as hassan sahih.
[81] Mohammad Hashim Kamali, Principles of Islamic Jurisprudence (Islamic Texts Society, 1991) p. 11.
[82] Ibid, pp. 264–70.
[83] See Qur'ān 4:6.

if a woman is permitted to enter into a contract of sale, then by analogy she should be competent to conclude a marriage contract on her own behalf without the need for a guardian. Nevertheless, other Muslim jurists have disagreed with the Hanafi school on this point, as they effectively distinguished between a marriage contract and business transactions where the former involves the family institution and to some extent the community, while the latter is a personal matter.[84]

There are various types of *qiyās* and some of them, based on the classification of the Shafi'i jurists, have shaped the nature of Islamic contract law. The classification, which is premised on whether the *qiyās'* effective cause is strong or weak comprises: *qiyās al-awlā* (analogy of the superior), *qiyās al-musāwi* (analogy of equals), and *qiyās al-adnā* (analogy of the analogy). In Islamic contract law, an example of analogy of equals is seen in the effective cause of Qur'ān 4:2 which is the prohibition on consuming the property of orphans. By extension, this analogy could be extended to all other forms of destruction, mismanagement, embezzlement, or even corruption, as all these dispositions will lead to the loss of property and hence will be forbidden under the law. Therefore, any contract that purportedly includes any term or condition that could lead to consuming the property of the other party will be considered invalid, subject to other principles underpinning Islamic contract law. **1.45**

Another example of *qiyās*, but in this case the analogy of the inferior, is seen in the *ribā* rules applicable to certain commodities. Islamic contract law prohibits the exchange of wheat and five other commodities unless the exchange is immediate, and the amounts are equal.[85] Muslim jurists have extended this rule to apples by analogy, while relying on the principle that both wheat and apples are edible and measurable accordingly. Despite the position of both Shafi'i and Hanafi jurists, other scholars have opined that the effective cause is quite weak in this example since apples are not a staple food. **1.46**

4.2.3 *Istiḥsān*

In any situation, circumstance, or contract that is not expressly regulated by law, the Muslim jurists may review such from the perspective of justice, fairness, and equity. This sometimes leads to the thought process of making an exception to the general rule on specific issues if the Muslim jurists are convinced beyond the slightest doubt that such a ruling would better serve justice and equity. The word *istiḥsān* simply means anything the jurists consider to be good as a form of preferential reasoning for a particular case. The Hanbali jurists Ibn Taymiyyah and Ibn Qudamah define *istiḥsān* as the thought process involving the abandonment of a legal ruling and preference for another which could be considered better based on general principles established in **1.47**

[84] Shaban, Zaki al-Din, and Muhammad al-Said Ali Abd, Usul al-fiqh al-Islami (Matbaat Dar al-Ta'lif, 1980) p. 134.

[85] The full *ḥadīth* states: 'Ubadah bin Al-Samit said: The Messenger of Allah said: "Gold for gold, of equal measure; silver for silver, of equal measure; salt for salt, dates for dates, wheat for wheat, barley for barley, like for like. Whoever gives more or takes more has engaged in *ribā*." ' *Ḥadīth* No. 4564, see Al-Nasa'i, *Sunan an-Nasa'i* (Al-Maktabah al-Tijariyyah al-Kubra, 1930) Vol. 7, p. 276).

the Qur'ān, Sunnah, or *ijmā'*.[86] A Hanafi jurist, Imam al-Karkhi, defines *istiḥsān* as a departure from existing legal precedents which involves taking decisions in a certain case that is different from a previous ruling made for a similar case due to a stronger reason in the present circumstances.[87]

1.48 Muslim jurists from the Hanafi school developed this principle to remove the rigidity in a point of law, as society continues to evolve, and new issues emerge that may require some concessions. The justification provided for this glaring departure from established law is found in both the Qur'ān and Sunnah.[88] Nevertheless, Muslim jurists have presented different opinions on the utilitarian value of *istiḥsān* as a source of Islamic law. While the majority of Muslim jurists believe that *istiḥsān* should be considered a valid source of Islamic law, a minority view—the Shafi'i school—disagree with this position and hold that *istiḥsān* should not be accorded the position of a source of Islamic law to avoid arbitrariness in rule-making.[89]

1.49 Examples of *istiḥsān* as a basis for Islamic contract law are seen in some contracts developed by Muslim jurists, which now are used in the Islamic financial services industry for structuring products. For the contract of hire (*ijāra*), even though there is no valuable consideration (both usufruct and wages) at the time of hire, this contract is validated based on analogy from the *ḥadīth* 'Give the labourer his wage before his sweat dries up',[90] which invariably allows the payment of the wages as well as the services provided to be deferred—a feature which cannot be adopted in other forms of contract. There cannot be double deferment of valuable consideration on both sides of the table, as this will lead to uncertainty and possibly result in future disputes. However, on the basis of *istiḥsān*, a contract of hire is valid in Islamic law as an exception to the general rule.[91]

1.50 Another example often quoted in Islamic jurisprudence is a forward sale contract (*bay' al-salam*). Unlike the conventional forward contract where payment and delivery of goods are deferred to a mutually agreed future date, Islamic contract law requires payment to be made in full in advance of delivery. In a *salam* contract, the object of the contract (*maḥal al-'aqd*), which is the commodity, does not exist at the time the parties conclude the contract. Ordinarily, such a contract will be prohibited since the object of contract is not in existence, as clearly stated in a *ḥadīth*: 'Do not sell what is not with you.'[92] However, beyond this general principle established in the *ḥadīth*,

[86] Ibn Qudamah, Raudat al-Nazir Wa Jannat al-Manazir (Muassat al-Rayyan, 2002) Vol. 1, p. 473.

[87] Abu al-Husain al-Basri, Kitab al-Mu'tamad fi Usul al-Fiqh (Al-Ma'had al-'Ilmi al-Faransi li al-Dirasat al-'Arabiyyah, 1964) Vol. 2, p. 840.

[88] For instance, Qur'ān 39:18 states: 'Who listen to speech and follow the best of it. Those are the ones Allah has guided, and those are people of understanding.' Similarly, Qur'ān 39:55 provides: 'And follow the best of what was revealed to you from your Lord [i.e., the Qur'ān] before the punishment comes upon you suddenly while you do not perceive.' In the Sunnah, Hanafi jurists have relied on the *ḥadīth*: 'What is considered good by the Muslims is also good in the eyes of God.' See Al-Amidi, al-Ihkam fi usul al-Ahkam (1914) Vol. 4, p. 214.

[89] Al-Shirazi, Abu Ishaq, Al-Luma' fi Usul al-Fiqh (Dar al-Kutub al-'Ilmiyyah, 2003) p. 121; Muhammad Salam Madkur, Madkhal al-Fiqh al-Islami (al-Dar al-Qawmiyyah, 1964) p. 84.

[90] *Ḥadīth* No. 2443. See Ibn Majah (n 80) Vol. 5, p. 510.

[91] Abu Talib Mohammad Monawer and Akhtarzaite Abdul Aziz, 'Dispute Over the Legality of Al-'ijārah Al-Mauṣūfah fi al-Dhimmah: A Survey of Fiqhi Opinions' (2015) 7(1) International Journal of Islamic Finance 59.

[92] *Ḥadīth* No. 2187, see Ibn Majah (n 80) Vol. 3, p. 308; *Ḥadīth* No. 4613, see Al-Nasa'i (n 85) Vol. 7, p. 289.

another *ḥadīth* provides an exception which Muslim jurists have relied on to validate a *salam* contract: 'Whoever concludes a *salam* (contract), let him do so over a specified measure, specified weight, and a specified period of time.'[93] Similarly, in a manufacturing contract (*istiṣnāʿa*), the object of contract is not present at the time of concluding the contract and hence should ordinarily be prohibited. However, from the perspective of *ijmāʿ*, no Muslim jurist has declared the contract prohibited in view of the fact that it has been practised in the Muslim community for centuries.

There is also a relationship between *istiḥsān* and the public interest in *muzāraʿa* (agricultural land tenancy contract).[94] In this case, the parties are the landowner and the farmer. The Hanafi jurists opine that the death of both contracting parties in a *muzāraʿa* (sharecropping) contract leads to an automatic termination of the contract. However, to mitigate the potential hardship the law may lead to if applied as it is, the Hanafi jurists have introduced an exception. The principle introduced in the exception provides that, in the event of the death of the landowner where the crops cultivated are yet to be ready for harvest, the contract will remain valid until the crops are ripe. This exception was introduced to ensure that the interest of the farmer is protected in the overall interest of the economy.[95] One final example of the application of *istiḥsān* is seen in a mortgage contract involving the property of a minor. Hanafi jurists allow the guardian of a minor to deposit the minor's property for safekeeping, but he or she is not allowed to pledge the property as a security for his or her own debt.[96] **1.51**

4.2.4 *ʿUrf*

One major secondary source of contract law is *ʿurf*, often interpreted as custom.[97] The word *ʿurf* is considered to indicate common practices in a given society, whether such practices are good or bad.[98] In essence, *ʿurf* is an established practice among the people which can be inferred from their statements, actions, or even inaction.[99] From the perspective of Islamic commercial law, *ʿurf* could be considered as all customary trade practices that do not contradict any rule established in the primary sources of Islamic law.[100] Therefore, what is regarded as *lex mercatoria*[101] in English law could be considered *ʿurf* provided such law merchant does not contradict or violate any established principle in the Qur'ān and Sunnah.[102] Numerous trade practices have been developed **1.52**

[93] *Ḥadīth* No. 2240, see Al-Bukhari, Al-Jami' al-Sahih (n 64) Vol. 2, p. 124.
[94] Al-Zuhaili (n 9) Vol. 6, p. 4701.
[95] Ibid.
[96] Mudasra Sabreen, 'Guardianship of Property in Islamic Law' (2021) 44(1) Hamdard Islamicus 129–33.
[97] Al-Zubaidi Mohammad Bin Mohammad Bin 'Abdu Al-Razzak, Taj al-'Arus min fawdhir al-Qamus (Wizarat al-I'lam, 1987) Vol. 16, p. 135.
[98] Ibn Manzur (n 11) Vol. 9, pp. 236–43.
[99] Khallaf (n 74) p. 89.
[100] Mohammad Akram Laldin, Introduction to Shariah and Islamic Jurisprudence (CERT, 2006) p. 120. See also Khallaf (n 74) p. 86.
[101] For a comprehensive discussion of this principle, see generally Orsolya Toth, The Lex Mercatoria in Theory and Practice (Oxford University Press, 2017).
[102] Hassan S. Khalilieh, 'The Lex Mercatoria Maritima: An Abridgement of the Jurisprudential Principles of the Early Islamic Maritime Qirad' (2020) 40(2) Comparative Studies of South Asia, Africa and the Middle East 266–76.

over the centuries and have eventually found their way into Islamic commercial law and as such have been adopted as part of the acceptable practices in Islamic contract law. One very recent example of *'urf* in Islamic contract law can be seen in the rules governing e-commerce and contracts concluded virtually through electronic means. As discussed above, electronic contracts are generally acceptable under Islamic law provided they are free from any prohibited element.

1.53 For any trade practice or even contractual disposition to be acceptable as part of the Islamic law of contract, such practice must fulfil the following conditions: first, the customary trade practice must be a common and recurrent phenomenon acceptable to every reasonable person;[103] secondly, the customary trade practice or contractual disposition must be, in practice, at the time of concluding the contract, as customary practices that were introduced or adopted after the contract is finalized will not be given any effect;[104] thirdly, the contractual disposition or customary trade practice must not violate any textual evidence (*naṣṣ*) or a definitive principle of law;[105] and, fourthly, custom cannot trump clear contractual stipulation, so parties can contractually derogate from a customary trade practice but as such must fulfil the requirement of the third condition mentioned earlier.[106] This reflects the inherent feature of dynamism in Islamic law, which allows for adaptation to the prevailing trade practices of any time or place.

4.3 Positive Law: A Tertiary Source?

1.54 The introduction of codified legislation in modern states, which has its historical basis in legal positivism, has introduced a new dimension to the construction of contract law from the Islamic perspective. A few Muslim majority countries such as Malaysia have grappled with the continuous tension between English common law and Islamic law in commercial transactions.[107] This has led to some sort of harmonization of laws in financial matters which has, to a large extent, shaped modern Islamic contract law, particularly in the Islamic financial services industry.[108] One major focus of the harmonization

[103] Al-Sabuni, 'Abdul Rahman, al-Madkhal al-Fiqhi wa—Tarikh al—Tashri' al-Islami (Maktabah Wahbah, 1982) pp. 139–40.

[104] Al-Jamal Mohammad Mahmud Muhammad, Tatbiqat al-'urf (Dar al-Fikr al-Jami'i, 2008) p. 47.

[105] Abu Zahrah, Usul al-Fiqh (Dar al-Fikri al-'Arabi, 1997) p. 127.

[106] Al-Shaqar 'Umar Sulaiman, *'Al-'urf baina al-Fiqh wa al-Qanun'*. Majallat Majm al-Fiqh al-Islami (International Islamic Fiqh Academy, 1988) Vol. 4, p. 3239.

[107] Some of the cases from the Malaysian courts where conflicts of jurisdictions between Islamic law and the English common law (often referred to as civil law in Malaysia) include *Bank Islam Malaysia Bhd v Adnan Bin Omar* Civil Suit No. S3-22-101-91(where the court held that the civil court has the exclusive jurisdiction to hear and determine Islamic financial disputes and Islamic commercial cases); *Mohd Alias Ibrahim v RHB Bank Berhad and another* [2011] 4 CLJ 654 (where the court emphasized that though Islamic law in Malaysia falls within the jurisdiction of the Sharī'ah Courts, when Islamic finance cases are brought before the court, they fall under the jurisdiction of the civil courts); and *Bank Kerjasama Rakyat Malaysia Bhd v EMCEEE Corporation Sdh Bhd* [2003] 1 CLJ 625 (where the court held that civil law applies to Islamic banking disputes).

[108] For the full report on the project, see Bank Negara Malaysia, Islamic Finance: Law Harmonisation Committee Report 2013 (Bank Negara Malaysia, 2013). As detailed in the report, the objectives of the Law Harmonisation Committee are:

- To position Malaysia as the reference law for international Islamic finance transactions;

of laws project was Islamic contract law where it was suggested that such contracts should be structured in a way that ensures certainty and enforceability under the law. This required some amendment to applicable legislation which was preceded by an in-depth analysis of non-Islamic elements in laws applicable to Islamic finance contracts. The ultimate result is a new set of laws and practices that do not contradict Islamic law principles. Legislative changes were made to ensure the enforceability of Islamic contracts while ensuring the feasibility of executing such contracts under positive legislation. The methodology adopted in the process involved both parliamentary legislation and *ijtihād* (legal reasoning).[109] While this approach could be considered as one of the ways of ascertaining valid customary law practices in the form of *'urf*, one might wonder whether the result of the process—positive legislation—could be regarded as a tertiary source of Islamic contract law.

5. An Overview of the Essential Elements of a Valid Contract

For a contract to be valid, there are certain requirements that must be fulfilled under Islamic law. These are conditions that must be met to have a valid contract in effect. Muslim jurists have expressed different views on the essential elements of a valid contract, particularly in Islamic commercial law.[110] The view of the majority of Muslim jurists is that there are four essential elements of a contract, namely, the form, the seller, the buyer, and the subject matter of the contract.[111] It is however interesting to note that the Hanafi school opines that the form or *ṣigha* is the only element of a valid contract. So, once there is the offer (*'ijāb*) and acceptance (*qabūl*) from both parties, the contract stands valid.[112] The implication of this singular element requirement for the validity of a contract intuitively implies the existence of other sub-elements, since an offer and a corresponding acceptance will only be made in relation to a particular subject matter. In addition, the offer and acceptance come from the seller and buyer who are the parties to the contract. The element of consent (*riḍā*) which is sometimes considered as a stand-alone requirement for the validity of a contract comes from a freely made offer and acceptance. **1.55**

- To achieve certainty and enforceability in the Malaysian law in regard to Islamic finance contracts; and
- For Malaysian laws to be the law of choice and Malaysian dispute resolution institutions as the forum for settlement of disputes for cross border Islamic financial transactions as part of creating a conducive legal system for Islamic finance industry.

[109] Kamali, Mohammad Hashim, 'Sharīah and Civil Law: Towards a Methodology of Harmonization' (2007) 14(3) Islamic Law and Society 391–420.

[110] Detailed analyses of each of the fundamental elements are provided in other chapters. This chapter only provides a general overview which introduces the general theories, principles, and rules.

[111] Al-Zuhaili (n 9) Vol. 5, p. 3309.

[112] Al-Marghinani, 'Ali bin Abu bakar, Al-Hidaya fi Sharh Bidayat al-Mubtadi (Dar Ihya al-Turath al-'Arabi, n.d.) Vol. 3, p. 23.

1.56 The Maliki jurists consider *ṣigha* as the first element of a valid contract which is executed through a freely made *'ijāb* and *qabūl* representing another fundamental element—consent.[113] In a similar vein, the Shafi'i and Hanbali jurists also consider *ṣigha* as the first element of a valid contract, which also comprises *'ijāb* and *qabūl*.[114]

5.1 Form of Contract (*ṣigha*)

1.57 From the views of all four schools of Islamic jurisprudence, the most essential element required for the validity of a contract is the form itself, which comprises the expression of the offer and a corresponding acceptance.[115] The form expresses the consent from both parties and represents the main instrument that gives validity to the contract. Therefore, the form of contract is everything that points to the consent of both parties. It involves the parties' intention to create legal relations voluntarily. The expression could be in form of speech, writing, a sign, an actual exchange, or any other disposition that represents consent.[116] It could also be ascertained through gestures or conduct, such as taking a commodity or giving it out without any verbal expression, for example buying a commodity whose price is known and taking it from the seller and in exchange giving the seller the price of it, which enables the buyer to take full possession.[117]

1.58 For a valid form of contract, it is required that the contract fulfil a number of conditions. First, the expression of the offer and acceptance should be clear and understandable by both parties. Both parties must fully understand the implication of their expressions and their respective obligations as consequences of such expressions. Parties are allowed to convey this in any way acceptable in the society and this could be by mere words, conduct, or even implied dispositions. The law gives effect to meanings and intentions in contracts rather than words and phrases. Secondly, the acceptance should correspond to the offer in perfect conformity which could be implied or expressed to conclude the contract. The offer and acceptance must conform to each other and should relate to the subject matter of the contract. In corresponding to the offer, the acceptance should be executed in accordance with the terms and conditions of the contract in an absolute and unconditional manner. Thirdly, it is required that offer and

[113] Al-Kasani, Abu Bakar, Badai al-Sanai (Dar al-Kutub al'Ilmiyyah, 2003) Vol. 5, p. 133.

[114] Imam Abu Zakariyya Al-Nawwawi, Rawdat ul-talibin wa umdat ul muftin (Al-Maktab al-Islami, 1991) Vol. 3, p. 338. See also Ibn Qudamah, al-Mughni (n 72) Vol. 3, 480.

[115] A detailed discussion on the form of contract is provided in Chapter 2.

[116] This requirement in Islamic jurisprudence has been adopted in modern civil codes. For instance, Art. 65 of the Qatar Civil Code regarding the requirement for consent for the validity of a contract states:

1. Will may be expressed verbally, in writing, a commonly used sign, an actual interchange indicating consent or by adopting any other attitude in respect of the connotation or intended fact the conditions of the situation do not admit of doubting.
2. Will may be also expressed implicitly unless the law, the agreement or the nature of the transaction does not require that such expression be explicit.

See Law No. (22) of 2004 Promulgating the Civil Code.

[117] Al-Juzairi, 'Abd Al-Rahman, Kitab al-Fiqh 'ala al-Madhahib al-Arba'ah (Dar al-Kutub al-'Ilmiyyah, 2003) Vol. 2, p. 142.

acceptance be made in immediate contemporaneity to ensure continuity in the chain. This emphasizes the significance of the contract session where the two contracting parties are present or where the absent party is aware of the offer and effectively communicates his or her acceptance.

5.2 Parties (*ʿāqidān*)

In Islamic contract law, there is a mandatory minimum requirement of two parties in any contractual arrangement.[118] The exception to this rule is a unilateral contract which takes the form of a deed such as a deed of gift (*hiba*). A unilateral promise cannot be regarded as a contract; there must be the presence of a minimum of two parties effecting a contract through the prescribed form. In a contract of sale, the parties are usually the buyer and the seller, where one transfers the ownership of the subject matter of the contract to the other party who effectively takes the possession. Such parties are required to have full legal capacity to conclude such contracts. The requirement of full legal capacity comprises sanity and maturity; hence, a child or an insane person cannot validly be considered as a party to a contract since they might not be able to appreciate the nature of the transaction and fully understand the terms and conditions of the contract. This restriction is premised on the need to protect such categories of people as part of the overall public intertest as they may not be able to distinguish between benefit or harm inherent in the contractual terms. Nevertheless, a child or an insane person can still enter a contract through an agent or guardian who concludes the contract on their behalf. **1.59**

5.3 Subject Matter of Contract (*maʿqud ʿalaihi*)

For a contract to be valid, there must be the subject matter (*maʿqud ʿalaihi*) of the contract or the object (*mabīʿ*) itself.[119] Whatever is exchanged in the contract as valuable consideration is considered the object or subject matter of the contract. This is similar to the common law concept of consideration in contract law.[120] However, in Islamic contract law, the consideration has to be lawful. Therefore, for the subject matter to be valid, it must fulfil five main conditions. Failure to fulfil the conditions will either lead to the contract being declared void *ab initio* or voidable at the instance of a party. Most of the conditions are stipulated to avoid speculative tendencies and terms (*gharar*) in the contract. **1.60**

[118] A detailed discussion on the parties to a contract is provided in Chapter 3.

[119] A detailed discussion on the subject matter of contract is provided in Chapter 5.

[120] A consideration under the English common law involves mutual promises between contracting parties where each promise is considered a sufficient consideration for the performance of the contract. The promises made must have some value appreciated by the parties making the promises. See Hugh Beale, Chitty on Contracts: General Principles (31st edn, Sweet & Maxwell, 2012) Vol. 1, para 3–004.

1.61 First, the subject matter must be *in existence* or should be capable of being in existence at a future date when the parties are concluding the contract. Subject to certain exceptions such as *salam* contract and *istiṣnāʿa* contract, a person cannot sell what he does not possess or own to avoid any future uncertainty that could spin out of control and lead to disputes between the contracting parties.[121] Failure to fulfil this condition will make the contract void. Secondly, the subject matter must be *capable of being delivered* to the buyer at the time the parties conclude the contract. Parties are not allowed to contract on straying animals, birds in the air, or even fish in the water since there could be the possibility of losing the subject matter before delivery.[122] Thirdly, the subject matter must be *specific and clearly known* to the contracting parties.[123] Fourthly, the subject matter of the contract *must be recognized as a legitimate asset* in Islamic law which is capable of being possessed.[124] In addition, any commodity that belongs to the public in its natural state cannot be a legitimate asset upon which parties can conclude a contract until it is domesticated and personalized through some concerted efforts. Fifthly, the subject matter must be *clean and pure* based on the requirements of Islamic law.[125] The majority of Muslim jurists hold that the subject matter must be clean and pure,[126] so items such as wine, blood, pork, and deceased bodies cannot be sold or constitute the subject matter of any contract.[127] It is worth noting that Hanafi and Zahiri jurists permit the selling of impurities on the condition that such a sale is not specifically prohibited by primary sources and it brings benefit to the people.[128]

[121] Al-Zuhaili (n 9) Vol. 5, p. 349.
[122] Ibid, Vol. 5, p. 349.
[123] Ibid, Vol. 5, p. 302.
[124] Al-Zarqa, al-Madkhal (n 13) Vol. 1, p. 426.
[125] Al-Zuhaili (n 9) Vol. 5, p. 343.
[126] Ibid.
[127] Ibid.
[128] Ibid.

2
Offer and Acceptance

1. Introduction

2.01 The foundations for a valid contract in Islamic law (*arkān*) consist of a contractual expression (*ṣīgha*), the existence of at least two contracting parties, and a valid subject matter.[1] This contractual expression is reflected in an exchange of offer (*ījāb*) and acceptance (*qabūl*) and its significance is reflected in subsequent codifications of Islamic contract law. For instance, the *Majalla* stipulates that a contract 'is composed of the combination of offer and acceptance'[2] and contracting entails 'the connection of an offer with an acceptance in a lawful manner which marks its effect on the subject of that connection'.[3] Similarly, the Kuwait Civil Code (1980) declares that a contract 'is the connection of an offer with an acceptance in view of producing an effect organised by law'.[4] In the Jordanian Civil Code, the contract is 'a connection and concurrence of an offer emanating from one of the contracting parties with an acceptance of the other party in a manner which affects the object of the contract and results in obligating each of the contracting parties with what was undertaken towards the other'.[5] It is clear therefore that the foundational elements of offer and acceptance in the Western legal tradition carry the same value in the Islamic legal tradition.

2. Types of *Ījāb* and *Qabūl*

2.02 Kāsānī and Ibn Qudāma contend that a contract is fundamentally an agreement expressed through words or actions[6] with clear evidence of *ījāb* and *qabūl*. In this manner, there are two modes for the expression of offer and acceptance. The first is through

[1] Kamāl al-Dīn Ibn Muḥammad ibn al-Humām, Fat'h al-Qadīr li Sharḥ al-Hidāya (Dār al-Fikr, n.d.) Vol. 3, p. 246; 'Abdul Karīm Al-Rāfī, Fatḥ al- 'Azīz fī Sharḥ al Wajīz (Dār al-Fikr, n.d.) Vol. 8, p. 394; Abū Ḥāmid Muḥammad ibn Muḥammad Al-Ghāzalī, Al-Wajīz fī al-Fiqh al-Shāfi'ī (Dār al abī Arqm bin al-Arqm, n.d.) Vol. 1, p. 273, Vol. 8, p. 396. *Majalla*, Art. 103.

[2] *Majalla*, Art. 103.

[3] *Majalla*, Art. 104.

[4] Kuwait Civil Code (1980) Art. 31.

[5] Jordan Civil Code (1976) Art. 87.

[6] Abū Bakr ibn Mas'ūd Al-Kāsānī, Badā'i' al-Ṣanā'i' fī Tartīb al-Sharā'i' (Dār al-Kutub al-'Ilmiyyah, 1986) Vol. 5, p. 133; Muwaffaq al-Din Abū Muḥammad 'Abd Allāh ibn Aḥmad ibn Muḥammad ibn Qudāma, Al-Mughnī (Maktabat al-Qāhira, 1968) Vol. 3, p. 560.

sigha qawliya (by means of words), whereas the second is *al-dalālāt al-ḥāliyya* (that which is understood from a situation or conduct), that is, *mu'āṭāt*.[7]

2.03 Anything which implies the consent of the parties may constitute *ījāb* and *qabūl*, such as a statement in writing (post, etc.), *ishāra* (gesture or indication), and *mu'āṭāt* from both or one of the parties. If such consent is obtained through *mu'āṭāt*—for instance, the buyer receives the *mabī'* and the seller his requested fee without any conversation or *ishāra*—the sale is concluded when consideration comes into the possession of the parties even if the subject matter is not an expensive item. *Mu'āṭāt* also occurs by the consumption of the subject matter. If *mu'āṭāt* indicates consent of the parties, Aḥmad bin Ḥanbal allows this as a means of conclusion of the contract. Abū Ḥanīfa allows conclusion only in respect of cheap subject matter and requires the existence of statements for agreements concerning expensive items (assuming that the contract is not suspended). Shafi'i does not allow *mu'āṭāt* at all and argues that the contract is concluded only through statements. The contract of sale is concluded if the *ījāb* or *mu'āṭāt* commences from either the buyer or seller.[8]

2.1 Express *Ījāb* and *Qabūl*

2.04 An express *ījāb* and *qabūl* is made through words—written or spoken[9]—that are normally employed in the locality where the contract is made.[10] As an instance of express *ījāb* and *qabūl*, when the Prophet was migrating, Abū Bakar made an offer to him as follows: 'take one of these two she-camels of mine' and the Prophet responded: 'with payment'.[11] Written express offers are permissible on the basis of the following *āya*: 'You who believe, when you transact a debt payable at a specified time, put it in writing . . .'[12]

2.1.1 The Concept of *Ījāb* and *Qabūl*

2.05 *Ījāb* is the first declaration or statement from a contracting party with which it intends to elicit and receive an acceptance, subject to an option for the offeree to accept it or reject it. Acceptance is the second or later statement from the second contracting party in response to *ījāb*.[13] In other words, in the sale contract, *ījāb* is the first statement, whether from seller or purchaser, and *qabūl* is the second statement, whether from seller or purchaser.[14] There is also an opinion that *ījāb* in a sale contract originates from

[7] Abdul Azīz Muḥammad Salmān, Al As'ila wal Ajwiba al-Fiqhiyya (n.p., 1988) Vol. 7, pp. 7–9; Zain alDīn Ibn Nujaim (Al-Nasafī), Al-Baḥr al-Rā'iq Sharḥ Kanz al-Daqā'iq (Dār al Kutub al 'Ilmiyya, 1997) Vol. 5, p. 431.

[8] Muḥammad ibn Aḥmad ibn 'Arfa, Al-Dusūqī, Ḥāshiyat al-Dusūqī 'alā al-Sharḥ al-Kabīr (Dār al-Fikr, n.d.) Vol. 2, p. 3.

[9] *Majalla*, Arts 173, 175.

[10] *Majalla*, Art. 168.

[11] Bukhārī, *Ḥadīth* 245.

[12] Al Baqara, 2:282.

[13] 'Abd Al-Raḥmān bin Sulaimān, Majma' al Anhur li al-Kalyūlī fī Sharḥ Multaqa al-Abḥur li al Ḥalabi wa ma' al Dur al-Muntaqā fi Sharḥ al-Multaqā (Dār al Kutub al 'Ilimiyya, 1998) Vol. 3, p. 5; Ibn 'Ābidīn, Radd al-Mu*ḥ*tār 'alā al-Durr al-Mukhtār (Dār al-Fikr, 1992) Vol. 7, p. 18; Al-Nasafī (n 7) Vol. 5, p. 440.

[14] Burhān al-Dīn al-Marghīnānī, Al-Hidāya fi Sharḥ Bidāyat al-Mubtadī fi Fiqh al-Ḥanafī (Makabat wa maṭba'at 'Ali Sibhi, n.d.) Vol. 5, p. 3; *Majalla*, Arts 101, 104.

the seller and *qabūl* from the purchaser[15] and that moreover *qabūl* preceding the *ījāb* is invalid.[16] In Hanbali tradition, there is an opinion that when *qabūl* precedes *ījāb*, no contract is created.[17] However, the Shafi'i tradition does not follow this approach.[18] More specifically, it is acceptable that *qabūl* precedes *ījāb* in the past positive tense, save if the *qabūl* preceding the *ījāb* is in an imperative sentence; in this case, the Malikis and Shaf'is allow it, whereas Abū Ḥanīfa does not.[19]

2.1.2 Form of *Ījāb* and *Qabūl*

The contract is normally concluded with the *ījāb* and *qabūl* even if they are expressed **2.06**
in the past, present, future, or imperative tense because significance is given to the meaning implied by the parties from their statements.[20] In this regard, Al-Kāsānī contends that offer and acceptance may be in the past tense as well as the present. In the past tense, the seller and buyer may say: 'I sold' or 'I purchased' respectively and with this, the elements of *ṣīgha* are satisfied. This is so because, despite being expressed in past terms, linguists and the jurists have customarily taken it as the *ṣīgha* of the present tense. The same is also true where the seller says: 'I have given this commodity for such amount' or 'this is yours for such amount' and the purchaser in response says: 'I accepted' or 'I have taken it' or 'I am pleased or content'. Such responses suffice for *ṣīgha* because each of these statements responds to the subject matter of the offer or acceptance respectively and importance is given to meaning and intention rather than apparent form. Similarly, offer and acceptance in the present tense are also valid. It is acceptable even if either *ījāb* or *qabūl* are expressed in the past tense and the other in the future tense with an intention to create the contract.

Al-Kāsānī argues that the contract is not concluded with statements in future or inter- **2.07**
rogative form, such as where the purchaser asks: 'Have you sold me this commodity for such amount?' and the seller says in response: 'I have sold'. Rather, the contract will be concluded only if the purchaser then says: 'I have purchased this commodity'. However, Shafi'i and Malikis suggest that the contract is concluded without such third statement from the purchaser. *Ṣīgha* in *amr* (imperative) is also sufficient to create the contract because the indication of the imperative tense on the contract is stronger than *muḍāri'* (present and future tenses). However, the same is also true with the types of imperative statements discussed above in respect of the interrogative form; that is, when the seller says: 'purchase this commodity from me for such amount' and the purchaser

[15] 'Alī bin Muḥammad ibn Khalaf, Kāfiyat al-Ṭālib al-Rabbānī al-Risālat ibn abī Zaid al-Qairwānī (Maṭba' al Madanī, 2002) p. 3.
[16] Ibn Mufleḥ, Al Nakt wa al-Fawā'id (Maktaba al M'ārif Riyāḍ, 1983) Vol. 1, p. 260.
[17] Qāḍī Abī Ya'lā al Baghdādī, Al Jāmi' al- Ṣaghīr fi al-Fiqh 'alā Madhhab al-Imām Aḥmad bin Ḥanbal (Dār Aṭlas li Inshār wa al-Taqḍi', 2000) p. 127.
[18] Al-Maghrabī, Mawahab al Jalīil li Sharḥ Mukhtaṣar Khalīl (Dār 'Ālam al Kutub, n.d.) Vol. 6, p. 14; Shahāb al-Din Aḥmad ibn Lu'lu Ibn al-Naqīb al-Rūmī al-Miṣrī, 'Umdat al-Sālik wa' Uddat al-Nāsik (Sha'ūn al-Dīniyya, 1982) Vol. 1, p. 150; Yaḥya ibn Sharaf al-Nawawī, Kitāb Al-Majmū' Sharḥ al-Muhadhdhab li Shīzarī (Dār al-Fikr, n.d.) Vol. 9, pp. 195, 201.
[19] Al-Mughnī (n 6) Vol. 6, p. 397.
[20] Al-Nasafī (n 7) Vol. 5, p. 443.

says: 'I have purchased'. In this case the contract is not concluded according to Al-Kāsānī, who argues that it will be concluded only after the seller says: 'I have sold'. Again, Shafi'i argues that for the conclusion of a contract the third statement from the seller is not required. The Shaf'is' rationale is that the interrogative or imperative statement is a mere (half) part of the contract. They contend that a statement from a person: 'marry your daughter with me' that is met with the response: 'I have married my daughter' suffices to create a marriage contract. As a consequence, it is argued that if this is indeed so, then why is a statement in the sale contract not considered a mere part (half), composed of two parts—*ījāb* and *qabūl.*

2.08 Hanafis, on the other hand, treat the imperative form of the *ījāb* and *qabūl* as an invitation. The Hanafi tradition contends that the statement: 'sell it' or 'purchase it' is in fact a demand from the other person for *ījāb* and *qabūl* and not in itself *ījāb* or *qabūl.* Therefore, such statement and any response thereto consist of only half of the *ījāb* and *qabūl*. The interrogatory form of the *ījāb* and *qabūl* encompasses the questions forming the content of *ījāb* and *qabūl*, but they are not *ījāb* and *qabūl* as such. Hanafis suggested that the same *ḥukm* should have been extended to the marriage contract by reason of analogy. In the context of the marriage contract, however, Hanafis relied on *isteḥsān* on the basis of a text narrated by Abū Yūsuf. In the relevant passage, Bilal sent an invitation for *nikāḥ* to a family of *Anṣār* who declined it. Bilal said: 'had the Prophet not directed me to send the message for the *nikāḥ* to you, I would have not sent this proposal to you'. Then they (persons to whom Bilal sent the message) said: 'you are made the owner' (implying their acceptance). Hanafis maintained that there is nothing in this exchange suggesting Bilal responded that he accepted the conclusion of the *nikāḥ*. Hanafis argued that the relevant analogy was meant solely for the marriage contract and that no similar analogy exists for the sale contract.[21]

2.1.2.1 Ṣīgha *by disabled persons and* ṣīgha *in sign language and* kināya

2.09 A person with speech and hearing impediments can create and revoke a valid contract (effectively offer and accept) through generally recognized signs, gestures, or indications.[22] Sign language, if understandable, is treated as no different from ordinary forms of communication.[23] The Malikis consider the use of signs by a non-disabled person as a valid offer in the same way as if it had come from a speech- and hearing-impaired person because such signs fulfil the need to communicate the offer.[24]

[21] Al-Kāsānī (n 6) Vol. 5, pp. 133–34. See also Al-Nawawī (n 18) Vol. 9, p. 198; Kamāl al-Dīn Ibn Muḥammad ibn al-Humām, *Al-Fatāwā al-Hindiyya* (also known as Fatawa al-'Ālamgiriya fil madhhab Imām Abū Ḥanīfa) (Dār al Kutub al 'Ilmiyya, 2000) Vol. 3, pp. 4–5; Al Sāwī, Balaghti Sālik li Aqrab al Masālik 'alā Sharḥ al-Saghīr li Dardīr (Dār al-Kutub al-'Ilimiyya, 1995) Vol. 3, p. 5; Al-Mughnī (n 6) Vol. 6, p. 397; Al-Mufleḥ (n 16) Vol. 1, p. 260; Abū al-Walīd Ibn Rushd, Bidāyat al-Mujtahid wa Nihāyat al-Muqtasid (Muṣtafā al-Ḥalabī, 1975) Vol. 3, p. 179; Ibn Qudāma, Al-Kāfī fī Fiqh al-Imām Aḥmad (Dār al-Kutub al-'Ilmiyya, 1994) Vol. 2, pp. 3–6; 'Abd Allāh ibn Mahmūd al-Mawṣilī, Al Ikhtiyār li Ta'līl al-Mukhtār (Al Ḥalbī Publications, 1937) Vol. 3, p. 71.

[22] *Majalla*, Art. 174; Al-Mughnī (n 6) Vol. 6, p. 14.

[23] Ibn Naqīb (n 18) Vol. 1, p. 150; Al-Rāfī (n 1) Vol. 8, p. 394; Al-Nawawī (n 18) Vol. 9, p. 201.

[24] Hasbullah Abd Raḥman, 'Offer and Acceptance in Islamic Law of Contract' (2008) 8 Journal Syriah 15, p. 16.

According to the Shafi'i tradition, there are certain contracts for the conclusion of which offer and acceptance need not be in words,[25] as is the case with gifts, *ṣadqa* (charity), etc.[26] The Shafi'is, however, mandate that both offer and acceptance be communicated in words in respect of contracts of sale, *salam*, *ṣarf*, *ṣulḥ*, mortgage, *iqāla*, *ḥawāla*, partnership, lease, *musāqāt*, will, etc. There are certain contracts for the conclusion of which words are needed only for the offer and not for the acceptance, such as agency, loan, *wadīʿa*, *juʿāla*, *ʿāriya*, etc. Some contracts, such as the one setting up a *waqf*, do not require offer and acceptance at all, according to Nawawī.[27] 2.10

2.1.3 Characteristics of *ṣīgha*

The form of the *ṣīgha* deals with its words and tense, whereas the characteristics (*ṣiffa*) of the *ṣīgha* pertain to its substantive dimension. 2.11

2.1.3.1 Conformity of Qabūl *with* Ījāb

Acceptance should be unconditional, absolute, and without any qualification.[28] The acceptance should conform with each term of the offer, such as the quantity and characteristics of the subject matter; cash or credit; and, time, place, and other conditions for delivery.[29] If the offeree provides his acceptance on terms other than those in the offer, or only on some terms of the offer, or where acceptance does not match the offer, such acceptance is not valid.[30] In this way, if the offeree varies the terms of the offer, qualifies any part of it, or accepts some part of the offer by rejecting other parts, there would be no acceptance. For instance, if the seller offers to sell two commodities but the offeree accepts one by rejecting the other, the contract is not concluded.[31] However, if the offer is made by the purchaser on some amount and the offeree accepts by lowering the amount or suggesting a decrease or if the offer is by the seller on some specific amount and the purchaser accepts it at a higher price, such variation in the terms of offer does not invalidate the acceptance and the contract is deemed concluded.[32] 2.12

2.1.3.2 Conditional offer

The Hanafis and Shafi'i contend that in order to form a binding contract, offer and acceptance should be communicated without stipulating any condition.[33] For instance, an offer stipulating: 'I sell you for a month' is an example of a conditional offer. If the contract is suspended by reference to the subject matter of the contract, the *ījāb* may 2.13

[25] Abū al-Faḍl 'Abd al-Rahmān ibn Abū Bakar ibn Muḥammad ibn Aḥmad Bakr Jalāl al-Dīn Al-Suyūṭī, Al-Ashbāh wa al-Naẓā'ir (Dār al-Kutub al-'Ilmiyya, 1990) p. 149.
[26] Muḥiy al-Dīn Al-Nawawī, Rauḍat al-Ṭālibīn wa 'Umdat al-Muftīn (Al-Maktab al-Islāmī, 1991) Vol. 3, p. 339.
[27] Ibid.
[28] *Majalla*, Art. 177; Al-Nasafī (n 7) Vol. 5, p. 432.
[29] Manṣūr Al-Buhūtī, Kashshāf al-Qināʿ 'an Matn al-Iqnāʿ (Dār al-Kutub al-'Ilmiyya, n.d.) Vol. 2, p. 459.
[30] Ibn 'Ābidīn (n 13) Vol. 7, p. 15.
[31] Al-Kāsānī (n 6) Vol. 5, pp. 136–37; Al Rāfʿī (n 1) Vol. 8, p. 394; Al-Mawsilī, Al Ikhtiyār li Taʿlīl al-Mukhtār li al-Mawsilī (Dār al-Risālat al-'Ilmiyya, 2009) Vol. 2, p. 7.
[32] Ibn al-Humām (n 21) Vol. 3, p. 3.
[33] Muḥammad ibn Muḥammad ibn Ahmad Al-Shirbīnī al-Qāhirī al-Khaṭīb, Mughnī al-Muḥtāj ilā Maʿrifat Alfāẓ al-Minhāj (Dār al-Kutub al-'Ilmiyya, 1994) Vol. 2, p. 10.

take the following form: 'I have sold this for such amount if you like.' Here 'if you like' is already a requirement of the contract, hence the *ījāb* is valid.[34]

2.1.3.3 Counter-offer

2.14 Varied or qualified acceptance is in fact deemed a counter-offer and a counter-offer generates a contract only after its acceptance by the offeror.[35] For instance, where offeror makes an offer to sell something for 1000 dinar in cash and the offeree accepts it for 1000 dinar on credit, the contract is not concluded. The same is true where the offer is for 1000 dinar on a month's credit, but the acceptance is for 1000 dinar for two months' worth of credit.[36] In these situations the contract is not concluded, save if the offeror provides express acceptance.

2.1.3.4 Fresh offer

2.15 If there is more than one *ījāb*, the contract will be concluded on the basis of the second one and the first one will be considered to have been revoked.[37] The later or fresh *ījāb* makes the offer *bāṭil* and acceptance is for the fresh *ījāb*. This is why, if there is a difference between offeror and offeree, the last statement determines conclusively whether the contract has been concluded. For instance, if the offeror offers to sell a commodity for one dinar and then before it is accepted utters: 'I have sold it to you for two dinar' and such utterance is accepted, such acceptance is for the second *ījāb*.[38]

2.1.3.5 Ṣafaqa wāḥida *and* ṣafaqa mutafarraqa

2.16 The offeree may not accept some part of the offer and reject the other. However, if the offeror makes an offer for two or three things with an intention that the offeree accept one without the other, there are two possibilities. If this is *ṣafaqa wāḥida*, this is not allowed. If it is deemed *ṣafaqa mutafarraqa*, then the offeree can accept one part without the other.[39]

2.17 To expand on the foregoing, when the offeror makes an offer for the sale or purchase of two or three commodities as one transaction (*ṣafaqa wāḥida*), the offeree cannot accept the *ījāb* in respect of one commodity only. If this *ījāb* is made in the form of separate transactions (*ṣafaqa mutafarraqa*), then the seller or the buyer, as the case may be, can accept the offer for one commodity without the other. Sarakhsi argues that if the offer is for the sale or purchase of one commodity and the offeree accepts the offer for part of such commodity, the contract would be concluded if the offeror then accepts such modified acceptance. Qaduri contends that if the part for which the offeree is giving his acceptance has been defined and specified, then the contact would be valid for that part

[34] Ibid, Vol. 2, p. 10.
[35] Al-Nasafī (n 7) Vol. 5, pp. 448–49; Al-Kāsānī (n 6) Vol. 5, pp. 136–37.
[36] Al-Nawawī (n 18) Vol. 9, p. 200.
[37] Al-Nasafī (n 7) Vol. 5, p. 444.
[38] Ibn 'Ābidīn (n 13) Vol. 7, pp. 20–21; Ibn Nujaim, Zain al-'Ābidīn ibn Ibrāhīm, Al Ashbāh wa al-Naza'ir (Dār al Fikr, 1983) p. 244; Ibn al-Humām (n 21) Vol. 3, p. 8.
[39] Al-Marghīnānī (n 14) Vol. 5, p. 6; Ibn al-Humām (n 21) Vol. 3, p. 12.

of the commodity. However, he cautions that if one price is quoted for more than two commodities, then acceptance for one of the commodities is not allowed.

To understand this discussion, it is important to understand the unity and differentiation of *ṣafaqa* (transaction). If the sale, the purchase, and the price are combined as one in situations where a single price is requested for all the subject matters, and there is one seller and one buyer, the *ṣafaqa* would be *muttaḥida* or *wāḥida*. If the price is different, such as where the offeror prescribes different prices for a group of different subject matters and one price for the other group of subject matters—the offer says: 'I have sold you these ten dresses and each dress costs ten (rupees)'—this is *ṣafaqa muttaḥida*. If there are two offerors or two offerees and one price is mentioned for the pertinent subject matters—for instance, the offeror says to the two offerees: 'I have sold this commodity to you two for this amount of money' and both offerees say 'we have purchased'—this offer amounts to *ṣafaqa wāḥida*. *Ṣafaqa* would become *mutafarraqah* if the specifications are different in the contract; that is, where there are different subject matters or different parts of a subject matter, then a specific price is ascribed to each subject matter or each part of the subject matter and there is repetition of the contract. For instance, the offeror says: 'I have sold you these dresses. I have sold you these dresses for ten (rupees) each and these dresses for five (rupees) each.' This is *ṣafaqa mutafarraqa*.[40] **2.18**

If there is one *ījāb* for two types of contracts, such as: 'I have sold this commodity for such amount and I have married with you for this amount of *mahr*' and the offeree accepts the sale and rejects the marriage, there is no contract. However, if the offeree accepts the marriage and rejects the sale, the marriage contract is valid. In response to one offer encompassing two contracts—for example, 'I have sold you this house and leased you this land', to which the offeree says 'I have accepted'—this would be considered acceptance for both contracts.[41] **2.19**

2.1.4 Words to be Used for a Contract

The Hanafis allow the conclusion of a contract by any words which carry the meaning of that contract.[42] It is not necessary to use the same words in *ījāb* and *qabūl*.[43] Any words implying a specific contract can be used because regard is given to the meaning and intentions and not to the words themselves.[44] **2.20**

Even so, the words of the *ījāb* and *qabūl* should be clear and precise.[45] They should clearly demonstrate the intentions of the parties[46] and provide evidence of their free **2.21**

[40] Ibn al-Humām (n 21) Vol. 3, pp. 15–16; Al-Nasafī (n 7) Vol. 5, pp. 448–49.
[41] Al-Nasafī (n 7) Vol. 5, p. 446.
[42] Al-Mawṣilī (n 21) Vol. 3, p. 71.
[43] Taqī al-Dīn Abū Bakar bin Muḥammad, Kifāyat al-Akhyār fi Ḥall Ghāyat al-Ikhtiṣār (Dār al Khabr, 1991) Vol. 1, p. 233.
[44] Ibn Nujaim (n 38) p. 242.
[45] Ḥawāshī al-Shirwānī and Ibn Qāsim al-'Abbādī, Ḥawāshī Tuḥfat al-Muḥtāj bi Sharḥ alMinhāj (Maktaba al-Tijāriyat al-Kubrā,n.d) Vol. 6, p. 224; Ibn Qudāma (n 21) Vol. 2, pp. 3–6.
[46] Al-Nawawī (n 18) Vol. 9, p. 195.

consent.[47] The expressions chosen should make clear the type of contract intended to be concluded and provide complete information about the subject matter and the money consideration involved.[48] If the words connote more than one meaning, the contract would not be binding unless one specific meaning is attributed to such words by custom (*'urf*).[49]

2.2 *Ījāb* and *Qabūl* through Conduct and *Muʿāṭāt*

2.22 An offer and acceptance may be implied from the parties' conduct.[50] Examples of offer or acceptance by conduct include the order by a customer to a butcher to cut meat from a specific part of an animal,[51] eating the commodity, riding and taking away a vehicle, putting on clothes after the seller's statement 'ride for 100 or put on for such amount', and by taking the commodity into possession without saying anything,[52] as well as consumption of the subject matter after *ījāb*.[53]

2.23 Mere conduct is sufficient to constitute a valid offer,[54] although Ibn Taymiyya emphasizes that conduct should be acknowledged in custom[55] because the employment of such conduct indicates that the offeror is aware of it.[56] In this regard, silence is interpreted as acceptance. For example, a purchaser tenders money to the shopkeeper and buys a melon. The silence of the vendor is his implied acceptance.[57] Abū Yūsuf and Muḥammad also argue that the taking of possession by the buyer in response to an offer from the seller is tantamount to acceptance of the offer.[58]

2.2.1 *Mu'āṭāt*

2.24 A sale may be consummated through taking and giving of the subject matter without a written or oral exchange between the parties; this is known *bay' al-ta'atī* or *mu'āṭāt*. The condition for this type of sale is the conferral of the contract's consideration by both the parties according to Halvani. The preferred opinion, however, on the basis of the text from Muḥammad is that the giving of a commodity by one party is sufficient to validly conclude such a contract.[59] The prime example of *mu'āṭāt* is where one person gives money and takes the commodity without any *ījāb* and *qabūl*.[60] For instance, the buyer

[47] Khalīl Ibn Ishāq al-Jundī, Mukhtaṣar Al Khalīl (Dār al-Ḥadīth, 2005) Vol. 3, p. 148.
[48] Al-Nawawī (n 18) Vol. 9, p. 202.
[49] Abū Al-Walīd al-Bajī, Al-Muntaqā (Dār al Kutb al-'Ilmi, 1999) Vol. 6, p. 24.
[50] *Majalla*, Arts 173, 175; Al-Mawṣilī (n 21) Vol. 3, p. 71.
[51] *Majalla*, Art. 175.
[52] Al-Nasafī (n 7) Vol. 5, p. 440.
[53] Ibn al-Humām (n 21) Vol. 3, p. 8.
[54] Al-Mughnī (n 6) Vol. 3, p. 562; Al-Kāsānī (n 6) Vol. 5, p. 134.
[55] Al-Karkhī, Uṣūl al-Karkhī (Javed Press Karachi, 2011) p. 173.
[56] Nabil Ṣaleḥ, 'Definition and Formation of Contract under Islamic and Arab Laws' (1990) 5 Arab Law 101.
[57] *Majalla*, Art. 175.
[58] Ibn al-Humām (n 21) Vol. 3, p. 6.
[59] Ibn al-Humām (n 21) Vol. 3, p. 10.
[60] Al-Nawawī (n 18) Vol. 9, p. 191.

asks: 'how much you are selling this meat?', to which the seller responds: 'three kilos per dinar'. To this the buyer says: 'OK, I have purchased, weigh for one dinar'. If the seller starts weighing the meat, he is deemed to have accepted the offer.[61]

In a sale conducted through *muʿāṭāt*, possession should occur with the permission of the owner.[62] A contract does not become binding when the person who knows the price of the commodity takes that commodity into their possession; rather, it becomes *lāzim* only after the price is paid.[63] **2.25**

2.2.1.1 Permissibility of muʿāṭāt

The subject of *muʿāṭāt* on the point of its permissibility has generated some discussion. The juristic opinions on the permissibility of a contract through *muʿāṭāt* can be summarized into three groups as follows.[64] **2.26**

First opinion: A contract is not possible without *ījāb* and *qabūl* and this is true for all kinds of contracts including sale, *ijārah*, *hibah*, *nikāḥ*, *waqf*, etc. This is the opinion of Shafi'i and Aḥmad bin Ḥanbal. According to them, the original rule is that the *ṣīgha* should be expressed through words. They base their opinion on the following *āyāt* of the Qur'ān: 'O believers! Do not devour one another's wealth illegally, but rather trade by mutual consent.'[65] They argue that the intentions in the mind of a person can be expressed only with words. *Muʿāṭāt* entails actions, and actions are of several kinds. They maintain that words for contracts are like prayers and supplications in *ʿibādāt* which require words for their expression. **2.27**

Second opinion: There are certain contracts that can be concluded by actions and hence the conclusion of such contracts by actions is allowed. This is true for sale, *waqf* (e.g. a person constructs a *masjid* and allows people to offer prayer in it or allows people to make burials on his land) and some kinds of *ijārah* (where a person gives clothes to a launderer for dry-cleaning or a tailor for sewing) and *hadiya*. If such contracts cannot be concluded through actions indicating such contracts, this is detrimental to commercial and ordinary life and, in any event, people have been entering into contracts through actions from the time of the Prophet. This is the preferred opinion among the Hanafis, Hanbalis, and Shafi'is. They do not allow *muʿāṭāt* in expensive commodities on the basis that there is no need to do so and also because there is no *ʿurf* allowing such *muʿāṭāt*. The determination of commodities as inexpensive or expensive is based on **2.28**

[61] Ibn al-Humām (n 21) Vol. 3, p. 11.
[62] Mussṭafā ibn-Saʿd Suyūṭī, Maṭālib ūlī al-nuhā fī sharḥ Ghāyat al-muntahā fī jamʿ al-Iqnāʿ wa-al-Muntahā (Wizārat al-Awqāf wa al-Shu-u ū n al-Islāmiyya, 2019) Vol. 3, p. 9.
[63] Khalaf (n 15) p. 3.
[64] Taqī al-Din Aḥmad ibn ʿAbd al-Ḥalīm Ibn Taymīya, Al-Fatāwa al-Kubrā (Dār al Kutub al ʿIlmiyya, 1987) Vol. 5, pp. 5–13; Al-Kāsānī (n 6) Vol. 5, p. 134; Al-Mughnī (n 6) Vol. 6, p. 397; Al-Nawawī (n 18) Vol. 9, p. 190; Ibn ʿĀbidīn (n 13) Vol. 7, pp. 17–18; Al-Maghrabī (n 18) Vol. 6, pp. 14–15; Zakariyyā al-Anṣārī, Ḥāshiya al-Sulaimān al Jamāl ʿalā Sharḥ al-Manhaj li Sheikh al-Islām al-Anṣārī (Dār al-Iḥyā al ʿArabī, n.d.) Vol. 3, pp. 8–9; Ibn Qudāma (n 21) Vol. 2, pp. 3–6.
[65] Nisā, 29.

'urf.[66] These three traditions share similar opinions on *mua'tat* in *ijārah*, *rehn*, *hibah*, etc., in respect of gifts and *ṣadqa*. The Shafi'is allow *mu'āṭāt*.[67]

2.29 Third opinion: The contract is concluded with anything, words or actions, that evidences the intentions of the parties. Anything broadly considered as a sale or *ijārah* suffices as such. If there is a difference among the various terms in the form of words or actions used by the parties for the conclusion of the contract, the meaning prevailing amongst the general public at the place of contract will be attributed to such terms. Neither the Sharī'ah nor language has placed constraints on terms because of the diversity of expression. For instance, *bay'* and *ijārah* are used in Arabic but not in many other languages or non-Arab countries. Therefore, this opinion regards the place where the contract is concluded as determining the validity of the parties' intent. This is the preferred opinion of the Malikis and Hanbalis. According to this opinion, *bay' al-mu'āṭāt* is allowed even if one party is using words whereas the other is using action. These schools also allow non-written conduct or action even if there are no words from either side, as where one person places down the price and takes a sack of goods. The same applies to other kinds of sale, such as *hibah* and *ijārah*. They base their opinion on several *āyāt* of the Qur'ān.[68] The proponents of the third opinion infer several principles as follows.

2.30 The first range of *āyāt* include: 'O believers! Do not devour one another's wealth illegally, but rather trade by mutual consent'[69] and 'Give women you wed their due dowries graciously. But if they waive some of it willingly (Or if they, of their own pleasure of heart remit something of it to you, or if they give up willingly to you anything of it), then you may enjoy it freely with a clear conscience.'[70] In these *āyāt*, no word or action has been specified to express consent for the contract. Secondly, there is no *ṣīgha* specified for different types of contract under the Sharī'ah and also there is no tradition narrated from the Companions of the Prophet or *tābi'īn* specifying any form of *ṣīgha*, or indeed that contracts may be concluded without *ṣīgha*. In such cases the role of *'urf* is paramount. Where the Sharī'ah and the parties' language are silent, resort is made to custom and usage.

2.31 Thirdly, the conduct and practices of human beings are of two kinds—*'ibādāt* (worship) to refine their *dīn* (religion) and *'ādāt* (conduct and worldly matters) which people need for their worldly life. *'ibāda* is made obligatory or permissible only by the Sharī'ah. In *'ādāt*, something is deemed permissible as long as it is not prohibited by the Sharī'ah. Therefore, sale, *hibah*, *ijārah*, etc., are considered *'ādāt* needed by the people. The Sharī'ah has come to refine the manners of life and has forbidden corrupt and immoral conduct and has in addition rendered things necessary for life. It has moreover

[66] Al-Nawawī (n 18) Vol. 9, p. 192.
[67] Ibid, Vol. 9, p. 194.
[68] Nisā, 3, 4, 29; Nūr, 32; Baqara, 231, 245, 261, 275, 276, 282, 283; Ṭalāq, 2, 6; Mujadala, 3.
[69] Nisā, 29.
[70] Nisā, 4.

disapproved of what is not appropriate and recommended the prevalence of *maṣlaḥa*. Through such rules, people can trade and contract as they wish, subject to the exceptions imposed by the Sharīʿah. Anyone who explores the narrations of the Prophet, his Companions, and *tābiʿīn* understands that *ṣīgha* has not been mandated for both the parties. The Prophet and those after him constructed mosques without claiming that they were *waqf*. Similarly, after purchasing a camel from Umar, the Prophet said: 'this is for you Abdullah bin Umar' and Abdullah bin Umar did not utter a word of acceptance. This has been used as the basis for suggesting that giving and taking becomes an effective and legitimate substitute for offer and acceptance.[71]

2.3 Mutual Assent (*tarāḍī*) and Intention to Contract

The consent of the parties is the foundation of contract.[72] The need for free mutual consent is established in the Qur'ān as follows: 'O you who believed, do not consume one another's wealth unjustly but only [in lawful] business by mutual consent.'[73] The mandatory element of mutual consent in *ṣīgha* is also established from the tradition of the Prophet who said: 'Transactions may only be done by mutual consent.'[74] Similarly, Abū Sa'id al-Khudri reported: **2.32**

> Allah's Messenger (may peace be upon him) forbade us (from) two types of business transactions . . . *munābadha* means that a man throws his garment to another and the other throws his garment, and thus confirming their contract without the inspection of mutual agreement.[75]

If there is no consent, the sale becomes *ghasb* in case there is transfer of possession.[76] *Tarāḍī* comes into being with the conjunction of offer and acceptance—express and implied.[77]

2.3.1 Intention to Contract

Ījāb has a purpose for every contract. For instance, in a sale contract, *ījāb* demonstrates the intention to transfer the ownership of the subject matter in return for its price[78] and the same is true with *qabūl* derived from the purchaser. The willingness to contract is something concealed which becomes revealed with the help of *ṣīgha*.[79] For this reason, if the offeror makes an offer, or the offeree accepts without any such intention, there is no contract. Intention is explored more fully in Chapter 4. **2.33**

[71] Ibn Taymīya (n 64) Vol. 5, pp. 5–13.
[72] Ibid, Vol. 3, p. 336.
[73] Qur'ān 4:20.
[74] Muḥammad bin Yazīd Ibn Māja, *Sunan Ibn Mājah* (Kitāb al Tijarāt, particularly the chapter on *bayʿ al-khiyār*) p. 2185.
[75] Muslim, *Ḥadīth* 3613.
[76] Al-Nasafī (n 7) Vol. 5, p. 431.
[77] Ibn Taymīya (n 64) Vol. 3, p. 411; ʿAbd al-Razzāq al-Sanhurī, Maṣādir al-Ḥaq (Beirut, n.d.) Vol. 1, pp. 84, 117.
[78] Al-Shirbīnī (n 33) Vol. 2, p. 6.
[79] Ibid, Vol. 2, p. 7.

2.3.2 Consent of the Coerced Party

2.34 Consent should be free and coupled with an intention to create the contractual relationship, which is not possible if one party is coerced (*mukrah*).[80] Consent through *ikrāh* (coercion) renders the sale *fāsid* and its validity is dependent on the approval of the coerced party[81] at whose option the subject matter and the price may be returned to the seller and the buyer respectively.[82] Coercion is justified only where the judge coercively sells the property of a person to pay back his debts. The contract for the sale of such person's property is valid even if he is not willing to make such contract.[83] A contract of sale under justified coercion arises also in circumstances where the coercer is a mortgagee, creditor, or judge (for the coerced is a hoarder or debtor).[84] This is so because *iḥtekār* (monopoly or hoarding) is forbidden and such hoarded property may be sold by the state to repel the collective harm cause to society.[85]

2.3.3 Consent of *Hāzil*

2.35 Impaired consent also arises in the event of *hāzil* whereby a person gives his consent in jest or for the sake of bargaining. Whether consent was given in jest or the party was just bargaining can be established either under oath (*yamīn*) or with other indications showing the jest.[86] There will be no need for *yamīn* where one party claims to have had no intention to contract, claiming further that his bargain was a mere inquiry about the quantum of price or the subject matter where there is an indication of *iltizām* (*binding nature*) of contract.[87]

2.3.4 Consent of Intoxicated Person

2.36 As above, no intention is attributed to an intoxicated person making an offer or acceptance.[88]

2.4 Communication of *Ījāb* and *Qabūl*

2.37 For the valid conclusion of a contract, the offer and acceptance must be communicated to the offeree and offeror respectively.[89] This section deals with different principles governing this subject.

[80] Al-Shirwānī (n 45) Vol. 6, p. 223.
[81] Ibn 'Ābidīn (n 13) Vol. 7, p. 18; Sulaimān (n-13)Vol. 3, p. 5.
[82] Al-Dusūqī (n 8) Vol. 2, p. 7.
[83] Muḥammad bin Abd al-Wahāb, Al-Durar al-Sunniyya fi al-Ajwabat al-Najdiyya (Musahaha, 1994) Vol. 6, p. 9; Al-Buhūtī (n 29) Vol. 2, p. 362.
[84] Al-Suyūṭī (n 62) Vol. 3, p. 10.
[85] Ibid, Vol. 3, pp. 62–64.
[86] Ibid, Vol. 3, p. 3; Al-Maghrabī (n 18) Vol. 6, pp. 15, 20, 24.
[87] Al Sāwī (n 21) Vol. 3, p. 6.
[88] Muḥammad bin Aḥmad Ramlī, Nihāyat al-Muḥtāj ilā Sharḥ il Minhāj fi fiqh 'alā Madhab Imām *Shāfi'ī* (Dār al Kutub al-'limiyya, 2002) Vol. 3, p. 380.
[89] Ibn al-Humām (n 21) Vol. 3, p. 3.

2.4.1 *Ījāb* and *Qabūl* from and to the Concerned Parties

The offer from the offeror should be communicated to the offeree after which the acceptance comes from the offeree.[90] The acceptance should be from the person to whom the offer is made. Therefore, if the offeree dies before accepting the offer, his legal heir or agent present in the *majlis* cannot accept the offer.[91] Some scholars from the Shafi'i tradition, however, contend that after an offer is made to the offeree who passed away before accepting it and, at the time of death, the legal heir of the deceased was present, they can accept the offer.[92] *Ījāb* and *qabūl* can be made by an agent.[93] **2.38**

2.4.2 Modes of Communication of *Ījāb* and *Qabūl*

The *ījāb* and *qabūl* may be communicated through instantaneous modes or postal transmission and dispatch. **2.39**

2.4.2.1 Instantaneous method

In face-to-face contracts, the offeree and the offeror should have physically heard the offer and acceptance respectively. For instance, in a sale contract, if the purchaser accepts the offer but the seller does not listen/hear such acceptance, there is no contract because the physical aspect of hearing is a *sine qua non* condition for the conclusion of the contract; it should be mentioned that Al Havi al Qudsi stipulates the conditions of listening and understanding.[94] If the seller makes an offer and the offeree accepts the offer and all those present in the session listen to the acceptance, but the offeror contends that he has not listened to the acceptance, without suffering from an auditory problem, the acceptance is considered to have been communicated.[95] **2.40**

2.4.2.1.1 Email, SMS, WhatsApp, and other forms of electronic communication There appears to be no obstacle in declaring an offer and acceptance communicated by a contemporary medium to be valid—such as through SMS, WhatsApp, and email—due to an Islamic maxim whereby 'contracts are formed from intentions', implying that so far as the intentions of the parties to create a contract are manifest, the medium for manifesting those intentions will be considered valid.[96] The parties who are physically distant from each other can also conclude the contract by calling each other.[97] All these modes may be included in the instantaneous modes of communication of offer and acceptance. **2.41**

[90] Al-Mufleḥ (n 16) Vol. 1, p. 260,

[91] Al-Shirbīnī (n 33) Vol. 2, p. 10.

[92] Yaḥya ibn Sharaf Al-Nawawī, Rauḍat al-Ṭālibīn wa 'Umdat al-Muftīn (Al-Maktab al-Islāmī, 1991) Vol. 5, p. 390 and Vol. 4, p. 8.

[93] Al-Nawawī (n 18) Vol. 9, p. 203.

[94] Al-Nasafī (n 7) Vol. 5, p. 446.

[95] Sirāj al-Dīn al-Awshī, Al- Fatāwā al-Sirājiyya (Dār ul 'Ulūm Zakariya, 2011) pp. 412–13.

[96] Mostafa Elssn and Muḥammad Subaty, 'Contract Formation Using Automated Message System: Survey of Islamic Contract Law' (2009) 23 Arab Law Quarterly 167.

[97] Al-Nawawī (n 18) Vol. 9, pp. 214–15.

2.4.2.2 Postal communication

2.42 A letter between absent parties is tantamount to a conversation in the present.[98] Therefore, a contract is also concluded through postal communication because writing and speaking produce the same legal effect;[99] communication in writing is valid by any reliable means. The offer may also be sent to the offeree through a messenger who can narrate the offer verbally. If the offeror makes an offer for the sale of a commodity to a person in his absence and such offer reaches this person who then accepts, this is not valid. If such an offer is communicated with the authority of the offeror, the acceptance of the offeree of such offer will generate a valid contract.[100]

2.5 When a Contract is Completed with the *Ījāb* and *Qabūl*

2.5.1 Direct Communication

2.43 A contract takes place with the completion of offer and acceptance,[101] and until such time the contract can be revoked.[102] As a result, the *qabūl* to the *ījāb* should be made before *ījāb* is revoked or has lapsed.[103] In a direct communication, the contract is complete with the meeting of offer and acceptance in the same *majlis* and the offeror listens to the acceptance, although some scholars such as Al Havi al Qudsi stipulate that the offeror should listen and understand the acceptance.[104] Therefore, the completion of offer and acceptance in direct communication is not a complicated phenomenon. For the time when the contract is concluded through *mu'āṭāt*, see Section 2.2 above.

2.5.2 Postal Communication

2.44 A contract can be concluded through postal communication.[105] Islamic law dictates that the contract is concluded when the offeree receives the offer letter and upon reading it verbally says: 'I have accepted', even if the offeree does not write back to the offeror to declare his acceptance. Taqi 'Usmāni derives this stance from a variety of juristic opinions. The Hanafis suggest that when the offer letter arrives with the offeree, this is tantamount to the offeror himself addressing the offeree,[106] thus making postal communication similar to verbal communication. Therefore, when the offeree reads, understands, and accepts the offer then the contract is concluded.[107] Some Hanbalis and Shafi'i scholars, such as Ghazali and Al-Buhūtī, also hold similar positions, arguing that in such cases, the offeree gets the *khiyār al-majlis* until he stays in the *majlis* and the offeror can also revoke the offer before the termination of such *majlis*.[108] Despite

98 Al-Mawsilī (n 31) Vol. 2, p. 23.
99 Ibn 'Ābidīn (n 13) Vol. 7, p. 26.
100 Ibn al-Humām (n 21) Vol. 3, p. 10; Al-Nawawī (n 18) Vol. 9, pp. 196–97.
101 Al-Nasafī (n 7) Vol. 5, p. 270.
102 Al-Kāsānī (n 6) Vol. 5, p. 134.
103 Al-Nawawī (n 18) Vol. 9, p. 199.
104 Al-Nasafī (n 7) Vol. 5, p. 446.
105 Al-Wahāb (n 83) Vol. 6, p. 5.
106 Al-Kāsānī (n 6) Vol. 5, p. 138.
107 Ibn al-Humām (n 21) Vol. 3, p. 9.
108 Al-Nawawī (n 18) Vol. 9, pp. 127–28; Al-Buhūtī (n 29) Vol. 3, p. 137.

these juristic opinions, modern scholars, including Taqi 'Usmāni and Sanhuri, opine that along with the declaration of acceptance from the offeree, the offeror's knowledge of such acceptance is also necessary. In this respect, they have reiterated the principle that the contract is concluded when the parties hear each other's communication (*ījāb* and *qabūl*) and that if the purchaser provides *qabūl* by saying 'I have purchased' which is not heard by the seller, no contract is created.[109]

Sanhuri suggests that the logic of this rule is based on the rationale that the offeror must hear the acceptance of the offeree when they are present in the same *majlis*, which further mandates the knowledge of the offeror to create the contract through postal communication. This is so because the exchanges taking place when the parties are present in a *majlis* are equivalent to the knowledge when one the offerees is absent.[110] Taqi 'Usmāni seconds this view, further arguing that the *āyāt* of the Qur'ān from where all juristic discussions emanate mandates only '*al-tarāḍī*'. He says that the time for getting this consent (*tarāḍī*) is when offer and acceptance meet with each other before the occurrence of any incident abolishing *ījāb*. If *qabūl* is signified while the *ījāb* was existent, the contract is completed. He goes on to explain that this is a religious rule whereby in postal communications the contract is concluded with the utterance: 'I accepted'. However, in order to declare a contract binding against the offeror, the communication of the acceptance letter to the offeror is mandatory. This is so because it is very difficult to prove the time of oral acceptance and of writing the letter in response to the offer letter. The acceptance letter may be lost on its way to the offeror. If the acceptance letter is delayed, the offeror may interpret such silence from the offeree as a rejection and conclude a contract with a third person. To eliminate these and many other impediments, the rule is that the contract should not be concluded before the acceptance of the offeree comes to the knowledge of the offeror and this knowledge is ascertained from the fact of delivery of the letter to him or her. Hence, the offeree becomes bound upon his declaration of acceptance and the offeror with the delivery of the acceptance letter.[111] **2.45**

2.6 Session and its Expiration

The *ījāb* and *qabūl* should coincide in the same session (*majlis*) as the contract does not conclude with the change of *majlis*.[112] Shafi'is' approach, in respect of postal communication, is that the session commences when the letter or the messenger reaches the offeree and lasts until the offeree responds to the offer in that session.[113] In this way, the *khiyār* of *majlis* for the offeree to whom the offer letter is addressed is the session in which he responds to the offer and the *khiyār* of *majlis* of the sender will continue **2.46**

[109] Ibn al-Humām (n 21) Vol. 3, p. 10.
[110] Al-Sanhurī (n 77) Vol. 2, p. 56.
[111] Taqi Usmani, Fiqh al Buyū' (Maktaba M'ārif al Qur'ān, 2015) Vol. 1, pp. 56–63.
[112] Al-Nasafī (n 7) Vol. 5, p. 432.
[113] Al-Kāsānī (n 6) Vol. 5, p. 138.

until the *khiyār* of the offeree is terminated, or if the sender revokes the offer before the offeree leaves the session.[114] The principle of offer and acceptance in the same *majlis* also applies where the sale is concluded through *mu'āṭāt*.[115]

2.47 Hanafis maintain, however, that abiding by this principle would close the possibility of sale because the offeree needs time to deliberate over the offer. Due to the need for deliberation, Hanafis have dispensed with the need for the meeting of offer and acceptance at the same time. Instead, they suggest that if in the course of the same *majlis* there is an interval between offer and acceptance, once the interval is over and as long as offer and acceptance are in the same *majlis*, offer would be assumed as standing and waiting for the acceptance and the session would complete when acceptance meets this offer.[116]

2.6.1 *Khiyār* Relating to the *Majlis*

2.48 From the *majlis* for the contract, the concepts of *khiyārāt* relating to such session along with the time of their termination and the possibility of contracting have emerged.

2.6.1.1 The basic concept of khiyār

2.49 For the offeror there is *khiyar al-rujū'* (option to revoke the offer before its acceptance) and for the offeree *khiyār al-qabūl* (option either to accept it in the *majlis* or reject it), both of which extend to the end of the session.[117] The sale becomes binding after the separation of the parties and there is no difference on this point among the various schools. What constitutes *tafarruq* (departure, separation) depends on custom (*'urf*).[118]

2.50 The unavailability of such *khiyār* entails the compulsion of the other party to accept the first party's offer or acceptance.[119] In other words, the absence of *khiyār al qabūl* will make the contract *lāzim* without the offeree's consent. The vitiation of *ījāb* before the ending of *majlis* is prejudicial to the offeree and its subsistence even after the termination of *majlis* is prejudicial to the offeror. Therefore, restricting its subsistence to the duration of *majlis* is beneficial for both the offeror and offeree.[120]

2.6.1.2 Justification

2.51 The Shafi'is and Hanbalis contend that the contracting parties possess sufficient *khiyār* to rescind the contract before the end of their session. However, the Malikis and Hanafis suggest that the contract becomes binding with the *ījāb* and *qabūl* alone and that the parties do not enjoy *khiyār al majlis*.[121] The Shafi'is and Hanbalis base their opinion on the following *aḥadīth*:

[114] Al-Nawawī (n 18) Vol. 9, p. 198.
[115] Al-Buhūtī (n 29) Vol. 2, p. 461.
[116] Al-Kāsānī (n 6) Vol. 5, p. 137.
[117] Al-Marghīnanī (n 14) Vol. 5, p. 6. *The khiyār al- Qabūl* cannot be inherited. See Al-Nasafī (n 7) Vol. 5, p. 456; Al-Mawsilī (n 31) Vol. 2, p. 7.
[118] Al-Mughnī (n 6) Vol. 6, p. 12.
[119] Al-Kāsānī (n 6) Vol. 5, p. 134.
[120] Al-Marghīnanī (n 14) Vol. 5, p. 5.
[121] Al-Mughnī (n 6) Vol. 6, pp. 8–11. For a *ḥadīth* relied on by Shāfi'ī to justify *khiyār al majlis*, see Al-Nawawī (n 18) Vol. 9, p. 219.

First *ḥadīth*: The Prophet said: 'The buyer and the seller have the option to cancel.'

Second *ḥadīth*: The Prophet said, 'The buyer and the seller have the option of cancelling or confirming the bargain unless they separate.'[122]

Third *ḥadīth*: The Prophet said: 'Both the buyer and the seller have the option of cancelling or confirming a bargain unless they separate, or the sale is optional.'[123]

Fourth *ḥadīth*: The Prophet said: 'Both the buyer and the seller have the option of cancelling or confirming the bargain, as long as they are still together; and unless they separate or one of them gives the other the option of keeping or returning the things and a decision is concluded then, in which case the bargain is considered final. If they separate after the bargain and none of them has rejected it, then the bargain is rendered final.'[124]

Taqi 'Usmāni points out that *khiyār al majlis* is possible where the parties are present before each other, but difficulties arise where they are located in different cities or countries and their exchange is through electronic means. Such contracts should be free from *khiyār al majlis* and that seems permissible from the *ḥadīth* being relied upon by the Hanbalis and Shafi'is. By establishing that the fourth *ḥadīth* is effectively a commentary to the third *ḥadīth*, it is suggested that that the *khiyār al majlis* can be waived in such circumstances.[125] **2.52**

2.6.1.3 Termination of khiyār al qabūl *and* khiyār al majlis

The contract session starts when the parties come together and ends with their separation, whereafter the offer lapses and cannot be accepted. Shafi'i tradition maintains that the separation is physical. There is also an opinion that *'urf* will ultimately decide the separation or departure terminating the session.[126] If the principal delegates the authority to some other person for acceptance, the *majlis* will be considered as pertaining to the circumstances of the agent.[127] The following incidents are deemed to terminate the contract session:[128] **2.53**

- The session will end after an offer proceeds from the offeror, if the offeree leaves the session or indulges himself in another business not relevant to the contract. This is so save where such separation is the result of coercion in which case the *khiyār* will remain until the coercion is removed. The same is true where they separate due to fear or necessity, such as a natural disaster.[129] If any person stands to leave

[122] Bukhārī 2110.
[123] Bukhārī 2111.
[124] Bukhārī 2112.
[125] Usmani (n 111) Vol. 1, pp. 63–66.
[126] Al-Nawawī (n 26) Vol. 9, p. 213.
[127] Ibn 'Ābidīn (n 13) Vol. 7, p. 47.
[128] Al-Kāsānī (n 6) Vol. 5, p. 137; Ibn Naqīb (n 18) Vol. 1, p. 150; Ibn al-Humām (n 21) Vol. 3, pp. 8–10; Al-Nasafī (n 7) Vol. 5, pp. 442, 456; Al-Hussainī (n 33) Vol. 1, p. 233; Al-Anṣārī (n 64) Vol. 3, p. 10.
[129] Al-Suyūṭī (n 62) Vol. 3, p. 85.

the *majlis*, the *ījāb* becomes *bāṭil* because this demonstrates the unwillingness of such party to make the contract and in case he leaves the *majlis*, *shaṭar-al-ʿaqd* (one part of contract, i.e. *ījāb* or *qabūl*) does not wait for the offer or the acceptance of the person who is absent.[130] Acceptance after separation does not create a contract.[131]

- A change of *majlis* before the acceptance is given.
- The *majlis* becomes very long or there is a long interval, or a significant lapse of time between the offer and acceptance. The permissible length of such interval is defined by *ʿurf*.
- The subject matter has changed or has been destroyed.
- The offeror revokes *ījāb* partially or fully.[132]
- The offeree rejects the offer by uttering: 'I do not accept'. Here, the rejection of the *ījāb* is by means of separation (*al-tafarraq*) as has been said in *al Mustaṣfā* and *Fatḥ al-Qadīr*. In *Ghāyat al* Bayān, it is argued that the separation (*al tafarraq*) occurs when the offeree accepts the offer and the *khiyār* ends. In this situation, *khiyār* ends and the sale becomes binding. Nakhaʿī is also of the same opinion due to the existence of all the *arkān* and conditions for the contract. In this situation, the *khiyār* for either party to rescind the contract may be harmful to the other party.[133]
- *Khiyār* also comes to end with the death of one of the parties. However, if a party becomes mentally incapacitated after the contract but recovers during the same session, the *khiyār* will remain available for that party.[134]

2.6.1.4 Contracting out of khiyār al majlis

2.54 If the parties have waived *khiyār al majlis* between them, the sale becomes *lāzim* and *khiyār* becomes *bāṭil*.[135] If the parties enter into a contract by expressly negating the right of *khiyār* of *majlis* there are three opinions according to Shafi'i tradition. The preferred one is that the sale will be void. The second opinion declares the sale valid and *khiyār* absent. However, the third opinion suggests that the sale is valid and the *khiyār* is not absent.[136]

2.55 As a result, *khiyār al-majlis* can be waived, as where the seller declares: 'I have sold you this for such amount with the condition that we do not have *khiyār*', to which the buyer responds: 'I have accepted'. In this case there is no *khiyār*. *Khiyār* can be waived before the separation of the parties if the party with the right to exercise such *khiyār* opts to waive it. It can also be waived after the sale is concluded.[137]

[130] Al-Mawsili (n 31) Vol. 2, p. 8.
[131] Suleimān (n 81) Vol. 3, p. 10.
[132] Al-Nasafī (n 7) Vol. 5, p. 447.
[133] Al-Mawsilī (n 31) Vol. 2, p. 8.
[134] Al-Suyūṭī (n 62) Vol. 3, p. 86.
[135] Al-Wahāb (n 83) Vol. 6, p. 52.
[136] Al-Nawawī (n 18) Vol. 9, p. 207.
[137] Al-Suyūṭī (n 62) Vol. 3, pp. 83, 85.

2.7 The Contract with *Khiyār al-majlis*

This *khiyār* is available according to the majority of Islamic jurists, save for the Malikis, in contracts such as *ṣulh*, *hibah*, *ijārah*, *ṣarf*, and *salam*. This is not available in contracts such as *nikāḥ*, *waqf*, *hiba bi ghair il-ʿiwaḍ*, *kafāla*, *ḥawāla*, and *shufʿa* because these contracts are *lāzim* and they are not subject to *khiyār*.[138] Similarly, there is no *khiyār* in *qarḍ*, *rehn*, *masāqāt*, *mazāraʿ*, *juʿāla*, *wakāla*, *sharika*, *muḍāraba*, *ʿariya*, or *wadiʿa*, because they are *ʿuqud jāiza*, which means they can be terminated by each party at any time.[139] **2.56**

2.7.1 Termination of Offer

The *qabūl* should be rendered before the *ījāb* lapses or terminated. The *ījāb* lapses or terminates in several ways, as follows. **2.57**

2.7.1.1 Rejection

An express or implied rejection of the offer by the offeree extinguishes the offer.[140] Acceptance by modifying the offer will also be tantamount to the rejection of the offer.[141] **2.58**

2.7.1.2 Revocation of Offer

Ījāb becomes *bāṭil* upon revocation.[142] Revocation of part of the *ījāb* amounts to revocation of the whole offer.[143] *Ījāb* may be revoked before its acceptance.[144] When *ījāb* and *qabūl* are complete, the contract becomes *lāzim*, in other words, the ownership of the parties is established, whereafter revocation is possible only on the basis of defect or absence of inspection at the time of contract. However, the Shafi'i tradition maintains that each party can revoke the contract so far as they are in the *majlis* and have not physically separated from each other. The Hanafi tradition contends that rescission of the contract in fact makes the right of ownership of the other party invalid.[145] However, an offer cannot be revoked if it is stated to remain for a fixed time or is otherwise accepted.[146] **2.59**

If any party leaves the *majlis* of the contract, the *ījāb* is revoked and becomes *bāṭil*.[147] Similarly, the fresh offer from the offeror before the original offer is accepted amounts to a revocation of the original offer.[148] For instance, an offeror offers to sell a commodity for one dinar and before it is accepted says: 'I have sold you for two dinar'. When the **2.60**

[138] Al-Wahāb (n 83) Vol. 6, p. 52; Al-Nawawī (n 18) Vol. 9, p. 207.
[139] Al-Suyūṭī (n 62) Vol. 3, p. 83.
[140] *Majalla*, Art. 183.
[141] Al-Buhūtī (n 29) Vol. 2, p. 460.
[142] Al-Nasafī (n 7) Vol. 5, p. 456.
[143] Ibid, Vol. 5, p. 447.
[144] Ibn al-Humām (n 21) Vol. 3, p. 3.
[145] Al-Marghīnanī (n 14) Vol. 5, p. 7.
[146] Liaquat Ali Khan Niazi, Islamic Law of Contract (Lahore Research Cell Diyal Sing Trust Library, 1990) p. 71; *Majalla*, Art. 187.
[147] Al-Nasafī (n 7) Vol. 5, p. 447.
[148] *Majalla*, Arts 184–185.

offeree responds: 'I accepted', this acceptance is for the second *ījāb* and not for the first one because the second *ījāb* is in fact the revocation of the first *ījāb*. This is same as if the offeror after making first offer says before the acceptance: 'I revoke the offer' and then makes the second offer.[149]

2.7.1.3 When the offer can be revoked

2.61 Hanafis maintain that an offer can be revoked before it is met with acceptance, whereafter there is no option of revocation. This outcome is in light of the *ḥadīth* narrated by Abū Huraira whereby 'both parties of the sale have a right of option before they separate from each other'.[150] Nakha'i suggests that when the offer is accepted, the contract becomes *lāzim* due to the existence of all the *arkān* and conditions for the contract. In this case, the *khiyār* for either party to rescind the contract may be harmful to the other party.[151]

2.62 The contracting parties have an option to rescind the contract before the termination of *majlis*.[152] The offeree has an option of revocation because of his right to deliberate over the offer.[153] This *khiyār* is available according to the majority of jurists, save for the Malikis, as already discussed above.[154]

2.7.1.4 Communication of the revocation

2.63 If the offeror revokes the offer but the offeree does not listen to such revocation and goes on to accept the offer, the contract is concluded. If acceptance and revocation of the offer reach the offeror and offeree respectively at the same time, revocation would be effective.[155]

2.7.2 Change of Subject Matter

2.64 Change in the subject matter brings the offer to an end. This is true where a perishable good no longer exists in the form originally intended to be sold. Acceptance for such good is no longer valid.[156]

2.7.3 Death of Party, Lapse of Time, and Non-Fulfilment of Condition Precedent

2.65 An offer comes to end with the lapse of time, death or insanity of the offeror, and the non-fulfilment of a condition precedent.[157]

[149] Ibn 'Ābidīn (n 13) Vol. 7, pp. 20–21; Al-Nasafī (n 7) Vol. 5, p. 444.
[150] Al-Kāsānī (n 6) Vol. 5, p. 134; Al-Nasafī (n 7) Vol. 5, p. 446.
[151] Al-Mawsilī (n 31) Vol. 2, p. 8.
[152] Al-Wahāb (n 83) Vol. 6, p. 51; Ibn al-Humām (n 21) Vol. 3, pp. 8–9; Ibn 'Ābidīn (n 13) Vol. 7, p. 47; 'Usmānī (n 111) Vol. 1, pp. 48–56.
[153] Al-Mawṣilī (n 31) Vol. 2, p. 7.
[154] Al-Wahāb (n 83) Vol. 6, p. 52. The contract is not concluded with the dispatch of the request to purchase some commodity even if such request is accompanied by a price consideration. Therefore, after the dispatch and receipt of such a request, the offeror can revoke the offer. See Ashraf al Thānavī, Imdād al Fatāwā (Zakariya Book Dipot India, 2014) 6:286.
[155] Ibn al-Humām (n 21) Vol. 3, p. 9; Ibn 'Ābidīn (n 13) Vol. 7, p. 46; Al-Nasafī (n 7) Vol. 5, p. 448.
[156] Al-Nasafī (n 7) Vol. 5, pp. 448–49.
[157] *Majalla*, Art. 187; Al-Nasafī (n 7) Vol. 5, p. 447; Al-Nawawī (n 18) Vol. 9, p. 199.

3

Legal Capacity (*Ahliyya*)

1. Introduction

The Qur'ān says that God only imposes on every man what he is capable of (*lā yukallifu llāhu nafs illā wus'ahā*).[1] *Taklīf* (the noun which derives from *yukallifu*) is generally understood to mean that someone has been ordered to do something that is hard to do (*ilzām mā fīhi kulfa*).[2] The term originates in theology, denoting God's imposition of obligations on his creatures who are then subject to His law. The passive participle of the term, *mukallaf*, refers to someone who is governed by this law. In a more general sense, it refers to every individual who has at his disposal the full and entire scope of the law.[3] A person considered *mukallaf* is capable of understanding the obligations imposed upon him/her (*khiṭāb al-taklīf*). He or she is an adult and rational person (*al-bāligh al-'āqil*). He or she must have the legal capacity which validates the imposition of legal obligations. Such capacity is an indication that he or she has reached the status of having obtained discretion or *compos mentis* (*'aql*).[4] 3.01

The topic of legal capacity is important for understanding Islamic law generally, but it has special significance for contract law and criminal law. In contract law, the topic with which we are primarily concerned, legal capacity is an essential element in each contract. 3.02

The following discussion examines the topic of legal capacity. It provides a general understanding of its definitions and legal bases and illustrates various legal impediments to capacity and the reasons and legal effects thereof. The chapter will also address women's legal capacity in view of jurists' unspoken and yet distinctive treatment of that capacity. An example of the varied approach by which jurists dealt with women's legal capacity is examined in the rules of testimony. 3.03

[1] Qur'ān 2:286; expressed similarly in 2:233; 6:152; 7:42; 23:62; 65:7; cf. D. Gimaret, 'Taklīf' in Peri Bearman, Thierry Bianquis, Clifford Edmund Bosworth et al. (eds), Encyclopaedia of Islam (2nd edn, W.P. Heinrichs) <http://dx.doi.org.ezproxy.soas.ac.uk/10.1163/1573-3912_islam_SIM_7344> accessed 20 September 2021.

[2] Ab al-Ma'ālī Abdul Malik al-Jūwaynī, al-Burhān fī Uṣūl al-fiqh (Dār al-Kutub al-'ilmiyyah, 1997) p. 14.

[3] Gimaret (n 1).

[4] 'Abd al-Karīm Zīdān, Wajīz fī Uṣūl al-Fiqh (Mu'assasat Qurṭuba, n.d.) p. 70.

1.1 Definitions

3.04 The Arabic word for legal capacity is *ahliyya*. The term can be defined as the competence of a human being to acquire rights and obligations. The three-consonantal root of *ahliyya* is *a-h-l* which is to be fit, suited, or qualified.[5] The jurists provide a number of different definitions of *ahliyya* but the core of their meaning is similar. For example, Al-Zarqā (d. 1999) states that *ahliyya* is 'a description presumed [to be] in a person rendering such a person a possible candidate to receive a legislative injunction'.[6] More generally, *ahliyya* can be defined as a set of required qualifications which, when met, allow the person to acquire rights, bear obligations, and conduct transactions with full legal effect.[7] Notably, Mālik's (d. 795) definition stresses the legal obligations which result from one's fitness or capacity to bear obligations so that he defines the concept as 'the fitness of the person to [fulfil] the laws [stipulated by] the Sharī'ah, [both those] he is entitled to and [those] he is subject to (*lahū wa-'alayhi*)'.[8] One can see that the fitness of the person is a necessary precondition for fulfilling the laws of the Sharī'ah and for confirming the validity of legal obligations. Therefore, legal capacity confirms the capacity of the human being to assume legal liability (*bi-l-dhimma*) or to fulfil one's legal obligations according to the Sharī'ah.

1.1.1 The Concept of *Al-Dhimma* (Human Accountability to God)

3.05 Prior to examining the legal bases of *ahliyya*, it is imperative to consider the term's theological foundations as these underscore the rights and obligations to which *ahliyya* gives effect. The concept of *al-dhimma* (human accountability to God) establishes the basis for *ahliyya* as legal capacity arises from the human obligation to God which has arisen in the primordial covenant between God and humanity. This relationship is described in the seminal Qur'ānic passage which deals with the covenant: 'And [remember] when your Lord brought forth from the Children of Adam, from their loins, their seed, and made them testify against themselves [saying]: Am I not your Lord? They said: Yes, verily. We testify. [This was] lest you should say at the Day of Resurrection: Lo! Of this we were unaware.'[9]

3.06 All obligations to which human beings are subject arise out of the covenantal encounter between God and humanity. The relationship with God is a vastly unequal one. God, the Lord, dictates the terms of the relationship. Humanity, the inferior party, must submit to those terms.[10] The covenant describes humanity's rights and responsibilities

[5] Hans Wehr, A Dictionary of Modern Written Arabic (Arabic-English), ed. J Milton Cowan (4th edn, Harrassowitz, 1979).

[6] Muṣṭafā Aḥmad Al-Zarqā, Al-Madkhal Al-fiqhī Al-'ām: Thalāthat 'aqsām fī Juz'aīn (Dār al-Qalam, al-Tab'ah 2, 2004) p. 781.

[7] Mahdi Zahraa, 'The Legal Capacity of Women in Islamic Law' (1996) 11(3) Arab Law Quarterly 245, p. 245.

[8] 'Izzudīn 'Abd al-Latīf, Ibn Mālik, Sharḥ al-Manār wa Hawāshīhi fī al-Uṣūl (al-Maṭba'a al-'Uthmāniyyah, 1897) p. 936.

[9] *Qur'ān*, trans. M.A.S. Abdel Haleem (Oxford University Press, 2008) 7:172.

[10] Bernard Weiss, The Spirit of Islamic Law (University of Georgia Press, 1998) p. 33.

and clarifies the consequences of both compliance and non-compliance. It is from the covenant that all other terms or specific commandments derive.[11] Fakhr al-Dīn al-Rāzī (d. 1209), a late twelfth-century jurist/theologian, describes the relationship between covenant and legal obligation thus: 'a covenant [*mīthāq*] occurs through the doing of those things that render obedience obligatory'.[12] The Lord's ushering of His creatures into an encounter with Him and making known to them His sovereignty over them and His creature's acknowledgement of His superiority are the things that render obedience obligatory.[13]

In the terminology of the divine law the concept of *dhimma* defines the person in terms of what is due to him and what is incumbent upon him, that is, a person's rights and obligations.[14] According to some jurists, *dhimma* is an attribute or quality which is attached to a human being. Other jurists such as al-Bazdawī (d. 1100) and Ibn Mālik argue that *dhimma* is not an attribute. Rather, it is an essence (*dhāt*) or soul and therefore the soul of a person bears responsibility through his covenant.[15] The majority of jurists argue that *dhimma* is the location or place of residence for legal capacity under Islamic law. It is the place where the rights and obligations reside in a human being and is a requisite condition for the existence of *ahliyya*. One scholar's way of thinking about *dhimma* is to view it as the balance sheet of a person, which highlights both assets and liabilities or rights and obligations.[16] In Islamic law, the term can only be assigned to a natural person, whereas the Western-style law equivalent is that of 'personality' which can be attributed to both natural and artificial persons or legal entities.[17] **3.07**

A human being is entitled to a contract of protection (*dhimma*) and consequently is defined as being subject to legal obligations due to him and incumbent upon him, in other words rights and obligations.[18] The basis, therefore, of establishing a person's legal capacity and therefore one's rights and obligations is life (*al-ḥayāt*) itself. Therefore, legal capacity is even attributed to the embryo (*li-l-janīn*) despite the embryo having deficient capacity until it develops into independent life. Indeed, that life is the basis of legal capacity indicates that it does not leave a person until death, and even in death some jurists take the view that legal liability remains attached to the person to some extent.[19] **3.08**

[11] Ibid.

[12] Fakhr al-Dīn al-Rāzī, al-Tafsīr al-Kabīr (Dār al-Kutub al-'Ilmiyyah, n.d.) Vol. 3, p. 106.

[13] Weiss (n 10) pp. 33–34.

[14] Mas'ūd b. 'Umar Taftāzānī, Sharḥ al-talwīḥ 'alā al-tawḍīḥ (Dār al-Kutub al-'ilmiyya, n.d.) Vol. 2, p. 161. *Dhimma* is defined in relation to *ahliyya* of *wujūb* only. The standard texts on *fiqh* discuss the definition of *dhimma* when discussing *ahliyya* of *wujūb* or as a separate topic.

[15] Ḥusain Khalaf Al-Jabūrī, 'Awāriḍ al-Ahliyya (Ma'had al-Buḥūth al-'ilmiyya wa Iḥiyā' (al-Turāth al-Islāmī, 1988)) pp. 95–97.

[16] Imran Ahsan Khan Nyazee, Islamic Jurisprudence: Usul al-Fiqh (The Other Press, The International Institute of Islamic Thought, 2000) p. 110.

[17] Ibid, p. 110. Nyazee argues that the idea of artificial legal personality or a fictitious person is incompatible with Islamic law since a fictitious person cannot enter into a covenant (*'ahd*) with God as it cannot perform religious duties. Modern Muslim writers have sought to acknowledge the existence of a fictitious personality as it underlies the socio-legal structure of the global economy.

[18] 'Alā' al-Dīn al-Bukhārī, Kashf al-Asrār fī Sharḥ Uṣūl al-Bazdawī (Dār al-Kitāb al-Islāmī, n.d.) Vol. 4, p. 237.

[19] 'Abd al-Karīm Zīdān (n 4) p. 93.

1.2 *Anwāʿ al-Ahliyya* (Forms of Legal Capacity)

3.09 The first type of legal capacity is *ahliyya al-wujūb*, which is an individual's capacity to acquire rights and obligations and therefore can be termed the capacity for acquisition (hereinafter, the capacity for acquisition or acquisitive capacity).[20] This capacity is rooted in the life of a human being (*insāniyya*), which the majority view as the legal basis. The second type of legal capacity is *ahliyya al-adā'*. This is the capacity to act or the 'capability of a human being to issue statements and perform acts to which the Lawgiver has assigned certain legal effects' (hereinafter, the capacity for performance or performative capacity).[21] *Ahliyya al-adā'* consists of two types: insufficient (*qāṣir*) and sufficient (*kāmila*). Insufficient *ahliyya* relates to an individual's intellect (*al-qudrāt al-qāṣira*). An individual must be able to understand God's commands, by means of reason. This is the *ahliyya* of mind. The second type concerns the individual's ability to act on a command and this requires the *ahliyya* of body. If a person's ability to act is sufficient or complete (*kāmila*), then one possesses complete *ahliyya al-adā'*. Complete *ahliyya al-adā'* denotes sufficient capacity for reason and a body sufficient in its ability to act (*al-qudrāt al-kāmila wa al-badan al-kāmil*).[22] In childhood a person lacks both abilities but has the potential for both. Gradually, bit by bit, the child matures and becomes discerning (*ṣabī ʿāqil*). The discerning child's body is weak but his intellect has the potential to become complete. In contrast, a mature person with a mental impediment (*al-maʿtūh al-bāligh*) possesses a weak mind even if his body is complete.[23] Therefore, *ahliyya al-wujūb* centres on the accountability of the individual which is rooted in the *dhimma*. The second type, *ahliyya al-adā'*, is concerned with the individual's ability to reason and their physical body.

1.3 Legal Bases or Foundations (*Nuṣūṣ Shariʿiyyah*)

3.10 Jurists arrived at the specific terminology of *ahliyya* by virtue of their reasoning (*ijtihād*). The primary legal texts (*nuṣūṣ shariʿiyyah*) provide the legal basis from which jurists exercised their *ijtihād*. Qur'ān 48:26 is said to provide a foundational legal basis for the concept: 'Allah sent down His tranquility to His Messenger and to the believers and made binding on them [their] promise to obey God, for that was more appropriate and fitting for them *(wa ahlahā)*.'

3.11 The word *ahl* used here is interpreted as implying rights and obligations relating to capacity.[24] According to other authors, the Qur'ānic verse 2:286 provides the definitive

[20] Imran Ahsan Khan Nyazee (n 16) p. 111.
[21] Muḥammad ibn Aḥmad al-Sarakhsī, Uṣūl al-Sarakhsī, ed. Lajnat Iḥyā' al-Maʿārif al-Nuʿmāniyya (Abū al-Wafā' al-Afghānā, n.d.) pp. 332–33.
[22] Ibn Abī Saʿīd ibn ʿUbayd Allāh al-Ḥanafī al-Ṣadīqī Jīwan, Nūr Al-Anwār Maʿa Ḥāshīyat Qamar Al-Aqmār (al-Bushra Publisher, 2008) Vol. 2, p. 149.
[23] Ibid.
[24] Ahmad Hassan, Principles of Islamic Jurisprudence (Adam Publishers & Distributors, 2007) p. 295.

basis for the concept of legal capacity.[25] It states: 'God does not burden any soul with more than it can bear: each gains whatever good it has done, and suffers its bad.'

Finally, the covenant (*'ahd*) into which the believer enters with God and from which all rights and obligations derive is established in the following verse (7:172): 3.12

> [Prophet], when your Lord took out the offspring from the loins of the Children of Adam and made them bear witness about themselves, He said, 'Am I not your Lord?' and they replied, 'Yes, we bear witness'. So you cannot say on the Day of Resurrection, 'We were not aware of this'.

1.3.1 *Ahliyya Al-Wujūb* and *Ahliyya Al-Adā'*

Jurists differentiate between the legal bases of *ahliyya al-wujūb* and *ahliyya al-adā'*. The 3.13
life of a human being (*insāniyya*), as described above, establishes the basis for *ahliyya al-wujūb* (the capacity of obligations due to and from the individual). The jurists unanimously agree on this point. Life makes a person eligible for the acquisition of a wide range of rights and obligations. The juristic basis for the capacity for performance (*ahliyya al-adā'*), on the other hand, is discernment or discrimination (*tamyīz*). In explaining the basic element of *ahliyya al-adā'*, Mullah Jīwan argues that reason (*'aql*), which is used synonymously with discernment, is the basis upon which this type of capacity functions, since to understand a command from God requires the ability to comprehend.[26] The Malikis, Hanafis, and Hanbalis define discernment as the ability to protect and manage one's property to one's benefit. Their definition, therefore, is clearly orientated toward obligations. They base this definition on Ibn Abbās's (d. 687) interpretation of the verse in [4:6] which he refers to a person's ability to use their property to their benefit.[27] The verse provides: 'Test orphans until they reach marriageable age; then, if you find they have sound judgement, hand over their property to them.'

In contrast, discernment according to the Shafi'i's is not only the ability to manage 3.14
one's property for one's own benefit. It also refers to the adherence to Islamic teachings. A person is considered non-discerning if his sins outweigh his good deeds, if he deals wastefully or excessively in his property, or transacts therein in forbidden ways.[28]

Every legal act is given effect through a 'discerning will' (*irāda mudrika*) or a human 3.15
being's ability to reason (*'aql*). A person who possesses the highest level of discernment is considered as possessing complete legal capacity, which entitles him to perform legal acts in the absence of impediment. On the other hand, persons who possess insufficient discernment are considered to possess deficient capacity for performance.[29] Both

[25] Mir Wali Ullah, Muslim Jurisprudence & the Quranic Law of Crimes (Taj Publishers, 1986) p. 68.
[26] Ibn Abī Sa'īd ibn 'Ubayd Allāh al-Ḥanafī al-Ṣadīqī Jīwan (n 22) Vol. 2, p. 149.
[27] Wahbah al-Zuḥaylī, Financial Transactions in Islamic Jurisprudence, trans. Mahmoud Al. El-Gamal (Dār al-Fikr, 2003) Vol. 2, p. 358.
[28] Muḥammad ibn Aḥmad Shirbīnī, al-Sirāj al-Munīr fī Ma'rifat ba'ḍ Ma'ānī Kalām Rabinā al-'alīm al-Khabīr (Maṭba'at Būlāq, 1285 Hijra (1868 AD)) Vol. 1, p. 282.
[29] Muḥammad Naim Omar, 'The Concept of Impediments to Legal Capacity ('Awāriḍ al-Ahliyya) in Islamic Law of Contract and the Egyptian Civil Code of 1948' (PhD Thesis, University of Wales, Lampeter, 2006) p. 23.

the capacity for acquisition and the capacity for performance may be either complete (*kāmila*) or deficient (*nāqiṣa*).

1.4 Impediments to Legal Capacity (*'Awāriḍ Al-Ahliyya*)

1.4.1 Definitions

3.16 Legal capacity is defined by considering the developmental stages of life that human beings experience until death, and by assessing the attributes of human beings that are acquired naturally from God as well as those which are acquired through life experience. The first eleven impediments map a progression in the maturity of the mind and body from childhood into adulthood and conclude in death. Importantly, it has been established that capacity for acquisition is deficient in the foetal stage of life, yet birth signifies complete capacity for acquisition as its legal basis is human life which exists from birth until death. Various contingencies of body and mind are interspersed throughout the course of life such as mental incompetence, unconsciousness, sleep, forgetfulness, slavery, terminal illness, menstruation, and post-partum bleeding. The remaining impediments are those which a human being may acquire throughout his or her lifetime. Together, these circumstances are known as impediments to the legal capacity of the human being (*'awāriḍ al-ahliyya*). *'Awāriḍ* can also be defined as a group of factors which restrict a person from enjoying rights according to his will (*irādah*).[30]

3.17 Pre-modern jurists, especially those of the Hanafi school, widen the scope of the concept to include matters that have effects on the establishment of legal rulings or which vitiate consent. Therefore, factors such as mistake, slavery, jest, and terminal illness are dealt with as impediments to legal capacity.[31] Contemporary jurists narrow the definition so that the concept refers to the circumstances which affect a person's mind (*'aql*) and/or discernment (*tamyīz*) or which place limitations on his acts.[32] Al-Zarqā, for example, takes a more systematic approach and centres his argument on the bases of the capacity for performance, namely, reason and discernment. Accordingly, any matter which does not influence the ability to reason or to discern is not viewed as an impediment.[33] In the same sense, Al-Nūrī restricts impediments to legal capacity as including insanity (*junūn*), imbecility (*'atah*), and prodigality (*safah*) as well as unawareness (*ghaflah*).[34] Yet the logic of modern scholars' reasoning is not always consistent. Al-Zarqā, contrary to his definition, adds indebtedness (*madyūnīyah*) and bankruptcy (*iflās*) as impediments, even though these characteristics do not influence a person's ability to reason or discern.

[30] Ibid, p. 32.

[31] Husayn Al-Nūrī, Dirāsah fī 'Awāriḍ al-Ahliyya fī al-Sharī'ah al-Islāmiyyah (Maṭba'at Lajnat al-Bayān al-'Arabī, 1953) p. 93.

[32] 'Abd al-Wahhāb Khallāf, al-Ahliyya wa 'Awāriḍuhā (Maṭba'at al-Naṣr, 1955) p. 23.

[33] Al-Zarqā (n 6) pp. 834, 853.

[34] Al-Nūrī (n 31) p. 96. Al-Nūrī offers a comprehensive discussion of the traditional views on impediments and why he thinks the categories are too numerous, ibid, pp. 93–100.

1.4.2 Types of Attributes

Despite these conceptual differences, in general, legal capacity is categorized into two types: heavenly or divine attributes (*samāwiyyah*) and acquired attributes (*muktasabah*). Divine attributes are those which are handed down by God and about which a person has no choice. The Hanafis include eleven 'given impediments' such as: minority (*ṣighar*), insanity (*junūn*), imbecility (*'atah*), forgetfulness (*nisyān*), sleep (*nawm*), faintness/unconsciousness (*ighmā'*), slavery (*riqq*), illness (*maraḍ*), menstruation (*ḥayḍ*), post-natal bleeding (*nifās*), and death (*mawt*).[35] **3.18**

Acquired attributes, on the other hand, are those which are acquired through choice and acquisition. Acquired attributes are further categorized according to: (i) attributes belonging to the self or ego of the person (*nafs*) such as ignorance (*al-jahl*), intoxication (*al-sukr*), prodigality (*al-safah*), and humour/jest (*al-hazl*); and (ii) attributes or effects by which another person affects the reason or discernment of another. This second category includes compulsion or duress (*al-ikrāh*), mistake, and ignorance (*khaṭa', jahl*).[36] The inclusion of these latter topics as relevant to legal capacity in the Islamic tradition reflects the pre-modern concern with factors which affect legal rulings in general or which have legal effects. It may be worth mentioning that, in contemporary law, duress, undue influence, and mistake are conceptually related to a party's vitiated consent and therefore are not dealt with under legal capacity. In sum, the impediments to legal capacity affect human beings' capacity to undertake legal acts such as contracts. Therefore, these impediments can be organized according to whether they affect the mind or the body:[37] **3.19**

- Impediments to the intellect: minority, insanity, imbecility, forgetfulness, sleep, prodigality, drunkenness, faintness/unconsciousness, duress, and mistake
- Impediments to the body: illness, menstruation, post-natal bleeding, and death
- Impediments to the body and intellect: minority, sleep, unconsciousness, drunkenness, and slavery

This categorization indicates that legal capacity in Islamic law is not a static concept. In fact, the individual can occupy multiple capacities at any one time as the individual progresses through life's manifold circumstances. Changes to the legal capacity of an individual represent the loss or gain of one or other of the forms of capacity in relation to the particular impediment. For example, a person may be simultaneously ill, insane, and suffer from drunkenness. These conditions produce specific legal effects with respect to prayer, fasting, bequest, contracting, and other social and religious acts.[38] **3.20**

[35] Muḥammad Amīn Ibn Maḥmūd Al-Bukhārī Amīr Bādshāh, Taysīr al-Taḥrīr (Musṭafā al-Bābī al-Ḥalabī, 1932) Vol. 2, p. 258; al-Ḥanafī al-Ṣadīqī Jīwan (n 22) pp. 156–83.

[36] For a discussion on the different types of ignorance '*jahl*', see al-Ḥanafī al-Ṣadīqī Jīwan (n 22) Vol. 2, p. 183. See also Nyazee (n 16) pp. 132–40.

[37] Fatima Seedat, 'Sex and the Legal Subject: Women and Legal Capacity in Hanafi Law' (PhD Thesis, McGill University) p. 124.

[38] Ibid, p. 141.

3.21 The following discussion first examines divine or heavenly attributes. In particular, the focus is on the most relevant factors to contemporary jurists, namely, minority (*ṣighar*), insanity (*junūn*), and imbecility (*ʿatah*).[39]

1.5 *Ḥajr* (Interdiction)

3.22 *Ḥajr* is the legal consequence of insufficient *ahliyya*. It is the positive law corollary to legal theory. While *ahliyya* is concerned with the available capacities of the legal subject, *ḥajr* deals with the limits imposed by those capacities and the ability of the individual to manage their own affairs. The Majalla defines interdiction (*ḥajr*) as 'prohibiting any particular person from dealing in his own property',[40] yet the focus on property is merely one legal consequence which can arise in the absence of *ahliyya*. *Ḥajr* prevents the imprudent distribution of property and limits oral statements related to marriage and divorce. Notably, children, slaves, and the mentally incompetent are automatically interdicted in view of the categories of persons as provided for in jurists' rulings regarding *ahliyya*.

1.6 Capacity of the Minor (*Ṣabī*)

3.23 In Islamic law minority is defined as the period in which a person has yet to reach the age of majority. Malikis and Hanafis categorized the developmental stages of a minor into two categories: namely, non-discerning (*ghayr mumayyīz*) and discerning (*mumayyīz*). The Shafi'is do not differentiate between a non-discerning and a discerning child in relation to the validity of a contract whereas the Hanbalis found that a discerning child's transactions were valid if authorized by his guardian (*walī*).[41]

[39] Al-Zarqā (n 6) p. 854 argues that minority, among others, should not be categorised as part of the so-called heavenly impediments. *ṣighar*, he says, is a natural stage of every human's life; it is an original state (*min al-aḥwāl al-ʾaṣliyya*) in the subject of *ahliyya*, and not part of the impediments (*laysa min al-ʿawāriḍ*).

[40] Majallat Al-Aḥkām Al-ʿadlīyyah, Art. 941. The Majalla refers to the civil code in force in the Ottoman Empire, and briefly in the Turkish republic, from 1285/1869 to 1926. The code covers contracts, torts, and some principles of civil procedure. It reflects Western-style law mainly in its organization into numbered books, sections, and articles, as in European codes. The Majalla was extremely important for several reasons. It represents the first attempt by an Islamic state to codify, and to enact as law of the state, part of the Sharīʿah. Further, the code did not always incorporate the dominant opinions of the Hanafi school of law, which governed the Ottoman Empire. Rather, the code incorporated those deemed most suited to the conditions of the times, in accordance with the principle of *takhayyur* (eclectic choice). While the justificatory memorandum (*esbāb-ī mūdjibe maḍbaṭasī*) submitted to the Council of Ministers said that the authors of the code 'never went outside the Hanafi rite', some of these opinions had in fact originated with non-Hanafi jurists. Such eclecticism became a major feature of later efforts at reform of the Sharīʿah and, by nature, provided added impetus for codification. Finally, since the Majalla was applied in the secular *niẓāmiyya* courts set up in the period as well as in the S̲h̲arīʿah courts, it applied to non-Muslim subjects of the empire as state law (*qānūn*), as well as to Muslims, on whom the code's *sharʿī* content would have been binding in any case; cf. C.V. Findley, 'Medjelle' in Bearman, et al. (eds) (n 1) <http://dx.doi.org.ezproxy.soas.ac.uk/10.1163/1573-3912_islam_SIM_5107> accessed 21 September 2021.

[41] Wahbah al-Zuḥaylī (n 27) Vol. 2, p. 358.

1.6.1 The Non-discerning Child

Upon birth, a child possesses complete capacity for acquisition but until he attains the age of majority, he lacks the capacity for performance. The capacity for acquisition establishes a liability for physical activities such as usurping or destroying property. A child who engages in such activities is liable for the damage. However, the absence of the capacity for performance means that liability for verbal dealings does not exist, as such dealings require a valid intent to establish legal consequences.[42] The Malikis and Hanafis categorize life according to stages in which different levels of the capacity for performance are present. The first stage lasts from birth until the attainment of partial discretion, which is set at seven years of age. During this stage, the child does not possess the capacity for performance as he lacks reason and discretion. He is therefore ineligible for the capacity for performance and as such is neither required nor able to perform any legally binding act. Legal acts can be performed on the child's behalf by a legal guardian according to the rules of the guardianship.[43] **3.24**

There is some disagreement about the period during which a child remains non-discerning. According to the Hanafis, a child is considered non-discerning from birth until he reaches the age of seven, at which time the child can be considered subject to the rulings of the Sharīʿah.[44] The majority of pre-modern jurists did not determine a specific age for the beginning of discernment. Jurists reasoned that intellectual capacity differed from one person to another and thus a standard was not seen as appropriate. The seven-year standard represented most prominently by the Hanafi school seems to have been introduced by modern scholars.[45] The basis of this age determination may lie in a *ḥadīth* which commands young children to pray: 'Command your children to pray when they become seven years old and beat them for it (prayer) when they become ten years old; and arrange their beds (to sleep) separately.'[46] **3.25**

A common interpretation of the *ḥadīth* is that a seven-year-old child can understand commands and thus can be taught. Therefore, a seven-year-old is considered a discerning child. Moreover, the standard is commensurate with the time at which children go to school, indicating that discernment is present (or is thought to be) in children at this age.[47] **3.26**

1.6.2 The Liability of the Discerning Child

Financial transactions are divided into three types for determining the liability of the discriminating minor.[48] The first category concerns purely beneficial acts such as the acceptance of a donation, gift, or charity but also includes the making of a last will and **3.27**

[42] Ibid, Vol. 2, p. 352.
[43] 'Abd al-Karīm Zīdān (n 4) pp. 94–95.
[44] Nyazee (n 16) p. 114.
[45] 'Abd al-Karīm Zīdān (n 4) p. 95.
[46] Narrated by Abū Dawūd, *Kitāb al-Ṣalāt*, chapter 26, *Ḥadīth* No. 495.
[47] Omar (n 29) p. 44.
[48] Nyazee (n 16) p. 118.

testament (*al-waṣiyya*).[49] According to the majority, the minor is eligible to perform these acts without having to acquire permission from the legal guardian.[50] The second category concerns legal acts which are harmful to the child, such as those which cause him to lose possession of something without gaining anything in return. This category includes the acts of giving (*hibah*), establishing a religious endowment (*waqf*), granting a divorce, manumission (*ʿitq*), giving a loan (*qarḍ*), or similar acts. The child is not entitled to perform these acts, nor is he entitled to give his permission to the legal guardian to perform these acts on his behalf. The legal guardian is restricted to the principle of safeguarding the child's best interests and avoiding any legal acts which may result in harm to the child. The third category concerns contracts that may result in benefit or harm. Contracts in this category include sale, hire, partnership, and similar Sharīʿah-based legal instruments. There is disagreement amongst the jurists as to the validity of this kind of contract. According to the Hanafis, a child is entitled to carry out this kind of contract subject to the guardian's approval.[51] The contract, although validly concluded, is said to be suspended (*mawqūfah*) until it has been approved. If the guardian remains silent as to his approval, the contract remains suspended until the child reaches puberty, at which time he has the right (*khiyār*) to ratify or nullify the contract.[52]

3.28 Unlike the majority, the Shafi'is do not differentiate between a non-discerning and discerning child in relation to the validity of a contract. A child has no capacity to conclude a contract whether he has been given consent by his guardian or not.[53] They base their ruling on the absence of 'prudence' (*rushd*) which, like discretion (*tamyyīz*), is viewed as a criterion of the capacity for performance. The difference of opinion stems from their interpretation of Qur'ānic verse 4:6: 'Test orphans until they reach marriageable age; then, if you find they have sound judgement, hand over their property to them.'

3.29 Al-Shāfiʿī (d. 820) argues the verse affirms that children will not gain any degree of the capacity for performance until they have reached puberty and demonstrate prudence. For Al-Shāfiʿī the nature of *rushd* relates not merely to financial acuity as Mālik argues. Rather, it also concerns sound religious behaviour. At its root, therefore, their disagreement is about whether the term *rushd* can be used to describe the non-righteous.[54]

[49] According to the Malikis, the Hanbalis, and one Shafi'i view, the bequest of a child is permissible and valid. The Hanafis, Shafi'is, and the Zahiris, on the other hand, argue that the bequest of a child is invalid. The latter's view centres on an authentic *ḥadīth* which provides that a child does not bear liability until puberty. This view categorizes bequests amongst the harmful acts because of the loss of property. Ibid. There is similar discussion on this topic in Al-Zarqā (n 6) 805 and Muḥammad Abū Zahra, Al-Milkiyyah wa Nazariyyat al-ʿAqd fī al-Sharīʿah al-Islāmiyyah (Dār al-Fikr al-ʿArabī, 1996) pp. 286–90.

[50] ʿAlāʾ al-Dīn Al-Kāsānī, Badāʾiʿ al-ṣanāʾiʿ (2nd edn, Dār al-Kutub al-ʿilmīyyah, 1986) Vol. 7, p. 171; see also al-Nūrī (n 31) p. 66 and al-Zarqā (n 6) p. 805.

[51] ʿAbd al-Karīm Zīdān (n 4) p. 97.

[52] ʿAlī Muḥyī al-Dīn Qarrah Dāghī, Mabdaʾ al-riḍā fī al-ʿuqūd: dirāsah muqāranah fī al-fiqh al-Islāmī wa-al-qānūn al-madanī al-Rūmānī ... wa-al-ʿIrāqi (Dār al-Bashāʾir al-Islamiyyah, 2002) p. 154.

[53] Al-Imām Abī Zakariyya al-Nawawī, Kitāb al-Majmūʿ al-Muhadhdhib (Dār iḥyaʾ al-Turāth Al-ʿArabī, n.d.) Vol. 9, pp. 147–48.

[54] Abū al-Walīd Ibn Rushd, Bidāyat al-Mujtahid wa Nihāyat al-Muqtaṣid, trans. Imran Ahsan Khan Nyazee (Garnet Publishing, 1994) Vol. 1, p. 337. In line with this reasoning, Al-Shāfiʿī argues, '*sufahāʾ* is women and minors'. Women's legal capacity is examined in para 3.86.

Further arguments, including one interpretation taken from Ibn ʿAbbās, provides that the meaning of *sufahā'* in Qur'ān 4:5 relates to both a child and the mentally infirm.[55] Therefore, the ruling which applies to the *sufahā'* is also applicable to the child. The verse commands: 'Do not entrust your property to the feeble-minded (*sufahā'*). God has made it a means of support for you: make provision for them from it, clothe them, and address them kindly.' 3.30

The majority, on the other hand, argue that the prohibition from passing on wealth to orphans until they reach puberty and prudence is undisputed, as is the meaning of the verse relating to the prodigal (*sufahā'*), yet these limits do not necessarily render void contracts which have been carried out with the consent of a child's guardian.[56] 3.31

As for criminal liability, it does not exist in the case of a person who has not attained their majority. Therefore, the *ḥudūd* and *qiṣāṣ* penalties are not applicable. Moreover, the guardian cannot stand as substitute for the child, since criminal offences as punishments are directed solely at transgressors. One important distinction is where a discerning child remains liable for blood money (*dīyyah*) because youth does not override the inviolability of the location of guilt in relation to murder and manslaughter.[57] Moreover, a discerning child may be liable to some suitable form of discipline (*ta'dīb*).[58] 3.32

Finally, acts of ritual and worship (*al-ʿibādāt*), which include not only acts of worship such as prayers but also the payment of *zakāt* (poor tax) as well as acts which combine the payment of money with physical acts such as the *ḥajj* (pilgrimage), are not incumbent on the child. The child does not possess the capacity for performance and such acts cannot be fulfilled by substitution as they are legal duties whose performance is based on free will.[59] Notably, there is some dispute amongst jurists concerning a child's payment of *zakāt*. Some jurists consider *zakāt* as a legal right of the poor and therefore oblige the rich, irrespective of age, to pay the tax. Those who do not consider the tax obligatory view it solely as an act of worship and therefore conditional upon being of mature age or mental development (*bulūgh*).[60] 3.33

1.7 The Age of Majority

Attaining the age of majority (*bulūgh*) is significant in Islamic law as it is the milestone at which full legal capacity is established according to the Hanafis, Hanbalis, and most Shafi'is.[61] It has been determined that the attribute of discernment is associated with 3.34

[55] Muḥammad bin Idrīs Al-Shāfiʿī, Aḥkām al-Qur'ān in 'Abd al-Ghanī 'Abd al-Khāliq (ed.), (Dār al-Kutub al-ʿIlmiyyah, 1990) Vol. 1, p. 138.
[56] Omar (n 29) p. 74.
[57] ʿAbd al-Karīm Zīdān (n 4) p. 96.
[58] Nyazee (n 16) p. 119.
[59] Masʿūd b. ʿUmar Al-Taftāzānī (n 14) Vol. 2, p. 164.
[60] Abū al-Walīd Ibn Rushd (n 54) pp. 283–84.
[61] The Malikis distinguish between the rulings for males and females. This distinction is complex and detailed, and while applicable in the pre-modern age, arguably it is no longer so. For further details, see Wahbah al-Zuḥaylī (n 27) Vol. 2, pp. 352–53.

the full development of a person's mental faculties and that the jurists associate discernment with the onset of puberty (*bulūgh*).

1.7.1 The Signs of Puberty

3.35 The natural signs of puberty are generally the indications by which the age of majority is determined. In the absence of these indications, jurists set a certain age at which time puberty is assumed to have transpired.

3.36 Ejaculation from wet dreams (*iḥtilām*) and female menstruation are unanimously viewed as indications that puberty has commenced.[62] Jurists base their opinion on a verse from the Qur'ān (24:59) in which God commands: 'When your children reach puberty, they should [always] ask your permission to enter, like their elders do. This is how God makes His messages clear to you: God is all knowing, all wise.'

3.37 Several *ḥadīths* support this interpretation. In one, the Prophet Muḥammad is to have said: 'There are three (persons) whose actions are not recorded (liability is exempted): a sleeper till he awakes, a boy till he reaches puberty (literally, has a wet dream), and a lunatic till he comes to reason.'[63]

3.38 In the absence of these signs, the majority of Hanafis stipulated that the age of fifteen is commensurate with the onset of puberty in both sexes, according to the majority. Notably, Abū Ḥanīfa (d. 767) elevates the age to eighteen for males and seventeen for females.[64] The minimum age, on the other hand, is twelve for boys and nine for girls.[65] The latter age stipulations are the law according to the Majalla. If a child has reached the age of fifteen and still shows no sign of puberty, the child is considered to have arrived at the age of puberty.[66]

1.7.2 Puberty and the Capacity for Performance

3.39 The presumption that puberty is an indication of intellect and discernment is rebuttable, however. If it is proved that a pubescent person has not yet reached full mental development, the capacity for performance can be withdrawn.[67] The legal basis for this determination is provided in the Qur'ān 4:6:

> Test orphans until they reach marriageable age; then, if you find they have sound judgement, hand over their property to them. Do not consume it hastily before they

[62] Jurists disagree on whether puberty can be determined by the appearance of pubic hair. In general, however, most jurists agree that it is a sign of puberty.

[63] Sunan Abī Dāwūd, Kitāb al-Ḥudūd, no. 4403 <https://sunnah.com/abudawud/40/53> accessed 15 February 2023.

[64] Nyazee (n 16) p. 113.

[65] The Shafi'is, Malikis, and Hanafis have each reached different rulings regarding the age of puberty and the signs of puberty. For a comprehensive discussion, see Yaḥyā ibn Sharaf Nawawī, Muḥammad Najīb Muṭīʿī, and Abū Isḥāq Shīrāzī, Kitāb Al-Majmūʿ: Sharḥ al-Muhadhdhab Lil-Shīrāzī (Dār Iḥyā' al-Turāth al-ʿArabī, 2001) pp. 360–69.

[66] Al-Majalla (n 40) Arts 986–987.

[67] Nyazee (n 16) p. 111.

come of age: if the guardian is well off, he should abstain from the orphan's property, and if he is poor, he should use only what is fair.

Note that the majority extrapolate the verse's specific reference to 'orphans' to human beings in general. Moreover, the verse indicates marriage (*nikāh*) which is viewed as commensurate with the age of puberty. Therefore, the majority stipulate that there are two conditions which must be fulfilled before the wealth of orphans is passed on to them: puberty (*bulūgh*) and discretion (*rushd*). When these conditions are present, complete capacity is established without the need for a court order.[68] However, before handing over his property to him, a youth must be tested for discernment. If he can show that he is of mature mind, his property should be handed over to him.[69] However, if he cannot, his property should not be handed to him, and he should be prohibited from dealing in it until such time as he has proved that he is of mature mind.[70] If property has been handed over to him by his guardian before it has been proved that the child is of mature mind, and such property is lost or the guardian destroys the property, the guardian is to be held liable.[71] 3.40

Notably, Abū Ḥanīfa takes a different position, maintaining that a person who attains the age of twenty-five must be able to have full disposal rights over his/her property irrespective of having attained discretion. A person at the age of twenty-five cannot be subject to interdiction (*ḥajr*) as doing so would his dignity. The argument is also based on the verse (17:34): 'Do not go near the orphan's property, except with the best [intentions], until he reaches the age of maturity (full strength).' A person of twenty-five years of age, it is argued, has attained full maturity or strength (*balagha ashuddahu*). 3.41

On the other hand, the majority subject a non-discerning person to interdiction irrespective of whether he has reached puberty. The same is the case in relation to persons who have attained discretion but subsequently lose it.[72] The principal jurists of all schools ruled that a child cannot be released from interdiction or cannot attain full legal capacity without attaining discernment irrespective of whether the onset of puberty has occurred.[73] 3.42

[68] A minority Shāfiʿī opinion ruled that a court order was necessary, since the removal of interdiction requires judgment and testing of the interdicted, by analogy with interdiction of the insane. See Shirbīnī, Muḥammad ibn Aḥmad, Mughnī al-muḥtāj (Dār al-Kutub al-ʿilmiyyah, 1994) Vol. 3, p. 140.

[69] Al-Majalla (n 40) Art. 981. Testing children is carried out by giving them temporary permission to deal or trade. The jurists differed in their rulings in relation to an underage child who is authorized to trade. This discussion is beyond the remit of this chapter. However, a good place to start is Wahbah al-Zuḥaylī (n 27) Vol. 2, pp. 366–68. See also Muwaffaq al-Dīn ʿAbd Allāh Ibn Aḥmad Ibn Qudāmah, al-Mughnī (Maktabāt al-Qahira, 1968) Vol. 4, p. 344.

[70] Al-Majalla (n 40) Art. 982.

[71] Ibid, Art. 983.

[72] Nyazee (n 16) p. 114.

[73] Wahbah al-Zuḥaylī (n 27) Vol. 2, p. 356. See also Al-Majalla (n 40) Art. 982.

1.8 Insanity (*Junūn*) or Mental Incompetence

1.8.1 Definitions

3.43 Jurists do not agree on the exact meaning of insanity despite the use of the term (*junūn*) in the Qur'ān and the Sunna. Some scholars view 'insanity' as a defective intellect, which hinders a person's ability to process acts and speech normally.[74] It is also known as an inability to distinguish between good and bad and to foresee the outcome of something.[75] Still others assign the term tangibility, considering it to be a 'pest' in the brain, causing a normal person to act against reason.[76] Despite these differences, the general meaning is that insanity is a kind of mental affliction which prevents the brain from functioning normally. This understanding is reflected in jurists' agreement of insanity's legal effects.

3.44 It is important to note that jurists' use of the term 'insanity' or what might now be termed 'mental impediment' was not distinguished from 'mental illness', which can come and go. Instead, two types of 'insanity' were established which, although medically inaccurate according to contemporary standards, relate to the permanence of 'mental impediment' and thereby acknowledge indirectly the difference between the two conditions. Notably, scholarly comment was concerned with the legal effects of these conditions and not the conditions themselves. The first type, known as *junūn aṣlī*, is when a person is afflicted with insanity from birth. The cause is thought to be a defective physical condition (of the brain) which impedes the brain's receptive capabilities. The condition is not considered curable. The second type, known as *junūn ṭāri'* concerns the person who has developed insanity with age, one who has attained majority with a sound mind but then develops 'insanity'. Two versions of this sudden-onset insanity are laid down. The first is when the normal function of the brain is interrupted, which is akin to an incidence of poor mental health. The second type is said to occur due to the 'Devil's control' over afflicted human beings, the effect of which causes a person to imagine something unreal. It is thought that this kind of insanity, the so-called satanic touch, can be cured by prayer.[77]

1.8.2 Interdiction (*Ḥajr*) of the Insane (Mental Incompetence)

3.45 The Majalla provides that 'minors, lunatics and imbeciles are ipso facto interdicted'.[78] The insane person is interdicted with automatic effect and without having to secure a court order.[79] However, the Malikis rule that the interdiction of an insane person requires the consent of his father, guardian, or a judge. Therefore, the meaning of interdiction in Islamic law is both the removal as well as the absence of the capacity for performance as in the case of the underage child. It is a legal condition which arises

74 Mas'ūd b. 'Umar al-Taftāzānī (n 14) p. 167.
75 Ibid.
76 Omar (n 29) p. 87.
77 Mas'ūd b. 'Umar al-Taftāzānī (n 14) p. 167.
78 Al-Majalla (n 40) Art. 957.
79 Omar (n 29) p. 105.

upon birth, but it is also an instrument which can be used to remove liability from certain types of persons.

The absence of the legal bases of active *ahliyya*, which are reason (*ʿaql*) and discretion (*tamyyīz*), result in interdiction of the insane person. The insane person is considered to be of unsound intellect (*fāsid al-ʿaql*) and devoid of discernment (*ʿadim al-tamayyīz*). Therefore, the absence of the capacity for performance of an insane person is analogous to that of the non-discerning child and he is treated in the same manner.[80] This means that an insane person lacks legal authority to trade, write wills, marry, or enter into any other type of contract. Notably, an insane person's capacity for acquisition is not affected by the condition as the legal basis for this type of capacity is human life. As with the non-discerning child, he is only liable for physical acts such as the fathering of children or the destruction of property.[81] His capacity for inheritance, for example, is undiminished as a result of his insanity. **3.46**

1.8.2.1 Distinctions between types of insanity and legal effects

The distinction between 'insanity from birth' and 'intermittent insanity' has legal consequences in civil transactions. The Majalla provides that the acts of the insane who are continuously mad, are considered to reflect deficient legal capacity as is the case with the non-discerning child. In relation to the intermittently insane, the Majalla provides that acts performed during periods of lucidity are given legal effect in the same way that the acts of sane persons are valid.[82] The interdiction is lifted without depending on a judge's order. This ruling is said to reflect consensus amongst the jurists.[83] However, there may be times at which an insane person's lucidity is imperfect so that he is not fully discerning. By analogy with the ruling for non-discerning children, his actions during this period are considered to be suspended until his guardian has given his approval.[84] According to the Hanafi and Maliki schools, such approval should be forthcoming if his dealings are beneficial, but equally approval should be withheld if they are harmful.[85] **3.47**

1.8.2.2 Legal bases of interdiction

Jurists arrived at many causes of interdiction, but insanity as well as minority, imbecility, prodigality, bankruptcy, sickness, marital ties, and pledge are agreed according to the different schools of law. The most direct evidence of this is the *ḥadīth* in which the Prophet was to have reported that: 'the pen is lifted for three persons: a sleeping person until he wakes up, a minor until he reaches puberty and an insane person until **3.48**

[80] ʿAbd al-Karīm Zīdān (n 4) p. 102.
[81] Wahbah al-Zuḥaylī (n 27) Vol. 2, p. 368.
[82] Al-Majalla (n 40) Art. 980.
[83] Muwaffaq al-Dīn ʿAbd Allāh Ibn Aḥmad Ibn Qudāmah (n 69) Vol. 4, p. 343.
[84] Mulla Khusrut, Mirʾāt al-uṣūl sharḥ mirqāt al-wuṣūl (Dār al-Kutub al-ʿIlmiyah, 2018) p. 439.
[85] Wahbah al-Zuḥaylī (n 27) Vol. 2, p. 368.

he recovers'.[86] It is argued that the lifting of the pen is to remove God's obligation (*taklīf*) from the insane person so that his actions have no legal effect.

3.49 Textual evidence from the holy sources illustrates the breadth of the interdiction's applicability. Notably, the word *ḥajr* (interdiction) does not appear in Qur'ānic verses, yet scholars cite these verses when developing their conceptual understanding of interdiction.[87] One of the first textual points of reference cited is Qur'ān 4:6 with which the reader is now familiar: 'Test orphans until they reach marriageable age; then, if you find they have sound judgement, hand over their property to them.'

3.50 God orders the guardian to test the orphan's judgement and should their judgement be sound, their properties can be released to them. Jurists' interpretation of this verse is that the child is put under interdiction until such a time as he attains puberty and can show discretion. Notably, this period of interdiction is commensurate with the absence of the capacity for performance.

3.51 In Qur'ān 4:5 God's commands are squarely directed at the mentally incompetent: 'Do not entrust your property to the feeble-minded. God has made it a means of support for you: make provisions for them from it, clothe them, and address them kindly.'

3.52 This verse is said to prevent the mentally incompetent from controlling property, but it also ensures their care and support. Notably, removing control of property from the mentally incompetent ensures that it will not be squandered.[88]

3.53 Furthermore, in Qur'ān 2:282 God exhorts: 'If the debtor is feeble-minded, weak, or unable to dictate, then let his guardian dictate justly.'

3.54 Al-Shāfi'ī's interpretation of the verse is that the feeble-minded refers to the prodigal, the weak refers to children, and the one unable to dictate refers to the 'insane'.[89]

1.9 Imbecility (*Al-Ma'tūh*)

1.9.1 Definitions

3.55 Imbecility is a closely related legal impediment. Indeed, many classical jurists discuss imbecility and insanity as one and the same.[90] An imbecile (*al-ma'tūh*) is defined as an individual who possesses a defect in the intellect which impacts his understanding, results in confused speech, and/or undermines his decision-making ability.[91] Other jurists view imbecility as intermittent. Mullah Jīwan defines the concept as a state in which a person's speech sometimes resembles a person of sound mind and at other

[86] Sunan al-Tirmidhī, No. 1423 (Book 15, Vol. 3). <https://sunnah.com/search?q=The\+pen\+has\+been\+lifted\+from\+three> accessed 11 May 2021.
[87] Muḥammad bin Aḥmed Al-Qurṭubī, Al-Jāmi' li Aḥkām al-Qur'ān (Dār al-Ḥadīth, n.d.) Vol. 5, p. 28.
[88] Omar (n 29) p. 104.
[89] Wahbah al-Zuḥaylī (n 27) Vol. 2, p. 347.
[90] Omar (n 29) p. 114. See also Wahbah al-Zuḥaylī (n 27) Vol. 2, p. 369.
[91] 'Abd al-Karīm Zīdān (n 4) p. 104.

times resembles an insane person.[92] The latter definition is more in keeping with the way in which modern jurists characterize the imbecile's condition. Namely, a person can be born an imbecile or can develop the condition because of illness.

1.9.2 Interdiction of the Imbecile

The jurists categorize imbecility in two forms. The first is an extreme degree of imbecility in which awareness and discernment are absent (*ma'tūh ghayr mumayyīz*).[93] The sufferer has no capacity for performance and therefore shares the legal status of the insane and the non-discerning child. All his dealings are invalid. **3.56**

The second category concerns an individual who shows some awareness and discernment, but his awareness is not of the same degree as persons with full intellectual capability.[94] An adult affected by this degree of imbecility is deemed to be like a child who has discernment and therefore possesses deficient legal capacity. Synonymous with the legal capacity of the discerning child, the legal acts of this type of imbecility are valid when they benefit the imbecile but are invalid when they only cause harm. Legal acts which may be beneficial or harmful are suspended subject to the guardian's permission.[95] Hanafi rulings derive from analogy with the discerning child in this regard.[96] **3.57**

1.10 Prodigality (*Safah*)

1.10.1 Definitions

The defining qualities of the *safīh*, according to the Maliki authority, Rabī'a b. 'Abd al-Raḥmān (d. 652), are as follows:[97] **3.58**

> One whose money does not produce a yield, either in his buying or in his selling; and the one who does not deprive himself of his pleasures, even though he engages in prodigality . . .; and the one who treats his wealth as if wealth were of no value; and the one who has no discretion in the administration of his financial affairs.

Therefore, two principal characteristics are present in Rabī'a's definition, namely, a character flaw which impedes one's ability to carry out beneficial monetary transactions, and prodigality, which is the squandering of one's money through excessive spending.[98] **3.59**

[92] Ibn Abī Sa'īd Ibn 'Ubayd Allāh al-Ḥanafī al-Ṣadīqī Jīwan (n 22) Vol. 2, p. 950.
[93] Muḥammad Abū Zahra, Al-Milkiyyah wa Nazariyyat al-'Aqd fī al-Sharī'ah al-Islāmiyyah (Dār al-Fikr al-'Arabi, 1996) p. 267.
[94] Zayla'ī, 'Uthmān Ibn Alī, Abd Allāh Ibn Aḥmad Nasafī, Aḥmad ibn Muḥammad Shalabī, and Aḥmad Azzū Ināyah, Tabyīn Al-ḥaqā'iq (Dār al-Kutub al-'Ilmīyyah, 2000) Vol. 6, p. 254.
[95] Ibid.
[96] Wahbah al-Zuḥaylī (n 27) Vol. 2, p. 369.
[97] Mālik ibn Anas, Al-Mudawwanah Al-kubrā Lil-Imām Mālik Ibn Anas Al-Asḥaḥī (al-Ṭab'ah 1., Dār al-Kutub al-'Ilmiyyah, 1994) Vol. 4, p. 72.
[98] Oussama Arabi, Studies in Modern Islamic Law and Jurisprudence (Kluwer Law International, 2001) p. 105.

3.60 Prodigality (*safah*) is regarded as one of the acquired impediments to legal capacity. However, juristic discussion is centred on the interdiction of the *safīh* (spendthrift) which, as previously highlighted, is used as a synonymous concept. Interdiction (*ḥajr*) in this sense is to block or prevent the non-discerning person from disposing freely of their wealth. All classical schools of law rule that the *safīh* is subject to interdiction because of his squandering of wealth in an unreasonable and irresponsible manner.

3.61 Arabic lexicographers determined that the trilateral root *s-f-h* signifies *khiffa al-ḥilm*, which, translated, is 'lightness in forbearance and/or understanding'. *Safah* is therefore the antonym of *ḥilm*, which indicates self-control and forbearance. Moreover, *safah* is 'caught in a web of multiple significations' so that it is also associated with *jahl* (ignorance) or silliness, 'foolishness . . . a deficiency in intellect or understanding'.[99] Moosa describes these associations of meaning as the *jahl-ḥilm/ʿilm/safah* complex which over time evolve in an unmistakable semiotic process so that meanings can be gradually sanitized.[100] Accordingly, there is 'a constant sliding of the signified under the signified', so that 'no constant or instant referent can be found for the word *safah* without carefully examining the context of signification and semiosis'.[101] Therefore, in Arabic usage, the meaning of *safah* has shifted according to the context in which meaning was to be signified. Yet Arabi argues that this ambiguity was 'seized upon' by the jurists who sought to affix a meaning to the term '*safīh*'. The result was the assignment of a technical legal significance for the purpose of legal discourse.[102]

3.62 According to Ibn Manzūr al-Ifrīqī (d. 1311–12), whose *Lisān al-ʿArab* (literally, tongue of the Arab) is the best-known dictionary of the Arabic language, *safah* relates to shallowness (*khiffa*), lack of depth or understanding (*naqs al-ʿaql*), or ignorance (*jahl*).[103] Yet the moral failings attributed to the concept differ markedly from jurists' usage of the term, which is centred on the preservation of property in Islamic law.[104] The *safīh* and the *mubadhdhir* (spendthrift) are semantically joined so that the concept came to describe a person who does not handle his property appropriately, or who overspends, or spends in unlawful ways.[105] Confirming the concept's focus on wastefulness, the majority held that as long as a person does not squander his property, his ability to handle his financial affairs and those of his family is not subject to interdiction. A Muslim whose behaviour is contrary to the rulings of Islam (*fāsiq*) cannot be interdicted because he or she is a sinner. They base this view on their ruling that interdiction was

[99] William Edward Lane, Arabic-English Lexicon (Williams & Norgate, 1863–93) Book 1, pt 4, pp. 1376–77.

[100] Ebrahim Moosa, '"The Sufahā" in Qur'ān Literature: A Problem in Semiosis' (1998) 75 Der Islam 1, pp. 9 and 10.

[101] Ibid, p. 11.

[102] Arabi (n 98) p. 102. Moosa argues that 'Islamic discourses show . . . a growing propensity towards logocentrism between the first and fifth centuries . . . Islamic discourses exhibit a longing for presence, for a constitutive reason (logos) and for an order of concepts claimed to exist in themselves, complete, self-referring and proper which regularly return to an origin.' See Moosa (n 100) pp. 2–4. The distinction between arguments is significant but is beyond the remit of this work.

[103] Muḥammad Ibn Manzūr al-Anṣārī al-Ifrīqī al-Miṣrī al-Khazrajī, Lisān al-ʿArab (Dār-Maʿārif, n.d.) Vol. 3, pp. 2032–34.

[104] Omar (n 29) p. 123.

[105] Wahbah al-Zuḥaylī (n 27) Vol. 2, p. 369.

legalized to prevent the inappropriate use of property and that there is no example in the early days of Islam in which sinners were interdicted solely by virtue of being sinners.[106]

1.10.1.1 The legal bases

The Qur'ān's exhortations in relation to prodigality are unequivocal but the term *safah* is not always present. In Qur'ān 6:141, the root of *isrāf* (intemperance, immoderateness, extravagance) is employed: 'And do not spend excessively (*tusrifū*), He does not love the excessive spenders (*al-musrifīn*).' And, in 17:26–7, the term *tabdhīr* (waste, squandering) is emphasized. God commands: 'And do not squander wealth (*wa lā tubadhdhir tabdhīran*), the squanderers (*al-mubadhdhirīn*) are the devil's brothers.' The terms *isrāf* and *tabdhīr* are used interchangeably in Arabic usage. **3.63**

However, Qur'ān 4:5 implies a connection between jurists' use of the term *safah* (plural, *al-sufahā'*) and the somewhat more technical meaning, namely, 'squanderer'.[107] God commands: 'Do not entrust your property to the feeble-minded (*al-sufahā'*). God has made it a means of support for you: make provision for them from it, clothe them, and address them kindly.' Therefore, the moral shallowness and ignorance attributed to *safah* is given a technical connotation in relation to a person who undervalues wealth and is wont to squander his wealth. Indeed, Arabi describes this semantic creativity as reflecting 'a creative episode of Islamic legal interpretation'.[108] Needless to say, jurists' creativity resulted in a diversity of views about the correct meaning of *safīh*, which contributed to jurists' disagreement about the interdiction (lack of legal capacity) of the spendthrift. **3.64**

1.10.2 Interdiction of the Prodigal (*Safīh*)

The jurists disagreed about the interdiction of mature and sane persons who squander their wealth. Mālik, Al-Shāfi'ī, the so-called seven jurists of Medina, and many jurists of Iraq found it permissible to interdict such individuals with the order of the ruler. This was also the opinion of Ibn 'Abbās and Ibn al-Zubayr.[109] There is little dispute amongst jurists that a minor is no longer to be interdicted, if, upon reaching majority, he shows discretion. Moreover, a majority of jurists from the Maliki, Shafi'i, Hanbali, and Hanafi schools held that interdiction should continue to be enforced on a prodigal person who, upon attaining majority, continues to exhibit prodigality.[110] However, once such persons have demonstrated discretion (*rushd*), interdiction is cancelled and their property is released to them according to Qur'ān 4:6: 'Test orphans until they reach marriageable age; then, if you find they have sound judgement, hand over their property to them.' **3.65**

[106] Ibid, p. 378.
[107] Arabi (n 98) p. 102.
[108] Ibid.
[109] Abū al-Walīd Ibn Rushd (n 54) Vol. 1, p. 334.
[110] Ibn 'Arafah al-Dusūqī, Ḥāshiyāt al-Dusūqī 'ala al-Sharḥ al-Kabīr (Dār al-Kutub al-'Ilmiyah, 2011) Vol. 3, p. 292.

3.66 The difference of opinion relates to the case where the prodigal, after reaching majority and exhibiting prudence for a time, then shows signs of prodigality. Again, the majority of jurists from the Maliki, Shafi'i, and some Hanafi ruled that interdiction is permissible when prodigality arises, irrespective of the individual having shown signs of prudence for time.[111] Their argument is that interdiction on those who have attained majority is analogous to the obligatory interdiction of minors due to prodigality. The same legal cause should give rise to the same legal effect (*ḥajr*).[112]

3.67 However, Abū Ḥanīfa and a faction of Iraqi jurists argued that interdiction cannot be initiated against mature persons of twenty-five years of age who display prodigality after a period of apparent prudence.[113] In such a case, the prodigal is not subject to interdiction and is free to dispose of his property. Abū Ḥanīfa argued that the non-discerning person's humanity (*Adamiyyah*) takes precedence over the interest in the preservation of property. Al-Marghinānī (d. 1135) of the Hanafi school comments on Abū Ḥanīfa's position as follows:[114]

> For Abū Ḥanīfa, the prodigal may not be interdicted because the rejection of his [active] legal capacity would constitute a loss of his humanity (Adamiyyah) and an identification with the beasts; this is a greater harm than the squandering of wealth; yet a greater [harm] may not be permitted to alleviate a lesser [harm].

3.68 The restriction of the prodigal's legal capacity would be to exclude him from participating fully in the 'sanctified human act' and hence would constitute an injury to his soul so grave that it overshadows any material benefits arising from interdiction.[115]

3.69 According to the majority of jurists, however, Qur'ān 2:282 provides evidence to support their ruling. The Qur'ān exhorts: 'If the debtor is feeble minded, weak, or unable to dictate, then let his guardian dictate justly.' The majority interpret this verse to indicate that God has imposed guardianship over the prodigal and the weak who are not able to dictate. The legality of guardianship indicates that the prodigal is interdicted and therefore incapable of concluding valid contracts.[116]

1.10.3 The Effects of Prodigality on Contract

3.70 Abū Ḥanīfa's disciples and the early masters of *fiqh* in the Hanafi school, Abū Yūsuf (d. 798) and al-Shaybānī (d. 805), ruled that the prodigal may be interdicted if he lacks discretion irrespective of the particular age of the individual. This is the accepted opinion of the Hanafi school. According to Abū Yūsuf, the judge (*al-qāḍī*) is to determine

[111] Marghinānī, Alī Ibn Abī Bakr, Al-Hidāyah: SharḥBidāyat al-Mubtadī (al-Ṭab'ah 1, Dār al-Kutub al-'Ilmiyyah, 2000) Vol. 4, p. 278.
[112] Abū al-Walīd Ibn Rushd (n 54) Vol. 1, p. 335.
[113] Ibid, Vol. 1, p. 335.
[114] Marghinānī (n 111) p. 278.
[115] Arabi (n 98) p. 113.
[116] Abū Bakr Ibn al-'Arabī al-Malikī, Aḥkām al-Qur'ān (Dār al-Kutub al-'Ilmiyyah, 1979) Vol. 2, p. 213. Qur'ān 4:5 is also cited as evidence that the prodigal should not be given control over wealth due to his squandering thereof. Furthermore, a number of *ḥadīths* are cited as evidence of the majority's ruling.

whether the adult lacks discretion and, if so, he is to interdict him.[117] A judicial ruling, it is argued, is necessary because the legality of interdiction is disputed. Moreover, prodigality is not easily observable, in contrast to insanity and imbecility. It can be a matter of opinion. A court ruling is said to resolve this dispute in accordance with the maxim: the ruling by a judge removes the disagreements (*ḥukm al- ḥākim yarfaʿ al-khilāf*).[118] A publicized court order is required to minimize the uncertainty and potential loss to those who may deal with such individuals on the assumption that they possess mental competence.[119] This is also the opinion of the Malikis, the Shafi'is, and the Hanbalis.[120] The interdicted person remains subject to interdiction until the judge establishes that he has attained prudence or discretion (*rushd*). In this sense, the judge assumes guardianship so as to protect society's interests from the prodigal's imprudent dealings. The Hanbalis add that a judge's interdiction should be witnessed and made public, so that others avoid dealing with the prodigal.[121]

For Abū Yūsuf, *rushd* is commensurate with financial aptitude (*wa-l-rushd ʿindahu al-ṣalāḥ fi-l-māl*). Should the judge find that the interdicted prodigal has attained financial aptitude, he is given access to his wealth.[122] Al-Shaybānī agreed with Abū Yūsuf in nearly all these principles. However, he differed in that he did not require a judge to give effect to interdiction or its voidance.[123] The majority opinion in the Hanafi school reflects that of Abū Yūsuf which, notably, differs from the school's ruling regarding the necessity of judicial interdiction of non-discerning children, insane individuals, and imbeciles.[124] In these latter cases, a judicial ruling is not necessary. **3.71**

1.10.3.1 The legal capacity of the prodigal (Safīh)

The majority of jurists such as the Hanafi, Maliki, and Hanbali schools assigned the prodigal a legal capacity similar to that of the discerning child.[125] The validity of the prodigal's contractual dealings is therefore suspended pending the permission of their guardians. If the guardian's permission is obtained, then the contract is deemed valid and enforceable. Should the trade turn out to be beneficial to the prodigal, then the ruler or judge may permit it (in the absence of the guardian's consent). If the trade is harmful, such as the giving of a gift, a guardian's consent does not validate an invalid act. Unlike the case of the discerning child, the prodigal's contract is only valid with the **3.72**

[117] Likewise, a court order is considered necessary for removing interdiction. See Ḥāshiyat Ibn ʿĀbidīn, Radd al-Muḥtār ʿalā al-Durr al-Mukhtār (Dār Ihya' al-Kutub, 2003) Vol. 9, p. 223.
[118] Muḥammad ʿAbd al-Raḥmān Alī Hawwārī, Baḥth fi al-Ḥajr (M.ʿA.al-R.ʿA. al-Hawwārī, 1989) p. 178.
[119] Wahbah al-Zuḥaylī (n 27) Vol. 2, p. 377.
[120] Ibid, Vol. 2, pp. 372–76.
[121] Ibid, Vol. 2, p. 375.
[122] Abū Jaʿfar al-Ṭahāwī, Mukhtaṣar al-Ṭahāwī in Abū al-Wafā al-Afghānī (ed.), (Dār al-Kitāb al-ʿArabī, 1950 (1370 AH)) p. 97.
[123] Ibid, p. 98.
[124] Wahbah al-Zuḥaylī (n 27) Vol. 2, p. 372.
[125] Several distinctions are worth pointing out. First, while a guardian is permitted to dispose of the child's property, the guardian of a prodigal is not allowed to do so. Secondly, divorce and manumission are valid acts of the prodigal whereas this is not the case with children. Thirdly, a prodigal's bequest is valid whereas a child's is not. See Muḥammad Abū Zahra, al-Aḥwāl al-Shakhṣiyyah (Dār al-Fikr al-ʿArabī, 1957) p. 480; and Muḥammad ʿAbd al-Raḥmān Alī Hawwārī (n 118) p. 191.

judge's consent. The Malikis, exceptionally, ruled that the dealings of an adult female prodigal, who has no guardian, are likewise suspended until she reaches menopause without getting married. If she does marry, her dealings are suspended until one year after the consummation of her marriage.[126]

3.73 In contrast, the Shafi'is ruled that the prodigal's contractual dealings are invalid even when authorized by the guardian. This opinion is analogous to the Shafi'is' ruling concerning the invalidity of acts undertaken by non-discerning children and the insane.[127] Some Hanbalis take this view on the basis that the prodigal's inability to make good financial decisions overrides the guardian's authorization, as financial dealings may turn out to be harmful.[128] The Shafi'is argue that the guardian's validation of a contract concluded by the prodigal contradicts the rationale and wisdom which underlies interdiction.[129]

3.74 The Malikis and Hanbalis make some allowance for the trivial expenditure of the prodigal, which in their view would not require the guardian's consent. This relates to requisites such as food, clothing, and the like. Their reasoning is that this kind of expenditure is insignificant and therefore permitting this type of expense does not undermine the rationale of interdiction which is to prevent the squandering of wealth.[130]

3.75 On the other hand, most Hanafis, Malikis, and Shafi'is considered marriage and divorce non-voidable activities and hence valid. They considered marriage a basic need so that the prodigal's invalid legal capacity was not permitted to void the contract. Although marriage also involves property, its primary purpose is to avoid sin and not to obtain a dowry. They balanced this right with the stipulation that should a prodigal marry a person and pay an unreasonably high dowry, the excess over the average value of dowries in similar marriages was to be voided.[131]

3.76 A *safih*'s will for one-third of the value of the testator's property was also deemed to be valid. This ruling is subject to the proviso that the third is designated for a good cause such as benefiting the poor, widows, or building schools and mosques, etc.

3.77 The *safih*'s receptive capacity, as in the case of the minor, remains intact. Therefore, he is liable for crimes with prescribed punishments (*ḥadd*) or retaliation (*qiṣāṣ*). Yet his financial liability, so long as he has been interdicted, is null and void. Therefore, if the prodigal commits murder, he may be punished for it. On the other hand, if the family of the victim demands financial compensation instead, they may not receive it because the prodigal's admission of guilt in financial dealings is invalid. The Shafi'is and the Hanbalis agree, however, that the financial compensation becomes payable once interdiction is removed. Indeed, all financial liabilities, including liability for damaged or

126 Wahbah al-Zuḥaylī (n 27) Vol. 2, p. 372.
127 Ibid, p. 373.
128 Ibid, p. 376.
129 Omar (n 29) p. 160.
130 Mālik Ibn Anas (n 97) p. 73.
131 Wahbah al-Zuḥaylī (n 27) Vol. 2, p. 371.

destroyed property, become binding upon the prodigal once his interdiction has been cancelled.[132] Notably, Abū Ḥanīfa argued that if the prodigal is liable for matters related to his body, he should not be restricted from acting in matters relating to financial affairs as life (*nafs*) takes priority over property in the Sharī'ah.[133]

The rights of other people are not prejudiced by the *safīh*'s foolishness. He is liable financially for the upkeep of his wife, child, and any other dependants. Moreover, he must pay the poor tax (*zakāt*) although he is not allowed to distribute *zakāt*. He is not allowed to engage in other acts of financial worship, for example charity (*ṣadaqa*), etc. **3.78**

1.11 Terminal Illness

1.11.1 Definitions

Terminal illness is a disease that cannot be cured or adequately treated and which is reasonably expected to result in the death of the patient. According to Al-Zarqā, terminally ill people lose their physical ability to perform their usual functions and duties.[134] The Majalla defines it as a sickness 'where in the majority of cases death is imminent, and, in the case of a male, where such person is unable to deal with his affairs outside his home, and in the case of a female, where she is unable to deal with her domestic duties'.[135] The Majalla stipulates further that terminal illness usually leads to death within one year. However, should the illness continue beyond one year, the person (for legal reasons) is regarded as being in good health and his financial dealings are valid. Should the condition change for the worse, resulting in death, he is considered to suffer from terminal illness from the time in which illness became worse.[136] Therefore, should the terminally ill person recover, he is not subject to the rulings for terminal illness. **3.79**

1.11.2 Interdiction of the Terminally Ill Individual

According to jurists of all the schools a terminally ill person is to be interdicted to protect the rights of his heirs.[137] The capacity for performance is therefore restricted (*ahliyya adā' nāqiṣah*) during terminal illness. The Malikis enlarged the category of persons subject to interdiction to include all individuals in situations in which death is a high probability including those on death row, and, reflecting the times, women in advanced pregnancy beyond six months.[138] Although terminally ill persons can conduct their own affairs, they are prohibited from entering into transactions that are in excess of one-third of the value of their estate after deducting debts or uncompensated contributions. This rule is derived from the rulings concerning wills (*waṣiyya*) and is **3.80**

[132] Ibid, pp. 374–76.
[133] 'Alī Muḥyī al-Dīn Qarrah Dāghī (n 52) Vol. 1, p. 319.
[134] Al-Zarqā (n 6) p. 836.
[135] Al-Majalla (n 40) Art. 1595.
[136] Ibid.
[137] Wahbah al-Zuḥaylī (n 27) Vol. 2, p. 379.
[138] Ibid, Vol. 2, p. 379.

designed to protect the rights of heirs.[139] If a terminally ill person's debts are equal to or more than their assets, they do not possess the right to dispose of their property.[140]

3.81 Therefore, gifts, charity, inheritance, selling at excessively low prices, or buying at excessively high prices cannot comprise more than one-third of the terminally ill person's estate. Anything in excess of one-third of his estate is suspended pending the permission of the would-be heirs. Should the terminally ill person recover from the illness, all his dealings are to be executed, according to the Hanafis, Shafi'is, and Hanbalis. However, if the terminally ill patient's debts exceed the full value of his estate, then he is interdicted in full, meaning that he has no disposition over the one-third share of his estate. This ruling is designed to protect the terminally ill person's creditors.[141] The Malikis qualify the majority's ruling by stipulating that the terminally ill person's dealings up to one-third of his estate are only valid if the value of the estate is unchanging. If variable in form or value, the Malikis ruled that the terminally ill person's transactions are suspended until he dies or recovers, irrespective of whether the person's dealings are within one-third of his estate. Upon death, the terminally ill person's transactions are executed up to one-third of his estate. If he lives, all his dealings are valid.[142]

1.11.2.1 The rights of heirs

3.82 To protect the rights of heirs a terminally ill person is prevented from engaging in transactions without a counter-value such as *hibah*, *waqf*, *ṣadaqah*, or those which exceed the market value or are less than the market value. In contrast, transactions with a counter-value such as financial contracts, leasing, silent partnerships, and crop-sharing are valid as they do not contain a contributory element which would affect the rights of heirs. This is the ruling of the Malikis and the Hanafis.[143] However, the Hanafis allow a terminally ill person to marry, provided that the dowry is not excessively high. A dowry which exceeded the social norm for similar brides is considered a voluntary contribution and subject to the rules regarding wills (*waṣiyya*). The Malikis also allow marriage subject to the one-third of the estate rule.[144]

1.11.2.2 Debts of the terminally ill

3.83 Acknowledgements of debt by the terminally ill person are similarly dealt with in view of the rights of heirs. Al-Shāfiʿī ruled that the terminally ill person's acknowledgement of debts is valid and not affected by rights of heirs or creditors as a person approaching death is inclined to tell the truth. The Hanafis, on the other hand, consider acknowledgements of debt from two perspectives. The first concerns the acknowledgement of debt in favour of an heir in which case it can be given effect subject to the heirs

[139] Nyazee (n 16) p. 129.
[140] Al-Zarqā (n 6) p. 838.
[141] Wahbah al-Zuḥaylī (n 27) Vol. 2, p. 380.
[142] Ibid.
[143] Ibid. See also Nyazee (n 16) p. 130.
[144] Wahbah al-Zuḥaylī (n 27)Vol. 2, p. 380.

permitting it. The second case concerns the acknowledgement of debt in favour of a third party which is considered valid. Such debts (*duyūn al-maraḍ*) are to be paid after all other existing debts have been paid.[145] The Majalla limits this type of debt acknowledgement to one-third of the property of the terminally ill individual.[146]

The Majalla sets out a debt ranking in which debts contracted in good health take priority over those contracted in ill health. Creditors, therefore, are reimbursed in relation to the health status of the terminally ill patient when he or she contracted the debt.[147] If, after having compensated creditors in relation to those debts incurred in healthier times, liabilities established during sickness and which can be ascertained clearly—for example, they relate to purchases, loans, even the destruction of property—are to be considered debts contracted in a state of good health and therefore paid out immediately.[148] **3.84**

Section 1.12 provides a brief overview of women's legal capacity. The analysis is necessarily limited to a technical understanding of women's legal capacity in relation to property and contract whereas a fuller analysis of the human rights of women is beyond the remit of this chapter. **3.85**

1.12 Women's Legal Capacity

Women's property rights are said to have vastly improved with the arrival of Islam. The first association between females and property in the Arabian Peninsula were found after the so-called birth of 'Islamic capitalism' in Mecca whereby the granting of individual property rights announced the end of the matrilineal system. Under that system women did not have the right to own property as this was held collectively by the family and administered by the woman's brothers.[149] Prior to this historical transformation women had been treated as childbearing chattels. Deprived of proprietary or other rights, they were sold into union with their husbands for a price to be paid to the female's father or other male relatives. The *nasab* (ancestral lineage) in tribal law under which the father was the sole basis of legitimacy was replaced by a system in which the maternal connection was given as much weight as that of the paternal one.[150] Prior to Islam a form of polyandry existed amongst the tribes of Ancient Arabia. Islam outlawed these practices and directed payment of the *mahr* (dowry) to the woman instead of to the father or nearest kinsman. Some argue that the marriage contract realigned the social structure by including both the man and wife as parties to the contract. This **3.86**

[145] Nyazee (n 16) p. 131.
[146] Al-Majalla (n 40) Art. 1601.
[147] Ibid, Art. 1602.
[148] Ibid.
[149] Maya Schatzmiller, Her Day in Court: Women's Property Rights and Islamic Law in Fifteenth Century Granada (Harvard University Press, 2007) p. 4.
[150] Noel J. Coulson, 'Regulation of Sexual Behavior Under Traditional Islamic Law' in Afaf Lutfi al-Sayyid Marsot (ed.), Society and the Sexes in Medieval Islam (Undena Publications, 1979) pp. 66–67.

lent women a degree of autonomy and volition in their affairs.[151] Yet others counter that a woman's position had hardly changed; that she was still regarded as property given the fact that the bridegroom had paid for her.[152] Indeed, whilst formal rules can sometimes change overnight due to political or judicial decisions, informal rules embodied in traditions, custom, and conventions are resistant to these changes. Such cultural constraints connect the past with the present and future.[153]

3.87 Despite the eventual improvements that Islam brought to women's position in Arabian society, it seems evident that at the time of the Prophet Moḥammad their position was hardly paramount.[154] Perhaps then it comes as a surprise that the *fiqh* on *ahliyya* and *ḥajr* is almost always gender neutral. There is no specific discussion of women's reason or the traits of femaleness or womanhood in relation to these topics.[155] Zahraa, a contemporary author, states that 'not one single Islamic jurist has stated or indicated that femininity is a defect of Islamic legal capacity' and that mature women have full legal capacity to conduct their own civil affairs and transactions whether they are single or married.[156] Moreover, a female's male relative or guardian (*walī*) does not possess the right to interfere in or even supervise a female's financial dealings or other civil affairs.[157] Al-Shāfiʿī confirms the veracity of these statements in the following passage:[158]

> [N]one of the jurists whom I have known have differed in opinion on the fact that both man and woman upon their attainment of the age of puberty and maturity [discernment] are alike in their ability to conduct their affairs by themselves . . . If someone says that the woman who has a husband cannot be given her properties unless upon permission from her husband, the answer, which refutes such a contention, will be that the word yatāmā [orphans] as mentioned in the Qur'ān denotes that it excludes both men and women from the institution of wilāyah [guardianship] upon satisfying the stated criteria. And that who is excluded by God Almighty from the institutions of wilāyah must not be subject to any form of guardianship except if there is an impediment such as spendthriftness or mental defect. This is supported by the Qur'ān, Sunna and reason.

[151] S. Haeri, 'Divorce in Contemporary Iran: A Male Prerogative in Self-Will' in Chibli Mallat and Jane Connors (eds), Islamic Family Law (Graham & Trotman, 1990) p. 56.

[152] See Reuben Levy, The Social Structure of Islam (2nd edn, Cambridge University Press, 1957) p. 95. Alongside these foundational reforms, the Qur'ān explicitly forbade the practice of burying alive unwanted female children, which counteracted the notion that female children meant a loss of prestige and status for the family. Qur'ān 17:31 commands: 'Slay not your children, fearing a fall to poverty. We shall provide for them and for you. Lo! The slaying of them is a great sin.' Qur'ān 6:151; 6:141, and 81:8 convey similar messages.

[153] Douglass C. North, Institutions, Institutional Change and Economic Performance (Cambridge University Press, 1990) p. 6.

[154] Ibid, p. 91. Levy describes the plight of women in the early Muslim era as one of 'subjection either to her nearest male kinsman—father, brother, or whoever he might be—or to her husband, whose right over her was regarded in the same way as his right over any other property. See ibid, p. 94.

[155] Seedat (n 37) p. 129.

[156] Zahraa (n 7) pp. 255–56.

[157] Ibid, p. 256.

[158] Muḥammad Ibn Idrīs al-Shāfiʿī and Maḥmūd Maṭrajī, Kitāb Al-Umm (Dār Al-Maʿrifah, n.d.) Vol. 3, p. 215.

It is also widely agreed that Islamic law possesses 'a core of spiritual equality' between men and women and that the voice of the Qur'ān is egalitarian and non-discriminatory.[159] Indeed, Qur'ān 39:6 is unequivocal on the subject: 'He created you all from a single being, from which He made its mate.'[160] Muslim men and women are considered equal before God and are accountable (*dhimma*) to the Lawgiver in relation to fasting, prayer, and pilgrimage, and with respect to property and associated contracts.[161] **3.88**

Moreover, as stated above, there is no specific reference to women having a different legal capacity due to the two criteria which distinguish *ahliyya al-adā'*. The argument is that two sex-specific impediments (these are grouped together in jurists' discussions) to legal capacity, which relate solely to women, namely menstruation (*ḥaiḍ*) and post-partum bleeding (*nifās*), do not diminish women's legal capacity for obligations or other acts. These states merely affect the ritual cleanliness required for prayer and fasting, and therefore in the absence of being able to fulfil this condition, prayer and fasting are not made compulsory.[162] Therefore, the temptation amongst some authors is to argue that *ahliyya* is addressed in a wholly gender-neutral manner but this is likely overstated, particularly when one takes a wider perspective on the issue. **3.89**

A wider perspective illustrates that spiritual equality diverges from equality in mundane affairs (*mu'āmalāt*), though, notably, not with respect to the disposition of property. The starting point for this discussion begins with the primary source of revelation, namely the Qur'ān. It is said that several verses of the Qur'ān which state that 'men are a degree above women' and that they are 'the guardians, i.e. protectors and maintainers, over women' perpetuate gender hierarchies.[163] The social implications of these verses are evident in the example of a leading commentator of the Qur'ān, Al-Ṭabarī (d. 310/923), whose interpretation of verse 4:34, led him to state:[164] **3.90**

> Men are in charge of their women with respect to disciplining (or chastising) them, and to providing them with restrictive guidance concerning their duties towards God and themselves (i.e. the men); by virtue of that by which God has given excellence

[159] Barbara Stowasser, 'The Status of Women in Early Islam' in Freda Hussain (ed.), Muslim Women (St Martin's Press, 1984) p. 25. Amongst many authors, this representation is made by Shaheen Sardar Ali in Gender and Human Rights in Islamic and International Law: Equal Rights Before Allah, Unequal Before Man? (Kluwer Law International, 2000) p. 43.

[160] Numerous Qur'ānic verses underscore this spiritual equality, such as 9:71–72:

> The Believers, both men and women, support each other; they order what is right and forbid what is wrong; they keep up the prayer and pay the prescribed alms; they obey God and His Messenger . . . God has promised the believers, both men and women, Gardens graced with flowing streams where they will remain; good, peaceful homes in Gardens of lasting bliss; and—greatest of all—God's good pleasure. That is the supreme triumph.

[161] Seedat (n 37) pp. 21–22.

[162] Ibn Abī Sa'īd ibn 'Ubayd Allāh al-Ḥanafī al-Ṣadīqī Jīwan (n 22) Vol. 2, p. 175. See also Al-Zarqā (n 6) p. 854. The Hanafis require the menstruating woman to make up the fast (*qaḍā'*) but she does not have to make up for the missed prayer. See Al-Qudūrī al-Baghdādī, Al-Mukhtaṣar (A Manual of Islamic Law According to the Hanafi School), trans. Ṭāhir Maḥmood Kiānī (Ta-Ha Publishers, 2015) p. 19.

[163] Qur'ān 2:228 and 4:34 respectively. Several further verses are said to perpetuate gender hierarchies, including 2:221, 2:282, 24:30, and 4:3. See Ali (n 159) p. 43.

[164] Muḥammad ibn Jarīr Ṭabarī and Maḥmūd Muḥammad Shākir, Tafsīr Al-Ṭabarī: Jāmi' Al-bayān 'an Ta'wīl Al-Qur'ān (al-Tab'ah 2., Dār al-Ma'ārif, 1969) Vol. 8, p. 192.

(or preference) to the men over their wives: i.e., payment of their dowers to them, spending of their wealth on them, and providing for them in full. This is how God has given excellence to (the men) over (the women), and hence (the men) have come to be in charge of (the women) and hold authority over them in those of their matters with which God has entrusted them.

3.91 The male's superiority in this passage can largely be explained by the economic superiority of men and their consequent responsibility for the household finances in early Islamic centuries.[165] Nonetheless, the extension of these interpretations to a woman's entire legal personality is the legal consequence.[166] A clear statement to this effect is given some 350 years after the death of Al-Ṭabarī by the scholar and theologian, Ibn 'Umar al-Baiḍāwī (d. 1286). He writes that:[167]

> Men are in charge of women, i.e., men are in charge of women as rulers are in charge of their subjects . . . God has preferred the one (sex) over the other, i.e., because God has preferred men over women in the completeness of mental ability, good counsel, complete power in the performance of duties and the carrying out of (divine) commands. Hence to men have been confined prophecy, religious leadership, saintship, the performance of religious rites: the giving of evidence in law courts, the duties of the holy war, and worship (in the mosque) on Friday, etc., the privilege of electing chiefs, the larger share of inheritance, and discretion in matters of divorce, by virtue of that which they spend of their wealth, in marrying (the women) such as their dowers and cost of their maintenance.

3.92 How are we to make sense of this inequality in view of Islam's egalitarian ethos? Let us consider Qur'ānic exegesis as some of its commentary relates to the way in which women's legal status was classified in the early Islamic centuries. The early authorities of *tafsīr* (exegesis) believed that the *sufahā'* (which the reader will recall was subject to interdiction due to an insufficient *compos mentis*) as revealed in Qur'ān 4:5 belonged to one of four categories: (i) women, (ii) children, (iii) women and children; or (iv) anyone who lacked discretion (*'aql*).[168] Al-Ṭabarī, who authored the famous commentary, *Jāmi' al-Bayān 'an Ta'wīl Āy al-Qur'ān* (Collection of Explanations for the Interpretation of the Qur'ān), recorded this history.[169] The leading scholars of early Islam, including the

[165] John L. Esposito, Women in Muslim Family Law (Syracuse University Press, 1982) p. 108. The Qur'ān is said to have vastly improved the social status and legal rights of women, which in pre-Islamic Arabia are depicted as almost non-existent. Yet a clean break with pre-Islamic tribal culture was clearly not possible. See Ali (n 159) p. 44.

[166] Ali (n 159) p. 69.

[167] 'Abd Allāh Ibn 'Umar Bayḍāwī and Muḥammad 'Abd al-Raḥmān Mar'ashlī, Anwār Al-tanzīl Wa-asrār Al-ta'wīl: Al-ma'rūf Bi-Tafsīr Al-Bayḍāwī (al-Ṭab'ah 1., Dār Ihyā' al-Turāth al-'Arabī: Mu'assasat al-Tārīkh al-'Arabī, 1998) Vol. 2, p. 92.

[168] Moosa (n 100) p. 13. Qur'ān 4:5 reads: 'And do not entrust to those who are *sufahā'* the possessions which *Allāh* has placed in your charge for their support; but let them have their sustenance therefrom, and clothe them, and speak unto them in a kindly way.'

[169] Ibn Jarīr al-Ṭabarī, Tafsīr al-Ṭabarī: al-Bayān 'an Ta'wīl Āy al-Qur'ān (Dār al-Ma'ārif, 1374–78 AH) Vol. 7, pp. 564–67. Al-Ṭabarī argued that these gender-biased interpretations were incorrect; that the term *sufahā'* is inclusive of both genders and to argue otherwise would be to displace its lexical meaning. Notably, Al-Rāzī argued to the contrary, that the plural of *sufahā'* can be gender specific in the Arabic language. Interestingly, Oussama Arabi's (n 81) interpretation of Ṭabarī's argument is that at the close of the third century a gender-neutral interpretation had

leading Companion, 'Abdallāh Ibn 'Umar (d. 73/693); the most famous commentator of the Qur'ān in the first generation, 'Abdallāh Ibn 'Abbās (d. 68/687); the well-known Basran authority, Ḥasan al-Baṣrī (d. 110/728); the Khurāsānī exegete, al-Ḍaḥḥāk bin Muzāḥim (d. 105/723); and other notable scholars believed that the term referred to women exclusively.[170] Al-Baṣrī and al-Ḍaḥḥāk are reported to have remarked that 'the woman is the most foolish of fools' (*al-mar'a asfah al-sufahā'*).[171] Ibn 'Umar was reported to have chastised a woman in passing, citing a *ḥadīth* narrated by Abū Umāma in which the Prophet was to have stated: 'Be warned that the fire has been created for the *al-sufahā'* (which he is to have repeated three times). And beware that the *sufahā'* are the women, except the woman who obeys her custodian (*qayyim*).' In Islamic law, a husband or male guardian acts as the custodian.[172] Fakhr al-Dīn al-Rāzī notes, furthermore, that *sufāhā'* referred to women of all categories, whether they are spouses, mothers, or daughters.[173] Al-Rāzī takes pains to justify the connection of women and *safah*. He notes apologetically that *safah* in women and children, or even men, for that matter, is not a quality of censure or derogation from the Sharī'ah nor would the term imply any disobedience to God. Rather, *sufāhā'* are people affected by a natural shallowness or intellect or an inability to discern harm from injury, rendering them unfit to manage property. Yet these qualities are not inherent features of women.[174]

Others argued to the contrary that *safah* indicates derogation from religion and substantiated their claims with a well-known tradition from the Prophet that women are deficient in intellect and religion: *nāqiṣāt fi-l 'aql, nāqiṣāt fi-l dīn*.[175] The Prophet is to have cited these deficiencies in view of the value of a woman's evidence, which is half that of a man's.[176] Moosa attributes this chauvinism to the narrative language of the Qur'ān and how it relates to the imaginary social consciousness—the so-called cultural imaginaire—of the Arabs. Hidden in the narrative language are the signifiers of chauvinism, sexuality, and economic power which characterize the discourse metonymically and metaphorically.[177] In contrast, however, *ḥadīth* literature also presents traditions that reflect complete equality such as the following tradition in which the Prophet is said to have remarked:[178] 'All people are equal, as equal as the teeth of a comb. There is no claim of merit of an Arab over a non-Arab or of a white over a black **3.93**

already become deeply entrenched in the *tafsīr* literature. Arabi's argument would seem to take a position unrelated to Ṭabarī's argument and therefore the evidence for this statement is unclear.

170 Ibn Jarīr al-Ṭabarī, Jāmi' al-Bayān 'an Ta'wīl Āy al-Qur'ān (Dār al-Fikr, 1984) Vol. 3, p. 245.
171 Ibid.
172 Fakhr al-Dīn al-Rāzī, Tafsīr al-Kabīr (3rd edn, Dār Iḥyā' al-Turāth al-'Arabī, n.d.) i/2, p. 68.
173 Ibid, Vol. 9, p. 175. Fakhr al-Dīn al-Rāzī is the author of *Mafātiḥ al-Ghayb* (*The Keys to the Hidden*), also referred to as *al-Tafsīr al-Kabīr* (*The Great Commentary*). Al-Rāzī was a leading commentator of classical Islam and, together with al-Ṭabarī, credited with having influenced the tradition of Qur'ānic commentary.
174 Moosa (n 100) p. 24.
175 Muḥammad b. 'Abdullāh ibn al-'Arabī, *Aḥkām al-Qur'ān* (Ḥalabī, 1968) Vol. 1, p. 318.
176 Ali (n 159) p. 70.
177 Moosa (n 100) p. 24.
178 cf. Ali (159) p. 50. The *ḥadīth* is said to have originated at the last address of the Prophet Muḥammad to the Muslims on the occasion of the *Ḥajjat al-Wadā'* (the farewell pilgrimage).

person: Only God-fearing people merit a preference with God. Thus, men and women are equal.'

3.94 It is difficult to reconcile these conflicting statements. The picture is even more muddled in view of women's largely unfettered capacity to deal in property. It is true that some followers of the Maliki school claimed that the eponym of that school, Mālik ibn Anas al-Aṣbaḥī (d. 795 CE), did not give married women the right to deal in their own property without the permission of their husband.[179] The Malikis are said to base this ruling on a *ḥadīth* which is said to be narrated by the five major narrators with the exception of Al-Tirmīdhī: 'A woman is not allowed to deal in her property if her husband is given inviolable marriage rights.'[180] The true position, however, is that a married woman is only restricted in relation to her charitable dispositions (gifts and guarantee) if they exhaust more than one-third of the married woman's property unless the husband has given his approval.[181] Elsewhere, the position of women under Maliki *fiqh* reveals few restrictions, if any. It is reported that if a woman who had property (*māl*) in the hands of a guardian (*waṣī*) gets married, she does not receive her property until her *waṣī* is satisfied of her situation (that she is now able to deal in it properly). If she consummated her marriage but is not considered to have reached *rushd* (maturity), her property will not be given to her (it remains with the guardian). Therefore, the husband has no say in his wife's property either before or after consummating the marriage.[182]

3.95 Notarial records from the fifteenth-century Maliki-governed Al-Andalus (contemporary Iberian Peninsula) and other Muslim-majority polities spanning different eras show that women regularly participated in buying and selling transactions.[183] Whilst notaries required the husband's witnessing of the document for 'fear that he might have rights to the property', married women did not require the explicit permission of their husbands to undertake these transactions.[184] Furthermore, the husband was not allowed to prevent her from selling by refusing to witness the transaction. The records indicate that the basic condition for making a sale transaction was ownership. The seller/buyer must also have attained majority and maturity of mind (*rāshid*).[185] Women's property rights, which were enforced by law and upheld socially, imbued women 'with

[179] Mālik is the eponym of the school that emerged in the Ḥijāz and in Medina where he became Medina's most accomplished jurist and tradition-recounter. A proverb was said to have been coined along the following lines: 'Could fatwas emanate from any other person while Mālik is in Medina?' See Ṣubḥī Maḥmaṣānī, 'Falsafat Al-Tashrī'fī Al-Islām, trans. Farhat J. Ziadeh (E.J. Brill, 1961) p. 25.
[180] Ibid.
[181] Wahba al-Zuḥaylī (n 27) p. 381.
[182] Al-Mudawwanah (n 97) p. 292.
[183] Al-Andalus was the Muslim-ruled area of the Iberian Peninsula. At its greatest geographical extent, its territory occupied most of the peninsula and a part of present-day southern France and, for nearly a century (ninth to the tenth centuries), extended its control over the Alpine passes which connect Italy to Western Europe. See Schatzmiller (n 149) p. 177. Schatzmiller draws these conclusions from her analysis of historical records originating from several Muslim-majority polities around the Mediterranean basin and over the course of many pre-modern centuries. Specifically, she examines documents from seventeenth-century Qayseri; nineteenth- to thirteenth-century Geniza (Cairo); seventeenth-century Aleppo; fourteenth-century Jerusalem; twelfth-century Sicily; and the thirteenth-century Red Sea port of Quseir.
[184] Ibid.
[185] Ibid.

a mentality that permitted women not only to feel secure about their ownership, but also to show entrepreneurial skills, to take advantage of financial opportunities with confidence, and to seize the moment and engage in commercial deals involving extensive finances'.[186] Yet women's involvement in private wealth decisions did not extend to commerce and trade in which credit and investment was necessary. Social pressures not to venture into the public sphere prevented women from engaging in this type of business which usually involved long-distance trade.[187] Women's lack of involvement in these activities is reflected in the silence of the documents with respect to women's participation in local trade. It is thought that their understanding of credit, as reflected in their personal disposal of wealth, is at odds with their lack of exposure to this wider aspect of economic life.[188]

The Hanafis, the Shafi'is, and a majority of the Hanbalis also do not restrict a discerning woman in relation to her dealings in her property, whether these are compensated or not.[189] The majority's ruling prioritizes the criteria of legal capacity as taken from the following Qur'ānic verse: 'If then you find them of sound judgment, release their properties to them' (4:6). They also ground their ruling in the established *ḥadīth* wherein the Prophet said: 'O women, give charity, even if it is from your jewellery, for indeed you will make up most of the people of hell on the Day of Judgment', and then the Prophet is said to have accepted their charity without inquiring for further details.[190] Despite the latter part of this verse, which is clearly prejudicial to women, it is important to contextualize the majority's ruling. During the Ottoman period, for example, Muslim women's capacity to deal in property was widely celebrated so that Christian and Jewish women pursued their inheritance rights through Islamic courts, seeking to avail themselves of the benefits of women's legal capacity which their own religious codes would not grant them.[191] Indeed, Al-Zuḥaylī, aware of this legacy, notes that 'all Muslims are proud of the fact that Islamic Law gave women full eligibility to own property and to deal in it'.[192] **3.96**

There is a juristic pattern of dealing separately with distinctive areas of law such as marriage, divorce, testimony, etc., whereby each topic addresses women's legal capacity separately. This makes the task of fully appreciating *ahliyya* more complex as the whole gamut of civil contracts must be evaluated to determine women's *ahliyya*.[193] Even the appreciation of women's property rights must include analysis of the laws affecting 'marriage, divorce, inheritance, guardianship, property rights, gifts, endowments, sales **3.97**

[186] Ibid, p. 181.
[187] Ibid, pp. 181, 191.
[188] Ibid, p. 189.
[189] Muwaffaq al-Dīn 'Abd Allāh ibn Aḥmad Ibn Qudāmah (n 69) Vol. 4, p. 561.
[190] Cited from Wahba al-Zuḥaylī (n 27) p. 382. See Jāmiʿ al-Tirmiḏī 'Ḥadīth No. 635' (Book of Zakat) <https://hamariweb.com/islam/hadith/jami-at-tirmidhi-635/> accessed 5 July 2021.
[191] Annelies Moors, Women, Property, and Islam: Palestinian Experience, 1920–1990 (Cambridge University Press, 1995) pp. 48–76.
[192] Wahba al-Zuḥaylī (n 27) p. 382.
[193] This introduction to the topic will deal with testimony, amongst the numerous positive law topics that consider women's *ahliyya*. Therefore, the purpose of this introduction is not to provide comprehensive coverage. Rather, some general principles concerning the treatment of women's *ahliyya* are outlined, while encouraging the interested reader to further investigate related areas of law.

and hirings'.[194] One finds that each topic brings forth different criteria or normative standards for the derivation of rules. For example, the technical criteria of legal capacity discussed above, which are discretion (reason) and puberty, are not definitive in relation to the rules of marriage and, as we shall see, other legal topics such as testimony. This leads to the conclusion that the law reflects what jurists felt was appropriate behaviour for men and women rather than solely the technical legal competencies necessary for an individual's legal capacity.[195]

3.98 The varied treatment of legal capacity may help to explain some contemporary orthodox jurists' perspectives on the issue. Imran Ahsan Khan Nyazee, whose textbook on Islamic jurisprudence represents the Ḥanafī tradition in contemporary South Asia, categorizes women's capacity for performance as imperfect (*nāqiṣah*).[196] Nyazee notes a woman's deficient legal capacity would:[197]

> Deny her the right to be the head of state, the right be a judge (*qāḍī*), the right to testify in cases being tried under *ḥudūd* and *qiṣāṣ* provisions (that is, duties where the right of God is involved). In addition to this, she does not have the right to divorce, like the right given to a man, she is given a share in inheritance that is equal to half the share of male heirs, and the *diyyah* paid in compensation of her death is half that of a man. These provisions have led certain Orientalists, like Joseph Schacht, to observe that in Islamic law 'a woman is half a man'.

3.99 We can see from this quotation that Islamic law restricts a woman's legal capacity in several fundamental areas of law including the right to lead or head a state, to adjudicate, and to testify in cases involving the 'right of God'. How can we account for the stark difference between the manner in which the doctrine of *ahliyya* is addressed and other areas of law or, indeed, in contrast to the ideas of Qur'ānic exegesis? The answer lies in the methodology with which legal capacity is addressed in *fiqh*. As Al-Zarqā points out, legal capacity is not a source of obligation by itself. Rather, it is a set of qualifications that enable a person to enjoy rights and acquire obligations. Each obligation in Islamic law has its own source(s) (*naṣ*) and conditions.[198] Viewed in this way, we can see that the various legal topics which Nyazee refers to each have their own legal basis (*naṣ*) and conditions, which is in keeping with the casuistic nature of the Sharīʿah. Yet, assigning unequal legal capacity to women is by no means automatic or the necessary interpretation of Islam's holy sources. On the contrary, the inferior status of women has been written into Islamic law. It is primarily a result of prevailing social conditions and norms rather than a reflection of the moral teachings of the Qur'ān.[199]

[194] Schatzmiller (n 149) p. 5. I argue that testimony (*shahādāt*) is also imperative in this analysis as the institution is essential to the validity of oral contracts. More broadly, a woman's ability to testify is clearly within the purview of legal capacity.

[195] Seedat (n 37) p. 205.

[196] I have defined *nāqiṣah* as deficient, whereas Nyazee chooses a synonym, imperfect.

[197] Nyazee (n 16) p. 120.

[198] Al-Zarqā (n 6) p. 855.

[199] Fazlur Rahman, 'The Status of Women in the Quran' in Guity Nashat (ed.), Women and Revolution in Iran (Westview Press, 1983) p. 37.

Therefore, the topic of legal capacity cannot be solely confined to the doctrine of *ahliyya* when examining female legal capacity. To do so would present a partial view of the complex, multiple, and 'expanded narrative of femaleness' which juristic texts embody.[200] In Section 1.13, a brief analysis of the *fiqh* of women's testimony (*ahliyya al-shahāda*) is examined to demonstrate this argument. 3.100

1.13 Women's Testimony (*Shahādah*)

The Qur'ān makes it incumbent on a witness to testify when called upon by a plaintiff,[201] yet a woman's responsibility to testify is unequal in relation to that of a man, highlighting an area of law where a woman's *ahliyya* is limited. Indeed, the Qur'ān establishes this inequality, and recalls the predominant idea that women are forgetful:[202] 'Call in two men as witnesses. If two men are not there, then call one man and two women out of those you approve as witnesses, so that if one of the two women should forget the other can remind her.' 3.101

1.13.1 Types of Evidence

Three types of evidence are accepted in Islamic law, namely, confession, testimony, and oaths.[203] Evidence is given orally in court. Written documents, on the other hand, are not generally viewed as evidence unless signed, witnessed, and affirmed in court. The reluctance to accept written documents as evidence centres on the fear of accepting forgeries whereas the veracity of the witness is considered to be more easily evaluated.[204] 3.102

1.13.2 The Number of Witnesses

The majority of jurists sanction testimony as the chief means of providing evidence in all cases, but the number of witnesses is determined by the particular case and schools differ herein.[205] For example, in the case of adultery the schools agree that the testimony of four men is required whereas the testimony of women in such cases is not accepted. One exception is the now extinct Ẓāhirī school which equated the testimony of two women to that of one man so that a total of eight women would be required in the case of adultery.[206] Notwithstanding adultery, penal matters with unalterable fixed punishments (*ḥudūd*) require the testimony of two just men. Women are not allowed 3.103

[200] Seedat (n 37) p. 140.
[201] Qur'ān 2:282: 'Let the witnesses not refuse when they are summoned.'
[202] Ibid.
[203] Christian Mueller, 'Judging with God's Law on Earth: Judicial Powers of the Qaḍī al-Jamā'a of Cordoba in the Fifth, Eleventh Century' (2000) 7(2) Islamic Law and Society 159, p. 165.
[204] Knut Vikor, Between God and the Sultan: A History of Islamic Law (Hurst & Company, 2005) pp. 176–77.
[205] Ṣubḥī Maḥmāṣanī (n 179) p. 177.
[206] 'Alī ibn Aḥmad Ibn Ḥazm and 'Abd al-Ghaffār Sulaymān Bindārī, Al-Muḥallā Bi-al-āthār (Dār al-Kutub al-'Ilmīyah, 1988) Vol. 8, p. 476.

to testify in these matters.[207] Al-Marghinānī explains that this ruling is based on the degree of doubt which accompanies women's testimony, which should be viewed as merely a substitute for evidence and therefore acceptable only when men's testimony cannot be obtained. Therefore, all non-property matters such as marriage, divorce, and similar matters are closed to women according to Mālik and Ibn Ḥanbal.[208] Al-Shāfiʿī is of the same opinion as his view was that the evidence of a woman was originally defective due to her deficient understanding, memory, and women's incapacity to govern. For these reasons women's evidence is not allowed in criminal cases.[209] All schools permit the testimony of one man and two women in matters concerning property and associated contracts of sale, loan, debts, and wrongful appropriation.[210] The Hanafis alone allow the testimony of one man and two women in all other cases, whether these relate to property or to other contractual rights such as marriage, divorce, agency, and so forth.[211] Al-Marghinānī goes on to explain the reasoning behind the law of women's testimony. The following passage merits quoting verbatim as Al-Marghinānī explains the underlying rationale for the law:[212]

> The reasoning of our doctors is that the evidence of women is originally valid; because evidence is founded upon three circumstances: namely, sight, memory, and a capability of communication; for by means of the first the witness acquires knowledge; by means of the second he retains such knowledge; and by means of the third he is enabled to impart it to the *Qaḍī*; and all these three circumstances exist in a woman; (whence it is that her communication of a tradition or of a message is valid); and with respect to their want of memory, it is capable of remedy by the junction of another; that is, by substituting two women in the room of one man; and the defect of memory being thus supplied, there remains only the doubt of substitution; whence it is that their evidence is not admitted in any matter liable to drop from the existence of doubt, namely, retaliation or punishment: in opposition to marriage, and so forth, as those may be proved notwithstanding a doubt, whence the evidence of women is admitted in those instances.

1.13.3 The Requirements of Testimony

3.104 Al-Marghinānī's commentary illustrates the requisites of testimony (*ahliyya al-shahāda*), which are sight, memory, and communication. Women's forgetfulness is raised as an impediment to this capacity which, however, can be ameliorated in some

[207] Muwaffaq al-Dīn ʿAbd Allāh ibn Aḥmad Ibn Qudāmah (n 69) Vol. 10, p. 170. The Ẓahīrī school is the exception, as noted earlier.

[208] Ṣubḥī Maḥmāṣanī (n 179) p. 178. Burhān al-Dīn al-Marghinānī (n 111) Vol. 3, p. 130.

[209] Burhān al-Dīn al-Marghinānī, Hidāya (A Commentary on the Mussulman Laws), trans. Charles Hamilton (Cambridge University Press, 2013) Vol. II, p. 667. Al-Marghinānī observes that Shafi'ī allows women to testify in cases that relate to property, which Al-Marghinānī finds curious. He then goes on to note that Shafi'ī's opinion that four women alone can validly testify in a case related to property is due to the fact that property transactions frequently occur whereas non-property transactions such as marriage are rare and of greater importance.

[210] Ṣubḥī Maḥmāṣanī (n 179) p. 178.

[211] Burhān al-Dīn al-Marghinānī (n 209) p. 667.

[212] Ibid, p. 668.

cases with the testimony of another woman. In other cases, which are considered too sensitive, women are excluded from testifying. Al-Marghinānī questions whether the evidence of four women alone should be admitted in view of the Hanafi ruling which allows the evidence of two women and one man in cases of property and other rights. He goes on to refute the logic of the analogy, however, and states that it is not accepted as it would require women to make regular public appearances which would not be suitable.[213]

A lone woman's testimony is valid solely in those cases where, according to a tradition of the Prophet, the subject matter relates to 'such things as it is not fitting for man to behold'.[214] Such cases relate to birth, virginity, or 'the defects of that part of a woman which is concealed from man'.[215] Al-Shāfi'ī ruled that four women are necessary even in such cases. Al-Marghinānī does not hesitate to object to this interpretation, however, as he states that the 'ocular examination of a woman, in these cases, is less indecent than that of a man; and hence also, as the sight of two or three persons is more indecent than that of one, the evidence of one woman is not insisted on as a condition in those instances'.[216] **3.105**

1.13.4 Conclusions

Seen from a contemporary perspective, the law relating to the testimony of women reveals the unmistakable gender bias of Islamic law.[217] Women's *ahliyya al-shahāda* reflects the social and ethical norms of the pre-modern past in which Islamic jurisprudence was developed. It is also the case that Islamic law was not dissimilar to Jewish law or even the legal codes of some Swiss cantons until the beginning of the nineteenth century, where the testimony of two women was counted as equivalent to that of one man. Even the Code Napoleon excluded the testimony of women in testamentary dispositions as well as several transactions related to personal status until the latter part of the nineteenth century,[218] yet it is notable that many influential jurists' interpretations of *fiqh* continue to propagate male-centric readings of the sources, which, one might argue, are no longer compatible with contemporary norms. For example, the venerated Lebanese lawyer, judge, politician, and authoritative Islamic jurist, Maḥmāṣanī (d. 1986), claims that 'it is an accepted social fact that women are less experienced than men in matters of practical life' and therefore, he intimates, the law relating to women's **3.106**

213 Ibid, p. 668.
214 Ibid.
215 Ibid.
216 Ibid, pp. 668–69.
217 Notably, the purpose of this section is not to dispute the rights of contemporary women. The primary purpose is to illustrate the pre-modern law of women's testimony and then to highlight how this law is propagated and contested.
218 Ṣubḥī Maḥmāṣanī (n 179) p. 179.

testimony is justified. Nyazee argues that women's lack of capacity to testify in matters of *ḥudūd* spares them the 'burden of this duty', which suggests women are not capable of dealing with such a burden.[219] An alternative argument is that women will remain 'inexperienced' so long as men do not treat them as their equal. Notably, men have given themselves the authority to decide who should be spared the 'burden'.

[219] Nyazee (n 16) p. 121.

4

The Role of Intent (*Niyya*)

1. Introduction

Every human action must derive from a person's will or his or her choice for the action. Intent is said to be given effect when the will is directed towards an act for a specific purpose.[1] Ṣubḥī Maḥmāṣanī, the contemporary Lebanese legal scholar (d. 1986), defines intention as 'the will directed towards the action, or the directing of the will towards the action'.[2] Intentions, in fact, are just one form of intentionality along with hope, fear, desire, belief, and many other mental states. If one has an intention, one has an intention to do something. Intentionality is the property of the mind by which it is able to represent other things.[3] Intentional states represent the mind's capacity to direct itself on things so that thoughts, hopes, desires, and beliefs are always directed on, or at, something.[4] **4.01**

In nearly every legal system, intention (hereinafter I will use 'intention' and 'intent' interchangeably) is 'a constitutive element of human actions', which is simultaneously a means by which those actions, whether those are religious acts or acts in general, can be assessed.[5] Yet intent is, by definition, an internal manifestation so that jurists, irrespective of background, face an interpretive problem in knowing it. Manifest signs and forms of legal expression, such as through individuals' speech acts and writings, are the primary means of discovering intent.[6] **4.02**

Apart from the belief in God, intent (*niyya*) is 'a fundamental concept of the whole Islamic religious law, be it concerned with worship or with law in the narrow sense'.[7] This significance is indicated by the opening placement of a *ḥadīth* in the authoritative *ḥadīth* compendium of al-Bukhārī which states that '[w]orks are only rendered efficacious by their intention' (*innamā al-aʿmāl bil-niyyāt*).[8] Wensinck describes the *ḥadīth* **4.03**

[1] Ṣubḥī Maḥmaṣānī, Falsafat Al-Tashrīʿ fī Al-Islām (The Philosophy of Jurisprudence in Islam), trans. Farhat J. Ziadeh (E.J. Brill, 1961) p. 159.

[2] Ibid.

[3] John R. Searle, Intentionality: An Essay in the Philosophy of the Mind (Cambridge University Press, 1983) p. 3.

[4] Tim Crane, 'Intentionality as the Mark of the Mental' in Anthony O'Hear (ed.), Contemporary Issues in the Philosophy of the Mind (Cambridge University Press, 1998) pp. 232–33.

[5] Paul R. Powers, Intent in Islamic Law: Motive and Meaning in Medieval Sunni Fiqh (Brill, 2015) p. 1.

[6] Brinkley Messick, 'Indexing the Self: Intent and Expression in Islamic Legal Acts' (2001) 8(2) Islamic Law and Society 151, p. 153.

[7] Joseph Schacht, An Introduction to Islamic Law (Clarendon Press, 1964) pp. 116–18.

[8] This *ḥadīth* is found in most major collections including al-Bukhārī, Muslim, al-Naʾī, al-Tirmidhī, and Ibn Māja. Quoted from Arent Jan Wensinck, 'Nīyya' in Peri Bearman et al. (eds), Encyclopaedia of Islam <http://dx.doi.org.ezproxy.soas.ac.uk/10.1163/1573-3912_islam_SIM_5935> accessed 20 August 2021.

as serving as a motto for the entire collection, which stresses the general significance Muslim jurists attributed to intention in relation to acts.[9]

4.04 The significance of intent (*niyya*) is particularly marked in relation to ritual acts, the so-called *'ibādāt*, such as prayer (*ṣalāṭ*), fasting (*ṣawm*), *zakāt*, and so on. Although Al-Ghazālī (d. 1111) required that *niyya* was declared prior to all such ritual acts ('ceremonial acts without *niyya* are not valid'), jurists were unanimous only regarding the *ṣalāṭ*.[10] Whilst the role of *niyya* in relation to *'ibādāt* is prominent and widely discussed in juristic manuals, the role of *niyya* in relation to *mu'āmalāt*, which regulates interactions amongst humans, is more varied and often discussed only in relation to some transactions.

4.05 Al-Qarāfī (d. 1285) observes that *mu'āmalāt* are legal commands which require the performance of an act for which a simple performance suffices to bring about the benefits thereto. The *'ibādāt*, on the other hand, require an external performance which does not on its own achieve the benefit of God's law.[11] The act of performing the *'ibādāt* primarily generates benefits in the hereafter and then only if the actor's *niyya* is sound. In contrast, performance of the *mu'āmalāt* brings almost immediate worldly benefits as well as rewards in the hereafter, sometimes irrespective of the parties' intentions.[12]

4.06 The role of intent in *mu'āmalāt*, which includes social interactions such as economic exchange, marriage, divorce, inheritance, and criminal law, varies across all these areas of law and even within a single legal text. Moreover, there is no general theory of intent or doctrine in Islamic law as this runs contrary to the casuistic nature of jurists' textualist hermeneutic.[13] Any attempt to synthesize a theory of obligations is superfluous given jurists' focus on finding solutions for individual cases.[14] In general, however, jurists treat intent as a means of understanding human actions. Intent provides a means by which jurists are able to define, categorize, and regulate the same.[15]

4.07 The following analysis focuses on the contracts of economic exchange, although reference to other areas of law, including ritual and family law, draws out the significance and conceptual contiguity which the concept of intention has been accorded in Islamic law.

[9] Ibid.
[10] Ibid.
[11] Shihāb al-Dīn al-Qarāfī, al-Umniyya fi idrāk al-niyya, Maktabāt al-Ḥaramaīn (ed.) (Qāsim al-Fāliḥ, Musā'id b., 1988) pp. 27–28.
[12] Powers (n 5) p. 32.
[13] For an enlightening overview of this methodology, the *uṣūl al-fiqh*, see Bernard G. Weiss, The Spirit of Islamic Law (University of Georgia Press, 2006).
[14] Chafik Chehata, Théorie Générale de l'obligation en droit musulman hanéfite (Éditions Sirey, 1969) p. 41.
[15] Powers (n 5) pp. 2–3.

1.1 The Role of Intent in the *Fiqh* of Worship (*Al-ʿIbādāt*)

Jurists' discussion of intent is notable for the wide range of terms used to define the concept. These terms range from *niyya*, which is used almost solely to discuss matters concerning *ʿibādāt*, to *qaṣd*, *irāda*, and *niyya* when dealing with commercial and family law. In relation to criminal law matters, the term *ʿamd* is employed. This variability is a telling characteristic of juristic discourse as the nomenclature reflects the diverse approaches and meanings in defining intent. *Niyya* in the context of *ʿibādāt*, for example, takes on a technical meaning which is examined below. In a commercial or family law context, however, *niyya*, along with related terms, connotes a more generalized meaning. In criminal matters, this shifts once again, where *ʿamd* connotes morally problematic or malicious intent. The variability of usage reflects the different meanings assigned to the areas of law in which the respective terms are used. Notably, words can have several meanings (*maʿān*, *madlūlat*) in language. Intending a meaning is the singling out of a particular meaning from other possible meanings, and even where a word produces a single meaning in the language, there must still be an intention to express that meaning. A meaning is always intended by the speaker, even in cases where a word gives rise to multiple meanings, so that the speaker's meaning 'comes alive in an actual speech situation'.[16] 4.08

Those aspects of *fiqh* manuals concerned with ritual and worship comprise the *fiqh al-ʿibādāt*, which is frequently translated as 'ritual law'. Ritual law includes the five pillars of Islam; the rules for ritual slaughter, hunting, diet, purification, *iʿtikāf* or the spiritual retreat to a mosque; as well as rules for washing and praying for the dead.[17] The term *niyya* is used almost exclusively in ritual law, taking on a technical meaning as it comes to define the acts of worship as required by God. *Niyya* in prayer (*ṣalāṭ*) is universally required whereas other ritual acts are treated as recommended (*mustaḥsan*). For example, jurists often require *niyya* in the performance of *wudu'* (ablutions) and *tayammum* (purification without water), whereas *niyya* is less prevalent in relation to the rules of *ghusl* (bathing).[18] However, there is a good deal of variability concerning the exact role of *niyya* in each text and amongst jurists in general.[19] 4.09

The term *niyya* derives from the Arabic root n-w-y. It appears just once in the Qur'ān in ṣurat al-Anʿām, 6:95, where the substantive of the root, *al-nawā*, is used. *Al-nawā* is 'at the heart of something'. It refers to a date pit or fruit kernel or core of something. In the canonical *ḥadīth* collections, *niyya* appears frequently yet these do not yet reflect the concept's technical meaning, which it came to possess from the second to the 4.10

[16] Weiss (n 13) p. 55.

[17] The five pillars of Islam are: profession of faith (*shahāda*), prayer (*ṣālāṭ*), alms (*zakāt*), fasting (*ṣawm*), and pilgrimage (*ḥajj*). A representative example of the *fiqh al-ʿibādāt* is presented in Burhān al-Dīn al-Marghīnānī's *Al-Hidāyah*. The *mukhtaṣar* of al-Qudūrī (Hanafi) provides that *ṣālāṭ* is required whereas *wudū'* is merely recommended. Therefore, there is no universal standard. See al-Qudūrī al-Baghdādī, Al-Mukhtahta (A Manual of Islamic Law According to the Hanafi School), trans. Ṭāhir Maḥmood Kiānī (Ta-Ha Publishers, 2015).

[18] Powers (n 5) p. 27.

[19] Ibid, p. 4.

eighth century.[20] Therefore, the legal meaning of *niyya* was not made clear in the textual sources. This epistemological opacity is evident in jurists' identification of the location of *niyya* in the heart (*qalb*), which was viewed as the site of the mind or intellect (*'aql*).[21] *Niyya* is therefore internal and largely inaccessible. It is an interior phenomenon, an action of the *qalb*, which lacks external or objectively observable characteristics. Jurists therefore face an interpretive problem in discovering the *niyya*. The solution is found in interpreting the outward manifestations of human activity including writing and speech acts.[22]

1.1.1 *Niyya* in Ritual Actions and Speech

4.11 The role of *niyya* in the *'ibādāt* reflects the set of actions including movements of the body and some speech required in ritual acts, although verbalization of *niyya* is at most a complement or confirming statement. Ibn Qudāmah (d. 1223) states, for example, that 'if one verbalises what he intends, this is by way of emphasis (*ta'kīdan*)'.[23] The texts provide rules for carrying out these actions, how and when the body is to be moved, and specific formulas to be uttered. Many jurists include *niyya* amongst the rules of *'ibādāt* so that the worshipper's intent plays a central role in constituting the act.[24] Ibn Rushd, for example, in discussing the acts of ablution (*wudū'*), expands on whether intention is a requisite condition. I quote the passage at length due to its explanatory capacity:[25]

> The jurists disagreed whether intention is a condition for the validity of ablution, although they had agreed on the stipulation of intention as a condition for worship (*'ibādāt*), because of the words of the Exalted, 'And they are ordered naught else than to serve Allah, keeping religion pure for Him', and because of the saying of the Prophet (God's peace and blessings be upon him), '*innamā al-a'māl bil-niyyāt* (Works are only rendered efficacious by their intention), which is a well-known tradition. A group of jurists, including Al-Shāfi'ī (d. 820), Mālik (d. 795), Ḥammād (d. 738), Abū Thawr (d. 854), and Dāwūd (d. 883/4), was of the opinion that it (intention) is a condition. Another group said it is not a condition, and this was the opinion of Abū Ḥanīfa (d. 767) and al-Thawrī (d. 778). The reason for their disagreement is the vacillation of the term *wudū'* between being a pure ritual *'ibāda*—I mean, not subject to rationalisation and intended only for the pleasure of Allah, like *salāh* and similar forms of mere ritual worship—and between an *'ibāda* that can be rational, like washing of dirt. They did not differ about pure *'ibāda* being in need of intention, and rational *'ibāda* not being in need of it.

[20] Wensinck (n 8).

[21] Ibid.

[22] Messick (n 6) p. 153.

[23] Muwaffaq al-Dīn 'Abd Allāh Ibn Aḥmad Ibn Qudāmah, *al-Mughnī* (Ri'āsat Idārat al-Buḥūth al-'Ilmīyah wa-al-Iftā' wa-al-Da'wah wa-al-Irshād, al-Mamlakah al-'Arabīyah al-Su'ūdīyah, 1981) Vol. 2, p. 132. Shīrāzī agrees with this statement. See al-Muhadhdhab fī fiqh Madhhab al-imām al-Shāfi'ī (Dār al-Qalam, 2001) Vol. 1, p. 69.

[24] Powers (n 5) p. 32.

[25] Abū al-Walīd Ibn Rushd, Bidāyat al-Mujtahid wa Nihāyat al-Muqtauqt, trans. Imran Ahsan Khan Nyazee (Garnet Publishing, 1994) Vol. 1, p. 3.

The *pure ritual ʿibāda* of which Ibn Rushd wrote are those rituals, similar to al-Qarāfī's bipartite definition discussed above, which benefit the worshipper in the hereafter. These acts do not possess any rational feature; they do not serve to bring about any earthly benefits. They are meant for the pleasure of Allah and hence require sincerity or intention whereas those acts possessed of rationalization are directed at earthly benefits. The role of intention in the performance of acts belonging to this latter category is disputed according to Ibn Rushd. 4.12

Although *niyya* is an internal and silent mental state, it defines a particular act of worship, and distinguishes acts from one another. Al-Qarāfī makes this argument:[26] '[*Niyya*] distinguishes that which is for God from that which is not . . . For example, bathing (*ghusl*) may accomplish cooling off and cleaning up, but can also fulfil a commanded act of worship . . . In the absence of *niyya* . . . fasting (*al-ṣawm*) is [merely] lack of nourishment.' 4.13

The requirement of *niyya* distinguishes acts of worship from ordinary actions and between levels of acts of worship such as required prayer and supererogatory prayer. According to Shīrāzī (d. 1291/92), the *niyya*, in relation to prayer, must be specified so that it distinguishes between evening prayer, noon prayer, and other prayers.[27] Jackson asserts that the distinguishing (*tamyīz*) between acts is the central thrust of Qarāfī's definition of *niyya*. Thus, its role is 'to isolate (*yumayyīz*) the specific objective for which a wilful act is performed'.[28] *Niyya* distinguishes between acts whose outward form is identical, thus lending them their identity.[29] Therefore, prayer (accompanied by *niyya*) can be differentiated from meditation. Without *niyya*, the latter, no matter how precisely performed, does not belong to the realm of worship.[30] 4.14

Section 1.2 redirects our focus to the role of intention in *muʿāmalāt*, which is the primary focus of this chapter. 4.15

1.2 Intent in Contract Law

Unlike the *fiqh al-ʿibādāt*, the law of social transactions, the *fiqh al-muʿāmalāt*, is to some extent morally neutral as they constitute the rules which regulate civil actions as opposed to those which are directed to the worship of God. Whereas *niyya* is often prescribed in ritual acts, it is largely assumed in civil acts. This bifurcation of the role of intent in Islamic law is widely recognized in the Ḥanafī *fiqh* of contract (*al-ʿaqd*), where the role of intent for the validity of contract was 'so little taken into consideration 4.16

26 Shihāb al-Dīn al-Qarāfī (n 11) p. 20.
27 Abū Isḥāq al-Shīrāzī, al-Muhadhdhab fī fiqh Madhhab al-imām al-Shāfiʿī (Dār al-Qalam, 2001) Vol. 1, p. 236.
28 Sherman Jackson, Islamic Law and the State: The Constitutional Jurisprudence of Shihab al-Qarafi (Brill, 1996) p. 200.
29 Powers (n 5) p. 45.
30 Ibid.

that the sale of an object is clearly considered to be valid even if the ends it serves are illegal'.[31] This understanding of the role of intent, where subjective intent was of no legal consequence, was also shared by al-Shāfiʿī, which the following passage from *al-Umm* (*The Mother*) makes clear.[32]

> No contract is nullified except due to its own terms [. . .] Sale contracts are not nullified on grounds of pretext or evil intention (*niyyat sūʾ*) . . . Thus if a man buys a sword intending to kill with it, the sale is permissible; though the intention is not admissible, it does not invalidate the sale. . . The book, followed by the Sunna and the general judgement of Islam, all indicate that contracts have legal effect according to their manifest content and are not invalidated by the intention of the parties.

1.2.1 The Schools' (*Madhāhib*) Approaches to Intent in Contract

4.17 The Hanafis and the Shafiʿīs are known to apply an objective approach to contract in which external elements such as speech acts, writing, or the circumstances in which the transaction takes place (to a limited extent) are given legal weight. The cause or motive does not affect the validity of the contract unless it is declared in the contract. For example, if the intention behind the contract is to commit a sinful act, but it was not made apparent in the contract, then the act is reprehensible (*makrūh*) for the Hanafis and prohibited (*harām*) for the Shāfiʿīs. Yet, save for these ethical remonstrations, the contract is valid (*saḥīḥ*).[33]

4.18 In contrast, the Malikis and Hanbalis lend more weight to the underlying motives or intentions of the contract even if these are not immediately apparent. They invalidate a contract whose cause (*qaṣd*) or *niyya* is prohibited on the condition that the opposing party knows about this intention or has strong evidence of it.[34] Al-Shāṭibī (d. 1388), the Andalusian jurist who followed the Maliki school, explains this approach:[35]

> Deeds are to be judged by intentions, and objectives are taken into account in dispositions, such as rituals and dealings. Roots of that are innumerable. Objective and motivating cause differentiate between a ritual and dealing—that is, contracts and dispositions. They also determine the validity, or invalidity, of these acts. Thus, when an ultimate objective of an act is unlawful, the act is also unlawful. For instance, when a sale is intended to be a means for *ribā* (usury), such sale is invalid.

[31] Chehata (n 14); cf. Oussama Arabi, 'Intention and Method in Sanhūrī's Fiqh: Cause as Ulterior Motive' (1997) 4(2) Islamic Law and Society 200, p. 200.

[32] Muḥammad b. Idrīs al-Shāfiʿī, Kitāb al-Umm, 8 vols (Dār al-Maʿrifa, 1990) Vol. 7, p. 297.

[33] Al-Kamāl Ibn Al-Humām, Fatḥ al-Qadīr (al-Maṭbaʿa al-Amīrīya, 1900) Vol. 8, p. 127; ʿAbd al-Raḥmān bin Aḥmad al-Zaylaʿī, Tabyīn Al-Ḥaqāʾiq Sharh al-Kanz (al-Maṭbaʿa al-Amīrīya, 1896) Vol. 2, p. 125.

[34] Abū al-Walīd Ibn Rushd, Bidāyat al-Mujtahid wa Nihāyat al- al-Muqtaṣid (Dār al-Maʿrifa, 1982) Vol. 2, p. 140; Muḥammad Ibn Muḥammad Ibn ʿabd al-Raḥmān Ḥaṭṭāb, Mawāhib al-Jalīl (Maṭbaʿat al-Saʿāda, 1911) Vol. 4, p. 404; Abū Isḥāq al-Shāṭibī, Al-Mawāfiqāt fī uṣūl al-Sharīʿah >>Sharīʿah (al-Maktaba al-Tijārīya al-Kubrā, 1985) Vol. 2, p. 261; Al-Mughnī (Dār al-Kitāb al-ʿArabī, n.d.) Vol. 4, p. 174; Ibn Qayyim al-Jawziyya, Iʿlām al-Mowaqiʿīn (Dār Ibn al-Jawzī, 2002) Vol. 4, p. 520.

[35] Al-Shāṭibī (n 34) Vol. 2, p. 324.

1.2.2 The Oral Nature of Contract Law

Further study of the role of intent in the *fiqh* texts must begin with the jurists' concern for speech acts which are the means for forming a contract. Before doing so, however, some historical background to contracts is apposite. Pre-modern contracts were primarily oral in nature and therefore required speech acts to form a contract. The role of written documents, however, was not insignificant even if jurists consistently favoured orally concluded contracts or informal contractual relations.[36] For example, contractual formulae, the *shurūṭ*, were widely used in formal, private transactions. Despite this, Islamic legal practice denied the validity of the use of written documents in court, whereas the Qur'ān commanded: 'When you contract a debt for a fixed term, record it in writing. Let a scribe record it in writing between you . . . Be not averse to writing down [the contract], whether [the amount] be small or great, with its term.'[37] Oral testimony was accorded greater evidentiary weight as the personal testimony of an upright Muslim was lent greater validity than a written document, which was seen as vulnerable to falsification. A private contract required at least two male witnesses, or two female witnesses for every male, whilst public documents required court-hired witnesses.[38] Every case heard in court required the use of witnesses, some who performed the role for the court regularly. The role of the witnesses, who usually numbered three or four in total, was to review the correctness of the legal procedures employed in the case and to retain memory of the case for the benefit of the community.[39] This distinctive procedure may have solidified the moral connection between the community and the court and contributed to consistency in judges' rulings. **4.19**

Despite the predominant historical practice of concluding contracts orally, the will (*irāda*) can be lawfully expressed by means other than the verbal utterance, such as in writing, by signalling, by exchange, and via any other means that implies consent.[40] **4.20**

Section 1.3 examines the role of intent in the formation of a contract. It begins with a short introduction to the theological background of contract in Islam, which is helpful for understanding the role of intention. **4.21**

[36] Jeanette A. Wakin, The Functions of Documents in Islamic Law (University of New York Press, 1972) pp. 6–7. Goitein documents eleventh-century Geniza records in which most transactions were concluded orally. See S.D. Goitein, *A Mediterranean Society: the Jewish Communities of the Arab World as Portrayed in the Documents of the Cairo Geniza* (University of California Press, 1967) Vol. 1, p. 196.

[37] Qur'ān 2:282.

[38] Ibid; Jonathan G. Ercanbrack, The Transformation of Islamic Law in Global Financial Markets (Cambridge University Press, 2015).

[39] Leslie P. Peirce, Morality Tales: Law and Gender in the Ottoman Court of Aintab (University of California Press, 2003) p. 97. Peirce explains that the use of witnesses (*shahādah* in the wider sense) was not an Islamic invention but was common throughout the pre-Islamic Near East. In pre-Islamic Arabia, the use of witnesses for giving evidence was almost certainly the most common form of proof, and ceremonies may have been performed for their reception.

[40] 'Abd al-Razzāq al-Sanhūrī, Manhūrī al-Ḥal- fī al-Fiqh al-Islāmī: Dirāsah Muqāranah bi-l-Fiqh al-Gharbī (Dār Iḥyā' al-Turāth al-'Arabī, 1998) p. 77. Ibn Taymiyya adds that valid contracts are those which achieve their objectives along with the other categories of contracts. See Ibn Taymiyya, Majmū' fatāwā Shaykh al-Islām Aḥmad ibn Taymīyya (1st edn, Maṭābi' al-Riyāḍ, 1961) Vol. 29, p. 7.

1.3 The Role of Intent in Contractual Formation

4.22 The theological background of contract law distinguishes the characteristics of an Islamic contract in important ways. Although the Muslim believer's ultimate commitment is to God, he or she has been given the right to decide (*irāda*) whether to enter a contract. He or she is the *ʿabd* (slave) of God (*rabb*) in the most literal meaning of the word. God is not merely the creator of all that he creates; He is the owner and thus possesses full property rights over all that He creates. God's slaves, in fact, have no original rights whatsoever apart from those bestowed by God, as it is He alone who possesses these rights. God's law is handed down from on high for the good of man; God makes provisions for humanity's well-being. He does not wish His slaves unwell. Indeed, humanity's well-being resides in the whole of nature or the very creation of God.[41] When God's subjects reach full maturity, God uses the powers of reasoning that he has given to all humanity to bring them into a covenantal encounter with Him. He addresses them with the words: 'Am I not your Lord?' His subjects answer, 'Yes, verily', impressing upon their consciousness His sovereignty. Humans, therefore, exist in a covenantal relationship with God, in which God has bestowed commandments and rules on his slaves that set out the obligations of His covenant. The so-called literature of commentary (*sharḥ*) of the Qur'ān describes the encounter as 'the covenant of sovereignty and subordination' (*ʿahd al-rubūbiyya wa al-'ubūdiyya*).[42] Fakhr al-Dīn al-Rāzī (d. 1209) confirms the legal obligations which derive from God's covenant with humans: 'A covenant occurs through the doing of those things that render obedience obligatory' (*al-mīthāq innamā yakūn fī al-umūr allatī tūjib al-inqiyād wa al-ṭāʿa*).[43] The covenant contains terms and conditions that must be fulfilled as they are the bedrock of all obligations and rights (in the mundane world). At the day of judgment, they cannot say: 'Of this [i.e. of your lordship and our obligation to obey you] we were unaware.'[44] Humans have testified to their acceptance of God's terms in the covenantal encounter and these terms must be obeyed.

4.23 Fulfilling the terms of God's covenant in the mundane acts of existence is paramount. The Qur'ān orders believers in this regard: 'You who believe, fulfil contracts (*awfū bil-ʿuqūd*)' (5:1); 'You who believe, be faithful to your contracts' (4:33); and 'Fulfil the covenant of God when you have entered into it, and break not your oaths after you have confirmed them' (16:91). Yet God's believers are not deprived of autonomy in contract or the freedom to agree the terms of a contract despite having submitted to God's covenant.

4.24 Indeed, the Qur'ān establishes consent as the foundation of contract in the mundane world: 'You who believe, do not wrongfully consume each other's wealth but trade by

41 Weiss (n 16) p. 24.
42 Ibid, pp 32–33, citing 7:172 of the Qur'ān.
43 See Fakhr al-Dīn al-Rāzī, al-Tafsīr al-Kabīr, 32 vols (Dār al-Fikr, 1981) Vol. 3, p. 114.
44 Weiss (n 13), citing 7:172 of the Qur'ān.

mutual consent.'[45] Numerous *ḥadīths* underscore this rule, such as where the Prophet is to have said: 'Transactions may only be done by mutual consent' or, elsewhere, 'Verily trade is based on mutual consent'.[46] Therefore, an individual's consent (*riḍā*) is necessary to form a valid contract.[47]

1.3.1 The Definition of Contract

Let us briefly recall the definition of contract to understand better the role which intent occupies in an individual's consent. The contract (*'aqd*) is 'the connection, and it's the attaching of two ends of two ropes and the like, and the binding of one to the other until they are connected and are like one piece'.[48] This definition emphasizes the connection of 'two ends of two ropes', underscoring the consensus or the meeting of the minds (*riḍā*) that is necessary to form a valid contract. The *Majalla* provides a more technical definition: 'the connection between offer and acceptance (*ījāb wa qabūl*) on a permitted way where the effect [of this connection] results in the objective [of the contract]'.[49] Here, the emphasis centres on the exchange of promises as well as what results from the exchange in a 'permitted way'. Therefore, one might suggest that a contract in Islamic law involves the exchange of promises which results in permissible legal effects.[50] **4.25**

1.3.2 Party Autonomy in Contract

Irāda is a term used to denote an individual's decision to enter into a contract. It consists of two elements. First, there is 'choice' (*ikhtiyār*). Choice in a contract is the intent to utter statements which establish the contract so long as one has the capacity and intent to utter these statements. Secondly, there is consent or satisfaction (*riḍā*), which is the complete satisfaction of one's objectives in having entered the contract. This latter element shows that party autonomy, or an individual's free will to make decisions, is a valid concept in Islamic law.[51] In the mundane world, an individual's will to decide the contracts he enters is unconstrained. **4.26**

For the Hanafis, these elements are conceptualized in three cases. The first is where the party intends the meaning that can be found in the contract and is content with its **4.27**

[45] Qur'ān 4:29.

[46] See Ibn Mājah, Sunan Ibn Mājah (Vol. 3, book 12, no. 2185) <https://sunnah.com/ibnmajah/12> accessed 23 September 2021.

[47] Al-Qurṭubī, Tafsīr al-Qur-īr (n.p., 1984) Vol. 5, p. 153.

[48] Muṣṭafā Aḥmad al-Zarqā, al-Madkhal al-Fiqhī (Dār al-Qalam, 1998) p. 384.

[49] The Majalla, Being an English Translation of Al-Majalla Al-Aḥkam Al-'Adliyyah and a Complete Code of Islamic Civil Law, trans. C.R. Tyser et al. (Law Publishing Company, 1967) Arts 103–104.

[50] Once parties have decided to enter a certain type of contract, the rules governing a particular contract follow as a matter of course. For an insightful overview of Islamic contract law in the English language, see Hussein Hassan, 'Contracts in Islamic Law: The Principles of Commutative Justice and Liberality' (2002) 13(3) Journal of Islamic Studies 257. Further exploration of the contract of sale (*bay'*), which, for some jurists, is the touchstone for all other commercial contracts, illustrates the emphasis placed on the items to be exchanged. Indeed, the *bay'* was simply defined as the exchange of one item for another. The Hanafis, for example, delimit the items that can be exchanged to those which are owned, and which qualify as property (*māl*). *Māl*, whilst defined differently according to the school, indicates a commodity that is desirable, and which it is possible to store for later use. See Wahbah al-Zuḥaylī, Financial Transactions in Islamic Jurisprudence, trans. Mahmoud Al. El-Gamal (Dar al-Fikr, 2003) Vol. 1, pp. 5–6.

[51] Abū Zahra, al-Milkīya wa Naẓarīyat al-'Aqd fī al-Sharī'a al-Islāmiya (Dār al-Fikr al-'Arabī, 1996) p. 192.

legal effects. The second case is where the party intends the utterance of the statements which establish the contract but does not intend that the legal effects come into being, as is the case of jesting. Abū Zahra, a contemporary Hanafi jurist (d. 1974), highlights a third case, where words are uttered under coercion. The Hanafis nonetheless consider this a choice.[52] Choice is viewed as the main pillar for entering a contract, whereas *riḍā* (contentment) is merely necessary for the validity of the contract (*ṣiḥḥa*). This indicates that the form and meaning of the utterance used to express the choice are the primary determinants of intent. A contract to which a party has assented via his or her utterance is considered binding albeit imperfect (*fāsid*). It becomes valid when the parties have reached consensus (*riḍā*). Uniquely, in addition to valid (*ṣaḥīḥ*) and invalid (*bāṭil*) contracts, a third category of contract (*fāsid*) adds a degree of flexibility to contract formation under Hanafi law and, arguably, allows the school's more objective approach to the interpretation of intent.

1.3.3 Revocable and Irrevocable Contracts

4.28 The objective approach to intent in the formation of contract is to treat revocable contracts, some of which can be used in finance, as contingent upon 'the wilful utterance of the contracting terms', whereas their validity depends on the contracting parties' contentment (*riḍā*).[53] Several contracts, known collectively as *'uqūd jā'iza* (contracts of licence) are capable of dissolution by unilateral revocation. These are non-binding contracts which permit unilateral revocation subject to notifying the other party of one's intent to revoke the contract. Revocation does not have retrospective effect so that the contractual effects remain valid until the point in time of its dissolution. Moreover, a court order is not required. Examples of non-binding contracts are the *wakāla* (agency), *wadī'a* (deposit), *rahn* (mortgage), *kafāla* (guarantee), *sharika* (partnership), etc.[54] Most non-binding contracts do not comprise an exchange of obligations. One party commits to doing something without the immediate exchange of price or detriment from a counterparty. In contrast, when a contract requires consent and immediate exchange has taken place, the 'demands of commutative justice' normally ensure that the contract is irrevocable.[55] However, this is not a failsafe principle as, for example, a gift (*hiba*) is primarily viewed as irrevocable unless made by a parent. The rule is that each contract must be evaluated for its own rules and legal effects.

4.29 In contrast, non-revocable contracts such as marriage, divorce, and *'itaq* (emancipation of slaves) are solely valid and legally effective based on choice alone. Once the parties have uttered their agreement to the terms of the contract, the issue of contentment does not arise. Therefore, in the Hanafi school, a divorce made in jest is a valid divorce.

52 Ibid.
53 See Muḥammad Wohidul Islam, 'Dissolution of Contract in Islamic Law' (1998) 13(4) Arab Law Quarterly 336, pp. 349–50.
54 Ibid.
55 Hassan (n 50).

The Shafi'is and other schools consider 'choice' an expression of what an individual really wants. The utterance of words is not an indication of what a person truly wants. Therefore, jesting should not be considered a choice, nor should coercion, mistake, and forgetfulness, as the words used in all these cases do not reflect a person's true wants. Choice and contentment are concomitant.[56] For these reasons, these schools consider both *ikhtiyār* (choice) and *riḍā* (contentment) essential to establish any contract, whether the contract is revocable or not.[57] **4.30**

1.3.4 Contemporary Jurists' Views of Intent

The modern purpose of revitalizing Islamic law in contemporary Muslim society is evident in contemporary jurists' view of *'irāda*. The contractual language they employ is much more familiar to the individual versed in Western-style law. The substance of their considerations, moreover, reflects their modernizing purpose. The modern Egyptian jurist and architect of Egypt's 1949 Civil Code, Al-Sanhūrī (d. 1971), is the standard setter in this regard. He defines a contract, not merely as the exchange of permissible commodities, but as the 'correspondence of two wills to establish an obligation' (*tawāfuq irādatayn 'alā inshā' iltizām aw naqlih*).[58] In this understanding of contract he is joined by many other notable jurists of his time.[59] A prominent Syrian contemporary of Sanhūrī, Al-Zarqā (d. 1999) takes a slightly different approach. He argues that it is not merely the meeting of the minds that establishes a contract under Sharī'ah. Rather, it is the agreement of two wills in satisfaction of the conditions of the Sharī'ah, which, contrary to Western-style law's subjectivity, endows the Islamic contract with a Sharī'ah objectivity.[60] In contrast, Sanhūrī argues that the will must be directed towards a permitted objective, which he defines as the 'cause' (*sabab*). The result is that a contract has two pillars: the agreement and the cause.[61] The legal cause is that which establishes the obligation (*al-sabab al-qānūnī aladhī ansha' al-iltizām*). However, this notion of cause (*sabab*) betrays Sanhūrī's goal of modernizing Islamic law for contemporary practice. Sanhūrī's desire to strengthen the methodological role of subjective intent in the interpretation of contracts is evident. At the time of his writing, Western-style law such as modern French law had developed a modern theory (of contract law) and Sanhūrī was impressed by the orientation of contemporary French jurisprudence to the demands of the judiciary. His theorizing of Islamic commercial law sought to modify Islamic principles 'to the satisfaction of the contemporary practicing judge'. Therefore, his development of the subjective 'cause' provided an answer to the relatively marginal role of *niyya* in *mu'āmalāt*. An important step towards this goal was to incorporate the French juridical notion of 'cause' as the subjective motive for contract.[62] **4.31**

[56] Ibid.
[57] Ibid, p. 196.
[58] 'Abd al-Razzāq al-Sanhūrī, al-Wajīz fī Naẓarīyat al-Iltizām (Dār al-Nahda al-'Arabiyya, 1966) p. 17.
[59] Ibrāhīm Aḥmad, Al-Iltizāmāt fī Al-Sharī'ah (al-Maktaba al-Azharīya li-l-Turāth, 2013) p. 41.
[60] Al-Zarqā (n 48) p. 384.
[61] 'Abd al-Razzāq al-Sanhūrī (n 58) p. 49.
[62] Arabi (n 31) p. 89.

4.32 However, a theory of cause in Islamic law is not found in pre-modern writings. Jurists understand 'cause' as an element of the obligation or a source of the obligation. This is reflected in the contractual forms (*shurūṭ*) wherein notaries list the cause of an obligation, such as that of a loan. Yet a theory of cause that reflects the subjective intent of an individual was not developed in *fiqh* manuals nor was it required for a valid contract.[63]

4.33 On the contrary, 'the real cause of the buyer's obligation is not the contract of sale, but the fact that ownership of a thing has been transferred to him'.[64] The price is the equivalent of the commodity. The refusal to pay the price is to upset the balance that the contract must ensure, the equilibrium in which equivalence or equality is the goal of contracting parties. Chehata, therefore, reduces the '"theory of cause" to a theory of equivalence'.[65]

4.34 Section 1.4 addresses the speech acts used in the formation of a contract. The focus is on understanding the weight that jurists ascribe to a party's intention as interpreted from the verbal utterances one performs in forming a contract.

1.4 Verbal Utterances in the Formation of Contract

1.4.1 Apparent or Hidden Intent

4.35 Intent can be apparent or hidden (*al-irāda al-ẓāhira wa al-irāda al-bāṭina*). Hidden will is closely connected to intention and thus is said to reflect what is wanted by the heart. Apparent will, in contrast, is the expression of intent by the tongue or one of its substitutes. The most authoritative method used to communicate contractual intent is to do so verbally.[66] However, other methods including writing, signalling, exchange, and implication are regarded as valid to varying degrees.[67]

1.4.2 Explicit or Allusive Speech

4.36 Hanafi jurists distinguish between speech that is explicit and direct (*ṣarīḥ*) or allusive or indirect (*kināya*). Explicit speech conveys a clear and definite meaning, whereas allusive speech is speech in which the intention of the speaker is hidden and requires explanation. The intention in this latter type of speech can be deduced from the wording of the text or from its references or implications.[68] The Shafi'i jurist Aḥmad Ibn Naqīb al-Miṣrī (d. 769) confirms this second category of speech acts:

> [U]nequivocal expressions (*ṣarā'iḥ*) . . . sales can likewise be effected by indirect expression with intention (*bi al-kināya ma' al-niyya*), such as 'take it for such-and-such

[63] Chehata (n 14) pp. 67–68.
[64] Ibid.
[65] Ibid.
[66] Ibrāhīm Aḥmad (n 59) pp. 76–77. Notably, Aḥmad requires verbal utterances for a valid contract although a written contract was also legally effective in the pre-modern era.
[67] 'Abd al-Razzāq al-Sanhūrī (n 40) p. 77. The schools took different positions on each of these means of conferring contractual intent. Sanhūrī discusses these in detail from pp. 77 to 98.
[68] Ṣubḥī Maḥmaṣānī (n 1) p. 164.

an amount,' or 'I consider it yours for such-and-such an amount,' intending thereby a sale which is accepted. If [the speaker] doesn't intend thereby a sale, it comes to nothing.[69]

The Hanbali jurist, Ibn Qayyim al-Jawziyya (d. 1350) categorizes the intentions of speakers in three cases. The first case resembles that of the Hanafi and Shafi'i jurists. This is the case where the correspondence between words and intentions is manifest and is graded in degrees of certainty. Ibn Qayyim's second category introduces examples of indirect speech where there is no correspondence between the words and intentions. This is the case where the speaker did not intend anything from his words, as in the case of a drunkard, an insane person, or a sleeping person. In this case, the utterance has no legal effect. In figurative speech, where a speaker intends something different from what his words ostensibly mean, the validity of words depends on the party's intention. If the person knows the meaning of the utterance, it has a legal effect. If the person does not intend the meaning, it is a question of what he or she intended. Should this intention amount to nothing, it is like a jester's utterance which is legally invalid. When he or she intends a different meaning, it is a question of whether the true intention is permissible or not.[70] 4.37

Ibn al-Qayyim's final category is where the words are clear but no discernible intention is evident and there is no evidence to assist in determining this.[71] This third category concerns speech which is entirely ambiguous, and therefore 'comes to nothing'.[72] 4.38

In an astute analysis Powers argues that the *fiqh* manuals demonstrate jurists' preoccupation with two broad categories of intent in speech acts. The first category is that of 'basic sincerity', which describes speech acts made in the process of contractual formation and 'complexity'.[73] The second category concerns the complex intentions that jurists consider in relation to the lawfulness of transactions. I adopt this methodology in the analysis below, using the work of the philosopher of intentionality, John Searle. 4.39

1.4.3 The Use of Verbal Tenses in the Formation of Contract

A valid contract requires the correspondence of the offer and acceptance in clear and explicit language.[74] Clarity of meaning or what constitutes such is given great consideration. The use of the past tense when making a contract implies the present—the here and now. The intentions of the parties are not relevant in this consideration. This is what may be described as clear, unequivocal speech (*ṣarīḥ*). The present tense, the imperfect in Arabic, may imply the present or the future tense and depends for its validity on the 4.40

[69] Aḥmad Ibn Naqīb al-Miṣrī, 'Umdat Al-Sālik (The Reliance of the Traveller: A Classic Manual of Islamic Sacred Law), trans. Noah Ha Mim Keller (Modern Printing Press, 1991) p. 378.

[70] Ibn Qayyim al-Jawziyya, I'lām al-Muwaqqi'īn 'an Rabb al-'Ālamīn (1st edn, Dār Ibn al-Jawzī, 2002) Vol. 4, p. 526.

[71] Ibid, Vol. 4, p. 519.

[72] Powers (n 5) p. 98.

[73] Ibid.

[74] Al-Zarqā (n 48) p. 405.

party's intention which is the inner will. According to the Hanafis, this type of speech requires clarification as it is allusive or indirect (*kināya*). If the offeror intended an immediate offer, and acceptance matches the offer, a valid sale is concluded. Otherwise, there is no valid offer capable of acceptance. The present tense that points exclusively to the future is not a valid offer.[75] Furthermore, commands or questions are seen as future-oriented and belong to the category of ambiguous speech, which has no legal effect.[76] The Hanafis, therefore, rely on the form and wording of the verbal expression to determine the expression of the inner will.[77]

4.41 The remaining schools of law agree with the Hanafis that the use of the past tense makes a contract binding, and that the intention must be concomitant with the present tense for a contract to be binding. The schools' disagreement concerns the command form (*ṣīghat al-amr*). According to the majority, the command form mostly implies the present tense and is therefore valid without inquiry into the intention. In those cases in which the command form may imply the future, the contract is validated when the intention is shown to indicate the present. Where a contracting party denies that his or her use of the command form is to have made an offer, he or she is required to take an oath to this effect.[78]

1.4.4 The Hanafis' Categorization of Speech Acts

4.42 Further examination of speech acts is useful to understand the categories discussed above. For example, beyond issues of verbal tense, what is meant by direct and unequivocal speech? The Hanafis provide a useful interrogation of language in this regard as they categorized speech acts according to the real, the metaphorical, and the derelict. The real refers to the meaning of a word which is used according to common usage. For example, when I refer to a lemon, I am referring to the yellow citrus fruit. Metaphorical usage, on the other hand, attaches meaning to common words which differs from the ordinary meaning. For example, I can also use the word 'lemon' to refer to a car or other mechanical device which is faulty or defective. The reader will recognize that the context in which this word is uttered helps to distinguish the different meanings. Finally, the final category of speech acts, the derelict, refers to language which is no longer in use and is void of meaning to all intents and purposes.[79]

4.43 The *Majalla* provides clear instructions for how these categorizations are to be interpreted. It states that 'in principle, words shall be construed according to their real meaning,'[80] yet 'when the real meaning cannot be applied, the metaphorical sense may be used'.[81] This would be the case when the real meaning or common usage of the word

[75] Ibn Nujaym, al-Ashbāh wa-l-Naẓā'ir (Dār al-Kutub al-'Ilmīyah, 1999) p. 20.
[76] Al-Kāsānī, Badā'i' al-Ṣanā'i' (al-Maṭba'a al-Jamālīya 1909) pp. 133–34.
[77] 'Abd al-Razzāq al-Sanhūrī (n 40) p. 70.
[78] Muḥammad b. Sa'īd b. Ḥabīb (Saḥnūn), al-Mudawwana al-Kubrā (al-Maṭba'a al-Khayrīya, 1907) Vol. 4, pp. 229–32.
[79] Ṣubḥī Maḥmaṣānī (n 1) p. 162.
[80] *Al-Majalla Al-Ahkām Al-'Adaliyyah* (n 49) Art. 12.
[81] Ibid, Art. 61.

would not make sense in the context of the speech act. Moreover, words are generally to be construed as laden with meaning, but 'if no meaning can be attached to a word it is disregarded altogether. That is to say, if a word cannot be construed in either a real or a metaphorical sense it is neglected as being devoid of meaning.'[82]

What interpretation is to be given to the situation in which the real and metaphorical meanings overlap, so that it is unclear what is being referred to? In this case there are divergent opinions amongst the schools. Abū Ḥanīfa believed that the 'real' meaning should be prioritized, whereas his two famous students, Abū Yūsuf and al-Shaybānī, along with other jurists ruled that the metaphorical and customary meanings should be given preference so long as these were continuous and predominant.[83] This latter view, which was included in the *Majalla*, is the majority view. Al-Shāfiʿī, along with other jurists, held that for the customary meaning to be given precedence, the underlying intentions of the parties must confirm this meaning.[84] **4.44**

1.4.5 The Malikis' Approach to Language

The Malikis are considered to have the least formalistic approach to language or contractual terminology, and rarely rely on it alone. They are also known for relying on implication, which requires a degree of subjectivity, rather than merely relying on objective implications.[85] Muḥammad Yūsuf Mūṣa, a contemporary Maliki jurist, confirms this characterization, which I quote at length:[86] **4.45**

> A contract, whatever its case and object, becomes binding by word or deed that unambiguously tells the wills of the contracting parties regardless of whether or not the contract in this state was customary or not. So whatever implied sale, it becomes binding; whatever implied hire, it becomes binding . . . The measure for those who follow this school is that whatever is used by the contracting parties whether word or deed, implies with certainty what they wanted from initiating the contract and establishing it regardless of the customary terminology and forms which made contracts binding. And so we see this view that takes informality to the limits; this is the dominant view in the Maliki school, and it is the apparent view in Ibn Ḥanbal's.

From this passage we see that the Malikis placed great emphasis on intent in contract, so much so that the approach to language categorizations discussed above (paras 4.43–4.45) could be displaced if the parties' intentions are or can be learned otherwise. Yet the Hanafis, whose formalism represents the opposing view, were not opposed to implication in certain situations, including those characterized by silence, presumption of fact (implication), or common usage. Indeed, most schools permit the *bayʿ al-taʿāṭī* (casual sale) in which the buyer and seller exchange the good and price without uttering **4.46**

[82] Ibid, Art. 62.
[83] Ṣubḥī Maḥmaṣānī (n 1) p. 163.
[84] Jalāl al-Dīn al-Suyūṭī, al-Ashbāh wa-l-Naẓā'ir (Dār al-Kutub al-ʿIlmīyah, 1983) p. 293.
[85] 'Abd al-Razzāq al-Sanhūrī (n 40) p. 93.
[86] Ibid.

a word. The offer and acceptance are implicit in this context.[87] Or the situational contract where someone leaves money in front of a group of people with the result that they become trustees of it. If they leave one by one, the last person remaining becomes liable.[88]

1.4.6 Signs, Customs, and Silence in Contractual Formation

4.47 Moreover, signs and customs are considered to provide additional observable indications about the apparent will upon which the contracting parties can rely instead of expressing their will in speech or in writing. In principle, however, there is no formalism in the formation of a contract. There is no need for special rituals of movements or gestures to form a valid contract.[89]

4.48 Silence is inconsequential unless it is supported by the facts of the situation. The *Majalla* confirms this Hanafi rule, which is shared by the other schools of law: 'No statement is imputed to a man who keeps silence, but silence is tantamount to a statement where there is a necessity for speech.'[90] Intent can be found in situations where the absence of speech provides clear indications, yet internal intentions alone do not establish a legal action. Until they have been expressed physically in a way which is discernible to the judge, they remain part of the unexpressed will.[91] One might say that they remain part of the unarticulated will or merely an unexpressed intentional state. Messick ascribes this to what he terms 'a kind of culturally specific foundationalism' which is the 'site of authoritative meaning-generation internally, within the self, and thus beyond direct observation.'[92]

4.49 Section 1.5 addresses what the philosopher John Searle calls complex actions. The relationship between complex actions and complex intentions is important for understanding complex transactions, particularly those in the modern economy.

1.5 Complex Actions and Intent

4.50 The discussion here centres on the degree to which parties' intentions are taken into consideration in relation to complex transactions for the purposes of determining whether such intentions invalidate a contract or transaction. One might refer to these complex transactions, following the philosopher John Searle, as so-called complex actions. Complex actions are the result of intentions which embody an intentional content or object. Searle differentiates between prior intentions and intentions in action. Prior intentions represent the whole intentional object, whereas intentions in action

87 Ṣubḥī Maḥmaṣānī (n 1) p. 164.
88 Al-Zarqā (n 48) p. 405.
89 Chehata (n 14) p. 109.
90 *Al-Majalla Al-Aḥkām Al-ʿAdliyyah* (n 49) Art. 67.
91 Al-Zarqā (n 48) p. 406.
92 Messick (n 6) pp. 153 and 161.

are directed at the movement alone. The prior intention represents the whole action as the conditions of its satisfaction (the conditions by which the intentional state is satisfied). In contrast, the intention in action presents, 'but does not represent, the physical movement and not the whole action as the rest of its condition of satisfaction.'[93]

An example is the intention to drive to the office. The prior intention is presented with several subsidiary acts that are necessary to satisfy the conditions of this intention. For example, the driver will need to start the engine; shift gears; pay attention to oncoming traffic, traffic lights, and cyclists; change lanes; park the vehicle, and so on. Numerous subsidiary acts are necessary to satisfy the intention but may not have been represented by the prior intention. Searle argues that these subsidiary movements are caused by the prior intention, given the intransitivity of intentional causation.[94] **4.51**

The significance of the concept of complex intentions in contract law becomes clear when considering that parties may wish to form a valid contract whilst simultaneously pursuing other commercial objectives. Searle's notion of complex intentions provides a framework for understanding these scenarios and for breaking down their constituent parts for further analysis. **4.52**

1.5.1 The Schools' (*Madhāhib*) Approaches to Complex Intentions

The *madhāhib's* approach to complex intentions resembles their respective approaches to the role of intent in the formation of a contract. The schools disagree about the legal validity of prior intentions and assess differently the intentions in action that are required to satisfy the intentional content of the same. The primary example is a contract that is valid in form (intention in action) but one or both parties' hidden intentions are for an illicit objective (prior intention). The schools' position on the so-called *muḥallil* or false betrothal contract (*zawāj al-muḥallil*) is a case in point. The objective of the *muḥallil* contract is for a man to marry a woman, have intercourse with her, and then divorce her. This allows a woman who has been divorced by her former husband to remarry him according to the law. The contract is based on the Qur'ānic rule which states: 'And if he (the former husband) divorces her, she will not be lawful for him until she marries a husband other than him, and if he divorces her, there is no sin upon them to remarry if they think that they can maintain Allah's bounds.'[95] **4.53**

For the Hanafis and Shafi'is, intent has no effect on the validity of the contract if such intent is not evident in the contractual terms. If the prior intention is to commit a sinful act, the act is reprehensible (*makrūh*) for the Hanafis and prohibited (*harām*) for the Shafi'is.[96] For both schools, however, the act remains valid.[97] In other words, the act is morally deficient but retains legal standing. The effect is to endow these formalistic **4.54**

[93] John R. Searle, Intentionality: An Essay in the Philosophy of the Mind (Cambridge University Press, 1983) p. 93.
[94] Ibid, pp. 93–94.
[95] Qur'ān 2:230.
[96] Wahbah al-Zuḥaylī (n 50) pp. 216–17.
[97] Ibrāhīm Aḥmad (n 59) p. 99.

interpretational methodologies with a secular capacity for distinguishing between objective acts and those hidden acts which are only known to God. These schools argue that one should not speculate on the intentions of others if these are not apparent. Only God knows the hidden intentions of his worshippers. Al-Shāfiʿī argued that:

> Rules (*aḥkām*) are based on appearance and Allah cares for the unseen. And whoever rules upon doubt, has given himself what Allah has made His exclusive prerogative . . . and He commanded his worshipers to accept what other people present in appearance and if anyone should have had the right to conjecture something unseen (*bātin*) it would have been the prophet peace be upon him.[98]

1.5.1.1 The lawfulness of the bayʿ al-ʿīna *(legal ruse)*

4.55 The lawfulness of the *bayʿ al-ʿīna* is dealt with similarly. Although a legal ruse (*ḥiyal*) designed to circumvent the prohibition of *ribā* (usury), the contract is valid for both the Hanafi and Shafi'i schools. The *bayʿ al-ʿīna* is one of the oldest legal stratagems of its kind: an object is sold on a deferred payment basis, then repurchased for a sum less than the original deferred price, payable on the spot.[99] One can utilize *ḥiyal* to make lawful that which is otherwise unlawful; to create what the Hanafis called '*makhārij*' (sing. *makhraj*) or 'exits'.[100] Devised by jurists to ease the difficulties presented by a legalistic adherence to the Sharīʿah in everyday life, *ḥiyal* provide flexibility or 'exits' which allow parties to achieve their commercial and other objectives. Therefore, *ḥiyal* represent a compromise between theory and practice, between ideals and reality.[101] How might this tendency towards ease be related to the way in which the Hanafis and Shafi'is view intent?

4.56 These schools' view of *ḥiyal* was regarded through the prism of their potential utility. *Makhārij* were devised to help the faithful seek remedies for 'oppressive' or inconvenient

[98] Al-Shāfiʿī, Muḥammad Ibn Idrīs, *Al-Umm* (al-Ṭabʿah 2, Dār al-Maʿrifah lil-Ṭibāʿah wa-al-Nashr, 1973) Vol. 4, p. 114.

[99] The transaction was so successful and widespread that Europeans of the Middle Ages adopted its use under the name of *mohatra* (from the Arabic, *mukhāṭara*, meaning risk or hazard). See Joseph Schacht, 'Ribā' in Martijn Houtsma, Thomas Arnold, R. Bassett, and Richard Hartmann (eds), Encyclopaedia of Islam, 1st edn (1913–1936) (Brill Online, 2014) <referenceworks.brillonline.com/entries/encyclopaedia-of-islam-1/riba-SIM_3700> accessed on 25 April 2014.

[100] Satoe Horii, 'Reconsideration of Legal Devices (ḥecon) in Islamic Jurisprudence: The Hanafis and Their "Exits" (makhārij)' (2002) 9 Islamic Law & Society 312, pp. 312–13.

[101] Schacht made the largest contribution to date to contemporary understanding of *makhārij* with his translation of four published works dedicated to expounding these 'ruses', as he called them; these included those by Abū Bakr Aḥmad al-Khaṣṣāf (d. 874), Abū Ḥātim Maḥmūd al-Qazwīnī (d. 440/1048–49), and Muḥammad Ibn al-Ḥasan al-Shaybānī (d. 189/805). See Joseph Schacht, Das Kitab Al-Hijal Fil-Fiqh (Buch der Rechtskniffe) *des* Abu Hatim Mahmud Ibn Al-Hasan Al-Qazuini (Orient-Buchhandlung Heinz Lafaire, 1924) p. 6. Three of the works are by Hanafis and the fourth by al-Qazwīnī, a Shāfiʿī jurist. Shaybānī was one of Abū Ḥanīfah's most brilliant disciples. His writings constitute some of the basic texts of Hanafi jurisprudence, which include the *Kitāb al-Aṣl*, *al-Jāmiʿ al-Kabīr*, and *al-Jāmiʿ al-ṣaghīr*—the so-called *ẓahir al-riwāya*, i.e. the authoritative and faultless transmission of Hanafi doctrine. The *ẓahir al-riwāya* contains the three major scholars of the Hanafi school: Abū Ḥanīfah (eponym of the school), Abū Yūsuf, and Shaybānī. See Horii (n 100) p. 319. The Hanafis' recommendation of their use stretches far beyond a limited exercise. Hanafis encouraged the faithful to utilize them, even to avoid merely undesirable situations, since the law provides for these exits for those who seek them. Ibn Qayyim al-Jawziyya confirmed this claim in his description of the Hanafi view regarding the Sharīʿah as a body of exits that envisioned the exigencies of human life.

situations that 'prejudiced' oneself. The diminished role of intent in these schools' interpretational methodologies does not reflect an amoral stance vis-à-vis the moralistic concerns of the Hanbalis and the Malikis. On the contrary, these schools' view of intent is grounded in a concern for the law's utility; the strictures of God's law could be overcome, whilst retaining its divine essence. The divine law could live on whilst society advances and requires legal flexibility.

1.5.2 The Hanafis' and Shafi'is' Formalistic Approach to Contractual Interpretation

Before turning our attention to the Hanbali and the Maliki approach to complex intentions, let us consider in greater detail the Hanafis' and Shafi'is' formalistic approach to contract. Once again, Al-Shāfiʿī is the most straightforward proponent of this methodology, which is evident in the following passage in his *Kitāb al-Umm*:[102] **4.57**

> The principle I follow is that any contract which is valid in appearance, I do not nullify (*Ana kull ʿaqd kāna ṣaḥīḥan fi'l-ẓāhir lam ubṭiluhu*) on grounds of suspecting the parties: I validate it by the validity of its appearance; I take their intention to be reprehensible (*akrah lahumā al-niyya*) if—were it made explicit—that intention would invalidate the sale. Thus, I reprehend the purchase of the sword by the man if he plans to kill with it. Yet its sale by the vendor to the man who kills unjustly with it is not prohibited, for he might not kill with it; consequently, I do not invalidate the sale. Similarly, I reprehend the sale of grapes by the vendor to a person whom he sees is making wine from it; but I do not void the sale of the grapes, because they were sold legally. Just as the buyer of the sword might not kill anybody with it, so the buyer of the grapes might not make wine.

Therefore, only when the sinful intention is a term of the contract (and hence apparent for all to see) would the sale be deemed null and void *ab initio*. Otherwise, such sales are reprehensible, but they are nonetheless valid. The quotation is striking for the manner in which it treats the individual sales as discrete steps. Each step is assessed for its lawfulness on its own terms with limited concern for how it is connected to the transaction as a whole. The prior intention, which is directed at the whole action, is disregarded in favour of the intentions in action, the discrete movements undertaken to satisfy the intentional objective. The intentions in action, when viewed as discrete actions by themselves, are objectively legal actions.[103] **4.58**

It is evident that the Shafi'is, like the Hanafis, incline towards giving more weight to the words of the contract rather than the motives and intentions.[104] A slightly more radical formulation of this approach is made by the authoritative Hanafi jurist, Ibn Nujaym (d. 1520), who argued that foundational contracts including sale *bay*ʿ (sale), *iqālah* (cancellation of contract), *hiba* (gift), and *ijāra* (lease) do not depend on intention for their **4.59**

[102] Muḥammad bin Idrīs Al-Shāfiʿī (n 32) Vol. 3, p. 65; cf. ʿAbd al-Razzāq al-Sanhūrī (n 40) Vol. 4, pp. 57–58; Powers (n 5) p. 114.

[103] Powers (n 5) p. 115.

[104] Abū Zahra (n 51) p. 216.

validity at all.[105] We can conclude, therefore, that both schools agree, more or less, that where the parties' intentions are unknown or difficult to ascertain and there is [apparent] divergence between these and the outward expression of the act, the external expression should be given effect. This is in line with the tradition of the Prophet which states: 'We give judgment on the basis of the apparent, God takes care of the inward intention.'[106] It is also confirmed in the *Majalla*, which provides that 'in obscure matters the proof of a thing stands in the place of such a thing. That is to say, obscure matters in which it is difficult to discover the truth are judged according to the obvious proof concerning their outward connotation.'[107]

4.60 The Hanafī approach to contractual interpretation, however, is not monolithic. Maḥmaṣānī, for example, challenges the sheer formalism often depicted of the Hanafī school. He argues that where a difference exists between the intention and the outward expression of an act, judgment should be made in view of the underlying intention so long as it can be ascertained. If there is a divergence between the words of an act and the meaning of those words, 'consideration should be given to the meaning and not the literal wording'.[108] Maḥmaṣānī offers us an example. The contract for the use of a thing with consideration is called a contract of hire (*al-istiṣnā'a*). If no consideration (price) is provided in the contract, one has contracted a gratuitous loan (*'ārīyah*). Therefore, if a party concludes a contract in which a tangible item has been lent albeit for a rental premium, the contract should be regarded as a contract of hire irrespective of whether the wording of the contract identifies it as a loan.[109] He emphasizes that the contractual modus of Islam aims at the 'search for meanings and real intentions'.[110] Maḥmaṣānī's subjectivist inclination diverges from his school's otherwise formalistic interpretational approach to intent in contract.

1.5.3 The Malikis' and Hanbalis' Subjectivist Approach to Contractual Interpretation

4.61 Let us shift our attention now to the subjectivist approach which is typified by the Malikis and Hanbalis. The Hanbali school is closely associated with the ethical and religious concerns of the Traditionalists (*muḥaddithūn*) as its eponymous founder, Ibn Ḥanbal, was a leading Traditionist or compiler of prophetic traditions as well as those of the Prophet's Companions.[111] The Hanbalis were accordingly pious and devoted to worship and asceticism. Therefore, the validity of legal acts in this school is

[105] Ibn Nujaym did not elaborate on the reasoning why these contracts should be classified as such. See Ibn Nujaym (n 75) pp. 20–21.

[106] Abū Isḥāq Shīrāzī (n 23) Vol. 2, p. 86.

[107] *Al-Majalla Al-Ahkām Al-'Adliyyah* (n 49) Art. 68.

[108] Ṣubḥī Maḥmaṣanī (n 1) p. 160. Additionally, al-Shawkānī argued against school doctrine and attempted to establish intention as the means by which a contract is validated. Although unsuccessful in his attempt, his example is instructive of the diversity of opinion. See Al-Kamāl Ibn Al-Humām (n 33) Vol. 5, pp. 84–85.

[109] Ṣubḥī Maḥmaṣānī (n 1) p. 161.

[110] Ibid, p. 163.

[111] Ibn Ḥanbal (d. 841) is one of the most highly respected intellectual figures in Islamic history. He was one of the foremost proponents of traditionalist (literalism-oriented) theology in Sunni Islam and compiled one of the most important collections of *ḥadith* called the *Musnad*. See the Introduction in Henri Laoust, Le *précis* de *droit* d'Ibn Qudāma (Institut Français de Damas, 1950) for an overview of this school's distinctive attributes.

made contingent on pious motivation.[112] Both the Malikis and Hanbalis consider the *muḥallil* contract void (*fāsid*).[113] If the *taḥlīl* (dissolution (of marriage)) is a term of the contract, it is considered null and void and the parties are to be separated without need for divorce. However, divorce (*ṭalāq*) is required if dissolution of the marriage was not included as a term of the contract but subsequently admitted. *Taḥlīl* is seen as violating a basic condition of marriage, namely, continued partnership. Therefore, it is essentially impermissible according to these schools, as the only means of 'permitting a *taḥlīl*' is to fulfil the conditions of a valid marriage with no intention of subsequently dissolving it.[114] We can see in this example that in cases where the dominant motive or intent of one of the parties is illegal, then the contract is deemed void. This is also the case in relation to the *bay' al-'aīna* where the Malikis and Hanbalis suspected that parties' intentions were to deal in *ribā*.[115] In a clear statement of these principles, the famous Hanbali jurist Ibn Taymiyya (d. 1328) explains that:[116]

> Allah has prohibited *ribā* and *zinā'* (adultery) and all forms of contracts that stem from these for the mischief they cause in society. He, on the other hand, permitted sale and marriage for the benefits entailed in them. There must be a real difference, therefore, between what is halāl and what is harām; otherwise, sale would be like *ribā*. The difference in form has no effect since it's the meanings and objectives that are considered. If the terms differed while the meaning was the same, the *ḥukm* (rule) will remain the same. And if the terms were the same while the meanings differed, the *ḥukm* will differ.

Ibn Qayyim al-Jawziyya, a disciple of Ibn Taymiyya, confirms the primacy of parties' intentions over words and terminology:[117] **4.62**

> Should the law take into account only the manifest meaning of expressions and contracts even when the purposes and intents (*al-maqāsid wa'l-nīyyāt*) appear to be otherwise? Or do aims and intents (*al-quṣūd wa'l-nīyyāt*) have an effect which requires paying attention to them and taking them into consideration? The evidence of the Law (*adillat al-shar'*) and its rules concur that intentions in contracts do count and that they affect the validity and invalidity of the contract (*annahā tu'aththir fī ṣiḥḥat al-'aqd wa fasādih*), determining whether the contract is legal or illegal.

The lawfulness of an act must be assessed for its aims and intents. Therefore, the form of an act and contract (*ṣūrat al-fi'l wa'l-'aqd*), although in itself lawful, is deemed illegal **4.63**

[112] Arabi (n 31) p. 95.

[113] The term '*fāsid*' is often translated as irregular or deficient. The majority of schools nonetheless consider a *fāsid* contract as one that is void (*bāṭil*). *It has no legal effects.* Only the Hanafi school maintains that a *fāsid* contract is one that is not void *ab initio*. Rather, it can become a valid contract (*ṣaḥīḥ*) if the offending condition, which is prohibited by the Lawgiver, is removed. Until such time as this is done, the contract remains in a state of suspension.

[114] 'Abd al-Raḥmān al-Jazīrī, Al-Fiqh 'alā al-Madhāhib al-Arba'a (Dār al-Kutub al-'ilmīyya, 2003) Vol. 4, pp. 74–80.

[115] Abū al-Walīd Ibn Rushd (n 25) 172. This is also the view of Ibn Taymiyya (n 40) Vol. 29, p. 30.

[116] Ibn Taymiyya, Bayan al-Dalīl 'alā Butlan al-ṭaḥlīl (al-Maktab al-Islāmī, 1988) pp. 246–47, 430.

[117] Ibn Qayyim al-Jawzyya, I'lām al-Muwaqqi'īn 'an Rabb al-'Ālamīn (al-Munīrīya Press, n.d.) Vol. 3, pp. 96–98, 496.

should a party's underlying intent be found unlawful. Ibn Qayyim provides several examples:[118]

> Thus, if a man buys a slave-girl intending that she be for his employer, then she is legally forbidden for the buyer; whereas if he buys her for himself, then she is permissible for him. Though the form of the act and the contract are distinct . . . Also if one sells a weapon to someone whom he knows will use it to kill a Muslim; then the sale is forbidden and invalid as it promotes crime and aggression; however, the sale is valid if he sells the weapon to someone engaged in holy war in God's way.

4.64 Recall Al-Shāfiʿī's description of the sale of a sword to someone whom he knows will use it to kill a Muslim. Al-Shāfiʿī found the sale valid as it satisfied the requirements of a valid sale. The unlawful intentions of the buyer are merely admonished in moral and ethical terms (*makrūh*). Ibn Qayyim takes the opposite position; the sale is invalid as the buyer's intent is unlawful. The form of the sale is irrelevant in this latter consideration. Arabi describes this legal reasoning as transcending 'formal adequacy into the domain of moral responsibility'.[119]

4.65 The Hanbali concern for moral responsibility has significant legal consequences for contracts, whether these are commercial or related to marriage. The *taḥlīl* marriage contract discussed above is considered null and void as are other *hiyal* such as the *bay' al-ʿīna*. The Hanbalis, and to a somewhat lesser extent, the Malikis, are prepared to draw legal consequences for unlawful intentions irrespective of whether these intentions are made plain in the terms of the contract. When one party has taken notice that the other party harbours unlawful intentions, such knowledge is sufficient to invalidate the transaction.[120] In other cases, where intentions are unrecognizable, the cause of the act (*sabab*) or the inducing motive as well as the circumstances are considered. Hanbali *fiqh* substitutes intent with cause in such a case. Should the cause not be identifiable, then the apparent meaning (*al-irāda al-ẓāhira*) of the act is to be given effect.[121]

118 Ibid. See also Wahbah al-Zuḥaylī (n 50) p. 218.
119 Arabi (n 31) p. 96.
120 'Abd al-Razzāq al-Sanhūrī (n 40) pp. 75–76.
121 Nabil Saleh, 'The Role of Intention (Niyya) Under Saudi Arabian Hanbali Law (2009) 23(4) Arab Law Quarterly 469, p. 475. Saleh argues that Hanbali fiqh diverges from Shafi'i and Hanafi fiqh only in theory, whereas in practice the rules of evidence in Hanbali law limit the investigation of intent, to some degree.

5

Maḥal Al'aqd

1. Introduction

The subject matter of a contract, also named *maḥal al 'aqd* or *ma'qūd 'alaih*, is an object/thing—movable or immovable and tangible or intangible—for which a contract is made. According to Islamic jurists (*fuqahā*), the determinants of the 'thing' allowed to become the subject matter of a valid contract are the following: (i) it should be *māl mutaqawwam* (legal); (ii) existent; (iii) owned by the seller; (iv) in the possession of the seller; (v) able to be delivered; and (vi) precisely determined (*ma'lūm*).[1] These conditions are discussed in detail in the chapter due to their importance; when met, they create contractual certainty, which is a foundational principle for an agreement to qualify as valid and for the ensuing rights and liabilities of the parties to be enforceable. The foregoing elements will be examined in the context of the contract of sale. Of course, the conditions pertaining to *mabī'* (subject matter in a sale contract) are also relevant in relation to other types of contract, such as *hiba* (gift), *ijārah* (lease; usufruct), *waṣiyya* (bequest), etc., and will be touched upon here as well. 5.01

In the course of this chapter it will become clear that there are certain elements that make the subject matter of a contract permissible for sale when originally it was not. In converting an impermissible subject matter into a permissible one, custom, benefit, and necessity play very important roles. 5.02

Impermissible subject matters, such as human organs or blood, are allowed on account of their necessity in surgery and medical treatment.[2] Subject matters originally thought to be non-existent are allowed for the facilitation of people's needs; for example, fruit and vegetables of which some have ripened and others have not yet ripened.[3] Similarly, 5.03

[1] Ibn 'Ābidīn, Radd al-Muḥtār Sharḥ Tanvīr al-Abṣār (Dār al-Fikr, 1412H/1992) Vol. 4, p. 505. See also Susan E. Rayner, The Theory of Contracts in Islamic Law: A Comparative Analysis with Particular Reference to the Modern Legislation in Kuwait, Bahrain and the United Arab Emirates (Graham & Trotman, 1991) p. 157. It should be noted that when Islamic law governs a particular transaction or contract, courts vested with jurisdiction will determine the legality of the subject matter under Islamic law. For instance, in *Golden Belt v BNP Paribas* [2017] EWHC 3182 (Comm), the Commercial Court of London held a sukuk bond to be compatible with the Sharī'ah, yet the sole arranger was found liable to a distressed fund because he had failed to ensure the proper execution of a promissory note.

[2] Ibn Qudāma, Al-Mughnī fī Fiqh al-Imīm Aḥmad bin Ḥanbal (Dār al-Fikr, 1405H) Vol. 4, p. 260; Abūbakr Al-Kāsānī, Badā'i' al-Ṣanā'i' fī Tartīb al-Sharā'i' (Dār al-Kutub al-'Ilmiyya, 1406H/1986) Vol. 5, pp. 138–40; Ibn 'Ābidīn (n 1) Vol. 4, pp. 501–05. It should be noted that the necessity in itself is not sufficient to make permissible an impermissible thing unless that situation is not included in some *qaida kulya*. See Ashraf Ali Thānwī, Imdād ul Fatāwā (Zikriya Book Depot Deoband Saharanpur year) Vol. 6, pp. 471–72.

[3] Fatāwā ibn Nujaim in the margin of Fatāwā al-Ghayāsiya (Maba'a Amīriya Egypt, 1922) p. 113.

some subject matters that are not *mutaqawwam* (legal) and have no value become permissible, if they are deemed beneficial according to custom.[4] Sometimes, the derived benefit from a *maḥal al-ʿaqd* permits the conclusion of a contract which would otherwise be prohibited.[5]

5.04 Custom plays a pivotal role not only in determining the point when possession is considered to have been delivered, especially regarding movable property such as vehicles, animals etc.,[6] but also in determining the *taqawam* (value) of a subject matter.[7] The prohibition of an object becoming the subject matter of contract may be excused by *ʿurf* (custom).[8]

5.05 On the other hand, *gharar* (contractual uncertainty; ambiguity) is a hurdle to a valid contract. *Gharar* in a transaction exists when the conditions of the *maḥal al-ʿaqd* are not clear and the contract's effects and results are not evident.[9] In other words, *gharar* exists in a thing when it is not certain whether that particular thing can be achieved/materialize or not.[10] *Gharar* is a broader concept than *jahāla* (ignorance; lack of knowledge); that is, every *majhūl* involves *gharar* but every *gharar* does not involve *jahāla*. There may be *gharar* without any *jahāla*, such as in the sale of a lost item or a stray animal whose qualities and nature are completely known, in which case there is no *jahāla*. However, *gharar* exists on the point of its delivery by the seller to the purchaser. Still, no *jahāla* can exist without *gharar*.[11] There are three degrees of *gharar* and *jahāla*. The first is excess lack of knowledge and uncertainty, which is forbidden by all schools of Islamic jurisprudence. An example may be drawn from the birds in the sky. The second degree is minor/trivial *gharar* and *jahāla*, which is permissible—for example, that which relates to the foundations of a house that is being sold. The third degree arises where *gharar* and *jahāla* are moderate or lie somewhere in the middle of the excessive and minor degrees described above. There is some difference if this kind of *gharar* is

[4] Al-Nawawī, Yaḥya ibn Sharaf, Al-Majmūʾ Sharḥ Al-Muhadhdhab (Dār al-Fikr, n.d.) Vol. 10, p. 286; Al-Ramlī, Shihāb al-Dīn, Nihāyat al-Muḥtāj ilā Sharḥ al-Minhāj (Dār al-Fikr, 1404H/1984) Vol. 3, p. 393 ff; *Al-Mughnī* (n 2) Vol. 4, p. 302.

[5] Al-Shīrāzī, Abū Ishāq Ibrāhīm, Al-Muhadhdhab fī Fiqh al-Imām al-Shāfiʿī (Dār al-Kutub al-ʿIlmiyya, 1995) Vol. 2, pp. 10–11.

[6] Muḥammad al-Dusūqī, Muḥammad ibn Aḥmad ibn ʿArfa, Ḥāshiyat al-Dusūqī ʿalā al-Sharḥ al-Kabīr (Dār al-Fikr, n.d.) Vol. 3, pp. 144–45.

[7] *Radd al-Muḥtār* (n 2) Vol. 7, pp. 241–42.

[8] Thānwī (n 2) Vol. 6, p. 458 and Vol. 3, p. 96. See also Haṣkafī, ʿAlā al-Dīn ibn Aḥmad ibn Muḥammad, Durr Mukhtār (Maktaba Zikriya Deoband, n.d.) Vol. 4, pp. 59, 186–89 and Vol. 7, pp. 75–77, 281–86; Haṣkafī, ʿAlā al-Dīn ibn Aḥmad ibn Muḥammad, Al-Dār al-Muntaqī ʿalā Majmaʿ al Anhur (Dār al Kutab al-ʿIlmiyya, n.d.) Vol. 3, p. 7; Ibn Nujaim, Al-Nahr al Fāʾiq (Maktaba Zikriya Deoband) Vol. 3, p. 360; Ibn Nujaim, Zain al-ʿĀbidīn ibn Ibrāhīm, Al-Baḥr al-Rāʾiq Sharḥ Kanz al-Daqāʾiq (Dār al-Kitab al-Islāmī, n.d.) Vol. 5, p. 507; Zailiʿī, Fakhr al-Dīn ʿUthmān ibn ʿĀlī ibn Mihjā al-Barīʿī ,Tabʾyīn al Haqāʾiq mʿa al Ḥāshiyat al-Shilbī (Maktaba Zakariya Deoband) Vol. 4, pp. 389–93; Ibn al-Ḥumām, Kamāl al-Dīn Ibn Muḥammad, Fatʾḥ al-Qadīr (Dār al-Fikr, n.d.) Vol. 5, p. 490; *Radd al-Muḥtār* (n 2) Vol. 7, pp. 86–88; Rāshid Aḥmad, Aḥsan al Fatāwā (H M Saeed Company, 2005) Vol. 6, pp. 486–90. Interestingly, in *Rainy Sky SA v Kookmin Bank* [2011] UKSC 50, paras 15–21, the UK Supreme Court held that where there are two possible constructions of a relevant document, the court may prefer that which is more consistent with business common sense rather than considering requirements under Islamic law.

[9] Al-Shīrāzī (n 5) Vol. 2, p. 12.

[10] Al-Qarāfī, Al-Furūq (Moʾassisāt al Risāla Nashiron, 2003) Vol. 3, pp. 403–04.

[11] Ibid, Vol. 3, p. 265; see also Nicholas C. Dau-Schmidt, 'Forward Productions: Prohibitions on Risk and Speculation under Islamic Law' (2012) 19 Indiana Journal of Global Legal Studies 533.

counted with the first or the second type.[12] *Gharar* may exist when the *ṣiffa* (qualities) and *qadr* (measurement, weight, number) of the subject matter, its deliverability or existence, are not known with precision.[13]

2. Legality of Subject Matter and Underlying Cause

The concept of *māl* or property is something which human nature desires and which may be accumulated or put aside for an hour of need.[14] The monetary or financial value (*māliyya*) of *māl* makes people wealthy and rich and establishes its value (*taqawam*). A commodity which, while permissible, is incapable of having a monetary value, or from which no benefit can be extracted, does not constitute *māl*.[15] There are two possible reasons why a commodity may not be susceptible of producing benefit. First, it may be of such low quantity that it cannot produce a benefit, as is the case with one or two grains of wheat, or a single raisin. Goods of such quantity are not considered *māl* and this would still be the case if the good in question were mixed with another good, or if it were used as bait for hunting, because this was not its original purpose. Secondly, objects such as insects, or beasts of prey, which cannot be used for hunting, or birds that are neither edible nor used for hunting, such as vultures and glede, do not produce benefit or a financial value.[16] The commodity that has the quality of making people rich but from which it is not permissible to benefit would be *māl*, as it will not have any value (*mutaqawwam*). Notably, sometimes both value and benefit are absent from a commodity.[17] **5.06**

To this end, *'ayn* (plural *a'yān*; determinate property) is classified twofold: *najas* (impure) and *ṭāhar* (pure). *Najas* are classified even further: first, *najas* that are intrinsically or in their own right impure, like a dog, a swine, wine, dung, and impurities along the lines of the following *ḥadīth*:[18] 'Allah has proscribed the sale of wine, dead animal, swine and idols.'[19] Secondly, there exist *najas* derived from the association of an object with another impure element, such as the affliction of an impurity, filth on garments, or used cooking oil.[20] *A'yān al-ṭahhara* (pure objects) are also of two kinds: (i) things in **5.07**

[12] Al-Qarāfī (n 10) Vol. 3, pp. 403–04; *Radd al-Muḥtār* (n 2) Vol. 4, pp. 528–30.

[13] Al-Nawawī (n 4) Vol. 9, pp. 346–48; Al-Shīrāzī (n 5) Vol. 2, p. 12 and Vol. 1, p. 262; ibn Muḥammad ibn Ahmad Al-Shirbīnī al-Qāhirī al-Khaṭīb, Mughnī al-Muḥtāj ilā Ma'rifat Alfāẓ al-Minhāj (Dār al Ma'rafa Beruit, 1997) Vol. 2, p. 18; Al-Sarakhsī, Al-Mabsūṭ (Dār al-Ma'rifah, 1414H/1993) Vol. 13, p. 192; Al-Kāsānī (n 2) Vol. 5, p. 163; Al-Qarāfī (n 10) Vol. 3, p. 265.

[14] *Majalla*, Art. 126; *Radd al-Muḥtār* (n 2) Vol. 4, p. 501.

[15] *Radd al-Muḥtār* (n 2) Vol. 4, pp. 501–02; see also *Riyad Bank v Ahli United Bank (UK) plc* [2005] EWHC 279 (Comm), per Mr Justice Moore-Bick, who took note of the restrictions under Islamic law concerning the subject matter of financial contracts.

[16] Al-Nawawī (n 4) Vol. 9, pp. 285–86; Al-Qarāfī (n 10) Vol. 3, p. 370; see Craig R. Nethercott and David M. Eisenberg (eds), Islamic Finance Law and Practice (Oxford University Press, 2012) p. 46.

[17] *Radd al-Muḥtār* (n 2) Vol. 4, p. 501; *Majalla*, Art. 211.

[18] Ibn e Māja, *Kitāb al-Tijārāt*, ch. 11.

[19] Al-Shīrāzī (n 5) Vol. 2, p. 9.

[20] Al-Nawawī (n 4) Vol. 9, pp. 269–70.

which there is some benefit, which may consist of immovable and movable objects such as edibles, drinks, clothes, perfumes, etc., and (ii) *aʿyān*, in which there is no benefit, as is the case with insects and beasts that cannot be used for hunting or a crow which cannot be eaten.[21]

5.08 Considering the above, *māl* is something which can be accumulated or put aside, even if its use is not permissible (e.g. wine). However, *māl* constitutes *mutaqawwam* when its use is also permissible by the Sharīʿah. Therefore, wine is *māl* but not *mutaqawwam*, so its sale by a Muslim would be invalid.[22] Property permissible by law and having some specific value is called *mutaqawwam* and may validly be sold.[23] *Māl* amounting to *mutaqawwam* or *ghair mutaqawwam* can be distinguished in two ways: first, on the basis of *ʿurf* (custom) and secondly, by means of declaring something as *mutaqawwam* by Sharīʿah,.[24]

5.09 A *māl* or property may be: (i) movable, namely, it can be transferred from one place to another, such as animals; merchandise; and things estimated in terms of their weight, number, or measurement, and; (ii) immovable, which cannot be transferred from one place to another, such as a house and land.[25] In a sale contract, the subject matter should be *māl mutaqawwam*, and what cannot be sold cannot be mortgaged,[26] donated, or gifted—that is,[27] given as *ṣadaqa* (charity),[28] *hiba*, *waqf*, or *iʿāra* (borrowing items).[29] By implication, the subject matter in these contracts should be *māl mutaqawwam*[30] and of a specific value.[31]

2.1 Permissible Subject Matters

5.10 Everything that is pure and beneficial can be sold.[32] For instance, movables, including books,[33] utensils made of gold or silver,[34] breast milk,[35] edibles, drinks, clothes, perfumes, etc., are allowed. Similarly, animals used for riding, eating, hunting, breeding,

[21] Al-Shīrāzī (n 5) Vol. 2, pp. 10–11.
[22] *Radd al-Muḥtār* (n 2) Vol. 4, pp. 501–05.
[23] Ibid, Vol. 7, p. 236; *Majalla*, Art. 199.
[24] Ibid, *Radd al-Muḥtār* (n 2) Vol. 7, pp. 241–42.
[25] *Majalla*, Arts 126, 128, 129.
[26] Al-Shīrāzī (n 5) Vol. 2, pp. 90, 334; *Al-Mughnī* (n 2) Vol. 4, p. 338.
[27] Ibn al-Humām, Al-Fatāwā al-Hindiyya (Dār al Kutub al ʿIlmiyya, 2000) Vol. 4, p. 417; Al-Shirbīnī (n 13) Vol. 2, p. 515; *Al-Mughnī* (n 2) Vol. 5, p. 598.
[28] Al-Shīrāzī (n 5) Vol. 2, p. 324.
[29] Ibid, Vol. 2, p. 322; *Majalla*, Art. 420. *Waqf* and *iʿāra* are allowed only for a thing from which benefit can be extracted on a long-term basis.
[30] Al-Shīrāzī (n 5) Vol. 2, p. 322; Al-Kāsānī (n 2) Vol. 5, p. 140; Al-Shirbīnī (n 13) Vol. 2, p. 11; *Al-Mughnī* (n 2) Vol. 4, p. 260; *Radd al-Muḥtār* (n 2) Vol. 4, pp. 501–05 and Vol. 7, pp. 241–42, 264.
[31] *Majalla*, Art. 709. See also Frank E. Vogel and Samuel L. Hayes, Islamic Law and Finance: Religion, Risk and Return (Martinus Nijhoff, 1998) p. 88.
[32] Al-Dardīr, Al Sharḥ al Saghīr annotated by Aḥmad bin Muḥammad al-Ṣāavī al Mālikī (Dār ul Muʿārif Cairo, n.d.) Vol. 3, p. 22; Al-Shirbīnī (n 13) Vol. 2, p. 16.
[33] Al-Nawawī (n 4) Vol. 9, p. 302.
[34] Ibid, Vol. 9, p. 307.
[35] Al-Shirbīnī (n 13) Vol. 2, p. 18; Al-Nawawī (n 4) Vol. 9, p. 254.

or for their wool may also validly be sold.[36] What people possess or accumulate from land and other immovable properties are permissible subject matters of a contract,[37] yet pure commodities, which do not carry any benefit allowed by the Sharīʿah, cannot be sold (note the aforementioned examples of insects, the beasts which cannot be used for hunting, a crow which cannot be eaten),[38] because the investment in what is not beneficial is a waste of money.[39]

If the pure thing becomes impure due to its contact/mixture with another impurity, if it may be purified by some process it can validly be sold; otherwise not. For instance, clothes, carpets, skin, utensils, even land, can be sold, for they can be purified. If the subject matter of the transaction cannot be purified (e.g. vinegar, molasses, processed milk, honey, etc.), it cannot be sold, as is the case with all other impure things.[40] **5.11**

Some rights cannot become the subject matter of sale—the right of pre-emption, the right of *qiṣāṣ*, and the rights of a potential legatee during the life of the legator.[41] However, there are certain rights the sale of which has become permissible by custom, as is the case with rights associated with immovable property. Normally these rights would be transferred along with their associated property. These may encompass, for instance, the right of passage/way, the right to water passage, or the right to use water and air rights, that is, the right to build a structure that occupies the vertical space above a property. These rights can be sold for a specific term on the basis of *ijāra* in isolation from the property with which they are associated. There is disagreement among scholars as to whether it may be sold on a permanent basis (*bayʿ al-ḥuqūq al-mujarrada*). Some schools, such as the Hanbalis, Shafi'is, Malikis, and modern Hanafis allow the sale of the right to benefit from property on a perpetual basis. Proponents of the Hanafis argue that, according to custom, when a right carries some monetary or financial value, it becomes *māl* and its sale is allowed if this is a personal/private right that has arisen and accrued in the person's favour. Moreover, the right should be transferrable, involve no *gharar*, and trade usages should also classify it as *ʿayn*.[42] The sale of the right to water is allowed by the Malikis, according to whom the sale of water that springs from a stream, is extracted from a well, or some other source of water collection is also allowed for a specific day or days in a month.[43] Similarly, the right of way or passage can be sold.[44] **5.12**

[36] Al-Shīrāzī (n 5) Vol. 2, pp. 10–11.
[37] Al-Nawawī (n 4) Vol. 9, p. 296.
[38] Al-Shīrāzī (n 5) Vol. 2, pp. 10–11; Al-Dardīr (n 32) Vol. 3, p. 22.
[39] Al-Ramlī (n 4) Vol. 3, p. 395.
[40] Al-Nawawī (n 4) Vol. 9, pp. 280–81; Al Dauūqī (n 6) Vol. 3, pp. 10, 11; Al-Shirbīnī (n 13) Vol. 2, p. 16; Al-Shīrāzī (n 5) Vol. 2, pp. 10–11.
[41] *Radd al-Muḥtār* (n 2) Vol. 7, pp. 33, 36.
[42] Al-Shirbīnī (n 13) Vol. 2, pp. 3, 6; Ibn al-Humām (n 8) Vol. 5, p. 206; *Radd al-Muḥtār* (n 2) Vol. 4, p. 132; Al-Buhūtī, Manṣūr ibn Yūnus ibn Ṣalāḥ al-Dīn, Kashshāf al-Qināʿ ʿan Matn al-Iqnāʿ (Dār al-Kutub al-ʿIlmiyya, n.d.) Vol. 3, pp. 391–92; *Al-Mughnī* (n 2) Vol. 5, pp. 35–36; Mālik bin Anas, Al Mudawanat al-Kubrā (Dār al Kutub al-ʿIlmiyya, 1994) Vol. 10, pp. 51, 121–22; Al Dasūqī (n 6) Vol. 23, pp. 170–71.
[43] Mālik bin Anas (n 42) Vol. 4, p. 470; *Majalla*, Art. 216.
[44] *Radd al-Muḥtār* (n 2) Vol. 7, pp. 272–74; Al-Shirbīnī (n 13) Vol. 2, p. 6. Right of way is the right of passing over real property held in absolute ownership and belonging to another. *Majalla*, Art. 142.

5.13 Some schools do not consider trademarks, goodwill, or the name of a business as *māl mutaqawam* and do not allow their sale. Even so, Shāmī opines that these rights can generally be transacted for consideration, or as compensation or substitution.[45] After completion of this process, such rights gain the same status as rights associated with a material thing. Thereafter, trademarks become rights over an *ʿayn* and their sale is allowed.[46] On the same basis, government-granted rights such as trade licences, patents, and copyright can be sold since they are considered property.[47]

5.14 Movable property such as merchandise and animals, as well as immovable property, can become the subject matter of a lease contract.[48] Personal services or skilled labour may become the subject matter of employment contracts for private and public sector employees, workmen, servants, craftsmen, and artisans.[49]

2.1.1 When a Permissible Subject Matter Becomes Impermissible

5.15 A subject matter permissible for a contract may become impermissible for several reasons. For instance, if the objective for which the subject matter is being sold is prohibited, its sale may also be prohibited. That would be the case when selling grapes, wheat, weapons, or leasing a house to someone who uses these things for purposes not allowed by the Sharīʿah. The Shafi'is declare such sale *makrūh*.[50] Similarly, if the nature of a property does not allow it to become the subject matter of a specific contract, a contract over that object/property will be void. An example of this category concerns goods that perish very quickly. Indeed, vegetables and fruit may not be pledged because they cannot be preserved until the maturity of mutual performance.[51] Furthermore, the sale of a pure commodity with which some kind of impurity, as described above, is associated and which cannot be purified is void (e.g. the sale of cooking oil). The majority of *fuqahā* consider that this oil cannot be purified and hence do not allow its sale. However, those who, like Hanafis, are of the opinion that the purification of such *maḥal al-aqd* is possible allow it to be sold, mortgaged, and disposed of for charity.[52] The same *ḥukm* (effect), namely, the voidance/annulment of the contract, is typically associated with the sale of impure water.[53]

5.16 The shares of a company can be sold and purchased, but if the company yields to any kind of usurious transaction then the sale of its shares is prohibited because the staff running the company are considered *wakīl* (agents acting on behalf of someone) of the shareholders and their conduct is attributed to the latter.[54] Thus, the sale and purchase

[45] Thānwī (n 2) Vol. 6, p. 529.
[46] Taqi Usmani, Islam aur Jadeed Mu'ashi Masa'il (Idāra e Islāmiyāt Publishers, 2008) Vol. 3, pp. 81–83.
[47] Ibid, Vol. 3, pp. 84, 85–88.
[48] *Majalla*, Arts 421, 534.
[49] *Majalla*, Arts 421–423, 562.
[50] *Al-Mughnī* (n 2) p. 318.
[51] Al-Nawawī (n 4) Vol. 10, p. 286; Al-Ramlī (n 4) Vol. 3, p. 393; *Al-Mughnī* (n 2) Vol. 4, p. 302.
[52] Al-Nawawī (n 4) Vol. 9, p. 284.
[53] Ibid, Vol. 9, p. 282.
[54] Thānwī (n 2) Vol. 6, p. 549.

of company shares is allowed subject to four conditions. First, the company should not be involved in any *ḥarām* (forbidden) business, for instance a winery. Secondly, if the company's assets are only liquid, then its shares may only be sold at face value, as otherwise the transaction will become usurious. If the company's assets comprise a mixture of liquid and fixed assets, then a share can be sold for more or less than its face value. Thirdly, if a company is conducting *ḥalāl* business but gets involved in usurious activities—for example, it borrows money on interest or places surplus amounts in a bank on *ribā* (interest)—the purchase of such shares, according to a group of scholars, is prohibited because the buyer will become part of those usurious activities. However, another group of scholars allows the purchase on the condition that the shareholder will raise his voice against such usurious activities in the company's annual general meeting. Finally, dividends paid from interest-based deposits should be classified as *ṣadaqa* (voluntary charity). Provided that these conditions are met, a person can purchase a company's shares for the sake of investment or capital gain.[55]

2.2 Impermissible Subject Matters

The sale of impure[56] and non-beneficial things is not allowed.[57] An analogy is pertinent for objects other than those discussed in previous sections.[58] The subject matter should be *mutaqawwam* (legal) under the Sharīʿah or deemed beneficial by custom, otherwise the contract is invalid. Muslim jurists count insects and reptiles such as snakes, scorpions, rats, ants, and other animals such as lions, wolves, buzzards, and ostriches as subject matters from which no benefits can be extracted. For instance, the use of animals as guards or for hunting (like a dog) produces a benefit. By contrast, the keeping of such animals to gain prestige in the local community is not a benefit.[59] Hence, these subject matters constitute *māl ghair mutaqawwam* (legally valueless property).[60] Furthermore, the sale of *waqf* property, that is, endowments to a religious, educational, or charitable cause, is not allowed.[61] **5.17**

The sale of a swine and its organs or parts of it, including its hair and skin, is not permissible.[62] The sale of a dead animal is equally not permissible. Yet, the parts of its body in which there is no life may validly be sold. These would be its skin (after tanning or dying),[63] muscles, wool, bones, hair, beaks, hooves, etc.,[64] since the Holy Prophet did **5.18**

[55] Usmani (n 46) Vol. 3, pp. 17–24.
[56] Al-Shīrāzī (n 5) Vol. 2, p. 9.
[57] Al-Qarāfī (n 10) Vol. 3, p. 370.
[58] Al-Shīrāzī (n 5) Vol. 2, pp. 10–11.
[59] Al-Nawawī (n 4) Vol. 9, p. 287.
[60] Ibid, Vol. 10, p. 286; Al-Ramlī (n 4) Vol. 3, p. 393; *Al-Mughnī* (n 2) Vol. 4, p. 302.
[61] Al-Nawawī (n 4) Vol. 9, p. 293; Al-Dardīr (n 32) Vol. 3, p. 22.
[62] Ibn Nujaim, *Al-Baḥr* (n 8) Vol. 6, p. 288; Taqi Usmani, Fiqh al Buyūʿ (Maktaba Maʿārif al-Qurʾān, 2015) Vol. 1, pp. 292 ff.
[63] Al-Nawawī (n 4) Vol. 1, p. 229 and Vol. 9, p. 274; Ibn Nujaim, *Al-Baḥr* (n 8) Vol. 1, pp. 185–86; *Radd al-Muḥtār* (n 2) Vol. 7, p. 267. For a different view, see Al-Dardīr (n 32) Vol. 3, p. 23.
[64] *Al-Mughnī* (n 2) Vol. 1, p. 66.

not object to their sale. The sale of blood is not permissible.[65] Nonetheless, on a general note, the Hanbalis allow the sale of *najas* if they are to be used as animal feed.[66]

5.19 The sale of wine and swine is prohibited for Muslims and non-Muslims according to Shafi'is, whereas for Hanafis, it is allowed for non-Muslims. The difference of opinion between the two rests in their differing views about whether non-Muslims are also addressees of the *aḥkām* of the Sharīʿah. The Shafi'is answer the question in the affirmative whereas Hanafis do not.[67] Hence the sale, *hiba*, *rehn*, *waqf*, or *waṣiyya* of a dead animal, blood, swine, and *waqf* property would be void because these subject matters are not *māl* and cannot be owned.[68] Other impermissible things that cannot be sold are pensions (they cannot even be sold to the government);[69] permits issued by the government for imports because they are not *māl*;[70] prize bonds because they are a combination of *ribā* and gambling;[71] commercial documents accompanying commodities/goods if the commodity/good is not simultaneously sold;[72] and opium, though it may be allowed as explained below.[73]

2.2.1 Permitting Impermissible Subject Matters

5.20 Subject matters which are impermissible may be allowed for a transaction on various accounts, including: where local custom allows; if necessity compels the use of that particular subject matter; if there is some permissible benefit in it; or if it is mixed with another permissible subject matter, and its essence is lost.

2.2.1.1 Benefit

5.21 If there is some benefit allowed by the Sharīʿah in a prohibited subject matter, the contract for that subject matter will be allowed for that purpose only.[74,75] Worms to be used as bait,[76] animal dung and manure for fertilizing land, reptiles and snakes in drug manufacturing,[77] donkeys for transport, dogs for hunting, monkeys as security guards, and birds captured for their beautiful voice and colours have been allowed for sale.[78] It should be noted that the subject matter allowed for sale by reason of the benefit derived therefrom should be used for that purpose only. Thus, a monkey sold with the purpose of being a security guard should only be used as such, not for playing or other

[65] Al-Nawawī (n 4) Vol. 9, pp. 277–78; *Al-Mughnī* (n 2) Vol. 4, p. 302.
[66] Al-Buhūtī (n 42) Vol. 3, p. 145.
[67] Al-Nawawī (n 4) Vol. 9, p. 271; Ibn Nujaim Al-Baḥr (n 8) Vol. 6, p. 288.
[68] *Al-Mughnī* (n 2) Vol. 4, p. 260; *Radd al-Muḥtār* (n 2) Vol. 4, pp. 501–05 and Vol. 7, pp. 241–42, 264; Al-Shīrāzī (n 5) Vol. 2, p. 90.
[69] Aḥmad (n 8) Vol. 6, pp. 521–22.
[70] Ibid, Vol. 6, p. 526.
[71] Ibid, Vol. 7, p. 26.
[72] ʿUsmānī (n 46) Vol. 3, p. 217.
[73] *Fatāwā* ibn Nujaim (n 3) p. 102.
[74] Al-Nawawī (n 4) Vol. 9, p. 276; Al-Shīrāzī (n 5) Vol. 2, pp. 10–11; Al-Buhūtī (n 42) Vol. 3, p. 152.
[75] *Al-Mughnī* (n 2) Vol. 4, p. 359. This treatise lists several things which are allowed due to their benefit.
[76] Al-Buhūtī (n 42) Vol. 3, p. 152.
[77] *Radd al-Muḥtār* (n 2) Vol. 7, pp. 236, 260; Al-Ramlī (n 4) Vol. 3, p. 395.
[78] Al-Shirbīnī (n 13) Vol. 2, p. 17; Al-Nawawī (n 4) Vol. 9, p. 272; Al-Ramlī (n 4) Vol. 3, pp. 397–98.

purposes.[79] The permissibility of animals as the subject matter of a sale depends on the benefits they can produce and on this ground all animals may be the subject matter of a contract, save for pork.[80] Opium and convolvulus plants, if they provide a benefit, are allowed to be sold.[81]

2.2.1.2 Necessity

As mentioned, the sale of blood is impermissible. However, contemporary scholars have allowed blood transfusion through sale and purchase as a means of medical treatment when no other treatment is available. Blood can also be sold in order to cover surgical needs within the framework of medical treatment. Interestingly, while it is permissible for the buyer to pay the purchase price, it is reprehensible for the seller to accept and receive it. Similarly, the Hanbalis allow the sale and purchase of human organs, such as the eyes and parts of skin when it is necessary to save the life of another human.[82] Moreover, breast milk is allowed by the Shafi'is and the Hanbalis (unlike Hanafis) on account of its necessity and benefit for humans.[83] In general, an object forbidden for sale is allowed on the basis of necessity. Sick persons can take urine, blood, and dead animals as medicine if a Muslim doctor has advised that there is cure in these and there is no *mubāḥ* (permitted) substitute as a viable alternative cure.[84] **5.22**

Wine, unfermented beverages of grapes, and all intoxicating drinks are forbidden.[85] Alcoholic and other non-intoxicating *ḥarām* products can be transacted for medical purposes if they are effective for a particular disease for which there is no other medicine.[86] **5.23**

2.2.1.3 Mixing of wine or other impurities with a pure subject matter

A *ḥarām* thing such as wine becomes permissible if it is not consumed by an individual but is instead used for external purposes such as the making of perfumes, dyes, ink, etc., because, according to Hanafis, the liquids produced would not become *najas* or *ḥarām* in this way.[87] The same *ḥukm* is attributed to edibles like ice-cream, biscuits, and chocolates after wine is mixed into them, even if the essence of wine is not changed. Hence, if wine is mixed with other substances and turns into vinegar, the sale of vinegar is allowed.[88] Yet, if the quantity of alcohol increases to a level that intoxicates its taker, the outcome of the mixture will be forbidden.[89] **5.24**

[79] Al-Buhūtī (n 42) Vol. 3, p. 153.
[80] *Radd al-Muḥtār* (n 2) Vol. 7, p. 260.
[81] Al-Shirbīnī (n 13) Vol. 2, p. 17; Al-Ramlī (n 4) Vol. 3, pp. 397–98.
[82] *Al-Mughnī* (n 2) Vol. 4, p. 260; *Radd al-Muḥtār* (n 2) Vol. 4, pp. 501–05 and Vol. 7, pp. 241–42, 264.
[83] Al-Nawawī (n 4) Vol. 9, pp. 304–05; *Radd al-Muḥtār* (n 2) Vol. 7, p. 264; Al-Qarāfī (n 10) Vol. 3, p. 371.
[84] *Radd al-Muḥtār* (n 2) Vol. 7, p. 480.
[85] Ibid, Vol. 6, p. 454.
[86] Ibid, Vol. 7, pp. 241–42, 480; Ibn al-Humām (n 8) Vol. 8, p. 160.
[87] Qurtubī, Aḥkām al-Qur'ān, Almā'ida, Verse 01 (Dār al-kutb al Miṣriyya, 1964) Vol. 6, p. 30. The majority opinion is that the inclusion of alcohol and all kinds of wine in perfumes renders them impure even if the quantity of the liquid is very large and even if its characteristics are changed. See Al-Nawawī (n 4) Vol. 1, p. 125.
[88] Shaybānī, Muḥammad ibn al-Ḥassan, Kitāb al-Ḥujat 'ala Ahl al-Madīna ('Ālam al-Kutub, n.d.) Vol. 3, pp. 8–14.
[89] *Radd al-Muḥtār* (n 2) Vol. 2, p. 349.

3. Existence of Subject Matter

5.25 Hanafis and the Shafi'is stipulate that all contracts, whether bilateral contracts of exchange (*muʿāwaḍāt*, e.g. sale, mortgage) or unilateral gratuitous contracts (e.g. gift), are *bāṭil* (void) if their underlying subject matter was not extant at the time of the conclusion of the contract. Exceptions are *salam*, *ijāra*, *masaqāt*, and *istṣsnāʿ* due to necessity and *ʿurf* (usage) among the people. By contrast, the Malikis opine that the existence of the subject matter is a necessary condition for contracts that result in exchange of goods or services for money and not for gratuitous contracts. In relation to the latter, Malikis provide that the expectation of a non-existent subject matter that is likely to materialize in the future would suffice.[90] On this point, the Hanbalis only declare a contract void if it involves *gharar* proscribed by the Sharīʿah and this includes the sale of a foetus (animal) in the womb of its mother without selling the mother, and the sale of milk in a mammal's udder. Without any differentiation between contracts of exchange and gratuitous contracts, a contract will be valid if there is certainty that the non-existent subject matter at the time of the contract's conclusion will come into existence in the future (e.g. the sale of a house based on its blueprint despite the fact that it has not yet been constructed). Neither the Qur'ān nor the Sunnah prohibit the sale of non-existent subject matters. It is the *gharar* which has been prohibited and it may occur in case of both existent and non-existent subject matters.[91]

5.26 The sale of a non-existent subject matter is definitely void.[92] The existence of the subject matter does not entail that the transacted object be present at the place where the contract is signed.[93] For instance, both the buyer and the seller should have knowledge of the house, which as an immovable object cannot be transported to the place where the contract is concluded.[94] The proscription of sale of non-existent subject matters is based on the tradition of the Holy Prophet wherein he prohibited the sale of the foetus in an animal's womb,[95] *a-maḍāmīn* (the foetus in the womb of a camel), and *al-malāqīh* (the breeding qualities of camels). Similarly, a commodity which is at risk of non-existence cannot become the subject matter of a contract. For example, in case of the sale of milk in the udder of an animal (which is prohibited), the udder may be consumed without any milk in it.[96]

[90] Ibn Rushd, Abū al-Walīd, Bidāyat al-Mujtahid wa Nihāyat al-Muqtaṣid (Dār al-Maʿrafa, 1981) Vol. 2, pp. 205, 247. See also Ibn al-Humām (n 27) Vol. 4, p. 417; Al-Shirbīnī (n 13) Vol. 2, p. 515; *Al-Mughnī* (n 2) Vol. 5, p. 598; *Majalla*, Arts 709, 856.

[91] Ibn Taimīya, Taqī al-Din Aḥmad ibn ʿAbd al-Ḥalīm, Nazriyat al-ʿAqd (Maktaba al-Sunna al-Muḥammadiyya) p. 224; *Al-Mughnī* (n 2) Vol. 4, pp. 200, 208; *Radd al-Muḥtār* (n 2) Vol. 7, p. 252.

[92] Shawkānī, Muḥammad ibn ʿAlī, Nīl al-Auṭār Sharḥ Muntaqa alAkhbār (Muṣṭafā al Bābi al-Ḥablī, 1928) Vol. 5, pp. 168–69; Al-Shīrāzī (n 5) Vol. 2, p. 12; *Majalla*, Arts 197, 205; Al-Nawawī (n 4) Vol. 9, p. 310.

[93] Mālik bin Anas, Al Mudawanat al-Kubrā (Dār al-Kutub al-ʿIlmiyya, 1994) Vol. 3, p. 260.

[94] Ibid, Vol. 3, p. 260.

[95] Bukhārī, *Kitāb al-Buyūʿ, Bab Bayʿ al-Gharar wa Ḥabl al-Ḥabla*, No. 2143.

[96] *Radd al-Muḥtār* (n 2) Vol. 4, p. 505 and Vol. 7, pp. 247, 516.

There is no difference of opinion on the prohibition of the sale of crops before and after fruition, or before their ripening, provided that they are still left on the tree. Similarly, there is consensus on the permissibility of selling unripe fruit on the condition that they will be cut or picked at the time of contract when some benefit can be extracted. Moreover, there is no disagreement as to the permission of sale after the commencement of ripening. It is important to note that the commencement of ripening, according to Hanafis, signifies the time when crops are safe from disease, while the Shafi'is denote the fruit's mellowness. Shafi'i, Aḥmad, and Mālik opine that selling fruit before the commencement of ripening is not allowed. Hanafis assert that when the fruit is in such a condition that benefit may be derived from it, such as to feed animals, it can be sold.[97] Where the clauses in the contract regarding the sale of the unripe fruit are silent on the precondition to collect the fruit when ripe, the Malikis and Shafi'is disallow such a sale, on the ground that it is prohibited to sell fruit before ripening has commenced, which they accept as generally applicable.[98] Hanafis allow such a sale when cutting the fruit, if its ripeness is generally implied in the contract to such a degree that it is as if it were expressly stated therein. For both schools the said prohibition obliges the seller to sell fruit as ripened before it has in fact ripened.[99] 5.27

The sale of a subject matter purchased by virtue of *salam* or *istaṣnā'* before it comes in the possession of the seller would constitute a sale of a non-existent subject matter, hence it is prohibited. For instance, the buyer of an apartment in a building whose design and floor plan were prepared but not constructed, cannot sell the flat.[100] A commodity that comes into being after a certain process takes place is considered non-existent before the employment of that process. Thereafter, its sale is forbidden—examples include flour, olive oil, juice, ghee, and meat produced only after a specific process is employed. On the other hand, the sale of the grain-bearing tip part of a cereal plant (ear) such as wheat is permissible because the seeds are existent at the time of the contract. However, the sale of hay (spikes of wheat) without the grains inside is not permissible because the hay cannot come into existence without being crushed. Therefore, prior to being crushed it is non-existent *māl*. 5.28

4. Certainty of Delivery of Subject Matter

The subject matter should be deliverable at the time of contract in order for the latter to be valid.[101] Such condition derives from the prohibition of sale involving *gharar*. What 5.29

[97] Muslim, *ḥadīth* 3913; Abi Dawūd, *ḥadīth* 3375; Bukhārī, *Ḥadīth* 3:101; *Radd al-Muḥtār* (n 2) Vol. 7, p. 85; Ibn Rushd, Al-Bayān wa al-Taḥṣīl (Dār al-Gharb al-Islāmī, 1988) Vol. 7, p. 243; Al-Kāsānī (n 2) Vol. 5, p. 138; Mālik bin Anas (n 93) Vol. 3, p. 188; *Al-Mughnī* (n 2) Vol. 4, pp. 148–49; Ibn al-Humām (n 8) Vol. 5, p. 489.

[98] Al-Nawawī, Ḥāshiyatān (Al-Qalyūbī and Amirah Rauḍat al-Ṭālibīn) (Sharika Maktaba wa Matba'a Muṣṭafā al-Bāb, 1956) Vol. 2, pp. 233–39; *Al-Mughnī* (n 2) Vol. 4, pp. 148–49.

[99] See also Shukānī (n 92) Vol. 5, pp. 193–201; Al-Sarakhsī (n 13) Vol. 12, p. 195.

[100] See the discussion in Chapter 11 on the contracts of *salam* and *istṣsnā'*.

[101] Al-Dardīr (n 32) Vol. 3, p. 22; Al Dusūqī (n 6) Vol. 3, pp.10,11; Al-Qarāfī (n 10) Vol. 3, p. 371; *Majalla*, Arts 198, 209.

cannot be delivered resembles a non-existent *māl* implicating *gharar*[102] and its sale is prohibited.[103] The seller's ability to deliver the subject matter is mandatory in contracts of exchange, according to all Muslim jurists. As far as gratuitous contracts are concerned, all *fuqahā*, except Mālik, disallow the contract. Examples could be *ijāra*, *rehn*, or a gift of a stray animal or a bird in the air or fish in the sea, due to the fac that these subject matters cannot be delivered.[104] Mālik allows gratuitous contracts on undeliverable subject matters on the basis that there is no apprehension of conflict between the parties if the subject matter is not delivered, since gratuitous contracts are acts of charity and, in case of non-delivery of the subject matter, the donee incurs no loss.[105]

4.1 Hurdles to the Delivery of the Subject Matter

5.30 The termination of the owner/seller's capacity to deliver the subject matter may be grounded in either *sharʿī* or *ḥissī*.[106] The seller should have *ḥissī* (physical) and *sharʿī* (juridical) capability to deliver the subject matter without exerting himself/herself to deliver/or making a huge effort to deliver.[107]

4.1.1 *Sharʿī* Capacity to Deliver

5.31 The owner is said to have *sharʿī* incapacity to deliver when the rights of another person are attached to the subject matter. This occurs in the sale of a mortgaged or trust property.[108] In this case the sale would not be valid. If a person owns something by intestate or testate succession and the property coming into his ownership is specified, he can dispose of it before possession is transferred to him. If X's property is in the possession of Y by virtue of *ʿāriya*, or *muḍāraba*, or because Y has been appointed as X's *wakīl*, X can sell that property to Y or anybody else because that property is deliverable and there is no fear of losing possession. It is as if he had actual possession of the subject matter. However, if his property is in the hands of some usurper, he can only sell it to that usurper and nobody else if he cannot ensure its delivery.[109]

5.32 Hence, a subject matter owned by others is in general undeliverable and cannot be sold, mortgaged,[110] leased,[111] or given to charity (*waqf*)[112] because the transfer of ownership, which is a constituent element for the validity of a sales contract, cannot be fulfilled.

[102] Al-Kāsānī (n 2) Vol. 5, p. 163; Al-Shīrāzī (n 5) Vol. 1, p. 262; Al-Qarāfī (n 10) Vol. 3, p. 265.
[103] Masnad Imām Aḥmad, Vol. 10, pp. 393, 475; Ibn e Māja, Vol. 2, p. 18 (No. 2195).
[104] Al-Kāsānī (n 2) Vol. 4, p. 187 and Vol. 5, p. 147; Ibn Rushd (n 90) Vol. 2, pp. 205, 247; Al-Shīrāzī (n 5) Vol. 1, p. 262; *Al-Mughnī* (n 2) Vol. 4, p. 200.
[105] Al-Dardīr (n 32) Vol. 4, p. 142.
[106] Al-Nawawī (n 4) Vol. 9, pp. 343–45.
[107] Al-Ramlī (n 4) Vol. 3, p. 399.
[108] Al-Nawawī (n 4) Vol. 9, pp. 343–45.
[109] *Al-Mughnī* (n 2) Vol. 4, pp. 191–92.
[110] *Majalla*, Art. 709.
[111] Al-Shīrāzī (n 5) Vol. 2, p. 92; *Majalla*, Art. 457.
[112] *Majalla*, Art. 775.

4.1.2 *Ḥissī* Capacity to Deliver

There may be some *ḥissī* (factual, material, or tangible) obstacle to the delivery of the subject matter by the owner—for example the sale of a lost thing:[113] a bird which flew from its cage, fish in water, a stray animal, usurped property,[114] the foetus in an animal's womb,[115] or a sunken boat that cannot be brought to the surface.[116] **5.33**

Obstacles to the physical possession of the subject matter raise the issue of *gharar* because the seller does not know whether he will be able to execute the delivery of a lost item or an item that he does not possess despite owning it. For *gharar* to be established, the emergence of the difficulty that renders the subject matter undeliverable suffices.[117] When the acquisition of the *māl* that is lost or usurped, and thereafter its delivery, is possible without causing great inconvenience to the seller or effort on his part, the subject matter is considered deliverable.[118] In the example of a fish that has fallen into a small pond and can be caught without tremendous effort, there is no *gharar* and the sale is allowed.[119] The opposite holds true when the fish has fallen into a very big pond and its recovery involves huge effort.[120] **5.34**

If the subject matter is not deliverable, even though the seller owns it, the contract will be void. As Hanafis argue, when the subject matter is undeliverable at the time the contract is concluded but becomes deliverable after its conclusion (e.g. the stray animal returns), there will be a new offer and acceptance; hence a new contract in relation to this subject matter will be concluded. Karkhī says that a new contract would be needed only if the initial contract were cancelled by a judge upon the buyer's application for the recovery of the subject matter and the judge could not enforce it. He contends, for example, that in the case of a stray animal, the seller is not deprived of ownership. Therefore, the sale is suspended at the stage of delivery but when the obstacles cease to exist, the contract will become valid once again. **5.35**

However, a contract concerning usurped property is suspended because the owner in this case has the possibility to deliver the property by appealing to the sultan, a judge, and the Muslim community. When ownership is recovered, the same contract will be enforced. **5.36**

113 Mālik bin Anas (n 93) Vol. 3, p. 254.
114 Al-Nawawī (n 4) Vol. 9, pp. 343–45; Al-Buhūtī (n 42) Vol. 3, p. 162.
115 Bukhāriī, *Ḥadīth* 2143; Al-Nawawī (n 98) Vol. 2, p. 176.
116 *Majalla*, Art. 209.
117 Al-Shirbīnī (n 13) Vol. 2, p. 18; Al-Nawawī (n 4) Vol. 9, pp. 343–45.
118 Al-Shirbīnī (n 13) Vol. 2, p. 19; Al-Buhūtī (n 42) Vol. 3, p. 162; Al-Shīrāzī (n 5) Vol. 2, p. 14.
119 Al-Kāsānī (n 2) Vol. 4, pp. 341–42; Al-Buhūtī (n 42) Vol. 3, p. 162.
120 Al-Nawawī (n 4) Vol. 9, pp. 343–45.

5. The Subject Matter Should Be Owned by the Seller

5.37 For the valid conclusion of a contract, the seller should either be the owner of the subject matter or have authority to sell it (*wakil* or *walī*) at the time of conclusion.[121] The condition of prior ownership is applicable to *hiba*,[122] lease,[123] gift,[124] *waqf*, and *ṣadaqa*.[125] The sale of objects or services not owned by the seller is considered *bāṭil* (void)[126] because the transfer of ownership does not take place where the subject matter is not owned by the seller.[127] The basis for the justification of of the described preconditions rests in tradition, specifically the exhortation 'sell not what is not with you'[128] and 'no man is bound by a transaction involving the sale of something that he does not own/possess'.[129]

5.1 Sale of Permissible Things

5.38 The sale of a public common good is not allowed because it is not owned by anyone. The Holy Prophet said that 'Muslims are partners in three things: water, pasture and fire, and their price is unlawful'.[130] However, partnership does not imply ownership; rather it means that benefiting from these three things is permissible (*mubāḥ*) for Muslims and non-Muslims equally. Examples are rivers, streams, wells, etc.[131]

5.1.1 Pasture

5.39 As mentioned, pasture is not susceptible to ownership[132] and its use is permissible to everyone. Therefore, its sale is not allowed even if the pasture lies within private land and the owner has not planted/grown the pasture.[133] However, when the owner of the land cuts the grass and takes it into his possession or plants it himself on his land or leaves his land uncultivated to allow grass to grow, the grass comes under his possession. He then becomes the owner and can sell the grass, which can further be inherited by his legatee or those to whom he has bequeathed it.[134] The same does not apply to the trees on private land. It does not matter if the landlord has planted the trees, because

[121] Al-Nawawī (n 98) Vol. 2, p. 176; Al-Buhūtī (n 42) Vol. 3, p. 157; Al-Kāsānī (n 2) Vol. 5, p. 146; Al-Dardīr (n 32) Vol. 3, p. 26; Al-Shīrāzī (n 5) Vol. 2, p. 13; Al-Qarāfī (n 10) Vol. 3, p. 371; *Majalla*, Arts 214, 446; Al-Nawawī (n 4) Vol. 9, p. 311.

[122] Ibn al-Humām (n 27) Vol. 4, p. 417.

[123] Ibid, Vol. 4, pp. 461–62.

[124] *Majalla*, Art. 857.

[125] Al-Shīrāzī (n 5) Vol. 2, p. 324.

[126] *Radd al-Muḥtār* (n 2) Vol. 4, p. 528.

[127] Al-Kāsānī (n 2) Vol. 5, p. 146.

[128] Al Tirmadhī, *Ḥadīth* 1232.

[129] Al-Nisā'ī, *Ḥadīth* 4612.

[130] Abū Abū Dāwūd, *Ḥadīth* 3477.

[131] Al-Sarakhsī (n 13) Vol. 23, pp. 164–65, 169.

[132] Al-Nawawī (n 98) Vol. 3, pp. 96–97; Abū Yūsaf, Kitāb al-Kharāj (Dār al-Maʿrafa, 1979) p. 102.

[133] Al-Sarakhsī (n 13) Vol. 23, p. 165; *Radd al-Muḥtār* (n 2) Vol. 10, p. 15; *Al-Mughnī* (n 2) Vol. 4, pp. 200–01; Mālik bin Anas (n 93) Vol. 4, pp. 469, 473; Al-Buhūtī (n 42) Vol. 3, p. 160; Ibn Rushd (n 97) Vol. 10, pp. 246–47.

[134] Mālik bin Anas (n 93) Vol. 4, pp. 469, 473; Ibn Rushd (n 97) Vol. 10, pp. 246–47; Al-Sarakhsī (n 13) Vol. 23, p. 165; *Radd al-Muḥtār* (n 2) Vol. 10, p. 15; Al-Nawawī (n 98) Vol. 3, p. 97. The author has drawn an analogy with its sale on water whose sale is permissible by the possessor.

the person who owns the land acquires ownership of the trees therein by default.[135] Yet again, if someone cuts the trees (e.g. the government) and sells them, this is permissible because this very act confers ownership of the trees (in this case, on the government).[136]

5.1.2 Water

Water may be found in different sources. First, there is river water and water in canals. Water in these cases is not owned by anyone and its use is permissible to everyone. It may be used to satisfy one's thirst or irrigate one's crops. Its sale is not allowed. Secondly, water may exist as a result of procurement. Naturally this is held in pipes (ducts) possessed by a public utility. In this case, the procurer owns it and can sell it.[137] Thirdly, water is concentrated in wells, ponds, streams, and channels, over which someone may exercise ownership rights. The legal nature of water in this case is contested. Different opinions have been expressed among scholars. Some Shafi'i supporters contend that ownership of the water in this case is determined in the same way as water procurement (*mamlūk*). Hanafis and the majority of the Shafi'is stipulate that such water constitutes a right and should not be considered property.[138] As Imām Yūsaf said, the owner of a well, pond, spring, or waterway (natural channel) cannot refuse humans or animals permission to drink its water, especially where it exists in excess quantity and the owner's needs are covered. Yet, the owner has the right to refuse to supply others with water for the purposes of irrigating their crops and trees. Nonetheless, he cannot sell the water because its quantity is not known (note: if it is known then sale thereof should be allowed). Yūsaf has also disapproved the sale of water accumulated in a factory or mill from a stream despite its quantity being known. However, a person can sell water stored in his or her utensils.[139] 5.40

5.1.3 Other Subject Matters

Similarly, the sale of wood, animals in the jungle, and free birds that have yet to be captured is not allowed.[140] In practice, governments confine the right to hunt animals to persons with a licence. However, the issuance of a hunting licence in return for a fee is prohibited because Allah has made the hunting of these animals permissible for everyone. Any restriction on the public is not allowed nor is it permissible for the government to seek money in order to issue the hunting licence.[141] A government takes into its possession the goods which have been smuggled illegally and sells them to the public, but the sale and purchase of these commodities is illegal since the government does not own the game.[142] 5.41

[135] Al-Sarakhsī (n 13) Vol. 23, p. 165.
[136] Thānwī (n 2) Vol. 6, pp. 561–62.
[137] Al-Sarakhsī (n 13) Vol. 23, pp. 164–65, 169.
[138] Shawkānī (n 92) Vol. 5, pp. 342–46.
[139] Abū Yūsaf (n 132) pp. 95–98; Taqi Usmani, Fiqh al-Buyū‘ (Maktaba Ma‘ārif al-Qur'ān, 2015) Vol. 1, pp. 336–38.
[140] *Radd al-Muḥtār* (n 2) Vol. 14, p. 22.
[141] Taqi Usmani, Fiqh al-Buyū‘ (Maktaba Ma‘ārif al Qu'ān, 2015) Vol. 1, p. 336.
[142] Aḥmad (n 8) Vol. 6, p. 527.

5.2 Perfect and Imperfect Title

5.42 The sale is valid only if the seller has perfect title of the property or has valid authorization to sell it. If an unauthorized person sells the subject matter in the presence of the actual owner and the owner remains silent, the silence of the owner would amount to his approval of the sale.[143]

5.2.1 Absence of Title

5.43 The sale of what is not owned by the seller at the time of contract but which he possesses as *wadīʿa* is not allowed, even if he later becomes the owner of the subject matter.[144] Property owned by others and which cannot be delivered, cannot be sold or mortgaged. The mortgage of a property by a person who wrongly believes that his predecessor has died and, thus, that he has inherited it, is invalid even if his predecessor dies afterwards and he eventually inherits the property; this is so because at the time of the mortgage he did not have authority to do so.[145] The mortgagee cannot sell, lease, or receive any other benefit from the mortgaged property. For instance, if an orchard was mortgaged, the mortgagee cannot sell the fruit to earn money as payment of the debt from the mortgagor. Even if there was a risk of damage to the mortgaged property, the mortgagee cannot undertake such actions because his possession of the property does not amount to ownership.[146]

5.2.2 Sale by a *Wakīl*

5.44 A sale by a *wakīl* is valid, whereas if undertaken by someone who is not the owner nor has authority to sell, the sale would constitute *mawqūf*.[147] The contract should be concluded by the person who has authority to do so. The person who lacks such authority is referred to as *faḍūlī*.[148] For instance, the borrower of the property may pledge it with the prior consent of the owner.[149]

5.2.3 Encumbrance on the Title of the Owner

5.45 If there is some kind of encumbrance or third-party rights are attached to property owned by the seller, the sale would be invalid, or would otherwise constitute *mawqūf*. The sale of leased property for which the lessor has received the money would be suspended if the property were sold before the expiration of the lease agreement.[150]

[143] Al-Buhūtī (n 42) Vol. 3, p. 157; Abū Ḥanifa, Hanbalis, and others claim that this is invalid. See Al-Kāsānī (n 2) Vol. 5, p. 146.
[144] Mālik bin Anas (n 93) Vol. 3, p. 270.
[145] Al-Shīrāzī (n 5) Vol. 2, p. 92; Al-Shirbīnī (n 13) Vol. 2, p. 22.
[146] Thānwī (n 2) Vol. 6, p. 528. See also Ḥaṣkafī, Durr Mukhtār (n 8) Vol. 10, pp. 83, 118; Ḥaṣkaf ī, Al Dar al Muntaqi (n 8) Vol. 4, pp. 273, 291.
[147] *Radd al-Muḥtār* (n 2) Vol. 7, p. 247; *Majalla*, Art. 447.
[148] Al-Nawawī (n 98) Vol. 2, p. 160. For discussion on contracts by a *faḍūlī*, see Chapter 11. Al-Ramlī (n 4) Vol. 3, p. 403.
[149] *Majalla*, Arts 726–727.
[150] Al-Shīrāzī (n 5) Vol. 2, p. 92; *Fatāwā* ibn Nujaim (n 3) p. 105; Ibn al-Humām (n 27) Vol. 3, pp. 117–18; Thānwī (n 2) Vol. 6, pp. 335–36.

Similarly, the sale of mortgaged property will be suspended until the mortgagee releases the mortgagor from his liability to pay the debt. If, however, it is acquiesced that the sale price or loan is paid back to the mortgagee, the sale will become complete and there would be no need for a new contract.[151] The trust property cannot be sold because ownership therein can be neither transferred nor acquired.[152] Furthermore, the property cannot be subject to another trust.[153]

5.2.4 Jointly Owned Property

An owner jointly owning an undivided parcel of land with another owner can sell his portion without the consent of the joint owner.[154] The joint owners may lease their property to a third party jointly.[155] Yet, each of the joint owners individually can lease out their share of the property only to the other co-owner and not to any other person.[156] 5.46

5.3 Establishment of Ownership

Governmental revenue records have greater probative value in proving ownership than the factual possession of the property at a given time.[157] Long-term possession (e.g. twelve years) does not confer ownership on the possessor; rather ownership is granted to the actual owner.[158] 5.47

6. Subject Matter Should Be in the Custody/Possession of the Seller

The subject matter should be in the possession or custody of the seller. The subject matter of a contract can be held either as *amāna* (trust)[159] or *maḍmūn* (guarantee).[160] Property kept as *amāna* can be sold before acquiring possession of it. Examples of this category are: property in possession of a *wakil*; a *musta'jir* after the time for *ijāra* is completed; or of a *walī* (guardian) after the minor, *safīh*, or *majnūn* acquire capacity to contract; and property inherited by a legatee in intestate or testate succession (bequeathed 5.48

[151] Al-Shīrāzī (n 5) Vol. 2, p. 92; Al-Nawawī (n 98) Vol. 2, p. 159; *Fatāwā* ibn Nujaim (n 3) pp. 107, 176; *Majalla*, Arts 745–747; Ibn al-Humām (n 27) Vol. 3, pp. 117–18.

[152] *Radd al-Muḥtār* (n 2) Vol. 7, p. 244.

[153] Al Tirmadhī, *Ḥadīth* 1232.

[154] *Majalla*, Art. 214; Al-Nawawī (n 4) Vol. 9, p. 309. Some require the prior consent of the partners. See *Fatāwā* ibn Nujaim (n 3) p. 106.

[155] *Majalla*, Art. 431.

[156] *Radd al-Muḥtār* (n 2) Vol. 6, pp. 47, 48; *Majalla*, Art. 429.

[157] Aḥmad (n 8) Vol. 7, pp. 216–17.

[158] Thānwī (n 2) Vol. 7, p. 324; Ḥaṣkafī, *Durr Mukhtār* (n 8) Vol. 9, p. 291; Al-Marghīnānī, Burhān al-Dīn, Al-Hidāya Sharḥ Bidāyat al-Mubtadī (Dār Iḥyā' al-Turāth al-'Arabi, n.d.) Vol. 3, p. 373.

[159] Trust or contract giving rise to fiduciary relationship and duties.

[160] This corresponds to the subject matter of the liability of the surety.

through a will), although in both cases the property may not have come into the legatee's possession.[161] *Al Maḍmūnāt* are of two types. First, *ḍamān al-yad* (liability arising from possession on trust), in which case the trustee is liable for compensation by value or price. By way of example, such compensation is given when a contract is revoked on account of *khiyār al-ʿayb*, or in the case of a *fāsid* (voidable) contract, as a result of which the commodity and the sale price are returned to the seller and buyer respectively. The seller can sell this subject matter anew before he recovers possession of the property. The second type *of al-maḍmūnāt is muaḍmūn bil ʿiwaḍ* (compensation or consideration) is *ʿaqd muʿāwaḍa* (contracts in which parties make an exchange). In this case, the sale of the subject matter of the contract is not permissible before its possession is recovered (e.g. the *mabīʿ* in a sale contract).[162]

5.49 The sale of movable and immovable property by the seller or by his agent is not allowed before the seller takes the property into his possession even if it is owned by him.[163] In every other case the sale would be *fāsid* (voidable).[164] The discussion on the need for possession of a subject matter is based on the *ḥadīth* of the Holy Prophet, specifically his admonition whereby 'he who buys foodstuff should not sell it till he is satisfied with the measure with which he has bought it'.[165] There is consensus that the sale of foodstuff before possession is not allowed. Whether in large amounts or otherwise, the sale of foodstuff prior to possession is not allowed according to Jamhur. Mālik allows the sale of foodstuff able to be sold by estimates in heaps, by reasoning that the *takhliya* is sufficient in heaps and keeping in possession (*al-istabqā*) is required in commodities which are sold in terms of measurement or weight.[166] There is a difference of opinion among the various *fuqahā* on the sale of non-food items.

5.50 Shafi'i and Muḥammad bin Hassan opine that the sale of everything—foodstuffs and non-foodstuffs, and both movable and immovable property—before acquiring possession is impermissible.[167] To generalize the prohibition, they have also relied on the *ḥadīth* narrated by Ibn e Umar who stated:

> I bought some oil in the market and while I had taken it (from the seller), a man approached me and offered to give me a good profit for it. As I was about to finalize the deal with him, a man caught hold of my forearm from behind. So, I turned around and found that he was Zaid bin Thabit (RA). He said, 'do not sell it [the oil] in the place where you bought it, till you take it to your dwelling. This is because Allah's Messenger

[161] Al-Nawawī (n 4) Vol. 9, pp. 320–21; Ibn al-Humām (n 27) Vol. 3, p. 15; Al-Shīrāzī (n 5) Vol. 2, p. 13; Al-Shirbīnī (n 13) Vol. 2, p. 92.
[162] Al-Nawawī (n 4) Vol. 9, pp. 320–21.
[163] Al-Nawawī (n 98) Vol. 2, p. 212; Al-Shirbīnī (n 13) Vol. 2, p. 90; *Majalla*, Art. 253.
[164] Usmani (n 46) Vol. 3, pp. 24–26.
[165] Bukhārīī, *Ḥadīth* 2136.
[166] Shawkānī (n 92) Vol. 5, p. 179.
[167] For the *ḥadīth* relied on for these opinions, see Al-Nawawī (n 4) Vol. 9, p. 326; Ibn al-Humām (n 8) Vol. 6, pp. 137–38; *Al-Mughnī* (n 2) Vol. 4, pp. 188–91.

has forbidden the sale of commodities in the place where they were bought, till the traders take them to their dwellings'.[168]

Similarly, the permission to sell a subject matter not in the possession of the seller would imply the earning of profit from a commodity which, in case of its destruction, he is not yet liable for because this remains the liability of the person who possesses it. The Holy Prophet forbade profit from a thing in which there is no liability for loss.[169] However, in this regard, Abū Ḥanīfa and Abū Yūsaf allow the sale of immovable property before the acquisition of possession because there is no fear of destruction. In this case, no question of liability arises, hence there is no need for the stipulation of prior possession as a condition of sale. By contrast, a plot situated on the coast or at altitude and on sliding land should be in the seller's possession before the sale due to the risk of destruction. As to this argument, two scholars disapprove of the sale of movable property before coming into the seller's possession.[170] **5.51**

Aḥmad bin Ḥanbal and Mālik argue that the prohibition of sale prior to possession is confined to foodstuffs only. They contend that the Holy Prophet explicitly referred to foodstuffs and if other things were also meant to be included in this prohibition, the specification of foodstuffs would become redundant.[171] The same argument is similarly deduced from the *ḥadīth* narrated by Ibn e Umar, according to which: **5.52**

> I would sell camels at *Al-Bāqī*; so, I would sell them for *dīnār* and take *dirham* in exchange; and I would sell for silver and take *dīnār* in return. So, I went to the Messenger of Allah and asked him about that and he said: 'there is no harm in that when the consideration equals the asking price'.[172]

The argument deduced from this *ḥadīth* is that an item's price is one of two possible considerations. Moreover, permissibility of sale before possession allows for the disposal of all subject matters before possession, save for foodstuffs. However, Hanafis and Shafi'is say this *ḥadīth* pertains to the contract of *ṣarf*[173] and is not relevant to the discussion concerning the sale of commodities. **5.53**

The rules governing the requirement of prior possession of movable and immovable property for subsequent sale also apply to the subsequent *hiba*, *ṣadaqa*,[174] **5.54**

[168] Abū Dāwūd, *Ḥadīth* 3499; Hākim, *Ḥadīth* 2:40. The other *ḥadīth* relied upon are: 'do not sell a thing until you take the possession of it', and in another narration 'when you have purchased something do not sell it until you have taken possession of it' (Al-Baihaqī, Vol. 5, p. 313; Aḥmad, Vol. 3, p. 402); 'It is not lawful to lend and sell, nor impose two conditions in a sale, nor to profit from what is not possessed, nor to sell what one does not have.' The Holy Prophet prohibited 'from selling what was not with me' (Al-Tirmadhiī 1234, 1235; Abū Dāwūd 3504; Al Nisā' ī 4611, 4612).

[169] Ibn Rushd (n 97) Vol. 7, p. 117.

[170] For the *ḥadīth* relied on for these opinions, see Al-Nawawī (n 4) Vol. 9, p. 326; Ibn al-Humām (n 8) Vol. 6, pp. 137–38; *Al-Mughnī* (n 2) Vol. 4, pp. 188–91; Al-Sarakhsī (n 13) Vol. 13, p. 8.

[171] For the *ḥadīth* relied on for these opinions, see Al-Nawawī (n 4) Vol. 9, p. 326; Ibn al-Humām (n 8) Vol. 6, pp. 137–38; *Al-Mughnī* (n 2) Vol. 4, pp. 188–91; Al-Sarakhsī (n 13) Vol. 13, p. 8.

[172] Al Tirmidhi, *Ḥadīth* 1242; Abū Dāwūd, *Ḥadīth* 3345; Al Nis ā'ī, *Ḥadīth* 4589; Ibn e Mājā, *Ḥadīth* 2462.

[173] *Al-Mughnī* (n 2) Vol. 4, pp. 189–90.

[174] *Radd al-Muḥtār* (n 2) Vol. 7, p. 98; Al-Shirbīnī (n 13) Vol. 2, p. 91; Ibn al-Humām (n 27) Vol. 3, pp. 14, 417. The objective of *hiba* is the transfer of ownership. Al-Shīrāzī (n 5) Vol. 2, p. 334. However, the *Majalla* states that no prior possession is required for a valid gift. See Arts 845, 846, and 861.

waqf,[175] *wadīʿa*,[176] and *Ijāra*.[177] The owner of a leased house can sell it to a person other than the tenant with the permission of the tenant. However, the possession of the buyer will be established according to the terms of the lease agreement.[178] The sale of a mortgaged property after possession is delivered to the mortgagee is not permissible. However, before the delivery of possession to the mortgagee or after delivery of possession to him but with his permission, the sale is permissible because the legal obstacle is removed.[179] Similarly, if a person has exercised his right of lien over a property that is in his possession, the owner cannot sell it.[180]

6.1 Transfer of Possession

5.55 Possession is the control exercised intentionally towards a thing by a person with the capacity to use it physically or otherwise dispose of it without any hurdles. Customarily, possession may be exercised upon the following categories of subject matter: (i) immovable properties and trees; (ii) tangible things which are normally transported (e.g. timber, grains, etc.); and (iii) tangible items such as *darāhim*, *dananīr*, clothes, small utensils, books, etc. How the transfer of possession takes place differs depending on the kind of subject matter involved in a transaction.

6.2 *Al-Takhliya*

5.56 The four schools of thought agree that possession is obtained by *al-takhliya*. *Takhliya* can be translated as removal of a hindrance, releasing or enabling the unrestrained disposal of the subject matter. In a contract of sale, it means that the buyer can obtain the object of the sale without any hindrance in relation to the object's disposal. For instance, when the seller abandons the subject matter of the sale to the buyer, such giving up of the property by the seller enables the buyer to use or dispose of the property without any obstruction by the seller or anyone else. In this way, the seller hands over possession of the property to the buyer.[181] Thus, the concept of *takhliya* implies possession consisting of the exercise of physical power over the subject matter without obstruction. Nonetheless, the nature of *takhliya* differs depending on the nature of the subject matter involved. Finally, it is important to note that capacity to obtain possession of such subject matter presupposes that there are no third-party rights associated with the

[175] Ibn al-Humām (n 27) Vol. 3, p. 14, who posits that the *waqf* is suspended until possession. Al-Nawawī (n 4) Vol. 9, p. 319 argues that the *waqf* requires acceptance and hence resembles a sale.

[176] Ibn al-Humām (n 27) Vol. 4, p. 372. The subject matter should be able to come into the possession of the buyer.

[177] Ibid, Vol. 3, p. 14.

[178] *Radd al-Muḥtār* (n 2) Vol. 14, p. 235.

[179] Al-Shirbīnī (n 13) Vol. 2, p. 20.

[180] Ibid, Vol. 2, p. 20.

[181] Al-Nawawī (n 4) Vol. 9, p. 333; *Al-Mughnī* (n 2) Vol. 4, pp. 181–84; Al-Dusūqī (n 6) Vol. 3, p. 145; Ibn al-Humām (n 27) Vol. 3, p. 18.

subject matter. For instance, if wheat (as the subject matter of sale) is in the bag of the seller or in the seller's house where he keeps his chattels, or on his land where the seller cultivates other crops, *takhliya* cannot be established because the concept necessitates the absence of any other rights of a person other than the buyer.[182]

6.3 Possession of Immovable Property

Immovable property can be a house or a piece of land and anything attached to it from a construction to trees.[183] Possession of immovable property is also established by *takhliya*. However, the nature of *takhliya*—delivery of the property—differs in the case of movable items, as will be explained in the next paragraph.[184] *Takhliya* of immovable property is possible with the delivery of the keys to the buyer by the seller, provided also that the house can be entered without any difficulty.[185] Moreover, if it is inferred by the circumstances that the delivery of the keys purports to be delivery of possession, it is not necessary that the intention to deliver the house is explicitly stated. *Takhliya* is established even if the buyer does not enter the house and even if the house is far from the buyer's residence.[186] Furthermore, for non-residential immovable properties *takhliya* is established with the delivery of the keys even if the seller has not vacated the property and removed his belongings. On the other hand, possession of a residential property is acquired when vacated by the seller; *takhliya* is not sufficient here.[187] Matters relating to the vacating of the property by the seller, including the time frame, are regulated by custom. Certainly, vacating may be completed gradually, especially when the seller's chattels are numerous. If the buyer allows the seller to keep possession of the house or retain his belongings there, then delivery will be affected because the seller's chattels would constitute *wadīʿa* (property for safekeeping) for the buyer.[188] If the seller does not have the keys, then the right of *taṣarruf* (disposition or activity on the property) is sufficient to establish *takhliya*. However, if the owner has conferred the right of *taṣarruf* without giving the keys to the buyer, even if the buyer possesses the keys, this does not amount to *takhliya*.[189] Trees and their fruit before being cut from the tree are included in the immovable property.[190] In the sale of land with fruit-bearing trees and/or crops, the fruit and crops respectively should be cut for the property's delivery of possession to be effectuated.[191] 5.57

[182] *Radd al-Muḥtār* (n 2) Vol. 7, pp. 94–96; Ibn al-Humām (n 27) Vol. 3, 18.

[183] Al-Nawawī (n 4) Vol. 9, pp. 333–36; Al-Dusūqī (n 6) Vol. 3, pp. 144–45; Al-Nawawī (n 98) Vol. 2, pp. 215–16; Al-Shīrāzī (n 5) Vol. 2, p. 14. A small ship is considered movable property whereas a large one is considered immovable. Al-Shirbīnī (n 13) Vol. 2, p. 96.

[184] *Radd al-Muḥtār* (n 2) Vol. 7, pp. 94–96; Ibn al-Humām (n 27) Vol. 3, p.18; *Majalla*, Art. 265.

[185] Ibn al-Humām (n 27) Vol. 3, p. 18; *Radd al-Muḥtār* (n 2) Vol. 7, pp. 94–96.

[186] Al-Nawawī (n 4) Vol. 9, pp. 333–36.

[187] Al-Dasūqī (n 6) Vol. 3, pp. 144–45; Al-Nawawī (n 98) Vol. 2, pp. 215–16; Al-Nawawī (n 4) Vol. 9, p. 274; *Majalla*, Art. 271.

[188] Ibn al-Humām (n 27) Vol. 3, p. 19.

[189] Al-Dusūqī (n 6) Vol. 3, pp. 144–45.

[190] Al-Shirbīnī (n 13) Vol. 2, pp. 94–95.

[191] *Majalla*, Arts 267–268.

5.58 If the purchaser/buyer is within the real estate, such as a house or an orchard, which can be locked, and is informed by the seller that the latter has delivered the property to him, delivery thereof has been effectuated. If the purchaser is outside the property but so near that he could immediately lock it, delivery is effectuated by the seller by merely stating that he has made the delivery. If he is not in close proximity to the property, however, delivery is effectuated after the expiration of such time as is necessary for him to arrive and enter therein.[192]

5.59 If two partners have divided their immovable assets, each partner can sell his share before obtaining possession of it.[193] The transfer of ownership of land from the seller to the buyer, which is proven by the government's revenue record, is considered transfer of possession because in this case the property is properly demarcated and, in the event that the seller does not abandon it, physical possession can be obtained through the intervention of the state.[194]

6.4 Possession of Movable Property

5.60 Movable property may consist of tangible things which are normally transported (e.g. timber, grains, etc.) or commodities.[195] These should be estimated by size or weight and sold on the basis of their weight or size. There is a difference of opinion as to when possession of these subject matters is established. Shafi'is and Hanbalis contend that possession is transferred when the subject matter is weighed (if it is measurable by weight), or when its size is measured.[196] Whether the commodity is still in the shop or the house of the seller is of no legal significance.[197] As far as countable things are concerned, the Shafi'is, Malikis, and Hanbalis stipulate that the completion of their counting signifies the completion of the transfer of possession.[198] If the commodity is sold in bulk estimates, possession thereof is obtained by its transfer from the seller's place to the buyer's.[199] Hanafis suggest that possession is transferred by *takhliya*. However, it is not permissible for the buyer to sell the subject matter of sale before its weight or size is measured. The justification for this lies in the *ḥadīth* of Ibn e ʿAbbass to which the Holy Prophet said: 'he who purchases foodstuff, should not sell it until it is weighed'.[200] For Hanafis, *takhliya* is sufficient[201] and the same would be the case when the commodity is sold in heaps (in estimates).[202]

192 *Majalla*, Art. 270.
193 Al-Nawawī (n 4) Vol. 9, p. 324.
194 Zaraqā, Muṣṭafā Aḥmad , Al-Madkhal al-Fiqh al-ʿĀm (Dār al-Qalam, 2004) Vol. 2, p. 706.
195 Al-Nawawī (n 4) Vol. 9, pp. 333–36.
196 *Al-Mughnī* (n 2) Vol. 4, pp. 186–87; Al-Dusūqī (n 6) Vol. 3, pp. 144–45; Al-Nawawī (n 98) Vol. 2, p. 217.
197 Ibn al-Humām (n 27) Vol. 3, p. 20.
198 Al-Nawawī (n 4) Vol. 9, p. 278; Al-Dusūqī (n 6) Vol. 3, p. 144.
199 *Al-Mughnī* (n 2) Vol. 4, pp. 181–84, 186–87.
200 Muslim, *Ḥadīth* 3814.
201 Al-Kāsānī (n 2) Vol. 4, p. 499.
202 *Al-Mughnī* (n 2) Vol. 4, pp. 186–87.

These principles are applied to various other situations. If the seller sells wheat stored in a house and gives the keys of that house to the buyer saying 'I am no more between you and the wheat', this act results in possession.[203] *Takhliya* can be established even by leaving the commodity in the house of the seller from where the buyer can take it whenever he wants.[204] In the case of cloth, its placement on a surface from which the buyer may easily recover it (e.g. by extending his arm) would amount to transfer of possession.[205] **5.61**

With regard to the sale of a sheep from a flock, pointing to a specific sheep would signify delivery of possession.[206] The prevailing custom (*urf*) plays a decisive role in determining when possession is transferred. For example, in the sale of a car or animals, delivery of the car keys or the bridle respectively denote transfer of possession.[207] **5.62**

The possession of movable items is established when transferred from the seller's place,[208] as for example where the buyer drives the vehicle or sits on the rug. *Takhliya* is sufficient with respect to the fruits on a tree before they are cut,[209] namely, if the fruit is sold while on the tree and the vendor gives permission to the purchaser to pick such fruit. In such cases delivery thereof has been effectuated.[210] **5.63**

The delivery of a commercial document by the owner to the buyer as proof of the sale of ascertained goods in a warehouse amounts to *takhliya*. If the goods are not ascertained, *takhliya* will not be established.[211] The importer of commodities can sell them only after obtaining their possession. In this regard, the delivery of possession of goods by the seller to the agent of the buyer will be considered transfer of possession to the buyer himself, even if the goods have not reached the buyer's country. If the buyer cannot appoint an agent, then he can only conclude an agreement to sell with a third party, which is not an enforceable contract.[212] Hence, the entrusting of property to an agent is considered delivery of possession to the principal himself.[213] In FOB (free on board); CIF (Cost, Insurance, and Freight); and CF (Cost and Freight) contracts, possession and *ḍamān* (liability) are transferred when the commodity is transferred to the shipping company, which is considered the agent of the buyer.[214] **5.64**

203 *Radd al-Muḥtār* (n 2) Vol. 7, p. 98.
204 Ibn al-Humām (n 27) Vol. 3, p. 18; *Majalla*, Art. 275.
205 *Radd al-Muḥtār* (n 2) Vol. 7, pp. 94–96. These principles are equally applicable to *hiba* and *ṣadaqa*. *Majalla*, Art. 274.
206 *Radd al-Muḥtār* (n 2) Vol. 7, p. 98; *Majalla*, Art. 272.
207 Al-Dusūqī (n 6) Vol. 3, pp. 144–45.
208 Al-Nawawī (n 98) Vol. 2, pp. 215–16; Al-Shīrāzī (n 5) Vol. 2, p. 14.
209 Al-Shirbīnī (n 13) Vol. 2, p. 95; *Majalla*, Art. 273.
210 *Majalla*, Art. 269.
211 Usmani (n 141) Vol. 2, pp. 410–15.
212 Aḥmad (n 8) Vol. 6, pp. 525–26.
213 Ibn al-Humām (n 27) Vol. 3, pp. 21–22.
214 Usmani (n 46) Vol. 3, pp. 204–05.

7. The Subject Matter Should Be *Maʿlūm*

5.65 According to all *fuqahā*, the subject matter should be *maʿlūm* (known, determined, ascertained, specified, apportioned, pinpointed, individualized, particularized, itemized, identified, and quantified) to both parties in order to avoid *gharar* due to *jahāla* (indefiniteness and ambiguity in the contract; ignorance) and conflicts between the parties. The Holy Prophet has prohibited the sale of *majhūl* and sales involving *gharar*.[215] Shafi'is and Hanbalis stipulate the applicability of the condition of a *maʿlūm* subject matter for both financial and non-financial contracts such as marriage contracts, as well as for gratuitous contracts such as *hiba*, *waṣiyya*, and *waqf*.[216] Hanafis confine the applicability of this condition to contracts of exchange—financial and non-financial. For instance, Hanafis contend that an act of charity is valid even where its subject matter is *jahāla*, since it would not lead to conflicts.[217]

7.1 Extent of Knowledge of Subject Matter

5.66 Knowledge of the subject matter need not cover in detail all characteristics of the *mabīʿ*. It suffices that the latter is adequately determined so that any possibility of conflict between the parties is eliminated. This may be achieved by describing the *jins* (nature of the subject matter or kind) and *qadr* (number, size, length, and quantity).[218] Therefore, lack of knowledge, which does not lead to disputes, is acceptable.[219] If a portion/part of the subject matter is exempted from the contract of sale, the condition that the subject matter should be defined applies also to the exempted part. To illustrate this point, consider one specific tree among many trees in a field, one floor from the many floors of a building, or one specific part of a piece of land; all should be adequately determined, otherwise the contract would be invalid.[220] Finally, in services contracts, the services should be specified too.[221]

[215] Al-Buhūtī (n 42) Vol. 3, p. 163; Al-Qarāfī (n 10) Vol. 3, p. 371. Some scholars contend that the ignorance of the seller of the *mabīʿ* does not invalidate the contract but that of the buyer does. See *Radd al-Muḥtār* (n 2) Vol. 4, pp. 528–30; Shawkānī (n 92) Vol. 5, pp. 147, 168–69; Al-Nawawī (n 98) Vol. 2, p. 176; Al-Shirbīnī (n 13) Vol. 2, p. 22.

[216] Al-Dardīr (n 32) Vol. 4, pp. 141–42; Al-Shīrāzī (n 5) Vol. 1, p. 263 and Vol. 2, p. 323; *Al-Mughnī* (n 2) Vol. 4, pp. 209, 234.

[217] Al-Kāsānī (n 2) Vol. 5, p. 158; Ibn al-Humām (n 8) Vol. 5, pp. 113, 222; Al-Shīrāzī (n 5) Vol. 2, p. 93; Nethercott and Eisenberg (n 16) 46.

[218] Al-Shirbīnī (n 13) Vol. 2, p. 22.

[219] Al-Kāsānī (n 2) Vol. 5, p. 157; Ibn Nujaim, *Al Baḥr al-Rāʾiq* (n 8) Vol. 5, p. 436.

[220] Shawkānī (n 92) Vol. 5, p. 171.

[221] *Majalla*, Art. 455.

7.2 Acquiring Knowledge of the Subject Matter

This knowledge of the subject matter can be acquired by pointing to the subject matter, by inspecting it, or by describing it.[222] **5.67**

7.2.1 Knowledge through Inspection or Examination

Inspection may involve examination of the subject matter as a whole. However, such a condition is not mandatory on all occasions. For instance, examination of some parts of the *mabīʿ* while excluding others will not invalidate the sale if all the inspected parts are in the same condition. Their state would be indicative of the subject matter's qualities in its entirety (e.g. inspection of some grains from a heap of wheat or the inspection of part of something stored in multiple pots). In this case, examination of some parts of the subject matter eliminates *gharar* concerning the entirety of the subject matter. Inspection should take place at the time of the contract's conclusion.[223] If the examined parts are not the same, but inspection of the rest involves great difficulty, the contract would be valid. If, however, no great obstacles to the inspection of other parts of the *mabīʿ* exist, there are two opinions as to how to proceed with the contract. The first allows the sale with the possibility of *khiyār*. The second view supports the argument that the contract should be disallowed because the buyer will not have the option of *khiyār* for what he has examined in the subject matter. He will have *khiyār* for what he has not inspected.[224] Normally, when the *qadr* (quantity, measurement) of the *mabīʿ* is not known, the sale is not allowed. Yet, the sale becomes permissible when *jahāla* is eliminated after examination of the subject matter.[225] Hence, when the subject matter is pointed out, named, or specified, then there is no need for the knowledge of its *qadr* or quality because *ishāra* (pointing out) is the most eloquent way of defining something.[226] However, if knowledge about the subject matter is not gained by pointing or naming, then it is imperative to describe its genre, kind, *qadr*, or quality so that the apprehension of conflict is eliminated.[227] **5.68**

7.2.2 Knowledge by Description

Sale by description is allowed if the description eliminates the *jahāla al-fāḥisha* (excessive and exorbitant lack of knowledge).[228] *Jahāla* (lack of knowledge) becomes *fāḥisha* (exorbitant) if it leads to conflicts and controversies. The contract is then voidable (*fāsid*), according to Hanafis, and void (*bāṭil*), according to other *fuqahā*.[229] An illustrative example of this kind of *jahāla* is the following: the seller tells the buyer: 'I have **5.69**

[222] Al-Buhūtī (n 42) Vol. 3, p. 163; Al-Qarāfī (n 10) Vol. 3, p. 265; Mālik bin Anas (n 93) Vol. 3, pp. 255, 260.
[223] Al-Buhūtī (n 42) Vol. 3, p. 163; Al-Qarāfī (n 10) Vol. 3, p. 265; Al-Nawawī (n 98) Vol. 2, p. 165; Al-Shirbīnī (n 13) Vol. 2, p. 27; Al-Shīrāzī (n 5) Vol. 2, pp. 15–16.
[224] Al-Shīrāzī (n 5) Vol. 2, pp. 15–16.
[225] Ibid, Vol. 2, p. 17.
[226] Thānwī (n 2) Vol. 6, p. 443; Al-Marghīnānī (n 158) Vol. 3, pp. 20, 21; Ibn Nujaim (n 8) Vol. 5, pp. 454–56.
[227] Thānwī (n 2) Vol. 6, p. 443.
[228] Al-Dardīr (n 32) Vol. 3, p. 22; *Radd al-Muḥtār* (n 2) Vol. 4, p. 506 and Vol. 7, pp. 48–51.
[229] *Radd al-Muḥtār* (n 2) Vol. 4, pp. 528–30 and Vol. 7, pp. 48–51; *Majalla*, Art. 213.

sold you everything in the village that belongs to me' and the buyer does not know what exactly the seller owns in that particular village.[230] *Jahāla* that does not lead to conflict is named '*jahāla al-yasīra*' (minimal or slight lack of knowledge). This is normally tolerated by contracting parties and is ordinarily allowed by the *fuqahā*;[231] for instance, the vendor sells his land by mentioning its boundaries while not providing its exact measurements (e.g. length and width), or when it is very well known in the area that the land being sold is owned by the seller.

7.2.2.1 Occasions when sale by description takes place

5.70 Sale by description:

(i) when the commodity is not present or if it is present it is hidden/covered/concealed (e.g. chattels packed in utensils or pots).[232] In this sale, if the subject matter does not live up to the original description, the contract will be rescinded/cancelled and the buyer cannot ask for an alternate commodity with the *ṣiffa* (quality/attributes) narrated in the contract. Even if the delivery of an alternative was foreseen in the initial contract, such agreement would be void;[233]

(ii) when the commodity is described but not specified. The sale would be allowed if the *sifāt* (qualities) are described in a way akin to the contract of *salam*, provided that the situation in which such sale is being conducted is such that it allows (or would allow) *salam*. The term *salam* or *salaf* should not be used at the time of contract. In this instance, if the seller delivers to the buyer the subject matter that was described and the buyer returns it because either some *ṣiffa* was missing or there was a defect in some of its qualities, the contract will not be cancelled, given that it was not concluded in relation to a specific subject matter.

This is a point of difference from the first case. For the second type, the inspection should precede the conclusion of the contract and the time/interval between them should not be so long that the subject matter of sale undergoes changes.[234]

7.2.2.2 Description of packaged goods

5.71 According to Shafi'is, Malikis, and Hanbalis, the sale of goods merely on the basis of their package description (e.g. on the box or carton that contains them) is binding on the buyer if he finds them to be in conformity with the description. Hanafis, however, suggest that there is an option for the buyer, which is very hard to follow. Hence, the sale of goods in utensils, jars, and other forms of packaging the weight of which is known is allowed by reference to custom.[235] The description of the commodity substitutes the need for examination, especially when the opening of the packaging and the display of

[230] *Radd al-Muḥtār* (n 2) Vol. 14, p. 104.
[231] Al-Qarāfī (n 10) Vol. 3, p. 265; *Radd al-Muḥtār* (n 2) Vol. 14, p. 104 and Vol. 4, pp. 528–30.
[232] Al-Buhūtī (n 42) Vol. 3, p. 163; Al-Shīrāzī (n 5) Vol. 2, pp. 14–15.
[233] Al-Buhūtī (n 42) Vol. 3, p. 163.
[234] Ibid, Vol. 3, p. 164; *Al-Mughnī* (n 2) Vol. 6, pp. 33–35.
[235] Mālik bin Anas (n 93) Vol. 3, p. 269.

the commodity causes great inconvenience to the seller,[236] or where the display may damage the goods.[237]

7.2.3 Need for Specification

Lack of specification of the subject matter is an obstacle to the validity of the contract if the subject matter differs substantially from others of the same kind. By way of example, if the seller says 'I have sold a sheep from this flock' without identifying the sheep, and there is excessive and exorbitant difference between the sold sheep and others, the sale is not valid although the price for each sheep may be the same.[238] The same would hold true if one of the shops leased to the lessee were sold to him with an option for him to take the one he or she preferred.[239] *Bayʿ al-ḥiṣāt*, whereby the seller sells a commodity among those of the same type/kind upon which a pebble has fallen,[240] is invalid. **5.72**

When no great difference among subject matters of the same type occurs, specification is not mandatory.[241] For instance, when the seller sells to the buyer one sack of wheat from a designated pile of sacks, the sale is valid[242] because as soon as the pile is specified, the sack becomes known and the possibility of *gharar* is eliminated.[243] The buyer has the option to take any sack he chooses.[244] The sale has become already binding for any one sack; civil liability (*ḍamān*) and ownership are transferred to the buyer with the specification of the sack. The sale of subject matter from a stockpile is allowed when both the seller and the buyer have *jahāla* about the weight or measurement of the subject matter. **5.73**

7.2.4 Immovable Property

The sale of a house by description is valid if the house conforms to the description given.[245] Necessary elements to be described include the city and the place where the house is located, its boundaries, its characteristics, its surface, etc. The house may also be described in terms of its structure, construction, situation, and its size (e.g. large, medium, or small).[246] If it is part of a joint property then the house should have been identified when the property was divided among the owners.[247] If the shares of the joint owners are defined and demarcated, then one joint owner can sell his share without prior permission from other joint owners; otherwise he cannot[248] because in an **5.74**

236 Al-Dusūqī (n 6) Vol. 3, p. 24.
237 Ibid, Vol. 3, p. 24.
238 Al-Nawawī (n 98) Vol. 2, p. 161; Al-Nawawī (n 4) Vol. 9, pp. 346–48.
239 *Majalla*, Art. 449.
240 Muslim, *ḥadīth* 3783; Jāmiʿ al-Uṣūl li Ibn al-Asir, *ḥadīth* Vol. 1, p. 528.
241 *Radd al-Muḥtār* (n 2) Vol. 4, p. 505.
242 Al-Kāsānī (n 2) Vol. 4, p. 359; *Radd al-Muḥtār* (n 2) Vol. 13, p. 146; *Al-Mughnī* (n 2) Vol. 4, pp. 207–09; Al-Dasūqī (n 6) Vol. 3, p. 17; *Majalla*, Art. 220; Al-Nawawī (n 4) Vol. 9, pp. 346–48.
243 Al-Shīrāzī (n 5) Vol. 2, p. 14.
244 Ibn al-Humām (n 8) Vol. 5, pp. 473–74.
245 Ibn Rushd (n 97) Vol. 7, p. 320.
246 Ibid, Vol. 7, p. 325.
247 Ibn al-Humām (n 27) Vol. 4, p. 417.
248 *Majalla*, Art. 215.

undemarcated property joint ownership extends to the property as a whole. The sale of an undetermined plot (piece of land) from many plots is not permissible according to Abū Ḥanīfa but permissible according to *Sāhibain*.[249]

5.75 A gift (*hiba*) to several persons without defining and identifying their shares is not valid. If the donees divide the property amongst themselves with the permission of the donor, the contract becomes valid.[250] If the *mawhūb* is adjacent to, or associated in some way with other things, then it should be clearly distinguished from these.[251]

[249] Ibn Nujaim (n 8) Vol. 5, pp. 487–88.
[250] Aḥmad (n 8) Vol. 7, pp. 261–62.
[251] Ibn al-Humām (n 27) Vol. 4, p. 417.

6

The Main Prohibited Elements in Contract

1. Introduction

As shown in Chapter 1, the general philosophy of Islamic contract law is premised on consent and mutual satisfaction when two or more contracting parties intend to establish legal relationship. This is often reflected as *consensus ad idem*, which emphasizes party autonomy or freedom in concluding any contract. However, beyond full party autonomy and given that all such relationships are governed by principles in the Qur'ān and Sunnah, there are a few prohibited elements which the parties are required not to undertake under the law. Such elements are specifically meant to prevent harm to either of the parties to the contract as well as to society as a whole. As will be discussed in Chapter 13, third parties are often impacted by contractual arrangements. Therefore, beyond the principle of privity of contract, Islamic law proactively contemplates and effectively anticipates the impact of any contractual arrangement on third parties. **6.01**

Against the above backdrop, this chapter examines the major prohibited elements in contractual arrangements. It begins with an examination of the theory of prohibition in contractual dealings which provides a general background on the underlying principles that underpin the prohibitions. Furthermore, the two major prohibited elements in contract—*ribā* and *gharar*—are examined from both theoretical and practical perspectives, with a number of examples from case law and some insights on drafting relevant commercial contracts with a view to guiding practitioners on how to contextualize these concepts in modern contractual arrangements. **6.02**

The chapter proceeds with the discussion on other prohibited elements in contract such as dealing in illegal commodities as the subject matter of contracts, gambling or games of chance, fraud, deception, coercion, usurpation, hoarding, and illegal profiteering. These are discussed in the light of relevant case law as well as practice guidance to drive home the idea of convergence of law from the perspective of vitiating elements in a contract. There are more similarities than differences between Islamic law and modern contract law in matters involving certain vitiating elements in contracts. These insights will be relevant to practitioners involved in drafting legal documentation for Islamic transactions since efforts have been made to identify some minor differences in some of the concepts with a view to providing meaningful guidance on the rules underpinning Islamic contract law. **6.03**

6.04 After discussing the prohibited elements, this chapter concludes with a rather interesting analysis on the other side of the coin when discussing prohibited elements in contract. This is where emphasis is placed on the positive dimension and impact of such prohibitions as well as an overarching principle of permissibility which forms the basis of all contractual arrangements in Islamic law. The principle of permissibility is inclusive in its scope rather than the exclusionary approach of the prohibited elements. In essence, these concluding thoughts have far-reaching implications in drafting legal documentation in Islamic transactions, as they would provide the basis for the adoption of global best practices that do not ordinarily contradict fundamental principles of Islamic law. Such an approach has been seen in the standardization of legal documentation for a number of Islamic finance transactions, which reflects a general adoption with some modifications or rather adaptation of conventional capital market documentation. Such a traditional approach dates back to the advent of Islam, and, although innovative, it allows for financial engineering that is targeted at sustainable development and socio-economic development.

2. The Theory of Prohibition in Contractual Dealings

6.05 The underlying philosophy of prohibition in Islamic law is based on the harmful effect of certain conducts, terms, dispositions, products, and even services. For instance, though oral contracts are allowed in Islamic law, the Lawgiver instructs contractual parties to document their terms and conditions.[1] This is similar to the four-corners rule in English law of contract where oral or implied terms cannot trump clear-cut provisions in a written agreement. It thus appears that the exceptions to the four-corners rule under English law could also be acceptable under the Islamic law.

6.06 There are numerous exceptions to the rule under English law but one exception that stands out is when the original contract itself is invalid or where an error is discovered in the contract. Such exceptions would also apply under Islamic law. This is reflected in a reported Prophetic precedent where Prophet Muhammad is reported to have said: 'Muslims are bound by all the contractual stipulations they have agreed upon.'[2] In another *ḥadīth*, it is reported that he emphasized that 'Muslims are bound by all the conditions they have agreed upon, unless the contractual conditions are against the principles of Islamic law where something that is unlawful is made lawful or lawful as unlawful.'[3] This clearly reflects the approach of Islamic law to contractual stipulations

[1] The longest verse of the Qur'ān (Qur'ān 2:282), which is generally called *aya al-dayn* (The verse on debt obligations) stipulates this rule. The opening part of the verse reads:

O you who have believed, when you contract a debt for a specified term, write it down. And let a scribe write [it] between you in justice. Let no scribe refuse to write as Allah has taught him. So let him write and let the one who has the obligation [i.e., the debtor] dictate. And let him fear Allah, his Lord, and not leave anything out of it.

[2] Al-Asqalāni, Ibn Hajar Ahmad bin 'Ali, Bulugh al-Marām min Adilat al-Ahkām (7th edn, n.p., 2003) p. 258 (hereafter Al-'Asqalāni, *Bulūgh al-Marām*).

[3] Related by Al-Tirmidhi. *Ḥadīth* No. 1352. See Al-Tirmidhi, Abu 'Isa Muhammad bin 'Isa, Al-Jami' Al-Kabir (Dar al-Gharb al-Islami, 1996) Vol. 3, p. 27 (hereafter Al-Tirmidhi, *Al-Jāmi' Al-Kabīr*).

and the possibility of going outside the four corners of an agreement in interpreting it, particularly when the cause of such an exercise is an element of prohibition.

In his views, Ibn Taymiyya explains the permissive spirit of Islamic law in its approach to contractual stipulations: 'The rule in contracts and the terms and conditions contained therein is that of admissibility, which makes them admissible unless there is a clear proof of prohibition.'[4] Therefore, if there is no prohibitive element in an agreement or even legislation from another jurisdiction or international convention, there is no harm in adopting it. This is the hallmark of legal transplant which is considered appropriate in Islamic law regardless of where such legislation or precedent emerges. This confers legitimacy on contracts and transactions of non-Islamic cultures or traditions such as English law and French law as well as contractual agreements concluded under those laws, provided they do not contain anything expressly forbidden in Islamic law. This is further justified by Ibn Taymiyya, who emphasized that 'Muslims agree that pre-Islamic contracts that were concluded by non-Muslims are valid after Islam to the extent that they are not specifically forbidden for Muslims'.[5] **6.07**

In order to understand this general theory of prohibition and the other side of the narrative somewhat better, this chapter will briefly examine the Saudi Arabian legal system, which is generally premised on the Hanbali interpretation of Islamic jurisprudence. It is well known that foreign laws and international conventions have been adopted by the Saudi legal system. The general principle is that such laws are considered part of Saudi law provided they do not contradict the Qur'ān and Sunnah.[6] For instance, in Saudi Arabia's Explanatory Memorandum to the Draft Regulations for Companies, the supremacy of sacred law is clearly identified, even though there is also some emphasis on the general overarching inclusive nature of Islamic law.[7] **6.08**

> In drafting these Regulations, it was imperative to rely primarily on the rules that have proved their worth in actual practice and have become customary among individuals, and to borrow suitable provisions from the regulations of other countries, in order to promote the harmony dictated by the international character of trade, which has always called for the unification of commercial regulations as a means of achieving prosperity for all. Any such rules or provisions as were inconsistent with the orthodox Shari'ah were excluded.[8]

[4] The principle is expressed in Arabic as: *al-aṣl fīha 'adam al-tahrīm*. See Ibn Taqi al-Din Ahmad ibn Taymiyyah, Fatawa Ibn Taymiyyah (Kurdistan Press, 1326–29 A.H.) Vol. 3, p. 334.

[5] Ibid, pp. 338–39.

[6] Oussama Arabi, 'Contract Stipulations (Shurūt) in Islamic Law: The Ottoman Majalla and Ibn Taymiyya' (1998) 30(1) International Journal of Middle East Studies 29–50, p. 41.

[7] Ahmad al-Samdan, Contracts' Conflict Rules in Arab Private International Law: A Comparative Study on Principles of Islamic and Civil Legal System (University Microfilms International, 1981) p. 76.

[8] See the Explanatory Memorandum to the Draft Regulations for Companies of Saudi Arabia issued under the Companies Act, Royal Decree No. M/6—dated 22 March 1385 A.H. amended under Royal Decree Nos: M/5 on 12 February 1387 A.H., M/23 on 28 June 1402 A.H., and M/46 on 4 July 1405 A.H., respectively.

6.09 The above Saudi approach to commercial law generally is quite instructive and is generally adopted even in common law jurisdictions like Malaysia where harmonization of laws has been at the forefront of legal reforms relating to Islamic financial services. This approach is no different from that which was adopted during the early days of Islam where the Prophet gave express, or in some cases tacit, approval to certain practices or obligations that were prevalent before the advent of Islam. Some other practices were modified based on the then ongoing revelation and are now considered generally as part of the Sharīʿah.[9]

6.10 Given the nature of general rules established in the Qurʾān and the explanatory nature of the Sunnah, a general prohibition of corruption or usurpation in the sacred text could easily be extended to other forms of violations involving proprietary claims.[10] As contractual dealings are sacrosanct, parties are expected to deal in good faith at all times and to avoid any prohibitory element specifically mentioned in the Qurʾān, explained in the Sunnah, or even extrapolated by the Muslim jurists from the primary texts. Nevertheless, the Lawgiver intends ease and not hardship for the subject of the law, which is why there are numerous concessions in even religious matters to facilitate things for people.

6.11 The general theory of prohibition in contractual transactions is premised on the basis of rulings in the principles of Islamic jurisprudence (*uṣūl al-fiqh*), which tends to establish a general permissibility rule with few prohibitive exceptions.[11] Although the word 'prohibition' is used in this chapter, there are situations where the ruling on certain conduct or omission would not be considered as a prohibition. There are even situations where conduct, a disposition, or a term which was originally considered as prohibited will become permissible, and vice versa, depending on the specific facts of a case or circumstances.

6.12 Rulings that are based on custom and tradition, particularly customary trade practices in contractual arrangements, could change according to time, place, and circumstance. This legal maxim is generally expressed thus: 'It is an accepted fact that the terms of law or rulings vary with the change in the times [and circumstance].'[12] This is the reason why Islamic financial transactions generally require a review and approval from learned Sharīʿah scholars, as such scholars do consider specific facts that are unique to the proposal presented to them. In essence, such practice could be likened to the practice of distinguishing facts while reviewing judicial precedents in an English court of law.[13]

9 Muhammad Yusuf Saleem, Islamic Commercial Law (John Wiley & Sons Singapore, 2013) p. 1.

10 For instance, Qurʾān 4:29 states: 'O you who have believed, do not consume one another's wealth unjustly but only [in lawful] business by mutual consent. And do not kill yourselves [or one another]. Indeed, Allah is to you ever Merciful.'

11 Ibn Taymiyyah, *Fatawa Ibn Taymiyyah* (n 4) Vol. 3, pp. 340–42.

12 Article 39 of Majallat al-Ahkām al-ʿAdliyyah al-Māddah (Ottoman Publisher, 1877). See Ahmad Ibn Shaykh al-Zarqa, Sharh al Qawaaʾid al-Fiqhiyyah (4th edn, Dar al-Qalam, 1996/1417) p. 227. It is on record that the French Civil Code rejected this principle.

13 This principle is also known as *stare decisis*. For a comprehensive analysis on how facts are distinguished in the court to avoid following past precedents, see generally C. Steven Bradford, 'Following Dead Precedent: The Supreme Court's Ill-Advised Rejection of Anticipatory Overruling' (1990) 59(1) Fordham Law Review 39–90.

Given the flexibility provided in Islamic law, particularly in contractual matters, there is considerable scope to structure new products based on new contractual arrangements, while identifying a few prohibited elements.

The entire spectrum of rulings or *aḥkām* in Islamic jurisprudence contemplates situations where particular conduct, or a particular term or omission, could be categorized under the following rulings: *wājib* (obligatory), *mandūb* or *masnūn* (recommended), *mubāḥ* (permissible), *makrūḥ* (disliked or detestable), and *ḥarām* (prohibited).[14] Each of these categories has its unique legal consequences and some of them, such as *ḥarām*, are further divided into additional categories. Since the main focus here is the discussion on prohibited elements in a contract, it is instructive to shed some light on the two main types of *ḥarām* in Islamic jurisprudence. The two types of *harām* are *ḥarām li dhātihi* (inherent prohibition) and *ḥarām li ghayrihi* (prohibition induced by external element).[15] 6.13

In contractual arrangements, *ḥarām li dhātihi* is an act, omission, or term prohibited because of its very essence as well as any resulting harm it causes to an individual or thing.[16] Examples of this type of *ḥarām* could be seen in usurpation of property or a contract that causes a direct harm to the environment which would negatively impact plant and animal life. On the other hand, *ḥarām li ghayrihi* is the prohibition induced by external factors which are not inherently harmful but are tainted with some prohibited elements. Examples of this category of *ḥarām* include ill-gotten wealth obtained through criminal activities or sin. This is the reason why money laundering, terrorism financing, dealing in illicit drugs, illicit financial transactions, and fraud are prohibited in Islamic law. In fact, most predicate crimes could be considered under the category of *ḥarām li dhātihi* as they are components of larger crimes. Since predicate crimes are usually components of larger crimes, they automatically become crimes and are prosecuted as such.[17] Whether a particular term in a contract or conduct falls under either of the two types of *ḥarām*, it will be considered prohibited in Islamic law. However, the ultimate authority for such determination is a qualified Sharīʿah scholar, a Sharīʿah advisory firm, or a Shariah Advisory Council (SAC).[18] 6.14

[14] Al-Saʿadi, ʿAbdur Rahman bin Nasir, Safwah Usūl al-Fiqh (Dar al-Sumaiʿi Publishers and Distributors, 2011) pp. 14–15.

[15] Al-Samʿāni, Abu Al-Muzafar, Al-Qawātiʿ fi Usūl al-Fiqh (Dar al-Faruq, 2011) pp. 231–32.

[16] *Al-Taftazāni, Masʿūd Ibn ʿUmar*, Sharh al-Talwīh ʿAla al-Tawdīh (Dar al-Kutub al-ʿIlmiyyah, 1996) Vol. 2, pp. 262–63.

[17] R.E. Bell, 'Abolishing the Concept of "Predicate Offence"' (2002) 6(2) Journal of Money Laundering Control 137–40.

[18] For a detailed analysis of the Sharīʿah governance framework in the modern Islamic financial services industry, see generally Zulkifli Hasan, Shari'ah Governance in Islamic Banks (Edinburgh University Press, 2012).

3. *Ribā* and *Gharar*: A Practical Approach

6.15 The first two fundamental elements one must watch out for in legal documentation for Islamic transactions are *ribā* (interest and usury) and *gharar* (excessive speculative risk). Though there are other prohibited elements described later in this chapter, these two fundamental elements are the most important and can be identified easily in a contract. This section provides a contextual and practical analysis of the two elements, with relevant examples from modern case law as well as documentation used in real-time Islamic contracts.

3.1 *Ribā*

6.16 Since the advent of Islam, one of the most important issues in any discussion involving contractual and commercial transactions is *ribā* and its different categorizations. Even though the word *ribā* is not defined in the Qur'ān, as it is generally believed that people understand the concept in its simple terms, its prohibitions are firmly established in the primary sources of Sharī'ah. In simple terms, the word *ribā* means any excess, increase, or addition over and above the amount of money borrowed or in the case of some specified commodities. It was common practice during the pre-Islamic era to stipulate certain excess amounts over and above the amount borrowed for a specified period.

6.17 In some of its earliest guidance, the prohibition of *ribā* in contracts underpinning commercial transactions is found in Qur'ān 2:275 where it states:

> Those who consume *ribā* (interest) cannot stand [on the Day of Resurrection] except as one stands who is being beaten by Satan into insanity. That is because they say, 'Trade is [just] like *ribā*.' *But Allah has permitted trade and has forbidden ribā*. So whoever has received an admonition from his Lord and desists may have what is past, and his affair rests with Allah. But whoever returns [to dealing in interest or usury]—those are the companions of the Fire; they will abide eternally therein.

6.18 Though the word *ribā* is loosely translated to mean both interest and usury, it implies any increase or excess amount paid over and above the money lent for a stipulated period. It is interesting to note Ibn Kathir's explanation of the phrase: '*But Allah has permitted trade and has forbidden ribā*.' In his exegesis of the verse, he explained that the ruling on trade is different from that which is applicable to *ribā*, as the former seeks to benefit all while the latter leads to harmful economic practices which could potentially lead to economic crisis.[19] The word *ribā* is a general term that means any increase or excess sought in the form of usury, bribery, excess profiteering, usurpation, and even fraudulent trading.[20] These prohibited practices have far-reaching effects on the overall

[19] Ibn Kathīr, Abu al-Fidā Ismail bin 'Umar, Tafsīr al-Qurān al-'Azīm (Dar al-Tayyibah, 1999) Vol. 1, p. 709.
[20] 'Abdullah Yusuf Ali, The Meaning of the Holy Qur'ān (10th edn, Amana Publications, 1999) p. 115.

economy, hence the need to prohibit them to ensure just and equitable distribution of resources in the society. Thus, *ribā* is often identified as economic injustice which is a threat to the entire society: 'Whatever loans you give, [only] seeking interest at the expense of people's wealth will not increase with Allah. But whatever charity you give, [only] seeking the pleasure of Allah—it is they whose reward will be multiplied.'[21]

The most recent experience of the grave impact of *ribā* on the world economic was witnessed during the Global Financial Crisis (GFC) in 2007–08 where Wall Street's giants were brought to their knees. In the years leading up to the GFC, lenders continued to offer more loans to borrowers who are ordinarily considered to be high risk, with a substantial increase in the number of subprime mortgages. There was also the issue of predatory lending, where lenders adopted fraudulent practices and deceptive measures to provide loans to borrowers who ordinarily could not afford such loans. This had a debilitating effect on investors in these mortgage securities.[22] Ultimately, when the bubble burst, financial institutions were left with illiquid and worthless investments in subprime mortgages worth trillions of dollars. Millions of people (borrowers) were left homeless, as most so-called homeowners realized that they owed more on their mortgages than their homes were worth. Foreclosures set in and many homeowners found themselves on the streets. An alternative to the subprime mortgage model would have been properly structured products based on partnership contracts where both the lender and borrower share the risk in the financed asset, as enunciated in Islamic commercial law. **6.19**

3.1.1 Two Broad Classifications of *Ribā*

In general, Muslim jurists classify *ribā* into two broad categories: *ribā al-faḍl*, which means any unlawful excess when countervalues are exchanged in a simultaneous transaction, and *ribā al-nasīʾa*, where unlawful gain is derived through deferment of the completion of exchange of countervalues. Muslim jurists also introduced a third category known as *ribā al-jāhiliyya*, simply called a pre-Islamic *ribā*.[23] The pre-Islamic *ribā* simply means a contractual arrangement where the lender gives the borrower an option at maturity date either to settle the debt or pay interest in excess of the original debt. The difference between the pre-Islamic *ribā* and the first two categories is that the two earlier categories apply to exchange of commodities whether deferred or concurrent due to the prevailing practice of trade by barter during the early days of Islam. Such exchange of countervalues often involved two precious metals, gold and silver, and four unique commodities—wheat, barley, dates, and salt, as established in the following *ḥadīth*: **6.20**

[21] Qur'ān 30:389.

[22] This far-reaching effect of *ribā* where interest is compounded until the whole economy is brought to its knees is considered one of the reasons for its prohibition. Qur'ān 3:130 states: 'O you who have believed, do not consume usury, doubled and multiplied, but fear Allah that you may be successful.'

[23] Muhammad Tāhir Ibn 'Ashūr, Maqāsid al-Sharīah al-Islamiyyah (Wazārat al-Awqāf Wa al-Shuūn al-Islamiyyah, 2004) Vol. 2, p. 461.

> Sell gold in exchange of equivalent gold, sell silver in exchange of equivalent silver, sell dates in exchange of equivalent dates, sell wheat in exchange of equivalent wheat, sell salt in exchange of equivalent salt, sell barley in exchange of equivalent barley, but if a person transacts in excess, it will be usury (*ribā*). However, sell gold for silver anyway you please on the condition it is hand-to-hand (spot) and sell barley for date anyway you please on the condition it is hand-to-hand (spot).[24]

In another *ḥadīth*, Abu Sa'id Al-Khudri narrated that the Prophet said:

> Do not sell gold for gold except when it is like for like, and do not increase one over the other; do not sell silver for silver except when it is like for like, and do not increase one over the other; and do not sell what is away [from among these] for what is ready.[25]

6.21 While the above principle established in the *ḥadīth* was initially restricted to the six items, the rule could be extended to products derived from such items if their exchange is tainted with elements of *ribā*. The reason behind the prohibition of the six items is premised on the nature of those items, which, at that time, and even in modern societies, constitute necessities of life and they are often subject to exploitative transactions. Muslim jurists such as Ta'us and Qatadah opine that *ribā al-faḍl* should be limited to the items expressly identified in the *ḥadīth*.[26] However, the majority of Muslim jurists argue that some other similar commodities could be included in the category, provided such other commodities have the same underlying features, which make them susceptible to exploitative contractual practices.[27]

[24] The variants of the *ḥadīth* are reported in Al-Nasa'i, Abu Abdul Rahman Ahmad bin Shuaib, Kitab al-Sunan al-Kubra (Muassasah al-Risalah, 2001) Vol. 6, pp. 44–46.

[25] The variants of this *ḥadīth* are related in Al-Bukhari, Muslim, Tirmidhi, Nasa'i, and Musnad Ahmad. There are other reported prophetic precedents about *ribā*, some of which include the following:

1. From 'Ubada ibn al-Samit: the Prophet said: 'Gold for gold, silver for silver, wheat for wheat, barley for barley, dates for dates, and salt for salt—like for like, equal for equal, and hand-to-hand; if the commodities differ, then you may sell as you wish, provided that the exchange is hand-to-hand.'
2. From Abu Sa'id al-Khudri: the Prophet said: 'Gold for gold, silver for silver, wheat for wheat, barley for barley, dates for dates, and salt for salt—like for like, and hand-to-hand. Whoever pays more or takes more has indulged in *riba*. The taker and the giver are alike [in guilt].'
3. From Abu Sa'id and Abu Hurayra: 'A man employed by the Prophet in Khaybar brought for him *janibs* [dates of very fine quality]. Upon the Prophet's asking him whether all the dates of Khaybar were such, the man replied that this was not the case and added that "they exchanged a sa' [a measure] of this kind for two or three [of the other kind]". The Prophet replied, "Do not do so. Sell [the lower quality dates] for dirhams and then use the dirhams to buy janibs. [When dates are exchanged against dates] they should be equal in weight." '
4. From Abu Sa'id: 'Bilal brought to the Prophet some barni [good quality] dates whereupon the Prophet asked him where these were from. Bilal replied, "I had some inferior dates which I exchanged for these—two sa's for a sa'." The Prophet said, "Oh no, this is exactly *riba*. Do not do so, but when you wish to buy, sell the inferior dates against something [cash] and then buy the better dates with the price you receive." '
5. From Fadalah ibn 'Ubayd al-Ansari: 'On the day of Khaybar he bought a necklace of gold and pearls for twelve dinars. On separating the two, he found that the gold itself was equal to more than twelve dinars. So he mentioned this to the Prophet who replied, "It [jewellery] must not be sold until the contents have been valued separately." '

See generally, Al-Nasa'i, *Kitab al-Sunan al-Kubr* (n 24) Vol. 6, pp. 40–46; Al-Bukhāri, Abu Abdullah Muhammad bin Ismai'l, *Al-Jāmi' al-Sahīh* (Al-Maktabah Al-Salafiyyah, n.d.) Vol. 2, pp. 108–09; Muslim, Al-Hajjaj Al-Qushairi Al-Nisaburi, Sahīh Muslim (Dar al-Tasil, 2014) Vol. 4, pp. 277–88 (hereafter Muslim, *Sahīh Muslim*).

[26] Wazārat al-Awqāf wa al-Shuūn al-Islamiyyah, Al-Mausū'ah al-fiqhiyyah al-Kuwaitiyyah (Dār Al-Salāsil, 1404–1427 A.H.) Vol. 22, p. 64.

[27] Ibid, Vol. 22, p. 63.

In the historic judgment on interest delivered by the Supreme Court of Pakistan in 1999, the Sharī'ah Appellate Bench of the court held that 'all the prevailing forms of interest, either in banking transactions or in private transactions, do fall within the definition of '*ribā*'. Similarly, any interest stipulated in the government borrowings, acquired from domestic or foreign sources, is *ribā* and clearly prohibited by the Holy Qur'ān.'[28] The court effectively declared all laws that provide for payment of interest void in Pakistan. Beyond the Muslim world, usury is generally prohibited in the laws of some countries even though the word 'usury' is defined differently in various jurisdictions. In most cases, usury laws cap the amount of interest that can be charged on loans. For instance, section 347 of the Canadian Criminal Code[29] stipulates that 60% is the maximum allowable annualized interest rate. Any interest charged over and above that level is usury and thus a criminal offence. A number of states in the United States have similar laws. However, in *Marquette National Bank of Minneapolis v First of Omaha Service Corporation*,[30] the US Supreme Court unanimously held that anti-usury laws of states regulating interest rates cannot be enforced against the category of nationally chartered banks operating in other states within the country. **6.22**

3.1.2 Is There Any Difference between Profit and Interest?

From the practical perspective in structuring products which are executed through modern contracts, the question however remains as to how profit is different from *ribā*, particularly in the modern sense where Islamic financial institutions become profitable in their business model as a result of what they call 'profit' while conventional financial institutions do charge interest or *ribā* since they are merely lending institutions. So, in performing the role of financial intermediary, are there any differences between Islamic financial institutions and conventional institutions in the way and manner in which they make money? It is pertinent to note that Islamic profit rates are often based on conventional benchmark rates. **6.23**

Profit or *ribḥ* is generally different from *ribā* as it is earned through proactive entrepreneurial efforts while assuming the associated risks. In commercial contracts, Islamic law envisaged the need to share risk and return. On the other hand, in *ribā*-based contracts, beyond advancing some funds, the lender does not do anything to earn interest. Islamic law places emphasis on investing in real economic activities to generate employment and promote the distribution of resources among people. On the contrary, lending institutions do not participate in any trading or investment beyond merely advancing funds, hence they do not undertake market risk since in most cases the loans are collateralized. Therefore, Islamic law allows contracting parties to stipulate terms and conditions on the responsibilities of each of the parties in a commercial contract **6.24**

[28] See para. 245 of the text of the judgment delivered by Justice Taqi Usmani. The text of the historic judgment on *ribā* (interest) given by the Supreme Court of Pakistan, 23 December 1999; section written by Muhammad Taqi Usmani.

[29] R.S.C., 1985, c. C-46.

[30] 439 U.S. 299.

and to share the underlying risk and return. In determining the pricing, they are allowed to utilize some external benchmarks or indicators to determine their profit rate.

6.25 According to the majority of modern Muslim jurists, the use of conventional benchmark interest rates such as the Secured Overnight Financing Rate (SOFR) and other similar benchmarks does not render the Islamic contract void on the basis of a prohibited element, that is, *ribā*, since there is no other alternative in pricing transactions. The use of such conventional interest rates as a benchmark in pricing Islamic products is considered a necessary evil that should be replaced with a more Islamic benchmark rate once available.

3.1.3 Loan Moratorium: Between Interest and Profit Rates

6.26 In recent times, particularly with the Covid-19 pandemic and the ensuing financial crisis, one major issue that emerged among experts was a loan moratorium in commercial contracts. A loan moratorium is the period during a loan contract in which the borrower is allowed to defer its repayment until a specified agreed period. Repayments would resume after the specified date. During the pandemic, many countries introduced both monetary and fiscal measures to cushion the effect of the crisis on financial consumers, many of whom have contracts stipulating interest payments. A similar experience was witnessed in Muslim-majority countries where Islamic banks granted profit payment moratoriums to financial consumers who had some financial dealings with them.

6.27 In times of economic crisis, Islamic law permits parties to enter a loan moratorium to defer repayment of the loan or financing. This rule is often interpreted as part of the overall ease granted by the law in forbidding interest-based transactions. The rule on a loan moratorium is expressly established in Qur'ān 2:280: 'And if someone is in hardship, then [let there be] postponement until [a time of] ease. But if you give [from your right as] charity, then it is better for you, if you only knew.'

6.28 It is worth noting that Ibn Kathir pointed out in his commentary on the above verse that during the pre-Islamic era, the lender often told the borrower at maturity that he should either pay immediately or interest would be added to the debt.[31] To mitigate this additional hardship on debtors, the above verse was revealed to encourage granting respite to debtors. This is further confirmed in a number of prophetic precedents, one of which was reported by Sulayman bin Burayda, who reported that he heard his father saying: 'I heard the Messenger of Allah say: "Whoever gives time to a debtor facing hard times, will gain charity of equal proportions for each day he gives." '[32]

6.29 In Malaysia, the central bank, Bank Negara Malaysia (BNM), allowed banks to restructure or reschedule loans and financing during the pandemic since many financial consumers were faced with serious economic hardship. In response to such exceptional

[31] Ibn Kathīr (n 19) Vol. 1, p. 717.
[32] Ahmad bin Hanbal, Musnad Ahmad (Muassasat al-Risālah, 2001) 23046, Vol. 38, p. 153.

circumstances, BNM issued the Policy Document on Credit Risk on 27 September 2019, which allows rescheduling and restructuring through the grant of a moratorium on financing and loan repayments.[33] The exercise requires amendment of the loan and financing agreements, and this goes to the very essence of the principal and interest/profit rates, particularly in the case of a restructuring exercise. While relying on key Islamic principles, one feature that clearly distinguishes the Islamic contract from the conventional contract in a loan/financing moratorium is seen in the resolution of BNM's SAC, where it stipulated that the financing period could be extended based on mutual agreement and that the sale price must not exceed the original sale price.[34] This implies that even when restructuring is done due to economic hardship, the sale price remains the same.

3.1.4 Interest and Late Payment Compensation

Another dimension to the discourse which has some practical implications is the concept of late payment compensation being introduced in Islamic contracts. This concept is not only relevant to Islamic finance contracts but to all types of Islamic contract, as there are always provisions for late payment. Loan defaults, late payments, and even judgment debts often attract interest in conventional practice. Since *ribā* is prohibited in Islamic law, the alternatives introduced by some modern Muslim jurists, which have been adopted in several jurisdictions, are the concept of *ta'wīdh* (fine or penalty) and *gharāma* (compensation). These two concepts are based on analogical deduction from some *ḥadīths* and legal maxims. For instance, intentional delay in payment is frowned on in Islam, based on the *ḥadīth* where the Prophet said: 'Delay by a rich person (in the payment of debt) is a tyrannical oppression.'[35] In a legal maxim derived from another *ḥadīth*, it is stated that '[t]here should neither be harm nor reciprocating harm'.[36] **6.30**

Based on the foregoing affirmative evidence, it is surmised that any delay in payment under a contract where the borrower or debtor is able to repay but refuses to settle the debt will result in a financial harm to the lender, supplier, vendor, or financial institution. This may lead to avoidable financial loss and economic hardship. So, in order to prevent such practice, which could be a loophole to be exploited in Islamic law by some contractual parties, modern Muslim jurists introduced the two concepts. Therefore, any harm in a contractual arrangement must be removed based on the legal maxim: 'Whatever harm (introduced by any party) should be removed'.[37] This will mitigate the losses associated with delayed payment and will help encourage financial consumers to settle their debts according to contractual stipulations. **6.31**

[33] See Bank Negara Malaysia, 'Credit Risk', issued on 27 September 2019. BNM/RH/PD 029-22. See para. 3 of Appendix 1 of the Policy Document.
[34] See the decision of the SAC of BNM in its 32nd meeting dated 27 February 2003.
[35] *Ḥadīth* No. 2400. See Al-Bukhari (n 25) Vol. 2, p. 175.
[36] Ahmad al-Zarqā', Sharh al-Qawā`id al-Fiqhiyyah (Dar al-Qalam, 1989) p. 165.
[37] Al-Suyūti, Jalaluddin Abdul Rahman bin Abu Bakr, Al-Ashbāh wa al-Nazā'ir (Dār al-Kutub al-`Ilmiyyah, 1983) pp. 83–84.

6.32 According to BNM's SAC resolution, late payment charges can be imposed by a financial institution in the financing contract based on the concepts of *ta'wīdh* and *gharāma* but subject to the following conditions:

a. *Ta`wīdh* may be charged on late payment of financial obligations resulting from exchange contracts (such as sale and lease) and *qarḍ*;
b. *Ta`wīdh* may only be imposed after the settlement date of the financing became due as agreed between both contracting parties;
c. An Islamic financial institution may recognize *ta`wīdh* as income on the basis that it is charged as compensation for actual loss suffered by the institution; and
d. *Gharāma* shall not be recognized as income. Instead, it has to be channelled to certain charitable bodies.[38]

The International Islamic Financial Market (IIFM) that publishes standard documentation on various Islamic financial products also includes a clause on the amount of late payment, including its calculation and utilization in its Master Murabahah Agreement.

6.33 In calculating the late payment amount, parties are allowed to determine the percentage, which is usually between 1% and 2% in practice. Therefore, the late payment amount is calculated thus: the unpaid sum multiplied by the sum of LIBOR for the applicable period plus a mutually agreed percentage, multiplied by the number of days in such applicable period, and finally divided by 360. In *Pan Northern Air Services Sdn Bhd v Maybank Islamic Bhd and another appeal*,[39] the Malaysian Court of Appeal was faced with the issue of whether an Islamic bank had imposed the correct *ta'wīdh* rate and amount following the customer's breach of repayment obligations under an Islamic contract known as *al-bayʿ bithaman ājil* (deferred payment sale contract) or BBA. In this case, Maybank granted an Islamic financing facility of RM41.016 million (*circa* US$10 million) to Pan Northern Air Services Sdn Bhd (the borrower) to finance the borrower's contractual obligations under its contract with the Government of Malaysia. The financing facility was based on an Islamic contract of BBA which included an asset sale agreement. Section 9.32 of the agreement states:

> If the Customer defaults in any payment on its due date of any one or more of the instalments or any other moneys herein covenanted to be paid, the Customer shall pay to the Bank ta'wīdh (compensation) at the compensation rate of 1% per annum on the overdue instalments calculated from the date of such default until the date of payment of the amount thereof and shall not be limited to the period of the financing or any method approved by Bank Negara Malaysia or at the Bank's discretion. The Ta'wīdh (compensation) on late payment may be varied by the Bank at its absolute discretion

[38] See the resolutions of BNM's SAC in its 4th meeting dated 14 February 1998, 95th meeting dated 28 January 2010, and 101st meeting dated 20 May 2010. Shariah Advisory Council, Bank Negara Malaysia, Sharīʿah Resolutions in Islamic Finance (2nd edn, Bank Negara Malaysia, 2010) pp. 129–30.
[39] [2021] 3 MLJ 408.

or upon receipt of advice from Bank Negara Malaysia upon written notification to the Customer.[40]

6.34 As a result of a premature termination of its contract with the Government of Malaysia, the borrower was not able to meet its payment obligations under the BBA agreements and this resulted in the termination of the BBA agreements by the bank before maturity. The bank took steps to appoint receivers and managers for the borrower. It was about to take further steps to enforce the borrower's securities when the latter requested for some time to allow it to arbitrate its dispute with the Government of Malaysia. Fortunately, the arbitration award was in the borrower's favour and it immediately sought to settle its debt with the bank. The borrower inquired about the total amount owed to the bank under the BBA agreements and it was informed that it was required to pay RM42.045 million (*circa* US$10.5 million) on the understanding that RM1 million (circa US$250,000) in *ta'wīdh* had been waived and in the event the borrower fails to pay that amount, the wavier will be revoked, and the borrower will be liable to pay the full outstanding amount. Even though the borrower was not satisfied with the bank's response to its request for details and statement of accounts on the outstanding amount owed, it paid the full sum demanded by the bank subject to its right to further question and ascertain the actual amount it should have paid as *ta'wīdh* and *ibra'* (rebate) and its right to seek a refund of any excess paid. The payment was accepted by the bank on the terms stipulated by the borrower. Subsequently, the borrower discovered that the bank used a different *ta'wīdh* calculation contrary to the calculation method stipulated in section 9.32 of the agreement. As a result, the borrower sued the bank for a refund of the excess amount paid to it and in a dramatic turn of events, the bank counterclaimed and requested the payment of the *ta'wīdh* discount it granted to the borrower in case the borrower succeed in its claim.

6.35 The High Court dismissed both the borrower's claim and the bank's counterclaim on the ground that the bank had followed the guidelines of BNM in charging its *ta'wīdh*. The court also held that the borrower was estopped from claiming any part of the settlement amount since the parties had reached a compromise on the payment earlier. The borrower was dissatisfied with the decision and therefore appealed to the Court of Appeal. At the same time, the bank also filed a consequential claim that in the event the borrower's claim was successful, it should be entitled to the *ta'wīdh* waiver it granted to the borrower. The Court of Appeal, while setting aside the decision of the High Court, unanimously allowed the borrower's appeal and the counterclaim brought by the bank. The Court of Appeal held that the borrower had paid an excess amount to the bank and that such amount should be refunded, and parties should stick to the contractually agreed rate of 1% *ta'wīdh* for the same period. The bank did not give any prior notice to the borrower on the variation in the *ta'wīdh* rate as required by section 9.32 of the agreement. On the counterclaim filed by the bank, the court agreed with the bank

[40] Ibid, para. 28, 420.

that discount or waiver of part of the *ta'wīdh* would no longer have any effect since the borrower's appeal was allowed.

3.1.5 Waiver of Interest Clause

6.36 In practice, the prohibition of *ribā* is enforced in Islamic contract through what is generally known as the *Waiver of Interest* clause. It is now considered as part of the boilerplate clauses in Islamic contracts. The clause states:

> The Parties recognise and agree that the principle of the payment of interest/usury is repugnant to Sharī'ah and accordingly to the extent that the applicable laws would but for the provisions of this clause, impose whether by contract or by statute an obligation to pay interest/usury or a sum in the nature of interest/usury, the Parties hereby irrevocably and unconditionally expressly waive and reject any entitlement to recover from the other interest/usury or sum in the nature of interest/usury.[41]

Other variations of the clause are:[42]

> The Parties acknowledge and agree that the principle of the payment of interest is repugnant to the principles of Shari'a and accordingly, to the extent that any legal system would impose (whether by contract, statute or court order) any obligation to pay interest, the Parties hereby irrevocably and unconditionally, expressly waive and reject any entitlement to recover interest from each other.
>
> The Bank and the Customer agree that to the extent that any court, contract or statute would impose any obligation to pay or recover interest, the Bank and the Customer each irrevocably and unconditionally waive any entitlement to recover interest from the other.
>
> Each party hereto acknowledges and agrees that, notwithstanding any other provisions of this Agreement, the principle of payment of interest is repugnant to the principles of Shari'a and to the extent that any law or provision would impose (whether by contract or statute) an obligation to pay interest to any other person in relation to this Agreement, each party hereto waives and rejects the entitlement to recover interest from another person.

6.37 Even before the modern prevalence of Islamic contracts in the form of documentation, parties were generally able to waive interest through contractual stipulations.

3.2 *Gharar*

6.38 *Gharar* can be described as ambiguities or excessive or speculative uncertainty in contractual terms and conditions. Such ambiguities in the contract could lead to untoward results. In order to prevent future disputes, the law prohibits such speculative

[41] Adapted from the IIFM Master Commodity Murabahah documentation.
[42] These are from various executed agreements reviewed by the author.

elements in the contract. A contract must clearly spell out the rights and obligations of parties to avoid future disagreements. While the Qur'ān general prohibits transactions tainted with ambiguities that could lead to injustice, the prohibition of *gharar* is firmly established in the Sunnah where certain types of transaction are explicitly prohibited.[43] However, in defining what constitutes *gharar*, Muslim jurists have provided some insights from their respective understanding. Al-Sarakhsi from the Hanafi school defines *gharar* as anything or any arrangement whose consequences are hidden or ambiguous.[44] Similarly, Al-Shirazi of the Shafi'i school defines *gharar* as that whose very nature and consequences are hidden.[45] In a similar fashion, Ibn Taymiyya of the Hanbali school and Al-Qarāfi from the Maliki school define *gharar* as that whose consequences are unknown.[46] In all the definitions, one common factor is the element of uncertainty which leads to ambiguities in the nature and consequences of the contract. In *Shetty v Al Rushaid Petroleum Investment Co*,[47] Lord Justice Floyd attempted to interpret the Saudi law applicable to damages for loss suffered and defined *gharar* thus: 'Shari'a has a doctrine knows as "*gharar*" meaning risk or uncertainty. Future activity is deemed "*gharar*" because it is uncertain to anyone except God.'[48]

3.2.1 The Legal Basis for the Prohibition of *Gharar*

Muslim jurists often cite Qur'ān 4:29 as the basis of the prohibition of *gharar*: 'O you who have believed, do not consume one another's wealth unjustly but only [in lawful] business by mutual consent.' In addition, Muslim jurists have relied on several *ḥadīths* to prohibit *gharar* in contracts. The Prophet has prohibited 'the sale of pebbles and the *gharar* sale', 'the sale of birds in the sky or the fish in the water', 'the catch of the diver', 'unborn calf in its mother's womb', and 'the sperm and/or unfertilized eggs of camels'.[49] **6.39**

3.2.2 Classification of *Gharar*

Gharar is divided into two categories: *gharar fāḥish* (major *gharar*) and *gharar yasir* (nominal *gharar*); while the former is prohibited, the latter is permissible as it is inevitable in contractual dealings. *Gharar yasir* is permissible where the uncertainty is trivial and where the contract is unilateral or has a charitable feature such as a gift. Muslim jurists have accepted some elements of *gharar* in contracts that promote public goods based on *maṣlaḥa*. An example of such a contract is *istiṣnā'a* (construction or **6.40**

[43] *Ḥadīth* No. 2752, see Ahmad bin Hanbal, *Musnad Ahmad* (n 33) Vol. 4, p. 480; *Ḥadīth* No. 6055, see Al-Nasa'i, *Kitab al-Sunan al-Kubr* (n 24) Vol. 6, p. 23.

[44] Al-Sarakhsi, Shams al-Dīn, Kitab al-Mabsūt (Dar al-Ma'rifah, 1985) Vol. 13, p. 194.

[45] Al-Shīrāzi, Ibrahim bin 'Ali bin Yusuf, al-Muhadhdhab fi Fiqh al-Imām al-Shāfi'i (Dār al-Kutub al-'Ilmiyyah, n.d.) Vol. 2, p. 12.

[46] Al-Qarāfi, Shihāb al-Din, Al-Furūq ('Ālim al-Kutub, n.d.) Vol. 3, p. 265; Ibn Taymiyyah, Ahmad bin Abdul Halim, Al-Qawa'id Al-Nuraniyyah al-Fiqhiyyah, Revised by Muhammad Hamid Al-Faqhi (Dar al-Ma'rifah, 1979) p. 116.

[47] [2013] EWHC 1152 (Ch); [2013] All ER (D) 86 (May).

[48] Ibid, para. 161.

[49] The text of the *ḥadīth* reads: 'The Prophet forbade buying what is in the wombs of domestic animals till they give birth; selling what is in their udders; buying a runaway slave; buying (something from) the spoils of war until they are divided; buying Sadaqat before they are received; and the unknown catch (find) of a diver. [Ibn Majah, al-Bazzar and ad-Daraqutni reported it with a weak chain of narrators].' See Al-'Asqalāni, *Bulūgh al-Marām* (n 2) p. 242.

manufacturing contract).[50] As business transactions and trade generally involve an element of risk, minor uncertainty is allowed and would not affect the validity of the contract. In contractual dealings, there could be *force majeure* where a party or both parties might not be able to perform their obligations under the contract. Such situations constitute uncertainty but the permissible type which is inevitable in commercial transactions.

6.41 Examples of major *gharar* include selling commodities that the seller does not own, and he or she is unable to deliver them according to contractual stipulations. For instance, a futures contract is not permissible in Islamic law as in most cases, the seller does not own the commodities at the time he or she promises to sell. The speculative element in derivative contracts is one of the reasons for their prohibition. *Gharar* could also emerge in a contractual arrangement that makes a particular contract contingent on an unknown event. For instance, a contract that provides that the seller would sell a house to the buyer if the value of the property increases to US$1 million within five years could be considered void based on *gharar* as it is speculative. In addition, in Islamic law, parties are not allowed to combine two or more contracts or make one contract contingent on the other. If this were to be allowed, the contracts would have become too complex which would lead to ambiguities and uncertainties resulting in future disputes. One other example of *gharar* is found in future sales where parties conclude a contract but defer the delivery of the commodity and the payment of the price.

3.2.3 *Gharar* Red Flags in Contracts

6.42 In drafting Islamic contracts, it is important to watch out for red flags that could potentially be regarded as *gharar*. These red flags are the main causes for the prohibition of *gharar* in Islamic contracts. Muslim scholars will always watch out for such elements while reviewing draft contracts sent to them for review. These include unascertainable ownership and/or possession of the underlying commodity; ambiguities in information, estimates, and pricing; interdependent and contingent contracts; and clauses relating to games of chance or gambling.

6.43 First, if at the onset it is not clear who owns or possesses the underlying property of the contract, then it is ambiguous and could be invalidated on the ground of *gharar*. The ownership and/or possession of the underlying property in a contract must be ascertained and free from all encumbrances at the time of contract. Future possession or ownership will not be regarded as full ownership and thus cannot lead to a valid transfer of property under a contract. In order to sell the property of someone else, it is important to obtain full power of attorney to execute the sale. If ownership and/or possession is not established, the contract will be tainted with uncertainties which could lead to the inability of the purported seller to deliver the property.

6.44 Secondly, one should check for ambiguities in information, estimates, and pricing. In particular, one needs to ascertain that the parties to the contract have the legal capacity

[50] M.A. Zarqā', Nizam al-Ta'mīn: Haqīqatuhu, Wa al-Ra'yu al-Shar'i fīhī (Mu'assasah al-Risālah, 1994).

to enter into the contract and that the information regarding the underlying property is clear and unambiguous. Information symmetry is paramount in concluding a contract. If the underlying property is not ascertained and the price is not yet determined, the parties will not be able to conclude the contract validly. In extreme cases where there is asymmetry of information, the disadvantaged party is given the right to rescind the contract at a future date.

Thirdly, when the legal relationship is premised on interdependent and contingent contracts, such will not be permissible as the arrangement will be considered speculative. The red flag here is the combination of two or more contracts or when one contract is made contingent on another contract. In addition, when the parties are uncertain whether or not the obligations under the contract will be performed, such legal arrangement will be considered void. Conditional terms and conditions are not permissible, particularly when this involves a sale contract where one sale is contingent upon the finalization of another, or even when one sale is conditional on the occurrence of an extraneous event such as if a party stipulates that they will sell some securities if there is a sudden market shutdown. And fourthly, clauses that have the semblance of a game of chance or gambling should immediately trigger a red flag and should be reviewed. To avoid elements of *gharar* in contracts, one needs to ensure the conditions laid down by Muslim jurists are clearly followed. It is pertinent to ensure that all conditions of a valid contract are present. **6.45**

3.2.4 Prohibition of *Gharar* in Civil Codes

Several countries in the Middle East expressly provide in their Civil Codes that the subject matter of a contract must be free from excessive *gharar*. In the Law No. 22 of 2004 Promulgating the Civil Code of Qatar, Article 150 states: **6.46**

1. The object of an obligation must be sufficiently defined or the contract shall be null and void.
2. If the obligation concerns an object, such object must be defined by itself, its kind, quantity, and degree of quality.

Similarly, and in more comprehensive terms, Article 203 of the UAE Civil Transactions Code, Law No. 5 of 1985 states: **6.47**

(1) In contracts of exchange, the subject matter shall be specified in such a manner as to avoid excessive *Jahala* (lack of knowledge): by reference to it or to the place where it is, if it exists at the time the contract is formed, or by stating its identifying description and quantity if it is an item that can be measured, or by any other means that minimize lack of knowledge.

(2) If the subject matter is known to both contracting parties, there is no requirement that it should be otherwise described or defined.

(3) If the subject matter is not specified as aforesaid, the contract shall be void.[51]

[51] Similar provisions are found in the Iraqi Civil Code, Law No. 41 of 1951, Art. 128; Jordanian Civil Code, Law No. 43 of 1976, Art. 161; Sudanese Civil Transactions Code 1984, Art. 79.

4. Other Prohibited Elements in Contract

6.48 Apart from *ribā* and *gharar*, there are other prohibited elements in contract which could render such contracts void or voidable at the instance of a party. These elements include impermissible subject matter; *qimār* and *maysir*; fraud, deception, and coercion; hoarding and illegal profiteering; and usurpation.

4.1 Impermissible Subject Matter

6.49 The property upon which parties conclude a contract must be permissible in the eyes of the law. A contract for the sale of illegal arms, drugs, alcohol, and even weapons of mass destruction would be invalidated based on impermissible subject matter. In addition, on the basis of such prohibition, one would be precluded from investing in stocks of companies promoting pornography, prostitution, pubs, abortion, casinos, or alcohol. In modern times, there is increasing emphasis on the protection of the environment, hence any contract that would lead to environmental contamination could be regarded as impermissible in Islamic law. If such contracts are upheld as valid, there could be consequences for damages or indemnification.

4.2 *Maysir* (Game of Chance) and *Qimār* (Gambling)

6.50 Both *qimār* (gambling) and *maysir* (game of chance) are discussed under the same heading, as they are used interchangeably by Muslim jurists.[52] Any game of chance could be regarded as *maysir* while *qimār* specifically refers to betting and wagering. Therefore, *maysir* is wider in scope as it includes all forms of gambling. *Maysir* has been defined as *qimār* due to the ease it provides for taking possession without any effort and wealth creation without any productive activity.[53] The prohibition of *maysir* and *qimār* is premised on the fact that one party takes it all while there is no exchange of countervalues between the parties. So, apart from Qur'ān 4:29 which generally prohibits taking the properties of others unjustly, *maysir* is specifically mentioned in Qur'ān 5:90–91.[54]

6.51 Muslim jurists have sometimes used *qimār* and *maysir* interchangeably and provided some insights into what constitutes gambling generally. For instance, Al-Jurjani describes *qimār* as the act of obtaining one thing after the other from another party in a

[52] See Al-Rāzi, Fakhr al-Dīn, al-Tafsīr al-Kabīr (Dār Ihyā al-Turāth al-'Arabi, 1420 A.H.) Vol. 6, p. 400.

[53] Al-Sayyid Salim, Abu Malik Kamal, Sahīh Fiqh al-Sunnah wa Adillatihi Wa Tawdīhi Madhahib al-Aimah (Al-Maktabah al-Tawfiqiyyah, 2003) Vol. 3, p. 292.

[54] Qur'ān 5:90–91 states: 'O you who have believed, indeed, intoxicants, gambling, [sacrificing on] stone altars [to other than Allah], and divining arrows are but defilement from the work of Satan, so avoid it that you may be successful. Satan only wants to cause between you animosity and hatred through intoxicants and gambling and to avert you from the remembrance of Allah and from prayer. So will you not desist?'

game. He also describes it as a winner-takes-all game.[55] Ibn al-'Arabi also defines *qimār* as a game where each of the contestants tries to outsmart his partner in action or statement for the purpose of taking over the prize set aside for the winner.[56] In his unique definition, Al-Shawqani defines *qimār* as a game where one of the players must win while the other loses.[57]

The Hanafi jurist Ibn Abidin described *qimār* and its etymological basis which comes from the word *qamar* that simply means something that increases at times and could decrease at other times. This implies there is the possibility that either of the gamblers could lose his or her wealth to the other party, and such a person may gain from the loss of the other party.[58] In essence, the pendulum could swing either way at any point in time without any productive effort. **6.52**

To consider any term or condition in a contract or transaction to be gambling, four features must be present. First, the transaction must consist of two or more parties. Secondly, a party places his or her wealth at stake with the intention of obtaining someone else's wealth. Thirdly, a stipulation that obtaining a gain of another party's wealth to be contingent upon an uncertain future event whose possibility of occurring is either feasible or not. Fourthly, the wealth which either party puts at stake is completely lost or the other party's wealth is obtained without providing anything in return. **6.53**

The prohibition of *maysir* is the reason for the prohibition of some financial products such as futures and options contracts and a range of other derivatives. In order to provide alternatives to Islamic financial institutions globally, the IIFM collaborated with the International Swaps and Derivatives Association (ISDA) to develop Sharī'ah-compliant contracts that can be used as suitable alternatives to conventional derivatives. The result of this collaborative effort is the ISDA/IIFM Tahawwut Master Agreement generally used by Islamic financial institutions and investors across the world. **6.54**

4.3 Fraud, Deception, and Misrepresentation

Three related prohibited elements in a contract are discussed here while identifying the different nature of each element and its consequence for the validity of the contract in Islamic law. Muslim jurists often use different terms to indicate fraud, deception, or misrepresentation in a contract. These terms are *ghabn*, *tadlīs*, or *taghrīr*, which have sometimes been used interchangeably. But for the purpose of this chapter, it is important to distinguish between the terms, given that their etymological as well as their juristic meanings could be different, something which has a significant implication on their effect on a contract. **6.55**

[55] Al-Jurjāni, 'Ali bin Muhammad, al-Ta'rīfāt (Dār al-Kutub al-'Ilmiyyah, 1983) p. 179.

[56] Ibn al-'Arabi, Muhammad b. 'Abd Allah, 'Aridat al-Ahwadhi fi Sharh al-Tirmidhi (Dār al-Kutub al-'Ilmiyah, 1353/1934).

[57] Al-Shawkāni, Muhammad ibn 'Ali, Nayl al-Awtār (Dar al-Ḥadīth, 1993) Vol. 8, pp. 107–08.

[58] Ibn 'Ābidīn, Muhammad Amin ibn 'Umar, Radd al-Muḥtār 'alá al-Durr al-Mukhtār (Maktabah Mustafa al-Bābi, 1966) Vol. 6, p. 403.

4.3.1 Nature and Meaning

6.56 The word *ghabn* or *ghubn* means fraud, deceit, cheating, or any act undertaken to defraud the other party.[59] The word *tadlīs* simply means deceit, fraud, or any act that is undertaken to swindle another party.[60] In this regard, fraud and deception will be regarded as *tadlīs*. From the lexical meaning of the word *taghrīr*, the word could mean deception or misrepresentation.[61] Another related word often used interchangeably with the terms is *ghash*[62] which also implies deception, deceit, fraud, and any act undertaken by a party to swindle another party.[63] From this lexical analysis, it appears *ghabn* and *tadlīs* can be used synonymously while *taghrīr*, even though it could also be used interchangeably with the two earlier terms as it also implies deception, would be less serious in its effect and thus could mean misrepresentation. Nevertheless, as will be seen below, Muslim jurists have used some of these terms interchangeably while they also differ on the definition and legal implications of some of them.

6.57 From the perspective of juristic usage of the terms and their analysis, a number of issues require further elaboration. Firstly, *ghabn* has been discussed from the perspective of gaining profit, which is the basis of every commercial contract, as both parties seek to maximize their gains (*mughābana*) at the expense of the other party. Even though Islamic law does not oppose profiting in commercial transactions and at the same time has not stipulated any percentage of profit for such transactions, it does however prohibit deception and fraud.[64] An example of this would be the deliberate false misrepresentation of facts (*ghabn fahish*) underpinning the underlying commodity for the contract by the seller. Also, when a seller conceals a defect in the commodity this would be considered deception or fraud. The Maliki jurists consider *tadlīs* and *taghrīr* as meaning the same thing.[65]

6.58 Secondly, another important implication of these terms is that they all lead to the introduction of unfair terms in a contract which is generally regarded as unconscionable behaviour in English contract law. The doctrine of unconscionability in English contract law applies to terms that are exceedingly unjust and operate to benefit one party who has superior bargaining power at the expense of the other party.[66]

[59] Hans Wehr, A Dictionary of Modern Written Arabic, ed. J. Milton Cowan (Spoken Language Services, Inc. 1976) p. 665.

[60] Ibid, p. 290.

[61] Ibid, p. 667.

[62] In the prophetic precedents, there is a *ḥadīth* that uses a derivative word of *ghash*: *man ghashsha falaisa minna* (Whoever deceives is not one of us). Al-Tirmidhi, Abu 'Isa Muhammad bin 'Isa, *Al-Jami' Al-Kabir* (n 3) 582. This *ḥadīth* is a *mutawatir ḥadīth* which implies the report was made by a substantial number of Companions of the Prophet, which makes it undeniably true. This *ḥadīth* was narrated in the context of what the Prophet witnessed in the market where he saw that the food sold was wet inside while being marketed as dry food. See Al-Suyūti, Jalaluddin, Qatf al-Azhar al-Mutanathirah fi al-Akhbār al-Mutawātirah (al-Maktabah al-Islāmi, 1985) p. 196.

[63] Wehr (n 60) p. 674.

[64] Al-Juzairi, 'Abd Al-Rahman, Kitab al-Fiqh 'ala al-Madhāhib al-Arba'ah (Dar al-Kutub al-'Ilmiyyah, 2003) Vol. 2, p. 255.

[65] S.E. Rayner, The Theory of Contracts in Islamic Law A Comparative Analysis with Particular Reference to the Modern Legislation in Kuwait, Bahrain and the United Arab Emirates (Graham & Trotman, 1991) p. 208.

[66] In the English case of *Lloyds Bank Ltd. v Bundy* [1974] EWCA 8, Lord Denning MR succinctly describes the doctrine thus:

> I would suggest that through all these instances there runs a single thread. They rest on 'inequality of bargaining power'. By virtue of it, the English law gives relief to one who . . . enters into a contract or

Thirdly, in understanding the nature of fraud, deception, or misrepresentation, it is pertinent to note that these acts can be perpetrated in different ways. This could be through a fraudulent statement to induce a party unduly to conclude a contract, through actual action, failure to disclose a fundamental term of the contract or commodity, and through the action of a third party which has direct implications on the transactions. 6.59

4.3.2 Elements

For fraud, deception, or fraudulent misrepresentation perpetuated through a positive act in order to induce another party to conclude a contract, four conditions must be met. 6.60

1. The defrauded party should have suffered material damage based on market practices which effectively induces such a party to conclude the contract.
2. The alleged fraud must be appealing to an extent as to induce a reasonable person.
3. One of the contracting parties must be aware of the fraud or defect and have effectively concealed it.
4. The defrauded party must be ignorant of the fraud without any proactive diligent means to be aware of it.[67]

Other Muslim jurists have stipulated that fraud, broadly defined to include misrepresentation, has four main elements: 6.61

1. Misrepresentation of a material fact or fundamental term of the contract (*ghabn fahish*). The misrepresentation must be shown to be false.
2. A clear intent (*niyya*) to deceive the other party. The maker must have known that such a fact is false. Wilful negligence to ascertain certain facts or recklessness will not absolve the maker of such facts from responsibility.
3. There must have been reliance (*'i'timād*) on the information. The innocent party must have relied on the misrepresentation of fact in agreeing to the contract.
4. The defrauded party must have suffered a material loss (*ḍarar*). The misrepresentation must have led to a material loss on the part of the defrauded party.[68]

The above elements of fraud are similar to the provisions found in several Civil Codes of Muslim countries. For example, Article 134 of the Qatari Civil Code states that a contract could be voidable on the ground of fraud by a person who had earlier given his or her consent to a contract. However, such a person needs to prove he would not have 6.62

transfers property for a consideration which is grossly inadequate, when his bargaining power is grievously impaired by reason of his own needs or desires, or by his own ignorance or infirmity, coupled with undue influences or pressures brought to bear on him by or for the benefit of the other. When I use the word 'undue' I do not mean to suggest that the principle depends on proof of any wrongdoing. The one who stipulates for his own excessive sum may be moved solely by his own self-interest, unconscious of the distress he is bringing to the other. I have also avoided any reference to the will of the one being 'dominated' or 'overcome' by the other, One who is in extreme need may knowingly consent to a most improvident bargain, solely to relieve the straits in which he finds himself.

[67] Noel J. Coulson, Commercial Law in the Gulf States: The Islamic Legal Tradition (Graham & Trotman, 1984) p. 86.

[68] M.T. Mansuri, Islamic Law of Contracts and Business Transactions (Adam Publishers and Distributors, 2010).

agreed to the contract if he had not been fraudulently induced to agree to the contract. Such fraudulent misrepresentation includes misrepresentation of facts of the contract or refusal to reveal a material fact when needed.

6.63 In the United Arab Emirates Civil Code, Articles 185, 186, and 187 state:

- Misrepresentation is when one of the two contracting parties deceives the other by means of trickery of word or deed which leads the other to consent to what he would not otherwise have consented to.
- Deliberate silence concerning a fact or set of circumstances shall be deemed to be a misrepresentation if it is proved that the person misled thereby would not have made the contract had he been aware of that fact or set of circumstances.
- If one of the contracting parties makes a misrepresentation to the other and it transpires that the contract was concluded by a gross cheat, the person so misled may cancel the contract.

4.3.3 Effects on Contract

6.64 The party who is defrauded may rescind the contract through the exercise of the option of fraud (*khiyār al-tadlīs*) and in other cases where the defect not identified was in the underlying commodity, it could be the option of defect (*khiyār al-ayb*). The main reason for the prohibition of fraud, deception, and misrepresentation is the implication of such conduct or term on the consent of one of the parties to the contract. Nevertheless, Muslim jurists have differed on the proper legal consequences of fraud, deception, and misrepresentation in a contract. Generally, for *tadlīs*, the buyer is given the option to revoke the contract and a maximum of three days is given to exercise such option.[69] In this case, *tadlīs* will only lead to a voidable contract at the instance of the buyer. On the other hand, *taghrīr* and *ghash* would lead to a void contract.[70]

6.65 Muslim jurists have also stipulated the possibility of an exercisable option for *ghubn* in sales contracts.[71] This has been discussed from two different perspectives: the seller and buyer in a contract of sale. First, *ghubn* that occurs from the perspective of the seller could be a situation where he or she sells a commodity for less than the actual amount unknowingly. Secondly, from the perspective of the buyer, there could be a situation where he or she unwittingly purchases a commodity above the market rate. Any party in a sales contract that finds himself or herself in such a situation where there is clear misrepresentation of facts is given the option of return (*khiyār al-rujū'*) in the sales contract and to void the contract accordingly. However, this is subject to the condition that he or she did not know the price of the commodity at the onset and there was no proper bargaining.

[69] Sayyid Sābiq, Fiqh al-Sunnah (Dar al-Ḥadīth, 2004) p. 923.
[70] Ibid, p. 924.
[71] Hanbali jurists agree with an exercisable option for *ghubn*, in contradiction with majority of the jurists. See Al-Tayyār, Abdullah, al-Fiqh al-Muyassar (Madār al-Watan, 2012) Vol. 6, p. 61.

4.4 Coercion

Coercion or duress (*ikrāh*) is not acceptable in contracts as it defeats the objective of free consent of the parties. It vitiates the legal capacity to conclude the contract. As discussed above, parties should conclude contracts freely. This is the essence of freedom of contract and party autonomy. In the absence of such freedom, a party may be given the option to rescind the contract. Ibn Hajar Al-Asqalani has defined coercion as compelling another person to do what he does not wish to do (such as to agree to certain terms and conditions of a contract).[72] Coercion could also mean a potential threat to induce another party to conclude a contract. Coercion can be carried out either directly against the coerced person or against her or her property or even a dependent. According to Al-Sarakhsi, the core elements of coercion are twofold: the coercer and the coerced.[73] In these two elements, there are other sub-elements which may be considered while ascertaining whether coercion is involved in the formation of a contract. These sub-elements include the possibility of a third party causing the coercion. In addition, the threat must be targeted at making the coerced party enter the agreement. Furthermore, the threatened act could either be physical or psychological with the intention of compelling the coerced party to enter the contract. 6.66

Coercion in contract can be classified into two types: unjust coercion (*ikrāh bi ghayr ḥaqq*) and just coercion (*ikrāh bi ḥaqq*). Under unjust coercion, the Hanafi jurists classified coercion into constraining (*mulji'*) and non-constraining (*ghayr mulji'*) coercion. It is pertinent to note that constraining coercion is also referred to as complete coercion, while the non-constraining type is also called incomplete coercion. While both types of coercion would nullify consent in a contract, it is only the constraining coercion that has the legal consequence of nullifying choice. On the other hand, the non-constraining coercion only negates consent but does not negate choice.[74] In this case, the Hanafis make a clear distinction between consent and choice. The example given for non-constraining coercion is when the threat is directed at a third party such as a family member. Bazdawi refers to this kind of coercion as moral coercion (*ikrāh adabi*) even though it is suggested that this type of coercion should be classified under the non-constraining coercion.[75] 6.67

While the majority of the jurists agreed with the Hanafis' broad classification of unjust coercion, they clarified the nature of the constraining coercion with additional emphasis on the fact that the coerced person must be in a situation where he has no power or choice in any manner to do otherwise. A general finding from juristic analysis reveals that due to the sanctity of a contract, the distinction between constraining and 6.68

[72] Al-'Asqalāni, Ibn Hajar, Fath al-Bāri (Beirut: Dār al-Ma'rifah, n.d.) Vol. 12, p. 311.
[73] Al-Sarakhsi (n 45) Vol. 11, p. 64.
[74] Al-Dubyān, Abu 'Umar Dubyān bin Muhammad, Al-Mu'āmalāt al-Māliyyah Asālah wa Mu'āsarah (Maktabah al-Malik Fahd Al-Wataniyyah, 1432H) Vol. 2, p. 53.
[75] Hafiz al-Din 'Abdullah Ibn Ahmad al-Nasifi, Kashf al-Asrār (Dār al-Kutub al-'Ilmiyyah, n.d.) Vol. 4, p. 1518.

non-constraining coercion will have no legal significance as consent is paramount in contractual relations.

6.69 Therefore, according to Hanafi and Maliki jurists, once it is established that a party has been coerced into a contract, whether constraining or non-constraining, the contract will be voidable at the instance of the coerced party. In essence, Hanafi jurists opine that the contract is *fāsid* or defective while the Maliki jurists argue that the contract could be considered valid but without any legal consequences (*ghayr lāzim*).[76] Interestingly, Maliki jurists also opined that the coercer could also rescind the contract upon an express approval from the coerced party. While the Hanafi jurists agreed with the Maliki position, they added a proviso that they would only allow the coercer to rescind the contract upon express consent of the coerced person, provided that the former had taken full possession of the subject matter of the contract. On their part, the Hanbali and Shafi'i jurists argue that such contract is void.[77]

6.70 The second type, which is justified coercion, is also known as legal compulsion (*ijbār sharʿī*) where the authorities or government compel a person to undertake a valid act. This could relate either to an issue affecting public interest or another person. Under this category, a person can be compelled by the authorities, including a competent court of law, to repay a debt.[78] The jurists unanimously agree that for such force to be used legally, what is being required of the subject of such compulsion must be permissible in the eyes of the law.[79] This type of coercion does not have much implication on the formation of contract but it could be relevant in legal enforceability of contracts, such as when a party defaults in a loan financing contract. In such a situation, the court may be able to compel the defaulting party to liquidate his or her own properties to settle the debt.

6.71 Muslim jurists have expressed different opinions on the validity of a contract made under coercion. The Maliki as well as some Hanafi jurists opined that a contract of sale made under coercion remains valid even though the effect of such contract will be suspended or contingent upon another condition (*mawqūf*).[80] On the contrary, the Shafi'i and Hanbali jurists held that when a contract is tainted with coercion, such contract is void *ab initio* (*bātil*), which means it has no legal effect whatsoever. This opinion is premised on the need for consent in every commercial contract as required by Qurʾān 4:29. In addition, a majority of the Hanafi jurists opined that a contract of sale concluded with some elements of coercion will not be considered void but defective and improper (*fāsid*). The effect of a defective contract, which remains improper, is that the contract could be ratified by the coerced party if he or she gives consent.[81]

[76] Al-Dubyān (n 75) Vol. 2, pp. 67–68.
[77] Ibid, Vol. 2, pp. 69–70.
[78] See Muhammad Shaqrah, Al-Ikrāh waatharuhu fi tasaarufat (Manar Islami, 1986).
[79] Ibid.
[80] Al-Dubyān (n 75) Vol. 2, pp. 67–69.
[81] Sābiq (n 70) p. 908.

4.5 Hoarding, Illegal Profiteering, and Price Fixing

Two related concepts, which are often considered as prohibitions within the general discourse on commercial contracts, are hoarding (*iḥtikār*) and illegal profiteering or price fixing (*tasʿīr*) that is occasioned by a cartel. In most cases, hoarding and monopoly lead to illegal profiteering, hence they are discussed under the same heading. Hoarding is also considered within the general context of market monopoly as it is defined as the practice of buying and storing essential commodities such as food while anticipating a price increase as a result of a shortage of such commodities in the market.[82] Just as competition law is used to regulate market practices, such as regulating anti-competitive conduct in modern economies, Islamic law had provided such standard guidance on the need to allow a free market, which effectively allows the market to determine prices of commodities. Therefore, any contractual term or condition that would have the legal consequence of hoarding, monopoly, or illegal profiteering will be prohibited in a contract.[83] This implies that Islamic law does not allow parties to conclude anti-competitive agreements. The Qur'ān explicitly prohibits hoarding and market monopoly.[84] Several prophetic precedents also point to the fact that such prohibited practices extend to illegal profiteering.[85] It is also important to add that the law does not stipulate the extent of the profit rate to be utilized in various contracts, but there is a clear prohibition of fraud and deception which could lead to profiteering. 6.72

[82] Mufti Muhammad Taqi Usmani, Fiqh al-Buyū ʿala Madhāhib al-ʿArbaʿa (Quranic Studies Publishers, 2015) Vol. 2, pp. 997–99.

[83] Ibid.

[84] For instance, Qur'ān 9:34 states: 'O you who have believed, indeed many of the scholars and the monks devour the wealth of people unjustly and avert [them] from the way of Allah. And those who hoard gold and silver and spend it not in the way of Allah—give them tidings of a painful punishment.' Also, Qur'ān 59:7 states: 'so that it will not be a perpetual distribution among the rich from among you.' In addition, Qur'ān 7:85 states: 'And to [the people of] Madyan [We sent] their brother Shuʿayb. He said, "O my people, worship Allah; you have no deity other than Him. There has come to you clear evidence from your Lord. So fulfil the measure and weight and do not deprive people of their due and cause not corruption upon the earth after its reformation. That is better for you, if you should be believers."' Other legal texts that have been used to support the prohibition of hoarding, monopoly and illegal profiteering are Qur'ān 5:8: 'O you who have believed, be persistently standing firm for Allah, witnesses in justice, and do not let the hatred of a people prevent you from being just. Be just; that is nearer to righteousness. And fear Allah; indeed, Allah is [fully] Aware of what you do.' Qur'ān 107:4–7: 'So woe then . . . those who want only to be seen and praised And deny and bar even the smallest items [to their fellow-men]!'

[85] The following represents a selected list of prophetic precedents that support the prohibition of hoarding and illegal profiteering:

1. 'Whoever hoards food is a sinner.'
2. 'Spend in charity and do not count it, lest Allah count it against you. Do not hoard it, lest Allah withhold from you.'
3. 'Whoever hoards food away from the Muslims, Allah will afflict him with leprosy and poverty.'
4. 'In hell there is a specific valley for the monopolizers, those addicted to alcohol and lusts.'
5. 'Verily the motive of food is to be prosperous and bestowed upon, whilst the monopolizer (by barring that) is accursed.'
6. 'Any person who buys food and withholds it forty days desiring to inflate the price then sells it and gives charity from its profit, there is no expiation of his sin for what he has done.'
7. 'The person who refuses to supply his neighbourly needs, on the Day of Judgment Allah will refuse to give him His goodness and leaves him to himself—and what a bad case it is for the one whom He leaves to himself!'

See Muslim, *Sahīh Muslim* (n 25) Vol. 4, p. 308; Taqi Usmani (n 83) Vol. 2, pp. 1000–02; Al-Tirmidhi, *Al-Jāmiʿ Al-Kabīr* (n 3) 1267, Vol. 2, pp. 545–46.

6.73 Profiteering through price fixing is generally prohibited in Islamic law. Anas reported that people once approached the Prophet and said to him: 'Prices have soared; kindly set the price for us.' Then the Prophet answered: 'Verily, Allah is the One who sets price, who holds back, who makes things easy, and grants sustenance. I definitely want to meet Allah without anybody claiming against me as a result of an oppression done as a result of blood matters or matters relating to their wealth.'[86] In interpreting this *ḥadīth*, Ibn Qudama explained that a proper understanding of the prophetic precedent could be garnered from two related perspectives. First, the Prophet was reluctant to fix prices even though his Companions had approached him to do so due to soaring prices of commodities in the market. It is thus clear that if fixing prices, which may not be as harmful as profiteering, were to be permitted by Allah, then he would have done so without any hesitation. However, due to the freedom given by Allah to human beings to transact as they wish within certain limits stipulated by law, such price fixing is not allowed. Party autonomy and freedom to determine a discounted price through mutual consent are encouraged rather than a top-down approach from the government. Islamic law believes in the role of market forces, including genuine demand and supply and the cost of production to determine the prices of commodities rather than an overwhelming state regulation. Secondly, it can be deduced from the *ḥadīth* above that price fixing could lead to acts of oppression forbidden in Islam.[87]

6.74 Imam Shawkani has emphasized that people should be free to exercise authority over their property and wealth generally, so price fixing is a glaring impediment to such freedom.[88] The state should be concerned about the overall welfare of the people and not the welfare or interest of the sellers alone, or, on the other hand, the welfare or interest of the buyers alone. Therefore, reducing the prices unnecessarily without taking into consideration the cost of production will be detrimental to the interest of the merchants. On the other hand, increasing the prices unnecessarily without taking into consideration market forces with the sole intent of protecting the interest of the merchants or sellers will be detrimental to the interest of the buying public and would ultimately lead to inflation. This also has the potential to deny the parties autonomy and the main element of consent will be missing in the sale contracts.

6.75 The nexus between profiteering and hoarding is seen in the fact that price fixing will always lead to hoarding, which ultimately results in high prices of commodities when the demand is high and supply is limited. High prices will cause untold hardship on the people, particularly the less privileged in society. The less privileged and the poor will not be able to buy essential commodities.

[86] Al-Tirmidhi, Al-Jāmiʿ Al-Kabīr (n 3) 1314, Vol. 2, p. 582.
[87] Ibn Qudāmah ʿAbdullah Ibn Muhammad, Al-Mughni (Dār ʿĀlim al-Kutub, 1997) Vol. 6, p. 312 (hereafter Ibn Qudāmah, *Al-Mughni*).
[88] Al-Shawkāni (n 58) Vol. 5, p. 260.

4.5.1 Permissible Price Control: Exception to the General Rule?

Regardless of the general rule on the prohibition of profiteering and price fixing, there are exceptions to the rule where price control may be introduced. Such is the case of a cartel among the sellers where they create unnecessary inflation by fixing prices of commodities. Such artificial market disruption is curtailed through state intervention to implement price control measures for the benefit of the masses. In allowing the state to step in, fundamental rights of people are protected and hoarding is prevented. This is the reason why a majority of jurists allow price control in particular circumstances.[89] Similarly, some Shafi'i jurists also permit price control on this basis, particularly in inflationary situations.[90] Therefore, price control would be allowed where such measure serves the general public interest.[91] Muslim jurists therefore allow price control measures to be implemented in the following situations: first, where entrepreneurs determine prices of essential commodities arbitrarily, the state is required to step in to control such prices;[92] secondly, price control measures can be introduced when there is an urgent general public need for manufactured goods;[93] thirdly, when a price increase is caused by hoarding, the state may compel hoarders to sell their stockpiles at a fair market price;[94] fourthly, also when there is price volatility as a result of anti-competitive practices such as monopoly, the state is required to step in to stem the tide;[95] fifthly, when there is a cartel among sellers or even, in extreme situations, among buyers, the state is required to enforce price control to stabilize the economy;[96] and sixthly, the state is required to step in and control prices and wages when certain essential services required by the community are in question.[97] 6.76

4.5.2 Effect of Profiteering on Contracts

Since profiteering, price control, and hoarding are generally forbidden in Islamic law, in the event that any clause is included in a contract that purports to lead to any of these, it may not be considered void provided the parties agree to the terms and the requirement for consent is fulfilled. To address this issue, many modern Muslim states have introduced competition laws which are part of the overarching frameworks for consumer protection. For instance, section 2 of the UAE Federal Law No. 4 of 2012 Concerning Regulation of Competition[98] states the objectives of the law as follows: 6.77

[89] See Al-Rāzi, Zayn al-Dīn, Tuhfat al-Mulūk (Dār al-Bashāir al-Islamiyyah, 1417 A.H.) p. 235; Ibn Abd al-Barr, al-Kāfi fi Fiqhi Ahl al-Madīnah (Maktabat al-Riyādh al-Hadīthah, 1980) Vol. 2, p. 730; Ibn Taymiyyah, Taqiy al-Dīn, Majmū' al-Fatāwa (Majma' al-Malik Fahad, 1995) Vol. 29, p. 254.

[90] Al-Nawawi, Yahya ibn Sharaf, Raudat al-Tālibīn Wa 'Umdat al-Muftīn (al-Maktab al-Islāmi, 1991) Vol. 3, p. 413.

[91] Sābiq (n 70) p. 920.

[92] Ibn Taimiyah, Al-Hisbah fi Al-Islam (Dar Al-Kutub Al-Ilmiyyah, n.d.) p. 22.

[93] Ibn 'Ābidīn (n 59) Vol. 6, p. 400.

[94] Ibn Taimiyah (n 93) pp. 21–22.

[95] Ibid, pp. 22–23.

[96] Ibn Qudāmah 'Abdullah Ibn Muhammad, Al-Turuq Al-Hukmiyyah (Maktabah Dar Al-Bayan, n.d.) p. 208.

[97] Ibid, p. 24.

[98] The Law was published on 23 October 2012.

1. Providing a stimulating environment for establishments in order to enhance efficiency, competitiveness and the interest of consumers and to achieve sustainable development in the UAE; and
2. Keeping a competitive market governed by the market mechanisms in accordance with the economic freedom principle through banning restrictive agreements, business and actions that lead to the abuse of a dominant position, controlling the operations of economic concentration and avoiding all that may prejudice, limit or prevent competition.

6.78 Similarly, Saudi Arabia has a Competition Law[99] which extends anti-competitive practices or arrangements to agreements and contracts among corporate entities containing clauses deemed anti-competitive. Such agreements or contracts will be considered void on the ground of violation of competition. Similar provisions, which were inspired by a mixture of Islamic law and the civil law, are seen in the Qatari Competition Law, which was enacted in 2006.[100] In order to oversee the overall implementation of the Law, the Competition Protection and Anti-Monopoly Committee was set up pursuant to Article 7 of the Law. One unique feature of the Qatari Law which is similar to the Saudi Competition Law is the prohibition on entering into any agreement or the conclusion of any contract whatsoever that violates rules of competition.[101] This is generally consistent with the views of Muslim jurists discussed above which prohibit restrictive agreements.

4.5.3 Has Islam Stipulated a Profit Limit?

6.79 In Islamic jurisprudence, there is no evidence that suggests a maximum limit in pricing goods generally. While there is no direct textual evidence in the Qur'ān to justify

[99] The Law was issued by Royal Decree no. M/75 dated 29/6/1440H (corresponding to 6 March 2019).

[100] Qatar Law No. 19 of 2006.

[101] Article 3 of the Qatari Competition Law states:

It is forbidden to enter into agreements, to conclude contracts or to undertake practices that violate the rules of competition, in particular the following:

1. Manipulating the prices of the products being handled, either by raising, lowering or fixing those prices, or by any other means.
2. Limiting the freedom of products to enter or exit markets, either completely or partially, by concealing them, refusing to handle them despite the fact that they are available, or stockpiling them without justification.
3. Deliberately provoking a sudden glut of products which causes them to circulate at a price that affects the economic performance of other competitors.
4. Preventing or hindering any person from practicing economic or commercial activity on the market.
5. Unjustifiably concealing from a particular individual, either completely or partially, the products available on the market.
6. Restricting production, manufacture, distribution or marketing of products; or limiting the distribution, volume or kind of services, or placing conditions or restrictions on their supply.
7. Dividing or allocating product markets on the basis of geographical area, distribution centres, type of customers, seasons or time periods, or goods.
8. Coordination or agreement among competitors with regard to presenting, or failing to present, bids in public tenders, negotiations and calls for procurement.
   This does not include joint offers previously announced by the participating parties, as long as this is not in any way intended to prevent competition.
9. Knowingly distributing false information about products or their prices.

seeking profit and its limits, some prophetic precedents may be instructive in this regard. In a *ḥadīth* narrated by 'Urwah Al-Bariqi, the Prophet gave him one dinar to buy a goat on his behalf. 'Urwah ended up using the money to buy two goats; he sold one of them for a dinar and finally delivered a goat and one dinar to the Prophet. While the Prophet was visibly surprised when 'Urwah briefed him on what transpired, he prayed for him by saying the sale should be blessed by God. The blessing the Prophet invoked on 'Urwah extends to all his business dealings to the extent that if he had bought dust, he could have made reasonable profit from it.[102] This *ḥadīth* provides general evidence on the permissibility of profit-making in business transactions but it does not purport to support any rate of profit or pricing policy in commercial transactions. This is seen in another prophetic saying where Jabir narrated that the Prophet said: 'May Allah show mercy to a man who is kind when he sells, when he buys and when he makes a claim.'[103]

Therefore, the principle in Islamic contract law is that Islam does not stipulate any profit rate or limit in business transactions. There is no limit on the amount of profit one can make in business dealings. Profit should be determined by a number of factors including cost of production or procurement, demand and supply factors, and scarcity of products. People are however encouraged to avoid taking advantage of others, hence reasonable profit should be stipulated when concluding sale contracts. A fair market price is encouraged, particularly if such a price is known. While there is no maximum limit in profit determination, parties should avoid profiteering. **6.80**

4.6 Usurpation (*Ghasb*)

Simply put, *ghasb* means usurpation, which is anything done to seize the property, or even a right of another person, unjustly. It is the illegal seizure of another person's property, wealth, or right forcefully. Etymologically, the word *ghasb* is derived from *gh-a-sa-ba* which literally means to tackle something away by force or illegally. It could also mean to extort something from someone through any means. The verb has also been used to refer to taking illegal possession of something, to seize unlawfully, or usurp.[104] This literal meaning appeared in a verse of the Qur'ān where, in a narration, a ship was said to be unduly seized by a king.[105] In Islamic law, the word *ghasb* means 'forcible, **6.81**

[102] This *ḥadīth* was reported by all the *ḥadīth* collections except Al-Nasa'i. The actual text of the *ḥadīth* is: 'Urwah al-Bariqi narrated, the Messenger of Allah gave him a Dinar to buy a sacrificial animal or a sheep. He bought two sheep and sold one of them for Dinar. Upon his return, the Prophet invoked Allah to bless his dealings of buying and selling. It was such that if he had bought (even) dust, he would have made a profit from it.' See Ibn Hajar Al-Asqalani, Bulugh Al-Maram min adilat al-ahkam: Attainment of the Objective According to Evidence of the Ordinances, trans. Nancy Eweiss, ed. Selma Cook (Dar Al-Manarah, 2003) pp. 301–02.

[103] Al-Nawawi, Riyādh al-Sālihīn (Al-Maktabah Al-Islāmi, 1996) p. 475.

[104] Wehr (n 60) p. 675.

[105] This story, in which the word '*ghasb*' was clearly mentioned, is narrated in Qur'ān 18:17 which states: 'As for the ship, it belonged to poor people working at sea. So I intended to cause defect in it as there was after them a king who seized every [good] ship by force.'

illegal seizure, extortion, usurpation, unlawful arbitrariness'[106] that seeks to deprive another party of his or her property or legal right in an unjust manner.[107]

4.6.1 Prohibition of *Ghasb*

6.82 Dispositions that lead to *ghasb* are prohibited in the Qur'ān and Sunnah as well as by the consensus of Muslim jurists. In the Qur'ān, Muslim jurists have relied on the following verse as the basis of the express prohibition of *ghasb*: 'And eat up not one another's property unjustly (in any illegal way, such as stealing, robbing, deceiving.'[108] The prohibition of *ghasb* stems from the general attitude of Islamic law to protection and preservation of the inalienable right to property and wealth. Therefore, any omission or commission that seeks to deprive individuals of their property rights in an unjust manner will be frowned on by the law. In essence, the prohibition is premised on the acquisition of any property or wealth through illegal means such as usurpation and other unjust means such as theft, corruption, illegal possession, and even benefit obtained through *riba*.[109]

6.83 Also, in the Sunnah, several prophetic precedents point to the prohibition or moral condemnation of dispositions that lead to *ghasb*. For instance, the Prophet said: 'Whoever seizes a handspan of land unlawfully, will surround him to the depth of seven earths.'[110] In another *ḥadīth*, it was reported that the Prophet said:

> Whoever has done any wrong to his brother, let him seek his forgiveness today, before there will be no dinar and no dirham [i.e., the Day of Resurrection], when if he has any good deeds, some of his good deeds will be taken and given to the one who was wronged, and if he does not have any good deeds, some of the bad deeds of the one who was wronged will be taken and thrown onto him, and he will be thrown into Hell.[111]

6.84 In his last sermon, the Prophet emphasized the sanctity of property and equated it with sanctity of life and Muslims were asked to ensure they respect each other's properties and avoid unnecessary and unjust interference with the property rights of others. Al-Bukhari reported that as part of the farewell sermon the Prophet said:

> O People! just as you regard this month, this day, this city as sacred, so regard the life and property of every Muslim a sacred trust. Return the goods entrusted to you to their rightful owners. Hurt no one so that no one may hurt you. Remember that you will indeed meet your Lord, and that he will indeed reckon your deeds.[112]

106 Wehr (n 60) p. 675.
107 Sābiq (n 70) p. 975.
108 Qur'ān 2:188.
109 Taqi Usmani (n 83) Vol. 2, p. 1006.
110 *Ḥadīth* No. 2453. See Al-Bukhāri (n 25) Vol. 2, p. 193.
111 Al-Bukhāri (n 25) Vol. 2, p. 197.
112 Ibid, Vol. 4, p. 248.

This *ḥadīth*, among numerous others, also points to the fact that usurpation is prohibited in Islamic law as it violates one of the five essentials identified as higher objectives of Islamic law: preservation of wealth (*hifẓ al-māl*).

4.6.2 What Happens to the Usurped Property?

It is therefore not allowed for the usurper who might have unjustly coerced the other party to conclude the contract to benefit from the usurped property or even deal in it contractually in whatever manner. What is required of the usurper is to return the property to the legal owner or, in the event that the owner is no longer alive, then the property will be returned promptly to his or her legal heirs. There are however extreme situations where the owner of the property or his heir can no longer be ascertained or cannot be easily reached; then, after exhausting all legal means to get to the legal owner, the usurper is allowed to donate the property to charity without the expectation of any reward whatsoever.[113] **6.85**

According to Imam al-Muwaffaq: 'The scholars agreed that it is obligatory to return the seized property if it is still in its original condition and has not changed.'[114] In addition to returning the seized property, any increase or benefit derived from such property while it was usurped must be returned to the original owner regardless of whether such increase or benefit was extraneous to the usurped property or directly connected to it. **6.86**

In the case of real estate, if the usurper has built any structure on the property or even plants crops on the land, the legal owner has the right to request that the usurper remove any structure built thereon as well as removing the crops planted.[115] Any property illegally obtained by a usurper will be forfeited without any compensation whatsoever. This seems to be the principle later established under the English law: *quicquid plantatur solo, solo cedit*, which simply means 'whatever is affixed to the ground, belongs to the ground'.[116] **6.87**

In the event that the usurper damages the property during its illegal possession, he or she is required to pay reasonable compensation to the legal owner after due assessment of the extent of damage done.[117] In addition, the compensation to the legal owner could also include rent payable for the period in which the property was usurped.[118] The usurper is required to pay the rent payable from the time the property was usurped up to the time it is returned to the legal owner. In determining the amount of rent payable, fair market value of rent payable for similar property will be utilized as a benchmark. **6.88**

[113] Taqi Usmani (n 83) Vol. 2, p. 1006.
[114] Ibn Qudāmah, *Al-Mughni* (n 88) Vol. 7, p. 401.
[115] Al-Zuhaili, Wahbah bin Mustafa, al-Fiqh al-Islāmi Wa Adillatuhu (Dār al-Fikr, n.d.) Vol. 6, p. 4813.
[116] This legal maxim has its origins in Roman law, and it is often traced to the Roman jurist Gaius. Blackburn J. in *Holland v Hodgson* (1872) LR 7 CP 328: 'There is no doubt that the general maxim of the law is, that what is annexed to the land becomes part of the land. . . .' See generally Peter Luther, 'Fixtures and Chattels: A Question of More or Less . . .' (2004) 24(4) Oxford Journal of Legal Studies 597–618.
[117] Al-Zuhaili (n 116) Vol. 6, p. 4801.
[118] Ibid, p. 4818.

The reason for this is that during the time the legal owner was deprived of the beneficial use of the property, the rent payable is a loss to him or her and, as such, the person is entitled to fair compensation.

6.89 The action for the recovery of usurped land is known as *istiḥqāq* in Islamic law and it is often brought by an interested party to ensure that usurped land is restored to the original owner. There is a rebuttable presumption in Islamic law that the original owner of a land continues to own it until the new claimant successfully rebuts the presumption by proving a better title. This presumption of legal title was later recognized and adopted in the English law as assize.[119] This explains the often-downplayed close relationship between Islamic law and English contract law discussed in the last section of this chapter.

6.90 Another question which could be relevant in today's financial markets where people buy and sell stocks on a regular basis is: if a person seizes another party's property, such as illegally obtained stocks, what happens if the price of such stocks suddenly drops in a highly volatile market? Muslim jurists have expressed different opinions on this issue, but the most correct opinion preferred by the majority is that in the event of a drop in price of the property usurped, the usurper must make it up to the fair market price to ensure no loss is recorded on the part of the legal owner.[120]

4.6.3 Effect on Contract

6.91 The effect of usurpation on the validity of the contract is essential to identify the implications of any clause that seeks to usurp another party's property in the terms contained in the agreement. This will determine the consequence of such a clause on the validity of the contract. When a contract of sale is concluded where the usurper intends to transfer the usurped property to another party through a sale, the applicable rule in Islamic law differs, depending on the nature of the usurped property. If the usurped property is a commodity or goods, it is not allowed for a third-party purchaser to buy such property. For instance, if the sale contract is concluded and the third-party purchaser without notice buys the property, the sale contract is considered *mawqūf* or an inactive sale contract which is pending approval as it involves others' rights. This is the view of Hanafi jurists, as such an inactive sale contract requires the approval of the legal owner for it to be effective.[121]

6.92 Therefore, if the legal owner refuses to give his or her consent and nullifies the contract, it then becomes void. And if a contract becomes void, the third-party purchaser without notice must promptly return the usurped property and the seller is also required to return the price to the buyer. On the contrary, if the legal owner permits the

[119] See a comprehensive analysis on the relationship between Islamic contract law and its far-reaching effect on modern English contract law in John A. Makdisi, 'The Islamic Origins of the Common Law' (1999) 77(5) North Carolina Law Review 1635, p. 1665.

[120] Taqi Usmani (n 83) p. 1006.

[121] Ibn Nujaym, Zayn al-Dīn, al-Bahr al-Rāiq Sharh Kanz al-Daqāiq (Dār al-Kitab al-Islāmi, n.d.) Vol. 6, p. 86; Ibn Qudāmah, *Al-Mughni* (n 88) Vol. 7, p. 399.

contract to take effect before any ensuing dispute, then the sale contract becomes valid. However, if the approval on the part of the legal owner comes after a dispute has arisen and the judge has delivered judgment on the issue, the sale contract will not be valid according to Abu Hanifah, but such a contract is considered valid according to other Hanafi jurists on the basis of the consent of the legal owner being the effective cause of the validity of the hitherto inactive sale contract.[122]

Conversely, if the usurped property is currency or money or any other negotiable instrument as commonly used in the modern day, different rules would apply. According to a unanimous opinion of the Muslim jurists, if the usurper intends to transfer the negotiable instrument or buys anything with the usurped property, such disposition will not be permissible under the law unless he or she posts a guarantee to that effect. But if the usurper purchases anything with the usurped money before posting the guarantee, Ibn Rushd has mentioned that such contract is not valid according to the views of Shafi'i jurists. Some other jurists opine that such a sale contract is valid but the deprived party who is the original legal owner would seek return of the purchased item from the usurper. The Maliki jurists opined that, in all situations, no one may purchase such a commodity from the usurper, probably because it was originally bought with usurped money.[123] **6.93**

5. Flipping the Coin: The Positive Dimension

As evident throughout this chapter, Islamic law, particularly its financial and commercial transactions, are often viewed from the perspective of strict prohibitions and negative screenings which generally smack of exclusions rather than promoting commercial transactions. This prohibitive feature is seen in the underlying theories of Islamic contract law. However, the other side of the coin is often obscured by preconceived prejudices against Islamic law generally. In essence, there is the positive dimension of the prohibited elements in financial and commercial contracts in Islamic law. The most important principle, which is the basis of Islamic contract law, is that all transactions, whether financial, commercial, or even non-contractual obligations, are permissible. **6.94**

In essence, the default rule in every transaction is permissibility. Such a wide ambit of permissibility allows counterparties to deal with each other in various ways whether such contracts were contemplated in the traditional Islamic law or not. This principle allows Muslim jurists of any time or clime to extend basic rules of Islamic law to any new or emerging contract. There are numerous modern transactions such as cryptocurrencies and other transactions carried out using Blockchain which were not known to traditional Islamic law. However, while relying on the principle of **6.95**

[122] Taqi Usmani (n 83) p. 1008.
[123] Ibid, p. 1009.

permissibility, such transactions could be regarded as valid in the eyes of Islamic law, provided all the boxes are checked. This does not portend that all cryptocurrency contracts are valid under Islamic law, but they could be reviewed for validity under the law by competent Muslim jurists who should opine on the legality of the individual product presented to them.

6.96 On the contrary, modern positive law provides for specific rules codified in statutes or handed down through judicial precedents with numerous regulations, which effectively state what the law is. In legal jurisprudence, the unique theories that are relevant to the modern legislative philosophy are premised on two schools of thoughts: positivist and realist schools. Rather than the general permissibility rule for commercial transactions in Islamic law, legal positivism would adopt a different approach. For instance, in legal positivism, the Austin's command theory has three main tenets: first, laws, whether commercial, criminal, or otherwise, are commands which are issued by the sovereign, often referred to as the 'uncommanded commander'; secondly, the commands are enforced through sanctions imposed by the sovereign; and thirdly, the sovereign is anybody who is obeyed by the majority.[124] This is, in part, the source of modern positive law made by a legislature, which comprises duly elected members.

6.97 Another relevant theory of analytical jurisprudence is the realist school, which itself did not give contracting parties the required freedom but focuses on how law operates in practice. In legal realism, law is determined by the action of judges and the relevant factors they consider in the process of judicial reasoning.[125] Undoubtedly, such an approach could deviate from the actual intent of the parties in contractual matters and thus may not perfectly reflect what the disputing parties originally intended. While contrasting these theories with the permissibility rule in Islamic law, one would conclude that the latter gives the parties more freedom as it upholds party autonomy and freedom to conclude contracts subject to few restrictions under the law.

6.98 The permissibility approach, which is often not prominent in discussions relating to Islamic law, has far-reaching effect in professional legal practice today, particularly among legal counsel who advise clients on Islamic transactions. Such an approach would guide even the drafting of relevant legal documentation, as Islamic law is more inclusive than the often-emphasized exclusionary approach. The permissibility principle allows the adoption of conventional finance documentation and adaptation of such legal documentation to suit the needs of Islamic contractual parties. In this regard, the IIFM has been spearheading the standardization of documentation widely used in the global Islamic financial services industry. While the IIFM develops some standardized documentation by itself, it sometimes partners with other industry

[124] For a comprehensive discussion of this theory, which built on previous conceptions of law by Hobbes and Bentham, see generally John Austin, The Province of Jurisprudence Determined (Cambridge University Press, 1995).

[125] See Keith J. Bybee, 'Legal Realism, Common Courtesy, and Hypocrisy' (2005) 1(1) Law, Culture, and the Humanities 76.

players globally to develop acceptable Islamic contract documentation. The IIFM has partnered with the ISDA and Bankers Association for Finance & Trade (BAFT) to develop some Islamic documentation. In some cases, it reviews available conventional templates based on general Islamic principles drawing significantly from leading law firms who advise on Islamic contract law as well as an eminent Sharīʿah Committee comprising leading Muslim jurists. The outcome of such rigorous efforts is standardized documentation for the global Islamic financial services industry, which has been widely adopted by financial institutions.

The permissibility principle extends to the benchmark rates used in Islamic financial transactions which are often incorporated into major contracts involving sukuk issuances or syndicated financing. As discussed in this chapter, most Islamic contracts, particularly the financial contracts used in the Islamic financial services industry, use conventional interest rates as benchmarks. In the absence of Islamic benchmark rates, this practice has been generally approved by modern Muslim jurists on the basis of the permissibility principle. It could also be argued that another related positive dimension of the prohibited elements in Islamic law is a legal principle that provides for circumstances where necessity could automatically render prohibited things permissible. This legal maxim has been widely used in structuring Islamic products and it is relevant in understanding Islamic contract law theory. **6.99**

7

Invalid Contracts

1. Introduction

7.01 There are three types of contract under Islamic law: *ṣaḥīḥ*, *fāsid*, and *bāṭil*.[1] Contracts whose essence and attributes are lawful and which have no defects in their elements (*aṣl*) or characteristics (*waṣf*) are termed valid.[2] It should be stated that in respect of *fāsid* contracts, only the *waṣf* may be defective, whereas in respect of *bāṭil* contracts the *aṣl* of the contract may also be defective.[3] *Fāsid* is a type of contract permitted by its intrinsic characteristics but not its features. Its irregularity negates its validity, which if cured would make this type of contract valid. The concept of *bāṭil* relates to a contract whose elements and characteristics are devoid of legality. This difference between *fāsid* and *bāṭil* results in a difference of effects.[4] Each of these contracts is divided into different types. Sometimes, the conditions incorporated in a contract also determine the nature of the contract as valid, irregular, or void. This chapter discusses these contracts, as well as the requirements pertaining thereto, and the types of terms which are included in a contract and their effect on its validity.

2. Valid Contracts

7.02 A *ṣaḥīḥ* contract complies with all the conditions regarding its *aṣl* and *waṣf*. As has been discussed in earlier chapters, a contract under Islamic law requires three elements, (*aṣl*) namely, the *ṣīgha* (form), which comprises the offer and acceptance; the subject matter; and the contracting parties.[5] Several conditions (*shurūṭ*) have been prescribed for each element. A contract is valid or *ṣaḥīḥ* if it contains all the required elements, along with

[1] Ibn Qudāma, Al-Mughnī fī Fiqh al-Imīm Aḥmad bin Ḥanbal (Dār al-Fikr, 1405H) Vol. 4, p. 189;; Mohammad Naseem and Saman Naseem, Islamic Law of Contracts (Kluwer, 2021) pp. 201–10.

[2] Ibn Nujaim, Al-Baḥr al-Rā'iq Sharḥ Kanz al-Daqā'iq (Dār al-Kitāb al-Islāmī, 1997) Vol. 5, p. 270; Ibn 'Abidīn, Radd al-Muḥtār Sharḥ Tanvīr al-Abṣār (Dār al-Fikr, 1412H/1992) Vol. 4, p. 518.

[3] *Radd al-Muḥtār* (n 2) Vol. 7, p. 234.

[4] Ibid, Vol. 5, p. 84; see Craig R. Nethercott and David M. Eisenberg (eds), Islamic Finance: Law and Practice (Oxford University Press, 2012) p. 2.

[5] Aḥmad Al-Dardīr and Muḥammad bin Arafa, Al-Sharḥ al-Kabīr (Dār al-Fikr, n.d.) Vol. 8, pp. 394–96.

the attendant conditions of each element, and moreover fulfils the requirements pertaining to all the external characteristics (*waṣf*), such as the rules on *ribā* and *gharar*.

7.03 In this way, several conditions have been prescribed for the validity of a contract. Some of these conditions are general in nature while others are specific. General conditions include all the requirements for *in'aqād* of a contract. Specific conditions include, among others, the absence of time restriction as well as information about the subject matter of the contract.[6] All relevant information required to make the transaction clear should be exchanged. Similarly, contracts involving future performance should delineate their time of maturity.[7]

2.1 Conditions for a Valid Contract

7.04 Hanafis (leading jurists from the Hanafi school) discuss the conditions pertaining to the formation, implementation, validity, and the binding nature (*luzūm*) of a contract. Their teachings will be explored more fully in Subsections 2.1.1 and 2.1.2.

2.1.1 Conditions for the Formation of a Valid Contract

7.05 The conditions for the formation (*in'aqād*) of a contract primarily relate to *ṣīgha*, contracting parties, and subject matter.[8]

2.1.1.1 Offer and acceptance

7.06 The *ṣīgha*[9] requires conformity between offer and acceptance issued in the same session, the existence of the *ījāb* until the issuance of *qabūl*, and the means and methods of their communication.[10] Consent should be freely provided free from fraud, misrepresentation, or coercion.[11] If the contract is found to have been made in jest, then it is deemed not to have been formed.[12]

7.07 Consent may be express or inferred from the conduct of the parties.[13] It should be noted that signs made by a person with a hearing and speech impediment are tantamount to

[6] *Radd al-Muḥtār* (n 2) Vol. 4, p. 500.
[7] Ibid.
[8] *Radd al-Muḥtār* (n 2) Vol. 4, p. 521; Al-Dardīr and bin Arafa (n 5) Vol. 8, p. 394; Al Rāf'ī, 'Abdul Karīm, Kitāb al-Dahab al-Ibrīz Sharḥ al-Mu'jam al-Wajīz (Dār al abī Arqm bin al Arqm, 2004) Vol. 1, p. 273; see also A. Zysow, 'The Problem of Offer and Acceptance: A Study of Implied in Fact Contracts in Islamic Law and the Common Law' (1985–86) 34 Cleveland State Law Review 77.
[9] See Chapter 2 for a comprehensive discussion on *ṣīgha*. The first requirement is consent, which is derived from verse 29 of the Nisā chapter in the Qur'ān; see also Nethercott and Eisenberg (n 4) 52.
[10] Al-Dardīr, Vol. 8, p. 394; Al-Mawṣilī, 'Abd Allāh ibn Mahmūd, Al Ikhtiyār li Ta'līl al-Mukhtār (Dār al-Kutub al-'Ilmiyya, 1937) Vol. 3, p. 71.
[11] Al-Qairwānī, Abi Zayd, *Risāla al-Qairwānī* (Dār Al-Fikar, n.d.) p. 140; Al-Māwardī, al-Hāwī al-Kabīr (Dār al-Fikr, 1994) Vol. 5, p. 17.
[12] Al Haṣkafī, 'Alā al-Dīn ibn Aḥmad ibn Muḥammad, Al-Durr al-Mukhtār (Dār al Kutb al-'Ilmiyya, 2002) p. 394.
[13] *Radd al-Muḥtār*, Vol. 4, p. 526; Khalīl Ibn Ishāq al-Jundī, Mukhtaṣar Al Khalīl (Dār al-Ḥadīth, 2005) Vol. 3, p. 148. It is stipulated that the formation of contracts through conduct is allowed only for trivial matters and not for major transactions. See Ibn Qudāma, Al-Kāfī (Dār al-Kutab al-'Ilmiyya, 1994) Vol. 2, pp. 3–6; Al-Karkhī, Uṣūl al-Karkhī (Javed Press Karachi, 2011) p. 173. According to another opinion, a sale by conduct is allowed in respect

the words spoken by a non-disabled person,[14] but these should be comprehensible and clear.[15] Where express, the consent should be in the past tense and not in the form of a question, thus eliminating the likelihood of ambiguity or uncertainty.[16] Shafi'i suggests that there are certain contracts which do not require offer and acceptance in the spoken or written word, such as those pertaining to gifts and *ṣadaqa* (charity).[17]

Offer and acceptance may precede each other. For instance, the buyer can say to the seller: 'sell it to me'.[18] However, in this case there should not be a long interval between offer and acceptance according to *'urf* (custom)[19] and the parties themselves should communicate both offer and acceptance directly to each other.[20] Ratification of a past offer or acceptance is also an effective way of giving consent to create a binding contract.[21] If any of the parties leaves its interlocutor before acceptance is communicated, then the offer stands revoked/annulled. If offer and acceptance are completed, then the sale becomes binding without the option of session.[22] **7.08**

2.1.1.2 Capacity of the parties

The *ṣaḥīḥ* contract also requires that the parties possess legal capacity and competence to contract.[23] Capacity requires prudence, pubescence, and ownership of the subject matter of the contract, or may otherwise be conferred through agency, while at the same time no interdiction is imposed on a party to the contract by reason of being a minor, or suffering from insanity, or imbecility (*ma'tūh*).[24] **7.09**

2.1.1.3 Subject matter

The subject matter of the contract must be *mutaqawwam* (pure, permissible, beneficial), existent, deliverable, known with specificity, and owned by the seller.[25] It should **7.10**

of both trivial and important issues. The description of cheap/trivial refers to objects such as bread, and expensive/important corresponds to a slave or whatever is more than the amount of *ḥad al sariqa* (fixed punishment for theft). See *Radd al-Muḥtār* (n 2) Vol. 4, p. 526.

[14] Shahāb al-Din Aḥmad ibn Lu'lu Ibn al-Naqīb al-Rūmī al-Miṣrī, 'Umdat al-Sālik wa' Uddat al-Nāsik (Sha'ūn al-Dīniyya, Qatar 1982) Vol. 1, p. 150.

[15] Abū Bakr ibn Mas'ūd Al-Kāsānī, Badā'i' al-Ṣanā'i' fī Tartīb al-Sharā'i' (Dār al-Kutub al-'Ilmiyya, 1406H/1986) Vol. 5, p. 133.

[16] See Chapter 5 for a discussion on conditions relating to the subject matter of contracts, including the use of benefit and necessity in legalizing a subject matter. Ibn Qudāma (n 13) Vol. 2, pp. 3–6; Abū al-Qurtubī Al-Bājī, Al-Muntaqā (Matba'at al-Sa'ādā, 1999) Vol. 4, p. 157 and Vol. 6, p. 24; Al-Mauṣilī (n 10) Vol. 3, p. 71.

[17] Al-Suyūṭī, Abū al-Faḍl 'Abd al-Rahmān ibn Abū Bakar ibn Muḥammad ibn Aḥmad Bakr Jalāl al-Dīn, Al-Ashbāh wa al-Naẓā'ir (Dār al-Kutub al-'Ilmiyya, 1411H/1990) p. 149; Al-Nawawī, Rauḍat al- Ṭālibīn (Al-Maktab al-Islāmī, 1412H/1991) Vol. 3, p. 339.

[18] Ibn Naqīb (n 14) Vol. 1, p. 150.

[19] Ibid.

[20] Al-Dardīr, Vol. 8, p. 394.

[21] *Radd al-Muḥtār* (n 2) Vol. 4, p. 524.

[22] Al-Mauṣilī (n 10) Vol. 3, p. 73.

[23] Al Ḥaṣkafī (n 12) Vol. 3, p. 96. See Chapter 3 for a comprehensive discussion on the capacity of parties to contract.

[24] Al Jundī (n 13) Vol. 3, p. 144; Abū Ibrāhīm Al-Muzanī, Mukhtaṣar al-Muznī (Dār al-Ma'rafa, 1990) p. 172; Al-Shāfi'ī, Al-Umm (Dār al-Ma'rifa, 1410H/1990) Vol. 3, p. 70; Fatāwā Al-Ghazālī, Al-Wasīṭ fi al-Maktab (Dār al-Islām, 1996) Vol. 3, p. 26; Al-Mauṣilī (n 10) Vol. 3, p. 71; Al-Kāsānī (n 15) Vol. 5, p. 133.

[25] *Al-Mughnī* (n 1) Vol. 3, p. 480; Ibn Naqīb (n 14) Vol. 1, p. 152; Al-Zarkashī, Al-Nahr li Muhīṭ (Dār al Kutab, 1994) Vol. 2, p. 26; Muḥammad Al-Sarakhsī, Al-Mabsūṭ (Dār al-Ma'rifa, 1414H/1993) Vol. 5, p. 8; Ibn Rushd, Abū

be specified through its measurement, weight, and counting, as well as other qualities. The sale of a subject matter ascertained by inspection or description is allowed. The disposition of non-existent objects or subject matters is not permitted because of *gharar*.[26] This is so because the existence of *khaṭar* (risk) or uncertainty (*gharar*) in the subject matter, price, or the time of performance/delivery of any contract is not permitted.[27] However, a subject matter susceptible to destruction, deterioration, or loss is valid if accepted by the purchaser.[28] Contracts for the sale of usufruct, such as a right of way, are valid.[29] Anything prohibited explicitly cannot become a valid subject matter, as is the case with wine, swine, and dead animals, among others.[30] There are certain commodities that may give rise to *ribā*-related consequences and hence need to be exchanged simultaneously.[31]

2.1.2 Conditions for *Nifādh* of a Contract

7.11 There are certain conditions for the enforcement, or *nifādh*, of a contract. These are ownership (*milkiyya*) and authority (*wilāya*). No person other than the owner possesses authority to make an offer, save through an agent, whether authorized or not (*faḍūlī*).[32]

2.1.3 Conditions for *Ṣiḥa* of a Contract

7.12 There are fifteen conditions for the validity, or *ṣiḥa*, of a contract. Among these there are both general and specific conditions. General conditions include all those required for the formation (*in'aqād*) of a contract because what is not formed cannot be validated.[33] Specific conditions relate to the time period for a deferred sale, possession (for a buyer), specific details about the exchange where commodities are prone to *ribā*, delivery in *ṣarf* (currency exchange) before the session ends, and information about the actual cost price in *murābaḥa*, *tawliya*, *ishrāk*, and *wadī'a* contracts.[34]

2.1.4 Conditions for *Luzūm* of a Contract

7.13 Conditions for *luzūm*, or rendering a contract binding, include all those mentioned above and additionally that the contract be free from options.[35]

al-Walīd, Bidāyat al-Mujtahid wa Nihāyat al-Muqtaṣid (Mustafā al-Bābī al-Ḥalabī, 1395H/1975) Vol. 3, p. 150; Al-Mauṣilī (n 10) Vol. 3, p. 71; Ibn Nujaim (n 2) Vol. 5, p. 279. See also Chapter 5 for a discussion of the subject matter and relevant conditions.

26 *Al-Mughnī* (n 1) Vol. 3, p. 480; Al-Buhūtī, Manṣūr ibn Yūnus ibn Ṣalāḥ al-Dīn, Kashshāf al-Qinā' 'an Matn al-Iqnā' (Dār al-Kutub al-'Ilmiyya, n.d.) Vol. 3, p. 162; Qādī Ibn Shujā', Al Ghayāb wa al Taqrīb (Dār Ibn Ḥazam, 1994) p. 153.

27 Al Qairwānī (n 11) p. 140.

28 Ibid.

29 Ibn Ḥajar 'Asqalānī, Al-Tahzīb fi al-Fiqh al-Aḥmad (Dār al-Kutb al- 'Ilmiyya, 1997) Vol. 3, pp. 282–85.

30 Ibn Qudāma (n 13) Vol. 2, p. 9; Al-Māwardī (n 11) Vol. 5, p. 17.

31 Ibn Mazāh, Muḥīṭ al-Burhānī fī al-Fiqh al-Nu'mānī (Dār al-Kutub al-'Ilmiyya, 2004) Vol. 6, p. 267.

32 *Radd al-Muḥtār* (n 2) Vol. 4, p. 521.

33 Ibid, p. 521.

34 Ibn Nujaim (n 2) Vol. 5, p. 281.

35 *Radd al-Muḥtār* (n 2) p. 526.

2.1.5 Conditions for External Attributes of a Contract

If the aforementioned elements are present and the conditions are met the contract comes into existence. However, a contract is not considered *ṣaḥīḥ* or legally enforceable (*mun'aqid*) unless it is free from externally prohibited defects such as *ribā* and *gharar*. If a contract contains such defects, Hanafis consider it *fāsid*. Hanafis define a *ṣaḥīḥ* contract as that which is lawful in terms of both *aṣl* and *waṣf*. 7.14

2.1.5.1 Gharar

For a contract to be valid, it must be free from *gharar*.[36] The characteristics of the subject matter should be obvious.[37] *Gharar* pertains to the subject matter of the contract and potentially also to the price. Therefore, knowledge of the price is considered as one of the two cardinal requirements of a *ṣaḥīḥ* contract. If a definitive price is determined then the contract is valid, whereas if it is merely mentioned, without specification of amount (or currency in transnational contracts), it will not be valid. If someone offers two prices in a single transaction, one for a spot sale and another in the event of a delayed sale, such an offer is invalid. This outcome is attributed to the Prophet Muḥammad who prohibited two sales in one because of the potential for creating a lack of clarity in the price and ultimately giving rise to *jahāla*.[38] 7.15

2.1.5.2 Ribā

Jurists generally agree that *ribā* prevails in two things: sale and liability arising out of sale, credit, or other transactions. *Ribā* incurred as a matter of liability is of two kinds. The first is *ribā al-jāhiliyya*, whereby the parties agree to the extension of the loan period against an increase in the amount of the loan. The second concerns discount and early payment and it is this that has caused most disagreement among jurists. Jurists agree that *ribā* in sale agreements is of two types, namely, delay and excess.[39] The rules of *ribā* can be categorized as follows: 7.16

- things in which neither excess nor delay is allowed;
- things in which excess is allowed, but not delay;
- things in which both are allowed; and
- things which are permitted in one category/genus but not in the other category.

Islamic jurists agree that neither delay nor excess (e.g. a person provides 1 kilogramme (kg) of wheat in order to receive 3 kg. In this case the 2 kg is considered an excess) is allowed on any of the commodities mentioned in the narration of Ubadah bin Samit, except what has been narrated by ibn 'Abbas. This is known as the *ḥadīth* of 7.17

[36] For *gharar* and how *gharar* is removed to make the contract valid, see Chapter 6. Al Qairwānī (n 11) p. 140; see Accounting and Auditing Organization for Islamic Financial Institutions (AAOIFI), 'Shari'ah Standard No. (31) Control on Gharar in Financial Transactions, 2/2' and AAOIFI, 'Shari'ah Standard No. (31) Control on Gharar in Financial Transactions, 5/1/2'.

[37] Al Qairwānī (n 11).

[38] Ibid.

[39] Ibid.

six commodities in recent writings. ʿUbāda bin Ṣāmit reported the Holy Prophet as saying: 'Gold is to be paid for by gold, silver by silver, wheat by wheat, barley by barley, dates by dates, and salt by salt, like for like and equal for equal, payment being made hand to hand. If these classes differ, then sell as you wish if payment is made hand to hand.'[40]

2.2 Types of Valid Contract

7.18 A *ṣaḥīḥ*, or valid contract, is a contract whose content and qualities are lawful and it suffers from no defects.[41] There are three types of *ṣaḥīḥ* contracts, namely, *nāfidh lāzim*, *nāfidh ghayr lāzim*, and *mawqūf*.[42] The *aṣl* and *waṣf* of a *ṣaḥīḥ* contract, as already noted, comply with the legality requirements of Islamic law. Such a contract should produce the effects ascribed under Islamic law. Some jurists maintain, however, that a contract whose effects are predicated on the occurrence of a future event is equally a species of *ṣaḥīḥ* contract. Such contracts are known as *mawqūf* contracts, that is, they are subject to a suspensive event. This is in line with the teachings of Hanafis and Malikis as well as some Ḥanbali jurists. Shafi'is and some Hanbalis are reluctant to concede that a suspensive delay continues to render the contract *ṣaḥīḥ*. Rather, their line of thinking suggests that in order for a contract to be considered *ṣaḥīḥ* its object/effects must materialize immediately, that is, it must be *nāfidh* (operative). *Mawqūf* or suspended contracts thus have no existence according to these jurists. As a result, a *mawqūf* contract is not immediately enforceable.[43]

7.19 The *nāfidh* (operative or immediate) contract is that in which all essential elements are found (e.g. contracting parties, subject matter, amongst others); pertinent conditions are met; external attributes are lawful (i.e. there are no defects); and the contract is not dependent upon ratification. In contrast, while the said essential elements may be found in a *mawqūf* contract, in addition to having met pertinent conditions, the effects of such contract are dependent upon ratification and hence it is not immediately enforceable.

2.2.1 The *Lāzim* Contract

7.20 A *nāfidh lāzim* contract is a contract which fulfils the aforementioned conditions pertaining to elements and external characteristics of contracts under Islamic law. Furthermore, it is not subject to rights of third parties or any option (*khiyār*). This

[40] Muslim, *Ḥadīth*, 10:3853 and 3069.

[41] Ibn Nujaim (n 2) Vol. 5, p. 293; *Radd al-Muḥtār* (n 2) Vol. 4, p. 516.

[42] Ibn Nujaim (n 2) Vol. 5, p. 284; Nethercott and Eisenberg (n 4) 50; Saba Habachy, 'The System of Nullities in Muslim Law' (1964) 13 American Journal of Comparative Law 61.

[43] Abū Yaʿlā al-Baghdādī, Al Riwāyatain wa al-Wajhain (Maktaba al-Maʿārif, 1985) Vol. 1, p. 349; ʿAbd al-Wahāb, Al-Ishrāf (Dār Ibn Hazm, 1999) Vol. 2, pp. 521–22.

contract itself is operative and susceptible to implementation. A contract becomes *lāzim* after its *in'aqād*, *nifādh*, and *ṣiḥa*, if there is no option attached to it, or if there is no cause of suspension, according to the Hanafis. On the other hand, Shafi'is stipulate that a contract becomes *lāzim* when the session ends and no *khiyār* (option) is available to the parties. The difference lies in the validity of *khiyār al-majlis* which is applicable to Shafi'is but not to Hanafis.[44] *In'aqād*, *ṣiḥa*, and *nifādh*, in addition to the absence of options, are required conditions for a contract to be considered *lāzim*. When a contract becomes *lāzim* it cannot be revoked by a party unilaterally, save with the consent of the other party.[45] For a contract to be considered *nāfidh* two requirements must be fulfilled. The first is *milkiyya* (ownership) and the second is *wilāya* (delegated authority), both of which are discussed in Subsection 3.3.3.[46]

2.2.2 The *Ja'iz* or *Ghayr Lāzim* Contract

A *nāfidh ghayr lāzim* contract is distinguishable from other contracts in that a party has **7.21** the right to revoke it without the consent of its counterpart. This right is bestowed by the conferral of a right of option. In this way, the contract is not binding for the party to whom the option is given. The contract may also become *ghayr lāzim* due to its nature, as is the case with *wakāla*, *wadī'a*, *sharika*, and *kafāla*, where both parties have the right to revoke the contract unilaterally.[47]

2.2.3 *Mawqūf*

Mawqūf is a suspended contract which is dependent or contingent on the occurrence of **7.22** a certain event, or a permission from a person with authority.[48] For instance, a contract by *faḍūlī* is suspended due to the possibility of acceptance,[49] or rejection from the concerned authority.[50] *Mawqūf* contracts have been classified by some scholars as a subcategory of *ṣaḥīḥ* contracts and some have included them as regular types of contracts. For instance, Al-Zayl'ī classified valid contracts into *ṣaḥīḥ*, *bāṭil*, *fāsid*, and *mawqūf*.[51] A contract procured by means of coercion has been discussed under the topic of *mawqūf fāsid* and is known as *bay' al-mukreh*.[52] This is because the coerced person has the choice to revoke or ratify the contract.

[44] Al-Kāsānī (n 15) Vol. 5, p. 160; see Nicholas P. Kourides, 'The Influence of Islamic Law on Contemporary Middle Eastern Legal Systems: The Formation and Binding Force of Contracts' (1970) 9 Columbia Journal of Transnational Law 407.

[45] Al-Kāsānī (n 15) p. 160; see also Muḥammad W. Islam, 'Dissolution of Contract in Islamic Law' (1998) 13 Arab Law Quarterly 336, p. 356.

[46] Al-Kāsānī (n 15) p. 180.

[47] Ibn al-Ḥumām, Kamāl al-Dīn Ibn Muḥammad, Fat'ḥ al-Qadīr (Dār al-Fikr, n.d.) Vol. 6, p. 246.

[48] Al-Kāsānī (n 15) Vol. 5, p. 180; Wahāb (n 43) Vol. 2, pp. 521–22.

[49] Al-Sarakhsī, Al-Mabsūṭ (Dār al-Ma'rifa, 1414H/1993) Vol. 12, p. 113.

[50] Al-Kāsānī (n 15) Vol. 5, p. 156; Muḥammad al-Dusūqī, Muḥammad ibn Aḥmad ibn 'Arfa, Ḥāshiyat al-Dusūqī 'alā al-Sharḥ al-Kabīr (Dār al-Fikr, n.d.) Vol. 3, pp. 3–7.

[51] Ibn Nujaim (n 2) Vol. 5, p. 293.

[52] Al-Nasafī, Kanz al-Daqā'iq (Dār al Bashā'ir al-Islāmiyya, 2014) p. 410.

2.2.3.1 Causes of suspension

7.23 The possible cause or causes due to which the effects of a *ṣaḥīḥ* contract are suspended may be summarized as follows.

7.24 Defective capacity: Minors with discretion (*ṣabī mumayyaz*) or under interdiction (*ḥajr*) due to *safah* (weakness of intellect) or *'atah* (lunacy or partial insanity) may be permitted to undertake certain kinds of transactions. These transactions are divided into three categories. The first category encompasses those that are purely beneficial for the person with defective capacity, such as acceptance of *hibba* and *ṣadaqa*. These transactions concern the conferral of ownership on the minor without anything being given in return. Purely beneficial transactions are allowed for minors without permission from their guardian. This is because the guardian is appointed to save the child from the pitfalls of damaging contracts and hence a contract that is beneficial for the minor requires no permission from their guardian.

7.25 The second category concerns transactions that are purely injurious to the minor, such as gifts, *waqf*, and others. These are transactions in which the minor suffers without any return or benefit. Minors may not enter into such transactions even with the permission of their guardian, on the ground that the guardian is not authorized to undertake these acts on behalf of the minor.

7.26 The third category concerns transactions oscillating between harm and benefit, such as *ijāra*, sale, and purchase. Minors can enter into these with the permission of their guardian.[53] Therefore, a transaction by a minor involving the likelihood of both benefit and harm is valid subject to ratification. Such ratification may be provided by the guardian after the transaction and before the minor attains puberty, or alternatively by the minor himself or herself after majority in case the guardian did not reject the contract before the minor attained majority. The *ḥukm* of such a contract is that before ratification it produces no effects, and ownership of goods or the agreed price is transferred once ratification is granted. The act of ratification in this case operates retrospectively and the effects of the agreement come into being from the date the contract is ratified. In the event that ratification is refused the contract becomes void.

7.27 Suspension due to lack of proper authority: The seller possesses authority to contract if he or she is the owner, guardian, or an authorized agent. If a person enters into a contract on behalf of another without authority or permission, the contract is considered valid, but its effects are considered suspended until ratified by the owner. If ratified by a person with the requisite authority, the contract becomes operative; otherwise it will be considered void. A *faḍūlī* is a person who acts without permission or an agent in breach of his mandate.[54] Where the *faḍūlī* has delivered the property and such delivery is not

[53] Al-Kāsānī (n 15) Vol. 5, p. 180.

[54] Al-Kāsānī (n 15) Vol. 5, p. 181. The preferred opinion for the Shafi'is and Hanbalis is that the contract by a *faḍulī* is void. See al-Suyūṭī (n 17) p. 150; *Al-Mughnī* (n 1) Vol. 4, p. 480; Al-Mauṣilī (n 10) Vol. 3, p. 71.

subsequently ratified by the owner, the *aḥkām* of *ghaṣb*[55] (usurpation) shall operate against the *faḍūlī*, namely, he or she must return the property or risk becoming liable for damages.

Suspension due to rights of third parties: If the owner sells the mortgaged property, it will be subject to the ratification of the mortgagee. Where a person has capacity and authority to act, for example in situations of ownership of the subject matter but subject to the rights of third parties, the contract is considered suspended and must be ratified by the third party in question. **7.28**

Shafi'is divide a contract into *ṣaḥīḥ* and *bāṭil/fāsid*. *Ṣaḥīḥ* can be *lāzim* or *Jā'iz*. Generally, *bāṭil* and *fāsid* are treated as the same, with the stipulation that *mawqūf* is a *bāṭil* contract, particularly where a *faḍūlī* is involved. In explaining this classification the Shafi'is distinguish between four discreet categories. **7.29**

First: contracts not binding on the parties and which are unlikely to become binding in the future. These contracts are *wakāla*, *mudāraba*, *mushārika*, *wadī'a*, and *'āriya*. Here, the option is available for both parties to declare the contract void. If an option is stipulated in such contract, it will become void because it renders it binding, although it is only *Jā'iz*. **7.30**

Secondly: contracts not binding on the parties but which are likely to become binding in the future upon the fulfilment of certain conditions. In this case, the parties have the option before the contract becomes binding, following which the option is lost to the parties. If the option is stipulated after the contract is binding or the option is removed prior to this, it becomes void. Five types of contracts fall within this typology, including *ju'āla* (emancipation on payment), *istihlāk al-amwāl bi ḍamān* (destruction of property with liability), and *qarḍ*. **7.31**

Thirdly: contracts binding on one party but not on the other under any circumstances. This category encompasses three sub-species of contracts, namely, *rehn*, *ḍamān*, and *kitāba* (emancipation). Hence, an option is granted to one party, the mortgagee, to whom the damages has to be paid. If a stipulation is included, which effectively removes the option from the abovementioned or grants it to the party not granted such option, it will be void. **7.32**

Fourthly: contracts binding on both parties. This has been divided into further subcategories. Where an option is not granted to any party (not an option of session or condition) the contract in question is *nikāḥ* and *rujū'*. The second sub-category concerns those contracts in which the option of condition is not applicable, as is the case with *ijāra*, *masāqāt*, and *ḥawāla*. The third sub-category consists of contracts whereby the option of session is applicable but a condition is not applicable. These contracts require delivery/possession before the contract can be considered as having come into **7.33**

[55] These are *aḥkām* which regulate a usurper's possession of property, which the usurper intends to encompass in a transaction.

being, as is the case with *salam* and *ṣarf*. There are contracts in which *khiyār al-majlis* is applicable (inbuilt) and where all possible options can be stipulated. This category further includes all sale contracts.[56]

3. *Fāsid* Contracts

7.34 *Fāsid* contracts are those whose elements (*aṣl*) are present and legal but in respect of which there may be a defect in characteristic (*waṣf*) that may be removed, upon which the status of *ṣaḥīḥ* can be attributed to it. However, not all jurists consider an irregular contract in the same sense; for Hanafis a *fāsid* contract can be validated by removing its defects, whereas the Shafi'is consider *fāsid* and *bāṭil* to be the same. The Hanbalis share the same view, although the Malikis have created a detailed categorization of irregular contracts on account of *ribā*, *gharar*, or other prohibitions.

3.1 Causes for *Fāsid* Contracts

7.35 The emergence of *fasād* (irregularity) in a contract may be due to several reasons. For instance, this is so where a commodity that is not *māl* for a Muslim is used in a contract in lieu of a price, for example wine or swine; where the agreed price is ambiguous; where the subject matter may lead to dispute; or where it has not been discussed at all. A sale in jest is considered *fāsid*, not *bāṭil*.[57] The sale of something that is not deliverable, beneficial, or pure is considered *fāsid* according to Hanbalis.[58]

7.36 The involvement of *ribā* in a contract makes it *fāsid*, according to Hanafis.[59] The contract also becomes *fāsid* by reason of *gharar*. *Gharar* may emerge in numerous ways, particularly where the price is ambiguous or not discussed at all.[60] In this case, the price or the consideration is unknown and hence may lead to conflict, as the likelihood of delivery is rendered impossible. Therefore, *bay' al-ghaib* is not allowed.[61] Nonetheless, in the event of uncertainty that does not lead to conflict it is considered permissible.[62] The contract becomes *fāsid* if consent is defective, where for instance it is procured by misrepresentation.[63] If there is a condition contradicting the essence of the contract this would render it *fāsid*.[64]

[56] Al-Māwardī (n 11) Vol. 5, pp. 342 and 375. See also al-Suyūṭī (n 17) p. 453; Al-Nawawī, Al-Majmū' Sharḥ Al-Muhadhdhab (Dār al-Fikr, n.d.) Vol. 9, p. 225; *Al-Mughnī* (n 1) Vol. 3, pp. 483, 493.

[57] *Radd al-Muḥtār* (n 2) Vol. 7, p. 234.

[58] Al-Madasī, Kitāb al-Sharḥ al-Kabīr (Dār al-Kitāb al-'Arabī, n.d.) Vol. 4, p. 7.

[59] For a discussion on *ribā*, see Chapters 6 and 7.

[60] *Radd al-Muḥtār* (n 2) Vol. 7, p. 234; Al-Samarqandī, Tuḥfat al-Fuqahā' (Dār al-Kutub al-'Ilmiyya, 1994) Vol. 2, p. 48.

[61] Al Ghazālī (n 24) Vol. 3, pp. 41–43; Ibn Ḥajar al-Haythamī, Tuḥfat al-Muḥtāj fī Sharḥ al-Minhāj (Al-Matba'a al-Maimaniyya, 1987) Vol. 4, p. 263.

[62] For a comprehensive discussion of *gharar*, see Chapter 6.

[63] al-Qurṭubī (n 25) Vol. 3, pp. 125–26.

[64] *Radd al-Muḥtār* (n 2) Vol. 7, p. 234.

3.2 The Effects of a *Fāsid* Contract and its Revocation

A *fāsid* contract has no legal effect[65] and no right of ownership is transferred.[66] Therefore, it is mandatory to remove all irregularities before taking possession.[67] A *fāsid* contract can be revoked (*faskh*), following which the underlying agreement is deemed extinguished.[68] There is no obstacle in revoking a *fāsid* contract.[69] For instance, a *fāsid nikāḥ* must be nullified because due to the irregulatity of the *nikāḥ* contract, the intercourse is not justified.[70] 7.37

3.3 Instances of *Fāsid* Contracts

3.3.1 *Bay' al-majhūl*

This pertains to the sale of a subject matter, the quantity (number, weight, or length), nature, or price of which is not known or is ambiguous as a result of *gharar*. There is little need to reiterate that contracts involving *gharar* are null and void.[71] 7.38

3.3.2 *Bay' al-īnā*

These types of contracts are employed to sell property on credit for a certain price with a view to repurchasing the same property at a price lower than the sale price, subject to prompt payment. It is required that both transactions take place simultaneously in the same session of the contract.[72] The Hanbalis consider these types of agreements as giving rise to *ribā al-nasiya*.[73] 7.39

3.3.3 Two Sales in One and Conditions in Sale

The Holy Prophet proscribed two sales in a single transaction. This entails a single contract relating to two sales, such as the sale of a single commodity for two prices, one in cash and the other on credit; or making a contract binding against one of the two prices. This sale is considered *fāsid* according to Hanafis,[74] because the price is indeterminate or uncertain. If this uncertainty is removed, then the contract becomes valid.[75] 7.40

[65] Badr Uddīn al-'Ainī, Al-Bināya Sharḥ al-Hidāya (Dār al-Kutb al-'Ilmiyya, 2000) Vol. 8, p. 202.

[66] Ibn Marrāh, Al Muhīṭ al- Burhānī fī Fiqh al-Nau'mānī (Dār al-Kutub al-'Ilmiyya Beirut, 2004) Vol. 3, p. 113; *Radd al-Muḥtār* (n 2) Vol. 7, p. 234. According to one Maliki tradition, *fāsid* contracts confer *shubhah* (doubt or impression) of ownership and therefore, if a commodity in a *fāsid* contract is destroyed in the hands of the buyer, compensation (*ḍamān*) is due by the seller. See Al-Mazrī, Shar' al-Talqīn (Dār al-Gharb, 2008) Vol. 2, pp. 431, 438.

[67] Al 'Ainī (n 65) Vol. 8, p. 202.

[68] Al Bābartī, Al Ināya Sharḥ al-Hidāya (Dār al-Fikr, n.d.) Vol. 2, p. 254.

[69] Al Mazrī (n 66) Vol. 2, p. 417.

[70] Al 'Ainī (n 65) Vol. 5, p. 180.

[71] *Gharar* may arise in a contractual relationship in several ways. For a comprehensive discussion see Chapter 6.

[72] Al-Ramlī, Shihāb al-Dīn, Nihāyat al-Muḥtāj ilā Sharḥ al-Minhāj (Dār al-Fikr, 1404H/1984) Vol. 3, p. 477; *Radd al-Muḥtār* (n 2) Vol. 5, p. 542; It is not permitted for an *istisna'* to be concluded on a sale and buy-back basis (*bay' al-īna*). Reference may be made to AAOIFI 'Shari'ah Standard No. (11) Istisna'a and Parallel Istisna'a, 2/2/4'.

[73] Ibn Qudāma (n 13) Vol. 2, p. 17.

[74] Al-Jaṣāṣ, Sharḥ Mukhtaṣar al-Ṭahāvī (Dār al-Bashā'ir al-Islāmiyya, 2010) Vol. 3, p. 100.

[75] Al Samarqandī (n 60) Vol. 2, p. 48.

7.41 *Bayʿ al-īnā* may take one of many forms.[76] The first is an exchange of two commodities (each with a different price) for two prices. This is prohibited by the consensus of jurists, chiefly because of the indeterminate price. Such illegality arises in two ways:

- If one says I will sell you my house at such price if you sell me your commodity at such price. This is not allowed in both form (i.e., if it constitutes a sale), as well as a type of condition,[77] or;
- If one says, I will sell this commodity for one dinar, or this other commodity for two dinars on the condition that the sale is binding in one of the transactions. This is equally invalid because it encompasses two contracts.

7.42 The second consists of an exchange of a priced commodity for two prices, one of which is in cash while the other is on credit. By way of illustration, a person might offer to buy a house from another for a price of 1000 dirham on the spot, or 2000 dirham through delayed payment, without however agreeing on the amount in the contract, leaving the specification of the amount to either party. There is no valid contract in this case because the price is not known.[78] *Bayʿ al-īnā* also falls in this situation, especially where one offers to sell a dress for cash on the condition that he buys it back from the initial buyer on credit, in such period, and at such price.

7.43 The third concerns situations where one person offers to sell to another one of two items for a price, without ultimately specifying which.

3.3.4 Sale with Defective Conditions

7.44 If a person attaches a condition in a sale intending to use the sold item for a month, then the sale is considered *fāsid*. This outcome is particularly relevant to commutative contracts, but not in respect of non-commutative contracts, as the former incur *ribā*, which is not applicable to the latter.[79] This is the case with forbidden conditions, but not with every stipulation.[80] For instance, some conditions do not render the contract *fāsid* or *bāṭil*, as is true with the requirement of the presence of a witness for the conclusion of a sale, the existence of a guarantor, the option of defect, spot payment/in currency, postponementof the price to a future time, the requirement of features in the commodity, the condition that it be returned if found defective, or a condition negating payment until the commodity is actually received. If a condition contradicts the essence of the contract or otherwise benefits one party against the other, then it is considered irregular.[81]

[76] Al ʿAinī (n 65) Vol. 8, p. 186; Al-Jaṣāṣ (n 74) Vol. 3, p. 100; Al Samarqandī (n 60) Vol. 2, p. 48; Ḥamad al-Ḥamd, Sharḥ Zād al-Mustaqnā li Aḥmad , Vol. 13, p. 67, available at <https://al-maktaba.org/book/852> accessed on 18 August 2021;; Al-Māwardī (n 11) Vol. 5, p. 342; Al Rāfʿī (n 8) Vol. 8, p. 194; Al Ghazālī (n 24) Vol. 3, p. 72; Al-Ramlī (n 72) Vol. 3, p. 150.

[77] Al ʿAinī (n 65) Vol. 8, p. 186.

[78] Al-Māwardī (n 11) Vol. 5, p. 342; Al Rāfʿī (n 8) Vol. 8, p. 194; Al Ghazālī (n 24) Vol. 3, p. 72; Al-Ramlī (n 72) Vol. 3, p. 150; Al ʿAinī (n 65) Vol. 8, p. 186.

[79] See Hassan Hussein, 'Contracts in Islamic Law: The Principles of Commutative Justice and Liberality' (2002) 3 Journal of Islamic Studies 257.

[80] *Radd al-Muḥtār* (n 2) Vol. 5, p. 84.

[81] Ibid.

3.3.5 *Bay' al-wafā*

Where the seller offers to sell a commodity against the buyer's loan to the seller upon condition that ownership to the buyer commences when he repays the loan, this is considered a sale guaranteed by the parties' consent and is called *bay' al-amāna*. It is assumed that the buyer will benefit from the commodity by means of usufruct, lease, use, or in some other way.[82] There is some difference of opinion between scholars who refer to this transaction as a *fāsid* sale, option, mortgage, or *ikrāh*. For instance, it is argued that the sold commodity in the hands of the buyer is tantamount to a pledge that cannot be used without the pledgee's permission. If any damage accrues it will be indemnified by him. When the loan is repaid the commodity is retrieved and there is no difference between *rehn* and this sale. This view is countered by those scholars arguing that if a transaction takes place under the term 'sale' it cannot be *rehn* (mortgage), and if the parties stipulated its revocation by using the word 'sale' or *wafā* it is not binding and hence is considered a *fāsid* sale. Similarly, others opine that it is a *ṣaḥīḥ* sale on the basis of *'urf*.[83] It is named *wafā* because the underlying promise also includes a condition/promise, whereby when the seller pays back the money the commodity will be returned to him. Certain jurists have allowed such a sale, probably because it avoids recourse to *ribā*.[84] 7.45

4. Invalid Contracts

Three schools do not differentiate between *fāsid* and *bāṭil* contracts and consider *fāsid* contracts as *bāṭil*. The Hanafi school treats the *fāsid* and *bāṭil* contracts discretely. As for *fāsid* contracts, only the *waṣf* of the contract is defective, whereas for a *bāṭil* contract, the *aṣl* of the contract is also defective.[85] Every sale is permitted, save for the type of transactions that are prohibited, which renders pertinent contracts void.[86] 7.46

4.1 Causes of Invalidity

4.1.1 Causes Associated with the Capacity of the Parties

According to the Shafi'is, a transaction by a *faḍūlī* is considered void, whereas Abū Ḥanīfa declared such transactions as falling within the scope of *fāsid* contracts.[87] 7.47

[82] Al-Buhūtī (n 26) Vol. 3, p. 149; Al Haitaimī (n 61) Vol. 4, p. 296; Al Mazrī (n 66) Vol. 2, p. 388; see also Nicholas H.D. Foster, 'The Islamic Law of Real Security' (2000) 15 Arab Law Quarterly 131.

[83] Ibn Nujaim (n 2) Vol. 6, p. 9.

[84] *Radd al-Muḥtār* (n 2) Vol. 5, p. 277.

[85] Ibid, Vol. 7, p. 234.

[86] Al Baqra, 275; Shāfi'ī (n 24) Vol. 3, p. 491.

[87] Al Ghazālī (n 24) Vol. 3, pp. 17–23.

4.1.2 Causes Associated with the Subject Matter

7.48 Ibn Āʿbidīn mentions that a difference between *bāṭil* and *fāsid* is that if the subject matter is not *māl* in any of the *dīn samāwī* (divine religions), then the sale is *bāṭil*, whereas if it is so (even if not *māl* under Islam) it is *fāsid*.[88] If wine is the subject matter, then the contract is void, albeit if the subject matter is the price of the sale or service then it is voidable. The rationale justifying this difference is that the subject matter is the object of the contract, while the price is just a means to achieve it. It is for exactly this reason that a sale is revoked if the subject matter (object) is destroyed and not because the price has been changed.[89] The sale of a non-existent or non-deliverable item, or an item that risks becoming non-existent, is void.[90] If the subject matter of a contract is *najas*, prohibited, or has no beneficial value, it will render a contract invalid.[91]

4.1.3 Illegality of the Object of the Contract

7.49 The object of a contract also determines the *ṣiḥa* of the contract. If the object of a contract over a permissible commodity is illegal, the contract is considered invalid. For instance, the Hanbalis and Malikis prohibit the sale of grapes, dates, or wheat to a person intending to make wine;[92] the same principle applies to the sale of weapons to a person intending to use them against others.[93] Although the Shafi'is[94] and Hanafis[95] permit such sale, the Shafi'is consider it *makrūh*. The Shafi'is also consider the sale of arms to rebels and dacoits *makrūh*, yet valid because such sale fulfils all the legal requirements needed for a valid contract. The Hanafis also allow the sale of land to one intending to cultivate it and make wine, but subject to *karāha* because it may lead a person to commit sins.[96]

4.2 Effect of an Invalid Contract

7.50 A void contract will have no legal effect whatsoever.[97] All schools agree that even if a buyer has taken possession of a commodity based on a void contract, he will not own it.[98] There is a difference of opinion as to whether the buyer will be liable for damages or other forms of compensation if the commodity is destroyed in his possession. One opinion is that the commodity will be treated as *amāna* by the consent of the seller, and if it gets destroyed without transgression then it will not be compensated. The second

88 Ibid; *Al-Kāfī* (n 13) Vol. 2, p. 4; *Al-Mughnī* (n 1) Vol. 4, pp. 159, 189; *Radd al-Muḥtār* (n 2) Vol. 5, p. 84; Shāfiʿī (n 24) Vol. 3, p. 70; Al-Māwardī (n 11) Vol. 5, pp. 13, 17; Al Ghazālī (n 24) Vol. 3, pp. 17–23.

89 Al Ḥaṣkafī (n 12) p. 420.

90 *Al-Kāfī* (n 13) Vol. 2, p. 4.

91 Ibid.

92 Ibn Rushd, Al-Bayān wa al-Tahsīl (*Dar al Gharb al Islami, 1988*) Vol. 18, p. 513; Ab ī Zaid al-Qairwānī, Al Nawādir wa al-Zaidāt (Dar Al Kotob Al Ilimiyah, 2010) Vol. 14, p. 295; Ibn 'Abdul Bar, Al-Kāfī fi Fiqh al-Ahl alMadīna (Maktaba al-Riyāḍ al-Ḥadīth, 1980) Vol. 2, p. 577.

93 Ibn Rushd (n 92) Vol. 18, p. 513.

94 Al Rāfʿī (n 8) Vol. 8, pp. 230–31. See also Al-Māwardī (n 11) Vol. 5, p. 270.

95 Al Jaṣāṣ (n 74) Vol. 6, p. 391.

96 Al-Sarakhsī (n 25) Vol. 24, p. 26.

97 Al-Zarkashī (n 25) Vol. 2, p. 26; Al Mazrī (n 66) Vol. 2, p. 438.

98 Al-Mauṣilī (n 10) Vol. 2, p. 23.

opinion is that compensation is due because possession by means of a void contract amounts to, or resembles, possession while a bargain is in progress.[99]

4.3 Instances of Invalid Contracts

A sale which lacks the conditions of a valid sale is an invalid sale. Every sale is permitted save those prohibited by the Prophet. Hence, every sale that has been prohibited is not allowed and considered as giving rise to a void contract.[100] **7.51**

4.3.1 Sale of Liabilities, Including Debts

The sale of credit for new credit arises where a person owes another against a commodity he bought (so he still has to pay the price for which he remains liable), or in the event of a debt sold to a third person or to the same person with delay. Scholarly consensus dictates that this type of sale is not allowed because there is prohibition against the sale of credit (one's liability) by means of further credit (something delayed)[101] as it involves *ribā al-jāhiliyya.*[102] This sale is not allowed in the same as well as different genus.[103] It has many forms[104] and the Malikis have identified three forms in which this sale may occur, as follows. **7.52**

The first concerns termination of credit by new credit or sale of credit by new credit, both of which give rise to *ribā al-jāhiliyya*, because credit is exchanged for another commodity or liability, or even by the very same commodity, but in excess of the original debt. **7.53**

The second type may assume two forms, namely, (i) sale of credit corresponding to the other person's debt; what X owes to A and Y owes to B each of these two (X and Y) sell to each other their respective debts; and (ii) a sale involving three persons, whereby X owes to A and goes on to sell the debt to a third person against credit. **7.54**

The third type involves delaying the price on *salam.*[105] Let us consider the following example. A person receives credit of 1,000 dirham and at the time of repayment he promises his creditor that he will offer him an equivalent amount of wheat at the end of year. In this manner, he has sold credit against wheat. Thereis also a famous pre-Islamic transaction that extends the time and amount of credit paid with excess or decrease (*haṭ wa ta'ajjul*).[106] Within the Shafi'i school, if a third person buys this credit then there is disagreement about its validity; one view allows it while another does not.[107] If X owes **7.55**

[99] Ibid, Vol. 2, p. 23; Al Mazrī (n 66) Vol. 2, p. 438; see Mahdi Zahra and Shafi Mahmor, 'The Validity of Contracts when the Goods are not Yet in Existence in the Islamic Law of Sale of Goods' (2002) 17 Arab Law Quarterly 379.
[100] Shāfi'ī (n 24) Vol. 3, p. 491.
[101] Al Sughdi, *Al Fatawa li Sughdi* (np an nd) Vol. 1, p. 475.
[102] Zaruq, *Sharḥ Matan al Risāla* (np. and nd)Vol. 2, p. 762.
[103] Sulaimān Al-Bujairimī, Tuḥfat al-Ḥabib 'alā Sharḥ al-Khaṭib (Dār al-Fikr, 1415H/1995) Vol. 3, p. 24.
[104] Al-Mardāwī (n 1) Vol. 12, p. 105.
[105] Al-Dusūqī (n 50) Vol. 3, pp. 61–62.
[106] Abd al-Raḥmān al-Maqdasī, Al-Sharḥ al-Kabīr (Dār al-kitāb al-'Arbī, n.d.) Vol. 12, p. 106.
[107] Al Jawainī, Nihāyat al-Maṭlab fī Darāyat al-Mazhab (n.p., n.d.) Vol. 5, p. 195.

Y 10 dirham and he buys from Z a cloth against these 10 dirham or says to Z: 'I bought from you against 10 dirham what X owes me', there is disagreement as to whether this is allowed.[108]

4.3.2 Sale of Impure Objects

7.56 The sale of impure objects or *najas*, such as blood, dead animals, and swine is prohibited. The discussion on impure objects, their permissibility, and the role of necessity and benefit in making them permissible subject matters of contract was addressed in Chapter 5.[109]

5. Types of *Shurūṭ* (Conditions)

7.57 There are four types of conditions which may have a direct impact on the *aṣl* or *waṣf* of a contract, or which may otherwise be opposite to the essence of the contract.[110]

7.58 The first type of condition is linked to the *muqtaḍā* of the contract and constitutes its essence and object and in addition stipulates the contractual liabilities which are in line with the essence of the contract. The contract will remain unaffected, irrespective of whether these are mentioned therein or not. For example, if the seller mentions in a deed of sale that he will retain absolute ownership of the commodity or that he is otherwise authorized to transfer or sell his property, such stipulations do not affect the contract.[111]

7.59 The second type of condition does not pertain to the essence of the contract; rather, its inclusion is beneficial to the contract and the parties. When a party does not fulfil these conditions, the other party may revoke the contract. For example, requiring witnesses to a contract or any guarantee in case of denial enhances the contract itself.[112] Under this condition, specific requirements or features may be demanded, such as that the land purchased have an agricultural value or the animal purchased be suitable for milking. If consent is given on the basis of any of these conditions, their non-fulfilment by one party entitles the other to *faskh* or to continue with mitigation of loss incurred due to non-conformity.

7.60 The third group includes conditions conflicting with the essence of the contract and which are not permissible even if they bring some benefits to the stipulator, on the ground that their incorporation renders the contract *bāṭil*. The legal implication of these conditions differs across contracts. For example, the existence of an option in

[108] Abū Muḥammad al-Baghwī, Al-Tahzīb fi Fiqh al-*Shāfiʿī* (n.p., n.d.) Vol. 3, p. 417.

[109] *Al-Kāf ī* (n 13) Vol. 2, p. 4; *Radd al-Muḥtār* (n 2) Vol. 5, p. 73; Al Rāfʿī (n 8) Vol. 8, p. 114; Al-Māwardī (n 11) Vol. 15, p. 159; Shāfiʿī (n 24) Vol. 3, p. 492.

[110] Nethercott and Eisenberg (n 4) 53; see generally Oussama Arabi, 'Contract Stipulations (shurūa) in Islamic Law: The Ottoman Majalla and Ibn Taymiyya' (1998) 30 International Journal of Middle East Studies 29.

[111] *Al-Mughnī* (n 1) Vol. 4, p. 480.

[112] Ibid.

a *nikāḥ* will make it *bāṭil*. Equally, the existence of a prohibition in a sale agreement whereby the buyer is required to further sell or lease the property, or put it to some other use, will render the sale contract *fāsid* but the debt or partnership will become void or *bāṭil*.[113]

The fourth type of condition goes against the essence of the contract but produces no adverse effect on it because while the condition itself is void the contract remains valid. For example, a stipulation by the seller that the sold commodity will be used for a specific purpose only by the buyer is *fāsid*, but such condition does not invalidate the contract. **7.61**

5.1 Valid Conditions

Valid conditions are those that have been validated by the *Sharʿ* and are moreover based on custom or predicated on the object or essence of the contract.[114] They have been classified into four distinct types. **7.62**

5.1.1 Conditions Which Are in Conformity with the Contract

These conditions concern the essentials, objects, or essence of the contract. Whether or not they are mentioned explicitly is irrelevant, as these requirements are already mandatory under the specific terms of the contract itself and nothing new is introduced. The subject matter of these conditions is an obligation to fulfil even if none of the parties has so stipulated expressly. This is true in respect of a condition stipulating that the seller deliver the commodity to the buyer; the buyer's right to return the commodity in the event of defects; the buyer's obligation to pay the price before possession;[115] and the buyer's right to own, use,[116] sell, gift, or mortgage the purchased commodity.[117] These conditions do not explain, enhance, or improve the nature of the contract.[118] **7.63**

5.1.2 Conditions Which Emphasize the Objectives of the Contract

These are not relevant to the purpose of the contract but confer a beneficial value on the object of the contract or the contracting parties. These conditions improve and complete the essence of the contract and eliminate the likelihood of denial and refusal. Examples include stipulations for guarantee or mortgage in a delayed sale, witness participation in a contract, as well as a stipulation of a particular quality in the goods.[119] **7.64**

113 Al Ḥaṣkafī (n 12) p. 394.
114 Ibn Humām (n 47) Vol. 6, p. 367.
115 Al Ḥaṣkafī (n 12) p. 413; Mālik ibn Anas, Al-Mudawwana al-Kubrā (Dār al-kutb al-ʿIlmiyya, 1994) Vol. 3, p. 185.
116 Al-Kalughātī, Al- Hidāya fil Mazhab al-Ḥanbalī (Ghīras Publications 2004) p. 239; Al Ghazālī (n 24) Vol. 1, p. 279.
117 Muṣṭafā al-Madanī, Al-Tazhīb fi Matan al-Ghāya wa al-Taqrīb (Dār Ibn Kathīr, 1989) pp. 125–27.
118 Al-Kalughātī (n 116) p. 239.
119 Al-Marḍāwī, Al-Tanqīḥ al-Mushab (Dār al Salfiyya, 2004) p. 127.

These conditions are binding on those to whom they are addressed and the contract is validated with these conditions. Moreover, the person who imposed these conditions will have a right to revoke or terminate the contract if these are not fulfilled. Some other examples include conditions describing the subject matter, as is the case with land required to be free of charge or mortgage,[120] or land which may be used for agriculture.[121]

5.1.3 Conditions Validated by the *Shar'*

7.65 These types of conditions are specified in the text of the contract or derived by a *ṣaḥīḥ qiyās*, such as the options granted to both parties, the option of a known time period, and the option of specification and cash.

5.1.4 Conditions Based on *'Urf*

7.66 If a condition is based on *'urf* then it may be relied upon. Although an *'urf*-based condition is binding, it is necessary that both parties are accustomed to it and that it is applicable in the place of work or residence of both parties. If it is foreign to at least one party it is not considered a valid *'urf*.[122] This is true, for example, where a buyer buying a lock stipulates that the seller will fix it on the door, or the seller will provide maintenance for a certain period for the sold commodity. If a practice does not amount to a custom in the jurisdiction where the contract is formed, then a condition based on an alien *'urf* is considered *fāsid* and so is the contract.[123]

7.67 An *'urf* by default is only valid where it does not contradict Islamic law. These types of conditions are prescribed by Hanafis and very much resemble the Hanbalis' wide scope of valid conditions, given their aim of *al-aṣl fi al-ashyā al-ibāḥa*.[124]

5.2 *Fāsid* Conditions

7.68 These conditions may give rise to a conflict as they encompass uncertainty (*gharar*) or incorporate a prohibited term or benefit one of the two parties.[125] Conditions carrying *gharar* cannot be determined with certainty.[126] If any prohibited matter is stipulated as a condition, this is considered a *fāsid* condition, for example the sale of an animal for fights as the Prophet has prohibited it.[127] According to the Hanafi school, if a *fāsid* condition is imposed in a commutative contract then the contract will become *fāsid*, but if the contract is non-commutative then it does not become *fāsid* merely because of the introduction of a *fāsid* condition. Rather, the condition will be void but the contract will

[120] Al-Madanī (n 117) pp. 125–27.
[121] Ibid, pp. 125–27; Al-Māwardī (n 11) Vol. 5, pp. 342, 375.
[122] Al-Ḥaṣkafī (n 12) p. 413.
[123] *Radd al-Muḥtār* (n 2) Vol. 5, p. 51.
[124] Ibid.
[125] Al-Kāsānī (n 15) Vol. 5, p. 139.
[126] Ibn Nujaim (n 2) Vol. 5, p. 300.
[127] Al- Zaili'ī, Tabyīn al-Sharḥ Kanz al-Daq ā'iq (Al-Maktba al Amīriyya, 1896) Vol. 4, p. 133.

remain valid. Ibn Āʿbidīn narrates that every *fāsid* condition leads to *ribā*. *Ribā* consists of any profit without liability and is applicable only in commutative contracts[128]

5.3 *Bāṭil* Conditions

These conditions are devoid of any characteristics pertaining to *ṣaḥīḥ* conditions and do not benefit any of the parties or any third party. These conditions do not emphasize the object of the contract, nor do they relate to the essence of the contract or to *ʿurf* (practice). When these conditions are abrogated and the contract is restored it becomes free of these conditions.[129] In *fatāwā Bazāziyya* it is mentioned that a *fāsid* condition will not void the contract if this is not of a commutative nature. Contracts pertaining to loans, gifts, charity, *nikāḥ*/marriage, divorce, *khulʿ*, and emancipation are not void by the insertion of a void condition; rather, the condition is void and once removed the contract is validated.[130] **7.69**

These conditions can be categorized into two groups. The first concerns conditions which negate/contradict the essence of the contract, or which negate and nullify the conditions necessary for the validity of the contract, which effectively vitiate it. This includes, for example, two sales in one.[131] Similarly, the stipulation that the buyer will not become the owner of property after the purchase vitiates the contract. The same is true with the condition that a partner will receive only a fixed amount from the profit of a partnership because this condition becomes an impediment to the object of the contract which intended to confer a share in the profit and here the predetermined/fixed amount is not a share in the profit.[132] **7.70**

The second concerns conditions which are void as such, albeit the contract remains valid. This consists of conditions which are in conflict with the essence of the contract, but which do not terminate it altogether because they have no effect on it. The rationale is that these conditions have no use, and thus by removing them from the contract nothing is lost, and the will/consent of the parties is not altered or affected.[133] This is the same as a condition imposed by the seller that the buyer will not sell, benefit, or donate the purchased commodity; such a stipulation hinders the buyer's right of use and ownership. Equally, in the event of *mudāraba* if the *rab al-māl* imposes on *al-āʿmil* (the person contributing capital) that he will give credit to the *rab al-māl* or dress him or indemnify the investment/money, such conditions are *fāsid*.[134] **7.71**

[128] *Radd al-Muḥtār* (n 2) Vol. 5, p. 49.
[129] Ibn Marraāh (n 66) Vol. 7, p. 130.
[130] *Radd al-Muḥtār* (n 2) Vol. 5, p. 80.
[131] Ibn Qudāma, ʿUmdah fi Fiqh (Al Maktabah al-ʿAsriyya, 2004) p. 241.
[132] Al-Mardāwī (n 1) Vol. 4, pp. 357–64.
[133] Ibid.
[134] Al Kalughātī (n 116) p. 239.

8

Contractual Terms

The Rights of Option (*Khiyārāt*) and Conditions (*Shurūṭ*)

1. Introduction

Contractual terms in Islamic law are governed by detailed rules, prohibitions, and exceptions in contrast to the civil and common law legal systems in which parties are generally free to agree terms according to their needs and interests. In the latter legal families, it makes less sense to speak of a highly regulated system of contractual terms since, in general, restrictions do not infringe party autonomy. The Sharīʿah places more extensive limits on parties' freedom to contract and these limits necessitate a jurisprudence which conceptualizes and organizes these limitations and, finally, provides legal justifications for them. We shall see that the schools differ markedly in some aspects of their jurisprudence concerning contractual terms. Whereas the Hanafis and Shafi'is take more lenient approaches to the rules concerning the rights of option (sing. *khiyār*; pl. *khiyārāt*), the Hanbalis and Malikis are decidedly liberal in relation to extrinsic options (sing. *sharṭ*, pl. *shurūṭ*). The reasons for these different approaches will be explored. 8.01

The rights of option are contractual terms which the schools of law have developed to ensure parties' consent to the contract. Options safeguard parties from making hasty decisions, in some cases and, in others, protect buyers from unscrupulous sellers in the case of fraud, defect, deception, and so on. A right of option provides the option holder with a unilateral choice to void (*faskh*) or conclude (*imḍā'*) a contract, underscoring Islamic law's interest in safeguarding the consent of the parties to the contract. Some options exist as a legal right and do not need to be incorporated whereas other options require agreement, rendering the contract non-binding (*ghayr lāzim*) and suspended until such time as the contract is concluded or rejected. When the option holder has decided to conclude the contract, the obligation becomes binding (*lāzim*). Should the option holder decide to rescind the contract, it is as though the contract had never existed, and the parties are returned to their pre-contractual positions.[1] 8.02

In contrast to the *khiyārāt*, which are developed and agreed intrinsically by the schools, the *shurūṭ* (conditions or stipulations) are the product of extrinsically produced stipulations which parties seek to include in their contract. In this category of contractual terms, the extent of contractual freedom is most visible. Our analysis centres on the 8.03

[1] Muṣṭafā Aḥmad Zarqā, *Al-Madkhal Al-fiqhī Al-ʿām: Thalāthat aqsām fī Juzʾaīn* (Dār al-Qalam, al-Ṭabʿah 2, 2004) p. 535. See also Susan E. Rayner, *The Theory of Contracts in Islamic Law* (Graham & Trotman, 1991) p. 305.

schools' varied approaches to these stipulations. Notably, the relevance of this analysis to modern contractual relations is unmistakable.

8.04 It is important to bear in mind that the use of the term 'conditions' refers to stipulations or terms wherein the existence of one thing depends on the existence of another thing (which is nonetheless existentially separated from the former).[2] 'Conditions' in the common law legal system refer to the classification of contractual terms as those fundamental terms which go to the root of the contract. Although we shall learn that Islamic law also categorizes contractual terms, it does so differently according to its own logic. The reader is advised to distinguish between these usages.

8.05 Sections 2 to 5 address the *khiyārāt* with the aim of providing a general overview of these types of terms which the schools developed endogenously. Sections 6 to 9 deal with *shurūṭ* and are focused on the schools' varying approaches to contractual freedom which these extrinsically developed stipulations underscore.

2. The Typologies of the Rights of Option

8.06 The typologies of *khiyārāt* can be distinguished in two categories. The first category contains options which require mutual consent for their validity. The parties must agree to these options before concluding the contract for these options to be valid. Examples are the option of contractual session (*khiyār al-majlis*), the option of specification (*khiyār al-ta'yīn*), and the option to defer payment within a specified time limit (*khiyār al-naqd*).[3]

8.07 The second category options are implied by operation of law. These types of options concern the substantive fairness of the contract such as the option for misdescription (*khiyār al-waṣf*), the option of inspection (*khiyār al-ru'ya*), and the option of defect (*khiyār al-'ayb*).

8.08 Our discussion begins with the first category of options, namely, those in which the parties' consent is necessary for the validity of the option. The default option of this category, the *khiyār al-sharṭ*, lays down some general principles and for this reason is given greater attention here. *Khiyār al-ta'yīn (specification)*, *khiyār al-ru'ya* (*inspection*), and (*khiyār al-'ayb*) (defect) are addressed in Chapter 15. In this section, they receive only general treatment.

[2] 'Abd al-Karīm Zīdān, *Wajīz fī Uṣūl al-Fiqh* (Mu'assasat Qurṭuba, n.d.) p. 59.
[3] Nicholas Kourides, 'The Influence of Islamic Law on Contemporary Middle Eastern Legal Systems: The Formation and Binding Force of Contracts' (1970) 9(2) *Columbia Journal of Transnational Law* 384, p. 407.

3. The Default Condition: *Khiyār Al-Sharṭ*

The Malikis recognized just two types of options: the so-called default option which allows the option holder to ponder the contract (*khiyār al-sharṭ*) and the option due to diminution (*khiyār al-naqīsa*). The Malikis also viewed this type of option as a legal right and so it is available to the affected party irrespective of whether it was stipulated in the contract.[4] 8.09

The *khiyār al-sharṭ* allows one or both parties to stipulate a condition in the contract which provides them with an option to rescind or affirm the sale within a fixed period.[5] The option allows the contracting party(ies) to determine any incidence of defect, fraud, mistake, or misdescription, or simply to determine the advantages of the transaction. However, the option disturbs the normal rules of the contract of sale, making the contract contingent on the expiry of an unlimited term, and opening the contract to the possibility of exploitation or fraud.[6] But options may not be contingent on some future, uncertain event as this would render the contract uncertain and void due to *gharar*.[7] 8.10

3.1 Duration of the Option

The Hanafis and Shafi'is and a majority of the Hanbalis generally agree that the option should not exceed three days.[8] The Majalla, on the other hand, leaves this to the parties to decide.[9] The famous students of Abū Ḥanīfa, Al-Shaybānī and Al-Sarakhsī, argued that the expiry of the term could be unlimited.[10] The Hanbalis and Shafi'is considered the 'eternal option' invalid whereas the majority of the Hanafis considered it merely defective and subject to rectification.[11] 8.11

The Malikis suggest an alternative by allowing the period of the option to last as long as necessity dictates. They categorized objects of sale according to such necessity so that fruit, for example, could not be sold with an option of more than one day whereas a house or similar object could be sold with an option of one month. The time afforded 8.12

4 Wahbah al-Zuḥaylī, *Financial Transactions in Islamic Jurisprudence*, trans. Mahmoud Al. El-Gamal (Dār al-Fikr, 2003) Vol. 1, p. 166.
5 Majallat Al-Aḥkām Al-'Adlīyyah, Art. 300.
6 Rayner (n 1) p. 311.
7 Ibid, p. 309.
8 Muḥammad Ibn Idrīs al-Shāfi'ī and Rif'at Fawzī 'Abd al-Muttalib, *Al-Umm* (al-Ṭab'ah 1, Dār al-Wafā' lil-Ṭibā'ah wa-l-Nashr wa-l-Tawzī', 2001) pp. 6–11; see also Muḥammad Abū Zahrah, *Al-Milkīyah Wa-naẓarīyat Al-'aqd fī Al-sharī'ah Al-Islāmīyah* (Dār al-Fikr al-'Arabī, 1996).
9 Majallat Al-Aḥkām Al-'adlīyyah, Art. 301.
10 Abūbakr Muḥammad b. Abī Sahal al-Sarakhsī, *Kitāb al-Mabsūṭ* (Dār al-Fikr, n.d.) Vol. 8, p. 72.
11 Abū Isḥāq al-Shīrāzī, *Al-Muhadhdhab fī Fiqh al-Imām al-Shāfi'ī* (al-Ṭab'ah 1, Dār al-Qalam, 1992) Vol. 3, p. 13; 'Abd al-Raḥmān al-Jazīrī, *Kitāb Al-fiqh 'alā Al-madhāhib Al-arba'ah* (Dār al-Kutub al-'ilmiyyah, 1998) Vol. 2, p. 161.

via this option allowed the parties to inspect the object of sale according to commercial exigencies.[12]

3.2 Extinguishing the Option

8.13 The option may be extinguished in the following ways:

1. When the option-holder elects to exercise the option, the option is no longer valid.[13] The affirmation or revocation of the contract must be expressed verbally or implicitly, and most jurists require that the other party be informed of the decision. However, contrary to Abū Ḥanīfa (d. 767) and his disciple, Shaybānī (d. 805), the Hanafi jurist Zaylaʿī (d. 1361) distinguished between revocation and affirmation, and this is the opinion which became the consensus opinion of the school. Ratification according to Zaylaʿī does not require notification as it is assumed that the other party is implicitly informed since he has not had the object of sale returned to him. Should the option-holder decide to rescind the contract, he must inform the other party of his decision. Failure to do so renders the contract binding on him.[14]
2. When the option has lapsed without having been exercised, the Hanbalis and Shafi'is view the contract as having been affirmed and made retroactively binding.[15] Notably, during the period of the option the contract is regarded as *ghayr lāzim* (non-binding). Imām Mālik required that the option-holder decide the time at which the option lapses. For this eponym, the lapse of time does not render the contract binding.[16]
3. Should the option-holder die prior to exercising the option, the option is invalidated, and the contract becomes binding according to the Hanafis. The conditional option is not inheritable for these schools. In contrast, Shafi'is and Malikis ruled that the option does not become void upon the death of the option-holder and can be inherited.[17]
4. Where loss or damage occurs to the object of sale during the period of the option, the option is invalidated. Loss or damage to the object and the effects on the contracting parties are discussed below.

[12] Abū al-Walīd Ibn Rushd, *Bidāyat al-Mujtahid wa Nihāyat al-Muqtaṣid (The Distinguished Jurist's Primer)*, trans. Imran Ahsan Khan Nyazee (Garnet Publishing, 1994) Vol. 1, p. 250.
[13] Abū Bakr Ibn Masʿūd al-Kāsānī, *Badāʾiʿ Al-ṣanāʾiʿ Fī Tartīb Al-sharāʾiʿ* (al-Qāhirah, 1909) pp. 267, 271.
[14] ʿUthmān Ibn ʿAlī, ʿAbd Allāh Ibn Aḥmad Nasafī Zaylaʿī, *Tabyīn Al-ḥaqāʾiq* (Maktabat Būlāq, 1896–97) Vol. 4, p. 15.
[15] Wahbah Muṣṭafā al-Zuḥaylī, *Al-Fiqh Al-Islāmī Wa-adillatuhu* (al-Ṭabʿah 2, Dār al-Fikr al-Muʿāṣir, 1985) Vol. 4, p. 542.
[16] See ibid, p. 542 who is referencing Mālik Ibn Anas (d. 795) et al., *Al-Mudawwanah Al-Kubrā Li-l-Imām Mālik Ibn Anas al-Aṣbaḥī* (al-Ṭabʿah 1, Dār al-Kutub al-ʿIlmīyah, 1994) Vol. 3, p. 233.
[17] Abū al-Walīd Ibn Rushd and Mājid Ḥamawī, *Bidāyat Al-mujtahid Wa-nihāyat Al-muqtaṣid* (Dār Ibn Ḥazm, 1995) Vol. 3, p. 1313.

3.3 Loss or Damage to the Object of Sale

If the object of sale has not been transferred to the buyer, that is, it is still in the possession of the seller, and the object of sale suffers damage or perishes, then: **8.14**

The option is extinguished, and the contract is invalidated.[18] The contract is invalidated as the object of the contract is incapable of delivery. **8.15**

If the object of sale has been transferred to the buyer, and the object suffers damage or perishes in the buyer's possession, then: **8.16**

If the seller has the right of option, the buyer is still liable to pay the equivalent value of the object, but he is released from paying the contractual price.[19] **8.17**

Where the buyer has the option, and the object of sale perishes, the contract is not invalidated, and the option is not extinguished. However, because the defect or absence of the object of contract prevents the buyer from returning the object to the seller, the result is that the option is rendered useless, and the sale becomes binding. The buyer is liable for paying the price as the contract has become binding.[20] **8.18**

Where the buyer has the option, and the object of sale is damaged through the actions of the seller or a natural event, the option is extinguished. This is the case whether the object of sale is in the possession of the buyer or the seller. The sale is voided for the damaged part of the object of sale, but the contract is also voided for the remaining part as the contract may not be partitioned after the contract has been concluded. **8.19**

Where the buyer or a third party has caused the damage to the object of sale, the contract is not voided. The seller has the right to proceed with the contract—indeed, the seller is incentivized to proceed in this manner—in which case the buyer or third party is liable for the diminution in value. In cases where the buyer has caused the damage to the object, he is personally liable for the loss. If the damage was caused by a third party, the buyer may impose a fine since the property belongs to the buyer, and third-party damage to such property renders the third party liable to damages.[21] **8.20**

4. Other Option Types

The Hanafis arrived at seventeen options. The *Majalla* recognized six of these. These are, in no particular order, the (i) *khiyār al-majlis* (option to withdraw offer/acceptance in the contractual meeting), (ii) *khiyār al-ru'ya* (inspection), (iii) *khiyār al-'ayb* (defect), (iv) *khiyār al-waṣf* (misdescription), (v) *khiyār al-naqd* (specified payment period), (vi) **8.21**

[18] Abūbakr Muḥammad b. Ibī Sahal al-Sarakhsī (n 10) Vol. 13, p. 44.
[19] Rayner (n 1); cf. Abū Bakr Ibn Mas'ūd al-Kāsānī (n 13) Vol. 5, p. 272; see also Jazīrī (n 11) p. 164.
[20] Abū Bakr Ibn Mas'ūd al-Kāsānī (n 13) Vol. 5, p. 272.
[21] Wahbah al-Zuḥaylī (n 4) Vol. 1, p. 191.

khiyār al-ta'yīn (specification/selection), (vii) *khiyār al-ghubn ma'a al-taghrīr* (injustice through excessive ignorance or uncertainty).[22] Let us examine these options in turn.

4.1 *Khiyār Al-Majlis*

8.22 The option to withdraw (*khiyār al-majlis*) an offer or acceptance while both parties are present in the contractual session provides either party in a contract with the freedom to withhold his acceptance after an offer has been made.[23] Traditionally, the Hanafi and Maliki jurists do not acknowledge the lawfulness of this type of option as their jurisprudence concludes that a contract is binding once the offer and acceptance have been exchanged. In contrast, the Shafi'is and the Hanbalis ruled that the parties have the right to withdraw from the contract if they have not parted ways or left the place where the archetypical sale is concluded.[24] The option is also extinguished by a party's renunciation of the option, whether express or implicit; the death of either of the contracting parties; the loss of the object during the *majlis*; or by agreeing to a *khiyār al-sharṭ*.[25] All schools agree that this option is not valid in unilateral contracts such as gift, *waqf* (endowment), *ḥawāla* (debt transfer), *shuf'a* (pre-emption), agency, *ju'āla* (reward), and partnerships (which are revocable by either partner). The Hanbalis include *muḍāraba* and *muzāra'a* amongst these partnerships.[26] They base this decision on the strong *ḥadīth* narrated by Abū Ḥanīfa and Abū Yūsuf (d. 798) that the Prophet was to have said: 'The two parties to a sale have the option as long as they have not parted or that one of them has given the other that option.'[27] Evidently, the Majalla adopted this option from these latter schools' jurisprudence as the Ottomans subscribed to the Hanafi school.

4.2 *Khiyār Al-Waṣf*

8.23 An option for misdescription (*khiyār al-waṣf*) arises when the vendor sells property on the condition that it contains certain desirable characteristics, and the delivered property proves to be devoid of that characteristic(s). In this instance the option allows the buyer to cancel the sale or affirm the contract for the full price.[28] This option applies to

[22] Ibid, Vol. 1, p. 165.
[23] Majallat Al-Aḥkām Al-'Adlīyyah, Art. 182.
[24] Muḥammad Ibn Aḥmad Shirbīnī, *Mughnī Al-muḥtāj Ilā Ma'rifat Ma'ānī Alfāẓ al-Minhāj* (al- Ṭab'ah 1, Dār al-Kutub al-'Ilmīyah, 1994) Vol. 2, p. 403; 'Abd Allāh Ibn Aḥmad Ibn Qudāmah al-Maqdisī, *Al-Mughnī* (al-Ṭab'ah 4, al-Amānah al-'āmmah li-l-iḥtifāl bi-murūr mi'at 'ām 'alā ta'sīs al-mamlakah, 1999) Vol. 4, pp. 10–17.
[25] Rayner (n 1) p. 308.
[26] 'Abd Allāh Ibn Aḥmad Ibn Qudāmah al-Maqdisī (n 24) p. 49. Ibn Qudāmah indicates in *Al-Mughnī* that he is undecided whether the option can be added to the *muzāra'a*.
[27] Muḥammad Ibn Ismā'īl Ṣan'ānī, *Al-'Uddah: Ḥāshīyat Al-'Allāmah Al-Sayyid Muḥammad Ibn Ismā'īl Al-Amīr Al-Ṣan'ānī Al-mutawaffā Sanat 1182 H 'alā Ihkām Al-Ahkām: Sharḥ'Umdat Al-ahkām Lil-'Allāmah Ibn Daqīq Al-'Īd Al—Mutawaffā Sanat 702 H* (Dār al-Kutub al-'Ilmīyah, 1999) Vol. 3, p. 428.
[28] Majallat Al-Aḥkām Al-'Adlīyyah, Art. 310.

sales where the object of sale is absent from the contractual session. The Shafi'is and the Hanbalis consider this option a sub-category of the defect option (*khiyār al-'ayb*) whereas the Hanafis approve it based on juristic preference (*istiḥsān*).[29]

The missing characteristic of the object of sale must be legally permissible or else the option is invalidated. Likewise, it must be customarily desired. If the characteristic does not meet this requirement, the option is invalidated, whereas the sale is validated. An example is the sex of an animal whereby the purchase of an animal under the assumption that it possesses a particular sex, contrary to fact, would not be seen as customarily desirable and hence the contract would be rendered valid.[30] Finally, the specification of the desired characteristic may not lead to uncertainty which results in dispute. If a dispute does arise from the specification, the condition and the sale are defective. An example is the condition that a purchased cow produce so many litres of milk, which is defective because it cannot be controlled.[31] **8.24**

4.3 *Khiyār Al-Naqd*

The parties may stipulate an option for payment (*khiyār al-naqd*) whereby the payment of the price is to be made by a certain deadline or else the sale is cancelled.[32] Normally, the sale is deemed void unless it has been paid within three days. However, Muḥammad Al-Shaybānī (d. 805), a leading disciple of Abū Ḥanīfa, allowed parties to stipulate any mutually agreeable period. If the price is paid within three days, there is a consensus that this type of option is permissible since it is modelled on the default condition option, the *khiyār al-sharṭ*. The condition option, unlike the payment option, is binding when the period of the option lapses without a party having exercised the option. In contrast, the default position for the price payment option is that unless the price has been paid within the three-day period, the sale becomes defective if the object of sale remains in its original condition. According to the Hanbalis, however, the sale becomes void.[33] **8.25**

[29] Wahbah al-Zuḥaylī (n 4) pp. 168–69.
[30] Ibid, p. 169.
[31] Ibid.
[32] Majallat Al-Aḥkām Al-'Adlīyyah, Arts 313–315.
[33] Manṣūr Ibn Yūnus al-Buhūtī and Ḥujāwī Mūsā Ibn Aḥmad, *Kashshāf Al-qinā' 'an Matn Al-iqnā'* (Maṭba't al-Ḥukūmah, 1974) Vol. 3, p. 184; Abūbakr Muḥammad b. Abī Sahal al-Sarakhsī (n 13) Vol. 13, p. 50; Muḥammad Ibn 'Abd al-Wāḥid Ibn al-Humām, 'Abd al-Razzāq Ghālib Mahdī, Aḥmad Ibn Maḥmūd Qāḍī Zādah, and 'Alī Ibn Abī Bakr Marghinānī, *SharẓFatḥ al-qadīr* (Dār al-Kutub al-'Ilmīyah, 1995) p. 281. See also Muḥammad Amīn Ibn 'Umar Ibn 'Ābidīn, Ḥusām al-Dīn Farfūr, 'Abd al-Razzāq Ḥalabī, and Muḥammad Sa'īd Ramaḍān Būṭī, *Ḥāshiyat Ibn 'Ābidīn* (al-Ṭab'ah 1, Dār al-Thaqāfah wa-l-Turāth, 2000) Vol. 14, p. 269.

4.4 *Khiyār Al-Ta'yīn*

8.26 A variation of the *khiyār al-sharṭ*, the option of selection (*khiyār al-ta'yīn*) allows a party at the time of contracting to reserve an option to select an object of sale from several objects within a stipulated period.[34] The option is implicitly directed at objects of sale whose complexities are avoided through onsite inspection.[35] The option holder may also elect to rescind the contract and the parties are placed in their pre-contractual positions. The reserve proposition allowed by this option allows the seller to give the buyer whichever object he chooses unless the buyer is absent, in which case there must be mutual consent. The Hanafis permit this option based on *istiḥsān* and the benefit it offers contracting parties, despite the ignorance or uncertainty concerning which object of sale will eventually be chosen. They argue that the option protects parties from the disadvantage which may result from a defect or some other cause. The option to choose the desired object on sight avoids this possibility. The sale becomes binding once the option-holder has made his choice of object.[36]

8.27 In contrast, the Shafi'is and the Hanbalis find this ignorance excessive and rule that the option is invalid as it does not conform to Islamic contractual principles.[37] These latter schools validate the *khiyār al-sharṭ*, but for this option they find proof in a *ḥadīth* of the Prophet and commercial expediency whereas the same, they argue, cannot be ascribed to the *khiyār al-ta'yīn.*[38]

4.4.1 Necessary Conditions for Validity

8.28 Anxious to prevent exploitation of the uncertainty brought about by the option of selection, the Hanafi and Maliki jurists enumerate several necessary conditions for its validity:[39]

1. The option is only applicable to bilateral contracts where property is transferred for consideration.
2. Both contractual parties may exercise the option whereas third parties may not.
3. The option must be described in detail and with accuracy.
4. A total number of three objects of sale may be stipulated for selection or else be ruled defective on grounds of *gharar*.

[34] Majallat Al-Aḥkām Al-'Adlīyyah, Arts 316–318.
[35] Abū Bakr Ibn Mas'ūd al-Kāsānī (n 13) Vol. 5, p. 261; Aḥmad Ibn Muḥammad Ṣāwī, Aḥmad Ibn Muḥammad Dardīr, and Muḥammad 'Abd al-Salām Shāhīn, *Bulghat Al-Sālik Li-Aqrab Al-masālik 'alā Al-Sharḥ al-Ṣaghīr Li-l-Quṭb Sayyidī Aḥmad Al-Dardīr* (Dār al-Kutub al-'Ilmīyah, 1995) Vol. 3, p. 89.
[36] Abū Bakr Ibn Mas'ūd al-Kāsānī (n 13) Vol. 5, p. 262; Muḥammad Ibn 'Abd al-Wāḥid Ibn al-Humām (n 33) Vol. 6, p. 300. (Ḥaṭṭāb is a Maliki scholar—the statement describes the Hanafi position.) See Muḥammad Ibn Muḥammad Ḥaṭṭāb (d. 1365), Khalīl Ibn Isḥāq al-Jundī, Muḥammad Ibn Yūsuf Mawwāq, and Zakarīyā 'Umayrāt, *Mawāhib Al-Jalīl Li-sharḥ Mukhtaṣar Khalīl* (al-Ṭab'ah 1, Dār al-Kutub al-'Ilmīyah, 1995) Vol. 6, p. 326.
[37] Muḥammad Ibn 'Abd al-Wāḥid Ibn Al-Humām (n 33) Vol. 6, p. 300; see also 'Abd Allāh Ibn Aḥmad Ibn Qudāmah al-Maqdisī and 'Abd al-Raḥmān Ibn Muḥammad Ibn Qudāmah, *Al-Mughnī* (Dār al-Fikr, 1984) Vol. 4, p. 33.
[38] Rayner (n 1) p. 320.
[39] Ibid, pp. 320–21. A detailed analysis of liability in relation to loss or damage of the objects of contract is provided in Chapter 15.

5. The Hanafis require that the objects of sale provided for selection be of the same class but differ from one another in quality or kind.
6. The Hanafis require that the price and period of delay be agreed prior to selection. The Malikis allow for a single price to be affixed for all objects. They employ the same liberal approach used in relation to *shurūṭ* to this option, ruling that delay will vary according to the nature of the transaction and according to customary practices.

4.5 *Khiyār Al-Ru'ya*

An option of inspection (*khiyār al-ru'ya*) provides the purchaser with the option to accept or reject the object of sale in sales where the buyer has not had the opportunity to inspect the object.[40] In contrast to the specification option, the inspection option is established by law (*shar'*) and is therefore implied into the contract. The Hanafis relied on the *ḥadīth* narrated on the authority of Abū Hurayrah (d. 678) and Ibn 'Abbās (d. 687) which stated: 'if someone buys an item without seeing it, then he has an option until he sees it'.[41] Furthermore, according to the Hanafis, the legality of this option is seen as one where consensus (*ijmā'*) has been established although other schools ruled that the sale based on this option is binding only if the characteristics of the object of sale match its description. Where there is a match, the buyer has an option.[42] Ibn Rushd (d. 1198), the Andalusian jurist and polymath, clarified the schools' opinions concerning the *khiyār al-ru'ya* in the following:[43] 8.29

> Items sold are two types: items that are present and observable, and there is no disagreement on the permissibility to sell these. And items that are not present (*ghā'ib*) and there is disagreement between scholars on this. Some say that selling unseen items is not allowed regardless of whether description is offered or not. This is the position of the Shafi'is . . . Mālik and the people of Madina say: it is permitted to sell unseen items based on their description if it is deemed unlikely that their described characteristics will change before it is delivered to the buyer. Abū Ḥanīfa says: it is permitted to sell a specified item without description, then when he sees it, he [the buyer] has the option to conclude the sale or rescind it . . . for Mālik, if the item matches its description, the sale becomes binding.

By analogy with the *salam* (forward sale), the Hanbalis deem this option valid, although hidden characteristics not included in the description of the object are excluded from 8.30

[40] Majallat Al-Aḥkām Al-'Adlīyyah, Arts 320–335.

[41] Al-Nawawī reported that amongst those who memorized *Aḥādīth* this is considered weak one. See Wahbah al-Zuḥaylī (n 15) p. 577.

[42] Muḥammad Ibn Aḥmad Ibn Juzayy, *Al-Qawānīn Al-fiqhīyah* (Dār al-Kitāb al-'Arabī, 1984) p. 256; 'Abd Allāh Ibn Aḥmad Ibn Qudāmah al-Maqdisī (n 24) Vol. 4, p. 84.

[43] Abū al-Walīd Ibn Rushd (n 17) pp. 1219–21.

the effects of the option.[44] Presumably, the buyer will reject an object where the characteristics do not match the description.

4.6 *Khiyār Al-'Ayb*

8.31 Finally, the option of defect (*khiyār al-'ayb*) is a legal right which provides the buyer with a right to reject the object of sale upon discovery of a defect.[45] Defects are defined as any characteristic not normally present in the object of sale and which would result in a difference in value in market trading.[46] This option is not conditional and therefore does not need to be stipulated in the contract for it to be given effect.[47] The legal effects of the defect option differ from the conditional option (*khiyār al-sharṭ*) in that it does not operate as a suspensive term. If the object of sale is defective, the binding nature of the contract is affected whereas the contract itself is valid and hence ownership will have passed to the buyer. For example, where the conditional option has been stipulated in the contract, it fundamentally affects the legal status of the contract, preventing the conclusion of the contract during the term of the option.[48] Early jurists' writings deal with defects in slaves after purchase. However, the option has been extended to all goods as enumerated in the Majalla.[49]

4.6.1 Buyer's Choices when Object of Sale is Defective

8.32 The buyer is given two choices when an object of sale is defective: (i) the buyer may affirm the contract in which case he is liable for the contract price; (ii) he may rescind the contract in which case he may recover the price or be relieved of payment if he has not already paid for the object. If the buyer has paid and received the item, and he chooses to rescind the contract, he must return the object as well.[50]

8.33 The Hanbalis take a stricter approach to payment for a defective object. Where the defect ensued while in the possession of the seller or arose through natural causes, the buyer is given the option to accept the defective object or to rescind the contract. Acceptance requires the payment of the full contractual price.[51]

[44] Wahbah al-Zuḥaylī (n 4) pp. 216–17.
[45] Majallat Al-Aḥkām Al-'Adlīyyah, Arts 336–355.
[46] Muḥammad Ibn 'Abd al-Wāḥid Ibn Al-Humām (n 33) p. 330; Abū Bakr Ibn Mas'ūd al-Kāsānī (n 13) p. 274; Aḥmad Ibn Muḥammad Ṣāwī (n 35) p. 91.
[47] 'Abd Al-Razzāq Al-Sanhūrī, *Maṣādir al-Ḥaqq* (Dār Iḥyā' al-Turāth al-'Arabī, 1997) Vol. 4, p. 216.
[48] Abū Bakr Ibn Mas'ūd al-Kāsānī (n 13) Vol. 5, p. 273.
[49] Muḥammad Ibn Muḥammad Ḥaṭṭāb (n 36) p. 332. Majallat Al-Aḥkām Al-'adlīyyah, Art. 336.
[50] Muḥammad Ibn 'Abd al-Wāḥid Ibn al-Humām (n 33) p. 327.
[51] Yaḥyā Ibn Sharaf Nawawī, 'Ādil 'Abd al-Mawjūd, 'Alī Mu'awwaḍ, and Jalāl al-Dīn Suyūtī, *Rawḍat Al-ṭālibīn* (al-Ṭab'ah 2, Dār al-Kutub al-'Ilmīyah, 2000) Vol. 3, p. 126; 'Abd Allāh Ibn Aḥmad Ibn Qudāmah al-Maqdisī (n 37) Vol. 4, p. 96.

4.6.2 Diminution in Value

The defect option is valid and effective when the defect is discovered both during the sale session (*majlis al-ʿaqd*) or afterwards, when the buyer has taken receipt of the object. The Hanafis agree that a defect is anything which results in a diminution of value as determined by commercial custom.[52] In contrast, the Malikis, who refer to this option as the *khiyār al-naqīṣa*, are more particular, requiring the diminution in value to be discernible or major; the diminution must render the object less suitable for its intended use.[53] The Shafi'is rule that the defect must have prevented the purchaser from carrying out his objectives in relation to the object for the option to rescind the contract.[54] These determinations are objectively ascertainable. **8.34**

4.6.3 Caveat Emptor?

The principle of caveat emptor does not apply here. If, however, the defect is one which may have occurred while in the possession of the buyer, then the judge must inquire with the seller as to the true origin of the defect. If the seller responds negatively, the onus of proof shifts to the buyer to prove that the defect originated in the seller's possession. If the buyer can produce such proof, the object may be returned to the seller unless the seller claims that the buyer was aware of the defect and accepted it. At this point, the buyer may require the seller to swear an oath that he sold the item free of defect. The oath must be unequivocal, for example 'I sold him this item and delivered it without this defect'. Should the seller not be able to swear such an oath, the object will be returned to the seller. There is disagreement as to whether this oath encompasses the period between the conclusion of the contract and the delivery of the object.[55] **8.35**

In cases where the defect is not customary in the respective category of goods, the object of sale can be returned to the seller without the buyer having to prove that the defect occurred whilst in the seller's possession. The seller's only recourse is to prove that the buyer was aware of the defect and accepted it. If the seller is unable to provide proof to this effect, the buyer is required to swear an oath that he was not aware of the defect. Failure to do so prevents the return of the object to the seller.[56] **8.36**

4.6.4 Liability

Furthermore, the liability for defect can be excluded by the parties' agreement. However, according to al-Shaybānī, such an exclusion can only apply to defects existing at the time of sale.[57] There is reluctance amongst the schools to allow parties to agree a term which seeks to exclude the seller's liability for a defect which arises after the conclusion of the sale. Rayner underscores that there is disagreement amongst the schools on this **8.37**

[52] Ibn Muḥammad Amīn Ibn ʿUmar Ibn ʿĀbidīn (n 33) pp. 383–89.
[53] ʿAbd Al-Razzāq Al-Sanhūrī (n 46) Vol. 4, pp. 270, 272. Aḥmad Ibn Muḥammad Ṣāwī (n 35) p. 91.
[54] Yaḥyā Ibn Sharaf al-Nawawī (n 51) p. 120.
[55] Ibn Muḥammad Amīn Ibn ʿUmar Ibn ʿĀbidīn (n 33) p. 416.
[56] Abū Bakr Ibn Masʿūd al-Kāsānī (n 13) pp. 279–80.
[57] Ibid, Vol. 5, pp. 276–77.

point and that disagreement centres on the Islamic aversion to validating contractual terms which are contingent on future exigencies. The nature of exceptions to this prohibition is so restrictive as to preclude the exclusion of liability for defects arising after conclusion of the contract.[58]

4.6.5 Proofs

8.38 Several *ḥadīths* establish proof for the lawfulness of the *khiyār al-ʿayb* including one where the Prophet is to have said: 'A Muslim is a brother to other Muslims. It is not permissible for a Muslim to sell a defective item to his brother without showing it to him.'[59]

8.39 Those are some of the principal *khiyārāt*, which are shared by the schools to varying extents. We now consider the Shafi'i and Hanbali categorizations before turning our attention to conditional stipulations (*shurūṭ*).

4.6.6 The Shafi's' Options

8.40 For their part, the Shafi'is enumerated sixteen valid options which they grouped into two types: (i) Those which allow the parties to choose (*khiyār al-tashahhī*). This group of options is focused on the sale session (*majlis al-ʿaqd*) or conditions which can be stipulated. (ii) The second category deals with options which the Shafi'is characterized as those which diminished or impacted the object of sale due to a defect or entitlement (*khiyār al-naqīṣa*). These options are a legal right which arise from verbal disagreement, purposive or active deception, or a conventional legal judgment. Examples of these types of options are the option based on defect (*khiyār al-ʿayb*); the option based on deception (*al-taṣriya*),for example, the udders of a she-camel or female sheep are tied so that the buyer is tricked into believing that the animal produces more milk than it actually does; options for disagreements about reality; and options meeting the caravans outside of town, amongst others.[60]

4.6.7 The Hanbalis' Options

8.41 The Hanbalis agreed upon eight types of option, including (i) *khiyār al-majlis* (contractual session); (ii) *khiyār al-ghubn* (deception); (iii) *khiyār al-tadlīs* (concealment of defect); (iv) *khiyār al-khiyānah* (betrayal); (v) *khiyār tafarruq al-ṣafqa* (sale partition option); (vi) *khiyār al-najash* (price-hiking option); (vii) *khiyār al-mustarsil* (sale or lease with unsound judgment); and (xiii) the *khiyār al-ʿayb* (defect).[61]

[58] Rayner (n 1) p. 332.
[59] Sunan Ibn Mājah, Vol. 3, Book 12, *Hadith* 2246 <https://sunnah.com/ibnmajah:2246> accessed 18 June 2022.
[60] Muḥammad Ibn Aḥmad Al-Shirbīnī (n 24) p. 402; ʿAbd Allāh Ibn Ḥijāzī Sharqāwī, Zakarīyā Ibn Muḥammad Anṣārī, and Musṭafā Ibn Ḥanafī Dhahabī, *Ḥāshiyat Al-Sharqāwī ʿalā Tuḥfat Al-ṭullāb Bi-sharḥ Taḥrīr Tanqīḥ al-Lubāb Li-Abī Yaḥyā Zakarīyā Al-Anṣārī* (al-Ṭabʿah 1, Dār al-Kutub al-ʿIlmiyah, 1997) Vol. 3, pp. 86–107.
[61] Manṣūr Ibn Yūnus Al-Buhūtī (n 33) pp. 166, 186–87, 190, 199, 201, 203, 217, 224.

5. Conditional Stipulations (pl. *Shurūṭ*; sing. *Sharṭ*)

5.1 The Role of Party Autonomy

Party autonomy is subject to three significant sources of restriction in Islamic law. First, parties may not deal in *ribā* (interest). Secondly, a variety of ritually and ethically illicit objects demarcate valid objects of sale. Thirdly, the validity of stipulations which parties seek to include in their contracts varies according to the school. This third category of potential restriction is the locus of much disagreement amongst the jurists. The majority of jurists do not allow contractual freedom where parties are free to agree to terms. The remainder of jurists who do allow parties a great deal of contractual freedom restrict such freedom only to those revealed texts which state prohibition unequivocally. This type of restriction concerns those mentioned in the first and second categories of restriction. **8.42**

5.1.1 The Schools' Policies Toward Freedom of Contract

The underlying difference between these two positions concerns the schools' policies towards contractual freedom and the role of the contracting parties' will or autonomy to draft terms according to their wishes. Those who favour restrictive rules argue that the Lawmaker is He who provides the legal effects of contracts. The Hanafis and Shafi'is are known for their adherence to the principle that the legal effects of every contract are God-given and hence arise naturally.[62] For these schools, the underlying principle in contracts and in relation to stipulations is prohibition/interdiction unless the textual evidence establishes permissibility (*al-ibāḥa*).[63] **8.43**

The overriding concern amongst Hanafis and Shafi'is in relation to their school doctrines concerning *shurūṭ* is the prohibition of interest (*ribā*). These schools prohibit parties from stipulating a benefit for one of the contracting parties which exceeds the primary effects of the contract. The Hanafis' formalistic approach to contractual interpretation is part and parcel of this jurisprudence. Parties' contractual stipulations are limited to avoid the appearance of *ribā* (*shibh al-ribā*) so that on any objective analysis of the contract including its terms and conditions, there is no unjustified return. If the language and cornerstones (contractual bases) of the contract are valid, contextual cues or even transactional matrices which may speak to an unlawful intent are not considered. These schools' approval and use of legal stratagems (*ḥiyal*) are an indication of this highly legalistic approach to the derivation of contractual rules and their eventual interpretation. **8.44**

In contrast, the Hanbalis and Malikis favour permissibility which goes hand in hand with the principle of sanctity of contract whereby parties are obliged to fulfil the terms **8.45**

[62] Rayner (n 1) p. 361.
[63] Muḥammad Abū Zahrah, *Ibn Taymīyah: Ḥayātuhu Wa-ʿaṣruhu - ārāʾuhu Wa-fiqhuhu* (Dār al-Fikr al-ʿArabī, 1977) p. 385.

which they have agreed. The Hanbalis elevate parties' consent to the status of a sufficient condition whereas the Hanafis view it only as a necessary condition and therefore insufficient to validate the transaction. Ibn Taymiyya, the Hanbali jurist, wrote that:

> The principal rule in contracts is the consent of the parties and the legal effect is what the parties committed themselves contractually [to undertake] . . . Since God does not command for commerce except mutual consent, mutual consent validates commerce . . .; thus, if the parties agree together the contract is valid, except if it contains what God and His Prophet forbid such as trading in wine and similar [forbidden] objects.[64]

8.46 The Lawmaker, according to these jurists, bestows parties with the will to create legal effects which entail liability and the promise to fulfil contractual terms. Unless specific textual evidence confirms prohibition and unlawfulness, these schools favour permissibility (*al-ibāḥa*).[65] The principle of non-prohibition (*'adam al-taḥrīm*) underlies all legal contracts and condition clauses with respect to business transactions and everyday transactions whereas those with respect to acts of worship (*al-'ibādāt*) are governed restrictively. The Qur'ān states unequivocally that '[Allah] has detailed for you [exactly] what he has outlawed to you' (Sūrat al-An'am, 119).[66] Ibn Taymiyya argues that this verse should be applied to all objects of material value (*'āmma fī'l-a'yān*), all customary acts, and all legal transactions (*al-Af'āl wa'l-taṣarrufāt*). Allah has not confirmed that a legal contract and/or a condition clause is unlawful except through a specific revealed text. If some act is not specified in the texts as being unlawful, then there is no wrongdoing in doing that thing because wrongdoing only issues from doing something that has been specifically outlawed.[67]

8.47 In modern contractual relations, where foreign contractual practices influence the contract law of Muslim-majority jurisdictions, the relevance of this jurisprudence is unmistakable. It paves the way for bestowing legitimacy on foreign contractual influences and for legal innovation.[68]

8.48 The Hanbali and Maliki approach to contractual intent (*niyya*) favours subjectivity and hence these schools' permissive attitudes towards stipulations are driven by their approach to parties' real intentions or motives underlying legal acts, in contrast to the language or effects of the contract alone. Ibn Taymiyya's disciple, Ibn Qayyim al-Jawziyya (d. 1350) distinguishes these contrasting approaches to contractual interpretation and the effect this has on the schools' determination of which stipulations are licit and which are not:

[64] Aḥmad Ibn 'Abd al-Halīm Ibn Taymiyyah, 'Abd al-Raḥmān Ibn Muḥammad Ibn Qāsim, and Muḥammad Ibn 'Abd al-Raḥmān Ibn Qāsim, *Majmū' Fatāwā Shaykh Al-Islām Aḥmad Ibn Taymiyah* (al-Ṭab'ah 1, Maṭābi' al-Riyāḍ, 1961) Vol. 29, p. 155.

[65] Ibid, p. 132.

[66] Ibid, p. 150.

[67] Ibid.

[68] Oussama Arabi, 'Contract Stipulations (Shurūṭ) in Islamic Law: The Ottoman Majalla and Ibn Taymiyya' (1998) 30(1) *International Journal of Middle East Studies* 29, p. 41.

> Should the law take account only of the manifest meaning of expressions and contracts even when the aims and intentions (*niyyāt*) appear otherwise? . . . Thus if a man buys a slave girl intending that she be for his employer, then she is legally forbidden for him. Whereas if he buys her for himself, then her possession is permissible for him. Though the form of the legal act and contract is the same in both cases, the intention and aim are different. Also, if one sells a weapon to someone whom he knows would be using it to kill a Muslim, then the sale is null and void as it promotes crime and aggression. But the sale is valid if he sells the weapon to someone engaged in holy war in God's way.[69]

Section 6 discusses the schools' respective approaches to *shurūṭ* and the rationales underlying them. **8.49**

6. The *Hanafis'* and *Shafi'is'* Approach to Conditions (*Shurūṭ*)

For these schools every stipulation which does not comply with the contractual rules as handed down by God is null and void. What might be termed the Hanafis' 'fundamental prohibition on stipulation' is attributed to the authority of the school's eponym, Abū Ḥanīfa and a related *ḥadīth* of the Prophet, wherein it is stated: 'I asked Abū Ḥanīfa about the sale contract with an attached condition (*al-bay' bi'l-sharṭ*). He said: "it is invalid (*bāṭil*) . . . 'Amr b. Shu'ayb related to me from his father, from his grandfather, that the Prophet forbade the sale with stipulation." '[70] **8.50**

6.1 Types of Conditions

Despite this far-reaching policy, the Hanafis elaborated several types of conditions which nonetheless reveal the strength of the prohibitive principle. The validity of the following types is subject to the strictly formalist mode of contractual interpretation which the Hanafis and Shafi'is favoured: **8.51**

1. *Shurūṭ* which are implied in the nature of the contract (*Shurūṭ yaqtaḍīhā al-'aqd*) such as the stipulation for the delivery of the object of sale are valid and binding.[71]
2. Stipulations which are appropriate to the contract (*Shurūṭ mulāi'ma al-'aqd*) are those which facilitate compliance with the contract's basic requirements. This allows the stipulation of the pledge of security (*rahn*) or the guarantee (*kafāla*), which are valid and binding. If the buyer does not meet the requirements of the

[69] Ibn Qayyim al-Jawziyya, *I'lām al-Muwaqqi'īn 'an Rabb al-'Ālamīn* (1st edn, Dār Ibn al-Jawzī, 2002) Vol. 4, p. 520.
[70] cf. Arabi (n 68) quoting Abūbakr Muḥammad b. Ibī Sahal al-Sarakhsī, *al-Mabsūṭ* (Al-Sa'āda Press, 1324 A.H.) Vol. 13, p. 13.
[71] Majallat Al-Aḥkām Al-'adlīyyah, Art. 186.

stipulation, the seller has the right to cancel the contract.[72] Al-Kāsānī justified the lawfulness of this stipulation in the following terms:

> The stipulation that is not inherent in the nature of the transaction, but which is appropriate to the contract (*mulā'im li'l-'aqd*) does not void the contract as it concords with its essential meaning and confirms it; so it rejoins the stipulation which is required by the transaction. This is the case if one sells an object on the condition that the buyer pledge a security (*rahn*) as a countervalue to the price, or on the condition that the buyer have a guarantor (*kafīl*) who stands security for the price. In these cases, the sale is legally permissible by virtue of juristic preference (*istiḥsānan*). For analogical inference (*qiyās*) does not permit the sale because, as a matter of principle (*fī'l-Aṣl*), any stipulation which differs from the primary contract invalidates it. Pledge and suretyship clauses, being extraneous to the primary terms of sale, have consequently a voiding effect on the contract. However, we have juristically opted to admit these stipulations because though formally (*ṣūratan*) different from the primary terms of the contract, they nevertheless agree with its essential meaning (*ma'nā*): the pledge of a security as a countervalue to the price is a consolidation of the price; the same holds for suretyship. Both stipulations reinforce the right of the vendor . . . and therefore do not invalidate the contract.[73]

8.52 Kāsānī's (d. 1191) explanation for validating this type of stipulation is remarkable in that it highlights the austerity of Hanafi jurisprudence which does not permit any addition to the primary contract which would bestow an advantage on one party to the detriment of the other. The pledge (*rahn*) or the guarantee (*kafāla*) are separate legal acts which are not intrinsic to the contract of sale, and which provide the seller with security in the event that the buyer defaults on his payment. Yet the need to safeguard the seller's right to the price for the thing sold justifies such an addition and is regarded as according with the basic nature of the sale contract. Juristic preference is the tool which allows the Hanafis to make this leap, overruling strict analogy, which would not permit this stipulation, in favour of a pragmatic solution that facilitates commerce and trade.

6.1.1 Customary Conditions

8.53 Similar reasoning, wherein *qiyās* is overruled in favour of pragmatism, is evident in the justification for allowing customary stipulations. These are:

1. Stipulations which have been established by custom (*sharṭ muta'āraf*) or agreed jurisprudentially such as *khiyār al-sharṭ* (the default condition) are valid and binding even though they are extrinsic to the terms of the contract. For example, if a seller sells cloth on the condition that he mend it or a lock on the condition that it is installed in a door, then these types of common practices are valid.[74] The

[72] Ibid, Art. 187.
[73] Abū Bakr Ibn Mas'ūd al-Kāsānī (n 13) Vol. 5, p. 171.
[74] Salīm Rustam Bāz, *Sharḥ al-Majallah* (Ṭab'ah 3, muṣaḥḥaḥa wa-mazīdah. al-Maṭba'ah al-Adabīyah, 1923) p. 88. See also Muḥammad Ibn 'Abd al-Wāḥid Ibn al-Humām (n 33) p. 406.

Hanafis favour pragmatism over rigid textual objectivity when commercial practice requires it.

2. A stipulation which does not provide a benefit to any of the contracting parties will not be given legal effect (*laghw*) despite the validity of the contract. For example, a stipulation that the object of sale not be sold on to a third party is void whereas the contract of sale is valid.[75] This type of stipulation, which is a negative covenant, is unenforceable according to the Hanafis.[76]
3. Notably, the Majalla is silent concerning the Hanafi policy of invalidating stipulations which benefit only one of the contracting parties.[77] The inclusion of an invalid stipulation has the effect of voiding the entirety of the contract.[78] In Hanafi *fiqh*, this is the *al-sharṭ al-fāsid* (the invalid stipulation) and it is arguably the most significant rule concerning stipulations given its nullifying effect on contracts.[79] In contrast, according to the Shafi'is, if the stipulation is one which is necessitated by the nature of the contract, such as returning a defective item, or a stipulation which contains a benefit to a party, such as the option of delay, the pledge (*rahn*) or guarantor (*ḍāmin*), this is accepted. However, any other stipulation which violates the objective of the contract, such as forbidding the buyer to sell the item or gift it, is void.[80] According to jurists of both schools, stipulations which benefit a party without requiring recompense are extraneous to the effects which naturally result from the sales contract and are usurious.[81]
4. Any one-sided advantage which is conditioned on the agreement of another, so-called combination contracts or 'two sales in one' is unlawful. The Prophet is to have forbidden a sale on condition of a loan.[82] Moreover, such transactions are seen as subject to *gharar* (excessive uncertainty) as the price for the object cannot be apportioned unambiguously.[83] For example, where a seller sells a house and stipulates that he be allowed to reside in the house for a period after the sale this renders the sale contract for the house invalid.[84]
5. Stipulations which delay delivery when goods are ascertained and in existence are invalid and thus invalidate a sale contract in which the immediate exchange of countervalues is the natural rule.[85] In the case of currency exchange, the immediacy is particularly important as it avoids *ribā al-nasī'a* (*ribā* of delay). Indeed, the imprecise deferment of any countervalue is invalid so that any deferment

[75] Salīm Rustam Bāz (n 74) p. 88.
[76] 'Alī Ibn Abī Bakr Marghinānī, 'Alī Ibn Abī Bakr, *The Hedaya: Commentary on the Islamic Laws* (2nd edn. Kitab Bhavan, trans. by Charles Hamilton, 1870) p. 273.
[77] Arabi (n 68).
[78] Joseph Schacht, *Introduction to Islamic Law* (Clarendon Press, 1964) p. 119.
[79] Arabi (n 68) p. 32. Wahbah Muṣṭafā Zuḥaylī (n 15) Vol. 5, p. 3473; Abū al-Walīd Ibn Rushd (n 17) pp. 1219–21.
[80] Muḥammad Ibn Aḥmad Shirbīnī (n 24) p. 381; Abū Isḥāq al-Shīrāzī, Zakarīyā 'Umayrāt, and Muḥammad Ibn Aḥmad Ibn Baṭṭāl al-Rakbī, *Al-Muhadhdhab fī Fiqh al-Imām al-Shāfi'ī* (al-Ṭab'ah 1, Dār al-Kutub al-'Ilmīyah, 1995) Vol. 2, p. 22.
[81] Abū Bakr Ibn Mas'ūd al-Kāsānī (n 13) p. 169; 'Alī Ibn Abī Bakr Marghinānī (n 75) p. 273.
[82] 'Alī Ibn Abī Bakr Marghinānī (n 76) p. 274.
[83] Ibid.
[84] Abū Bakr Ibn Mas'ūd al-Kāsānī (n 13) p. 169.
[85] Schacht (n 78) p. 119.

must be agreed and brought home to the parties to the contract for the condition to be valid.[86]

8.54 The demands of strict analogy to contractual rules, on the one hand, and the pragmatic concessions to market practice, on the other, characterize Hanafi reasoning concerning stipulations. The desire to legalize as many transactions as possible is in constant conflict with the theory of the invalidating condition.[87] The border at which the lawful stipulation merges into the invalid one (*al-sharṭ al-fāsid*) by virtue of an added benefit to one party must be considered on a case-by-case basis. In general, however, it can be concluded that Hanafi concessions to juristic preference and custom do not outweigh the school's restrictive policy on the freedom to contract. The Hanafis' distinctive position concerning the invalid stipulation showcases the school's limitations to party autonomy. This policy is magnified by the ethical and ritual interdictions common to all schools of law.

7. The *Hanbalis*' and *Malikis*' Approach to Conditions (*Shurūṭ*)

8.55 Hanbali jurisprudence concerning stipulations is decidedly permissive in contrast to the Hanafi school. The Hanbalis recognize prophetic traditions concerning the prohibition of 'sales combined with loan contracts' or 'two sales in one' but they liberate the sale contract from Hanafi restrictions by invoking the authority of Ibn Ḥanbal (d. 841), the eponym of the Hanbali school, whose jurisprudence argued that: 'whereas two stipulations in a sale are inadmissible, a single stipulation is permissible'.[88] The justification which Ibn Ḥanbal cites for this ruling is a prophetic *ḥadīth* in which Jābir Ibn ʿAbdallah was to have sold a camel to the Prophet, who consented to the condition that the camel first transport Jābir to his home.[89] Therefore, the prophetic tradition forbids two stipulations whereas one stipulation is permissible according to the Hanbalis. Moreover, Ibn Ḥanbal denied the validity of the Hanafi tradition, claiming that it was 'not mentioned in any certified tradition collection', emphasizing Ibn Ḥanbal's expertise as an expert *ḥadīth* compiler (*muḥaddith*).[90]

7.1 The Juristic Foundation

8.56 The Hanbali *ḥadīth* is widely cited, underscoring its authority as the ideological framework concerning the school's policy toward *shurūṭ*. Al-Khiraqī's (d. 945–46)

[86] ʿAlī Ibn Abī Bakr Marghinānī (n 76) p. 274.
[87] Arabi (n 68) p. 33.
[88] ʿAbd Allāh Ibn Aḥmad Ibn Qudāmah al-Maqdisī (n 24) p. 308.
[89] Ibid.
[90] Arabi (n 68) p. 40.

mukhtaṣar[91] sets out the lawfulness of the single attached condition bestowing benefit on one of the parties. Confirming the rightfulness of this opinion, the Hanbali scholar Ibn al-Bannā' (d. 1097) cites the *ḥadīth* in support of a benefit being passed on to only one of the contracting parties, as in: 'The single stipulation is admissible. The seller may stipulate the usufruct of the sold item for a determined period such as: "I sell you this slave on the condition that he serve me for one month or so. Both the sale and the stipulation are admissible, contrary to the opinion of Abū Ḥanīfa and in accordance with Jābir's report." '[92]

7.1.1 Permissible Terms

8.57 The juridical basis for extending the permissibility of stipulations allows these schools to develop conditions which diverge markedly from the Hanafis and Shafi'is. The Hanbalis and Shafi'is validate those stipulations as set out above, all of which the former schools agree are compatible with the natural effects of the contract, but they recognize a stipulation which benefits one party or indeed a third party to the exclusion of the counterparty. It is this distinctive policy which radically alters these schools' jurisprudence on *shurūṭ* and, indeed, the nature of the terms which parties are allowed to incorporate into their contracts. Examples are a condition for the sale of a house where the seller is allowed to reside in the house for a period. Both schools uphold the validity of this type of stipulation. Another is the sale of land where a condition stipulates that the buyer must build a mosque on that land or bequeath it to a *waqf* (trust).[93]

8.58 The Malikis qualify this one-sided advantage, whether for the counterparty or a third party, to stipulations which are 'reasonable' or 'not excessive', whereas the Hanbalis allow the stipulation without limitation.[94] The Maliki qualification to this permissive jurisprudence is related to this school's concern for restricting the extent of advantage provided by the one-sided stipulation so that exploitation (*Istighlāl*) can be avoided.[95] If the stipulation prevents the buyer from dealing with his items, such as selling or gifting them, the stipulation and sale are void. However, if the seller stipulates some benefit for himself from the item he sold, such as riding the camel or residing in the house for a limited time, this is allowed based on the *ḥadīth* of Jābir. If the seller stipulates something that entails the appearance of *gharar* or *ribā*, the Malikis will allow both sale and stipulation if the risk of these two affecting the contract was slight. However, they disallow the sale and stipulation if the risk was great, and allow the sale but disallow the stipulation if the risk was somewhere in between.[96]

[91] Abū al-Qāsim al-Khiraqī was one of the earliest authorities on Hanbali *fiqh*. His writings were destroyed by fire but his legal manual, *al-Mukhtaṣar* (the Digest), is an important reference work for the Hanbali school.

[92] Abū Alī al-Ḥasan Ibn al-Bannā', *Kitāb al-Muqni' fī Sharḥ Mukhtaṣar al-Khiraqī* (Maktabat al-Rushd, 1993) Vol. 2, pp. 697–98.

[93] Ibid.

[94] 'Abd Allāh Ibn Aḥmad Ibn Qudāmah al-Maqdisī (n 24) p. 308.

[95] Rayner (n 1) p. 359.

[96] Abū al-Walīd Ibn Rushd (n 17) p. 176.

8.59 Where a seller stipulates that he must have first refusal at the cost price should the buyer wish to sell the object, all schools deem this condition invalid except the Hanbalis. Importantly, the ethical and ritual prohibitions including stipulations which result in uncertainty (*gharar*) such as a sale combined with a loan or indeed those which contain interest (*ribā*) are invalid in all schools of law.[97]

7.1.2 The Hanbalis' Freedom to Contract

8.60 The legal writings of the later Hanbali jurists are characterized by even more progressive reflections on *shurūṭ* creating a jurisprudence that most closely approximates the freedom to contract. Ibn Qudāma (d. 1223) and Ibn Taymiyya (d. 1328) and Ibn Taymiyya's disciple, Ibn Qayyim al-Jawziyya, are the most influential jurists of later Hanbali jurisprudence whose works appeared more than one century after the primary Hanafi treatises by al-Sarakhsī and al-Kāsānī. Arabi attributes this temporal distance and the reflection it allowed as having partly contributed to the relative liberalism of these Hanbali authors.[98]

8.61 Ibn Taymiyya's approach to conditional stipulations, which, amongst jurists, extends furthest in its approach to contractual freedom, is premised on his interpretation of the Holy Qur'ān and its bedrock principles regarding the obligation to fulfil contracts. In the Qur'ān, Allah exclaims: 'O you who believe, fulfil [your] legal contracts' and 'Fulfil your legal agreements with Allah', and 'Fulfil [your] legal contract, for indeed the legal contract is a thing [you will be] held to account for'.[99] Therefore, every stipulation or term is an agreement and is binding. Whoever does not fulfil his contracts contravenes this textual stipulation of the Qur'ān.[100]

8.62 Ibn Taymiyya buttresses these Qur'anic proofs with authentic traditions which emphasize the prohibition of breaching agreements. The Prophet is to have said that '[a]of those you sit with are complete hypocrites or a cluster of them (*khuṣla min hunna*) have a cluster of hypocrisy [in them], until he calls them [by name]. If something happens, he lies/rejects it, if he promises to [do something] he goes back on his word; if he contracts [a legal agreement with someone] he breaches it; and if he contests [something in a law case] he acts immorally.'[101] Moreover, 'there will be raised on the Day of Resurrection for everyone who breaches [his legal agreements] a banner by which the degree of his perfidy will be known [to all]', reinforcing the sinfulness of breaching contracts and the punishment for doing so.[102]

8.63 Ibn Taymiyya shows a remarkably modern sensibility for parties' autonomy to contract freely. The underlying principle in contracts, he argues, is the satisfaction of the two contracting parties who have bound themselves legally [to their contractual promises].

97 Ibid.
98 Arabi (n 68) p. 30.
99 The Qur'ān, Surat al-Mā'ida, v. 1; Surat al-Baqara, v. 2:177.
100 Muḥammad Abū Zahra, *Ibn Taymiyah* (n 63) p. 390.
101 Ibid.
102 Ibid.

Allah has declared: 'O you who believe, do not consume each other's property unless there be business transactions among you out of [your own] satisfaction' (*Surat al-Nisā'*:29). Yet Ibn Taymiyya's proofs extend beyond the holy sources to include humanitarian and pragmatic concerns. He states that contracts [and conditional stipulations] are what people need and argues that if people did not need [additional] stipulations, they would not seek to include them in their contracts. He rounds out his argument by restating that legal acts which have not been outlawed should be presumed to be permissible.[103]

[103] Aḥmad Ibn 'Abd al-Halīm Ibn Taymiyya (n 64) p. 156.

9

Bilateral Contracts

1. Introduction

There are two main types of contracts in Islamic law: unilateral and bilateral contracts. Building on the earlier extensive discussions on key aspects of Islamic contract law, this chapter examines key contracts recognized in Islamic law based on several classifications according to Muslim jurists. The chapter covers bilateral contracts for a consideration, with special focus on sales-based contracts and other similar agreements in Islamic jurisprudence. **9.01**

The very essence of a contract in Islamic law is a disposition involving two or more parties. In a typical contract, one party makes the offer while the other provides a corresponding acceptance and this makes the contract a two-party transaction.[1] However, it is important to note that the word *'aqd* is also used for other contracts such as gifts, bequests, and guarantees which are generally considered unilateral contracts.[2] **9.02**

Bilateral contracts with a consideration involve bilateral promises from parties to the contract which is often considered sufficient in concluding the contracts.[3] As discussed earlier, the consent of the parties is a key element in every contract, particularly in bilateral contracts. Without the consent of the parties involved, a bilateral contract is not valid. **9.03**

In Islamic commercial jurisprudence, bilateral contracts are called *'uqūd al-mu'āwaḍāt*, which also implies that such contracts are commutative in their real essence.[4] In commutative contracts, ownership is conferred on either of the parties through an exchange which is often called a consideration. A commutative contract could be a simple sale contract, lease contract, or even a contract of currency exchange. Therefore, the consideration in such commutative contracts is often called *'iwaḍ*. **9.04**

Bilateral contracts often reflect parallel, corresponding, and conforming promises made by the parties; hence, there is always the element of mutual **9.05**

[1] Ibn 'Āshur, Maqasid al-Sharīah al-Islamiyyah (Wizarah al-Awqaf wa al-Shu'un al-Islamiyyah, 2004) Vol. 2, p. 438 (hereafter Ibn 'Ashur, *Kitab Maqasid*).
[2] Ibid.
[3] Nazih Kamal Hammad, Mu'jam al-Muṣṭalaḥāt al-Iqtiṣādiyyah fī Lughah al-Fuqahā' (Dār al-'Alamiyyah li al-Kitāb, 1995) p. 83.
[4] For a detailed analysis on commutative contracts in Islamic financial contracts, see Mahmud Al-Hadir, 'Uqūd al-mu'awadat al-Maliyyah wa mada tahul al-Aham fiha (Dar al-Furqan lil-Nashr wa al-Tawzi'i, 2013).

promises[5] with the intention to create a binding legal relationship. Even though there are different juristic views regarding the binding nature of bilateral promises,[6] there is general unanimity among jurists that commercial and financial contracts with consideration while the parties have the intention of creating a legal relationship are binding on the parties.[7] This is contextualized within the modern-day contract laws and the increasing interactions between the Islamic legal system and other world legal systems such as the civil law and the English common law.[8]

2. Classification of Bilateral Contracts

9.06 In Islamic commercial jurisprudence, various Muslim jurists have provided different classifications of bilateral contracts. A common classification is as follows: general contracts of exchange (*'uqūd al-mu'āwaḍāt*), contracts of security (*tawthīqāt*), contracts of partnership (*shirka*), contracts of safe custody (*wadī'a*), contracts relating to the utilization of usufruct (*manfa 'a*), and ancillary contracts of services.[9] However, for a proper context, this chapter will adopt another classification that takes into account the popular classifications adopted by jurists. For the purpose of this chapter, Figure 9.1 provides a classification that will guide rest of the chapter.

9.07 Due to the nature of Islamic commercial jurisprudence and some interrelated topics, some contracts pertaining to the above classification have been discussed in other chapters. So, to avoid repetition, the reader's attention will be drawn to such aspects and appropriate cross-referencing will be provided. Though the types of commutative contracts are quite extensive, this chapter provides a high-level analysis of the most commonly used contracts.

3. A General Contract of Sale

9.08 General contracts of sale are bilateral legal arrangements, which are often between two contracting parties with a valid offer (*'ijāb*) and a corresponding acceptance

[5] Bilateral promises are known as *muwa'adah*. See Ibn Manzur, Lisan al-'Arab (3rd edn, Dar Ihya' al-Turath al-'Arabi, 1999) Vol. 5, pp. 341–42. Also see Abul-Hasan Ahmad ibn Faris Zakariyya, Mu'jam al-Maqayis fi al-Lughah (Dar Ihya' al-Turath al-'Arabi, 1422/2001) p. 1058.

[6] See Al-Ghazali, Ihya' 'Ulum al-Din (al-Maktabah al-Tijariyyah al-Kubra) Vol. 3, p. 133; and Ibn Rajab, Jami' al-'Ulum wa al-Hikam (Dar al-'Ulum al-Hadithah, Baghdad: Dar al-Sharq al-Jadid) p. 404.

[7] For a discussion on how Islamic law has adapted to modern legal systems, with particular reference to financial development, see Habib Ahmed, 'Islamic Law, Adaptability and Financial Development' (2006) 13(2) Islamic Economic Studies 80–101.

[8] For a comprehensive discussion of the Islamic origins of the English common law, including significant aspects of English contract law, see John A. Makdisi, 'The Islamic Origins of the Common Law' (1999) 77(5) North Carolina Law Review 1635.

[9] Mohd Daud Bakar, 'Contracts in Islamic Commercial and Their Application in Modern Islamic Financial System' (2003) 4(1) Iqtisad Journal of Islamic Economics 1–42.

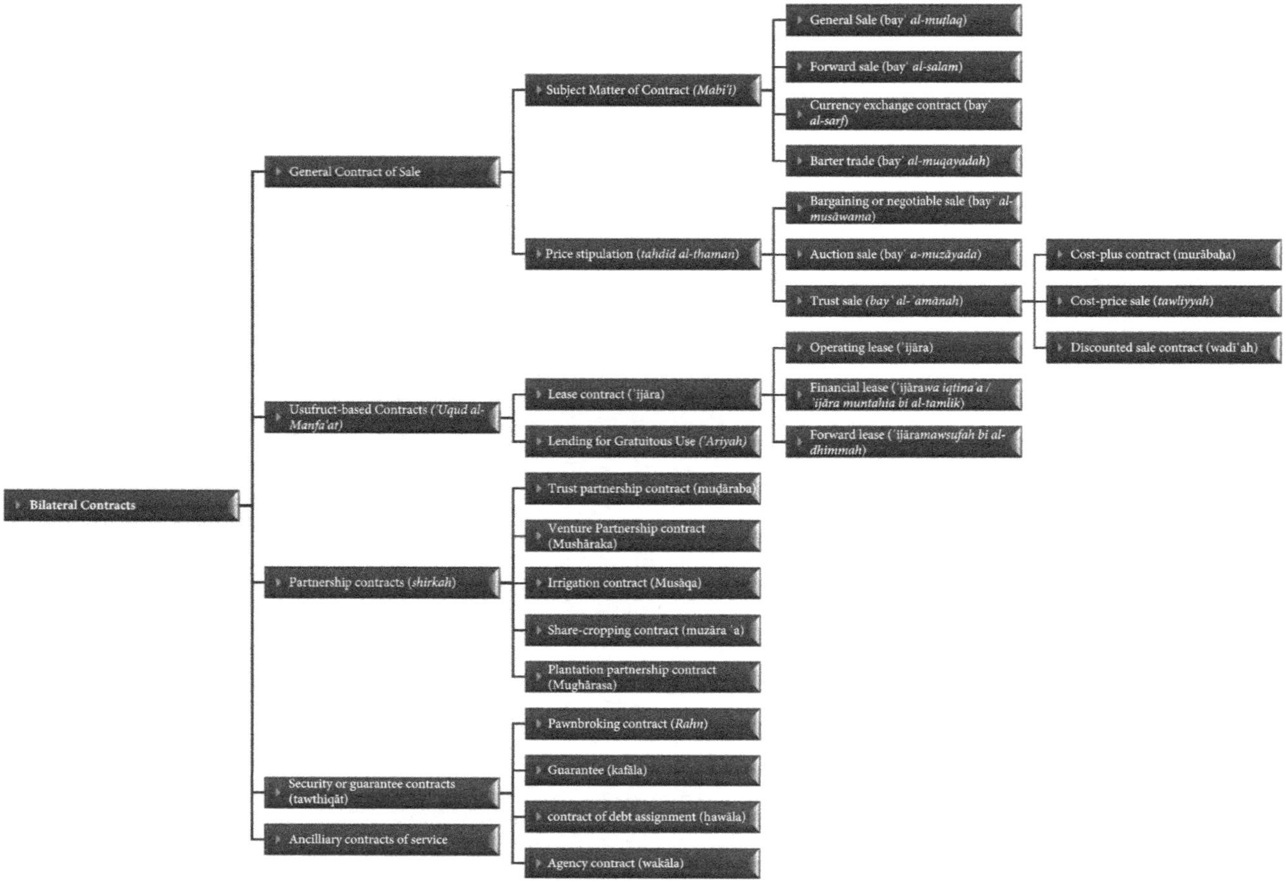

Figure 9.1 Classification of commutative contracts in Islamic lawSource: Author.

(*qabūl*).[10] A general contract of sale is the hallmark of commutative contracts in Islamic law.[11] In the literal sense, a contract of sale generally means an exchange, whether or not it involves proprietary consideration.[12] A typical exchange involves giving a subject matter of sale and receiving another in replacement, such as a barter trade.[13] However, in the juristic sense, a contract of sale can be defined as the exchange of one property for another voluntarily by two parties with the intention of creating a legal relationship.[14] Such an exchange will generally avoid all prohibited elements such as usury (*ribā*) or the involvement of any speculative tendencies that could lead to uncertainties (*gharar*). Therefore, in a typical sale contract, while the vendor sells an item in order to be entitled to the price of the commodity, the buyer becomes the owner of the sold item which hitherto belonged to the seller. The consideration for the transaction must be morally and legally acceptable and the parties must undertake the exchange based on mutual consent in order to ensure the contract is legally valid.

3.1 Elements

9.09 For a contract of sale to be valid, the majority of Muslim jurists stated that there are three fundamental elements that must be present: the parties (typically the buyer and the seller); the language (which could be words, verbal description, gesture, writing, or other acceptable way of expressing contractual intention); and the subject matter.[15] However, Hanafi jurists specifically stipulated that the essential elements required for the validity of a sale contract are the *'ījāb* and *qabūl* which encompass all other elements such as the parties, language, and subject matter since all these other elements appear in any valid offer and acceptance.[16]

9.10 It is pertinent to add that for valid offer and acceptance, parties to a contract of sale are required to have the requisite legal capacity.[17] The intention to enter into a valid legal relationship is often expressed through the language in any manner acceptable to the parties subject to prevailing market practices.[18] Finally, the subject matter of the contract is the main point of reference for the parties in a contract of sale, as it represents the reason why the parties are expressing their respective intentions to deal.[19]

[10] Al-Kāsānī, Abū Bakr ibn Mas'ūd, Badā'i' al-Sanā'i' fī Tartīb al-Sharā'i' (Sharikat al-Maṭbū'āt al-'Ilmīyah, 1910) Vol. 5, p. 133.
[11] Ibid, pp. 133–34.
[12] Al-Zarqā, Ahmad Mustafa, Al-Madkhal al-Fiqhi Al-'ām (Dar al-Qalam, 2004) Vol. 1, pp. 382–84.
[13] Ibid, p. 383.
[14] Al-Sābūni, Abd Al-Rahman, Al-Madkhal Lidirasat Al-Fiqh Al-Islami (4th edn, Damascus: Al-Matba'ah Al-Jadidah, 1978) Vol. 2, p. 116.
[15] Wahbah Al-Zuhaili, al-Fiqh al-Islāmi wa adillahtuhu (Dar al-Fikr, 1997) Vol. 4, p. 2930.
[16] See Chapter 2 for a detailed analysis of the various principles underlying the offer and acceptance and high-level consideration of the views of Muslim jurists.
[17] See Chapter 3 for the discussion on legal capacity which is applicable in sale contracts.
[18] Chapter 4 discusses the role of intention in contracts in Islamic law, as applicable to a contract of sale.
[19] Chapter 5 discusses the subject matter of a contract and all its underlying principles.

3.2 Classification

Being a commutative contract, a sale contract may be understood from two different perspectives in Islamic law. First, from the perspective of the subject matter of the contract; and secondly, from the perspective of price stipulation. Under the first category, there are four unique sub-categorizations, and these are: general sale (*bayʿ al-muṭlaq*), forward sale (*bayʿ al-salam*), currency exchange contract (*bayʿ al-ṣarf*), and barter trade (*bayʿ al-muqāyaḍa*).[20] 9.11

3.2.1 Classification on the Basis of the Subject Matter of Contract

Bayʿ al-muṭlaq or a general sale contract is the generic mode of buying and selling and it is the most prevalent commutative contract used in markets generally. It usually involves the sale of a commodity with a fixed price. Prices of goods are determined quite easily in a fair and mutually acceptable manner, thus making this form of contract a preferred mode of trading. This form of contract of sale is often referred to as an outright sale with a corresponding price which could be paid on the spot or deferred depending on the agreement of the parties. The reason why it is referred to as a general or absolute sale is that it does not include any condition. There is never an option to rescind the contract of sale, as it is considered final, conclusive, and binding on the parties.[21] 9.12

Bayʿ al-salam or forward sale is a sale contract where the buyer pays the full price for the subject matter of the contract in advance (typically agricultural products) while the parties agree on the future delivery of specific goods at a future date.[22] The underlying principles of *bayʿ al-salam* and the conditions for its validity are discussed in Chapter 11. 9.13

Bayʿ al-ṣarf or contract of exchange, often used for currency exchange in modern-day transactions, involves the buying and selling of money where money is exchanged for money, which includes the sale of gold for gold or silver for silver. This kind of sale contract could also involve other staple foods as documented in the relevant prophetic precedents. The conditions for the validity of the exchange contract are immediate possession, equality in quantity or equal-for-equal transaction, absence of any option of condition except for option of defect, and non-deferment of the delivery of the countervalues.[23] 9.14

Bayʿ al-muqāyaḍa or barter trade (or commodity exchange) is one of the oldest forms of commutative contract. Barter trading involving the exchange of one commodity for another between willing parties is valid in Islamic law. It is often called *bayʿ al-ʿayn bi al-ʿayn* as it involves the exchange of one commodity for another without the need for the payment of any form of money. The objects of the contract must be exchanged on a spot basis without any deferment. In a situation where one of the underlying objects of 9.15

[20] Al-Zarqā (n 12) pp. 539–40.
[21] Al-Kāsānī (n 10) p. 134.
[22] Ibid, p. 135.
[23] Ibid.

exchange is money paid and exchanged on a spot basis, the sale will be regarded as *bayʿ al-muṭlaq*, as explained above.[24] In addition, if one of the objects is money and the delivery of the non-monetary object is deferred, then the sale contract is regarded as *bayʿ al-salam*, as explained above and in more detail in Chapter 11.

3.2.2 Classification on the Basis of Price Stipulation

9.16 The second classification on the basis of price stipulation is further categorized into three unique forms of contract: bargaining or negotiable sale (*bayʿ al-musāwama*), auction sale (*bayʿ al-muzāyada*), and trust sale (*bayʿ al-ʾamāna*).

9.17 *Bayʿ al-musāwama* or bargaining sale is premised on the negotiation of the ultimate selling price between the parties without any reference to the original cost price or marked-up profit. Once the parties to the sale contract agree on the price, the sale is finalized without any disclosure obligation on the part of the seller to reveal the original cost price and the profit rate component of the price.[25] Therefore, parties to the contract bargain and agree on the final price. In a situation where the seller does not want to disclose the actual cost price and the profit margin, as in the case of a *murābaḥa* contract, it is permissible to proceed on the basis of a *musāwama* contract where a lump-sum price is disclosed and negotiated for the purchase of the underlying asset.

9.18 *Bayʿ al-muzāyada* or auction sale involves the sale of a commodity in the open market where numerous buyers, often called bidders, are invited to compete on the price. The buyer offering the highest proposed price gets the commodity once the seller approves it. While there are bases for the validity of auction sale in Islamic law, Muslim jurists express different views due to the nature of the contract. The majority of jurists supported the validity of the contract, but there is a minority opinion stating that an auction sale is not valid in Islamic law on the basis of the *ḥadīth* which expressly prohibits a person from bidding on another person's bid.[26] However, the opinion of the majority of jurists is preferred, as it has its firm basis in prophetic precedents. According to Al-Kāsānī, the Prophet practised *muzāyada* and hence it is permissible.[27] This is also the opinion of the Maliki jurists, as Ibn Juzay emphasized that *muzāyada* is different from bidding on another person's bid. According to the majority of jurists, a *muzāyada* contractual arrangement is different from the prohibited bidding on another's bid since the contract process involves bidding before the determination of the final price. The prohibition of bidding on another person's bid kicks in after the price determination.[28]

9.19 There is another contract that somewhat resembles the *muzāyada* contract, but operates as a reverse auction and is generally known as *bayʿ munāqaṣa* in Islamic jurisprudence.

[24] Al-Kāsānī (n 10) p. 134.
[25] See Susan E. Rayner, The Theory of Contracts in Islamic Law (Graham and Trotman, 1991) p. 104.
[26] Mufti Muhammad Taqi Usmani, Fiqh al-Buyu ʿala al-madhahib al-arbaʿah (Maktabah Maʿarif al-Qurʾān, 2015) Vol. 1, pp. 124–25 (hereafter Taqi Usmani, *Fiqh al-Buyu*).
[27] Al-Kāsānī (n 10) p. 134.
[28] Ibid.

A reverse auction is a bidding process where numerous sellers present their proposals to a single prospective buyer with a view to winning the business from such a buyer. In such competitive bidding, prices tend to trend down while the potential sellers or suppliers compete, hence the name *munāqaṣa* which implies a reduction or discounted price.[29] The permissibility of the *munāqaṣa* contract is similar to that of *muzāyada*.

Bayʿ al-ʾamāna or trust sale is any form of sale contract that either imposes some forms of disclosure obligation on the seller with respect to the cost price and desired profit rate or outright safe-keeping of the underlying object of the contract. This type of sale contract is premised on good faith, trust, and confidence. A trust sale contract is divided into three sub-categories: *murābaḥa* (cost-plus contract), *tawliya* (cost-price sale contract), and *wadīʿa* (discounted sale).[30] First, the *murābaḥa* contract involves the sale of a commodity or asset at a mark-up cost, that is, cost price plus a profit margin to reflect the services performed in procuring the commodity. Both the buyer and seller agree on the cost price and the applicable profit margin at the time of concluding the contract which implies that the marked-up cost is predetermined and agreed by the parties. Secondly, the *tawliya* contract involves the sale of the commodity at its original acquisition price without any profit margin or discount. Thirdly, in a *wadīʿa* contract the commodity is sold below the cost price, that is, at a discounted rate, which makes this form of trust contract the direct opposite of the *murābaḥa* contract.[31] **9.20**

Classification on the basis of price stipulation or mode of payment could also involve distinguishing between sale contracts involving a spot payment or deferred payment. Both forms of payment are allowed in Islamic law subject to the general principles underpinning commutative contracts.[32] For the spot sale, payment for the commodity is made in full at the time of purchase without any deferment whatsoever of any aspect of the consideration. This form of immediate payment and spot delivery of the underlying commodity is the most common form of sale contract in business transactions. On the other hand, the deferred payment sale contract is also permissible in Islamic law on the condition that price is predetermined by the parties at the time of concluding the contract. In this latter case, spot delivery of the subject matter or object of the contract is made while payment is deferred or paid over a period of time in instalments as may be agreed by the parties. The deferred payment sale contract can be in the form of an instalment purchase contract or *bayʿ al-taqsīṭ*, where the deferred purchase price is paid over a period of time in equal or unequal instalments as agreed by the parties.[33] **9.21**

29 Taqi Usmani, *Fiqh al-Buyu* (n 26) pp. 132–35.
30 Abdullah Al-Tayyār, al-Fiqh al-Muyassar (Madar al-Watan, 2012) Vol. 6, p. 23.
31 ʿAli Haydar, Kitab Durar al-Hukam fi Sharh Majalat al-Ahkam (1st edn, Dar al-Jail, 1991) Vol. 1, p. 337.
32 Al-Kāsānī (n 10) pp. 134–36.
33 Ibid.

4. Usufruct-Based Contracts

4.1 Lease Contract

9.22 Though the lease contract will be discussed in sufficient detail in Chapter 11, it is pertinent to introduce this form of commutative contract briefly since it involves a bilateral transactional arrangement with consideration. The consideration in a lease contract is quite unique and usually has the usufruct element which is different from the general sale contract.

9.23 In Islamic jurisprudence, *ijāra* simply means the conferment of benefit or usufruct (*manfa'a*) in a property on another person for valuable consideration in kind, debt, or money. In this form of commutative contract, a party who owns a property transfers the benefit of, right in, or usufruct of, such a property to another party for an agreed consideration for a specified period of time.[34]

9.24 The subject matter of an *ijāra* contract is the usufruct or benefit derived from the use of the underlying asset since ownership of such asset still lies with the owner/lessor. The lessee only acquires possession for the purpose of deriving benefit of the underlying asset which does not confer immediate ownership. Therefore, the subject matter of a lease contract comprises the rental amount being paid by the lessee to the lessor and the usufruct of the underlying asset by the lessee, and these together form the consideration of the contract.[35]

9.25 The purpose of a lease contract is seen in the fulfilment of a common need of people in a manner that helps to achieve justice among them. People's needs are numerous and may not be easily achievable, hence the need for interrelationships through contractual prescriptions by the Lawgiver. The lease contract therefore confers beneficial ownership on a person which allows him or her to fulfil his immediate needs for valuable consideration.[36]

9.26 The majority of Muslim jurists are of the opinion that *ijāra* has three main pillars which are further divided into six sub-pillars. The three main pillars are: first, the form, which comprises the offer and acceptance, just like any other contract; secondly, the parties, which are the lessor (who owns the asset) and the lessee (who is legally entitled to the usufruct or benefit derived from the asset); and thirdly, the subject matter of the lease contract which is in the form of consideration: the rent which is paid to the lessor and the usufruct enjoyed by the lessee for the duration of the *ijāra* contract.[37]

[34] Manṣūr ibn Yūnus Al-Buhūtī, Kashshāf al-qinā' 'an Matn al-Iqnā' (Dar al-Kutub al-'Ilmiyah, 2009) Vol. 4, p. 23.

[35] Ibid, p. 24.

[36] Ibid.

[37] Al-Juzairi, 'Abd Al-Rahman, Kitāb al-Fiqh 'ala al-Madhahib al-Arba'ah (Dar al-Kutub al-'Ilmiyyah, 2003) Vol. 2, p. 98.

However, the Hanafi jurists restrict the pillars of *ijāra* to just the form of the contract which comprises the offer and acceptance.[38] Other pillars such as the contracting parties and the subject matter of the contract are part of the overall contract which has been duly constituted by the valid offer and acceptance between the lessor and the lessee.[39] In all cases, *ijāra* involves the utilization of the benefit derived from the asset or usufruct while the underlying asset remains intact and owned by the lessor except where the parties have structured the transaction to confer ownership on the lessee at the end of the lease period, as explained below.[40] **9.27**

The lease contract in Islamic jurisprudence is divided into three main categories: first, the operating lease (typical lease contract); secondly, the financial lease (*ijāra wa iqtinā'a* or *ijāra muntahiya bi al-tamlīk*); and thirdly, the forward lease (*ijāra mawsūfa bi al-dhimma*).[41] **9.28**

The operating lease is the typical lease contractual arrangement where the owner of a property leases the property to another person for a specified period of time and at an agreed price.[42] In this lease contract, the lessor remains the owner of the property at every point in time. The lessee only enjoys the beneficial use or usufruct of the property without any promise by the lessor to sell the property to the lessee. The underlying principle of an operating lease, which is the generic form of *ijāra*, is that the lease must be immediate, and consideration for the contract is provided by the contracting parties without further delay.[43] **9.29**

The financial lease is a modern form of *ijāra* which was developed by modern Muslim jurists based on Islamic contract principles discussed earlier. Once parties to a lease contract mutually agree that even though the contractual arrangement begins with a simple lease agreement, the ultimate purpose is to confer ownership on the lessee at the expiration of a specified period of time, then such a contract will be regarded as a financial lease (*ijāra wa iqtinā'a* or *ijāra muntahiya bi al-tamlīk*).[44] With respect to this method of ownership transfer, a financial lease can lead to the transfer of legal title of the underlying property through a gift (*hiba*) which means the lessee does not need to make any additional payments at the expiration of the lease period and automatically becomes the legal owner of the property. On the other hand, a financial lease that is executed through a sale will require the lessee to pay the lessor a specific amount at the end of the lease period in order to validly transfer the legal title in the property to the former.[45] **9.30**

[38] Al-Tayyār (n 30) Vol. 6, p. 180.
[39] Al-Juzairi (n 37) Vol. 2, p. 98.
[40] Al-Samarqandi, 'Alā al-Dīn, Tuhfat al-fuqahā (Dar al-Kutub al-'ilmiyyah, 1994) Vol. 2, p. 529.
[41] Ibid. For the modern application of some of these new types of *ijāra*, see Al-Buhūtī (n 34) Vol. 3, pp. 560–62.
[42] Ibid, Vol. 3, p. 560.
[43] Ibid, Vol. 3, p. 561.
[44] Abdul-Sattar Abu Ghuddah, 'Practical Application of al-Ijarah al-Mawsufah fi al-Dhimmah (Forward Ijarah)' 28th Al-Baraka Symposium on Islamic Economics (Al Baraka Banking Group, 2007) p. 13.
[45] Nurdianawati Irwani Abdullah and Asyraf Wajdi Dusuki, 'A Critical Appraisal of Al-Ijarah Thumma Al-Bay (AITAB) Operation: Issues and Prospects', Paper presented at 4th International Islamic Banking and Finance Conference, Monash University of Malaysia, Kuala Lumpur, 13–14 November 2004, p. 15.

9.31 The forward lease or *ijāra mawsūfa bi al-dhimma* is another type of lease contract introduced by Muslim jurists to facilitate modern transactions, particularly in the Islamic finance industry.[46] This is a form of an *ijāra* contract which involves deferring part of the consideration, in other words an *ijāra* for a future date. In a forward lease, the usufruct of the property is deferred as the property is not yet in existence. The underlying property in this case, whose usufruct is the subject matter of the contract, will only be available at a future date commonly known as the forward delivery date.[47] The payment of advance rentals can begin at the contract date and the lessor uses such funds received from the lessee to construct the property.[48]

9.32 The majority of the Muslim jurists are of the opinion that this form of *ijāra* is valid and binding on the parties once they conclude the contract. However, the Hanafi jurists opine that a forward lease is not binding on the parties, as they consider only the operating lease, which takes effect immediately, as binding. This minority opinion does not suggest that the forward lease is not permissible, as the permissibility of the contract among the four major schools of in Islamic jurisprudence is not in question. The only issue on which they differ is the binding nature of the contract.[49]

4.2 Lending for Gratuitous Use

9.33 Another contract involving the use of the usufruct of an asset is *'āriya* which involves lending for gratuitous use of an asset, as reflected in the opinions of the Muslim jurists.[50] In this bilateral contractual arrangement, a party lends his or her property to another party for the use of its usufruct for an indefinite period. It is a gratuitous contract because it is concluded without a fee.[51] Unlike *ijāra* which involves the transfer of usufruct with consideration, *'āriya* does not involve any consideration—only the usufruct is transferred in this latter case. This gratuitous contract is highly encouraged as it seeks to benefit people. People are dependent on one another in different ways and this contract allows them to assist one another by borrowing some assets at a time of need without necessarily seeking to own them.[52]

[46] Al-Buhūtī (n 34) Vol. 3, p. 560.

[47] Ali Muhyiddin Al-Quradaghi, 'al-Ijarah 'ala Manafi al-Ashkhas: Dirasah Fiqhiyyah Muqaranah fi al-Fiqh al-Islami wa Qanun al-'Amal', Paper presented at 18th session of European Council for Fatwa and Research, Paris, 1–5 July 2008, p. 14.

[48] Al-Buhūtī (n 34) Vol. 3, p. 560. Also see generally Abdul-Sattar Abu Ghuddah, 'Practical Application of al-Ijarah al-Mawsufah fi al-Dhimmah (Forward Ijarah)', 28th Al-Baraka Symposium on Islamic Economics (Al Baraka Banking Group, 2007).

[49] Monzer Kahaf, 'Use of Usufruct Bonds in Financing Public Utility' in Ausaf Ahmad and Tariqullah Khan (eds), Islamic Financing Instruments for Public Sectors Resource Mobilization (The Islamic Research and Training Institute, 1997) pp. 286–87.

[50] This refers to the definitions proffered by the Maliki, Hanafi, and Shafi'i jurists. See Al-Juzairi (n 37) Vol. 3, pp. 237–38.

[51] Ibid.

[52] Ibid, Vol. 3, p. 239.

Some of the fundamental rules applicable to the *ʿāriya* include the right of the lender to request that the underlying asset be returned at any time. The asset must have some usufruct which is the subject matter of the contract itself. While the borrower takes possession, he or she is only entitled to the usufruct and cannot claim full ownership. However, while the borrower enjoys the usufruct, he or she must be responsible for the maintenance of the asset.[53] **9.34**

There are situations where the *ʿāriya* contract contains some restrictions relating to time, place, and nature of use. Such restrictions must be observed in line with contractual stipulations. In addition, once the borrower takes the possession of the asset, he or she is not allowed to let or even pledge the asset to another party. The borrower holds the asset in trust for the lender.[54] **9.35**

The *ʿāriya* contract can be divided into various categories by Muslim jurists depending on their respective perspectives. For instance, the Hanafi jurists classify *ʿāriya* contracts into the following four unique categories: unlimited lending without time or beneficial use restrictions, restricted lending in time and beneficial use, restricted lending in time but unlimited beneficial use, and restricted lending in beneficial use without time limitation.[55] The Hanbali jurists, for their part, classify *ʿāriya* contracts into two categories: unlimited gratuitous lending and limited gratuitous lending based on time or beneficial use limitations.[56] The Maliki jurists provide three different categories as follows: limited gratuitous lending according to time, limited gratuitous lending according to beneficial use, and unrestricted gratuitous lending.[57] Finally, the Shafi'i jurists provide two broad categories: unrestricted gratuitous lending and restricted gratuitous lending limited by time.[58] **9.36**

5. Partnership Contracts

Though partnership contracts are discussed in Chapter 10, it is important to provide a general overview of such contracts within the context of bilateral contracts as they also involve some form of consideration. Even though these forms of contract often involve the sharing of risk and returns, parties frequently receive some form of consideration for their involvement in such contractual arrangements. As suggested by the original word '*shirka*', partnership contracts involve sharing risk and returns.[59] **9.37**

[53] Al-Samarqandi, *Tuhfat al-fuqahā* (n 40) Vol. 3, pp. 177–80.
[54] Al-Juzairi (n 37) p. 249.
[55] Ibid, Vol. 2, p. 244.
[56] Ibid, Vol. 2, pp. 245–46.
[57] Ibid, Vol. 2, pp. 246–47.
[58] Ibid, Vol. 2, p. 247.
[59] Al-Buhūtī (n 34) Vol. 3, p. 496.

9.38 Partnerships (*shirka*) are generally of two major types: *shirka 'amlāk* (joint ownership partnership) and *shirka al-'uqūd* (contractual partnership or business partnership).[60] For the purpose of this chapter, the focus is primarily on business partnership which often involves contractual arrangements and clear-cut stipulations that guide the business relationship.

9.39 The most common partnership contracts are *mushāraka* (venture partnership contract) and *muḍāraba* (trust partnership contract). However, there are numerous other bilateral partnership contracts in Islamic jurisprudence which are intended for specific purposes, particularly agricultural cultivation, and there is always the element of valuable consideration in such contracts. These contracts include: *musāqa* (irrigation contract), *muzāra'a* (share-cropping contract), and *mughārasa* (plantation partnership contract).[61]

9.40 Without going into specific details, it is sufficient here to provide a high-level overview of both *muḍāraba* and *mushāraka* contracts. Even though they are not sale contracts, the consideration element is in the form of profit-sharing for the joint ventures.[62]

9.41 Partnership contracts, with specific reference to *shirka*, can be divided into two major categories[63]: first, *shirka al-'uqūd* (joint enterprise or business partnership contract); and secondly, *shirka al-milk* (joint ownership). For the first category, *shirka al-'uqūd* can be further divided into three sub-categories: *shirka al-wujūh* (partnership in goodwill), *shirka al-'amal* (partnership in services), and *shirka al-'amwāl* (joint venture partnership). On the other hand, *shirka al-milk* could be optional by voluntary dispositions of the parties in establishing joint ownership over a property, or by operation of law which is compulsory in its effect.

9.42 *Mushāraka* or venture partnership contract is a form of *shirka al-'amwāl* which is a sub-category of *shirka al-'uqūd*. In this form of partnership, the parties invest some capital in the joint enterprise where they share both the business risk and return. Parties in this form of partnership are required to predetermine their profit rates by determining the ratio of profit. They are also expected to share any loss associated with the business enterprise in accordance with the ratio of their respective investments in the enterprise.

9.43 With respect to the capital being invested by the partners, the majority of Muslim jurists are of the opinion that any capital to be invested in a *mushāraka* contract should be in liquid form, that is, financial investment and not goodwill, commodities, or investment in kind. Imam Ahmad bin Hanbal and Imam Abu Hanifah clearly argued that the investment capital for *mushāraka* cannot be made in kind.[64] On his part, Imam Malik permits contribution in kind to a *mushāraka* partnership since liquidity of capital is not

60 Al-Samarqandi (n 40) Vol. 3, p. 5.
61 Al-Buhūtī (n 34) Vol. 3, p. 499.
62 Ibid.
63 Al-Zuhaili (n 15) Vol. 5, p. 3877.
64 Al-Kāsānī (n 10) Vol. 6, p. 59.

one of the fundamental conditions for the validity of the contract. However, whatever contribution in kind made by a partner will be evaluated on the basis of the prevailing market rate at the time of contract to ascertain the financial value.[65] In a way, the Maliki view partially agrees with the position of Imam Abu Hanifah and Imam Ahmad.

Furthermore, Imam Shafi'i's position introduces a new dimension into the analysis. The Shafi'i position is premised on the classification of commodities into two groups: those that can be replaced by similar items in both quality and quantity in case the original ones are destroyed (*dhawā al-amthāl*), and those that cannot be replaced (*dhawā al-qīma*).[66] Those commodities that can be replaced easily with the same amount of quality and quantity could be considered liquid assets and are thus eligible to be contributed as a form of capital to a *mushāraka* arrangement. On the other hand, those that cannot be replaced or compensated by similar commodities are considered not liquid and as such cannot be contributed as share capital to a *mushāraka*.[67] **9.44**

Muḍāraba or trust partnership contract is also known as *qirāḍ* or *muqāraḍa* among the Hanafi and Hanbali jurists.[68] This is partnership in profit where the capital provider (*rabb al-māl*) entrusts his or her capital to an entrepreneur (*muḍārib*) who trades with the funds with the sole objective of making enough profit to be shared between the partners. The capital provider in this contractual arrangement is a sleeping partner while the entrepreneur who has the requisite business acumen and skills exclusively manages the business enterprise professionally.[69] **9.45**

There two major types of *muḍāraba*: restricted and unrestricted.[70] For the restricted *muḍāraba*, the capital provider specifies the kind of business in which he or she wants to invest the funds, and the *muḍārib* is bound by such contractual terms and conditions. The *muḍāraba* becomes restricted if there is limitation on the place or time of transaction or even the type of product to deal in. On the other hand, the unrestricted *muḍāraba* involves a situation where the capital provider leaves it open to the *muḍārib* to invest in any legitimate business that will ensure good returns. In this latter type, the entrepreneur is not bound by time or place, nor even the type of trade or limited to dealing with a particular buyer or seller.[71] **9.46**

Profit distribution in *muḍāraba* is based on predetermined ratios at the time of contract based on mutual consent.[72] Beyond the agreed profit ratios, the *muḍārib* cannot earn a salary or any other remuneration for managing the business enterprise.[73] While there is general unanimity amongst Muslim jurists on this point, the Hanbali jurists do allow **9.47**

65 Abdullah bin Ahmad Ibn Qudāmah, Al-Mughni (Dar 'Alam al-Kutub, 1997) Vol. 6, p. 196.
66 Abu al-Ma'ali Al-Juwaini, Nihayat al-Matlab fi Dirayat al-Mazhab (Dar al-Minhaj, 2007) Vol. 7, pp. 175–76.
67 Ibn Qudāmah (n 65) Vol. 6, p. 196.
68 Ibn 'Ashur (n 1) Vol. 2, pp. 446–47.
69 Ibid, Vol. 2, p. 447.
70 Ibid.
71 Ibid.
72 Al-Zuhaili (n 15) Vol. 5, p. 3931.
73 Muhammad bin Ahmad Al-Sarakhsi, Al-Mabsut (Dar al-Ma'rifah) Vol. 22, pp. 149–50.

the *muḍārib* to draw reasonable expenses incurred on food from the *muḍāraba* enterprise.[74] The Hanafi jurists allow for the *muḍārib* to deduct from the *muḍāraba* accounts any out-of-pocket expenses relating to any business trip outside the city where the business is being carried out and this may include food and accommodation, provided this is related to the business.[75]

9.48 *Musāqa* or the irrigation contract is a bilateral contract where a farm owner contracts the services of another person for the irrigation and tending of the plants, fruits, and crops. The consideration for such contract is a predetermined share in the produce once this is harvested.[76] In other words, the owner of agricultural land shares the harvest or produce with another person as consideration for the latter's efforts in irrigating the crops.[77]

9.49 According to the Hanafi jurists, the subject matter of the *musāqa* contract comprises fruitful trees such as palm trees, vines, and the roots of eggplants due to people's needs for such produce. Some other jurists within the Hanafi school have broadened the scope to include non-fruiting trees such as willows and other trees typically used for firewood if they require watering and preservation. If the latter category of non-fruiting trees and willows do not require watering and preservation, then they can form the subject matter of a *musāqa* contract.[78]

9.50 The Maliki jurists allowed a *musāqa* contract to be concluded on crops generally, and fruit trees with firm roots such as grapevines, palm trees, and apple trees. Ibn Ashur allowed this type of bilateral contract in any cultivation of crops just like the case of fruit trees if they require watering and preservation. However, the Hanbali jurists restricted this contract to edible fruit trees only, while excluding willows, walnuts, and roses. For the Al-Shafi'i jurists, *musāqa* contract is limited to the cultivation of palm trees and grapes.[79]

9.51 *Muzāra'a* or a share-cropping partnership contract is an agricultural cultivation arrangement between two or more parties whereby they agree to contribute land, labour, and other relevant agricultural products with a view to sharing the crop yield after harvest based according to a pre-agreed ratio. Abu Hanifah emphasized that a *muzāra'a* contract is only valid if the parties clearly stipulate the following in their contract: virgin land, legal capacity of the contracting parties, duration of contract, the seed owner and provider, type of seeds, predetermined shares of each party, distinction between the landowner and the worker, and finally external partnerships outside the contract, if any.[80]

[74] Ibn Qudāmah (n 65) Vol. 5, p. 186.
[75] Al-Kāsānī (n 10) Vol. 6, p. 109.
[76] Ibid, Vol. 6, p. 185.
[77] Ibn 'Ashur (n 1) Vol. 2, p. 450.
[78] Ibid, Vol. 2, p. 451.
[79] Ibid.
[80] Ibid, Vol. 2, p. 455.

The Maliki jurists are of the view that a *muzāra'a* contract is permissible subject to two key conditions, as explained by Ibn al-Qasim: first, the land to be cultivated must not be leased land; and secondly, parties should share equally in all inputs.[81] The Hanafi and Shafi'i jurists generally regard *muzāra'a* as impermissible or defective, but some Shafi'i jurists later allowed it in times of need as a derivative of a *musāqa* contract.[82] So, the majority of Muslim jurists are of the opinion that *muzāra'a* is permissible, relying on the prophetic precedent relating to the experience of the Prophet where he shared in the crops and fruits with the people of Khaybar.[83] 9.52

There are different types of *muzāra'a* contract. The first, which is considered valid, is where a party provides the land for cultivation and also provides the seeds to be planted. The other party, who is the worker, only provides his expertise in terms of requisite labour and livestock, if necessary. The second type of valid *muzāra'a* is where a party provides the land to be cultivated and the other party provides the requisite labour, seeds, and animals, if required. Furthermore, the third type of valid *muzāra'a* is where a party provides the land, seeds, and animals, if required, while the other party provides the requisite labour to cultivate the land. There is another type that is considered invalid or, better put, defective, and that is where a party provides the land and animals to aid cultivation, while the other party provides the seeds and the requisite labour to cultivate the land.[84] 9.53

Mughārasa or the plantation partnership contract is a bilateral contract where a landowner gives another person a piece of land for the cultivation of useful trees in return for a known amount of royalties, share in the produce, or even land. The landowner may assign a share of the plantation or orchard's harvest to the worker as consideration for the work done in cultivating the fruit-bearing trees.[85] The Hanbali jurists also referred to this type of agricultural contract as *munāṣaba*.[86] 9.54

The plantation partnership contract can take two different forms. First, a contractual arrangement where the landowner provides all the necessary materials required for cultivating the plantation and all other related expenses. In this case, the only contribution of the other party who is the worker is his expertise in cultivating the plantation and tending the trees for a fixed period as agreed by the parties. At the expiration of the contractual period, the consideration the worker receives is a fixed wage or an identified portion of the plantation or orchard. The majority of jurists regard the first form as impermissible, except Maliki jurists with certain conditions.[87] The second form could 9.55

[81] Al-Kalbi Ibn Juzay, Al-Qawanin al-Fiqhiyyah fi Takhlis Madh-hab al-Malikiyyah wa al-Tanbih 'ala Madh-hab al-Shafi'iyya wa al-Hanafiyyah wa al-Hanbaliyyah (Dar Ibn Hazm, 2013) p. 470.
[82] Ibn al-Rif'ah, Kifayat al-Nabīh fi Sharh al-Tanbīh (Dar al-Kutub al-'Ilmiyyah, 2009) Vol. 11, p. 200.
[83] Ibn Juzay (n 81) pp. 470–71.
[84] Al-Kāsānī (n 10) Vol. 6, pp. 179–80.
[85] Muhammad bin Ahmad Ibn Rushd, Al-Muqadimat Al-Mumahadat (Dar Al-Gharb Al-Islami, 1988) Vol. 2, pp. 236–37 (hereafter Ibn Rushd, *Al-Muqaddimat*).
[86] Ibid, Vol. 2, p. 236.
[87] Al-Zuhaili (n 15) Vol. 6, p. 4726.

be a contractual arrangement where the worker provides all materials required to cultivate the plantation or orchard and also bears all associated expenses related to the cultivation while the landowner only provides the land. As consideration, the worker only receives a share of the harvest which is required to be predetermined.[88] This second form of *mughārasa* is often likened to a *muzāraʿa* contract. The second form is permissible only according to Hanafi and Hanbali jurists.[89]

6. Security or Guarantee Contracts

9.56 The underlying principles of security or guarantee contracts otherwise known as *tawthiqāt* are discussed in sufficient detail in Chapter 12 and partly in Chapter 13. Nevertheless, a general overview is provided here to situate these forms of contract properly within the general purview of bilateral contracts. The *tawthiqāt* contracts include guarantee contract (*kafāla*), pawnbroking contract (*rahn*), debt assignment (*ḥawāla*), and agency contract (*wakāla*). Though some of these contracts involve third-party rights, they often begin with a bilateral contractual arrangement with or without valuable consideration.

9.57 In the modern application of the *tawthiqāt* contracts, one unique feature of such contract structures is their inherent nature as accessory or subordinate contracts, as they are often used in structuring other financial contracts. That is, these forms of contracts require other substantive contracts before they can be used as accessory contracts to facilitate the original contracts. They serve a unique objective of safeguarding the rights of the contracting parties.

9.58 *Kafāla* is a contract of guarantee where a guarantor jointly assumes the obligations of a principal debtor in a specified debt obligation. Therefore, both the guarantor and the debtor become jointly liable for the settlement of the underlying debt obligation. The beneficiary of the guarantee is the creditor. In strict legal terms, the guarantor underwrites any claim against the debtor so that when the latter fails to fulfil his or her debt obligation when due, the guarantor will be obliged to make good such obligation.[90]

9.59 *Rahn* or pledge contract is a bilateral contract where a party pledges an asset as collateral for a debt to be paid in future, and failure to pay the debt could prevent the creditor from fulfilling the debt obligation from the pawned asset.[91] The *rahn* contract is one of the major means of protecting and preserving wealth in Islamic law.[92] This contract can

88 Ibn Rushd, *Al-Muqaddimat* (n 85) Vol. 2, p. 236.
89 Al-Zuhaili (n 15) Vol. 6, p. 4727.
90 Al-Kāsānī (n 10) Vol. 6, pp. 2–3.
91 Al-Buhūtī (n 34) Vol. 3, p. 321.
92 Yusuf Hamid al-ʿAlim, Al-maqasid al-ʿammah li al-Shariʾah al-Islamiyyah (Al-Dar al-ʿAlamiyyah li al-kitab al-Islami, 1994) p. 496.

also facilitate public needs where immediate individual needs can be fulfilled without hardship through credit transactions and deferred payment sales.[93]

Ḥawāla or the contract of debt assignment involves the transfer of a debt obligation from one party to another, that is, the liability to settle a debt is transferred from the principal debtor to a third party who is required to fulfil the debt obligation to the original creditor. Even though it is a bilateral contract, it inherently involves third-party rights. Once a valid *ḥawāla* contract is concluded, the existing debt between the creditor and the debtor is cancelled, as the transferee now assumes the debt obligation which is then between the transferee and the original creditor.[94] 9.60

Wakāla or the agency contract is a bilateral contract where a principal authorizes another party who is the agent to undertake certain well-defined business activity on his behalf. Such business activity must be permissible in Islamic law. Even though the *wakāla* contract begins with a bilateral contractual arrangement, its third-party implication allows the agent to establish contractual relations between his principal and a third-party entity or individual depending on the actual terms of the original agency contract. Even though the agent may perform the task voluntarily, there is always a fee for the agency relationship, but the delegated business matters must be such as are capable of delegation under the law. A *wakāla* contract has two unique forms: the general agency or unrestricted agency contract and the specific or restricted agency contract.[95] 9.61

7. Other Ancillary Contracts of Service and Supply

Apart from the *tawthiqāt* contracts briefly explained above, there are other ancillary contracts that are generally used in structuring Islamic products. The focus here will be contracts for service and the following three ancillary contracts have been selected for a brief overview: *ju'āla* (commission), *'ajr* or *'ujr* (fees), and *bay' al-'istijrār* (supply) contracts. 9.62

Ju'āla or commission is a bilateral contract where a party undertakes to provide a specific reward, compensation, or commission to anyone who is able to achieve a specified task or result which may be uncertain at the time of the promise.[96] This form of contract is also called a promise with a corresponding reward or *wa'd bi al-jā'iza*. The subject matter of a *ju'āla* contract is the specified work or task that is expected to be carried out. As an ancillary contract, *ju'āla* can be utilized in the modern-day Islamic finance industry for debt collection in cases involving overdue debts as well as brokerage services. 9.63

[93] Abu Muhammad 'Izz al-Din 'Abd al-'Aziz b. 'Abd al-Salam al-Silmi, Qawa'id al-Ahkam fi Masalih al-Anam (Dar al-Ma'rifah, n.d.) Vol. 2, pp. 58–59.
[94] Al-Kāsānī (n 10) Vol. 6, p. 15.
[95] Ibid, Vol. 6, pp. 19–20.
[96] Al-Buhūtī (n 34) Vol. 4, p. 225.

9.64 *ʾUjr* or fees is a form of compensation or wage paid for certain work or services. For instance, in a contract of agency, the agent may be paid fees for undertaking to perform some tasks on behalf of the principal. Similarly, in a contract for hire for services, the price paid by the hirer to the hired party is the consideration for services rendered. Another example of *ʾujr* or *ʾajr* is seen in an employment contract where a party hires another to perform certain tasks. The salary or wage received by the employee from the employer is the consideration for the work performed by the former.[97] Charging a service fee for work performed is permissible in Islamic contract law. When such charges are reasonable, they could easily replace the usurious charges which are forbidden in Islamic law.

9.65 *Bayʿ al-ʾistijrār* or a supply contract is a sale and purchase contractual arrangement where parties agree to buy and sell certain commodities from time to time in different quantities without the need to repeat the offer and acceptance requirement in a typical contract.[98] In modern parlance, this type of sale contract is often covered by what is known as a master framework agreement or a master service agreement.[99] Sometimes, it is simply called a framework agreement where there are repeated sales which could be on the spot or based on deferred payment terms. Delivery of the sold commodities could also be staggered across a certain agreed period of time.

8. Types of Contracts of Sale and Applicable Legal Principles

9.66 In the classifications of contract of sale by Muslim jurists, a unique categorization that has a fundamental effect on the extent of validity, the binding nature and executability of the terms of contract are essential in understanding bilateral contracts. The categorization of contracts of sale according to their legal effect is as follows:

1. *Bayʿ munʿaqid* (enforceable) and *bayʿ bāṭil* (void)
2. *Bayʿ ṣaḥīḥ* (valid sale) and *bayʿ fāsid* (defective or voidable sale)
3. *Bayʿ nāfidh* (immediately effective) and *bayʿ mawqūf* (contingent or withheld sale)
4. *Bayʿ lāzim* (binding sale) and *bay ghayr lāzim* (non-binding sale).[100]

9.67 A brief overview of the above categorization will help in understanding the legal effect of such sales within the context of bilateral contracts.

[97] Al-Zuhaili (n 15) Vol. 5, p. 386.

[98] Muhammad Taqi Usmani, Buhuth fi Qadaya Fiqhiyya Mu'asirah (Dar al-Qalam, 1998) p. 58.

[99] For a general discussion on framework agreement in modern global trade, see generally Torsten Müller, Hans-Wolfgang Platzer, and Stefan Rüb, International Framework Agreement: Opportunities and Limitations of a New Tool of Global Trade Union Policy (Friedrich-Ebert-Stiftung, Internat. Entwicklungszusammenarbeit, Globale Gewerkschaftspolitik, 2008).

[100] See Al-Zuhaili (n 15) Vol. 5, pp. 393–95.

Bay' mun'aqid (enforceable) and *bay' bāṭil* (void). An enforceable contract of sale is a contract that meets all conditions stipulated for the validity of a contract. Once all conditions are met, the contract of sale is considered valid and enforceable with immediate effect. **9.68**

On the other hand, a void contract is a contract that does not fulfil one of the essential conditions for the validity of a contract and/or contains an illegal term or condition. In most cases, both the substance and form of such a contract render it void. An example of a void contract is an agreement where two parties agree to a loan contract with the payment of interest (*ribā*), which is illegal in Islamic law. It is also possible to render a contract void on the ground of excessive speculation, for example in a contract involving the sale of birds in the sky. The legal effect of such sales is that the contract is void and cannot be cured by any further step than to invalidate the contract.[101] **9.69**

Bay' ṣaḥīḥ (valid sale) and *bay' fāsid* (defective or voidable sale). In Islamic contract law, a valid contract of sale is a contract whose essence and fundamental attributes are in accordance with Islamic law. This makes it enforceable without the need for any remedial step from either of the parties to the contract. While Muslim jurists have used the words *'aṣl* (origin) and *waṣf* (description) as two key benchmarks for the determination of a valid contract of sale, one may consider those two elements from the perspectives of both substance and form. For a contract of sale to be considered valid, it must fulfil the economic substance of the transaction as well as the form required under Islamic law. For a proper determination of the validity of a contract, three key conditions need to be met: first, all elements or conditions required by Islamic law must be met; secondly, any additional condition required to be fulfilled must be met; and thirdly, the purpose and subject matter of the contract must comply with principles of Islamic law.[102] **9.70**

On the other hand, a defective sale involves a contract that is lawful in its actual substance, such as the offer and acceptance as well as the subject matter, but unlawful in its true description, such as any key feature that supports its enforceability, for example the price of the subject matter. In this situation, if the parties have fulfilled all other conditions and are yet to agree on the price, then the contract remains voidable, but its substance remains enforceable. Though voidable, *bay' fāsid* can be rectified by addressing the defect.[103] **9.71**

Bay' nāfidh (immediately effective) and *bay' mawqūf* (contingent or withheld sale). Whether a contract of sale is effective immediately or contingent upon the positive action of a third party has been considered as one of the key classifications of a contract of sale with reference to its legal effect. As for *bay' nāfidh*, it is effective immediately and enforceable by the contracting parties. It does not involve or require any validation, **9.72**

[101] Ibid, Vol. 5, p. 393.
[102] Ibid, Vol. 5, pp. 393–94.
[103] Malik bin Anas, Al-Mudawanah (Dar al-Kutub al-Ilmiya, 1994) Vol. 3, p. 185.

intervention, or approval by a third party. This form of contract is enforceable upon the fulfilment of all conditions of the contract without further delay.[104]

9.73 On the other hand, *bayʿ mawqūf* is a contingent contract which is withheld pending the consent of a third party. In this form of contract, both the substance and description are lawful, but it requires the ratification of a third party due to certain features relating to the parties such as issues relating to full legal capacity. An example of *bayʿ mawqūf* is a sale contract concluded by an unauthorized agent (*bayʿ fuḍūlī*).[105] In this case, the agent may be acting on behalf of the principal in other matters, but in this specific undertaking the agent has not been specifically authorized to represent the principal. Such a sale contract will be considered valid, but it is contingent upon the approval of the principal.[106]

9.74 It is pertinent to emphasize that under the Sharīʿah, the default rule is that nobody can deal with the property of another without prior authorization.[107] As exceptions to this general rule, the Hanafi and Maliki jurists are of the opinion that any act carried out by an unauthorized person may be ratified and approved by the true owner of the property and that makes the action valid in the eyes of the law. However, the Shafi'i and Hanbali jurists do not consider such a contract valid.[108]

9.75 *Bayʿ lāzim* (binding sale) and *bayʿ ghayr lāzim* (non-binding sale). This is the classification of contract in accordance with its binding nature between the parties. Whether a contract of sale will be legally binding on the parties will depend on certain factors. In the first instance, a binding sale contract is a valid sale where neither of the parties can unilaterally rescind the contract without the express consent of the other party except when the terms and conditions of the contract include an inherent optional condition (*khiyār al-sharṭ*).[109] On the other hand, a non-binding sale contract is that in which either of the parties has the right to rescind the contract unilaterally and without the consent of the other party. In such non-binding contracts, options are provided in the contract which can be invoked by either party. The termination or rescission by either party is based on conditions or options provided in the contract itself.

9. Prohibited Contracts of Sale

9.76 The general principle in Islamic contract law is that all contracts are permissible in the eyes of the law except when there are elements of injustice between the contracting

[104] Al-Zuhaili (n 15) Vol. 5, pp. 393–97.
[105] Muhammad ibn ʿAbd al-Wahid Ibn Humam, Sharh Fath Al-Qadir (Dar al-Kutub al-Ilmiya, 2009) Vol. 6, pp. 401–02.
[106] Shams al-Din Muhammad Al-Sharbini, Mughni al-Muhtaj ila Ma'arifah Ma'ani alfaz al-Minhaj (Dar al-Kutub al-Ilmiya, 1994) Vol. 2, p. 15.
[107] Ali bin Ahmad Ibn Hazm, Al-Muhallā bi'l Athār (Dar al-Fikr, n.d.) Vol. 7, pp. 313–14.
[108] Al-Buhūtī (n 34) Vol. 2, p. 11.
[109] Malik bin Anas (n 103) Vol. 3, pp. 208–09.

parties.[110] Such exploitative elements gradually change the essence of the contract from permissibility to abhorrence and, ultimately, prohibition. So, anything that involves excessive risk, deception, cheating, mistake, and fraud will invalidate a contract that is ordinarily permissible in its real essence.[111] These prohibitory elements are mostly contained in clear legal texts of the Qur'ān and Sunnah.

Although Chapter 6 examines the main prohibited elements in a contract, it is important to briefly examine certain contracts of sale that are prohibited in Islamic law. The discussion begins with reasons for the prohibited sales and continues with the different types of prohibited contracts of sale identified by the Muslim jurists. As will be noticed in the analysis below, some of the contracts of sale, even though prohibited, may not be invalidated under the law.[112] **9.77**

There are also some contracts that have been accepted by some modern Muslim jurists in certain jurisdictions which are considered forbidden in other jurisdictions based on differences of opinion on such transactions. Though these kinds of contract of sale are many, a few have been selected here for analysis. Beyond just prohibited sales, any term or condition in a valid contract that inherently reflects or subtly mirrors any of the prohibited sales in substance or in form will either render the bilateral contract defective or illegal depending on the nature and extent of the issue involved. **9.78**

9.1 Reasons for Prohibition

As a general rule, as discussed in Chapter 6, all contracts of sale involving any element of *ribā*, *gharar*, *maysir*, or illegal subject matter are prohibited in Islamic law. In most of such transactions, there is an element of economic injustice as well as deception where a few people enrich themselves at the expense of a larger population in the society. Islamic law abhors such practices, as it seeks to promote fair distribution of resources through distributive justice and economic empowerment. This is primarily targeted at combating the ills of an oligarchic society where plutocracy prevails.[113] **9.79**

The exploitative tendencies in most prohibited transactions do not promote partnership in contracts. The general philosophy of Islamic contract law is the promotion of progressive economic partnerships. That is why mutual consent or meeting of minds is a cardinal condition for the validity of a contract in Islamic law. As will be seen below, most of the prohibited contracts contain elements of greed and selfishness with the **9.80**

[110] Abu Malik Kamal bn. Al-Sayyid Salim, Ṣaḥīḥ Fiqh Al-Sunnah wa Adilatuh wa tawdih madhahib al-A'imah (Al-Maktabah Al-Tawfikiyyah, 2003) Vol. 4, p. 290.
[111] Ibid.
[112] Al-Juzairi (n 37) Vol. 2, p. 245.
[113] This cardinal objective of economic justice and fair distribution of resources has its origin in the Qur'ān where Allah commands in Qur'ān 59:7: 'As for gains granted by Allah to His Messenger from the people of "other" lands, they are for Allah and the Messenger, his close relatives, orphans, the poor, and ⌜needy⌝ travellers *so that wealth may not merely circulate among your rich*. Whatever the Messenger gives you, take it. And whatever he forbids you from, leave it. And fear Allah. Surely Allah is severe in punishment' (emphasis added).

general tendency to outsmart the other party. Such a zero-sum game tendency is the hallmark of *maysir* and *qimār* which are prohibited in Islamic contract law.

9.81 Any contract that does not entail the sharing of risk in any business or investment is deemed exploitative. In most cases, such forbidden contracts do not have any direct impact on the real economy. Capital is completely misallocated, hence there is no underlying business transaction that will create economic value which could have led to job creation and the economic empowerment of the people. In such situations, capital does not flow into the real economy. One major economic problem that most of the forbidden contracts cause is stagflation—a situation where high inflation and economic stagnation occur at the same time.[114] This is an economic term usually used to refer to inflation-induced recession.[115] Three major problems occur when there is stagflation: high inflation, slow economic growth, and a steady high rate of unemployment.

9.2 Types of Prohibited Sales

9.82 There are various types of prohibited contracts. Some of them are not prohibited outright but could be defective according to the views of some Muslim jurists. A few of the contracts that are either prohibited or could contain some defective elements are explained below.

9.83 *Bayʿ al-ḥāḍir li bād*. Though this sale literally means the sale of an urbanite on behalf of the nomad or Bedouin, in the juristic sense it is a type of contractual arrangement that was prevalent during the time of Prophet Muhammad whereby a party (broker) goes to meet the Bedouin farmers who cultivate grains in the rural areas and buy their grains at a very low price, then sell those grains at a relatively high price to buyers in the city. In this type of contract of sale, the agent therefore earns significant profit from both the seller and the buyer, thereby disrupting the market price of such essential commodities. In order to curtail inflationary trends and to avoid exploitative tendencies, the Prophet Muhammad prohibited this type of sale arrangement and encouraged sellers and buyers to deal with each other directly without the intermediation of the agents who exploit the parties' ignorance of the real market price of the commodities.[116]

9.84 For the prohibition of this contract of sale, three conditions must be present or else it will be considered a permissible market practice. First, the urbanite must have intended to sell the commodities on behalf of the Bedouin; secondly, the Bedouin must be ignorant of the market price of the commodities; and thirdly, the price of the commodities must have been unduly increased beyond the market rate.[117] The reason for

[114] This term is generally attributed to Iain Macleod. See Edward Nelson and Kalin Nikolov, 'Introduction' in Bank of England Working Paper (Report) (Bank of England, 2002) p. 9. SSRN 315180. Also see John Helliwell, 'Comparative Macroeconomics of Stagflation' (1988) 26(1) Journal of Economic Literature 4.

[115] N. Gregory Mankiw, Principles of Macroeconomics (Cengage Learning, 2008) p. 464.

[116] Al-Tayyār (n 30) Vol. 6, p. 33.

[117] Ibn Qudāmah (n 65) Vol. 6, pp. 308 and 310.

the prohibition of this type of sale is that if the Bedouin farmer is allowed to sell his commodities to the people directly, people will buy them cheaply, and things will be easy for them. However, if a broker is introduced into the value chain, the price will increase for the people in the city and things may be difficult for people generally.[118] This is in line with the general objective of Islamic economic policies which tend to promote ease for the people and prevent every avoidable harm or difficulty, including economic hardships.

Bayʿ talaqy al-rukbān. This is a business practice where one purchases products from farmers at a relatively low price while keeping them ignorant of the actual market prices. This betrays the good faith element in business contracts, as the buyers capitalize on the ignorance of the farmers by buying at very low prices. When the seller approaches the market to sell his commodities, a buyer meets him just before he gets to the market and buys all the commodities without informing the seller of the market price of the commodities. The buyer does this so that he can sell them commodities at a very high price in the market. **9.85**

Such exploitative business arbitrage harms the entire economy as prices of commodities are manipulated. This contract of sale was prevalent during the pre-Islamic era where a buyer purchased a full caravan load of goods before it entered the market. It is however important to emphasize that if the buyer buys all the commodities before they get to the market, the seller may be given the option of voiding the contract of sale in the event that the latter gets to the market and discovers that he was deceived. In such a situation, he is given the option of rescinding the contract on the ground of deception.[119] **9.86**

Bayʿ al-muzābana. This is a barter trade involving dried and fresh fruits. This contract of sale was prevalent during the pre-Islamic era and the early days of Islam. In this contractual arrangement, a party exchanges fresh fruits for dried fruits where the measurement of the latter is precisely determined and that of the former is estimated since they are still on the trees.[120] Since this type of transaction involves *gharar* which could lead to a dispute, Islamic law prohibits it in its entirety. Muslim jurists are unanimous in the prohibition of this form of sale.[121] **9.87**

Bayʿ al-muḥāqala is another contract of sale that has some resemblance with *bayʿ al-muzābana.* It involves the sale of grains that are still in ears in exchange for dry or processed grains. Another form of it is seen in a contract between a landowner-lessor and farmer-lessee where the later pays rent to the former using the produce derived from the land, for example wheat produced from the land. Regardless of whichever form the **9.88**

[118] Ibid, Vol. 6, p. 309.
[119] Ibid, Vol. 6, p. 312.
[120] Al-Tayyār (n 30) Vol. 6, p. 28.
[121] Ibid.

transactions take, it is impermissible due to the exchange of two unequal amounts in a contract involving produce (wheat or barley) that is subject to *ribā*.

9.89 *Bayʿ al-munābadha* or toss sale. This contract of sale involves tossing whatever is in the hands of both contracting parties, which often involves throwing of a piece of cloth, pebbles, or any object. Once both parties throw to each other what is in their hands, the sale is concluded and each of them goes away with whatever it got. In simple terms, a party tells the other to give him what he has in his hands in return for what he has in his own hands. This form of sale is forbidden as a result of its excessively speculative nature. While barter trade is permissible, there is excessive uncertainty in the subject matter of this form of barter trade; hence, it is impermissible.[122]

9.90 *Bayʿ al-kālī bi al-kālī* or sale of a debt for a debt is also called *bayʿ al-dayn bi al-dayn*. A contract of sale involving the sale of a debt for another debt is not permissible in Islamic law. When the countervalues of a bilateral contract are both deferred, then it is deemed to be an exchange of debt for debt.[123]

9.91 *Bayʿ al-talji'a* or a fictitious contract of sale. In this contract of sale, the seller pretends he is selling his property to another person even though there is no actual sale. This is one of the tactics utilized by some defaulting debtors who try to dispose of their assets fictitiously to a third party, usually a close family member, to avoid any legal action by the creditors to claim such property. It is also possible to execute such a sale for fear of confiscation of one's property even though, in the true sense of it, the seller does not intend to sell the property.[124]

9.92 Muslim jurists expressed different opinions on the legal rule applicable to *bayʿ al-talji'a*. Abu Hanifah and a popular view among Hanbali jurists are of the opinion that such a contract of sale is void because it appears to be fictitious and thus deceptive, which negates the requirement of mutual consent in contracts.[125] As such, the contract of sale is not executable. However, the Shafi'i jurists, as well as some reports from the Hanafi and Hanbali jurists, argued that such a sale is *ex facie* permissible given the express agreement between the parties and it fulfils all conditions for the validity of a contract of sale. Based on the foregoing analysis, the preferred opinion appears to be that *bayʿ al-talji'a* is not a valid contract of sale since the element of consent is missing.[126]

9.93 *Bayʿ al-wafā'* or sale with the right of redemption (or sale and buy-back contract at the same price). This is a contract of sale that contains a fundamental term legally obliging the buyer to agree to return the goods purchased once the agreement is executed. In this sale, the buyer honours the obligation to sell the purchased goods back to the original seller at the same price and on a spot basis. Therefore, it is a spot sale and immediate

122 Ibn Rushd, Bidayat al-mujtahid wa nihayat al-muqtasid (Dar Al-Ma'rifah, 1997) Vol. 3, p. 167.
123 Al-Tayyār (n 30) Vol. 6, pp. 40–41.
124 Ibid, Vol. 6, pp. 38–39.
125 Ibid, Vol. 6, p. 39.
126 Ibid.

buy-back transaction. It is important to note that the prices of both the original sale and the subsequent repurchase are the same and are paid in full on a spot basis. The Maliki jurists refer to this contract of sale as *bay' al-thanāya*, while the Shafi'i jurists call it *bay' al-'uhda* and the Hanbali jurists identify it as *bay' al-'amānah.*[127]

In terms of the legal validity of *bay' al-wafā'*, different jurists proffer various views. The Maliki and Hanbali jurists as well as early Hanafi and Shafi'i jurists are of the opinion that the contract of sale is defective (*fāsid*) because of the seller's contractual stipulation that compels the buyer to return the subject matter of the contract once he refunds the price earlier paid to him. According to this view, such an act contradicts the requirement for a valid contract of sale because the buyer fully owns the sold property once the contract is duly executed.[128] **9.94**

Some of the later jurists among the Hanafi and Shafi'i schools are of the opinion that *bay' al-wafā'* is a valid contract due to some of its underlying principles, one of which relates to the benefit the buyer derives from the property sold. According to them, this justifies the repurchase of it by the original seller so that it is not sold to a third party.[129] Furthermore, some Hanafi jurists introduce another dimension to the contract by considering *bay' al-wafā'* as a *rahn* (pledge) contract. So, they do not consider it as a sale but rather as a pledge contract which leads to the application of the legal principles underpinning a pledge contract.[130] **9.95**

Bay' al-najsh. This contractual arrangement involves a fraudulent sale or manipulative overpricing. In this contractual arrangement, a person or group of persons collude with a seller to influence the price of an ongoing auction through higher bids in order to entice genuine bidders to increase their own bids and finally get stuck with the final price of the subject matter. Such manipulative overpricing leads to an artificial price as compared to the normal market price. The end result is that the fair market price is distorted, and the unsuspecting bidder is made to pay a much higher price as a result of numerous fake bids during the auction.[131] **9.96**

Despite the prohibition mentioned above, one wonders whether such a manipulative contract of sale is valid. The majority of Muslim jurists are of the opinion that the contract of sale is valid because the act of manipulation was carried out by the fraudulent person who may be external to this specific contract of sale. The contracting party should not be blamed for the act of an external party who seeks to disrupt the market price of commodities. The contract of sale is valid, as in the case of *bay' talaqy al-rukbān*, where it is considered voidable at the instance of the innocent party against the deceptive party. Therefore, *bay' najsh* can be enforced against the fraudulent person but could be voidable at the instance of the innocent party.[132] **9.97**

[127] Ibid, Vol. 6, p. 42.
[128] Al-Mawsu'at al-Fiqhiyyah Al-Kuwaitiyyah (Dar al-Kutub al-Ilmiya) Vol. 9, p. 260.
[129] Ibid.
[130] Ibid.
[131] Ibn Qudāmah (n 65) Vol. 6, p. 304.
[132] Al-Tayyār (n 30) Vol. 6, p. 35.

9.98 *Bay' al-'ina* or sale and buy-back agreement. This is a contract of sale where a person sells a commodity to another party for a price to be paid at a future date, though with spot delivery. Then, at the same time, the seller immediately buys back the commodity for a price lower than the original price at which he initially sold it,[133] but this later price is paid immediately.[134] On the face of it, this gives the buyer immediate liquidity, but it appears to be a loan since the buyer is paying a higher amount than he should have paid.[135] In other words, it is a spot transaction involving the sale of a commodity at a deferred price which is followed straight away with a buy-back for immediate cash, which is often lower than the original price. At the end of the period specified in the first leg of the transaction, the buyer is obliged to pay the original deferred price, which is higher.[136]

9.99 The Hanafi, Maliki, Hanbali, and even some Shafi'i jurists opined that *bay' al-'ina* is not permissible in Islamic law. This prohibition of *bay' al-'ina* by the majority of Muslim jurists is premised on the ban on *ribā*-based transactions and any form of contract that has some resemblance to *ribā*, as proscribed by the Qur'ān.[137] Prophetic precedents also contain similar prohibitions.[138] The main essence of the prohibition is seen in the difference between the original deferred price and the spot cash price for the same commodity in a contract between the same parties in the same contractual session.[139]

9.100 However, it is pertinent to note that some Muslim jurists are of the opinion that *bay' al-'ina* is permissible. This is seen among some Shafi'i jurists, Abu Yusuf, Abu Daud, and Abu Thur, who argued that *bay' al-'ina* is a valid contract of sale and does not contradict Islamic legal principles when properly concluded by the parties, that is, when it fulfils some mandatory conditions.[140] Some of these conditions include that the parties should not intend a loan contract, all elements of contracts must be present, the two

[133] Muḥammad ibn Muḥammad Ḥaṭṭāb, Mawahib al-Jalil Sharh Mukhtasar Khalil (Dar al-Fikr, 1992) Vol. 4, p. 391.

[134] Al-San'aani, 'Abd al-Razzaaq, Al-Musannaf (Dar Al-Kutub al-Ilmiya, 2000) Vol. 8, p. 184.

[135] *Al-Mawsu'at Al-Fiqhiyyah* (n 128) Vol. 9, p. 96.

[136] Ibn Humam (n 105) Vol. 7, p. 213.

[137] Muhammad bin Abu Bakr Ibn Qayyim al-Jawziya, I'lam al-Muwaqi'in 'an Rabb al-'Alamin (Dar al-Kutub al-Ilmiya, 1996) Vol. 3, p. 166.

[138] For instance, the following narration is often quoted to support the prohibition of *bay' al-'inah*:

> "Ma'mar and al-Thawri told us, from Abu Ishaq, from his wife, that she entered upon 'Aishah among some other women and a woman asked her: O Mother of the Believers, I had a slave girl. I sold her to Zayd ibn Arqam for eight hundred to be paid at a later date, then I bought her from him for six hundred, and I gave him six hundred in cash, but it was recorded as eight hundred. 'Aishah said: What a bad transaction you have done, by Allah! What a bad transaction he has made, by Allah! Tell Zayd ibn Arqam that he has cancelled out his jihad with the Messenger of Allah (peace and blessings of Allah be upon him) unless he repents. The woman said to 'Aishah: Do you mean that I should take my capital and return the extra amount to him? She said: "So whosoever receives an admonition from his Lord and stops eating *ribā*, shall not be punished for the past; his case is for Allah (to judge); but whoever returns (to *ribā*), such are the dwellers of the Fire—they will abide therein' [al-Baqarah 2:275]. Or she said: 'but if you repent, you shall have your capital sums. Deal not unjustly (by asking more than your capital sums), and you shall not be dealt with unjustly (by receiving less than your capital sums)."

See Ibn 'Abd al-Haadi, Tanqih tahqiq ahadith al-ta'liq (Dar al-Watan lil-Nashr, 2000) Vol. 2, p. 558, who classified the chain of the *ḥadīth* as good.

[139] Al-Kāsānī (n 10) Vol. 5, p. 198.

[140] Muhammad Amin Ibn 'Abidin, Radd Al-Mukhtar wa Hashiyah Ibn Abidin (Dar Al-Fikr, 1992) Vol. 5, p. 325.

separate contracts must be clearly distinguished from each other, and they must take place consecutively.[141]

Tawarruq or monetization. This is a sale contract where a person who is in need of liquidity purchases a commodity from a seller on a deferred payment basis, in other words on credit, and sells the same commodity to a third party for a lower price, although on a cash basis.[142] The majority of Muslim jurists are of the opinion that *tawarruq* is permissible based on the permissibility of sale as provided for in the Qur'ān.[143] The fundamental difference between *tawarruq* and *bay' al-'ina* is seen in the nature of the two sales. In the former, the buyer sells the commodity to a third party, while in the latter, the buyer sells back the commodity to the original seller though at a lower price. 9.101

While the majority of Hanbali jurists are of the opinion that *tawarruq* is permissible, there are scholars such as Ibn Taimiyya[144] and Ibn Al-Qayyim[145] who held that it is impermissible in Islamic law. In addition, since the Shafi'i jurists permit *bay' al-"inah*, it goes without saying that they consider that *tawarruq* is permissible as a valid sale contractual arrangement. For the Maliki jurists, even though they do not approve of *bay' al-'ina*, they do allow *tawarruq*. While most Hanafi jurists agreed that *tawarruq* is permissible, there are some later jurists of the same school of jurisprudence who opine that *tawarruq* has some resemblance with *bay' al-'ina* and therefore it is at best considered *makrūḥ* or discouraged and reprehensible.[146] 9.102

While the majority of the jurists are of the opinion that the classical *tawarruq* described above is permissible and this seems to be the preferred opinion, there is another type of *tawarruq* in modern business practice which most modern jurists consider forbidden. This new form of *tawarruq* is known as the organized *tawarruq* or *tawarruq munazzam*, which is often called *tawarruq*, through the banks. In this new form of *tawarruq*, a person buys a commodity from a bank based on deferred payment terms and immediately requests the bank to sell it for a lower spot price. The Islamic Fiqh Council have declared that this form of organized *tawarruq* is not permissible.[147] 9.103

141 Amir Shaharuddin, 'The bay' al-'Inah Controversy in Malaysian Islamic Banking' (2012) 26(4) Arab Law Quarterly 499–511.

142 Al-Buhūtī (n 34) Vol. 3, p. 186.

143 Al-Tayyār (n 30) Vol. 6, p. 25.

144 See Taqiuddin Ibn Taymiyah, Al-Fatawa Al-Kubra (Dar al-Kutub al-Haditha, 1964) Vol. 5, p. 392.

145 al-Jawziyah Ibn Al-Qayyim, Tahdhib al-Sunan (Maktabah al-Ma'arif lil-Nashr wa al-Tawzi', 2007) Vol. 5, p. 801.

146 Muhammad Al-Shawkani, Nail al-Awtar (Dar Ibn Hazm, 1441 AH) Vol. 5, p. 206.

147 International Islamic Fiqh Academy, 'Resolutions and Recommendations of the International Islamic Fiqh Academy', English translation of the Arabic Issue, Session 2-24, Resolutions 1–238, 1985–2019, Second Issue, 2021, p. 410. The Islamic Fiqh Academy resolved thus:

1. In Fiqh terminology, Tawaruq refers to the act of a person (the *mustawriq*) buying a commodity on credit and sells it to someone other than the original seller, at a cash price (in most cases) lower than the purchase price, in order to obtain cash. This form of *tawaruq* is permitted by Shariah, provided that it satisfies Shariah-acceptable conditions of sale.
2. Structured *tawaruq* in contemporary terminology means the case of a person who buys a good on credit from local or international markets. Then the seller (the financer) arranges selling of the good, either directly or through an agent or in collusion with the buyer (the *mustawriq*), at a cash price, which is (in most cases) lower than the purchase price.
3. Inverse *tawaruq* takes the same form of structured *tawaruq* except that the *mustawriq* is the institution, and the financer is the client.

10

Equity-Based Partnership Contracts

1. Introduction

The notion of *sharika* or *mushāraka*, which is effectively an equity-based partnership predicated on a contractual relationship, is used interchangeably in this chapter. The term literally means mixing, yet technically its meaning differs in accordance with the type of *sharika* applied in a particular context. A *sharika* may be categorized under three broad categories, namely, *sharikat al-ibāḥa*, *sharikat al-milk* (co-ownership) and *sharikat al-ʿaqd* (partnership). *Sharikat al-ibāḥa* is probably the most difficult to locate anywhere at present and hence it will not be discussed here. *Sharikat al-milk* also has little relevance to the commercial world; therefore this chapter will primarily focus on *sharikat al-ʿaqd*. Since the development of *sharikat al-ʿaqd* by the Hanafi school is far more comprehensive than its treatment by other schools, the analysis in this chapter is primarily based on Hanafi scholarly output,[1] although the opinions of other schools are also explained where relevant and necessary. 10.01

Sharikat al-ibāḥa is defined as the 'common right of the people in ownership by acquisition or gathering of things that are *mubāḥ* (permissible for such acquisition) and which are not originally owned by anyone'.[2] The general public has common rights over some subject matters and, in this sense, are considered partners. The person who acquires said assets converts them into his or her ownership, as is the case with water and pasture. In practice, such partnership is not conferred as a matter of individual ownership and is instead exercised by the state. 10.02

2. Co-ownership (*Sharikat al-amlāk*)

The Majalla defines *sharikat al-amlāk* as 'the existence of a thing in the exclusive joint ownership of one or more persons due to any reason of ownership, or it is the joint claim of two or more persons for a debt that is due from another individual arising from a single cause'.[3] The reasons for ownership indicated here include: 'purchase, or taking 10.03

[1] For instance, see Abūbakr Al-Kāsānī, Badāʾiʿ al-Ṣanāʾiʿ fī Tartīb al-Sharāʾiʿ (Dār al-Kutub al-ʿIlmiyya, 1986) Vol. 6, pp. 56–78; Muḥammad Al-Sarakhsī, Al-Mabsūṭ (Dār al-Maʿrifa, 1993) Vol. 11, pp. 151–220; Al-Samarqandī, Tuḥfat al-Fuqahāʾ (Dār al-Kutub al- ʿIlmiyya, 1994) Vol. 3, pp. 5–18.

[2] Majalla, Art. 1045.

[3] Majalla, Art. 1045. See also Ibn ʿĀbidīn, Radd al-Muḥtār Al-Durr al-Mukhtār Sharaḥ Tanvīr al-Abṣār (Dār al-Fikr, 1992) Vol. 6, p. 466.

by way of gift, or by acceptance of a bequest, or inheritance, or by mixing or causing to mix one property with another, that is to say, by uniting them in such a way that they cannot be distinguished or separated.[4] In this way, the element of co-ownership is the mixing of the *'ain* or *dayn* in such a way that each may not be distinguished or separated from the other.[5]

2.1 Types of Co-ownership

10.04 Co-ownership may be *'ayn* (specific property in existence)[6] and *dayn* (something to be received).[7] The co-ownership of both may be optional (*sharikat al-ikhtiyār*)[8] or obligatory (*sharikat al-jabr*).[9] The parties themselves create voluntary co-ownership by their acts, as is the case with the purchase or acceptance of a gift or a bequest, or by mixing property together.[10] Conversely, obligatory or compulsory co-ownership is created by 'some cause other than the acts of the joint owners, such as through inheritance'.[11]

2.2 Rights of Co-owners

10.05 Co-owners have an undivided co-ownership of each element of the property as well as the fruit of the co-owned property.[12] The profit or access to the capital of co-ownership is shared according to the ratio of ownership of the capital.[13]

10.06 The co-owners are not agents of each other. Therefore, a co-owner can use or sell the share of other co-owners only with prior permission or agreement. An unauthorized disposal of another partner's share to a third party resulting in destruction of property would subject him to the payment of compensation. The said co-owner will also be liable for compensation if his authorized use results in harm to the property. In this way, the co-owner possesses that share as *wadī'a*.[14]

[4] Majalla, Art. 1060; Al-Kāsānī (n 1) Vol. 6, p. 56.
[5] Majalla, Art. 1060; Ibn al-Humām, Al-Fatāwā al-Hindiyya (Dār al Kutub al-'Ilmiyya, 2000) Vol. 2, p. 320.
[6] Majalla, Art. 1067. For instance, the co-ownership of a single sheep or a flock of sheep.
[7] Majalla, Arts 1066, 1068; *Radd al-Muḥtār* (n 3) Vol. 6, p. 467.
[8] Majalla, Art. 1063; Al-Kāsānī (n 1) Vol. 6, p. 56; *Al-Fatāwā al-Hindiyya* (n 5) Vol. 2, p. 320; 'Abd Allāh Al-Mauṣilī, Al-Ikhtiyār li Ta'līl al-Mukhtār (Dār al Risālat al 'Ālamiya, 2009) Vol. 2, p. 440.
[9] Majalla, Art. 1064; Al-Kāsānī (n 1) Vol. 6, p. 56; *Al-Fatāwā al-Hindiyya* (n 5) Vol. 2, p. 320; Al-Mauṣilī (n 8) Vol. 2, p. 440.
[10] Majalla, Art. 1063.
[11] Majalla, Arts 1064, 1092.
[12] Majalla, Art. 1073.
[13] *Al-Fatāwā al-Hindiyya* (n 5) Vol. 2, p. 320; Al-Marghīnānī, Al-Hidāya Sharḥ Bidāyat al-Mubtadī (Dār Iḥyā' al-Turāth al-'Arabī, n.d.) Vol. 4, p. 393.
[14] Majalla, Arts 1069, 1071, 1075. Dwelling in a jointly owned house is an exception (Majalla, Art. 1070); *Al-Fatāwā al-Hindiyya* (n 5) Vol. 2, p. 320; Al-Mauṣilī (n 8) Vol. 2, p. 440; Al-Kāsānī (n 1) Vol. 6, p. 65.

The right to demand the recovery of a debt vests each co-owner jointly and severally.[15] A co-owner cannot postpone the joint debt without prior permission of the other owner(s).[16] The same rules govern *'ayn* and *dayn* possessed by one co-owner. 10.07

3. *Sharikat al-'aqd* (Partnership)

Muslim jurists have defined *sharikat al-'aqd* in different ways. The Malikis stipulate that this partnership is established when each partner confers upon another a right of disposition of capital on its behalf and also retains such a right for itself.[17] For Hanafis, this is a contract between two or more people with a view to common participation in capital and its profits.[18] The Hanbalis define partnership as 'a participation of two or more persons in the entitlement of a thing and its disposition'.[19] Shafi'i defines it as 'an establishment of an undivided right in a single thing held in common between two or more persons'.[20] 10.08

These definitions are not useful due to their inherent limitations. None of the four definitions covers certain kinds of partnership, as is the case with *muḍāraba*. For instance, the Hanafi and Maliki definitions do not include wealth as a basis to form this partnership and therefore they do not encompass certain partnerships which do not require wealth for their establishment, like *muḍāraba*, *sharikat al-wujūh*, and *sharikat al-a'māl*.[21] Similarly, the Hanbali and Shafi'i definitions do not indicate the purpose of those partnerships intended to make a profit.[22] A comprehensive definition is provided by the Accounting and Auditing Organization for Islamic Financial Institutions (AAOIFI) in that '*Sharikat al-'Aqd* (contractual partnership) entails an agreement between two or more parties to combine their assets, labour, or liabilities for the purpose of making profit'.[23] 10.09

3.1 Types of *Sharikat al-'aqd*

There is considerable difference of opinion among the various *fuqaha* on the classification of *sharikat al-'aqd*. Maliki, Shafi'i, and Hanbali jurists divide it into: 10.10

[15] Majalla, Art. 1100.

[16] Majalla, Art. 1112.

[17] Ibn Qudāma, Sharḥ al-Kabīr (Dār al-Fikr, 1984) Vol. 3, p. 348; Al-Kharshī, Sharḥ al-Kharshī 'alā Mukhtaṣar Khalīl (Dār al-Fikr, n.d.) Vol. 4, p. 270.

[18] Majalla, Art. 1329; Al-Kāsānī (n 1) Vol. 6, p. 56.

[19] Ibn Qudāma, Al-Mughnī fī Fiqh al-Imām Aḥmad bin Ḥanbal (Dār al Kutub al-'Ilmiyya, 1994) Vol. 5, p. 1.

[20] Shihāb al-Din al-Ramlī, Nihāyat al-Muḥtāj ilā Sharḥ al-Minhāj (Dār al-Fikr, 1984) Vol. 5, p. 1; Al-Shirbīnī, Mughnī al-Muḥtāj ilā Ma'rifat al-Alfāẓ al-Minhāj (Dār al-Kutub al-'Ilmiyya, 1415H/1994) Vol. 2, p. 274.

[21] The Hanbali and Shafi'i definitions do not cover *muḍāraba* because the delivery of *muḍāraba* capital to the *muḍārib* and non-participation by *rab al-māl* constitute mandatory conditions of the *muḍāraba*.

[22] Imran Nyazee, Islamic Law of Business Organizations Partnerships (IRI, 1999) pp. 18–20.

[23] 'Shariah Standard No. (12), Sharikah (Musharakah) and Modern Corporations (Revisited Standard), 2/1'.

1. *Sharikat al-'inān*
2. *Sharikat al-mufāwaḍa*
3. *Sharikat al-a'māl*
4. *Sharikat al-wujūh*

10.11 The *Hanbalis* contend that *muḍāraba* constitutes a species of *sharikat al-'aqd*, whereas the Shafi'is and Malikis consider it as an independent contract.[24] Conversely, the Hanafis distinguish *sharikat al-'aqd* into *amwāl*, *a'māl*, and *wujūh*, with each type established as either *'inān* or *mufāwaḍa*.[25] They provide the following categorization:

1. *Sharikat al-amwāl* (*mufāwaḍa* and *'inān*)
2. *Sharikat al-a'māl* (*mufāwaḍa* and *'inān*)
3. *Sharikat al-wujūh* (*mufāwaḍa* and *'inān*)
4. *Muḍāraba*

3.2 Formation of a *Sharikat al-'aqd*

10.12 All schools save for the Hanafis hold that *sīgha*, the parties, *maḥal al-'aqd* (capital), and labour to be performed with the capital constitute the necessary elements of a partnership.[26] For the Hanafis there is only one element necessary for the contract and that is *sīgha*, namely offer and acceptance.[27] All other schools require elements other than *sīgha* as necessary conditions. This in turn entails that the absence of a condition or a violation thereof renders the underlying contract *bāṭil*, whereas an issue in the condition makes it *fāsid*. An otherwise *fāsid* contract is unenforceable unless the problem with the missing condition is rectified. Conversely, a *bāṭil* contract cannot be rectified and a new contract must instead be concluded.[28]

10.13 Partnership in its formation also involves various agreements. Agreements of trust (*amāna*) and agency (*wakāla*) exist in partnerships established by way of *'inān* and *mufāwaḍa*, with the stipulation that a partnership by way of *mufāwaḍa* also encompasses a surety agreement (*kafāla*).[29] Each contract has a different function in the operation of the partnership. For instance, under the contract of trust, a partner holds the

[24] *Al-Mughnī* (n 19) Vol. 5, p. 1; Al-Ramlī (n 20) Vol. 5, pp. 4–5; Muhammad al-Shafi'i, Al-Umm (Dār al-Ma'rifa, 1410H/1990) Vol. 4, p. 487; Abū Ibrāhīm Al-Muzanī, Mukhtaṣar al-Muzanī fi Furū' al Shāfi'iyya (Dār al-Kutub al-'Ilmiya, 1998) p. 150.

[25] Al-Samarqandī (n 1) Vol. 3, p. 5; Al-Kāsānī (n 1) Vol. 6, p. 56; Kāmāluddīn Ibn al-Humām, Fat'ḥ al-Qadīr wa bi hāmisha sharḥ al 'ināya 'alā al-Hidāya (Matba'a al Kubrā al-Amīriya, 1897) Vol. 5, p. 5; *Radd al-Muḥtār* (n 3) Vol. 6, p. 475; *Al-Fatāwā al-Hindiyya* (n 5) Vol. 2, p. 320.

[26] Ibn Rushd, Bidāyat al-Mujtahid wa Nihāyat al-Muqtaṣid (Muṣṭafā al-Bābi al-Ḥalabī, 1975) Vol. 2, p. 179; Al-Ramlī (n 20) Vol. 5, p. 5.

[27] Al-Marghīnānī (n 13) Vol. 4, p. 484; Al-Sarakhsī (n 1) Vol. 11, p. 168; Ibn Nujaim, Al-Baḥr al-Rā'iq Sharḥ Kanz al-Daqā'iq (Dār al-Kutub al-'Ilmiyya, 1997) Vol. 5, p. 282; Al-Kāsānī (n 1) Vol. 6, pp. 56–57.

[28] Al-Kāsānī (n 1) Vol. 6, p. 56.

[29] Al-Marghīnānī (n 13) Vol. 4, pp. 398, 406; *Al-Fatāwā al-Hindiyya* (n 5) Vol. 2, pp. 328, 335.

property of another partner (owner) in trust and is not liable to the owner if the property is destroyed in his hands without negligence.[30]

3.3 Entitlement to Profit

Profit is the sole purpose of a partnership and there are three bases for the entitlement to profit. First is the contribution of wealth (*māl*) because profit is an accrual over the capital and hence would belong to the owner of the capital. The other two bases are *amal* and liability for loss (*ḍamān*). By way of illustration, in *muḍāraba*, the *muḍārib*'s entitlement to profit is due to his work and the *rab al-māl's* entitlement is due to his wealth and liability for loss. This is because wealth becomes the basis for profit only after it is combined with liability for loss on account of the tradition of the Prophet whereby it was held that 'entitlement of profit is based upon the corresponding liability for loss'.[31] **10.14**

3.4 Legal Nature of Partnership

A partnership is considered a *jāiz* (*ghair lāzim*) contract and each partner can rescind it unilaterally, which will be effective if rescission is made in the presence of the other partner or communicated to the other partner if that other partner was absent at the time of rescission.[32] **10.15**

3.5 *Sharikat al-amwāl*

In *sharikat al-amwāl*, the partners contribute wealth or capital as investment to earn and share profit that is to be distributed amongst them. For the Hanafis, *sharikat al-amwāl* can be concluded even without mention of *sharika*, as long as the contract as a whole implies the existence of a valid offer and acceptance.[33] **10.16**

3.5.1 Conditions for *Sharikat al-amwāl*

There are certain conditions governing *sharikat al-amwāl*, particularly the existence of 'inān and *mufāwaḍa*, as discussed below.[34] **10.17**

[30] Al-Marghīnānī (n 13) Vol. 4, pp. 397–98, 406, 415; Ibn Nujaim (n 27) Vol. 5, p. 283; Al-Kāsānī (n 1) Vol. 6, p. 60.

[31] Ibn al-Humām (n 25) Vol. 5, p. 10; Al-Kāsānī (n 1) Vol. 6, pp. 62–63, 69; Nyazee (n 22) pp. 69–75. The Shafi'is count wealth as the sole basis of any entitlement to profit and hence disapprove of *sharikat al-wujūh* and *sharikat al-abadān*. See Al-Shirbīnī, Mughnī al-Muḥtāj ilā Ma'rifat Alfāẓ al-Minhāj (Dār al-Kutub al-'Ilmiyya, 1994) Vol. 2, pp. 275.

[32] Al-Kāsānī (n 1) Vol. 6, p. 77.

[33] Ibid, Vol. 6, p. 56.

[34] Al-Samarqandī (n 1) Vol. 3, p. 5; Nyazee (n 22) p. 125 ff.

3.5.1.1 Presence of capital

10.18 The capital should be in the form of *'ayn* (ascertained or specific property). It should neither be *dayn* (receivable) nor wealth which is absent, otherwise neither*'inān* nor *mufāwaḍa* are allowed because the purpose of achieving profit from the partnership based on *dayn* becomes impossible. However, the capital is not required to be present at the time of the contract setting up the partnership; rather, it should be present when the contract of partnership will become effective and that point comes upon transaction with the capital. For instance, A gives B $1000 and asks him to contribute the same amount to purchase and sell a commodity upon which profit will be shared between them equally, and B performs the activity accordingly. This would be considered a partnership despite the fact that the capital from B was not present at the time of the conclusion of the contract.[35]

3.5.1.2 Mixing of capital

10.19 Under the Shafi'i school, *sharikat al-'aqd* can be constituted only after the capital becomes indistinguishable and inseparable from the parties' initial contribution, because *sharikat al-'aqd* is based upon *sharikat al-milk* for which the existence of indistinguishable assets is mandatory. If capital is lost before becoming indistinguishable, potential liability would lie with each owner.[36] The Hanbalis opined that the capital is assumed to be mixed/indistinguishable with the conclusion of the contract and if, after the contract and prior to actual mixing of the assets, the capital belonging to one partner is destroyed, both partners would incur liability.[37]

10.20 The Hanafis do not consider the mixing of capital as well as the delivery of capital by one partner to the other as prerequisites for the conclusion of a partnership agreement. Their scholarship clearly suggests that *sharikat al-'aqd* is based on an agency agreement, which itself is valid without the mixing of capital contributions. In *sharikat al-'aqd*, a partner, being an agent, makes purchases with ascertained capital and hence the prerequisite is the ascertainment of capital at the time of conclusion of the contract or at the time of purchase. For the Hanafis, it is only the wealth purchased and the profit generated in which mixing is mandatory. If capital from one partner is destroyed before mixing it with the capital of other partner, its owner will be solely liable because the partnership is not established before the transaction is made on these forms of capital.[38]

[35] For Hanafis, see Al-Kāsānī (n 1) Vol. 6, p. 60; Al-Samarqandī (n 1) Vol. 3, p. 5; *Al-Fatāwā al-Hindiyya* (n 5) Vol. 2, p. 324; Sirāj al-Dīn, Al-Fatāwā al-Sirājiyya (Dār al-Kutub al- 'Ilmiyya, 2011) p. 367. The Hanbali school also suggests that the capital should be available for each transaction. See Manṣūr Al-Buhūtī, Kashshāf al-Qinā' 'an Matn al-Iqnā' ('Ālam al-Kutub, 1997) Vol. 3, p. 191. Shafi'i supporters also contend that the presence of the partners at the time of a transaction is mandatory. See Al-Shafi'i (n 24) Vol. 4, p. 487; Al-Muzanī (n 24) p. 150.

[36] Al-Kāsānī (n 1) Vol. 6, p. 60; Al-Shafi'i (n 24) Vol. 4, p. 487; Al-Muzanī (n 24) p. 150.

[37] *Al-Mughnī* (n 19) Vol. 5, p. 13; Al-Buhūtī (n 35) Vol. 3, p. 192.

[38] Al-Kāsānī (n 1) Vol. 6, p. 60; Al-Samarqandī (n 1) Vol. 3, p. 6; *Al-Fatāwā al-Hindiyya* (n 5) Vol. 2, p. 324; Al-Mauṣilī (n 8) Vol. 2, p. 443.

3.5.1.3 Form of capital to establish a partnership

The capital or investment in *ʿinān*-based *sharikat al-amwāl* (as well as that based on *mufāwaḍa*) should be in the form of money or currencies.[39] If goods of the same species that are estimated by measurement, weight, or number are mixed with each other, the *sharikat al-ʿaqd* is also allowed.[40] **10.21**

A partnership may not be based on *ʿurūḍ* (goods or property) or immovable property because their value at the time of contract is uncertain and is prone to sudden fluctuations; hence the ratio of profit which is based on the contribution of the partners cannot be ascertained with precision at the time of distribution of the property. However, if some commodity is used due to its liquidity as a basis for a partnership under customary practice it may exceptionally be allowed.[41] **10.22**

3.5.2 Kinds of *Sharikat al-amwāl*

Sharikat al-amwāl is based either on *inān* or *mufāwaḍa*. These will be examined in more detail in the following sections. **10.23**

3.5.2.1 ʿInān sharikat al-amwāl

The term *ʿinān* refers to the reins used for riding and controlling an animal. In the legal realm, it refers to a contract 'between two or more persons to work in any particular trade with determined capital and to share profit and loss with determined rates'.[42] There is consensus among all Muslim jurists on the validity of *ʿinān*.[43] **10.24**

3.5.2.1.1 Formation of *ʿinān* partnerships If only the words '*sharika*' or '*inan*' are used in the agreement, the resultant partnership would be *ʿinān* based on agency because an *ʿinān* contract encompasses only an agency agreement without surety.[44] According to the Shafi'is, *ʿinān* would imply special *ʿinān*, with a special agency contract incorporated therein. This would entail that, in the case of *ʿinān* with special agency, the partner requires special permission to enter into credit transactions. However, for the Hanafis, this would still be a general *ʿinān*[45] whereby the partner concerned is granted an implied permission in respect of all transactions. The Hanafis stipulate that *ʿinān* becomes special only through the explicit intention of the parties, as this is clearly expressed in **10.25**

[39] Al-Kāsānī (n 1) Vol. 6, p. 59; Al-Marghīnānī (n 13) Vol. 4, pp. 401–02; Al-Samarqandī (n 1) Vol. 3, pp. 5–6; *Al-Fatāwā al-Hindiyya* (n 5) Vol. 2, p. 324; Al-Mauṣilī (n 8) Vol. 2, p. 445.

[40] Dāwūd ibn Yūsaf, Fatāwā Ghayāsiyya (Al Matbaʿa al Amīriya, 1904) p. 127; Al-Kāsānī (n 1) Vol. 6, p. 60; However, *Mālik* allows it if they are of the same kind because profit can be earned from them. See Al-Zailaʿī, Tabyīn al-Ḥaqāʾiq Sharḥ Kanz al-DAqāʾiq (Matbaʿat al-Kubrā al-Amīriya, 1895) Vol. 3, p. 317 and Vol. 5, p. 55.

[41] Al-Kāsānī (n 1) Vol. 6, p. 59; ʿAli al-Ḥaddād, Al Jawhara al-Nayyara ʿalā Mukhtaṣar al-Qudūrī (Maktabah Ḥaqqāniya, n.d.) pp. 345–46; *Al-Mughnī* (n 19) Vol. 5, p. 12.

[42] Tahir Mansoori, Islamic Law of Contracts and Business Transactions (5th edn, Shariah Academy IIUI, 2009) p. 254.

[43] *Sharikat al-amwāl* based on *ʿinān* is the only form of partnership allowed by the Shafi'is. Al-Shafi'i (n 24) Vol. 4, p. 487.

[44] Ibn Nujaim (n 27) Vol. 5, p. 282; Al-Marghīnānī (n 13) Vol. 4, p. 406.

[45] Al-Sarakhsī (n 1) Vol. 11, pp. 155–56.

their agreement.[46] However, in *ʿinān*, additional conditions can be stipulated, such as that all partners may be granted surety for each other (agreement of surety).[47]

10.26 3.5.2.1.2 Types of *sharikat al-ʿinān* The *ʿinān* partnership may be general or special in nature. Both of these types will be explored in the subsequent sections.

3.5.2.1.2.1 General *ʿinān*

10.27 In general *ʿinān*, there is no restriction on the partner to conduct any type of legitimate commercial activity to earn profit.[48] In special *ʿinān*, the categories of commodities or the territory in which he is allowed to trade are prescribed for the transacting partner. Such a partner may be allowed to conduct only one transaction or series of transactions in such a commodity. Both general and special *ʿinān* may be based on agency and may also have surety agreement between them.[49]

10.28 3.5.2.1.3 Basics of the *ʿinān* partnership It is important to set out the key characteristics of *ʿinān* as they arise in the scholarship of Islamic law. The effects of a contract of *ʿinān* are described in the following subsections.

3.5.2.1.3.1 Agency between partners

10.29 The existence of agency is a necessary component of a partnership. Even if it is not mentioned in the partnership contract, each partner becomes an agent for all other partners and acts on their behalf. It is clear that in order for such agency to operate, each partner should possess appropriate legal capacity for entering into the contract of agency.[50] Hence, for *ʿinān sharikat al-amwāl* only with agency (*wakāla*) and without guarantee (*kafāla*), the partners should 'be of sound mind and perfect understanding' and 'a minor who has received authority may also enter into' *ʿinān sharkat al-amwāl*. If *kafāla* (including the authority of *istadāna*) is also included in *ʿinān*, then it cannot be concluded by a minor, even if the said minor has received prior permission from the guardian.[51]

10.30 Where an agent concludes a contract (e.g. a sale), the *ḥukm* of the contract automatically passes to the principal and the *ḥuqūq* of the contract is retained by the agent. *Ḥukm* refers to the primary effects of the contract, such as transfer of ownership, and *ḥuqūq* refers to the means by which to achieve those effects, as is the case with delivery of the commodity, stipulation of the option, its price, etc. Only the transacting partner, rather than the principal, can bring a legal action or be sued for his or her performance.

[46] Al-Kāsānī (n 1) Vol. 6, p. 56.
[47] Majalla, Art. 1335; *Al-Fatāwā al-Hindiyya* (n 5) Vol. 2, p. 315; Ibn Nujaim (n 27) Vol. 5, pp. 290–91; Ibn al-Humām (n 25) Vol. 5, p. 20; Sirāj al-Dīn (n 35) p. 359.
[48] Al-Kāsānī (n 1) Vol. 6, p. 62.
[49] Ibid, Vol. 6, p. 62.
[50] Ibid, Vol. 6, pp. 58–59, 62; *Al-Fatāwā al-Hindiyya* (n 5) Vol. 2, p. 336. For legal capacity to contract, see Chapter 3.
[51] Majalla, Arts 1333–1335.

However, if a surety contract is also included as in *mufāwaḍa*, *ḥuqūq* is transferred to both partners.[52] In Maliki scholarship, the concept of agency requires that all partners can sue and be sued severally and jointly.[53] The Hanbalis stipulate that *ʿinān* is based on agency and trust, thereby providing authority to the other partner to conduct all trade that is specified. Partners possess all powers given to them in *ʿinān sharikat al-amwāl*. Each partner can sue and be sued for the liabilities arising from the partnership.[54]

3.5.2.1.3.2 Equality in contribution of capital and distribution of profits

The partners are free to establish this partnership even with the unequal contribution of capital[55] and distribution of profit that is not equal to the contributed capital even if the work to be undertaken concerns one or all partners.[56] The conditions regarding the distribution of profit should be clearly expressed (as ambiguity as to profit vitiates the *sharika*)[57] and be strictly observed by the parties.[58] **10.31**

However, the Hanbalis contend that the partners can agree to award a larger share of profit; in any event, losses will be apportioned according to the share of the capital contributed. Conversely, the Shafi'is and Malikis argue that profits must be in strict accordance with the ratio of capital contributed by each partner,[59] whereas Shafi'is take the position that the amount of work exacted from the partner is of no consequence.[60] The apportionment of profit should be specified in the agreement in terms of fractions such as a third, a half, or three-quarters, and needs to be aligned in accordance with the ratio of the capital contributed.[61] **10.32**

It should be noted that after the vitiation of a partnership, any condition stipulating unequal profit is also subject to vitiation and the distribution of profit is made according to the amount of capital contributed.[62] To determine profit, the price of the capital at the time of contract would be taken into consideration.[63] **10.33**

[52] Nyazee (n 22) p. 59; Al-Sarakhsī (n 1) Vol. 11, pp. 155–56; *Al-Fatāwā al-Hindiyya* (n 5) Vol. 2, p. 331; Al-Kāsānī (n 1) Vol. 6, pp. 70, 72; Al-Marghīnānī (n 13) Vol. 4, pp. 398–99.
[53] Al-Kharshī (n 17) Vol. 4, p. 283.
[54] *Al-Mughnī* (n 19) Vol. 5, p. 14; Al-Buhūtī (n 35) Vol. 3, pp. 192–94.
[55] Majalla, Art. 1365; *Al-Mughnī* (n 19) Vol. 5, p. 13; Al-Buhūtī (n 35) Vol. 3, p. 192; Al-Kāsānī (n 1) Vol. 6, p. 62.
[56] Al-Kāsānī (n 1) Vol. 6, p. 62; Al-Samarqandī (n 1) Vol. 3, p. 7; *Al-Fatāwā al-Hindiyya* (n 5) Vol. 2, p. 336; Sirāj al-Dīn (n 35) p. 369.
[57] *Al-Fatāwā al-Hindiyya* (n 5) Vol. 2, p. 320; Al-Kāsānī (n 1) Vol. 6, pp. 63–64; Al-Marghīnānī (n 13) Vol. 4, p. 407; Muḥammad Ibn Ḥabīb (Sahnūn), *Al-Mudawwanat al-Kubrā* (Matbʿat -Saʿāda, 1905) Vol. 5, p. 62.
[58] Majalla, Art. 1367.
[59] Abū Isḥāq Al-Shīrāzī, Al-Muhadhdhab fī Fiqh al-Imām al-Shāfiʿīi (Dār al Shāmiya, 1992) Vol. 3, p. 335; *Al-Mughnī* (n 19) Vol. 5, pp. 20–21; Sahnūn (n 57) Vol. 5, p. 62.
[60] Muḥy al-Dīn Al-Nawawī, Rauḍat al-Ṭalibīn wa ʿUmdat al-Muftīn (Al-Maktab al-Islāmī, 1991) Vol. 3, pp. 516–17.
[61] Al-Buhūtī (n 35) Vol. 3, p. 191; *Al-Fatāwā al-Hindiyyah* (n 5) Vol. 2, p. 320.
[62] Ḥaddād (n 41) Vol. 1, p. 349; Imām Al-Maḥbūbī, Sharḥ al-Wiqāya maʿ Muntahā Niqāya (Al-Wāriq, 2006) Vol. 3, p. 284.
[63] *Al-Fatāwā al-Hindiyya* (n 5) Vol. 2, p. 325.

3.5.2.1.3.3 Rights of partners in an *'inān* partnership

10.34 Each partner alone or through their agent can sell the property of the partnership or purchase by offering cash, as well as by loan, for the price they deem fit without prior permission from the other partners. However, the price cannot be lower than that prevailing in the market because this negates the purpose of a partnership, which is to earn profit. The property purchased by him will be considered his own if he makes a purchase for the partnership as a result of flagrant misrepresentation or he transacts with his own funds while not in possession of partnership funds to purchase property in which the partnership does not actually deal.[64] If the partner has been specifically prohibited by other partners from making such transaction, the said partner will make good any loss accruing from this prohibited transaction.[65]

10.35 In the event of an *'inān* encompassing only an agency contract, a partner (acting as an agent) can buy on credit, but the amount of credit should not exceed the total capital of the partnership. Such a partner can exceed this limit only subject to express authorization from the other partners (authority or *wilāyat al-istadāna*). The transacting partner would be personally liable for purchases made beyond the total capital and conducted without the authority of *istadāna*.[66]

10.36 It is generally agreed that all partners have the right to *ibdā'* (giving capital of the partnership to another person without making that other person a partner in profit).[67]

10.37 Each partner may invest the capital of the partnership in *muḍāraba* and appoint agents, mortgage, lease, or deposit the capital as *wadī'a* because all these transactions are encompassed within the limits of the partnership agreement and are legitimate ways of conducting trade. But he cannot invest the partnership capital in another partnership.[68]

10.38 Since the contract of partnership is based on agency, according to Hanafis, the partner making the transaction is saddled with pertinent contractual rights and obligations. For instance, if a partner makes sales or purchases, hires, or delivers property, all these transactions are binding on him alone and it is he who will sue and be sued for all claims related to this particular transaction. In equal measure the transacting partner must use his right of option to reject the goods. However, if the partnership is also based on *kafāla* as well, a third party can sue the other partners, but the other partners cannot sue the said third party.[69]

[64] Majalla, Arts 1373–1376; Al-Samarqandī (n 1) Vol. 3, p. 8; *Al-Fatāwā al-Hindiyya* (n 5) Vol. 2, p. 337; Al-Kāsānī (n 1) Vol. 6, p. 68.

[65] Majalla, Art. 1383.

[66] *Al-Mughnī* (n 19) Vol. 5, p. 14; Al-Buhūtī (n 35) Vol. 3, pp. 192–94; Al-Samarqandī (n 1) Vol. 3, p. 8.

[67] Al-Zaila'ī (n 40) Vol. 3, p. 319; Al-Kāsānī (n 1) Vol. 6, p. 68.

[68] Al-Samarqandī (n 1) Vol. 3, p. 9; Sirāj al-Dīn (n 35) p. 370; Al-Mauṣilī (n 8) Vol. 2, p. 452; Al-Kāsānī (n 1) Vol. 6, p. 69. The Hanbalis do not allow a partner to establish another partnership or *muḍāraba*. See *Al-Mughnī* (n 19) Vol. 5, p. 14; Al-Buhūtī (n 35) Vol. 3, pp. 192–94.

[69] Majalla, Arts 1377 and 1378.

It is generally agreed that any of the partners can travel with the capital of *sharika*.[70] It is also generally agreed that a partner cannot mix partnership capital with his own,[71] nor can he pledge any part of the partnership property for his personal loans except with prior permission from all other partners.[72] Finally, it is generally accepted that a partner cannot give a *qarḍ* nor can he gift the property of the partnership as a gift.[73] **10.39**

3.5.2.1.4 Dissolution of the *ʿinān* partnership There are several ways in which *ʿinān*-based *sharikat al-amwāl* may be vitiated. Apart from the circumstances discussed below, several conditions can have a vitiating impact on *sharika*. It should be emphasized that some conditions do not invalidate the partnership, even if they are invalid in and of themselves. Some conditions, however, serve to invalidate the partnership as a whole, such as monopoly-type conduct by one of the partners.[74] After a *sharikat al-ʿaqd* (partnership) collapses or becomes *fāsid* or *bāṭil*, the rules of *sharikat al-milk* govern the division of profits and property. It should also be noted that death, insanity, or migration of a partner to enemy land constitute vitiating factors for all kinds of partners.[75] **10.40**

Recession of the contract by either party: the *sharikat al-ʿinān* is based on an agency contract[76] and is *jāiz* and *ghair lāzim*, which means that it can be terminated by either party at will.[77] In this regard, the denial by any party of the *sharika* produces a recessionary effect on the *sharika* itself. If one partner says to another that he no longer desires to fulfil the aims of the *sharika* with him, this would amount to denial and result in vitiation of the *sharika*.[78] **10.41**

Loss of capacity of either party: the loss of capacity, death, or insanity of a partner renders the agency agreement as well as the partnership based on it *bāṭil*.[79] However, if there are three (or more than two) partners and one of them passes away, the partnership remains intact for the surviving partners.[80] When a partner is an apostate and migrates to enemy land, the *sharika* is also invalidated. However, such migration without any judicial verdict on the apostasy will suspend the partnership.[81] **10.42**

Expiration of period: the partnership also comes to end after the time for which the partnership was established expires or the venture for which it was constituted is accomplished. **10.43**

70 *Al-Fatāwā al-Hindiyya* (n 5) Vol. 2, p. 338.
71 Al-Kāsānī (n 1) Vol. 6, p. 69.
72 *Al-Fatāwā al-Hindiyya* (n 5) Vol. 2, p. 337.
73 Al-Kāsānī (n 1) Vol. 6, p. 69.
74 Al-Kāsānī (n 1) Vol. 6, p. 78. For valid and invalid conditions and their effect on contract, see Chapter 7.
75 Ibid, Vol. 6, p. 77.
76 Al-Ramlī (n 20) Vol. 5, p. 6.
77 Ibid, Vol. 5, p. 10; Al-Shīrāzī (n 59) Vol. 3, p. 383; Al-Kāsānī (n 1) Vol. 6, p. 78.
78 Ibn al-Humām (n 25) Vol. 5, p. 34; *Al-Fatāwā al-Hindiyya* (n 5) Vol. 2, p. 346; Al-Mauṣilī (n 8) Vol. 2, pp. 450–51.
79 Al-Kāsānī (n 1) Vol. 6, p. 78. The period of insanity invalidating the agreement should be one month according to Abū Yūsuf and one complete year according to Muhammad, during which time the partnership will remain suspended.
80 *Al-Fatāwā al-Hindiyya* (n 5) Vol. 2, p. 346.
81 Al-Kāsānī (n 1) Vol. 6, p. 38; *Al-Fatāwā al-Hindiyya* (n 5) Vol. 2, p. 346.

10.44 Destruction or loss of capital: the destruction or loss of capital, even of one partner, will end the *sharikat -al-ʿinān*, and liability will lie with the owner of the capital if it is lost before a purchase was intended with the lost capital. If assets have been mixed in the partnership's capital, then the loss would be shared by all partners, and what is saved from the destruction will be shared by them.[82] If one partner has made a purchase with his capital and after that the capital of the other partner is destroyed, all partners will be entitled to the purchased commodity because the *sharika* was established at the time of purchase and the purchasing partner was acting as agent. If the capital of one partner is destroyed and the other partner made a purchase with his capital, such commodity would belong to him exclusively because with such destruction, the *sharika*, including the underlying agency contract, came to an end.[83]

3.5.2.2 Mufāwaḍa sharikat al-amwāl

10.45 The literal meaning of *mufāwaḍa* is participation in each thing with equality.[84] Technically, *mufāwaḍa* is 'a contract of participation between two or more persons, with the condition of complete equality with respect to capital, profit and status, for working with their own wealth or with their labour in another's wealth, or on the basis of their creditworthiness so that each partner is surety for the other'.[85] The Malikis defined it as a partnership where a partner gives his permission to the other partner to make transactions generally in trade or in relation to a specific trade, and this permission is continuous in nature, that is, the other partner need not seek permission anew.[86] *Mufāwaḍa* may be for a trade in general as well as for a specific trade.[87] *Mufāwaḍa* encompasses an agency component and surety agreements.[88]

10.46 3.5.2.2.1 Legitimacy of *mufāwaḍa* Hanafis allow the practice of *mufāwaḍa* on account of *istiḥsān*.[89] The foundation of *istiḥsān* is the tradition of the Holy Prophet who exhorted people to 'engage in *mufāwaḍa* for it is full of blessings'. People also used to practise *mufāwaḍa* at the time of the Prophet, who did not refute its validity with divine will. Further, *jahāla* involved in *mufāwaḍa* is no different from that found in *muḍāraba*.[90] However, according to Shafi'i and Maliki, *sharikat al-mufāwaḍa* is void.[91]

[82] Al-Samarqandī (n 1) Vol. 3, p. 8; *Al-Fatāwā al-Hindiyya* (n 5) Vol. 2, p. 336; Al-Shaybānī, Al Jāmiʿ al-Kabīr (Matbaʿat al Istāqama, 1937) p. 267.
[83] Al-Mauṣilī (n 8) Vol. 2, pp. 450–51; Al-Naṣafī, Kanz al-Daqā'iq (Dār al Bashā'ir al Islāmiya, 2014) p. 399; Al-Zailaʿī (n 40) Vol. 3, p. 319.
[84] *Radd al-Muḥtār* (n 3) Vol. 6, pp. 475–76.
[85] Nyazee (n 22) p. 161.
[86] Al-Dusūqī, Ḥāshiyat al-Dusūqī ʿalā al-Sharḥ al-Kabīr (Dār al-Fikr, n.d.) Vol. 3, pp. 351–52.
[87] Ibn Nujaim (n 27) Vol. 5, pp. 282–83.
[88] Al-Samarqandī (n 1) Vol. 3, p. 9; Sirāj al-Dīn (n 35) p. 386.
[89] *Istiḥsān* refers to the discretion offered to jurists or judges to find the best possible solution to a juristic or theological problem. See Ahmad Hasan, 'The Principle of istiḥsān in Islamic Jurisprudence' (1977) 16 Islamic Studies 347.
[90] Al-Marghīnānī (n 13) Vol. 4, p. 396; Ibn al-Humām (n 25) Vol. 5, p. 7.
[91] Al-Shafi'i (n 24) Vol. 4, p. 487; Al-Shīrāzī (n 69) Vol. 3, p. 333; Al-Ramlī (n 20) Vol. 5, pp. 4–5; Al-Zailaʿī (n 40) Vol. 3, p. 313.

3.5.2.2.2 Formation of the *mufāwaḍa* partnership In order for the lawful formation of a *sharikat al-mufāwaḍa*, the term *mufāwaḍa* must be mentioned,[92] otherwise the *sharika* would be considered a general *'inān*. This is because people are assumed to have no knowledge of all the rules pertaining to *mufāwaḍa* and knowledge can be assumed only after a *mufāwaḍa* is expressly incorporated in the agreement. However, if only the conditions of *mufāwaḍa* are included without any mention of the term *mufāwaḍa*, this would be still be deemed as encompassing *mufāwaḍa* because the conditions are more important than the words.[93] If some of the conditions of *mufāwaḍa* are not met, as is the case with *mufāwaḍa sharikat al-amwāl*, the wealth of the partners becomes unequal at any point in time (partner X contributed dirham and partner Y contributed dinar both equal in value but the value of dinar increases by making the contribution of capital unequal), it is converted into *'inān* (general) because the *mufāwaḍa*, which is based on agency and surety, is predicated on *'inān*, which itself is a creature of agency. In other words, vitiation of *mufāwaḍa* does not vitiate *'inān*.[94] **10.47**

3.5.2.2.3 Conditions of a *mufāwaḍa* partnership All the conditions relating to capital, contractual capacity, and disposition of partners in the *'inān* partnership are equally applicable to *mufāwaḍa* because a *mufāwaḍa*, just like *'inān*, is a type of *sharikat al-amwāl*. The conditions making an *'inān fāsid* will also make a *mufāwaḍa fāsid*.[95] There are however certain conditions which are peculiar to the *mufāwaḍa* partnership, all of which are discussed in the following subsections. **10.48**

Agreements of agency and surety: since there is a contract of surety in *mufāwaḍa*, all partners must enjoy majority as adults (*bāligh*). Minors, even if they enjoy the permission of their guardian, cannot conclude this contract.[96] **10.49**

Equality in capital, profit, and loss: partners contribute equal capital and share profits and losses equally. This equality should remain intact at every moment of *sharika*.[97] If there is some disparity in any of these, the *mufāwaḍa* will convert into *'inān*.[98] Even the contribution by one partner of excess work does not entitle him to extra profit.[99] According to the preferred opinion of the Hanafis, capital of different species with equal value would be allowed for *mufāwaḍa*.[100] Knowledge about the amount of capital is not required at the time of contract.[101] **10.50**

[92] Ibn Nujaim (n 27) Vol. 5, p. 282; Al-Mauṣilī (n 8) Vol. 2, p. 441; Al-Kāsānī (n 1) Vol. 6, p. 62.
[93] Al-Marghīnānī (n 13) Vol. 4, p. 396; Al-Kāsānī (n 1) Vol. 6, p. 62.
[94] Al-Kāsānī (n 1) Vol. 6, pp. 62, 69; Ibn Nujaim (n 27) Vol. 5, pp. 287, 291; *Al-Fatāwā al-Hindiyya* (n 5) Vol. 2, p. 326; Sirāj al-Dīn (n 35) p. 368; Al-Mauṣilī (n 8) Vol. 2, p. 441; Ibn al-Humām (n 25) Vol. 5, p. 20.
[95] Al-Samarqandī (n 1) Vol. 3, p. 9.
[96] Al-Kāsānī (n 1) Vol. 6, pp. 60–61.
[97] Al-Marghīnānī (n 13) Vol. 4, p. 395.
[98] Al-Samarqandī (n 1) Vol. 3, p. 9; Al-Kāsānī (n 1) Vol. 6, pp. 61–62.
[99] The Malikis contend that equality of capital or labour is not a condition for the formation of *mufāwaḍa*. See Sahnūn (n 57) Vol. 5, pp. 68–69.
[100] Al-Kāsānī (n 1) Vol. 6, p. 61.
[101] Ibid, Vol. 6, p. 63.

10.51 Incorporation of the term '*mufāwaḍa*' in the agreement: to conclude a *mufāwaḍa* agreement, the term '*mufāwaḍa*, should be expressly used in the offer. If only the word '*sharika*' is used in the agreement, the resultant partnership would be deemed merely an *'inān* or *wakāla*.[102]

10.52 Generality of trade: there should be a general permission for trade of every type because the restriction of *mufāwaḍa* to a specific type of trade negates the concept of equality which lies at the heart of *mufāwaḍa*.[103]

10.53 3.5.2.2.4 Rights and duties of partners in *mufāwaḍa* partnerships *Mufāwaḍa* partners possess all the rights which they have in *'inān* because the *mufāwaḍa* is more general than *'inān*.[104] The Malikis contend that a partner can sell the partnership's goods without the permission of the other partners. By extension, a partner can purchase on credit only if permission is granted and the goods to be purchased are ascertained and this rule will also apply to purchases on credit beyond the capital of the partnership.[105] The Hanafis argue that any partner in a *mufāwaḍa* can buy and sell on credit but cannot purchase at a price that is excessively higher than prevailing market rates.[106] Along with the underlying agency agreement, a surety agreement is also built into the *mufāwaḍa*, which automatically confers on the transacting partner the authority of *istadāna*. Therefore, other partners are liable even if the credit purchase exceeds the total capital of the partnership. Even if a partner incurs a liability, the other partner(s) will also be liable for this.[107]

10.54 A partner cannot undertake *hibba* or *ṣadaqa* of property forming part of a *mufāwaḍa* partnership, nor can he provide *qarḍ*, as this is only available to all partners acting jointly. However, a partner can pledge the property of the *mufāwaḍa* for the debts of the *sharika*.[108] A partner cannot include a third party in *mufāwaḍa* as a partner without the permission of other partners.[109] A partner cannot further conclude a *mufāwaḍa* contract with third parties but may conclude an *'inān* contract with third parties.[110] If one of the partners has extended the time originally set out for the payment of receivables, this would be binding on the other partners.[111] One partner may discharge the contract concluded by the other partner(s).[112] A partner cannot purchase anything solely for himself. If this occurs it will be considered as being owned by both or all of the partners unless it is necessary for his livelihood.[113]

[102] Al-Marghīnānī (n 13) Vol. 4, p. 396; Al-Sarakhsī (n 1) Vol. 11, p. 154; Ibn Nujaim (n 27) Vol. 5, p. 293.
[103] Al-Kāsānī (n 1) Vol. 6, p. 61.
[104] Al-Samarqandī (n 1) Vol. 3, p. 9; Al-Kāsānī (n 1) Vol. 6, p. 72.
[105] Al-Dardīr, Al-Sharḥ al-Saghīr 'alā Aqrab al-Masālik ilā Madhhab al-Imām Mālik (Dār al Ma'ārif, n.d.) Vol. 3, pp. 464–65; Al-Kharshī (n 17) Vol. 4, pp. 275, 277; Sahnūn (n 57) Vol. 5, p. 71; Al-Dusūqī (n 86) Vol. 3, p. 352.
[106] *Al-Fatāwā al-Hindiyya* (n 5) Vol. 2, p. 329.
[107] Al-Kāsānī (n 1) Vol. 6, p. 72; Nyazee (n 22) pp. 61–62.
[108] *Al-Fatāwā al-Hindiyya* (n 5) Vol. 2, pp. 328–29, 331.
[109] Al-Kharshī (n 17) Vol. 4, p. 276; *Al-Fatāwā al-Hindiyya* (n 5) Vol. 2, p. 329.
[110] Al-Sarakhsī (n 1) Vol. 11, pp. 182–83.
[111] *Al-Fatāwā al-Hindiyya* (n 5) Vol. 2, p. 331.
[112] Ibid, Vol. 2, p. 331.
[113] Sirāj al-Dīn (n 35) p. 369.

It is accepted that a partner can travel with the capital of a *mufāwaḍa* without prior permission from other partners and the expenses of the travel would be borne by the partnership.[114] **10.55**

3.5.2.2.5 Dissolution of *sharikat al-mufāwaḍa*. The *sharikat al-mufāwaḍa* comes to an end when the parties' equality and surety agreements are absent. It is equally vitiated under the same set of reasons which vitiate *ʿinān*, such as the migration of a partner to enemy territory, denial of *sharika*, death, etc.[115] **10.56**

3.6 *Sharikat al-abdān*

In this partnership, persons contributing their personal labour participate in the acceptance of work, as is the case with tailors or bleachers, and who go on to perform manual labour (hence is called *sharikat al-abdān* or *sharikat al-ṣanāiʿ*). Their capital is their skill (hence it is also called *sharikat al-ṣanāiʿ*).[116] According to Shafi'i, *sharikat al-abdān* is void.[117] **10.57**

3.6.1 *Inan sharikat al-abdān* and its Conditions

The *sharikat al-abdān* based on the *ʿinān* contractual model will be explored in the following subsections. **10.58**

3.6.1.1 Nature of the subject matter

This kind of *sharika* cannot be established in respect of commodities, the ownership of which is transferred upon their acquisition on the basis of actual possession, such as hunting, mining, or the collection of wood, because a partnership requires agency, and agency in the acquisition of these is not allowed.[118] This is so because the person who takes them into his possession becomes the owner. Even if partners participate in this activity with the condition of agency, the agency would be *fāsid*, because it cannot be granted in these things, and the matters in which no agency is allowed cannot become the subject matters of *sharika*.[119] **10.59**

If one partner furnishes a shop and the other contributes his skill (tailoring, etc.) under the condition of sharing profits equally, Muhammad allows this contract on the basis of *istiḥsān* due to necessity and social need, as well as because this constitutes common practice among those for whom denial would create hardship and for whom this contract is vital for several reasons.[120] The *Majalla* also allows a *sharika* between two persons, one of whom supplies the shop and the other contributes tools and implements, **10.60**

[114] *Al-Fatāwā al-Hindiyya* (n 5) Vol. 2, p. 329.
[115] Sirāj al-Dīn (n 35) p. 369; Al-Kāsānī (n 1) Vol. 6, p. 72.
[116] Al-Sarakhsī (n 1) Vol. 11, p. 152.
[117] Al-Shafi'i (n 24) Vol. 4, p. 487; Al-Shīrāzī (n 69) Vol. 3, p. 333; Al-Ramlī (n 20) Vol. 5, pp. 4–5.
[118] Al-Samarqandī (n 1) Vol. 3, p. 17; Sirāj al-Dīn (n 35) p. 370.
[119] Al-Kāsānī (n 1) Vol. 6, p. 63; Al-Buhūtī (n 35) Vol. 3, p. 216.
[120] Al-Kāsānī (n 1) Vol. 6, p. 64; Al-Sarakhsī (n 1) Vol. 11, p. 161.

or only labour,[121] in which case they can divide the profit equally between them because 'the right of the owner of the shop to a half share accrues merely by reason of having guaranteed and undertaken the work, and this includes his right to make use of the shop'.[122]

3.6.1.2 Similarity of profession

10.61 To constitute this *sharika*, similarity of profession is not a prerequisite because this *sharika* is based on the *ḍamān al-ʿamal* (liability arising from the performance of work accepted by the partners) and both are liable for their work irrespective of the similarity of their professions.[123] The Zufr and Malikis stipulate similarity of profession as a prerequisite.[124] The reason for this difference of opinion lies in the fact that Hanafi's supporters contend that this partnership is based on *ḍamān al-ʿamal* (liability arising from works) whereas others count *khalṭ* (mixing) as a requirement of the *sharika* and argue that the mixing is not possible between two different professions.[125] The other reason for this difference is that, for Hanafis, the partnership is allowed in two different capitals as well as two different professions whereas Zufr disallows partnership in two different capitals as well as two different professions.[126]

3.6.1.3 Acceptance of work and liability thereof

10.62 As discussed earlier, a partner is an agent of other partners and the *ḥuqūq* of contract (performance, delivery, or price and goods, etc.) remains with the transacting partner, whereas the *ḥukm* (primary objective of the contract, such as transfer of ownership) immediately passes to the principal partner. The effect of the application of this rule would be that it is only the partner obtaining the work who should be liable for its performance and not the other partners, yet this rule has been declared inapplicable in *ʿinān*-based *sharikat al-abdān*. Consequently, customers may demand the performance of the work from either partner and also each partner can insist on payment or remuneration from the customer.[127] Therefore, each partner in *sharikat al-abdān* can accept work and perform it. It is also allowed if one of them accepts work and the other performs it.[128] The Malikis contend that even if the work is accepted by one partner, both partners will be liable for its performance and also for the goods if destroyed.[129]

10.63 If the partners have accepted a property to work on and this is destroyed, the partners would be jointly liable to the customer according to the shares of work stipulated for them in the agreement, for example liability will be equal if an equal share of work was

121 Majalla, Arts 1395 and 1396.
122 Majalla, Art. 1346.
123 Al-Kāsānī (n 1) Vol. 6, p. 64.
124 Al-Kharshī (n 17) Vol. 4, p. 283.
125 Al-Mauṣilī (n 8) Vol. 2, p. 452.
126 Al-Kāsānī (n 1) Vol. 6, p. 65.
127 Nyazee (n 22) pp. 150–54; Al-Kāsānī (n 1) Vol. 6, p. 76; Majalla, Art. 1387; Al-Marghīnānī (n 13) Vol. 4, p. 417.
128 Majalla, Art. 1386; *Al-Fatāwā al-Hindiyya* (n 5) Vol. 2, pp. 141–44.
129 Al-Kharshī (n 17) Vol. 4, p. 286.

stipulated; alternatively, liability would be calculated in the ratio of 1:3 if the partners had agreed to contribute the work according to this ratio. The customer can choose to sue either of the partners.[130]

3.6.1.4 Distribution of profit

The partners can agree on the equal or unequal amount of work to be contributed by them and the share of the profit proportionate or disproportionate to the share of work contributed; for example, a partner performing less work may be assigned a larger share of profit due to, for instance, his greater expertise, etc.[131] Hence, the profit will be shared according to the agreement between the parties even if one of them does not offer labour due to some genuine excuse, such as illness, or without any excuse because a partner becomes entitled to profit in *sharikat al-abdān* with the incorporation of such stipulation in the agreement.[132] **10.64**

3.6.2 *Mufāwaḍa Sharikat al-abdān*

In this partnership, which is based on agency and surety agreements (needing contractual capacity for a surety agreement), all the partners accept the work and are equally liable for work, losses, and profit (compensation for the work done) and the *ḍamān al-ʿamal* would be stipulated in equal terms for all partners. Apart from these, all the conditions pertaining to *ʿinān sharikat al-abdān* would apply.[133] **10.65**

3.7 *Sharikat al-wujūh*

According to Shafi'i, *sharikat al-wujūh* is void[134] because the intermingling of capital is a condition for the formation of the *sharika*.[135] The Malikis also consider it to be void.[136] **10.66**

3.7.1 *Inan Sharikat al-wujūh*

Persons who do not have wealth to create a partnership may buy commodities on credit and sell them for cash. Since only a creditworthy person can purchase on credit, or in other words, their creditworthiness is their capital, this partnership is termed a partnership with creditworthiness.[137] **10.67**

The Shafi'i school does not allow this because they base *sharika* on *sharikat al-milk*, which is not possible in *sharikat al-wujūh*. However, Hanafi's supporters allow it **10.68**

[130] Majalla, Art. 1393.
[131] Majalla, Arts 1391–1392; Al-Mauṣilī (n 8) Vol. 2, p. 453; Al-Marghīnānī (n 13) Vol. 4, p. 416. For an opposite opinion of the Malikis, see Al-Kharshī (n 17) Vol. 4, p. 283.
[132] Al-Kāsānī (n 1) Vol. 6, p. 63.
[133] Al-Samarqandī (n 1) Vol. 3, p. 12; Al-Kāsānī (n 1) Vol. 6, pp. 63–76.
[134] Al-Sāfiʿī Shafi'i (n 24) Vol. 4, p. 487; Al-Shīrāzī (n 69) Vol. 3, p. 333; Al-Ramlī (n 20) Vol. 5, pp. 4–5.
[135] Al-Zailaʿī (n 40) Vol. 3, p. 322.
[136] Sahnūn (n 57) Vol. 5, pp. 40–41.
[137] Al-Samarqandī (n 1) Vol. 3, p. 10.

because it is based on agency wherein each partner is an agent of others in respect of all purchases and distributions according to their agreement. Profit stipulated in the partnership agreement must be according to the ratio of partners' ownership, and such ownership will be determined on the basis of the price of the goods. This would be so even if one of the partners contributes extra work in the partnership and any condition assigning extra profit to one partner will be void because such condition would entitle a partner to benefit from the profit of another. The partners would be liable according to this share in the price of the goods purchased on credit (*ḍamān al-thaman*).[138] This *sharika* is based on *ḍamān* (liability for the loss) and this *ḍamān* creates the entitlement to profit, in other words the amount of profit is equal to the amount of liability and amount of liability is equal to the amount of ownership of the commodities. Therefore, if the amount of profit due is calculated as being higher than the amount of liability (share of ownership), this is not allowed.[139] The partners are agents of each other for the duration and purposes of the partnership's activities, as well as standing surety for each other in respect of payments to be made.[140]

3.7.2 *Mufāwaḍa Sharikat al-wujūh*

10.69 If this is based on *mufāwaḍa*, the partners constitute surety for each other, they should have capacity for the contract of surety, and there should be equality in their ownership of the purchased commodity. There should be equality in the liability of partners in the price of commodity and profits but only under the condition that they include the word '*mufāwaḍa*' in the agreement or mention the conditions clearly implying *mufāwaḍa*. If they do not mention this term, then this would be *'inān*.[141]

4. *Muḍāraba*

10.70 *Muḍāraba* is also termed *muqāraḍa* and *qirāḍ* and in it one partner contributes the capital and the other supplies the labour. The partner who supplies capital is *rab al-māl* (owner of the capital) and the person who performs the labour is called *muḍārib* (workman). The basis of this partnership is offer and acceptance.[142]

[138] Majalla, Arts 1399–1403; Al-Kāsānī (n 1) Vol. 6, p. 65; Al-Samarqandī (n 1) Vol. 3, p. 11; *Al-Fatāwā al-Hindiyya* (n 5) Vol. 2, p. 341; Al-Marghīnānī (n 13) Vol. 4, pp. 418–19; Nyazee (n 22) pp. 154–56.
[139] Ḥaddād (n 41) Vol. 1, p. 349.
[140] Al-Naṣafī (n 83) p. 400.
[141] *Al-Fatāwā al-Hindiyya* (n 5) Vol. 2, p. 341.
[142] Al-Kāsānī (n 1) Vol. 6, pp. 79–80.

4.1 Justification of *Muḍāraba*

Allah says in the Qur'ān: 'He knows that there are among you those who are sick and others who are journeying in the land in quest of Allah's bounty' (*yuḍāribūn a fil arḍ*).[143] The Holy Prophet worked on a *muḍāraba* basis for Khadīja prior to his marriage with her. The Prophet said: 'there is great blessing in three things: the credit sale, *muqāraḍa* and mixing wheat and barley for domestic consumption, not sale.'[144] **10.71**

The Governor of Kūfa gave some money to the two sons of Caliph Umar who then used the money to conduct trade. Umar then gathered many Companions of the Prophet and took half the profits earned by his sons and the initial amount given to them by treating this as *muḍāraba ipso post facto*.[145] Nobody objected to this and hence it became *ijmā' sukūtī*. **10.72**

Muḍāraba is also allowed by virtue of *istiḥsān* on the basis of need. The rationale is that a person with money may not be able to invest for profit, whereas a person with skills may not have sufficient wealth to use his skills profitably. Hence, it makes sense for both to come together with money from one side and work from the other to create profit for both.[146] **10.73**

4.2 Elements of *Muḍāraba*

The Hanafis argue that offer and acceptance is the single element of a *muḍāraba* contract. Shafi'i supporters, on the other hand, require six elements, namely, the existence of contracting parties, contribution of labour, profit, wealth, and *sīgha* (offer and acceptance).[147] A *muḍāraba* can be concluded with the use of word '*muḍāraba*' in *sīgha* and also without using it, as when *rab al-māl* says to the *muḍārib* 'take this money and trade with it and we will share the profit equally or so' and then this is accepted by the *muḍārib*. All this clearly implies that *muḍāraba* is concluded.[148] **10.74**

4.3 Relation between the Parties

A *muḍārib* views the capital of *rab al-māl* as held in trust with no liability if this is destroyed in his possession. He transacts with it as an agent of the *rab al-māl*. After profit is generated, he becomes a partner and, due to the partnership agreement, co-owner with the *rab al-māl* of the capital. After vitiation, the *muḍāraba* converts into *ijāra*, and the **10.75**

143 Qur'ān 73:20.
144 Al-Shawkānī, Nayl al-Awtār min Asrār Muntaqā al-Akhyār (Dār ibn al-Jawzī, 2006) Vol. 10, p. 377.
145 Ibid, Vol. 10, p. 376.
146 Ibid, Vol. 22, p. 19.
147 Al-Ramlī (n 20) Vol. 5, pp. 202–21; *Al-Fatāwā al-Hindiyya* (n 5) Vol. 4, p. 311.
148 Al Dusūqī (n 86) Vol. 3, p. 517; *Al-Mughnī* (n 19) Vol. 5, p. 17; Al-Buhūtī (n 35) Vol. 3, p. 198; *Al-Fatāwā al-Hindiyya* (n 5) Vol. 4, p. 311.

muḍārib becomes *ajīr* in which case he is entitled to reasonable wages for his work after the profit due to the *rab al-māl*. After vitiation of the *muḍāraba*, if capital is lost while in the possession of the *muḍārib*, he will have no liability. Where the *muḍārib* contravenes a condition of the *muḍāraba*, he becomes a usurper and is liable for any diminution in the capital.[149]

4.4 Conditions of *Muḍāraba*

10.76 The conditions for *muḍāraba* pertain to the capacity of the parties, the capital contributed, and accrued profit. These are explored in the following subsections

4.4.1 Capacity of Parties for *Muḍāraba* Agreement

10.77 The *rab al-māl* and *muḍārib* should possess sufficient capacity to become principal and agent respectively.[150] For a fuller discussion on the law of agency and capacity as this applies to classical and modern Islamic contract law the reader is directed to Chapter 3 of this volume.

4.4.2 Capital of *Muḍāraba*

10.78 All capital allowed for the constitution of *sharika* can become capital of a *muḍāraba*.[151] The capital should be in the form of absolute currencies. Property or financial papers which are to be sold and whose sale proceeds are to be invested in *muḍāraba* are also permissible. Receivables of *rab al-māl* from a third party can also become the capital of the *muḍāraba*.[152] The amount of capital should be known and be delivered to the *muḍārib* because the *muḍāraba* business is to commence after such delivery.[153] There should not be any control of *rab al-māl* over such capital, which should be solely disposed of by the *muḍārib*.[154] Any stipulation for *rab al-māl* to work for the *muḍārib* will render the *muḍāraba fāsid*.[155]

4.4.3 Profit-Sharing in *Muḍāraba*

10.79 The share of profit should be clearly specified as any ambiguity thereof or any condition leading to ambiguity in profit-sharing will vitiate the *muḍāraba*.[156] For instance, if the agreement stipulates that the *rab al-māl* will give to the *muḍārib* the amount he

[149] Al-Naṣafī (n 83) p. 522; Al-Shirbīnī (n 20) Vol. 2, p. 406; *Radd al-Muḥtār* (n 3) Vol. 8, p. 444; *Al-Mughnī* (n 19) Vol. 5, pp. 27, 34–35, 45–47; Al-Samarqandī (n 1) Vol. 3, pp. 22–23, 25; *Al-Fatāwā al-Hindiyya* (n 5) Vol. 4, p. 314; Al-Mauṣilī (n 8) Vol. 2, pp. 459–60.

[150] Majalla, Art. 1407. See agency agreements in Chapter 11 in respect of the conditions to become principal and agent.

[151] Sirāj al-Dīn (n 35) p. 531.

[152] Majalla, Arts 1338 and 1339; *Al-Mughnī* (n 19) Vol. 5, pp. 11–13; Al-Ramlī (n 20) Vol. 5, p. 221; Al-Shaybānī, Kitāb al-Hujja ʿalā Ahl al-Madīna (ʿAlam al-Kutub, 2006) Vol. 3, p. 20; Al-Samarqandī (n 1) Vol. 3, p. 21; *Al-Fatāwā al-Hindiyya* (n 5) Vol. 4, p. 311.

[153] Al-Kāsānī (n 1) Vol. 6, pp. 82–83; Al-Shaybānī (n 152) Vol. 3, p. 29.

[154] Al-Mauṣilī (n 8) Vol. 2, p. 461.

[155] Ḥaddād (n 41) Vol. 1, p. 351; *Al-Fatāwā al-Hindiyya* (n 5) Vol. 4, p. 311.

[156] Al-Mauṣilī (n 8) Vol. 2, p. 460; Al-Naṣafī (n 83) p. 522.

wishes, the *muḍāraba* becomes *fāsid*.[157] Profit should be specified as a portion of the total profit, such as a quarter, a half, a third, two-thirds, etc., and not as a fixed amount, such as 100 dirham for the *muḍārib*. Profit should be distributed after clear calculation of the capital and the amount of profit accrued from the capital.[158] If shares of the profit are not mentioned in the agreement, there is a presumption in favour of equal distribution of profit.[159]

The assignment of profit to one party will invalidate the *muḍāraba* agreement as if the entire profit were to be conferred upon the *muḍārib*, in which case this would amount to a *qarḍ* (loan agreement) and conferment of the whole profit for *rab al-māl* will make it *biḍaʿa* (to give goods to another for trading without any wages or profit).[160] The *muḍārib* is entitled only to a share from the profit and not the capital.[161] What is destroyed from the *muḍāraba* would be deducted from its accrued profit and not from the capital of the *muḍāraba*.[162] **10.80**

4.4.4 Types of *Muḍāraba*

A *muḍāraba* can be categorized into restricted and unrestricted (absolute) *muḍāraba*. If an absolute *muḍāraba* is subject to some condition or limitation it will transform into a restricted or limited form. Limitations are of three kinds. First, restrictions concerning a specific city or territory. Secondly, specifications relating to the person with whom the *muḍārib* is allowed to deal. Thirdly, specifications as to the kinds of trade activities in which the *muḍārib* is allowed to engage, for example dealing only in foodstuff, etc. If no limitation as to place, time, type of business, or seller/purchaser, etc. is stipulated, the *muḍāraba* is considered absolute. For example, the *rab al-māl* says to the *muḍārib*: 'I have given this wealth to you on *muḍāraba* on the condition that we will distribute profit equally.' In a restricted *muḍāraba*, the *muḍārib* has to follow all the limitations imposed on him. Both absolute and restricted *muḍāraba* generate the same legal effects as regards the powers and liabilities of the *muḍārib*.[163] **10.81**

4.4.4.1 Permissible acts for the muḍārib *under absolute* muḍāraba

In the case of an absolute *muḍāraba*, the *muḍārib* can perform all the acts related to the *muḍāraba* partnership, including the following,[164] unless he is specifically denied these powers. If he conducts a transaction in violation of a prohibition or without prior permission where such was needed, he or she would be personally liable. **10.82**

157 *Al-Fatāwā al-Hindiyya* (n 5) Vol. 4, p. 315.
158 *Al-Mughnī* (n 19) Vol. 5, p. 20; Sahnūn (n 57) Vol. 5, p. 90; Shaybānī (n 152) Vol. 3, p. 30; Ḥaddād (n 41) Vol. 1, p. 351.
159 Al-Kāsānī (n 1) Vol. 6, pp. 83–85; *Al-Fatāwā al-Hindiyya* (n 5) Vol. 4, p. 314.
160 Al-Shirbīnī (n 20) Vol. 2, p. 406; *Al-Fatāwā al-Hindiyya* (n 5) Vol. 4, p. 311.
161 *Al-Fatāwā al-Hindiyya* (n 5) Vol. 4, p. 313.
162 Ḥaddād (n 41) Vol. 1, p. 357.
163 Majalla, Arts 1406 and 1407; Al-Kāsānī (n 1) Vol. 6, p. 98; Shaybānī (n 152) Vol. 3, p. 23; Al-Samarqandī (n 1) Vol. 3, pp. 20–21, 23; *Al-Fatāwā al-Hindiyya* (n 5) Vol. 4, p. 325; Al-Mauṣilī (n 8) Vol. 2, pp. 463–64.
164 Majalla, Art. 1414. See also Al-Kāsānī (n 1) Vol. 6, p. 82; Al-Samarqandī (n 1) Vol. 3, p. 23.

- He can undertake to sell and purchase, on cash and credit, as he sees fit. He cannot purchase at a price exorbitantly higher than the prevailing market value.[165] The *muḍārib* does not have *istadāna*. If the *rab al-māl* grants authority of *istadāna*, the debt would be distributed equally between the *muḍārib* and the *rab al-māl*.[166]
- He may appoint an agent. If the capital is lost while in the possession of the *muḍārib* or his agent before the commencement of any activity on that capital, no liability would accrue against the *muḍārib* because this money was in its possession as a matter of trust. Therefore, the *rab al-māl* would be liable.[167]
- He may accept payment through the transfer of debts on the basis of *ḥawāla*.
- He needs specific permission from the *rab al-māl* before making a gift of property or giving capital on further *muḍāraba*, or as a loan. Such authorization may be in the form of express permission or a general statement from the *rab al-māl* to the *muḍārib* in the sense of 'do with it as you see fit'.[168] But if he (first *muḍārib*) gives the capital to another person (second *muḍārib*) on *muḍāraba*, the first *muḍārib* will become liable only after the second *muḍārib* uses that capital in a commercial activity and not before that.[169] He can give the partnership commodity as a pledge, for hire, investment, and safekeeping[170] because the aim of the *muḍāraba* is to earn profit and the *muḍārib* may be in need of any of these to earn profit.[171]
- The *muḍārib* can travel outside the territory of business with the capital of the *muḍāraba*.[172] When the *rab al-māl* stipulates that the *muḍārib* should conduct business in a certain territory, he cannot go beyond that territory, nor can he give the capital to a person outside that territory, otherwise he would be liable to the *rab al-māl* in case of loss.[173]

4.4.5 Dissolution of the *Muḍāraba*

10.83 The *muḍāraba* comes to an end in one of following ways. It should be noted that after the *muḍāraba* is vitiated, it converts into *ijāra*.[174]

4.4.5.1 Unilateral termination

10.84 The *muḍārib* is an agent and possesses sufficient authority to terminate the *muḍāraba* when he sees fit.[175]

165 But he cannot go beyond the limit of its capital, except with prior permission, because otherwise this would be considered his personal debt. See Al-Kāsānī (n 1) Vol. 6, p. 91; *Al-Mughnī* (n 19) Vol. 5, pp. 25–27; Shaybānī (n 152) Vol. 3, pp. 28–29, 32–33; *Al-Fatāwā al-Hindiyya* (n 5) Vol. 4, p. 325.
166 Al-Samarqandī (n 1) Vol. 3, p. 8; *Al-Fatāwā al-Hindiyya* (n 5) Vol. 4, p. 332.
167 Al-Kāsānī (n 1) Vol. 6, p. 107.
168 Shaybānī (n 152) Vol. 3, pp. 34–35; Al-Samarqandī (n 1) Vol. 3, p. 23; *Al-Fatāwā al-Hindiyya* (n 5) Vol. 4, pp. 326–27; Sirāj al-Dīn (n 35) p. 531; Al-Mauṣilī (n 8) Vol. 2, p. 461.
169 Al-Zaila'ī (n 40) Vol. 5, p. 63.
170 Al-Kāsānī (n 1) Vol. 6, pp. 110–11; Al-Naṣafī (n 83) p. 522.
171 Al-Zaila'ī (n 40) Vol. 5, p. 57.
172 *Al-Fatāwā al-Hindiyya* (n 5) Vol. 4, p. 320.
173 Ibid, Vol. 4, p. 324.
174 Al-Samarqandī (n 1) Vol. 3, p. 17.
175 Shaybānī (n 152) Vol. 3, p. 23.

4.4.5.2 By expiry of a fixed time

If the *rab al-māl* prescribes a date or a period for the termination of the *muḍāraba*, this will stand terminated on such date or on the passage of such period.[176] **10.85**

4.4.5.3 By death or insanity of the partners

If either the *rab al-māl* or the *muḍārib* dies, or is afflicted with madness without any lucid interval, the partnership is deemed to be cancelled.[177] **10.86**

4.4.5.4 By violation of agreement or directions of the rab al-māl

If the *muḍārib* acts *ultra vires*, violates a condition in the agreement, misappropriates property, disobeys directions of the *rab al-māl*, for example not to travel with the capital of partnership outside the territory of business or sell on credit, the *muḍāraba* may be cancelled.[178] After such cancellation, the *muḍārib* will be considered a usurper of the capital in his possession and if he purchases something after this violation, such purchase is considered as having been made on his personal account. However, in order for these legal effects to become operative, the restriction should be stipulated in express words; for instance, 'trade in this market only and not in any other'.[179] **10.87**

4.4.5.5 By destruction of capital

Destruction of the capital before the *muḍārib* could undertake any purchases with it will render the *muḍāraba* void and the *muḍārib* will incur no liability.[180] **10.88**

5. Financing through *Sharika* and *Muḍāraba*

In light of the general principles outlined above, the *muḍāraba* and *sharika* can be used as modes of financing so long as they do not violate any of the abovementioned principles, that is, ownership of assets according to the ratio of financing, liability for loss, and freedom to agree on profit disproportionate to the investment. Therefore, the *muḍāraba* and *mushāraka* individually, or jointly, may be used for the purpose of project financing.[181] **10.89**

[176] Majalla, Art. 1423; Al-Mauṣilī (n 8) Vol. 2, p. 464; Ḥaddād (n 41) Vol. 1, p. 353.
[177] Majalla, Art. 1429; Al-Samarqandī (n 1) Vol. 3, pp. 24–25.
[178] Majalla, Arts 1421 and 1422.
[179] Al-Zaila'ī (n 40) Vol. 5, pp. 58–60.
[180] Al-Samarqandī (n 1) Vol. 3, p. 25.
[181] For more details, see Muhammad Taqi Usmani, An Introduction to Islamic Finance (Maktaba Ma'ariful Qur'ān, 2008) pp. 56 ff.

5.1 Diminishing *Mushāraka*

10.90 In the context of a diminishing *mushāraka* 'one of the partners promises to buy the equity share of the other partner gradually until the title to the equity is completely transferred to him'.[182] The vehicle of a diminishing *mushāraka* is used as a mode of financing in several ways, for instance house finance, vehicle finance, and business finance.[183]

10.91 In house finance, the customer and institution become partners in order to purchase a house by contributing 20% and 80% of capital (in the form of cash or tangible liquid assets)[184] respectively, with a promise from the customer to buy the institution's share by making payments periodically. The institution grants its share to the customer on lease.[185] To make this purchase, the institution's share in the house is divided into a certain number of equal units, say ten units, and the 80% contribution of the institution is divided into ten equal instalments.[186] The customer after the first three months pays the price of the institution's one-tenth share, whereafter the customer's share increases to 30% and the institution's share diminishes to 70%. In this way, at the end of the agreed period the customer becomes the owner of the house, and throughout this period the customer continues to pay the rent and the price of the unit purchased by him.

10.92 In the same way, the customer and the institution jointly purchase a car, which the customer retains by using the share of the institution on lease by paying the rent amount and the price of the share units of the institution to diminish its ownership. Similarly, in a partnership business established by the customer and the institution through the contribution of 20% an 80% of the capital respectively, the parties' agreement as to the specific amount of profit to be paid to each partner, including the division of the institution's ownership into a certain number of units which the customer periodically purchases to diminish the ownership of the institution, ultimately renders the customer sole owner at the end of a specific time period.

182 AAOIFI, 'Shariah Standard No. 12, 5.1 (2017)', pp. 346, 347. To establish the enforceability of such promise, see Usmani (n 181) pp. 88–89.

183 Usmani (n 181) p. 82.

184 AAOIFI, 'Shariah Standard No. 12, 5.4 (2017)', p. 347; e.g. 'land for construction, or equipment required for the operation of partnership'.

185 AAOIFI, Shariah Standard No. 12, 5.9 (2017)', p. 347, which emphasizes that 'it is permissible for either of the partners to rent or lease the share of the other partner for a specified amount and for whatever duration'.

186 AAOIFI, 'Shariah Standard No. 12, 5.8 (2017)', p. 348, which stipulates that 'the subject matter of the partnership may be divided into shares in which case the Institution's partner can purchase a particular number of these shares at certain intervals until the partner becomes the owner of the entire shares and consequently becomes the sole owner of the subject matter of the partnership'.

A purchase by the customer of the institution's share should not be stipulated in the contract, but rather the first joint purchase and subsequent purchase by the customer should be independent of each other.[187] However, the diminishing *mushāraka* contract should not give any partner the right to withdraw its capital.[188] The profit should be clearly agreed and stipulated in the contract, which may be disproportionate to the equity ownership of the partners. However, the allocation of loss should be equal to the equity share of ownership.[189] **10.93**

[187] Shariah Standard No. 12, 5.1 (n 182) pp. 346–47.
[188] AAOIFI, 'Shariah Standard No. 12, 5.2 (2017)', p. 347.
[189] AAOIFI, 'Shariah Standard No. 12, 5.5 (2017)', p. 347.

11

Ancillary Contracts

1. Introduction

11.01 This chapter will explore so-called ancillary contracts under Islamic law. While some contracts of this type resemble their counterparts in Western legal systems, such as agency (*wakāla*), most others do not, and their existence is based on the ideals of a fair and just Islamic society. Besides *wakāla* this chapter will also examine the regulation of *ju'āla* contracts, which are effectively contracts for remuneration for an agreed task; *ijāra*, which correspond to lease contracts; *ṣarf*, which focus on the sale of money for money; the somewhat controversial *salam* contracts, which are of a *sui generis* nature; *istiṣnā'*, which are contracts for manufacturing; and *tawarruq* contracts, which represent a complex string of financing transactions at the end of which the lender receives cash derived from the financier's sale of commodities. While all these types of contracts may at first hand seem disparate, their grouping as ancillary contracts under Islamic law has been standard among Muslim jurists. The reader will come to appreciate that the source for the creation of these types is the Qur'ān itself, as later developed on the basis of *fiqh*.

2. *Wakāla* (Agency)

11.02 Agency comprises 'one person (principal) empowering some other person (agent) to perform an act for him, whereby the latter stands in the stead of the former in regard to such act'.[1] Allah says in the story of the people of the cave in the Qur'ān: 'So send one of you with this silver coin of yours to the city and let him look to which is the best of food and bring you provision from it and let him be cautious.'[2] This is said to be the foundation of agency.[3] This permission for agency is also based on the *āya*: 'send an arbitrator from his people and an arbitrator from her people. If they both desire reconciliation, Allah will cause it between them. Indeed, Allah is ever Knowing and Acquainted [with all things].'[4] It is opined that arbitrators are agents of the

[1] Majalla, Art. 1449; Al-Maidanī, Al-Lubāb fī Sharḥ al-Kitāb (Dār al-Kitāb al-'Arabī, n.d.) Vol. 1, p. 202; Shams al-Dīn al-Ḥaṭṭāb, Mawāhib al-Jalīl fī Sharḥ Mukhtaṣar Khalīl (Dār al-Fikr, 1992) Vol. 5, p. 181; Al-Ramlī, Nihāyat al-Muḥtāj ilā Sharḥ al-Minhāj (Dār al-Fikr, 1984) Vol. 5, p. 15; Al-Buhūtī, Kashshāf al-Qinā' 'an Matn al-Iqnā' (Dār al-Kutub al- 'Ilmiyya, n.d.) Vol. 3, p. 461.

[2] Qur'ān 18:19.

[3] Ibn Qudāma, Al-Mughnī fī Fiqh al-Imām Aḥmad bin Ḥanbal (Dār al-Fikr, 1405H) Vol. 5, p. 87; Ibn al-Humām, Fat'ḥ al-Qadīr (Dār al-Fikr, n.d.) Vol. 8, p. 4.

[4] Qur'ān 4:35.

spouses.[5] The Holy Prophet appointed Hakīm bin Huzām (or 'Urwah al-Bāriqī)[6] as an agent to purchase for him a ram for the feast of sacrifice (*ʿīd al-aḍḥā*).[7] There is broad and undeniable consensus over the legality of the contract of agency.[8]

2.1 Essential Elements of *Wakāla*

11.03 The following sections spell out in more detail the essential elements of the *wakāla* contract and consider its legal implications.

2.1.1 Parties to the *Wakāla* Contract

11.04 The parties to the contract of agency are constituted by the principal (*aṣīl*) and the agent (*wakīl*).

2.1.1.1 Principal

11.05 The principal is the person who delegates or transfers his authority to undertake a known disposition to another person. Thus, it is a requirement for the principal to have the power of disposition and capacity to delegate.[9] Therefore, persons considered as suffering from insanity, imbecility, the frail, and infants that have not reached the age of discretion (*tamyīz*, i.e. someone seven years old who understands the nature of contracts) cannot be principals.[10] Jurists allow a child that has reached the age of discretion to appoint an agent to act on its behalf in purely beneficial dispositions such as the receipt of gifts, bequests, etc. They have also agreed that appointing an agent to act in a purely detrimental disposition is not permissible. However, there is disagreement as to whether dispositions vacillating between benefit and detriment are also legal. The Hanafis, Malikis, and Hanbalis have opined that such appointment is lawful with the leave of the guardian.[11] The Shafi'is are, however, of the view that a minor may not act in the capacity of principal and any appointment is void.[12] A prodigal person whose disposition has been suspended cannot appoint an agent to perform acts that he cannot otherwise perform himself.[13]

[5] Muḥammad Al-Shirbīnī, Mughnī al-Muḥtāj ilā Maʿrifat Alfāẓ al-Minhāj (Dār al-Kutub al-ʿIlmiyya, 1994) Vol. 3, p. 231.

[6] Al-Tirmidhī 1258.

[7] Al-Tirmidhī 1257.

[8] Ibn ʿĀbidīn, Radd al-Muḥtār Sharḥ Tanvīr al-Abṣār (Dār al-Fikr, 1992) Vol. 5, p. 509; Ibn Hummām (n 3) Vol. 8, p. 3; Al-Dusūqī, Ḥāshiyat al-Dusūqī ʿalā al-Sharḥ al-Kabīr (Dār al-Fikr, n.d.) Vol. 3, p. 377; Al-Ramlī (n 1) Vol. 5, p. 15; Ibn Qudāma (n 3) Vol. 5, p. 201; Al-Qurṭubī, Al-Jāmiʿ li Aḥkām al-Qur'ān (Dār al-Kutub al-Miṣriyya, 1964) Vol. 10, p. 376.

[9] Ibn Nujaim, Al-Baḥr al-Rā'iq Sharḥ Kanz al-Daqā'iq (Dār al-Kitāb al-Islāmī, n.d.) Vol. 7, p. 140; Al-Balkhī, Al-Fatāwā al-Hindiyya (Dār al-Fikr, 1310H) Vol. 3, p. 561; Al-Ḥaṭṭāb (n 1) Vol. 5, p. 182; Al-Buhūtī (n 1) Vol. 3, p. 462.

[10] *Radd al-Muhtār* (n 8) Vol. 5, p. 509; Al-Kāsānī, Badā'iʿ al-Ṣanā'iʿ fī Tartīb al-Sharā'iʿ (Dār al-Kutub al-ʿIlmiyya, 1986) Vol. 6, p. 20; Al-Ramlī (n 1) Vol. 5, p. 32; Ibn Qudāma (n 3) Vol. 5, p. 202.

[11] *Al-Fatāwā al-Hindiyya* (n 9) Vol. 3, p. 561; Al-Buhūtī (n 1) Vol. 3, p. 463; Al-Mardāwī, Al-Inṣāf fī Maʿrifat al-Rājiḥ min al-Khilāf (Dār Ihyā al-Turāth al-ʿArabī, n.d.) Vol. 5, p. 355; Al- Ṣāwī, Ḥāshiyat al- Ṣāwī ʿalā al-Sharḥ al- Ṣaghīr (Dār al-Maʿārif, n.d.) Vol. 3, p. 384.

[12] Al-Shirbīnī (n 5).

[13] Al-Ramlī (n 1) Vol. 5, p. 31; Ibn Nujaim, Al-Baḥr al-Rā'iq Sharḥ Kanz al-Daqā'iq (Dār al-Kitāb al-Islām, n.d.) Vol. 7, p. 149; Ibrāhīm bin Mufliḥ, Al-Mubidiʿ fī Sharḥ al-Muqniʿ (Dār al-Kutub al-ʿIlmiyya, 1997) Vol. 4, p. 320.

2.1.1.2 *Agent*

The agent is the person to whom the principal entrusts the execution of his objective in the contract of agency. Just like the principal, an agent must not be insane or an infant that has not reached the age of discretion.[14] As to the appointment of a minor with discretion as an agent, the Hanafis and Hanbalis consider it valid.[15] The Hanafis have, however, stipulated that the rights in such a contract should be shouldered by the agent if he is an adult; where he is a minor these should be shouldered by the principal that appoints him.[16] Shafi'is count such appointment void on the basis that a minor does not have the legal capacity to undertake matters regarding his or her own rights.[17] Agent and principal should be known to each other with specificity and clarity, otherwise the contract will be void.[18] The appointment of an indeterminate person is thus void.[19] The agent is recognized as a trustee who shall be liable only if he acts *ultra vires*, or is negligent in the undertaking of his duties.[20] **11.06**

2.1.2 *Ṣīgha*

Consent is mandatory in order to conclude the contract of agency and is expressed though offer and acceptance. **11.07**

2.1.2.1 *Offer*

The majority of jurists contend that only the principal can initiate an offer,[21] whereas Hanafis maintain that both principal and agent can do so.[22] The offer may be through express words, such as the utterance: 'you are my agent in a particular affair', or 'I have handed this over to you',[23] or 'sell it to him'.[24] Utterances similar to these are sufficient to create an offer.[25] However, statements like 'I am depending on you' do not create an agency due to the uncertainty about the intentions of the principal.[26] The principal may signify his verbal offer directly to the agent, or through other persons.[27] **11.08**

[14] Ibn Qudāma (n 3) Vol. 5, p. 88.
[15] Al-Kāsānī (n 10) Vol. 6, p. 20; Ibn Nujaim (n 13) Vol. 7, p. 142; Al-Buhūtī (n 1) Vol. 3, p. 463; Al-Mardāwī (n 11) Vol. 5, p. 355.
[16] Al-Kāsānī (n 10) Vol. 6, p. 20; Ibn al-Humām (n 3) Vol. 8, p. 14.
[17] Sulaimān al-Jamāl, Futūḥāt al-Wahhāb bi Tauḍīḥ Sharḥ Manhaj al-Ṭullāb or Ḥāshiyat al-Jamāl (Dār al-Fikr, n.d.) Vol. 3, p. 402.
[18] Al-Dusūqī (n 8) Vol. 3, p. 378; Al-Ramlī (n 1) Vol. 5, p. 34; Muṣṭafā al-Suyūṭī, Maṭālib al-Nuhā fī Sharḥ Ghāyat al-Muntahā (Al-Maktab al-Islāmī, 1994) Vol. 3, pp. 429–30; Al-Suyūṭī, Al-Ashbāh wa al-Naẓā'ir (Dḥr al-Kutub al-'Ilmiyya, 1990) p. 251.
[19] Al-Dusūqī (n 8) Vol. 3, p. 378.
[20] Sayyid Sābiq, Fiqh al-Sunna (Dār al-Kitab al-'Arabī, 1997) Vol. 3, p. 233.
[21] Al-Dardīr, Bulghat al-Sālik li Aqrab al-Masālik (Dār al-Ma'ārif, n.d.) Vol. 3, p. 506; Al-Ramlī (n 1) Vol. 5 p. 32. Al-Buhūtī (n 1) Vol. 3, p. 461.
[22] Al-Kāsānī (n 10) Vol. 6, p. 20.
[23] Ibid, Vol. 6, p. 20; Al-Ramlī (n 1) Vol. 5, p. 55; Al-Māwardī, al-Ḥāwī al-Kabīr (Dār al-Fikr, 1994) Vol. 6, p.1108; Al-Buhūtī (n 1) Vol. 3, p. 461; Al-Kharshī, Sharḥ al-Kharshī 'alā Mukhtaṣar Khalīl (Dār al-Fikr, n.d.) Vol. 6, p. 70.
[24] Muḥammad Khasro, Sharḥ Majallat al-Aḥkām (Dār Iḥyā' al-Kutub al-'Arabi, n.d.) Vol. 2, p. 289; Al-Mardāwī (n 11) Vol. 5, p. 353; Al-Nawawī, Rauḍat al-Ṭālibīn (Al-Maktab al-Islāmī, 1991) Vol. 4, p. 300.
[25] *Al-Fatāwā al-Hindiyya* (n 9) Vol. 3, pp. 564–65.
[26] Al-Māwardī (n 23) Vol. 6, p. 1107; Al-Shirbīnī (n 5) Vol. 2, p. 243.
[27] 'Ali Ḥaidar, Sharḥ Majallat al-Aḥkām (Dār al-Jīl, 1991) Vol. 3, p. 527; Ibn Ābidīn (n 8) Vol. 5, p. 526.

The communication of the offer may be in writing,[28] for example through a letter,[29] or through understandable gestures.[30] An offer may also be implied from the words, actions, or conduct that confer authority on an agent.[31] Even so, the Malikis contend that the form of such words or conduct should constitute custom at the time offered.[32] For instance, if the husband disposes of his wife's property when she is silent, he would be considered as her agent.[33] However, neither the Hanafis nor the Shafi'is count such silence as tacit approval.[34]

2.1.2.2 Acceptance

11.09 Like offer, acceptance can also be verbal, as articulated by words such as 'accepted' or any other similar phrase indicating acceptance. It may be written in a note, correspondence, letter, etc.[35] It may also arise on account of conduct,[36] for example where the agent remains silent but performs an action demanded by the principal.[37] Acceptance may also be inferred by known and understandable gestures,[38] although the Hanafis and Shafi'is confine this permission to mute persons only.[39] The Malikis even allow for non-mute persons, arguing that gestures are referred to as speech in the Qur'ān, where Allah says: 'He said, "Your sign is that you will not [be able to] speak to the people for three days except by gesture".'[40] Subsequent ratification has the same effect as a previous authorization to appoint an agent.[41] Agency is created by immediate acceptance as well as delayed acceptance.[42]

2.2 When Agency Takes Effect

11.10 The agency can be executory, attached to a condition precedent, linked to the future, as well as temporary:[43]

[28] Ibn Nujaim (n 18) p. 403; Aḥmad Al-Zarqā, Sharḥ al-Qawā'id al-Fiqhiyya (Dār al-Qalam, 1989) p. 349; Muḥammad al-Borno, Al-Wajīz fī Īḍāḥ Qawā'id al-Fiqh al-Kulliyya (Mu'assasat al-Risāla, 1996) p. 302.
[29] Ḥaidar (n 27) Vol. 3, p. 527.
[30] Al-Shirbīnī (n 5) Vol. 3, p. 380; Al-Zarkashī, A-Manthūr fī al-Qawā'id al-Fiqhiyya (Ministry of Endowment, Kuwait, 1985) Vol. 1, p. 164.
[31] Al-Sīsāwī, Sharḥ Fat'h al-Qadīr (Dār al-Fikr, n.d.) Vol. 6, p. 166; Al-Ramlī (n 1) Vol. 5, p. 55; Vol. 2, p. 461; Al-Dusūqī (n 8) Vol. 3, p. 380; Muḥammad al-Mālikī, Sharḥ Mukhtaṣar Khalīl (Dār al-Fikr, n.d.) Vol. 6, p. 70; *Al-Mughnī* (n 3) Vol. 5, pp. 208–09; Al-Rahaibānī (n 18) Vol. 3, p. 429; Mufli*ḥ* (n 13) Vol. 4, p. 325.
[32] Al-Kharshī (n 23) Vol. 6, p. 70.
[33] Al-Ṣāwī (n 11) Vol. 3, pp. 505, 506; Al-Dusūqī (n 8) Vol. 3, p. 380.
[34] Ibn Nujaim (n 18) pp. 154, 155; Al-Shirbīnī (n 5) Vol. 2, p. 15.
[35] Ibn Nujaim (n 18) p. 293; Al-Sayyid Ḥusain, Al-Wakāla fī al-Sharī'ah al-Islāmiyya (Assembly of Muslim Jurists in America, 2004) p. 136.
[36] Ali Haidar (n 27) Vol. 3, pp. 526, 527; Al-Ḥaṭṭāb (n 1) Vol. 3, p. 430; Al-Shirbīnī (n 5) Vol. 2, p. 222; Al-Buhūtī (n 1) Vol. 3, pp. 461–62.
[37] Ali Haidar (n 27) Vol. 3, p. 528; *Al-Mughnī* (n 3) Vol. 5, p. 93; Al-Ḥaṭṭāb (n 1) Vol. 5, p. 190; Al-Buhūtī (n 1) Vol. 3, pp. 461, 462; Al-Kharshī (n 32) Vol. 6, p. 70.
[38] Ibn Nujaim (n 18) p. 343; Al-Ḥaṭṭāb (n 1) Vol. 4, p. 229; *Al-Mughnī* (n 3) Vol. 3, p. 566.
[39] Al-Kāsānī (n 10) Vol. 5, p. 135.
[40] Qur'ān 3:41; Al-Ḥaṭṭāb (n 1) Vol. 4, p. 229.
[41] Majalla, Arts 1452 and 1453.
[42] Al-Nawawī, Al-Majmū' Sharḥ Al-Muhadhdhab (Dār al-Fikr, n.d.) Vol. 14, p. 106.
[43] Majalla, Art. 1456.

- When there is no condition precedent for making agency effective, nor is agency made contingent on any future event, the agency takes effect immediately.[44]
- The agency may be dependent on a condition precedent. For example, where someone says, 'whenever the pilgrim returns, sell this food item or whenever my family asks for something give it to them'. The Hanafis, Hanbalis, and Shafi'is consider such agency valid on the basis of the *ḥadīth* whereby the Prophet appointed Zaid bin Ḥaritha as commander of the Muslim army in the Battle of Mu'tah and then he said: if Zaid is killed, then Ja'far (should take over), and if Ja'far is killed, then Abdullah bin Rawāhah (should take over).[45] However, some Shafi'is and Hanbalis maintain that linking agency to conditions invalidates the contract.[46]
- Sometimes an agency is made contingent on a future event or time, as where the principal appoints his agent to sell certain properties during the month of Ramadan or sell them the next day. These are valid agencies.[47]
- Agency may be temporary, for instance, where the agent is appointed for a month. This type of agency agreement is valid.

2.3 Object of Agency

The principal confers authority on the agent to achieve an objective, target, or task that is the object of the agency and which 'must be sufficiently well known to enable it to be carried out'.[48] On the basis of its object, an agency is classified into general and specific. The mandate of a specific agency must be specific, such as the sale of a particular property. The agent cannot go beyond this mandate. If the agent contravenes its mandate and purchases any other building, this belongs to the agent and not the principal.[49] In general agency, the agent is appointed to do everything on behalf of the principal. The Hanafis and Malikis allow both general and specific agencies.[50] However, there is a difference of opinion concerning the scope of the conferment of the agency by words of a general nature. According to Hanafis, the expression: 'you are my agent on everything or on large and small things' implies the protection of interests of the principal only.[51] However, if the principal appoints a person saying: 'you are my agent on any permissible thing that I will direct you to do', such agent shall represent the principal in all pecuniary dispositions like buying, selling, and giving gifts and alms. However, as to whether divorce, emancipation, and declaration of *waqf* are also covered by this **11.11**

[44] Ali Haidar (n 27) Vol. 3, pp. 534, 535; Al-Rahaibānī (n 18) Vol. 3, p. 428; Al-Kāsānī (n 10) Vol. 6, p. 20.

[45] Bukhārī 4261; *Radd al-Muḥtār* (n 8) Vol. 5, p. 252; Al-Kāsānī (n 10) Vol. 6, p. 20; *Al-Mughnī* (n 3) Vol. 5, p. 93; Al-Shirbīnī (n 5) Vol. 2, p. 223.

[46] Al-Māwardī (n 23) Vol. 8, p. 190.

[47] Al-Kasānī (n 10) Vol. 6, p. 20; Al-Rahaibānī (n 18) Vol. 3, p. 428; Al-Ramlī (n 1) Vol. 5, p. 56; Al-Ṃāwardī (n 23) Vol. 8, p. 190.

[48] Majalla, Art. 1468.

[49] Majalla, Art. 1479.

[50] Ibn al-Humām (n 3) Vol. 7, p. 501; Ibn Nujaim (n 13) Vol. 7, p. 139; Ibn Rushd, Bidāyat al-Mujtahid wa Nihāyat al-Muqtaṣid (Muṣtafā al-Bābī al-Ḥalabī, 1975) Vol. 2, p. 302.

[51] Ibn Nujaim (n 3) Vol. 7, p. 140.

declaration, certain scholars agree, whereas others state that it is included only if there is previous evidence or a statement suggesting this fact.[52] The Malikis argue that the statement: 'you are my agent on all my affairs' would include anything that will serve to increase the principal's financial interest or earnings, excluding non-financial matters like manumission, donations, and alms, unless the principal specifically confers these upon the agent.[53] Shafi'is and Hanbalis maintain that general agency is not valid.[54] They consider knowledge of the object of the agency in every aspect as a prerequisite, which is not known in general agency. However, they allow generality in agency to some extent, for instance where the principal appoints an agent to receive all debts owed to the principal. In such a case, the agency is valid even if the specific amount is not disclosed.[55]

2.4 Things Allowed to Be Delegated in an Agency

11.12 Jurists are unanimous on the permissibility of delegation of certain tasks and functions to the agent, while disagreeing on others. Tasks and functions unanimously permitted are discussed below.

2.4.1 Contracts

11.13 Jurists have agreed over the permissibility of agency by which to buy or sell on behalf of the principal,[56] because the Prophet appointed Urwa al-Bāriqī to purchase him a ram[57] and also gave Hakīm bin Hizām *dīnār* to purchase for him a ram for the feast of sacrifice.[58] Jurists have also agreed that agency is lawful in *ḥawāla* (transfer of debt); *rehn* (security for loan); *kafāla* (guarantee), *sharika* (partnership); *wadīʿa* (entrustment); *muḍāraba* (entrepreneurship); *juʿāla* (reward for defined task); *musāqāt* (irrigation); *ijāra* (leasing); *qarḍ* (loan); *waṣiyya* (bequest); *faskh* (annulment of contract); *ibrāʿ* (absolution); *iqāla* (mutual rescinding of contract); *shufʿa* (right of pre-emption);[59] and matters relating to liability, conciliation, and gifts.

2.4.2 Pecuniary Acts of Worship

11.14 Agents can carry out pecuniary acts of worship on behalf of their principal, such as *zakāt* (recommended alms), as well as the fulfilment of vows and expiations (*kaffāra*)[60]

[52] *Radd al-Muḥtār* (n 8) Vol. 4, pp. 399–400; Ibn al-Humām (n 3) Vol. 7, p. 500.
[53] Al-Dasūqī (n 8) Vol. 3, p. 380.
[54] Al-Ramlī (n 1) Vol. 5, p. 25; *Al-Mughnī* (n 3) Vol. 5, p. 211; Al-Shirbīnī (n 5) Vol. 2, pp. 217–19.
[55] Al-Ramli (n 1) Vol. 5, p. 25; *Al-Mughnī* (n 3) Vol. 5, p. 211.
[56] Al-Kāsānī (n 10) Vol. 6, p. 21; Al-Dusūqī (n 8) Vol. 3, p. 377; Al-Ramlī (n 1) Vol. 5, p. 22; *Al-Mughnī* (n 3) Vol. 5, p. 88.
[57] Tirmidhī 1258.
[58] Ibid, 1257.
[59] Al-Kāsāni (n 10) Vol. 6, p. 21; Al-Dusūqī (n 8) Vol. 3, p. 377; Al-Ramlī (n 1) Vol. 5, p. 23; Al-Buhūtī (n 1) Vol. 3, p. 461; *Al-Mughnī* (n 3) Vol. 5, p. 203.
[60] Al-Kāsānī (n 10) Vol. 6, p. 21; Ṣāleh al-Azharī, Jawāhir al-Iklīl (Al-Maktaba al-Thaqāfiyya, n.d.) Vol. 2, p. 125; Al-Ramlī (n 1) Vol. 5, p. 23; Al-Buhūtī (n 1) Vol. 3, p. 461.

because the Prophet sent his representatives to collect *zakāt* and disperse it to those entitled to it.[61]

2.5 Matters Which an Agent Cannot Undertake on Behalf of the Principal

Jurists generally agree that the following matters cannot be undertaken by an agent on behalf of a principal. **11.15**

2.5.1 Testimony, Oaths, and Vows

A principal cannot delegate his testimony to his agent because this relates to what the principal knows, sees, or hears and none of this can properly be undertaken by the agent. Similarly, agents cannot swear an oath or make a vow on behalf of their principal, because both are similar to bodily acts of worship which are personal in nature. This impressibility is also applicable to actions like *li'ān* (mutual imprecation), *īlā* (a husband's vow not to have sexual intercourse with his wife), and *qasāma* oaths.[62] **11.16**

2.5.2 Sinful Actions and Crimes

The commission of sinful or criminal conduct, such as usurpation, purchase of alcohol, murder, theft, etc., cannot be delegated because the commission of these acts is unlawful for the principal himself.[63] **11.17**

2.5.3 Bodily Acts of Worship

The principal cannot delegate obligatory acts that consist purely of worship and are personal in nature and which possess no monetary value, as is the case with prayer, fasting, and purity.[64] **11.18**

2.6 Matters Delegated upon which Jurists Disagree

2.6.1 *Ḥajj* and *'Umra*

Persons able to perform *ḥajj* cannot delegate to another person the performance of *ḥajj* on their behalf. However, those unable to perform *ḥajj* may according to the Hanafis, Shafi'is, and Hanbalis allow such delegation,[65] whereas Mālik contends **11.19**

[61] Bukhārī 1496; Muslim 29.

[62] Ali Al-Simnānī, Rauḍat al-Quḍat wa Tarīq al-Najāti (Mu'assasāt al-Risāla, 1984) Vol. 2, p. 636; Al-Azharī (n 60) Vol. 2, p. 125; Al-Qarāfī, Al-Furūq ('Ālam al-Kutub, n.d.) Vol. 4, p. 26; Al-Ramlī (n 1) Vol. 5, p. 23; Al-Shirbīnī (n 5) Vol. 2, p. 220.

[63] Al-Kharshī (n 32) Vol. 6, p. 70; Al-Dusūqī (n 8) Vol. 3, p. 380; *Al-Mughnī* (n 3) Vol. 5, p. 205; Al-Ramlī (n 1) Vol. 5, p. 23; Al-Shirbīnī (n 5) Vol. 2, p. 220.

[64] Al-Kāsānī (n 10) Vol. 2, p. 212; *Radd al-Muḥtār* (n 8) Vol. 2, p. 238; Al-Nawawī (n 42) Vol. 7, p. 116; Al-Rahaibānī (n 18) Vol. 2, p. 273.

[65] Al-Kāsānī (n 10) Vol. 2, p. 212; *Radd al-Muḥtār* (n 8) Vol. 2, p. 241; Al-Shirbīnī (n 5) Vol. 1, p. 469; *Al-Mughnī* (n 3) Vol. 3, p. 228.

otherwise.[66] Jurists are generally in agreement that *'umra* can be performed through agency.[67]

2.6.2 Woman Marrying through an Agent

11.20 The majority of jurists agree that it is not permissible for a woman to appoint an agent to contract marriage on her behalf. The reason is that she does not have the power to contract her marriage.[68] The Hanafis are of the view that a free, adult, sane woman has the power to contract her marriage and, as a result, she can delegate it through an agency.[69]

2.7 Legal Effects of Agency

11.21 The legal effects of agency depend on the type of agency contracted. In this segment, agency in sale, purchase, and litigation is discussed.

2.7.1 Agency in Sale

11.22 Agency to sell may be both absolute and limited (qualified) in nature. Both of these are discussed in the following subsections

2.7.1.1 Absolute power or with no express limitation on the power of an agent

11.23 According to Abū Ḥanīfa, the power of an agent appointed to sell is absolute and shall not be limited, unless there is suspicion regarding his conduct. Thus, he can sell at a high or a low price, or by immediate or delayed payment, as the term absolute (*mutlaq*) takes all of these forms.[70] The Malikis, Shafi'is, and Hanbalis subject this to certain limitations. The sale should be subject to a currency (Malikis, Shafi'is, and Hanbalis)[71] that is dominant in the town (Shafi'is).[72] It is not permissible for an agent with absolute power to sell at a price less than the prevailing price, especially in the presence of a buyer who is willing to pay more (Shafi'is, Hanbalis, and Malikis).[73] In such cases, the principal will have an option (Malikis) or the agent will be liable for the difference in the price (Shafi'is and Hanbalis), or if the property is obtainable, the agent will recover it for the principal (Shafi'is).[74]

[66] Al-Ḥaṭṭāb (n 1) Vol. 2, p. 543; Al-Dusūqī (n 8) Vol. 2, p. 17.

[67] Al-Kāsānī (n 10) Vol. 2, p. 213; Al-Shirbīnī (n 5) Vol. 1, p. 28; *Al-Mughnī* (n 3) Vol. 3, p. 243.

[68] Jalāl al-Dīn ibn Shās, 'Aqd al-Jawāhir al-Thamīna fī Madh'hab 'Ālam al-Madīna (Dār al-Gharb al-Islāmī, 2003) Vol. 2, p. 492; *Al-Mughnī* (n 3) Vol. 6, p. 449.

[69] Al-Kāsānī (n 10) Vol. 6, p. 20.

[70] Ibid, Vol. 6, p. 27.

[71] Ibn Juzaī, *Al-Qawānīn al-Fiqhiyya* (n.p., n.d.) p. 216; Al-Mardāwī (n 11) Vol. 5, p. 379; Al-Kāsānī (n 10) Vol. 6, p. 27.

[72] Al-Dusūqī (n 8) Vol. 3, p. 382; Al-Mardāwī (n 11) Vol. 5, p. 378; Sulaimān al-Jamāl, Ḥāshiyat al-Jamāl bi Tauḍīḥ Sharḥ al-Minhāj (Dār al-Fikr, n.d.) Vol. 3, p. 408.

[73] Al-Mardāwī (n 11) Vol. 5, pp. 379–80; *Ḥāshiyat al-Jamal* (n 72) Vol. 3, pp. 408–09; Al-Dusūqī (n 8) Vol. 3, pp. 382–83.

[74] Al-Mardāwī (n 11) Vol. 5, p. 389; *Al-Mughnī* (n 3) Vol. 5, pp. 255–56; Ḥāshiyat al-Jamāl, (n 72) Vol. 3, pp. 408–09.

11.24 Since the sale is undertaken by one person to another, an agent is prohibited from selling the property to himself,[75] even if the principal has directed the agent to become the buyer of such property.[76] But the Malikis and Hanbalis allow an agent to become the buyer if the principal so permitted,[77] especially where he is purchasing it at a price higher than that offered by another potential purchaser or it is consistent with the market price.[78]

2.7.1.2 Agent with qualified power to sell property

11.25 An agency with limitations is valid if the limitations are not ambiguous (Hanafis, Malikis, and Hanbalis). The Hanafis have relied on *istiḥsān* for validating such qualification and refer to the *ḥadīth* in which the Prophet gave a dinar to Hakim bin Hizam to buy a ram for the feast of sacrifice without describing the type of ram to be purchased. This was a minor or simple ambiguity which did not lead to dispute between the principal and his agent and is allowed.[79]

11.26 There is consensus that agents must adhere to the limitations prescribed by the principal because they are acting within the right of the principal. An infraction of any limitations by the agent would attract his liability. For instance, where the principal directs an agent to sell at no less than a particular price, any sale at a lesser price would entitle the principal to rescind the sale.[80] However, such a sale is suspended until accepted or rejected by the principal.[81]

2.7.2 Agency to Purchase a Property

11.27 According to the Hanafis and Malikis, the principal can provide absolute authority to the agent to purchase on their behalf through utterances such: 'buy me whatever you want or whatever you think appropriate, or any suitable house' and such agency is valid despite the ambiguity regarding the type, description, and price, provided that the agent does not purchase at a price higher than the prevailing market price.[82] However, the Shafi'is and some Hanbalis insist that such agency is invalid.[83]

2.7.3 Agency in Litigation

11.28 Generally, jurists have agreed on the basis of consensus of the Companions concerning the permissibility for agents to represent their principal in litigation.[84] 'Alī ibn Abi Ṭālib conferred upon his brother 'Aqīl bin Abi Tālib the authority to represent him before

[75] *Radd al-Muḥtār* (n 8) Vol. 4, p. 406; *Al-Fatāwā al-Hindiyya* (n 9) Vol. 3, p. 589; Al-Mardāwī, ibid, Vol. 5, p. 375; Al-Rahaibānī (n 18) Vol. 3, p. 463; Ibn Juzaī (n 71) p. 216; *Al Mughnī* (n 3) Vol. 2, p. 224.

[76] *Radd al-Muḥtār* (n 8) Vol. 4, p. 406; *Al-Fatāwā al-Hindiyya* (n 9) Vol. 3, p. 589; *Al Mughnī* (n 3) Vol. 2, p. 224.

[77] Al-Mardāwī (n 11) Vol. 5, p. 375; Ibn Juzaī (n 71) p. 216.

[78] Ibn Juzaī (n 71) p. 216; Al-Dusūqī (n 8) Vol. 3, p. 387.

[79] Al-Kāsānī (n 10) Vol. 6, p. 23; *Al-Mughnī* (n 3) Vol. 5, p. 213; Al-Shirbīnī (n 5) Vol. 2, p. 222. Shafi'is and some Hanbalis and Hanafis suggest that such ambiguity invalidates the contract.

[80] Al-Kāsānī (n 10) Vol. 6, p. 27; Al-Dusūqī (n 8) Vol. 3, p. 385; *Al-Mughnī* (n 3) Vol. 5, pp. 251–52.

[81] Al-Zuhailī, Al-Fiqh al-Islāmī wa Adillatuhū (Dār al-Fikr, 1997) Vol. 5, p. 4098.

[82] Al-Kāsānī (n 10) Vol. 6, p. 23; Al-Dusūqī (n 8) Vol. 3, p. 344.

[83] *Al-Mughnī* (n 3) Vol. 5, p. 212; Al-Shirbīnī (n 5) Vol. 2, pp. 221–22.

[84] *Al-Mughnī* (n 3) Vol. 5, p. 51.

Caliph Abubakar by saying: 'a judgment in his favour is a judgement in my favour and a judgement against him is a judgment against me.'[85] This representation in litigation on behalf of the principal includes arguing a case[86] and admission (except matters that relate to retribution and *ḥudūd* punishments).[87] Zufr, Mālik, Shāfiʿī, and Aḥmad bin Ḥanbal are of the opinion that even if the agency is absolute, the agent cannot confess, settle, or offer absolution (*ibrāʾ*) because the authority to represent does not include authority to bring suits to an end.[88]

11.29 Zufr contends that in the event of judgments in favour of the principal, the agent cannot take possession of property because his mandate to represent in court was to guide the principal, while taking possession of property will transform an agent into a trustee. However, the Shafi'is seem to allow it if permitted by custom or by the principal expressly. The Hanafis allow the agent to acquire possession by arguing that when the principal appointed the agent to represent him in litigation, he had effectively trusted him to receive it as well, because the litigation does not end until the subject matter of the dispute is possessed by the owner through his agent. Thus, appointment as legal representative is also an appointment to receive the property.[89]

2.8 Agency with Consideration

11.30 The essence of *wakāla* is that it is a gratuitous contract and as a result the agent is not paid for the service he provides to the principal. For this reason, it is considered as a non-binding contract (*ʿaqd jāiz*).[90] The legal basis of this is the *ḥadīth* in which the Prophet appointed Unais bin Marthad al-Ghanawī to execute *ḥadd* punishment[91] and ʿUrwah al-Bāriqi to purchase a ram for him.[92] In both these cases, the agents were not paid for the service they provided.

11.31 Where a contract of agency stipulates paying the agent, then it turns into a contract of exchange (*ʿaqd al-muʿāwaḍa*) and jurists have generally agreed over its legality.[93] The Prophet used to send his employees to collect *zakāt* to distribute to its rightful owners

[85] Al-Māwardī (n 23) Vol. 6, p. 1098.

[86] Ibn Nujaim (n 13) Vol. 7, pp. 143–44; *al-Fatāwā al-Hindiyya* (n 9) Vol. 3, p. 564. The Malikis contend that where the agent is the opponent's enemy, the agency shall only be permissible if the opponent has consented to its enemy's representation. See Al-Dusūqī (n 8) Vol. 3, p. 378; Al-Ramlī (n 1) Vol. 5, p. 53; Al-Shirbīnī (n 5) Vol. 2, p. 222; *Al-Mughnī* (n 3) Vol. 5, p. 205, Vol. 3, p. 442; *Radd al-Muḥtār* (n 8) Vol. 5, p. 512; Al-Kāsānī (n 10) Vol. 6, p. 22.

[87] Al-Kāsānī (n 10) Vol. 24, p. 6; Al-Sarakhsī, Al-Mabsūṭ (Dar al-Ma'rifa, 1993) Vol. 4, p. 19; *Radd al-Muḥtār* (n 8) Vol. 4, p. 430.

[88] Ibn Rushd (n 50) Vol. 4, pp. 85–86; Al-Shīrāzī, Al-Muhadhdhab fī Fiqh al-Imām al-Shāfiʿī (Dār al-Kutub al-ʿIlmiyya, n.d.) Vol. 2, p. 163; *Al-Mughnī* (n 3) Vol. 5, p. 91.

[89] Al-Kāsānī (n 10) Vol. 6, p. 24; Al-Shīrāzī (n 88) Vol. 1, p. 167; *Al-Mughnī* (n 3) Vol. 5, p. 91.

[90] Al-Kāsānī (n 10) Vol. 7, p. 460; Ibn Shās (n 68) Vol. 2, p. 497; Al-Nawawī (n 24) Vol. 4, p. 332; Al-Buhūtī (n 205) Vol. 2, p. 317.

[91] Bukhārī 2314; Muslim 1697.

[92] Bukhārī 3642.

[93] Al-Sarakhsī (n 87) Vol. 19, p. 91; Al-Qarāfī (n 62) Vol. 1, p. 188; Al-Ramlī (n 1) Vol. 5, p. 52; *Al-Mughnī* (n 3) Vol. 7, p. 204.

and paid them for the service rendered.[94] However, an agency with consideration assumes the form of *ijāra* (contract of service provision).[95] Thus, the agent will be entitled to pay whenever he undertakes what is required of him or delivers it.[96]

According to all four schools, in the event of an agency with consideration the agent has the same status as an employee or labourer (*ajīr*). In this way, the agent is bound to undertake the business of agency and cannot unilaterally withdraw from the contract.[97] However, the Shafi'is argue that unless the terms of the contract stipulate that it is *ijāra* (labour or employment contract), an agency with consideration is still a non-binding contract for both parties and either of them can withdraw from it and terminate the agency. Thus, the agent shall be a trustee regarding what he receives.[98] The disagreement centres on whether regard is given to terms and their construction or to objectives and meanings of contracts.[99] **11.32**

2.9 Termination of Agency

2.9.1 Dismissal or Resignation

Agency is a non-binding contract and either party may validly withdraw from it.[100] Any action after termination will be void. In order for this outcome to materialize (i) the other party should be aware of the termination by the first party;[101] (ii) no third-party rights should be attached to the agency; and (iii) the agency must be without consideration.[102] **11.33**

2.9.2 Death

An agency is also terminated by the death of either the principal or the agent.[103] However, there is disagreement on the termination of the agency by reason of insanity, sickness, restriction of the power of disposition (*ḥajr*), apostasy, intoxication, loss of power of disposition by the principal in the object of the agency, where the agent exceeds his limit, denial of the agency, the end of partnership that creates the agency, performance of the requirement of the agency, and withdrawal from the agency. **11.34**

94 *Al-Mughnī* (n 3) Vol. 5, p. 210.
95 Al-Nawawī (n 90) Vol. 4, p. 332; *Al-Mughnī* (n 3) Vol. 5, p. 210.
96 *Al-Mughnī* (n 3) Vol. 5, p. 210.
97 Al-Ḥaṭṭāb (n 1) Vol. 5, p. 188; *Al-Mughnī* (n 3) Vol. 7, p. 205; Al-Nawawī (n 24) Vol. 4, p. 332.
98 Al-Nawawī (n 24) Vol. 4, p. 332; Al-Ramlī (n 1) Vol. 5, p. 52.
99 Al-Sarakhsī (n 87) Vol. 22, p. 22; Al-Qarāfī (n 62) Vol. 1, p. 39, Vol. 3, p. 143; Al-Suyūṭī (n 18) p. 212; Al-Zarkashī (n 30) Vol. 2, p. 371; Aḥmad al-Sālūs, Mausū'at al-Qaḍāyā al-Fiqhiyya al-Mu'āṣira wa al-Iqtiṣād al-Islāmī (Dār Umm al-Qurā, 2001) Vol. 30, pp. 203–06.
100 Al-Kāsānī (n 10) Vol. 6, p. 51; Al-Dusūqī (n 8) Vol. 3, p. 396; Al-Shirbīnī (n 5) Vol. 2, p. 231; *Al-Mughnī* (n 3) Vol. 5, p. 242.
101 Al-Kāsānī (n 10) Vol. 6, p. 51; Al-Dardīr (n 33) Vol. 3, p. 396; Al-Shirbīnī (n 5) Vol. 2, p. 232; *Al-Mughnī* (n 3) Vol. 5, p. 242; Al-Mardāwī (n 11) Vol. 5, p. 372.
102 Al-Dusūqī (n 8) Vol. 3, p. 357; Muḥammad 'Illīsh, Fat'ḥ al-Aliyy al-Mālik fī al-Fatwā 'alā Madh'hab Malik (Dār al-Ma'rifa, n.d.) Vol. 2, p. 327; Al-Azharī (n 60) Vol. 2, p. 132; Al-Nawawī (n 24) Vol. 4, p. 332; Al-Haithamī, Ḥāshiyat al-Sharwānī ma' Tuḥfat al-Muḥtāj (Al-Maktaba al-Tijāriyya, 1938) Vol. 5, p. 337.
103 Al-Dusūqī (n 8) Vol. 3, p. 396; Al-Shirbīnī (n 5) Vol. 2, p. 408; *Al-Mughnī* (n 3) Vol. 5, p. 213.

3. *Juʿāla*

11.35 In *juʿāla* an individual promises a defined reward to another, payable only after the execution of the specified task.[104] Despite the fact that *juʿāla* is analogically invalid due to its uncertainty, it becomes lawful as a concession[105] on the basis of pertinent authorities from the Qur'ān and Sunnah. Allah says in the Qur'ān: 'And for he who produces it is [the reward of] a camel's load.'[106] When the Companions conducted a treatment (exorcism) of the people and the latter, on the demand of the Companions, gave a herd of sheep as reward for their treatment, the Holy Prophet allowed the Companions to take the sheep as reward.[107] Hanafis do not, however, allow this due to uncertainty. Also, in *juʿāla* that is not offered to a named individual, the promise is not offered to an offeree, which negates the nature of the contract.[108]

3.1 Elements of *Juʿāla*

11.36 There are four elements in *juʿāla*: *ṣīgha*, the contracting parties, the required work, and the consideration (*juʿl*).

3.1.1 *Ṣīgha*

11.37 The offeror (*jāʿil*) should express his intention to give a certain reward to an offeree in return for undertaking a certain task.[109] The offeree may be the general public, such as 'whoever returns my lost animal will get this reward' or may be a particular individual.[110]

3.1.2 Parties to the Contract of *Juʿāla*

11.38 According to the Shafi'is and Hanbalis, the conditions applicable to the capacity or authority to enter into a contract of exchange apply here.[111] An agent or guardian acting on behalf of another can become *jāʿil* but he cannot promise an amount above the ordinary, otherwise the difference in amount would count as his liability. A determinate offeree cannot further delegate his work to another person unless permitted by the offeror, expressly or impliedly. In case of an offer to the general public in which a person has not been identified, he can make such a delegation.[112]

104 Al-Kharshī (n 32) Vol. 7, p. 59; Muḥammad al-Māliki, Sharḥ Ḥudūd Ibn ʿArafa (Al-Maktabah al-ʿIlmiyyah, 1350H) Vol. 1, p. 402.
105 This is argued by the Malikis, but both the Shafi'is and Hanbalis allow this contract. See Muḥammad Illish, Minahj al-Jalīl Sharḥ Mukhtaṣar Khalīl (Dār al-Fikr, 1989) Vol. 8, p. 59.
106 Qur'ān, Yūsuf, 72.
107 Bukhārī 5736; Muslim 2201.
108 Al-Sarakhsī (n 87) Vol. 11, p. 17; Al-Kāsānī (n 10) Vol. 6, p. 203.
109 Al-Ramlī (n 1) Vol. 5, p. 467.
110 Ibid, Vol. 5, p. 466; Zakariyya Al-Anṣārī, Asnā al-Maṭālib fī Sharḥ Rauḍ al-Tālib (Dār al-Kitāb al-Islāmī, n.d.) Vol. 2, p. 439.
111 Al-Haithamī (n 102) Vol. 6, p. 365.
112 Ibid, Vol. 6, pp. 365–94; Al-Ramlī (n 1) Vol. 5, p. 467.

3.1.3 Subject Matter of *Ju'āla*

The subject matter of the *ju'āla* is the work for which *jā'il* (the offeror) declares a reward.[113] This work can be teaching a discipline, craft, or provision of information, serving as a tourist guide, or the provision of a cure. It can also consist in the return of lost property, such as a runaway camel. The subject matter of *ju'āla* should not be unlawful, nor should it be work or a duty that is obligatory for the worker.[114] The Shafi'is and Hanbalis argue that the task to be performed may be both particularly defined and ambiguous.[115] 11.39

Ijāra and *ju'āla* look similar but their effects on an act are often different. For example, *ijāra* is invalid if the conduct or work which is difficult to define or is qualified becomes its subject matter, but *ju'āla* on such ambiguous work would be valid. This is the case with finding and returning runaway camels, despite the fact that the whereabouts of the camel are not known. It is argued that if similar ambiguity concerning increments as profit in *muḍāraba* is allowed without any necessity then tolerating such an ambiguity to achieve wealth or property out of necessity should be accepted even more readily. However, the work should be defined if this is easy to do, as is the case with erecting a structure: the place, length, breadth, and height as well as the place where it is to be erected should be stated. Similarly, *ju'āla* is valid for work in respect of which *ijāra* is valid, for instance where the offeror says: 'whoever returns my run-away camel will receive a fair reward'.[116] 11.40

The *ju'āla* becomes invalid with the specification of a time for the performance of work according to the Malikis and Shafi'is, as for example returning a camel in one month. However, the Malikis argue that limiting the contract to a particular time is valid if the worker is to be paid at the end of the time, irrespective of whether he has completed the task or not, but such an outcome will transform the *ju'āla* contract into one of *ijāra*.[117] The Hanbalis allow stipulation of time, saying that if the contract is valid without a clearly defined time, it should be valid where the time for the duration of the contract is known.[118] 11.41

3.1.3.1 Consideration in Ju'āla

The amount of consideration must be known in terms of form as well as quantity. However, the Malikis have opined that there is nothing wrong with ambiguous payments, as the Prophet said: 'whoever kills a fighter (in the battlefield) and has evidence 11.42

[113] Al-Ḥaṭṭāb (n 1) Vol. 5, p. 455; Muḥammad Al-Abdarī, Al-Tāj wa al-Iklīl li Mukhtaṣar Khalīl (Dār al-Fikr, 1398H) Vol. 5, p. 452; Al-Shirbīnī (n 5) Vol. 3, p. 618; Al-Buhūtī (n 1) Vol. 4, p. 204.

[114] Al-Haithamī (n 102) Vol. 3, p. 366; *Al-Mughnī* (n 3) Vol. 6, p.143.

[115] Sulaimān al-Bujairimī, Ḥāshiyat al-Bujairimī 'alā Sharḥ al-Manhaj—Al-Tajrīd li Naf' al-'Ābīd (Matba'at al-Ḥalabī, 1950) Vol. 3, p. 238.

[116] Al-Haithamī (n 102) Vol. 6, p. 367; Ibn Juzaī (n 71) p. 182; *Al-Mughnī* (n 3) Vol. 6, p. 351; Al-Buhūtī (n 1) Vol. 4, p. 206; Al-Qāsim al-Abdarī (n 113) Vol. 5, pp. 454–55.

[117] Al-Dusūqī (n 8) Vol. 4, p. 66; Al-Qurṭubī, Al-Muqaddimāt al-Mumahhidāt (Dār al-Gharb al-Islāmī, 1988) Vol. 2, p. 177.

[118] Mansūr Al-Buhūtī, Sharḥ Muntahā al-Irādāt ('Ālam al-Kutub, 1993) Vol. 2, p. 373.

thereto, the fighter's possession shall be his.'[119] The fighter's possessions are normally unknown.[120] The consideration must be pure, owned, and deliverable at the end of the contract by the offeror.[121] Consideration should not be made before the work is completed and any stipulation for advance payment will render the contract invalid.[122]

3.2 Effects of *Juʿāla*

11.43 According to the Shafi'is, Hanbalis, and Malikis, *juʿāla* is a non-binding contract before the commencement of labour if there is no obligation upon them.[123] Some of the Malikis declare *juʿāla* binding upon both parties even before commencement of the labour, just like *ijāra*.[124] However, jurists have agreed that the contract becomes binding after the completion of the task.[125]

11.44 The *jāʿil's* property that has fallen into the possession of a worker after fulfilment of the task is considered trust property[126] and the judge can award expenses for the maintenance of such property[127] even if the property could not be delivered to the owner. This is so because such expenses are permitted as a necessity to protect the property recovered.[128]

3.3 Termination of *Juʿāla* Contract

11.45 The insanity of a determinate worker as well as the death of either party will terminate the *juʿāla*. The Malikis contend that death should occur before the commencement of work.[129] *Juʿāla* shall also be terminated after a worker completes the work and receives payment. The Malikis support the view that the right of rescission is available to a worker before or after the commencement of the work, whereas the *jāʿil* can rescind it only before commencement of the work.[130] The Shafi'is allow rescission for either of the parties so long as the work has not been completed.[131] The Accounting and Auditing Organization for Islamic Financial Institutions (AAOFII) Standards stipulate

[119] Bukhārī 42; Muslim 1751.
[120] Al-Kharshī (n 32) Vol. 7, p. 59; Al-Ramlī (n 1) Vol. 5, p. 467; Al-Shirbīnī (n 5) Vol. 3, p. 620; Al-Buhūtī (n 1) Vol. 4, p. 203.
[121] Al-Ramlī (n 1) Vol. 5, p. 472; Aḥmad Al-Dardīr and Muḥammad bin Arafa, Al-Sharḥ al-Kabīr maʿa Ḥāshiyat al-Dusūqī (Dār al-Fikr, n.d.) Vol. 4, p. 63; Al-Ṣāwī (n 11) Vol. 4, p. 79.
[122] Al-Ramlī (n 1) Vol. 5, p. 476; Al-Dusūqī (n 8) Vol. 4, p. 63.
[123] Al-Kharshī (n 32) Vol. 7, p. 60; Al-Anṣārī (n 110) Vol. 2, p. 442; Al-Buhūtī (n 1) Vol. 4, p. 203.
[124] Al-Ramlī (n 1) Vol. 5, p. 476; Al-Qurṭubī (n 117) Vol. 2, p. 179; Al-Buhūtī (n 1) Vol. 4, p. 203.
[125] Al-Ṣāwī (n 11) Vol. 4, p. 83; Al-Ramlī (n 1) Vol. 5, p. 466; *Al-Mughnī* (n 3) Vol. 6, p. 375.
[126] Al-Ramlī (n 1) Vol. 5, p. 472; Al-Anṣārī (n 110) Vol. 2, p. 442; Al-Dusūqī (n 8) Vol. 4, p. 63; Al-Buhūtī (n 1) Vol. 4, p. 207.
[127] Al-Dusūqī (n 8) Vol. 4, p. 67; Al-Ramlī (n 1) Vol. 2, p. 442, Sulaimān Al-Bujairimī, Tuḥfat al-Ḥabīb ʿalā Sharḥ al-Khaṭīb - Ḥāshiyat al-Bujairimī alā Manhaj al-Tullāb (Dār al-Fikr, 1995) Vol. 3, p. 222.
[128] Al-Buhūtī (n 1) Vol. 4, p. 205.
[129] Ibid.
[130] Al-Dusūqī (n 8) Vol. 4, p. 68.
[131] Al-Haithamī (n 102) Vol. 5, p. 66.

that the worker is entitled to reasonable wages if the offeror rescinds the contract after the commencement of the work, but if such rescission originates from the worker after the commencement of the work, he will not be entitled to wages.[132]

3.4 Difference between *Ju'āla* and *Ijāra*

Ju'āla is different from *ijāra* because the former is a non-binding contract without any need for acceptance and is valid despite the uncertainty and existence of an unknown party.[133] **11.46**

3.5 Contemporary Applications of the *Ju'āla* Contract

Ju'āla contracts can be used as an incentive for economic development, such as enhancing agricultural lands or the discovery of mineral resources and petroleum, regardless of the amount of labour required or the time it takes.[134] Banks can declare *ju'āla* for recovery of bad loans and provide a predetermined reward for anyone that helps in their recovery.[135] *Ju'āla* can be used to secure permissible financing facilities and brokerage activities.[136] **11.47**

4. *Ijāra*

Ijāra entails 'giving something on rent' and is used for securing both human labour (*ijārat al-ashkās*) and usufruct (*ijārat al-ashyā*).[137] The term *ijāra* is employed in two different places. First, service contracts in which the employer engages the services of another person (*ajīr*) in return for wages, for example lawyers and doctors.[138] Secondly, in *ijāra* a usufruct of properties and assets is exchanged for a consideration. *Ijāra* in this sense is similar to a lease and here the lessor is called the *mu'jir* and the lessee is called the *musta'jir*.[139] **11.48**

Ijāra is a lawful contract.[140] This is based on the provisions of the Qur'ān, the Sunnah, and consensus. Allah says in the Qur'ān: 'And if they breastfeed for you, then give them their payment.'[141] The Prophet said: 'whoever that hires an *ajīr* (labourer) he should **11.49**

[132] AAOIFI Standard No. 15, p. 6.
[133] Ibid, p. 7.
[134] Hai'at al-Muhāsaba wa al-Murāja'a li al-Mu'assasāt al-Māliyya, *Mi'yār* (n 97) p.15.
[135] Ibid.
[136] AAOIFI Standard No. 15, p. 9.
[137] Al-Ṣāwī (n 11) Vol. 4, p. 5; Al-Dardīr (n 121) Vol. 4, p. 2.
[138] Taqi Usmani, An Introduction to Islamic Finance (Maktaba Ma'arif al-Qurān, 2008) pp. 157–58.
[139] Al-Sarakhsī (n 87) Vol. 15, p. 74; Muḥammad Al-Shafi'ī, Al-Umm (Dar al-Ma'rifa, 1990) Vol. 4, p. 26; Al-Dardīr (n 21) Vol. 4, p. 5.
[140] Al-Sarakhsī (n 87) Vol. 15, p. 74; Al-Kāsānī (n 10) Vol. 4, p. 201; Ibn Rushd (n 50) Vol. 2, p. 220.
[141] Qur'ān 65:6.

inform him his payment'[142] and instructed to 'give a labourer his wage before his sweat dries'.[143] He said: 'I will be a litigant against thee on the day of resurrection and among them he mentioned a man who hires another man and demands his obligation to be fully met but did not pay him his wage.'[144] There is also consensus among jurists from the time of the Companions of the Prophet up to the present time on the permissibility of *ijāra*.[145]

4.1 Nature of the *Ijāra* Contract

11.50 *Ijāra* is a binding contract (*'aqd lāzim*) as Allah says in the Qur'ān: 'And fulfill all obligations.'[146] Hence, it cannot be rescinded unilaterally without legal justification, for example that the subject matter of *ijāra* is defective or inaccessible,[147] destroyed, or stolen.[148]

4.2 Elements of *Ijāra*

11.51 As in other contracts, the majority of scholars contend that the existence of *ṣīgha*, parties, and subject matter constitute the three quintessential elements of *ijāra* contracts.[149] For Hanafis, there is only one element—*ṣīgha*—because the existence of parties and subject are implied in *ṣīgha*.[150]

4.2.1 *Ṣīgha*

11.52 An *ijāra* contract can be formed by using any term or statement clearly suggesting *ijāra*,[151] such as 'I am lending this house to you' or 'This is a gift to you in exchange for so and so amount', or 'I am selling or giving the usufruct of this house to you for a period of three months in exchange for so and so amount',[152] or 'I am transferring ownership of the usufruct of this house to you'. Hanafis and Shafi'is justify the validity of *ijāra* concluded with the term 'sell' by arguing that, in *ijāra*, ownership is transferred in return for consideration.[153] However, some of the Shafi'is and Hanafis oppose this by contending that 'sell' involves transferring the actual property and not its usufruct,[154]

[142] Baihaqī 11651, Vol. 6, p.198; Vol. 8, p. 235.
[143] Abū Dāwūd 2443.
[144] Ibn Māja 2442; Bukhārī 2114.
[145] Al-Sarakhsī (n 87) Vol. 15, p. 74; Al-Ṣāwī (n 11) Vol. 4, pp. 5–6; Ibn Rushd (n 50) Vol. 2, p. 221; Al-Ramlī (n 1) Vol. 5, p. 261.
[146] Qur'ān 5:1.
[147] Ibn Rushd (n 50) Vol. 2, p. 229.
[148] *Al-Mughnī* (n 3) Vol. 6, pp. 20, 21; Ibn Rushd (n 50) Vol. 2, p. 229; *Al-Fatāwā al-Hindiyya* (n 9) Vol. 4, p. 410.
[149] Al-Abdarī (n 113) Vol. 5, p. 389; Al-Nawawī (n 24) Vol. 5, p. 173; Al-Buhūtī (n 1) Vol. 3, p. 146.
[150] Al-Kāsānī (n 10) Vol. 4, p. 174.
[151] Al-Buhūtī (n 1) Vol. 3, pp. 457–58.
[152] *Al-Fatāwā al-Hindiyya* (n 9) Vol. 4, p. 409; Al-Haṭṭāb (n 1) Vol. 5, p. 390; Al-Dasūqī (n 8) Vol. 4, p. 2; Al-Ramlī (n 1) Vol. 5, p. 261.
[153] Al-Shīrāzī (n 88) Vol. 2, p. 244; *Al-Fatāwā al-Hindiyya* (n 9) Vol. 4, pp. 409–10.
[154] Aḥmad al-Qalyūbī, Ḥāshiyat al-Qalyūbī (Dār al-Fikr, 1995) Vol. 3, p. 68.

and also usufruct comes into existence only at the time it is enjoyed and not at the time of conclusion of the contract. Hence, this would be a sale of a non-existent object and by extension would be void.[155] *Ijāra* can be concluded through conduct and gestures by mute persons.[156] Acceptance must be unqualified.[157]

4.2.2 Parties to the Contract

Ijāra by insane persons is invalid. The majority of jurists with the exception of the Shafi'is have opined that the contract of a child with discretion is valid if his guardian has so allowed.[158] A person without any authority (*faḍūlī*) cannot conclude *ijāra*.[159] **11.53**

4.2.3 Object of the Contract

The subject matter of *ijāra* can either be the usufruct of real property (*ijārat al-ashyā*) or a service to be provided by a person (*ijārat al-ashkās*).[160] **11.54**

- *ijārat al-ashyā*, enjoyment of the property, must not exhaust its source.[161]
- The usufruct must be a valuable thing and jurists, save for the Hanbalis, argue that anything freely available cannot be the subject matter of *ijāra* as this will be a waste of money.[162]
- Enjoyment of the usufruct must not be unlawful, such as adultery, alcohol, etc.[163] It should not be an obligatory act of worship which every individual has to perform personally nor a prohibited sinful action.[164]
- There must be legal and factual ability to enjoy the usufruct. Therefore, a stray animal or property which is usurped or is not accessible by the lessor cannot be leased.[165]
- The subject matter of a contract must be clearly defined and known, such that any ambiguity that can lead to dispute is avoided.[166]
- Anything that can serve as payment in a contract of sale can serve as payment in a contract of *ijāra*, and all conditions required in the sale price are also required in the price of *ijāra*.[167] Usufruct can become consideration because usufructs in *ijāra*

[155] *Radd al-Muḥtār* (n 8) Vol. 5, p. 3.
[156] Al-Kāsānī (n 10) Vol. 5, p. 134; Ibn ʿĀbidīn (n 52) Vol. 5, p. 4; *Al-Fatāwā al-Hindiyya* (n 9) Vol. 4, p. 409; Al-Ṣāwī (n 11) Vol. 4, p. 8; Al-Ḥaṭṭāb (n 1) Vol. 5, p. 390; Al-Ramlī (n 1) Vol. 5, p. 263; *Al-Mughnī* (n 3) Vol. 4, p. 4.
[157] Al-Kāsānī (n 10) Vol. 5, pp. 136–38.
[158] Al-Sarakhsī (n 87) Vol. 10, p. 207; Al-Kāsānī (n 10) Vol. 5, p. 154; Al-Qarāfī (n 44) Vol. 5, p. 373; Al-Nawawī (n 24) Vol. 5, p. 250; *Al-Mughnī* (n 3) Vol. 6, p. 51.
[159] Al-Kāsānī (n 10) Vol. 4, p. 176; *Al-Fatāwāh al-Hindiyya* (n 9) Vol. 4, pp. 410–11.
[160] Al-Dusūqī (n 8) Vol. 4, p. 3; *Al-Mughnī* (n 3) Vol. 6, p. 8.
[161] Al-Kāsānī (n 10) Vol. 4, p. 175; Al-Dusūqī (n 10) Vol. 4, p. 20; *Al-Mughnī* (n 3) Vol. 5, p. 404. Ibn Rushd has narrated the opinion that allows such exhaustion. Ibn Rushd (n 50) Vol. 2, p. 224.
[162] *Al-Fatāwā al-Hindiyya* (n 9) Vol. 4, p. 411; Al-Kāsānī (n 10) Vol. 4, p. 175; Al-Dusūqī (n 8) Vol. 4, p. 20; Al-Shīrāzī (n 88) Vol. 2, p. 244; *Al-Mughnī* (n 3) Vol. 6, p.143.
[163] Al-Kāsānī (n 10) Vol. 4, pp. 184, 191; Al-Ṣāwī (n 11) Vol. 4, p. 36; Al-Nawawī (n 24) Vol. 1, p. 159; *Al-Mughnī* (n 3) Vol. 6, pp. 134, 136. The *ḥadīth* in which the Prophet cursed alcohol and those carrying or using it was transmitted by Tirmidhī 1295; Abū Dā'ūd 3674.
[164] Tirmidhī 209.
[165] *Al-Fatāwā al-Hindiyya* (n 9) Vol. 4, p. 411; Al-Shīrāzī (n 88) Vol. 2, p. 246.
[166] *Al-Fatāwā al-Hindiyya* (n 9) Vol. 4, p. 411; Al-Kāsānī (n 10) Vol. 4, p. 180; Ibn Rushd (n 50) Vol. 2, p. 230; *Al-Mughnī* (n 3) Vol. 5, p. 357.
[167] Al-Ṣāwī (n 11) Vol. 4, p. 159; Al-Kāsānī (n 10) Vol. 5, p. 322; *Al-Fatāwā al-Hindiyya* (n 9) Vol. 4, p. 412.

are treated as real property and can be exchanged as real property. A house can be leased for another house.[168] The Hanafis stipulate that the usufruct should be of a different kind, as where consideration for leasing a house may be to undertake some defined labour.[169]

- The Hanafis, Malikis, and Shafi'is do not allow the consideration to be part of the product of the service or work performed because where the product is lost, the labourer loses his pay. This is true with skinning a sheep where the pay is the skin as it is unknown whether the skin will be properly extracted.[170] The Prophet prohibited paying the flour grinder from the flour he grinds.[171] The Malikis allow this where the pay is well defined, such as where one asks another to harvest the crops on his farm and be entitled to half of the harvest.[172]

4.3 Effect of *Ijāra*

11.55 The execution of *ijāra* should not be associated with future indefinite time. Failure to mention such time will make it effective immediately.[173] However, the association of *ijāra* to a definite or specific time is valid in both *ijārat al-ashyā* (*ijāra* over entity) as well as *ijārat al-ashkās*.[174] Al-Kāsānī stated that *ijāra* shall not be executed within the period of the right of option (*khiyār*) as it is a barrier to the formation of the contract.[175] The Hanafis and Malikis maintain that the lessor becomes entitled to the consideration only after the subject matter of *ijāra* is transferred and enjoyed. However, there are some notable exceptions to this general rule entitling the lessor to payment at the time of conclusion of an *ijāra* contract or before the transfer and enjoyment of the subject matter. This is true where the lessee himself furnishes payment to the lessor, or the parties themselves agree to that effect, as the Prophet said: 'Muslims are subject to stipulations they agreed';[176] or where custom allows, for example leasing houses as well as hiring transport; or where the consideration has been specified and pinpointed, such as saying this garment shall be the pay.[177] The Shafi'is and Hanbalis stipulate that where a contract is silent on the time for payment of consideration, the consideration should be paid when the property is transferred to the lessee whether he has enjoyed it or not.[178]

[168] Al-Shīrāzī (n 88) Vol. 2, p. 251; Ibn Rushd (n 50) Vol. 2, p. 226; Al-Buhūtī (n 1) Vol. 3, p. 556.
[169] *Radd al-Muḥtār* (n 8) Vol. 5, p. 52.
[170] Al-Sarakhsī (n 87) Vol. 16, p. 79; Al-Ṣāwī (n 11) Vol. 4, p. 18; Al-Nawawī (n 24) Vol. 5, p. 158.
[171] Al-Dārquṭnī 3029.
[172] Al-Ṣāwī (n 11) Vol. 4, pp. 24–25.
[173] Al-Ruhaibānī (n 18) Vol. 3, p. 77; Al-Kāsānī (n 10) Vol. 5, p. 133.
[174] *Al-Fatāwā al-Hindiyya* (n 9) Vol. 4, p. 410; Al-Ṣāwī (n 11) Vol. 4, p. 30; Al-Nawawī (n 24) Vol. 5, p. 182.
[175] Al-Kāsānī (n 10) Vol. 4, p. 176; *Al-Fatāwā al-Hindiyya* (n 9) Vol. 4, p. 411; Ibn Rushd (n 50) Vol. 2, p. 228; Al-Shīrāzī (n 88) Vol. 2, p. 244.
[176] Abū Dāwūd 3594; Al-Tirmidhī 1352; Al-Kāsānī (n 10) Vol. 4, p. 202.
[177] Al-Ṣāwī (n 11) Vol. 4, p. 161; Al-Dusūqī (n 8) Vol. 4, p. 4.
[178] Al-Ramlī (n 1) Vol. 5, p. 266; *Al-Mughnī* (n 3) Vol. 5, p. 329.

4.4 Obligations of the Lessor

4.4.1 Surrender of Possession of the Leased Property

In *ijāra* for work, the *ajīr* is obliged to perform the work required from him under the *ijāra*. In *ijārat al-ashyā*, the lessor will deliver the leased property to the lessee to allow him unhindered and full enjoyment therefrom for the duration of the *ijāra*.[179] However, the title remains with the lessor.[180] An option is available if there is a defect that affects the usufruct for which the contract is formed or for the absence of a particular quality in *ijāra* for work.[181] **11.56**

4.4.2 Guaranteeing the Usurped Property from Usurpation

The majority of scholars have opined that where the leased property is usurped, the lessee has the option to continue or annul the contract or wait for the recovery of the property for a short period within which he shall not be required to pay. If he annuls the contract, he shall be obliged to settle what he has already enjoyed. However, if the usurper is the lessor, he has no right to claim the payment. In *ijāra* concerning works, the *musta'jir* will be entitled to annul the contract only if the *ajīr* cannot arrange a substitute for the subject matter.[182] **11.57**

4.5 Obligations of the Lessee

The Hanafis, Malikis, and Shafi'is, but not the Hanbalis, stipulate that the lessor is entitled to prevent the lessee from enjoying the property until payment is made (after it becomes due).[183] Every artisan, such as painters, can apply their right of lien on the property until payment is made to them.[184] The lessee should enjoy the property in accordance with the stipulated term or custom as well as taking proper care thereof. For instance, if he hires a vehicle for his personal transportation, he cannot use it for the transportation of another person.[185] The lessee holds the leased property on trust and is not liable if it is damaged or destroyed without transgression or failure to follow instructions, or without negligence in care.[186] The lessee is bound to surrender the leased property after the expiry of the lease.[187] **11.58**

179 *Al-Fatāwā al-Hindiyya* (n 9) Vol. 4, pp. 413, 437–38; Al-Buhūtī (n 1) Vol. 2, p. 565.
180 Al-Kāsānī (n 10) Vol. 4, p. 201.
181 Ibid, Vol. 4, p. 223; Al-Nawawī (n 42) Vol. 13, p. 321.
182 Al-Kāsānī (n 10) Vol. 4, p. 223; Al-Nawawī (n 42) Vol. 13, p. 321.
183 Al-Kāsānī (n 10) Vol. 4, p. 203.
184 Al-Ḥaṭṭāb (n 1) Vol. 5, p. 431; Al-Nawawī (n 42) Vol. 13, p. 321.
185 Al-Shīrāzī (n 88) Vol. 2, p. 256.
186 Ibid, Vol. 2, p. 256–57; Al-Buhūtī (n 118) Vol. 2, p. 270; *Al-Mughnī* (n 3) Vol. 6, p. 36; Al-Kāsānī (n 10) Vol. 4, p. 204; Al-Ṣāwī (n 11) Vol. 4, p. 14.
187 Al-Kāsānī (n 10) Vol. 4, p. 205; Al-Shīrāzī (n 88) Vol. 2, p. 256; *Al-Mughnī* (n 3) Vol. 5, p. 396.

4.6 Termination of *Ijāra*

11.59 *Ijāra* can be terminated either by the lapse of the period of the lease,[188] loss of the subject matter in *ijārat al-ashyā*,[189] or by mutual agreement. In *ijārat al-ashkās*, destruction or reversal of the work done will result in an obligation to repeat the work.[190] The Hanafis contend that the death of either party terminates *ijāra*. This is a position with which the majority of scholarly opinion disagrees, arguing that after the conclusion of *ijāra*, ownership is transferred. In the lease of land, after the death of the lessor, the family of the deceased lessor has no right to remove the lessee until the expiration of the lease.[191]

11.60 Long-term *ijāra* contracts, such as construction of large structures, farming, and mining, can be annulled by the lessee in the face of public emergency, such as war, natural disaster, escalation of prices, etc., making usufruct of the contract unattainable. This would be the case where land leased for farming from rainwater is unproductive due to drought,[192] as well as in situations where public insecurity prevents residence in leased premises.[193] *Ijāra* cannot be terminated on unimportant grounds like personal fear of the lessee (or proximity to his enemies)[194] and return of the lessor's family to live in the building leased by the lessor because of their absence.[195]

4.7 Application of *Ijāra* by Islamic Banks

11.61 Islamic banks frequently use *ijāra* in various finance leases but with the same structures and features. These mechanisms are created for the transfer of the asset to the lessee at the end of the leasing period, normally through another contract implicated at the end of the lease tenure. This has been achieved in various ways, such as:

1. The bank unilaterally promising to make a gift of the asset to the client at the end of the period, provided that the client pays all instalments fully.
2. A promise to sell the asset to the client at an agreed price, upon payment of the remaining instalments.

[188] Al-Shīrāzī (n 88) Vol. 2, p. 260; *Al-Fatāwā al-Hindiyya* (n 9) Vol. 4, p. 416.
[189] Al-Kāsānī (n 10) Vol. 4, p. 233; Al-Sarakhsī (n 87) Vol. 16, p. 2; Al-Ṣāwī (n 11) Vol. 4, p. 51.
[190] Al-Nawawī (n 24) Vol. 1, p.162; *Al-Mughnī* (n 3) Vol. 5, p. 342.
[191] Al-Kāsānī (n 10) Vol. 4, p. 200; Al-Ṣāwī (n 11) Vol. 4, p. 179, Al-Dusūqī (n 8) Vol. 4, p. 32; *Al-Mughnī* (n 3) Vol. 6, p. 38.
[192] Ibn Rushd (n 50) Vol. 4, p. 16.
[193] *Al-Mughnī* (n 3) Vol. 8, p. 31.
[194] Ibid, Vol. 8, p. 31.
[195] Al-Nawawī (n 24) Vol. 5, p. 240; Resolution 23 (5/7) of the Council of Fiqh Academy on Effects of Emergencies on Contractual Rights and Obligations. See Al-Qarārāt al-Mujamma'iyyah fī al-Mu'āmala al-Māliyya alā al-Abwāb al-Fiqhiyya, pp. 105–08. Available at <www.alukah.net/sharia/0/0137836/> accessed on 21 February 2023.

3. The client is allowed to purchase the asset, and the final instalment is considered the price for purchasing the asset.[196]

4.8 The Application of *Ijāra* in Personal Financing

There are three steps used in *ijāra* related to personal financing services. Some examples include the following applications: **11.62**

1. The bank does not normally provide cash. Perhaps banks will identify the need of the customer in the first place. For instance, the client may be in need of money to finance his services, such as travel (*ḥajj* and *'umra*) or education fees or marriage ceremonies or other services.
2. The bank will buy a package of tickets for the travel agency or buy a place at a university which includes tuition fees, accommodation fees, and an allowance for students, or otherwise provide travel services for those in need of money to travel.
3. The bank will offer services to the client based on an agreed rental contract price (capital + profit). The customer will pay the full amount to the bank either in a lump sum or in instalments.

5. *Salam*

Salam refers to the sale of a prescribed commodity with a defined quality and quantity in exchange for an advance payment of consideration. Allah says in the Qur'ān: 'O ye who believe! When ye deal with each other, in transactions involving future obligations (*dayn*) in a fixed period of time, reduce them to writing.'[197] Ibn 'Abbās said that this ā*ya* permits *salam* (*salaf*).[198] Ibn al-'Arabī states that every transaction where one of the considerations is immediately paid while the other is delayed is *dayn* (term used in this ā*ya*).[199] The Prophet said: 'whoever wants to do *salam* in dates, he should do it based on a defined measure, weight and time of delivery.'[200] Ibn Qudāma says that *salam* is permitted by every scholar.[201] The majority of jurists among the Hanafis, Malikis, Shafi'is, and Hanbalis are of the view that *salam* is contrary to the method of analogy as it concerns the sale of a non-existent object, which is prohibited by the Sharī'a. While the Prophet did exhort: 'do not sell that which you do not have',[202] *salam* is otherwise **11.63**

[196] Mohammed A. Ishak, 'An Appraisal of the Position of Islamic Law on Personal Financing' in Islamic Banking and Finance the Nexus with the Real Economy (Proceedings of 2nd International Conference conducted by International Institute of Islamic Banking and Finance, Bayero University Kano Nigeria, 28–29 April 2015) p. 446.
[197] Qur'ān 2:282.
[198] Muḥammad Al-Shāfi'ī, Musnad al-Imām al-Shāfi'ī (Dār al-Kutub al-'Ilmiyya, 1951) Vol. 2, p. 171.
[199] Muḥammad al-Ma'āfirī, Aḥkām al-Qur'ān (Dār al-Kutub al-'Ilmiyya, 2003) Vol. 1, p. 327.
[200] Muslim 4202. See also Bukhārī 2240.
[201] *Al-Mughnī* (n 3) Vol. 4, p. 339.
[202] Abū Dāwūd 3505.

allowed on the basis of the express *ayah* of the Qur'ān and *ḥadīth* of the Prophet as well as *ijmā'* (consensus) due to necessity.[203] To explain the necessity, for instance a farmer with no money to take care of his farm and unable to secure a loan can finance his business through a *salam* transaction.[204]

5.1 Essential Elements of *Salam*

11.64 The Hanafis consider *ṣīgha* as the only element of *salam*, while the majority require three elements: *ṣīgha*, existence of parties, and a subject matter.

5.1.1 *Ṣīgha*

11.65 Jurists have agreed that any term implying *salam*, including sale, can be used to signify an offer and acceptance for a *salam* contract if its conditions are met.[205] However, Zufr and some Shafi'is opine that *salam* cannot be formed with the mere word 'sale'.[206] The majority of jurists suggest that *salam* cannot be subject to an option of condition because the payment is transferred to the *muslam ilaihi* before the parties separate from each other, which negates the option of a condition.[207] In the Maliki school, the right of option is available for three days on the condition that the consideration paid is not lost because the loss of cost would render the contract invalid.[208]

5.1.2 Parties to the Contract of *Salam*

11.66 Each party should have attained the age of discretion and have power to enter into the contract,[209] through ownership or agency.[210] Terminally ill persons do not have capacity to give consent.[211]

5.1.3 Object of *Salam*

5.1.3.1 Conditions applicable to both commodity and consideration

11.67 Both the commodity and the price to be paid must have a value.[212] The exchanged commodities should not be such as to involve *ribā al-nasī'a* in their exchange. This is to avoid one of the qualities of usury of increment (*ribā al-faḍl*) as the *muslam fīhi* (subject matter of *salam*) is a credit to be delivered in the future. Thus, if the price also has the

[203] Ibn Nujaim (n 13) Vol. 6, p. 169; Muḥammad 'Illīsh, Minah al-Jalīl Sharḥ Mukhtaṣar Khalīl (Dār al-Fikr, 1989) Vol. 5, p. 231; Al-Anṣārī (n 110) Vol. 2, p. 122.

[204] *Al-Mughnī* (n 3) Vol. 4, p. 339.

[205] This opinion is common to all schools. See Al-Kāsānī (n 10) Vol. 5, p. 201; Al-Ramlī (n 1) Vol. 4, p. 182; 'Illīsh (n 203) Vol. 4, p. 435; Al-Buhūtī (n 118) Vol. 2, p. 88; Al-Shīrāzī (n 88) Vol. 2, p. 72; Al-Ḥaṭṭāb (n 1) Vol. 4, p. 538.

[206] Shīrāzī (n 88) Vol. 2, p. 72.

[207] Al-Kāsānī (n 10) Vol. 5, p. 201.

[208] 'Illīsh (n 203) Vol. 5, p. 231.

[209] 'Ali al-Qarahdaghī, Muqaddimāt fī al-Mālī wa al-Milkī wa al-'Aqd, in Haqībat al-Qaradāghī al-Iqtiṣādiyya, Book 3, p. 251.

[210] Al-Zuhailī (n 81) Vol. 4, p. 2985.

[211] Al-Sarakhsī (n 87) Vol. 29, p. 38.

[212] 'Uthmān al-Zaila'ī, Tabyīn al-Ḥaqā'iq Sharḥ Kanz al-Daqā'iq (Al-Matba'a al-Kubrā al-Amīriyya, 1313H) Vol. 5, p. 235; Al-Sarakhsī (n 87) Vol. 13, p. 25; Al-Sālūs (n 99) Vol. 25, p. 199; Al-Zuhailī (n 81) Vol. 4, p. 2879.

quality of *ribā al-faḍl*, there will be usury of delay (*ribā al-nasī'a*) and this, jurists agree, will make the contract void.[213] This is based on a *ḥadīth* of *ribā* narrated by 'Ubāda bin al-Sāmit.[214] The majority of jurists, save for Hanafis, consider as usufruct any property from which the usufruct is derived. They further maintain that a usufruct can become the subject matter of *salam* as well as its payment. For instance, allowing a person to live in a house in return for a commodity to be delivered in the future.[215]

5.1.3.2 Requirements of salam *payment (*Ra's Māl al-Salam*)*

The consideration/payment should be known just as in any other contract of exchange **11.68**
in terms of its currency and amount. In case of a commodity being used as payment, its type and *qadr* (measurement, weight, or number) should be known.[216] The majority of jurists contend that payment should be transferred at the contract session before the parties separate, otherwise the contract is invalid.[217] This is based on the tradition of the Prophet, whereby 'whoever that wants to enter into the contract of *salam*, his *salam* should be for the [acquisition of] defined measure, known weight and a known time of delivery' (*ḥadīth* of *salam*).[218] The separation of the parties without payment of consideration would transform the contract into a sale of credit for credit in which both exchanged commodities are delayed. This is prohibited.[219] The Malikis allow the delay of payment for two or three days but no more than that. For them, this slight delay may be pardoned.[220]

5.2 Requirements or Conditions of the Commodity

The subject matter of *salam* must be known with accurate description and quantity, **11.69**
such that it eliminates ambiguity and any possibility of dispute between the parties at the time of delivery and also demonstrates the possibility of its delivery. Therefore, the parties have to state the genus of the commodity, in addition to its sub-particular types, if any. If the subject matter becomes defective before its delivery, the recipient of the advanced payment can opt for a different subject matter meeting the agreed quality.[221] Hence, it should not be identified as a particularly pinpointed commodity,[222] such as products of a specific tree or piece of land because they may be destroyed by the time

213 Ibn Juzai (n 71) p. 177; Al-Buhūtī (n 118) Vol. 2, p. 71; Ibn Rushd (n 50) Vol. 2, p. 227; Al-Buhūtī (n 1) Vol. 3, p. 306.
214 Muslim 4145.
215 Al-Kharshī (n 32) Vol. 5, p. 203; Al-Ansārī (n 110) Vol. 2, p. 123; Al-Ramlī (n 1) Vol. 4, p. 182; Al-Buhūtī (n 118) Vol. 2, p. 252.
216 *Radd al-Muḥtār* (n 8) Vol. 5, p. 210; Ibn Juzaī (n 71) p. 177; Al-Nawawī (n 42) Vol. 13, p. 97.
217 Al-Kāsānī (n 10) Vol. 5, p. 202; *Al-Umm* (n 139) Vol. 3, p. 95; Al-Nawawī (n 42) Vol. 13, p. 97; Al-Buhūtī (n 118) Vol. 2, p. 97; *Al-Mughnī* (n 3) Vol. 4, p. 328.
218 Muslim 4202. See also Bukhārī 2240.
219 *Al-Mughnī* (n 3) Vol. 5, p. 57; Majalla, Art. 387.
220 Al-Kharshī (n 32) Vol. 5, p. 220; Al-Qurṭubī (n 117) Vol. 2, p. 28.
221 Al-Buhūtī (n 1) Vol. 3, p. 292; Al-Anṣārī (n 110) Vol. 2, p. 124.
222 Ibn Juzaī (n 71) p. 178; Al-Ḥaṭṭāb (n 1) Vol. 4, p. 534; Al-Nawawī (n 24) Vol. 4, p. 6; Al-Ramlī (n 1) Vol. 4, p. 183.

of delivery.[223] Based on this, jurists have stated that the subject matter of *salam* should encompass fungibles, such as things whose weight and length can be measured, and countables or valuables that can be definitively qualified.[224] According to Al-Shīrāzī, it is permissible to contract *salam* on anything that can be sold and whose qualities can be definitively described, such as currencies, and grains,[225] any other farm produce as well as industrial or mechanical products.[226]

11.70 All schools, save for the Shafi'is, agree that the delivery of a commodity must be suspended or delayed[227] by relying on the *ḥadīth* of *salam*.[228] These jurists argue that the specific instruction concerning the future delivery creates an obligatory command that the delivery must be in the future.[229] The Shafi'is however allow the immediate delivery of the subject matter by arguing that if delayed delivery is lawful, then immediate delivery must be lawful on the basis of *qiyās al-aulā*[230] because this will remove uncertainty.[231]

11.71 The time of delivery must be known as is ordained in the *ḥadīth* of *salam* which stipulates 'a known time of delivery'.[232] Ignorance as to the quantity and time will render a *salam* contract invalid irrespective of whether the defect is serious or simple.[233] The time of delivery can be specified as the beginning or middle of *Muḥarram*, a particular day of the month, etc.[234]

11.72 Jurists have disagreed on the stipulation of the place of delivery. The Hanbalis contend that the place of delivery is not obligatory because in the *ḥadīth* of *salam* the Prophet did not mention it.[235] The Malikis also consider it preferable and not mandatory to mention the place in the contract.[236] The Shafi'is argue that if the contract is concluded at a place which is not suitable for delivery, like the desert, or where extra costs will be incurred for delivery, then failure to mention the place of delivery will make the contract invalid.[237]

11.73 The possession of the subject matter should be deliverable at the agreed place.[238] The majority of jurists, except for the Hanafis, stipulate that the availability of the subject

[223] Al-Qurṭubī (n 117) Vol. 2, p. 27.
[224] Ibn Nujaim (n 9) Vol. 6, p. 169; Al-Kharshī (n 32) Vol. 5, p. 212; Al-Anṣārī (n 110) Vol. 2, p. 128; Al-Buhūtī (n 1) Vol. 3, p. 276.
[225] Al-Shīrāzī (n 88) Vol. 2, p. 72.
[226] Mujama' al-Fiqh al-Islāmī, 9th Session.
[227] Ibn Juzaī (n 71) p. 178; Al-Kāsānī (n 10) Vol. 5, p. 212; *Al-Mughnī* (n 3) Vol. 4, p. 355.
[228] Bukhārī 2239; Muslim 1604.
[229] See also Ibn Rushd (n 50) Vol. 3, p. 219.
[230] Al-Ramlī (n 1) Vol. 4, p. 185; Al-Anṣārī (n 110) Vol. 2, p. 124.
[231] Al-Shīrāzī (n 88) Vol. 2, p. 79; Al-Shāfī'ī (n 139) Vol. 3, p. 95.
[232] Al-Kharshī (n 32) Vol. 5, p. 210; *Al-Mughnī* (n 3) Vol. 4, p. 338; Ibn Juzaī (n 71) p. 178; Al-Ramlī (n 1) Vol. 4, p. 186.
[233] Al-Kāsānī (n 10) Vol. 5, p. 213.
[234] Al-Mughnī (n 3) Vol. 4, p. 357; Al-Ramlī (n 1) Vol. 4, p. 187; Al-Nawawī (n 24) Vol. 4, p. 8.
[235] Al-Buhūtī (n 1) Vol. 3, p. 306; Al-Mughnī (n 3) Vol. 4, p. 366.
[236] Ibn Rushd (n 50) Vol. 2, p. 229; Abū al-Qurṭubī Al-Bājī, Al-Muntaqā Sharḥ al-Muwaṭṭā (Matba'at al-Sa'āda, 1332H) Vol. 4, p. 299.
[237] Al-Anṣārī (n 110) Vol. 2, p. 128; Al-Nawawī (n 24) Vol. 4, pp. 12–13.
[238] Al-Kharshī (n 32) Vol. 5, p. 218; Al-Nawawī (n 24) Vol. 4, p. 11; Al-Buhūtī (n 1) Vol. 3, p. 290.

matter is not required at the time of conclusion of a *salam* contract[239] because in the *ḥadīth* of *salam*, the Prophet did not make availability of subject matter mandatory and did not exclude from *salam* non-existent subject matters. The Hanafis argue that the subject matter should be available in the market at the time of the contract.[240]

5.3 Ownership of the Exchanged Commodities

With the contract of *salam*, the seller acquires title over payment received. Although the ownership of the subject matter of *salam* (*muslam fīhi*) has become credit in favour of the buyer, its ownership has not yet become definitive because it is susceptible to loss or the inability of the seller to deliver it, which will then lead to its voidance[241] and, hence, according to the Hanafis, Shafi'is, and Hanbalis, the buyer cannot sell it.[242] The prohibition on selling it is also based on the saying of the Prophet: 'whoever enters into a *salam* contract, he should not dispose it until he receives it.'[243] The Malikis allow the sale of the subject matter to anyone other than the original seller if it is not a food item which is prohibited from sale before its possession.[244] **11.74**

5.4 Delivery of the Subject Matter (Commodity of *Salam*)

The seller is obligated to make delivery of the subject matter according to the stipulations of the contract, whereupon the buyer is obligated to accept delivery.[245] In case of the buyer's refusal to accept delivery, the judge can accept it on his behalf and the seller shall not be liable for the commodity.[246] However, the purchaser has no right to demand delivery before the agreed date of delivery.[247] Jurists disagree on the outcome arising from the seller's delivery before its due date and the purchaser's refusal to accept it. The Shafi'is and Hanbalis suggest that if such delivery is harmful for the buyer, he will not be bound to accept, since the commodity may be spoilt before the date, or the older commodity may be more valuable than the new one. On the other hand, the buyer will be required to accept delivery if this is not harmful, as in the case of steel whose value does not change, and its receipt will involve no extra cost. The Malikis contend that the acceptance of such delivery is permissible but not obligatory for the buyer. However, the Malikis agree that slightly earlier delivery must be accepted by the buyer.[248] **11.75**

[239] Al-Bājī (n 236) Vol. 4, p. 300; *Al-Mughnī* (n 3) Vol. 4, p. 326.
[240] Al-Kāsānī (n 10) Vol. 5, p. 211.
[241] Al-Suyūṭī (n 18) p. 326.
[242] *Radd al-Muḥtār* (n 8) Vol. 5, p. 318; Al-Zailaʿī (n 212) Vol. 4, p. 118; Al-Anṣārī (n 110) Vol. 2, p. 84; *Al-Mughnī* (n 30) Vol. 4, pp 372. There is disagreement on the lawfulness of other applications of *salam*. See Al-Kāsānī (n 10) Vol. 5, p. 214; Al-Nawawī (n 42) Vol. 13, p. 154.
[243] Al-Darquṭnī 2977; Ibn Māja 2283.
[244] Ibn Rushd (n 50) Vol. 2, p. 205.
[245] Al-Nawawī (n 24) Vol. 4, pp. 29, 30.
[246] *Al-Mughnī* (n 3) Vol. 4, p. 374.
[247] Al-Nawawī (n 24) Vol. 4, p. 30.
[248] Ibn Juzaī (n 71) p. 178.

5.5 Seller's Inability to Make the Delivery

11.76 If the seller fails to make the delivery on the due date, the Hanafis, Malikis, and some of the Shafi'is argue that the buyer has the option to either rescind the contract and take back his payment or wait for the seller's performance. This is so because the contract concerned the purchase of a defined commodity as credit and therefore it shall remain as such. This is not a prerequisite that the commodity be delivered among the agricultural produce of that year; rather, it is what the purchaser stipulated. Therefore, he shall have the option to either continue to wait or rescind the contract.[249] Ibn Rushd says that continuing such a transaction would be a sale of credit for credit. Shīrāzī is of the view that the subject matter is presumed to be the produce of that year and its loss would annul the contract.[250]

5.6 Security as to the Obligation in *Salam*

11.77 The majority of jurists, except the Hanbalis and the international Fiqh Academy, stipulate that there is nothing wrong with the buyer demanding security or a guarantor for his payment in a contract of *salam*.[251] It has also been narrated that taking security in *salam* was disfavoured by some Companions of the Prophet, such as ʿAlī, Ibn ʿUmar, Ibn ʿAbbās, al-Ḥasan, Saʿīd bin Jubair, as well as al-Auzāʿī.[252]

5.7 Modern Applications of the *Salam* Contract

11.78 According to the International Fiqh Academy, *salam* is today considered a highly effective financing instrument in the Islamic economy and in the activities of Islamic banks, given its flexibility and responsiveness to the needs of various sectors of the economy, such as agriculture, construction, and even trade, whether the financing need is short-, medium-, or long-term.[253] The Academy has enumerated the following as areas of application of the *salam* contract:

11.79 *Salam* contracts may be used to finance agricultural activities where Islamic banks deal with farmers who expect to have their commodity available during a particular season, either from their own crop or from that of others, particularly where their crops are insufficient to honour an expected delivery. The bank would thus have extended a benefit

[249] Al-Buhūtī (n 205) Vol. 2, p. 95; Ibn Juzaī (n 71) p. 178; Al-Nawawī (n 24) Vol. 4, p. 11.

[250] Muḥammad Sams al-Dīn, Al-ʿInāya Sharḥ Al-Hidāya (Dār al-Fikr, n.d.) Vol. 9, p. 279; Ibn Juzaī (n 71) p. 178; Al-Nawawī (n 42) Vol. 13, p. 158; Ibn Rushd (n 50) Vol. 2, p. 230.

[251] Resolution No. 85/2/9, International Fiqh Academy in its 9th Round in Abu Dhabi, 1–6 April 1995; ʿIllīsh (n 203) Vol. 5, p. 329; *Radd al-Muḥtār* (n 8) Vol. 5, p. 217; *Al-Mughnī* (n 3) Vol. 4, p. 277; Al-Shafiʿi (n 139) Vol. 3, p. 90.

[252] *Al-Mughnī* (n 3) Vol. 4, p. 374; Al-Buhūtī (n 118) Vol. 2, p. 96.

[253] Resolution No. 85/2/9.

of great value and protected the farmers against failure to achieve their own production targets.

A *salam* contract may be used to finance agricultural or industrial activities, particularly financing the stages before the production and export of the marketed goods, by means of buying them under a *salam* contract and marketing them again at profitable prices. **11.80**

A *salam* contract may be applied in financing artisans, small-scale manufacturers, farmers, or industrialists, by providing them with the necessary production needs in the form of tools, equipment, or raw material as forward capital against access to some of their produce and remarking them.[254] **11.81**

As mentioned in the above resolution of the Fiqh Council, Odeduntan has observed that as the bank or financing institutions have little or nothing to do with farm produce, they serve to benefit from the products in any of the following ways. First, by purchasing the commodity through *salam*, the bank can sell the commodity through a parallel contract of *salam* for the same date of delivery. Since the period of *salam* in the second parallel contract is short-term and the price is higher than in the first contract, the difference between the two prices represents the profit accruable to the bank. In this scenario, the shorter the period of *salam*, the higher the price and greater the profit. As a result, institutions can manage their short-term financing portfolios. Secondly, the bank can obtain a promise to purchase from a third party. Such a promise must be unilateral from the expected buyer. In this case, the buyer need not pay the price in advance. When the bank receives the commodity, it usually reserves the right to sell it at a predetermined price to a third party in line with the terms of the promise.[255] **11.82**

6. *Istiṣnāʿ*

Istiṣnāʿ means to ask for something to be made for the requester.[256] The Hanafis have defined it as a contract to purchase a commodity stipulated to be made or manufactured in the future.[257] Al-Zarqa has defined it as a contract in which a buyer purchases from a manufacturer a thing to be manufactured based on specific qualities subject to a specific price.[258] Examples include: the making of shoes, garments, weapons of war and ships, aeroplanes, rockets, household furniture, construction materials, and other items. **11.83**

[254] Ibid.
[255] Akeem K. Odeduntan, 'Financing Agriculture through Salam' in Islamic Banking and Finance the Nexus with the Real Economy (Proceedings of 2nd International Conference conducted by International Institute of Islamic Banking and Finance, Bayero University Kano Nigeria, 28–29 April 2015) pp. 150–51.
[256] Muḥammad al-Thānawī, Mausūʿāt Kashshāf Iṣṭilaḥāt al-Funūn wa al-ʿUlūm (Maktaba Lubnan, 1996) Vol. 1, p. 155.
[257] Al-Kāsānī (n 10) Vol. 6, p. 2677; Al-Sarakhsī (n 87) Vol. 12, p. 138.
[258] Muṣṭafā al-Zarqā, *'Aqd al-istiṣnāʿ Mujallāt Mujamaʿ al-Fiqh al-Islāmī*, No. 2/8.

6.1 Defining the Rule of *Istiṣnāʿ*

11.84 The Hanafis allow *istiṣnāʿ* as an independent contract on the basis of *istiḥsān* (juristic preference)[259] as the Prophet asked for the making of a ring.[260] According to them, there has always been consistent practice of *istiṣnāʿ* since the time of the Prophet which has never attracted any criticism.[261] However, other schools contend that *istiṣnāʿ* is valid if the conditions of *salam* are present. The *salam* shall be voided if the raw material of the work, such as steel, or the worker, is not identified.[262]

6.2 Essential Elements of *Istiṣnāʿ*

11.85 Essential elements of *istiṣnāʿ* are *sīgha*, the parties to the contract, and the object of *istiṣnāʿ* which includes both the commodity and its cost.

6.2.1 *Ṣīgha* of *Istiṣnāʿ*

11.86 The contract of *istiṣnāʿ* is concluded with whatever indicates the consent of its parties to enter into the said contract.[263] All conditions required in contracts of exchange must be met as it constitutes a contract of mutual obligation.

6.2.2 Parties to the Contract of *Istiṣnāʿ*

11.87 There are two parties in *istiṣnāʿ*: the party asking for production of the desired item (*mustaniʿ*) and the producer, maker, or supplier of the product (*ṣāniʿ*). The basic requirements for the parties in any contract are full legal capacity to perform transactions and the power to contract.[264]

6.2.3 Object of *Istiṣnāʿ*

11.88 The majority of scholars in the Hanafi tradition are of the opinion that the subject matter of *istiṣnāʿ* is the actual product to be produced. The buyer can reject the product only on the basis of a right of option to see and inspect. If the contract is based on the work by the producer alone, the contract would not have been valid if the work was done by another person.[265] In this way, *istiṣnāʿ* requires the product to be produced as well as the labour for the production. Both will be supplied by the *ṣāniʿ*. The type of product must be a transaction allowed by custom.[266]

[259] Al-Kāsānī (n 10) Vol. 6, p. 2678; Ibn al-Humām (n 3) Vol. 5, p. 355.
[260] Bukhārī 5876.
[261] Al-Kāsānī (n 10) Vol. 6, p. 2678.
[262] 'Illīsh (n 203) Vol. 5, p. 386; Al-Shāfiʿī (n 139) Vol. 3, p. 133; Al-Mardāwī (n 11) Vol. 4, p. 300.
[263] Al-Ṣāwī (n 11) Vol. 3, p. 14; Al-Nawawī (n 42) Vol. 9, p. 149; Al-Buhūtī (n 1) Vol. 3, p. 146.
[264] Al-Zuhailī (n 81) Vol. 4, pp. 2960–94.
[265] Al-Sarakhsī (n 87) Vol. 12, p. 139; Al-Kāsānī (n 10) Vol. 5, p. 2. Some among the Hanafis believe that *istiṣnāʿ* refers to work or production. Ibn al-Humām (n 8) Vol. 7, p. 155.
[266] Ibn al-Humām (n 8) Vol. 7, p. 166.

6.3 Effect of *Istiṣnāʿ*

The Hanafis are unanimous that *istiṣnāʿ* is non-binding before the commencement of work and susceptible to termination by either party. Where the contract is completed, the producer has the right to sell it before the party that demands the production sees it. This is because the contract is not targeted at that particular product but rather at a product that has the same qualities.[267] Abū Yūsuf is, however, of the view that where the product is consistent with the qualities required and agreed upon by the parties, it becomes a binding contract and there would be no right of option.[268] 11.89

6.4 Types of *Istiṣnāʿ*

6.4.1 Traditional or Normal *Istiṣnāʿ*

This involves only two parties, namely, the *mustaṣniʿ* and *ṣāniʿ* without anyone mediating between them. The object is to make that which is demanded by the *mustaṣniʿ* based on the agreed price. The raw material is supplied by the producer. This form of *istiṣnāʿ* is the most common as it is used to acquire their basic needs, as well as by companies to secure their supplies through manufacturers that have the capacity to produce said needs. It is also used by governments for infrastructural development through contractors in opening bids.[269] 11.90

6.4.2 Parallel or Investment *Istiṣnāʿ*

This form of *istiṣnāʿ* is developed by banks and consists of two contracts as follows. In the first stage, the bank enters into a contract with its customer who demands the production and supply of a particular product. Here, the bank will be the assumed producer. The price will usually be a credit to be settled by the customer in the future. The bank will then enter into a second contract with the producer mentioned in the first contract as described by their customer. The bank will usually settle with the producer immediately at a price normally less than that agreed by the bank with its customer because the margin will be their profit. When the bank receives the product and this enters into its possession, it will transfer it to the customer as fulfilment of the first contract. The bank's profit will be the margin of the production price over the price agreed with the customer due to the fact the bank has guaranteed the product between its reception and transfer to the customer. Where the product is lost before its transfer to the customer, the customer shall not be liable for the loss. Similarly, any damage to the product or where the product does not satisfy the requirement of the customer, the bank will shoulder the liability. All these risks justify the profit the bank is making. 11.91

[267] Al-Kāsānī (n 10) Vol. 5, p. 3.
[268] *Radd al-Muḥtār* (n 8) Vol. 5, p. 224.
[269] Aḥmad Balkhair, 'Aqd al-istiṣnāʿ wa Taṭbīqātuhu al-Muʿāṣirah (LLM Thesis, Alhaj Lakhḍar University Faculty of Sharia, Department of Economics, 2008) pp. 20–21.

11.92 Contemporary jurists have opined that this sort of contract is permissible. They argue that it is not conditional that the contract of *istiṣnāʿ* is entered into by the person that manufactures the product. Thus, there is nothing wrong with entering into the contract with a non-manufacturer who will then seek the manufacturer to make the products and bring them to the party requiring the product. According to Al-Kāsānī, this is because the contract's effect is not applied to the particular item produced or manufactured; rather, it is a subject matter prescribed to possess the required qualities. It is enough that the manufacturer purchases the product from another person and supplies it to the customer.[270] It is also stated in *Hidāya* that even if the final product is brought but produced by another person before the contract and the party that demands the product accepts it, it is lawful.[271]

6.5 Difference between *Istiṣnāʿ* and *Salam*

11.93 *Istiṣnāʿ* is different from *salam* because the former contract is concluded only for a thing which is to be manufactured, whereas *salam* can be about anything, whether manufactured or not. The consideration in *salam* should be paid in advance, whereas this is not mandatory in *istiṣnāʿ*. *Salam* is binding, whereas *istiṣnāʿ* is not binding.[272]

6.6 Difference between *Istiṣnāʿ* and *Ijāra*

11.94 In *istiṣnāʿ* the manufacturer uses his own material to produce the commodity. If uses the raw material of the customer, this would become *ijāra* and the manufacturer will receive remuneration.[273]

6.7 Termination of *Istiṣnāʿ*

11.95 An *istiṣnāʿ* contract is terminated by producing the requested product and delivering it, as well as acceptance along with the settlement of its cost.[274] Similarly, the contract is terminated if one of the parties dies, in the same manner that the death of a party in the course of an *ijāra* contract serves to terminate it.[275]

270 Al-Kāsānī (n 10) Vol. 5, p. 3.
271 Al-Marghīnānī, Al-Hidāya Sharḥ Bidāyat al-Mubtadī (Dār Ihyā' al-Turāth al-'Arabī, n.d.) Vol. 3, p. 77.
272 Usmani (n 138) p. 196.
273 Ibid, pp. 196–97.
274 Al-Sālūs (n 99) Vol. 3, p. 329.
275 *Radd al-Muḥtār* (n 8) Vol. 7, p. 166.

7. *Ṣarf*

Ṣarf has been technically defined as selling *thaman* for *thaman*. *Thaman* (plural *athmān*) is anything designated to serve as the price for payment of an object or service that is accepted to serve as currency, whether it is silver, gold, copper, or brass coins.[276] The Malikis argue that this is sale of cash (*naqd*) for other forms of cash (*naqd*), such as selling gold for silver.[277] In modern times, it is any legal tender that serves as money in different countries. 11.96

7.1 Legality of *Ṣarf*

The sale of *athmān* is permissible subject so some conditions.[278] Allah has permitted it in the Qur'ān as follows: 'But Allah has permitted trade and has forbidden interest.'[279] 'Ubādah bin al-Ṣāmit narrates that the Prophet said that '(exchanging) gold for gold, silver for silver, barley for barley, wheat for wheat, date for date, salt for salt should be same for same, equal for equal, hand to hand. If any of these elements differ, sell either of them as you wish if it is hand to hand (i.e. immediate transfer of possession)' ('First *Ḥadīth*' hereinafter).[280] The meaning of equal for equal is in terms of quantity not form; as the Prophet has said, high quality and low quality are all the same.[281] The Prophet has also said 'do not sell gold for gold unless it is equal for equal; do not increase one over the other. Do not sell silver for silver unless it is equal for equal; do not increase one over the other' ('Second *Ḥadīth*' hereinafter).[282] 11.97

7.2 Conditions for the Validity of *Ṣarf*

As the contract of *ṣarf* involves exchange of currencies (traditionally gold and silver) to get profit which involves usury, jurists have prescribed several conditions that distinguish usurious transactions from *ṣarf*: 11.98

- Parties should transfer the possession of the subject matter at the same contract session without separation.[283] The basis of this is the Second *Ḥadīth*;[284] the *ḥadīth*

276 Ibid, Vol. 5, p. 257; Al-Kāsānī (n 10) Vol. 5, p. 215; Al-Shirbīnī (n 5) Vol. 2, p. 364; *Al-Mughnī* (n 3) Vol. 4, p.134.
277 Al-Dusūqī (n 8) Vol. 3, p. 2; Al-Ḥaṭṭāb (n 1) Vol. 4, p. 226.
278 Al-Dusūqī (n 8) Vol. 3, p. 2.
279 Qur'ān 2:275.
280 Muslim 1587.
281 Muḥammad al-Bābartī, Al-Ināya Sharḥ al-Hidāya (Dār al-Fikr, n.d.) Vol. 7, p. 4.
282 Bukhārī 2177; Muslim 1584.
283 Al-Kāsānī (n 10) Vol. 5, p. 215; Ibn Juzaī (n 71) p. 166; Al-Shīrāzī (n 88) Vol. 2, p. 28; *Al-Mughnī* (n 3) Vol. 4, p. 192; Al-Buhūtī (n 1) Vol. 3, p. 266.
284 Al-Bābartī (n 281) Vol. 7, p. 4.
Bukhārī 2177; Muslim 1584.

exhorting to 'sell gold with silver however you want it hand to hand';[285] and, another *ḥadīth* '(selling) gold with silver is usurious unless it is hand to hand'.[286] A separation invalidating the *ṣarf* contract is physical separation; for instance, if they both sleep at the place of contract session or if they go together to the house of one of them and transfer the possession of subject matter there, *ṣarf* is valid.[287] This is so for the *ṣarf* involving same usurious commodities such as selling gold for gold or different commodities like sales of gold for silver.[288]

- No right of option is available to any party in *ṣarf*[289] because delivery of currency is a condition for the validity of *ṣarf* and the right of option undermines the purpose of possession and thus impedes confirmation of ownership and the conclusion of a contract.[290] If the right of option is dropped in the contract session, the contract is validated.[291]
- It is not permissible to delay transfer of possession of commodities or cash in a *ṣarf* contract to a future date, as the entitlement of the exchanged commodity is established before separation.[292] If the stipulation for delayed transfer is rescinded in the same contract session and possession is delivered there before separation, *ṣarf* becomes valid.[293]
- If commodities of the same type are exchanged, for example gold for gold or silver for silver, both the exchanged commodities must be equal in weight even if the quality of their moulding differs.[294] This is on the basis of the Second *Ḥadīth*.[295]

7.3 Legal Effects of *Ṣarf*

11.99 Generally, the option of a condition (*khiyār al-sharṭ*) does not apply in the contract of *ṣarf* because this has to be concluded and executed immediately.[296] However, the option of defect does not prevent conclusion of the contract or its execution as the absence of defect is a typical requirement just as in any contract of sale.[297] Hence, the Hanafis maintain that if the exchanged commodity is found to be defective the contract shall be voided, but if it is replaced the *ṣarf* can be allowed.[298] Where the defect is discovered

[285] Tirmidhī 1285.
[286] Bukhārī 2134.
[287] Al-Kāsānī (n 10) Vol. 5, p. 215; Ibn al-Humām (n 3) Vol. 6, p. 259; Al-Shirbīnī (n 5) Vol. 2, p. 29; Al-Buhūtī (n 1) Vol. 3, p. 266.
[288] Al-Kāsānī (n 10) Vol. 5, p. 216.
[289] Ibid, Vol. 5, p. 219; Al-Azharī (n 60) Vol. 2, p. 14; Al-Buhūtī (n 118) Vol. 2, p. 73.
[290] Ibid, Vol. 5, p. 219.
[291] Ibid; Ibn al-Humām (n 3) Vol. 7, p. 132; Al-Buhūtī (n 118) Vol. 2, p. 73.
[292] Al-Kāsānī (n 10) Vol. 5, p. 219; Al-Shirbīnī (n 5) Vol. 3, p. 24; Al-Buhūtī (n 1) Vol. 3, p. 264.
[293] Al-Kāsānī (n 10) Vol. 5, p. 219.
[294] *Radd al-Muḥtār* (n 8) Vol. 4, p. 234; Ibn Juzaī (n 71) p. 251; Al-Azharī (n 60) Vol. 2, p. 10; Al-Shirbīnī (n 5) Vol. 2, p. 24; *Al-Mughnī* (n 3) Vol. 4, p. 39.
[295] Bukhārī 2177; Muslim 1584.
[296] Al-Sarakhsī (n 87) Vol. 14, p. 3; Al-Ḥaṭṭāb (n 1) Vol. 6, p. 137; Al-Nawawī (n 42) Vol. 9, p. 188; Al-Buhūtī (n 1) Vol. 4, p. 250.
[297] Al-Sarakhsī (n 87) Vol. 13, p. 193; Al-Buhūtī (n 1) Vol. 3, p. 268; Al-Ḥaṭṭāb (n 1) Vol. 6, p. 164; Al-Nawawī (n 42) Vol. 12, p. 183.
[298] Al-Kāsānī (n 10) Vol. 5, p. 220.

in some of the exchanged commodity, the contract shall be void to the extent that the defective commodity can be returned back to the seller.[299] The Malikis argue that if the buyer approves the defective commodity, then he will be compensated for the reduction in value. If the buyer rejects, the contract shall be voided, and each party shall take back what it gave.[300]

[299] *Radd al-Muḥtār* (n 8) Vol. 4, p. 236.
[300] Al-Sawī (n 11) Vol. 3, p. 59; Al-Azharī (n 60) Vol. 2, p. 13; similarly, for the Shafi'is and Hanbalis, see Al-Anṣārī (n 110) Vol. 2, p. 76; Al-Buhūtī (n 1) Vol. 3, pp. 267–68.

12

Unilateral Contracts

1. Introduction

12.01 The requirement of offer and acceptance to create a contract implies the existence of two parties, thus excluding the unilateral formation of a binding agreement.[1] Examining the verb *ʿaqada* which is the root of the word *ʿaqd* (contract) leads to a different conclusion. *ʿAqada* means tying a rope or any other tangible or intangible object.[2] This term also denotes covenants and agreements which bind people through their mutual consent.[3] In its broader sense, *ʿaqd* means every *iltizām* (obligation) or *taṣarruf* (disposition), unilateral or bilateral, that initiates a legal effect.[4] Al-Ḥaṭṭāb has defined *ʿaqd* as obliging oneself with something that is not binding and which upon approval becomes binding.[5] For this reason, *ʿaqd* (contract) is synonymous with *iltizām* in the general sense, given that in its stricter sense the term *ʿaqd* covers a specific type of obligation (*iltizām*) which emanates from transactions involving at least two persons, such as purchase, sale, and lease. *Iltizām*, in its wider sense, also includes unilateral actions, such as the declaration of *waqf*, vowing, oaths, etc.; or transactions emanating from two persons as in the case of contracts of exchange.[6] *Taṣarruf* (disposition) refers to any conduct that emanates from an individual with his volition and upon which a ruling of Sharī'ah applies.[7] The concept of *taṣarruf* is much wider than *ʿaqd* in both its general and specific senses. This is true, for instance, where a right is created, transferred, amended, or discharged, irrespective of whether such actions emanate from one person, as is the case with *waqf* and *ibrāʿ* (absolution), or from two persons, such as sales and lease.[8] The standard definition among the Malikis, Shafi'is, and Hanbalis is that a contract consists of 'every conduct from which a legal obligation emanates'.[9]

[1] Al-Dusūqī, Ḥāshiyat al-Dusūqī ʿalā al-Sharḥ al-Kabīr (Dār al-Fikr, n.d.) Vol. 4, p. 71; Ibn Rushd, Bidāyat al-Mujtahid wa Nihāyat al-Muqtaṣid (Muṣṭafā al-Ḥalabī, 1975) Vol. 2, pp. 171–355; Majalla, Arts 103, 104; Wahba Al-Zuhailī, Al-Fiqh al-Islāmī wa Adillatuhu (Dār al-Fikr, 2007) Vol. 4, p. 2918.

[2] ʿAbd Allāh Bayḍāwī, Anwār al-Tanzīl wa Asrār al-Ta'wīl (Dār Iḥyā' al-Turāth al-ʿArabī, 2012) Vol. 3, p. 201.

[3] Muʿjam Maqāyīs al-Lugha, Vol. 4, p. 86; Lisān al-ʿArab, Vol. 3, p. 296; Tāj al-ʿArūs, Vol. 8, p. 394.

[4] Ibn Taimiyya, Nazariyyat al-ʿAqd (Sunna al-Muḥammadiyya, 1949) pp. 18–21; Al-Jaṣṣāṣ, Ahkām al-Qur'ān (Dār al-Iḥyā' al-Turāth, 1984) Vol. 2, p. 294.

[5] Abū al-Ḥaṭṭāb, Taḥrīr al-Kalām fī Masā'il al-Iltizām (Dār al-Gharb al-Islāmī, 1984) p. 68.

[6] Al-Zuhailī (n 1) Vol. 4, p. 2918.

[7] Aḥmad Al-Sālūs, Mausūʿāt al-Qaḍāyā al-Fiqhiyya al-Muʿāṣira wa al-Iqtiṣād al-Islāmī (Dār Umm al-Qurā, 2001) Vol. 12, p. 71.

[8] Al-Shaibānī, Al-Ḥujja ʿalā Ahl al-Madīna (ʿĀlam al-Kutub, 1403H) Vol. 2, p. 734; Al-Dusūqī (n 1) Vol. 3, p. 71; Ibrāhīm Farḥūn, Tabṣirāt al-Ḥukkām fī Uṣūl al-ʿAqḍiya wa Manāhij al-Aḥkām (Maktabat al-Kulliyyāt al-Azhariyya, 1986) Vol. 3, p.71.

[9] Maḥmūd Ṣāleh, ʿUqūd Idh'an wa al-Mumārasāt al-Ma'ībʿa lahā (n.p., 2004).

12.02 Thus, contracts are classified based on an individual's ability to undertake the underlying obligations independently. This has given rise to two general types of contracts, unilateral and bilateral. In unilateral contracts, such as vows and *waqf*, according to Al Zarakhshī there is no requirement that the conduct be accepted by another party.[10] These contracts are also known as *'uqūd tabarru'āt* (gratuitous contracts) because they are concluded without consideration.

12.03 This chapter discusses the leading instances of unilateral contracts, that is, promise, gift, loan, will, and endowment. As discussed in the preceding segments, Islamic legal theory sets out necessary conditions for the validity of a unilateral contract. These concern the quality of the offer, the contracting parties, and the subject matter of the unilateral contract.

2. *Wa'ad* (Binding Promise)

12.04 *Wa'ad*, or promise, is a notification whereby the promisor seeks to convey something to another person, or creates an obligation in favour of another with a promise to perform in future.[11] The promise without an intention to perform is not a *wa'ad*,[12] although this has been termed a promise in a *ḥadīth* by the Prophet as follows: 'The signs of a hypocrite are three: when he speaks, he lies; when he promises, he breaks it; and when he was entrusted, he cheats.'[13] Most jurists have interpreted the promise mentioned in this *ḥadīth* as one made with the intention of not fulfilling it without any plausible excuse.[14]

2.1 Permissibility of *Wa'ad*

12.05 A promise is generally lawful in Islam. Allah says in the Qur'ān: 'Also mention in the Book (the story of) Ismā'īl. He was (strictly) true to what he promised, and he was an apostle (and) a prophet.'[15] This *āya* implies that fulfilling a promise is a virtuous act and makes a promise lawful. Similarly, Jabir bin 'Abdullah has narrated that once the Prophet said: 'If the money of Bahrain comes, I will give you a certain amount of it. The Prophet had breathed his last breath before the money of Bahrain arrived. When the money of Bahrain arrived, Abū Bakr announced: "Whoever was promised by the Prophet should come to us." I went to Abū Bakr and said: "The Prophet promised me so and so." Abū Bakr gave me a handful of coins and when I counted them, they were five

[10] Al-Zarkashī, Al-Manthūr fī al-Qawā'id al-Fiqhiyya (Ministry of Endowments, 1985) Vol. 2, pp. 397–98.
[11] Al-'Ainī, 'Umdat al-Qārī fī Sharḥ Ṣaḥīḥ al-Bukhārī (Al-Munīriyya, n.d.) Vol. 1, p. 220; Muḥammad Al-Anṣārī, Sharḥ Ḥudūd ibn 'Arafa - al-Hidāya al-Kāfiya al-Shāfiya li Bayāni Ḥaqā'iq al-Imām ibn 'Arafa al-Wāfiya (Al-Maktabah al-'Ilmiyyah, 1350H) p. 428.
[12] Al-Anṣārī (n 11) p. 429.
[13] Bukhārī 33; Muslim 107.
[14] Al-Ghazālī, Iḥyā al 'Ulūm al-Dīn (Dār al-Ma'rifa, 1982) Vol. 3, p. 133.
[15] Qur'ān 19:54.

hundred in number. Abū Bakr then said: "Take twice the amount you have taken (besides)." '[16] This *ḥadīth* demonstrates the legality and permissibility of promises.

2.2 Lawfulness of Actions Invoking Promises

Muslim jurists generally agree that fulfilment of a promise to perform unlawful acts is **12.06** not permissible.[17] The Prophet said: 'there shall be no (fulfilment of) vowing (*nadhr*) a sinful act.'[18] This *ḥadīth* implies that where a Muslim is not allowed to undertake a prohibited act promised between him and Allah, he is also prohibited from performing such acts promised with other persons.

If a person promises to perform obligatory actions (taking care of one's parents, **12.07** maintaining one's wife, or paying debts), he would be obligated to perform them.[19] The promise to perform lawful or *mubāḥ* actions is recommended.[20] It seems that the promise to perform what is already obligatory as well as otherwise recommended actions has not added to the binding nature of these actions.

2.3 Is a Promise Binding on the Promisor?

While there is disagreement as to whether a promise is binding, there is no dispute re- **12.08** garding its preference as good conduct on which every believer must aspire to reach. In the Qur'ān it is stated that Allah has said: 'Also mentioned in the Book (the story of) Ismā'īl. He was (strictly) true to what he promised, and he was an apostle (and) a prophet.'[21] Allah says: 'And fulfil (every) commitment. Indeed, the commitment is ever [that about which one will be] questioned.'[22] In another verse, He says: 'And fulfil the covenant of Allah when you have taken it, [O believers], and do not break oaths after their confirmation while you have made Allah, over you, a security [i.e., witness]. Indeed, Allah knows what you do.'[23] The Prophet himself is quoted as saying: 'The signs of a hypocrite are three: when he speaks, he lies; when he promises, he breaks it; and when he was entrusted, he cheats.'[24]

Regarding whether a promise is binding or strongly recommended, jurists have ex- **12.09** pressed diverging views, as follows.

[16] Bukhārī 2296 and Muslim 2314.
[17] Al-Jaṣṣāṣ (n 4) Vol. 5, p. 334.
[18] Muslim, *Ḥadīth* 1641.
[19] Ibn Hazm, Al-Muḥallā (Al-Tibā'a al-Munīriyya, 1374H) Vol. 8, p. 29; Al-Jaṣṣāṣ (n 4) Vol. 3, p. 442.
[20] Al-Jaṣṣāṣ (n 4) Vol. 3, p. 442 and Vol. 5, p. 334; Al-Ḥaṭṭāb (n 5) p. 160; Abū Mūsā Al-Qurṭubī, Al-Istidhkār al-Jām'i li Madhāhib Fuqahā al-Amṣār (Dār Qutaiba, 1993) Vol. 14, p. 349.
[21] Qur'ān 19:54.
[22] Qur'ān 17:34.
[23] Qur'ān 16:91.
[24] Bukhārī 33; Muslim 107.

2.3.1 Non-obligatory Nature of the Promise

12.10 According to the majority of jurists (Shafi'is, Hanbalis, and some Malikis), the fulfilment of a promise is not binding, whether by reference to religion or law, even if the promisee has incurred some liability or committed to some cause by relying on such a promise. Instead, the promise being superogatory (*sunna*), its performance attracts a reward, and there is no sin for failure to fulfil it.[25] For instance, if a person promises another to give him a specified or unspecified amount of money or to appoint him to a particular position, this would be a non-binding promise. However, failure to fulfil such a promise is disliked.[26] This opinion is based on an *āya* of the Qur'ān:

> And never say of anything, 'Indeed, I will do that tomorrow;' Except [when adding], 'If Allah wills.' And remember your Lord when you forget [it] and say, 'Perhaps my Lord will guide me to what is nearer than this to right conduct'.[27]

This verse implies that making a promise without subjecting it to Allah's will is a sinful act and is prohibited. Similarly, if a promisor has made a promise by subjecting it to Allah's will and is unable to perform it, he would not be in breach of the promise, which exemplifies the non-binding nature of the promise.[28] However, some scholars argue that subjecting a promise to Allah's will without any intention to perform it is a lie, and its non-fulfilment will be deemed a breach of the promise.[29]

12.11 Another basis for holding a promise non-binding is derived from a *ḥadīth* of the Prophet as follows: 'If a man promises his brother and it is his intention to fulfil that promise but was unable to fulfill the promise and did not come on the appointed day, there shall be no sin upon him.'[30] The proponents of the non-binding nature of promises have interpreted this *ḥadīth* to mean that the prohibition against breaching a promise applies only to the promise made without any intention to perform.[31] Others have, however, rejected this view because the *ḥadīth* is weak (*ḍa'īf*). Even if the *ḥadīth* is sound, it does not indicate that fulfilling a promise is not obligatory; rather, the absence of sin or religious liability is assumed only to be applicable where there is a legally acceptable excuse for not fulfilling the promise.[32]

[25] Abā Zakariyya Al-Nawawī, Rauḍat al-Ṭālibīn wa 'Umdat al-Muftīn (Al-Maktab al-Islāmī, 1991) Vol. 5, pp. 390; Al-Mardāwī, Al-Inṣāf fī Ma'rifat al-Rājiḥ min al-Khilāf 'alā Madh'hab al-Imām Aḥmad bin Ḥanbal (Maṭba'at al-Sunna al-Muḥammadiyya, 1956) Vol. 11, p. 152; Ibn Rushd, Al-Bayān wa al-Taḥṣīl wa al-Sharḥ wa al-Taujīh wa al-Ta'līl li Masā'il al-Mustakhraja (Dār al-Gharb al-Islāmī, 1988) Vol. 8, p. 18; Muḥammad bin Muflih Faraj, Al-Furū' fī Fiqh al-Imām Aḥmad bin Ḥanbal (Mu'assasāt al-Risāla, 2003) Vol. 11, p. 92.

[26] Ibn Ḥazm (n 19) Vol. 8, p. 28.

[27] Qur'ān 18:23–24.

[28] Ibrāhiīm Muflih, Al-Mubdi' Sharḥ al-Muqni' (Dār al-Kutub al-'Ilmiyya, 1997) Vol. 8, p. 138; Ibn Ḥazm (n 19) Vol. 8, pp. 29–30.

[29] Zain al-Dīn Al-Ḥanbalī, Jāmi' al-'Ulūm wa al-Ḥikam (Mu'assasāt al-Risāla, 1999) Vol. 2, p. 482.

[30] Abū Dāwūd 4995. Al-Bānī has however declared the *ḥadīth* as *ḍa'īf* (weak).

[31] Shihāb Al-Qarāfī, Al-Dhakhīra (Dār al Garb al Islāmī, 2008) Vol. 6, p. 199.

[32] 'Ali al-Harāwī Al-Qārī, Murqāt al-Mafātīḥ Sharḥ Mushkāt al-Maṣābiḥ (Dār al-Fikr, 2002) Vol. 9, p. 103.

2.3.2 Binding Nature of the Promise

According to the second opinion, fulfilling a promise is unconditionally binding on the promisor, both religiously and legally. If the promisor fails to perform his promise, he commits a sin, and the court can enforce such promise. This is the opinion of the Malikis[33] as well as some Hanbalis, including Ibn Taimiyya.[34] They base their opinion on an *āya* of the Qur'ān as follows: 'And fulfil (every) commitment. Indeed, the commitment is ever [that about which one will be] questioned.'[35] They also rely on the following verse in the Qur'ān: 'And fulfil the covenant of Allah when you have taken it, [O believers], and do not break oaths after their confirmation while you have made Allah, over you, a security [i.e., witness]. Indeed, Allah knows what you do.'[36] In their opinion, these verses suggest that Allah has commanded fulfilment of commitments and covenants, which includes promises and contracts which a man has obliged upon himself with an individual or Allah.[37] **12.12**

The significance attached by the Prophet to the fulfilment of promises implies that any breach thereof is prohibited.[38] However, others have disagreed, contending that the mere criticism of non-fulfilment of a promise does not render the breach a prohibited act.[39] In justification, this school cites the *ḥadīth* of the Prophet whereby if a man makes a promise intending to perform it but was unable to fulfil it, there shall be no sin upon him.[40] This *ḥadīth* indicates that non-performance of a promise made without any intention to perform it would attract sin.[41] **12.13**

Even so, Al-Subkī and Ibn Ḥajar al-Asqalānī, both of the Shafi'i school, have opined that a promise is binding religiously (non-performance will render it sinful) but not unlawful (i.e. a judge cannot enforce it).[42] Ibn al Arabi of the Maliki school says that if there is an excuse, the promise would not be binding, and for this he based his opinion on the *ḥadīth* of the Prophet whereby: 'If a man promises his brother and it is his intention to fulfil that promise but was unable to fulfill the promise and did not come on the appointed day, there shall be no sin upon him.'[43] This opinion is also based **12.14**

33 Ibn Rushd (n 25) Vol. 8, p. 18; Al-Ḥaṭṭāb (n 5) pp. 160–64; Abū al-Qāsim Al-Shāṭ, Ibn al-Shāṭ, Idrār al-Shurūq 'alā Anwā' al-Furūq (Dār al-Kutub al-'Ilmiyya, 1998) Vol. 4, p. 57.

34 Al-Mardāwī (n 25) Vol. 11, p. 152. It has also been narrated that 'Umar bin 'Abdul 'Azīz, as narrated by Ibn Rushd, Ibn al-Ashwa', Ibn Ḥajar, Ibn Shubruma, and Ibn Ḥazm, all enforced promises as binding in their judgments. See Ibn Rushd (n 25) Vol. 15, p. 317; Ibn Mufliḥ (n 25) Vol. 11, p. 93. Al-'Asqalānī, Fatḥ al-Bārī bi Sharḥ Ṣaḥīḥ al-Bukhārī (Dār al-Ma'rifa, 1379H) Vol. 5, p. 290; Ibn Ḥazm (n 19) Vol. 8, p. 28.

35 Qur'ān 17:34.

36 Qur'ān 16:91.

37 Jamāluddīn al-Faraj, 'Abdurraḥmān Al-Jauzī, Zād al-Maṣīr fī 'Ilm al-Tafsīr (Dār al-Kitāb al- 'Arabī, 1422H) Vol. 3, p. 24.

38 Al-Qarāfī (n 31) Vol. 6, p. 299.

39 Ibid.

40 Abū Dā'ūd 4995. Al-Bānī has however declared the *ḥadīth* as ḍa'īf (weak).

41 Muḥammad Mubārak Fūrī, Tuḥfat al-Aḥwadhī bi-sharḥ Jāmi' al-Tirmidhī (Dār Iḥyā' al-Turāth al-'Arabī, 2009) Vol. 7, p. 321.

42 Tāj al-Dīn Al-Subkī, Tabaqāt al-Shāfi'iyya al-Kubrā (Dār Iḥyā' al-Kutub al- 'Arabiyya, n.d.) Vol. 10, p. 232; Ibn Ḥajar Al-'Asqalāni, Fath al-Bārī fī Sharḥ Ṣaḥīḥ al-Bukhārī (Dār al-Kitāb al-Jadīd, 1969) Vol. 5, p. 290.

43 Abū Dā'ū 4995.

on jurisprudential reasoning (*qā'ida uṣūliyya*) that the Sharī'ah does not oblige that which is impossible to perform. Thus, if an excuse prevents the promisor from fulfilling the promise and it is beyond his choice, execution of such promise shall not be obligatory.[44]

2.3.3 Promise Becomes Binding Only if There is a Condition Precedent

12.15 According to this line of thinking, the fulfilment of the promise is not binding unless it is attached to a condition precedent. Thus, if A tells B 'sell this to C and if he does not pay you, I will pay it', the fulfilment of such a promise is binding upon A. However, where it is an abstract promise and is not attached to a condition precedent, it shall not be binding. Thus, if A promises to pay B's indebtedness without attaching any condition, it shall not be binding upon A, even though it is religiously recommended for him to fulfil such a promise. This opinion is held by the Hanafis[45] and is based on the verse of Qur'ān in which Allah says: 'O you who have believed, why do you say what you do not do? Great is hatred in the sight of Allah that you say what you do not do.'[46]

12.16 It has been argued, however, that the verse is generally applicable to anything that one says but does not perform, regardless of whether the promise is contingent on a condition precedent. As a result, limiting the application of the verse to this particular category cannot be recognized as a strong inference.

2.3.4 Promise Becoming Binding When Linked with a Cause and the Promisee's Reliance on Promise

12.17 The fulfilment of a promise is binding only when it is linked to a cause (*sabab*). Thus, if A asks B to give him a loan to get married and he agrees, such a promise is binding. However, where the promise is not linked to a cause, it shall not be binding, such as where A asks for a loan without stating the cause and B accepts to grant the loan. This opinion is the preferred opinion among Malikis and it is a narration of Aṣbugh.[47]

12.18 However, according to a famous narration among the Malikis, which is also preferred by Ibn Qāsim and Saḥnūn, in order for a promise to be considered binding, in addition to a cause, the promisee should have relied on that promise. For instance, where A promises B to give him a dowry if he gets married or provides him a loan to build his house if he demolishes it, the fulfilment of such a promise is binding upon the promisor,

[44] Muḥammad al-Khādimī Al-Ḥanafī, Barīqa Maḥmūdiyya fī Sharḥ Tarīqa Muḥammadiyya wa Sharī'a Nabawiyya fī Sīra Aḥmadiyya (Maṭba'at al- Ḥalabī, 1384H) Vol. 2, p. 284.

[45] Ibn Nujaim, Al-Ashbāh wa al-Naẓā'ir 'alā Madhahb Abī Hanīfa (Dār al-Kutub al- 'Ilmiyya, 1999) p. 247.

[46] Qur'ān 61:2–3.

[47] Ibn Rushd (n 25) Vol. 15, p. 343; Abū Muḥammad Al-Qairawānī, Al-Nawādir wa al-Ziyādāt 'ālā mā fī al-Mudawwana min Ghairihā min al-Ummahāt (Dār al-Gharb al-Islāmī, 1999) Vol. 12, pp. 205–06; Al-Qarāfī (n 31) Vol. 6, pp. 2978, 298; Muḥammad Al-Abdarī, Al-Tāj wa al-Iklīl li Mukhtaṣar al-Khalīl (Dār al-Fikr, 1978) Vol. 7, p. 301.

and a judge can enforce it after the promisee takes the proposed actions and not before that.[48] The requirement of the promisee's reliance on the promise in order to be considered binding may be that the promisor has incited the promisee to spend something or incur some liability, and it is the inciting party that should bear the burden so that no harm or counter-harm be caused (*lā ḍarara wa lā ḍirāra*).[49]

2.4 Conditions Applicable to the Binding Promise

Apart from the conditions mentioned above as to the condition precedent, as well as the cause and reliance of the promisee on the promise, there may be several other conditions regulating the binding nature of promises. These other conditions are determined by the form the promise takes. For instance, A tells B that if he gives him his car he in turn promises to give him something else. Alternatively, A tells B that if he forgives a loan owed to C, he promises to give him some property in return. This is a contract of exchange to which the conditions of the contract of sale would apply. These include the absence of *jahāla* (ambiguity) on the subject matter of the contract and the consideration and absence of *gharar* (ambiguity).[50] Where the promisor promises to give something for the enjoyment of the promisee's property, such promise shall be treated as a rent agreement, and all conditions applicable in *ijāra*, such as defined time and usufruct as well what is promised as consideration, must all be known. The subject matter of the promise is conduct to be performed in favour of the promisor; for example, if you bring back my lost camel, I will give you a specific amount; or if you find water while digging a well, I will give a certain amount of money. Such a promise shall be treated as *juʿāla* and it only becomes binding if the stipulated conduct is performed.[51] **12.19**

2.5 Revocation of Promise

The promisor cannot revoke a legally enforceable binding promise after the promisee has taken action by which he or she has relied on such promise, as in this case its revocation would be detrimental to the promisee. If the promisee has not taken or initiated action by relying on the promise or where the condition precedent did not materialize, the promisor can revoke the promise. **12.20**

[48] Ibn Rushd (n 25) Vol. 15, p. 343; Al-Qairawānī (n 47) Vol. 12, p. 204; Al-Qarāfī (n 31) Vol. 6, pp. 297–98; Al-Ḥaṭṭāb (n 5) pp. 161–62.

[49] Muḥammad al-ʿAzīz, Juʿaiṭ, Majālis al-Irfān wa Mawāhib al-Ra ḥmān (Mediterranean Publisher, n.d.) Vol. 2, p. 34.

[50] Al-Ḥaṭṭāb (n 5) p. 200.

[51] Ibid, p. 203.

3. Gift (*Hiba*)

3.1 Nature and Validity of Gift

12.21 The notion of gift under Islamic law signifies the transfer of ownership of lawful property to another person without exchange for any benefit in return.[52] A gift is a valid contract that is approved by both the Qur'ān and *ḥadīth* in several texts. The Qur'ān used the word *yahabū* (derived from *hiba*), meaning gift. It is stated therein: 'He (Allah) gives female (offspring) upon whom He wills and gives male (offspring) to whom he wills.'[53] At another place, Allah says: 'but if they, of their own pleasure, give/remit any part of it to you, take it and enjoy it without fear of any harm (as Allah has made it lawful).'[54] The Prophet said: 'give presents to one another for this would increase your mutual love.'[55] 'Āisha related that the Prophet used to accept gifts and give something in return.[56] The Prophet said: 'give present to one another for present removes rancour from the heart.'[57]

12.22 A gift to relatives is preferable to one given to neighbours, and a gift to relatives and neighbours is preferable to a gift to other non-relatives.[58] A grantee can sell the subject matter of a gift after he has accepted it and when he dies it becomes the subject of inheritance.[59] Modern Shafi'i scholars allow the association of gift to a specific time span, that is, a gift for the lifetime of the grantee only that can be enjoyed only by the grantee while he or she is alive. Older juristic opinion holds such gift void.[60]

3.2 How the Gift is Different from Other Transactions

12.23 When a gift is made with the intent of having a reward from Allah, it becomes *sadaqa*, which is allowed even for the rich. If no reward is intended, then it is just a gift.[61] The point of difference between gift and sale concerns the effects of revocation. After revocation, the grantee of a gift holds the property in trust, while in the case of a sale, the buyer holds it as guarantor.[62]

[52] Al-Abdarī (n 47) Vol. 10, p. 389; Muḥammad Al-Shirbīnī, Al-Mughnī al-Muḥtāj ilā Ma'rifat Alfāẓ al-Minhāj (Dār al-Kutub al-'Ilmiyya, 1994) Vol. 10, p. 194.
[53] Qur'ān 42:49.
[54] Qur'ān, Nisā 4:4.
[55] Imām Muslim, Sunan Muslim (Dār al-'Arabiyya, 2010) Vol. 2, p. 857.
[56] Ibid.
[57] Imām Tirmidhī, Sunan Tirmidhī (Dār Al-Hadīth, 2010) Vol. 4, p. 441.
[58] Al-Shirbīnī (n 52) Vol. 10, p. 194.
[59] Ibid, Vol. 10, p. 87.
[60] Al-Shirbīnī (n 52) Vol. 3, p. 571.
[61] Ibid, Vol. 3, p. 558.
[62] Ibid, Vol. 3, p. 571.

3.3 Requirements of a Valid Gift

The conditions for a valid gift are offer and acceptance, the existence of the parties, valid subject matter, and the delivery of the gift to the grantee.[63] **12.24**

3.3.1 Offer and Acceptance

The gift is valid once there is an offer and acceptance, and the donor will not be allowed to deny it.[64] All the standard conditions concerning *ṣīgha* are relevant to gift contracts. The offer can be made in the form of 'I give you' or 'I grant you ownership'.[65] The acceptance can take the form of 'I accept', or 'I agree'. Acceptance is a requirement for the validity of a gift, but sometimes acceptance may not be required. For example, when a person asked another: 'free your slave for me'. If the grantor frees the slave, there will be no need for acceptance.[66] Similarly, an announcement by the father of a gift to his son is tantamount to acceptance of the gift.[67] A delay in acceptance does not serve as a rejection of the offer.[68] A gift with a condition will not invalidate the gift; rather, the condition shall be rejected while the gift remains valid.[69] **12.25**

If a gift of a property is made to two persons, the one present can accept on behalf of his absent co-donee.[70] However, if the absent person accepted after the death of his partner, the acceptance is not valid.[71] Hence, consent is a *sine qua non* requirement for a gift, and a guardian cannot gift the property of a woman without her consent,[72] nor can a partnership gift its property without the consent of its partners.[73] Consent for the gift should be free and without the exercise of any duress.[74] **12.26**

3.3.2 Parties

Every Muslim that has reached the age of maturity and is mentally sane can make a gift.[75] The donor must have ownership of the property and the power to dispose. For instance, a guardian cannot gift his ward's property, as is the case with property inherited by a child.[76] The grantee should have the capacity to accept the gift. Gifts to a foetus or an animal are invalid, but the guardian can accept the gift on behalf of his ward.[77] **12.27**

[63] Al-Mardāwī (n 25) Vol. 8, p. 87; 'Abdullah Al-Mauṣilī, Al-Ikhtiyār li Ta'līl al-Mukhtār (Dār al-Kutub al-'Ilmiya, 1937) Vol. 3, p. 54; Ibn al-Humām, Fat'ḥ al-Qadīr Sharḥ al-Hidāya (Dār al-Fikr, n.d.) Vol. 6, p. 507.
[64] Al-Abdarī (n 47) Vol. 10, p. 389.
[65] Al-Shirbīnī (n 52) Vol. 3, p. 558.
[66] Ibid; Al-Samarqandī, Tuḥfat al-Fuqahā' (Dār-al-Kutub al- 'Ilmiyya, 1994) Vol. 3, p. 159; Ibn Nujaim, Al-Baḥr al-Rā'iq Sharḥ Kanz al-Daqā'iq (Dār al-Kitab al-Islāmī, n.d.) Vol. 7, p. 284.
[67] Al-Sarakhsī, Al-Mabsūṭ (Dār al-Ma'rifa, 1993) Vol. 12, p. 85.
[68] Al-Qarāfī (n 31) Vol. 6, p. 255.
[69] Al-Samarqandī (n 66) Vol. 3, p. 159.
[70] Mālik ibn Anas, Al-Mudawwana al-Kubrā (Dār Kutub al- 'Ilmiyya, 1994) Vol. 4, p. 289.
[71] Al-Sarakhsī (n 67) Vol. 12, p. 87.
[72] Ahmad Tha'alabī, Kashf al-Bayān 'an Tafsīr al-Qur'ān (Dār Iḥyā al-Turāth al-'Arabī, 2002) Vol. 2, p. 193.
[73] Al-Marghīnānī, Hidāya fi Sharḥ Bidāyat al-Mubtadī fi Fiqh al-Ḥanafī (Matkabat wal matba'a 'Ali Sibhī, n.d.) Vol. 1, p. 184.
[74] *Adamu v Ibrahim* (2016) Pt 1 SQLR 143, at p. 148.
[75] Ibid, p. 148.
[76] Ibn Anas (n 70) Vol. 4, p. 289.
[77] Al-Shirbīnī (n 52) Vol. 3, p. 558.

Therefore, gifts can be made in favour of any living person capable of holding the property.[78] Knowledge or specification of the gift are not necessary. Equally, a gift to an unknown beneficiary is valid.[79]

3.3.3 Subject Matter

12.28 Everything that can be sold may be made the subject of a gift. Therefore, the subject matter must be *ḥalāl*,[80] lawful,[81] and pure. Hence, gifts concerning impure objects, such as pigs,[82] lost property, services, or property that aids in disobedience to Allah,[83] or property gifted by the guardian of a woman's dowry,[84] is void. A gift of debt is allowed if made to the debtor and not to a third party[85] because of uncertainty in its delivery. The payment of *zakāt* owed by a poor person in the form of a gift is not permissible.[86] Gift of a property that is undivided or which has not been demarcated is not void but becomes complete only after its demarcation and delivery to the donee. Abūbakar made a gift to his daughter, ʿĀisha, but did not separate this from the rest of his other properties and did not hand it over to her. During his last hours and knowing fully well that it is not allowed to make a gift to some heirs, he announced his revocation of the gift despite his love for his daughter.[87] The subject matter of a gift does not necessarily have a precise monetary value.[88] The gift is valid even if the donor does not know the actual amount or value of the property he is giving.[89]

3.3.4 Possession (*Hauzi*) in a Gift

12.29 Delivery of the subject matter to the grantee or his agent is a requirement for the validity of the gift.[90] In a gift to a child, actual delivery to the father or guardian of the child is necessary.[91] In the Nigerian case of *Adamu v NDA*, the appellants sued to recover real estate gifted to them by their late grandmother *inter vivos*. The gift was made in the presence of witnesses. However, the deceased grantor had insisted she would collect the rent to sustain herself, and the grantees were to assume possession after her death. The respondent, the only surviving son, continued to collect the rent even after the grantor's death. When the appellants demanded possession, they were asked to wait. The Court of Appeal held that there is no valid gift and that a gift takes effect when there is delivery of possession.[92]

[78] *Adamu v Ibrahim* (n 74) at 148.
[79] Al-Abdarī (n 47) Vol. 10, p. 389.
[80] Al-Shirbīnī (n 52) Vol. 10, p. 194.
[81] Ibn Nujaim (n 66) Vol. 20, p. 129.
[82] Ibid,.
[83] Al-Shirbīnī (n 52) Vol. 10, p. 194.
[84] Thaʿalabī (n 72) Vol. 2, p. 193.
[85] Al-Shirbīnī (n 52) Vol. 3, p. 558.
[86] Ibid.
[87] Al-Sarakhsī (n 67) Vol. 12, p. 87.
[88] Ibn Nujaim (n 66) Vol. 7, p. 284.
[89] Al-Abdarī (n 47) Vol. 10, p. 389.
[90] Ibid, Vol. 10, p. 389. If the donor does not possess capacity to deliver the subject matter of the gift to the donee, the donation is not finalized. See Al-Sarakhsī (n 67) Vol. 11, pp. 39–66; Ibn al-Humām (n 63) Vol. 6, p. 507.
[91] Al-Zakzakī, Fat'ḥ Al-Jawād Fī Sharḥ Al-Irshād (n.p., 1982) Vol. 2, p. 191; Ibn Anas (n 70) Vol. 4, p. 408.
[92] *Adamu and Three Others v NDA* (2014) Pt 2 SQLR 101, p. 104.

Abū Yūsuf maintained that the transfer of possession must be actual.[93] If a piece of clothing locked in a box is gifted and the box is in the possession of the donee, but its keys are with the donor, delivery is not effective. The gift is completed only when the box is opened and the grantee takes possession of the clothing.[94] However, the Court of Appeal in Nigeria has held that a gift would be valid by delivery of possession, whether actual or constructive. There are several Maliki jurists who argue that transfer of possession is not a necessary condition for a valid gift. All that is necessary, according to these voices, is that the donor divest himself completely of all ownership and dominion over the subject matter of the gift.[95] 12.30

The acquisition of possession by the grantee should be with the permission of the grantor.[96] Gifts without transfer of possession or possession without the consent of the donor are not valid. In the event of the grantor's death before the delivery of the subject matter, the property reverts to the grantor and is inherited by the grantor's legal heirs.[97] The same applies where the donor dies before the donee takes over possession of the subject matter of the gift.[98] 12.31

3.4 Witnessing a Gift

Witnessing a gift is not a condition for its validity; rather, it is needed to avoid potential conflict. For instance, in the case of a gift by a father to his son, the act of witnessing was originally intended as a means of avoiding trouble with other heirs after the father's death.[99] Different evidentiary requirements are prescribed in each jurisdiction. In Nigeria, for example, in the case of *Buriye v Kurama*,[100] the Sharia Court of Appeal of Borno State held that a gift can be established in any of the following ways: 12.32

1. Admission by the defendant;
2. Two unimpeachable male witnesses who witnessed the gift;
3. A male witness and two female witnesses;
4. A male witness and the claimant's oath.

93 Ibn Nujaim (n 66) Vol. 7, p. 284.
94 Ibid.
95 Al-Samarqandī (n 66) Vol. 3, p. 159.
96 Al-Sarakhsī (n 67) Vol. 12, p. 99; Ibn al-Humām (n 63) Vol. 3, p. 558. Some scholars opined that if it is at the place of the gift, the donee can take the property even without the consent of the donor so long as there is valid offer and acceptance. However, if it is not at the place of the gift, then the donee cannot take the property without the consent of the donor. See Al-Mauṣilī (n 63) Vol. 3, p. 54.
97 Al-Qarāfī (n 31) Vol. 6, p. 255; Al-Qairawānī, Risāla al-Fiqhiya (Dār al-Fikr, 2002) p. 362.
98 Al-Mardāwī (n 25) Vol. 8, p. 87.
99 Ibid, Vol. 8, p. 89.
100 *Buriye v Kurama* (2015) 3 Pt 1 SQLR 105, p. 106.

3.5 Gift by a Father to his Children

12.33 A father can make a gift of his property to his children, all or specific, both males and females[101] and can lawfully withdraw a gift he has made to his children, whether to a minor or an adult.[102] When a father announces a gift to his minor child (or husband to his wife) that satisfies the requirement of delivery and can keep it in trust,[103] he must not use this to his benefit. He is not allowed to keep the gift when the child becomes an adult.[104] There is disagreement about whether a father can gift his entire property to one child or make gifts unequally between his children. Nuʿmān Bin Bashīr narrated that his father took him to the Prophet and asked the Prophet to witness the gift of a house the father made to him. The Prophet asked the father: 'Have you made a similar gift to all your children?' The father replied 'no'. The Prophet then said: 'Fear Allah and be just between your children' and as a result the father revoked the gift.[105] This *ḥadīth* is interpreted to mandate equality between male and female children.[106] Some scholars have said that such equality is only recommended and is not obligatory because the Prophet said: 'let another person be the witness, I cannot be a witness to injustice.' This is assumed by several scholars as reflecting the validity of the gift. Similarly, the Companions of the Prophet gave preference to some children over others. For example, Abūbakar gave preference to Aisha over his other children, while 'Umar gave preference to 'Abdullah. Some scholars also opine that this relates to treatment between children, just like in inheritance when a male child is given twice the share of females.[107] Other than inheritance, a person is allowed to make a gift of his entire estate to a poor person.[108]

3.6 Revocation of the Gift

12.34 Revocation of gifts is allowed but disfavoured.[109] Ibn 'Abbās reported the Prophet saying that he who makes a gift and revokes it is like a dog that vomits and eats back what it has vomited.[110] Some scholars added that in order for revocation to be valid it must be supported by the custom of the people.[111] Hence, revocation is valid before the delivery of the subject matter to the grantee.[112] Similarly, where a gift is made to two

[101] *Usman v Kareem* (2013) 1 Pt 1 SQLR 91, p. 99; *Muḥammadu v Secretary and Another v Adamu* (2013) 1 Pt 3 SQLR 44, p. 50; Ibn Anas (n 70) Vol. 4, p. 289; Ibn Qudāma, Al-Mughnī fī Fiqh al-Imām Aḥmad bin Ḥanbal (Dār al-Fikr, 1405H) Vol. 6, p. 309.
[102] Al-Qarāfī (n 31) Vol. 5, p. 201; Al-Qairawānī (n 97) p. 362.
[103] Al-Sarakhsī (n 67) Vol. 11, p. 350 and Vol. 12, p. 83.
[104] Al-Qairawānī (n 97) p. 362; Al-Sarakhsī (n 67) Vol. 11, p. 89.
[105] Imām Bukhārī, Al-Jāmiʿ Sahih (Dār Al-Shaiʿabī, 1987) *Ḥadīth* 2586.
[106] Al-Shirbīnī (n 52) Vol. 3, p. 558.
[107] Ibid, Vol. 3, p. 558; Al- Ṣanāʾiʿ, Subul al-Salām (Al-Sharika al-Quds, 2007) Vol. 3, p. 124.
[108] Al-Qairawānī (n 97) p. 362.
[109] Al-Qarāfī (n 31) Vol. 5, p. 201; Ibn Nujaim (n 66) Vol. 20, p. 21.
[110] Bukhārī 2587.
[111] Al-Mardāwī (n 25) Vol. 8, p. 87.
[112] Ibn Anas (n 70) Vol. 4, p. 414.

persons and one has accepted, the grantor can validly revoke the gift before the acceptance from the second grantee.[113] If a donor dies[114] or becomes bankrupt[115] before the gift is accepted, the gift stands revoked automatically.

Revocation is exceptionally not disfavoured in respect of fathers making gifts to their children.[116] Even so, such revocation is generally disliked, especially where the distribution of the gifts was fair among the children.[117] Revocation of a gift made by a father to his son must satisfy the following conditions before it can be accepted: **12.35**

1. The subject matter is still in the possession of the child and is deliverable to the father. For example, the child has not sold it, or the subject matter has not been divulged to the legal heirs of his son after his death.
2. Other rights have not been associated with the subject matter. For example, the child has not invested the gifted money in business with a third party. If the father withdraws the gift, it will harm the son or even third parties and the messenger of Allah has said: 'Do not harm and do not be harmed.'
3. There must be no increment on the subject matter of the gift, for example, growth in the gifted animals, construction on the gifted land. In this case, Shafi'is allow revocation whereas Hanafis do not.[118]

Ali believed that when a woman revokes a gift she has made to her husband and claims she was compelled to make the gift, it shall be accepted, but a husband will not be allowed to revoke a gift made to his wife. This is because it is possible and normal for a husband to compel his wife, but it is unusual for a wife to compel her husband.[119] **12.36**

4. Loan (*Qarḍ*)

4.1 Concept of *Qarḍ*

Lexically, the word *qarḍ* means cutting out and it has come to denote the money given to another person to pay back. Technically, it is defined as money given out of kindness to another person to enjoy it and subsequently return its substitute.[120] Thus, the money given out, in other words the loan is referred to as *qarḍ* and the party that gives it, is **12.37**

113 Al-Sarakhsī (n 67) Vol. 12, p. 66.
114 Yūsaf Al-Qurṭubī, Al-Kāfī fii Fiqh ahl al-Madīna (Maktabat al-Riyadh al-Hadītha, 1980) Vol. 2, p. 1010.
115 Al-Abdarī (n 47) Vol. 10, pp. 389–402.
116 Ibn Nujaim (n 66) Vol. 7, p. 284; Al-Shirbīnī (n 52) Vol. 3, p. 560; *Zarami and Another v Maina Kafa* (2015) 3 Pt 1 SQLR 143, pp. 87, 89.
117 Al-Shirbīnī (n 52) Vol. 10, p. 201.
118 *Al-Mughnī* (n 101) Vol. 6, p. 309; Al-Shirbīnī (n 52) Vol. 3, p. 572, Vol. 10, p. 201.
119 Al-Sarakhsī (n 67) Vol. 12, p. 92.
120 Ibn 'Ābidīn, Radd al-Muḥtār Sharḥ Tanvīr al Abṣār (Dār al-Fikr, 1992) Vol. 4, p. 534; Aḥmad al-Haithamī, Tuḥfat al-Muḥtāj Sharḥ al-Minhāj ma'a Ḥāshiyat al-Sharawānī wa al-Abādī (Al-Maktaba al-Tijāriyya al-Kubrā, 1983) Vol. 1, p. 340, Vol. 4, p. 407; Al-Buhūtī, Kashshāf al-Qinā' 'an Matn al-*Iqnā'* (Dār al-Fikr, 1412H) Vol. 3, p. 312.

called *muqriḍ*. The recipient is referred to as *muqtariḍ*, while the money that is paid back is known as *'iwaḍ al-qarḍ* (consideration of the loan). The loan itself is known as *iqtirāḍ*. This is known as the real *qarḍ* (loan) by the majority of jurists, while the Shafi'is consider it as one of two types of loan, the other being an assumed loan (*al-qarḍ al-ḥukmī*), for which they outlined specific rulings. Examples include cost of maintenance of a lost but found child, feeding the hungry or clothing the naked if they are not poor and with the intention of making that a loan, or where a person acted on behalf of another by paying for a debt or service based on the directive of such person.[121]

4.2 Legal Nature of *Qarḍ*

12.38 There is no dispute among jurists that giving a loan to the loanee is *mandūb* (recommended).[122] This opinion is based on the following saying of the Prophet:

> Whoever relieves a believer of distress from the distresses of this world—Allah will relieve him of distress from the distresses of the Day of Resurrection. And whoever facilitates [a matter] for one in financial difficulty—Allah will facilitate for him [matters] in this world and the Hereafter.[123]

Nevertheless, circumstances under which the loan is sought can turn such recommendation into an obligation, unlawful act, disfavoured act, or even a prohibited act.

4.3 Essential Elements of Loan and their Requirements

12.39 The majority of jurists recognize three elements comprising the loan contract, namely, *ṣīgha*, the parties, and the subject matter of the loan, whereas for the Hanafis, the *ṣīgha* is the only element of the loan.[124]

4.3.1 Offer and Acceptance

12.40 Jurists have agreed that the contract of loan can be formed using the terms of *qarḍ* (loan) or *salaf* or any term representing the parties' intention to that effect and can also be formed by the parties' conduct.[125] Abū Yūsuf and Muḥammad of the Hanafi school[126] as well as the Shafi'is have stated that offer and acceptance are the sole conditions for the validity of *qarḍ*, just like other contracts of exchange (*mu'āwaḍāt*). This

[121] Al-Ramlī, Nihāyat al-Muḥtāj ilā Sharḥ al-Minhāj (Dār al-Fikr, 1984) Vol. 4, p. 218; Muḥammad Zakariyyā Al-Anṣārī, Asnā al-Maṭālib fī Sharḥ Rauḍ al-Tālib (Dār al-Kitāb al-Islāmī, n.d.) Vol. 2, p. 141.
[122] Al-Ramlī (n 121).
[123] Muslim 2699.
[124] Al-Sālūs (n 7) pp. 113–14.
[125] *Radd al-Muḥtār* (n 120) Vol. 4, p. 181; Al-Kāsānī, Badā'i' al-Ṣanā'i' fī Tartīb al-Sharā'i' (Dār al-Kutub al-'Ilmiyya, 1986) Vol. 7, p. 395; Al-Buhūtī (n 120) Vol. 3, p. 299; Al-Maqdisī, Al-Mughnī ('Alam al-Kutub, 1997) Vol. 6, p. 430.
[126] Al-Kāsānī (n 125) Vol. 7, p. 394.

condition does not apply to the presumptive or assumed loan (*al-qarḍ al-ḥukmī*),[127] for example, feeding the hungry, clothing the naked, feeding a lost but found child, or a situation where one directs another to give money to a third person like a poet, transgressor, or feeding the poor.[128] In all these cases, there is no need for offer and acceptance, according to the Shafi'is, and the presumptive obligation is assumed to be created between the loaner and the loanee. The Shafi'is are of the view that consent for the loan should be free. For instance, consent procured through illegal coercion makes the loan contract invalid. But where the coercion is lawful, such as where there is a dire necessity on the part of the loanee, the loan shall be valid under such conditions.[129]

Al-Nawawī opined that offer and acceptance are not requirements for a valid loan agreement. Thus, if a man sends another person a messenger and he sends back the money, the loan is valid. Similarly, if the loaner tells the loanee that he is giving him a sum of money as a loan and hands it to him, the loan is deemed as established and is valid.[130] **12.41**

4.3.2 Contracting Parties

There is no dispute among jurists that a loaner must have the capacity to enter into a gratuitous contract.[131] This is because it is a contract of kindness (*irfāq*) and gratuity (*tabarruʿ*) with no immediate consideration.[132] For the Hanafis, a loan made by the father from the minor's assets[133]—and for the Hanbalis a loan by the guardian from the ward's money and by the administrator from *waqf* property[134]—are invalid. The Shafi'is, however, contend that the guardian can give a loan if there is a necessity and the guardian is empowered (especially through a court judgment) to loan under such necessity.[135] As to the capacity of the loanee, the Shafi'is stipulate the existence of general conditions needed for a contract.[136] The Hanbalis argue that he must have a *dhimma*, which can contain a debt and, for that reason, there can be no loan in favour of a mosque or school as, according to them, these are entities without *dhimma*.[137] **12.42**

[127] Al-Haithamī (n 120) Vol. 5, p. 40; Al-Anṣārī (n 121) Vol. 2, p. 141.
[128] Al-Ramlī (n 121) Vol. 4, p. 218.
[129] Al-Haithamī (n 120) Vol. 5, p. 41.
[130] Al-Nawawī (n 25) Vol. 4, p. 32.
[131] Niẓām al-Din al-Balkhī, Al-Fatāwā al-Hindiyya (Dār al-Fikr, 1310H) Vol. 3, p. 206; Al-Ramlī (n 121) Vol. 4, p. 219; Al-Buhūtī, Sharḥ Muntahā al-Irādāt (ʿĀlam al-Kutub, 1993) Vol. 2, p. 225.
[132] Al-Buhūtī (n 120) Vol. 3, p. 300; Al-Kāsānī (n 125) Vol. 7, p. 394, Vol. 2, p. 140; Al-Haithamī (n 120) Vol. 5, p. 41.
[133] Al-Kāsānī (n 125) Vol. 7, p. 394.
[134] Al-Buhūtī (n 131) Vol. 2, p. 225.
[135] Al-Haithamī (n 120) Vol. 5, p. 41.
[136] Al-Anṣārī (n 120) Vol. 2, p. 140.
[137] Al-Buhūtī (n 120) Vol. 3, p. 300 and Vol. 2, p. 225.

4.4 Can the *Bait al-Māl* (Public Treasury) Take a Loan?

12.43 There is no disagreement among jurists that the *Imām* (ruler) can take a loan on behalf of the *bait al-māl*. But there are certain conditions for such permission, including that the loan would be sought during times of crisis or in the public interest and the *bait al-māl* has lost its income;[138] *bait al-māl* must have an expected income to settle these loans,[139] which should be taken to meet the obligation which if left unmet would be detrimental;[140] and the ruler and his family have paid back all that they owe to the *bait al-māl*.[141]

12.44 Taking a loan on behalf of a *waqf* due to *maṣlaḥa* is lawful.[142] Jurists differ on the requirements for taking such a loan. The Hanafis contend that this is permitted only subject to the *wāqif's* (endower) permission, and assuming there exists some need, such as repairing trust property for which there is no income. If these conditions are met, the loan may be taken if the court so allows and there is no possibility of leasing out trust property to get a loan.[143] The Malikis and Hanbalis maintain that there is no need for a judge's permission if there is no income to undertake a repair because the administrator, being a trustee, is vested with absolute permission to manage the property.[144]

4.5 Subject Matter of Loan

12.45 The following are a set of necessary conditions which the subject matter of the loan must satisfy and in respect of which there is agreement among jurists.

4.5.1 Fungible

12.46 According to the Hanafis, a loan must involve fungibles (*mithliyyāt*), encompassing properties with the same value, such as currencies and other measured, weighted, and countable properties. Non-fungibles (*qīyamiyyāt*) with different values, such as animals and land properties, cannot be given out as loans.[145] Kāsānī reasons that it is not possible to return the same property or its value because different valuers will value it differently, ultimately leading to conflict.[146] Ibn 'Ābidīn also supports this view by arguing that a loan is borrowing at the beginning, an exchange contract at the end, when

[138] Al-Juwainī, Ghiyāth al-Umam fi al-Tyāth al-Zulam (Maktabat Imām al-Ḥaramain, 1401H) p. 279.
[139] Al-Shāṭibī, Al-I'tiṣām (Dār Ibn 'Affān, 1992) Vol. 2, p. 620.
[140] Abū Ya'lā, Al-Aḥkām al-Sulṭāniyya (Dār al-Kutub al- 'Ilmiyyah, 2000) p. 253.
[141] Al-Subkī (n 42) Vol. 8, p. 215.
[142] Al-Buhūtī (n 120) Vol. 3, p. 300, Vol. 2, p. 225.
[143] *Radd al-Muḥtār* (n 120) Vol. 3, p. 419.
[144] Al-Ḥaṭṭāb, Mawāhib al-Jalīl fī Sharḥ Mukhtaṣar al-Khalīl (Dār al-Fikr, 1992) Vol. 6, p. 40; Al-Buhūtī (n 120) Vol. 3, p. 300, Vol. 2, p. 225.
[145] *Radd al-Muḥtār* (n 120) Vol. 4, p. 171; Abū Ja'far Aḥmad Al-Ṭaḥāwī, Sharḥ Ma'ānī al-Āthār ('Ālam al-Kutub, 1994) Vol. 4, p. 60.
[146] Al-Kāsānī (n 125) Vol. 7, p. 395.

no benefit may be derived from it and it is instead consumed, which is why the obligation to return must be a credit in *dhimma*, which is possible only if it is fungible.[147]

The Malikis and Shafi'is have allowed non-fungibles by expanding the category of things that can become the subject matter of a loan. They suggest that anything that can be a subject matter of *salam* (advance payment sales), whether it is an animal or something else, even if it is non-fungible (*qiyamī*), but which can be recognized as credit in *dhimma*, is allowed for a loan contract.[148] The basis for this is that the Prophet took the loan of a young camel.[149] Thus, a useful analogy may be made to expand the category of objects. The Hanbalis are even more liberal and suggest that anything that can be sold can also be the subject matter of a loan, whether it is fungible or not and whether it can be adequately described or not.[150] **12.47**

4.5.2 Real Property

The subject matter of a loan must be real property (*'ayn*). According to the Hanafis[151] and the prevailing opinion among the Hanbalis,[152] a usufruct (*manfa'a*) cannot be given out as a loan. The Hanafis stipulate that a similar thing is returned among the parties to a loan, which is not possible in the case of usufruct,[153] on the ground that they do not consider it as property. The Hanafis define property as something to which the mind is attracted and which can be kept for subsequent use, which is not the case with usufruct. The Hanbalis disallow usufruct.[154] For the Shafi'is and Malikis, usufructs clearly described with definitive features can become the subject matter of *salam* contracts, just like real property, and hence can become the subject of loan agreements.[155] **12.48**

4.5.3 The Requirement of Being 'Known'

There is no dispute among jurists that a loan must be known clearly in terms of its amount and features, and must be subject to a definitive description.[156] Ibn Qudāma has rationalized this condition by saying that if the loanee does not know the exact amount received, redemption will not be possible. Similarly, it is not permissible to loan things measured or weighed in bulk as that which is to be returned cannot be definitively known.[157] **12.49**

[147] *Radd al-Muḥtār* (n 120) Vol. 4, p. 171.
[148] Ibn Jauzī, Al-Qawānīn al-Fiqhiyya (n.p., n.d.) p. 293; Al-Ḥaṭṭāb (n 144) Vol. 4, p. 545; Muḥammad 'Illīsh, Minaḥ al-Jalīl Sharḥ Mukhtaṣar al-Khalīl (Dār al-Fikr, 1989) Vol. 3, p. 47; Abū Isḥāq Al-Shīrāzī, Al-Muhadhdhab fī Fiqh al-Imām al-*Shafi'i* (Dār al-Kutub al-'Ilmiyya, n.d.) Vol. 1, p. 310; Al-Ramlī (n 121) Vol. 4, p. 222.
[149] Transmitted by Muslim, *Ḥadīth* 1600.
[150] Al-Buhūtī (n 120) Vol. 3, p. 300 and Vol. 2, p. 225; *Al-Mughnī* (n 101) Vol. 6, p. 432.
[151] *Radd al-Muḥtār* (n 120) Vol. 4, p. 171.
[152] Al-Buhūtī (n 131) Vol. 2, p. 225; Mufliḥ (n 28) Vol. 4, p. 205.
[153] *Radd al-Muḥtār* (n 120) Vol. 4, p. 171.
[154] Al-Buhūtī (n 120) Vol. 3, p. 300.
[155] Al-Nawawī (n 25) Vol. 4, p. 27; Ibn Jauzī (n 148) p. 280.
[156] Al-Nawawī (n 25) Vol. 4, pp. 33–34; Al-Ramlī (n 121) Vol. 4, p. 223; Al-Buhūtī (n 131) Vol. 2, p. 225 and Vol. 3, p. 300.
[157] *Al-Mughnī* (n 101) Vol. 6, p. 434.

4.6 Types of Loans

12.50 Loans can be classified as matured and non-matured. A matured loan is a loan which the loaner has the right to demand back, while a suspended or non-matured loan is that which the loaner has no right to demand. Such a loan is to be paid at a future date or partitioned in accordance with the loanee's ability to pay.[158] A loan can also be a shared loan when it is paid back by more than one loanee.[159] Sometimes, a loan is determined at the time when it becomes the liability of the loanee; for instance, a debt admitted while the loanee was healthy and a loan admitted while the loanee was terminally ill.[160]

4.7 Interest in Loan

12.51 Any interest on a loan or an increment to that which is given at the time of return is tantamount to usury, which serves to invalidate the contract of *qarḍ*.[161] This is so because the objective of the contract of *qarḍ* is kindness and seeking Allah's pleasure. Thus, where the loaner stipulates that the loanee must return more than was given, the objective of the contract has been contradicted and, for this reason, it shall be invalidated.[162] For further discussion on *ribā*, readers are directed to Chapter 6.

4.8 Termination of a Loan

12.52 There are specific ways to discharge the loan agreement, as follows:

1. A loan contract comes to an end with the payment of the loan by the loanee or his agent to the loaner or his agent.[163]
2. The loan agreement is also discharged through *al-ibrā'*, that is, the loaner has forgiven the loan and absolved the loanee from liability.[164] The offer of the loaner to make an effective *al-ibrā'* does not require acceptance from the loanee, albeit the loanee's rejection will render it ineffective.[165]

[158] Al-Sarakhsī (n 67) Vol. 25, p. 173; Muḥammad al-Kharshī, Sharḥ al-Kharshī 'alā Mukhtaṣar Khalīl (Dār al-Fikr, n.d.) Vol. 5, p. 263; Al-Nawawī, Al-Majmū' Sharḥ Al-Muhadhdhab (Dār al-Fikr, n.d.) Vol. 6, p. 6; Al-Buhūtī (n 120) Vol. 3, p. 325; Badruddīn Al-Zarkashī, A-Manthūr fī al-Qawā'id al-Fiqhiyya (Ministry of Endowment, 1985) Vol. 2, p. 158.
[159] Al-Kharshī (n 158) Vol. 2, p. 197; Al-Mardāwī (n 25) Vol. 9, p. 213; Ibn Ḥazm (n 19) Vol. 4, pp. 221–22.
[160] Al-Anṣārī (n 11) Vol. 5, p. 23; Al-Dusūqī (n 1) Vol. 3, p. 399; Al-Shafi'ī, Al-Umm (Dār al-Ma'rifa, 1990) Vol. 7, p. 27; Ibn Mufliḥ (n 25) Vol. 6, p. 609.
[161] Al-Kāsānī (n 125) Vol. 7, p. 395; Abū Al-Adawī, Ḥāshiyat al-Adawī 'alā Kifāyat al-Tā'ib al-Rabbānī (Dār al-Fikr, 1994) Vol. 2, p. 149; 'Ali Al-Tusūlī, Al-Bahjah fī Sharḥ Al-Tuḥfa (Dār al-Kutub al-'Ilmiyyah, 1998) Vol. 2, p. 287; Ibn Jauzī (n 148) p. 293; Al-Anṣārī (n 121) Vol. 2, p. 142; Al-Nawawī (n 25) Vol. 4, p. 34; Al-Buhūtī (n 120) Vol. 2, p. 227 and Vol. 3, p. 304.
[162] Al-Kāsānī (n 125) Vol. 7, p. 395.
[163] Muḥammad Qadrī Bāshā, Murshid al-Hairān (Būlāq, 1891) Arts 195, 196.
[164] Ibn Nujaim (n 45) p. 389; Majalla, Arts 1062–1064; Al-Dusūqī (n 1) Vol. 3, p. 411.
[165] Majalla, Art. 1068; *Murshid al-Hairān* (n 163) Arts 246, 236, 224.

3. *Al-muqāṣṣa* is another way to bring a loan agreement to an end, whereby the parties to the loan contract agree to absolve the loanee's liability upon condition that he also absolve the loaner of a loan owed to him.[166] Al-Dasūqī is of the view that *muqāṣṣa* can be obligatory in some circumstances, including where both loans have matured; or the two loans share the same repayment period; or the party whose loan has matured demands it, whereby a ruling to that effect shall be obligatory.[167]
4. Where the *dhimma* of the loaner and the loanee becomes one. This arises where A, being the brother of B owes $1,000 to B and B subsequently dies and has no heir but A. Thus, A will become both the loaner and the loanee as the *dhimma* of his brother along with all liabilities and obligations conferred to him.[168]
5. A loan terminates where the loaner agrees that the loanee transfers liability to another party, in which case both the *muḥīl* (transferor) and his guarantor (if any) shall not be liable if he consented to such transfer. The loaner will therefore demand payment of the loan from the transferee.[169]

5. Will (*Waṣiyya*)

5.1 Meaning and Nature of Will

Waṣiyya is a noun derived from *al-tauṣyatu*, which means granting ownership to another after death.[170] For instance, if a person declares that he gives one-third of his estates to another person, Muslim scholars consider this a gift 'and not a will. In order to render it a will the will writer must state the words "after my death"'.[171] Where the will writer stipulates that the ownership of particular property be bequeathed to a particular person and that person rejects it or dies, then it may be bequeathed to another person and the will is valid.[172] **12.53**

5.2 Conditions of a Valid Will

5.2.1 Parties

The maker must be capable of making the will and hence a child or persons deprived of legal capacity, particularly those who do not understand the consequences of their actions or a person upon whom injunction (*ḥajr*) has been imposed, cannot make **12.54**

166 *Murshid al-Hairan* (n 163) Art. 224; Ibn Jauzī (n 148) p. 293; Al-Shafi'ī (n 160) Vol. 8, p. 59; Al-Zarkashī (n 158) Vol. 1, p. 391; *Al-Mughnī* (n 101) Vol. 9, pp. 447–448; Al-Dusūqī (n 1) Vol. 3, p. 227.
167 Al-Dusūqī (n 1) Vol. 3, p. 227.
168 Al-Sālūs (n 7) Vol. 21, p. 140.
169 *Radd al-Muḥtār* (n 120) Vol. 4, pp. 291–92.
170 Ibn Nujaim (n 66) Vol. 24, p. 90.
171 Ibid, Vol. 24, p. 109.
172 Ibid, Vol. 24, p. 98.

a will. The beneficiary of the will must be in existence before the will is made in his favour. To that end, some scholars argued that if the beneficiary is alive, it suffices if the will is made for the benefit of a foetus more than six months in the womb. Similarly, the beneficiary must not be the legal heir of the maker who is already entitled to inherit the maker. A will made to such a beneficiary can be made only with the permission of the other heirs. Moreover, the beneficiary must not have been convicted of the murder or manslaughter of the maker.[173]

5.2.2 Quantum of Will

12.55 The will must not exceed one-third of the deceased's estate after debts and funeral expenses have been covered.[174] This is based on a *ḥadīth* where the Prophet stated: 'Allah has allowed you to make gifts in respect of one-third of your estate.' Similarly, Sa'ad ibn Abī Waqās told the Prophet that he was sick and had just one daughter, so he wanted to give her his entire estate. The Prophet said 'no'. Sa'ad then said 'half?', the Prophet said 'no'. Sa'ad then said 'one-third?' The Prophet approved the one-third but stated that even that is too much and that it is better to leave your heirs wealthy than leaving them in a state of poverty.[175] It is reported in a *ḥadīth* that wills exceeding one-third of the deceased's estate and granted to a single person constitute the gravest of sins.[176]

5.3 Conditional Will

12.56 If the maker has made his will contingent on some condition, it will become effective after fulfilment of that condition. If the will fails, the property will return to the heirs for inheritance. For instance, if the maker makes a will stating that X inherits so long as she does not remarry or leave town, the beneficiary will be entitled to the property if she keeps to the terms and conditions stated.[177]

5.4 Revocation of the Will

12.57 The maker can rescind the will during his lifetime. For instance, when a person makes a will and hands it over to another during sickness but the maker collects back the will after recovering from the sickness and dies while the will was in his own possession, Mālik opined that the retrieval of the document by the maker is an indication of rescission of the will.[178] Similarly, Mālik maintains that if a person makes a will in a state of good health and dies, the will is valid even if he keeps the document with him. Ibn

[173] Ibid, Vol. 24, p. 94; Ibn al-Humām (n 63) Vol. 24, p. 128; Ibn Anas (n 70) Vol. 4, p. 450.
[174] Ibn Nujaim (n 66); Al-Sarakhsī (n 67) Vol. 12, p. 27.
[175] Mālik ibn Anas, Muwattā Mālik (Dār Iḥyā Turāth al-'Arabī, n.d.), referring to *Ḥadīth* 1456, Vol. 2, p. 763.
[176] Ibn Nujaim (n 66) Vol. 24, p. 96.
[177] Ibid.
[178] Ibn Anas (n 70) Vol. 4, p. 330.

Qāsim stated that if a person makes a will in a state of sickness or wellbeing but has not put any condition, such as 'when I die from this sickness', then the will becomes binding and enforceable.[179] When a person makes a will in favour of a foetus and dies, and there is a miscarriage, the foetus is not entitled to anything.[180]

When a person is asked if he has made a will and denies doing so, such denial does not constitute revocation of the will already made. If the maker intends to revoke a will, he should expressly state so. When the maker makes a will for the benefit of two people but rescinds in respect of one of them, without specifying which one, all heirs have the right to revoke any one of the two beneficiaries. Suppose a man makes a will in respect of land and then digs the land. This action serves as a revocation. When he plants trees, it is also a form of revocation, but when he plants wheat, that is not considered revocation.[181] **12.58**

5.5 Invalid Wills

When a person declares that upon his or her death two of their commodities should be bequeathed to X and one of the commodities is destroyed and the testator also dies, the will becomes void.[182] If a testator makes a will and declares that he gives X a sheep from his farm and a sheep is born after the testator's death, the beneficiary is only entitled to the original sheep without its offspring. However, if the testator has mentioned a specific farm, then the beneficiary is entitled to both the sheep and its offspring.[183] When a person says to another that upon his death he forfeits money borrowed, there is consensus among scholars that no valid will exists; exceptionally, Abū Qāsim opined otherwise.[184] Abū Laith opined that a will made by a sick person through signs is void because he cannot express himself clearly. Even so, some scholars maintain that such a will is valid so long as it can be understood because a will can be made expressly by word of mouth or by sign language.[185] **12.59**

A will in favour of a beneficiary who later kills the testator is void.[186] After the death of a person, the Prophet always starts with the settlement of debts before wills.[187] **12.60**

179 Ibid.
180 Ibid, p. 337.
181 Ibn Nujaim (n 65) Vol. 24, p. 112.
182 Ibid, p. 100.
183 Ibid, p. 104.
184 Ibid, p. 109.
185 Ibid, p. 111.
186 Al-Sarakhsī (n 67) Vol. 12, p. 47.
187 Ibid, p. 262.

6. Endowment (*Waqf*)

6.1 Meaning and Nature of *Waqf*

12.61 *Waqf* means stopping or withholding, for example, withholding a house.[188] The Qur'ān says: 'Stop them, they will be questioned.'[189] From a theoretical perspective, *waqf* is the act of keeping or withholding the ownership of a property while allowing another person to enjoy the usufruct.[190] Jurisprudentially, it is the act of retaining the property with the giver and allowing others to benefit from it. Abū Ḥanīfa defined it to mean keeping property with rules from Allah. In *Fatḥ al-Qadīr* the meaning of 'keeping property with rules from Allah' was interpreted as those rules which benefit the person chosen by the giver. 'Umar asked the Prophet about a farm/land he had in the territory of Khaibar as to whether he should give it out in charity and the Prophet said to him: 'make a gift of its root, it cannot be sold, given as gift nor inherited but the fruits will be given as gift.' 'Umar made a gift of it for Allah's sake, to be used to get freedom for slaves, feed guests, poor people and travellers.[191] A *waqf* is to be undertaken for the sake of Allah with no intention for the property to return to the maker.[192]

6.2 Creation of a *Waqf*

12.62 Scholars generally agree that using words like 'I have agreed that this should be a *ṣaqada* in the form of *waqf* in perpetuity for the poor' validly creates a *waqf*. Abū Yūsuf and several others have also approved the use of words 'this is *ṣaqada* in the form of *waqf*, arguing that by mentioning *ṣaqada* the intention is understood.[193]

6.3 Conditions for a Valid *Waqf*

6.3.1 *Waqf* Associated with Conditions

12.63 Sometimes, a condition is attached to the *waqf*, and the effect of a condition on a *waqf* depends on the nature of that condition. Some conditions render a *waqf* void. For instance, where the donor retains the right to sell *waqf* property at any time for his benefit[194] or makes himself the beneficiary of the *waqf*,[195] or associates a *waqf* to a future event,[196] or declares 'if I die, my house should be used as *waqf*,'[197] such conditions

[188] Ibn Nujaim (n 66) Vol. 14, p. 249.
[189] Qur'ān, Assāfāt: 24.
[190] Al-Sarakhsī (n 67) Vol. 12, p. 47; Ibn al-Humām (n 63) Vol. 14, p. 61.
[191] Al-Sarakhsī (n 67).
[192] Al-Samarqandī (n 66) Vol. 3, p. 375.
[193] Ibid.
[194] Ibid, Vol. 14, p. 257.
[195] Ibid, Vol. 3, p. 375.
[196] Ibid, Vol. 14, p. 275.
[197] Ibid.

are void without any adverse impact on the *waqf*. This is true, for example, when the donor gives himself an option to rescind the *waqf* or says the mosque he gave as *waqf* shall be used only by certain people.[198] In both cases, the condition is rejected, and the *waqf* remains valid. Certain conditions are valid. This is true, for instance, in respect of a condition that the donor can change the property of the *waqf*[199] or that the *waqf* shall operate after the death of the *wāqif*.[200]

6.3.2 Conditions for the Subject Matter

When a trust is established during sickness, it must not exceed one-third of the estate.[201] **12.64** When a person makes a *waqf* from the assets of its property (e.g. date trees) to the poor during sickness and dies without handing them over, the *waqf* will be enforced if it does not exceed one-third of his estate. Otherwise it will be treated like a will (*waṣiyya*). If he established it during a state of good health, the *waqf* will be considered a failure because handing over the property is a condition precedent to its validity.[202]

6.3.2.1 Nature of subject matter

It is advised that the *wāqif* should give one of his best properties for the *waqf* as stated in the **12.65** Qur'ān: 'You cannot attain piety until you give from what you like.'[203] The Qur'ān further says: 'Do not give the filthy.'[204] Accordingly, 'Umar made a gift of his beloved farm in compliance with these Qur'ānic verdicts as encouraged by the Prophet.[205]

The subject matter should be a lawful, transferable asset that is susceptible to own- **12.66** ership and of lasting duration. The subject matter must also be identifiable and specific,[206] or, in other words, known. When a person sets up a *waqf* from his or her assets without identifying that property, there is no valid *waqf*. It is valid if the *wāqif* says he has given everything in his house as *waqf* without mentioning the exact quantity.[207] However, Ibn Rushd opined that where the exact amount is not known the *waqf* is disfavoured.[208] In this manner, clothes, armoury,[209] animals,[210] real estate or land (whole or part thereof),[211] books,[212] and other similar assets can become the subject matter of *waqf*. *Waqf* of money for use in perpetuity as capital is also allowed. The beneficiary will

198 Al-Sarakhsī (n 67) Vol. 12, p. 72.
199 Al-Samarqandī (n 66) Vol. 14, p. 257.
200 Al-Shirbīnī (n 52) Vol. 3, p. 567.
201 Al-Samarqandī (n 66) Vol. 3, p. 375.
202 Ibid, Vol. 3, p. 424.
203 Qur'ān, Āl 'Imrān: 92.
204 Qur'ān, Baqara: 264.
205 Al-Sarakhsī (n 67) Vol. 12, p. 53.
206 Al-Samarqandī (n 66) Vol. 3, p. 375; Al-Abdarī (n 47) Vol. 7, p. 626.
207 Al-Samarqandī (n 66) Vol. 14, p. 253.
208 Al-Abdarī (n 47) Vol. 7, p. 626.
209 Al-Shirbīnī (n 52) Vol. 3, p. 567.
210 Ibid, Vol. 3, p. 419.
211 Al-Sarakhsī (n 67) Vol. 12, p. 64.
212 Ibid, Vol. 10, p. 312.

always provide any amount that is lost from the capital.[213] The *waqf* property cannot be given as a gift, sold, owned, or used as security in a mortgage.[214]

6.3.2.2 Delivery

12.67 The *waqf* is not considered complete until delivery takes place.[215] When a person makes a *waqf* but does not surrender the subject matter, following his death the property reverts to his heirs.[216] There may be different modes to effectuate the delivery. In the case of a mosque, when congregational prayer is conducted inside or, according to some scholars, with the prayer of one person in that mosque, it is deemed that delivery has taken place. In respect of a graveyard, delivery takes place with the burial of a dead body.[217] However, Mālik is of the view that a public announcement is sufficient for the delivery and that is the practice in Madina.[218]

12.68 Mālik stated in the *Mudawwana* that if a person makes a *waqf* to his son and dies indebted, and there is no evidence as to which of the two—waqf or the debt—came first, the son must provide evidence that the *waqf* preceded the debt; otherwise, the *waqf* will be declared void. There is another view that if possession has been delivered before the *wāqif's* death, the *waqf* will be given preference.[219]

6.3.3 Capacity and Authority of the Parties

6.3.3.1 Wāqif

12.69 The person making the *waqf* must not be a minor, lack capacity, be bankrupt, or be under interdiction/injunction to deal with his or her property (*ḥajr*).[220] A *waqf* can only be set up by a person that owns the property. Therefore, a *waqf* before acquiring ownership of property or usurped property is void.[221] A non-Muslim can make *waqf* exclusively for people of his faith or even to his children so long as this is counted as an act of piety.[222] It is lawful for the *Imām* (ruler) to make *waqf* of a land in *bait al-māl* (public treasury).[223]

6.3.3.2 Beneficiary

12.70 The beneficiary of the *waqf* must be spelt out and be alive. For instance, the *waqf* would be void if a person makes *waqf* for the poor amongst his children while none of them is poor.[224] There is no condition for the beneficiary to accept it before it becomes binding,

[213] Al-Abdarī (n 47) Vol. 7, p. 626.
[214] Al-Qarāfī (n 31) Vol. 10, p. 427.
[215] Al-Sarakhsī (n 67) Vol. 12, p. 53; Ibn Nujaim (n 66) Vol. 14, p. 260; Ibn Anas (n 70) Vol. 4, p. 419.
[216] Al-Samarqandī (n 66) Vol. 3, p. 375; Ibn Anas (n 70).
[217] Al-Sarakhsī (n 67) Vol. 12, p. 59.
[218] Abū Ḥanīfa and Muḥammad made it a condition, while Abū Yūsuf did not consider it a condition. Al-Samarqandī (n 66) Vol. 3, p. 375.
[219] Ibid, Vol. 3, p. 319.
[220] Ibid.
[221] Ibn Nujaim (n 66) Vol. 14, p. 249.
[222] Ibid, Vol. 14, p. 268.
[223] Al-Shirbīnī (n 52) Vol. 3, p. 567.
[224] Ibid, Vol. 3, p. 567.

hence the beneficiary of the *waqf* may be unborn (but the *waqf* fails if the beneficiary is not ultimately born).[225] Non-Muslims (poor Christians and Jews) can also become beneficiaries.[226]

A *waqf* set up by a person for personal benefit is void. Ibn Arfa'a stated that even if he has partners and the co-partner has taken over possession, then it shall be valid only for the co-partner and not for himself.[227] Abū Yūsuf, however, opined that if in the end the property returns to the *wāqif*, the *waqf* is valid because what is important is the pleasure of Allah and the Prophet has stated that 'the act of feeding yourself is *ṣaqada*' and to 'start with yourself and then people you care for'.[228] Abū Yūsuf opined that a person can make a *waqf* for his wives to enjoy certain things after his death as long as they do not remarry. This is intended for their benefit and the care of his children.[229] The beneficiary of the *waqf* cannot be transferred or comingled with the property of another person.[230] 12.71

6.4 Life of *Waqf*

The *waqf* must be set up as a permanent mechanism and no time should be fixed for its expiration.[231] For that reason, the *waqf* will be invalid if a person says: 'I give out my house as *waqf* for a day or week' or says: 'the property will return back to me'.[232] 12.72

6.5 Purpose of *Waqf*

The purpose of the *waqf* should be delineated before it becomes valid. For instance, when a person says 'I hereby make a *waqf* of this house' it is not a valid *waqf* until he adds 'for the beneficiaries' purpose'.[233] This purpose should be lawful.[234] The *waqf* is void when it is meant for any act of disobedience to Allah, or where it involves some kind of illegality.[235] The *waqf* property should be used for the purpose for which the *waqf* is created. For instance, a mosque dedicated as *waqf* cannot be used as a private residence.[236] Mālik said that if an animal is given as *waqf* for the course of Allah, it must be used for that course until it becomes so weak that it can no longer serve its purpose. It may then be sold and the amount realized should be used to buy another animal that 12.73

225 Al-Abdarī (n 47) Vol. 7, p. 626.
226 Ibid, Vol. 7, p. 633.
227 Al-Abdarī (n 47) Vol. 10, p. 319.
228 Al-Sarakhsī (n 67) Vol. 12, p. 72.
229 Ibid, Vol. 12, p. 80.
230 Al-Abdarī (n 47) Vol. 7, p. 626.
231 Al-Samarqandī (n 66) Vol. 3, p. 375.
232 Ibid, Vol. 3, p. 260.
233 Al-Sarakhsī (n 67) Vol. 12, p. 55.
234 Al-Shirbīnī (n 52) Vol. 3, p. 567.
235 Al-Abdarī (n 47) Vol. 10, p. 312.
236 Ibn al-Humām (n 63) Vol. 6, p. 236.

will serve the original purpose of the *waqf*. Ibn Qāsim added that if the amount realized does not suffice to buy another horse, it should be added to other amounts from other sources to buy another animal or be given as charity.[237]

6.6 Administration of *Waqf* Property

12.74 The donor will appoint or allow a person to administer the *waqf* property.[238] Even in the case of a mosque, someone must be responsible for cleaning, locking, and opening it.[239] The administrator of the *waqf* is generally allowed to eat from the *waqf* even if not expressly permitted but he cannot feed people outside his immediate family. 'Umar allowed eating and making *ṣaqada* from it.[240] The Qur'ān states in connection with the management of the property of orphans:

> Test the orphans until they reach the marriageable age. Then, if you perceive in them proper understanding, hand their property over to them, and do not consume it extravagantly and hastily, lest they should grow up. Whoever is rich should abstain (from using it for himself), and whoever is poor may have from it (to the extent of his necessary need) with fairness. So, when you hand their property over to them, make witnesses upon them. Allah is sufficient for reckoning.[241]

In all circumstances, the administrator is not allowed to sell the property.[242]

6.7 Things Associated with the *Waqf* Property

12.75 When a person makes a *waqf* of a graveyard, his heirs have the right to cut the trees in the graveyard because the trees are not part of the *waqf*. Abū Ḥanīfa accepts this. Similarly, a person who makes a *waqf* of his house does not include the buildings in the property.[243] If it is land that is given as *waqf*, then that includes the trees. But if it was planted after the *waqf*, then the trees belong to the person that planted them. However, if the person that planted the trees is unknown, then it shall be for the judge to do what is appropriate in the circumstances.[244] When the *waqf* consists of a house where the deceased donor's children live and one of his children makes an improvement or keeps some items in the house, except where a contrary intention is made known, the improvement or new items are deemed part of the *waqf* property. Al-Mukhzuumī opined

[237] Al-Abdarī (n 47) Vol. 7, p. 631.
[238] Ibn al-Humām (n 63) Vol. 6, p. 236.
[239] Ibid, Vol. 6, p. 236.
[240] Al-Sarakhsī (n 67) Vol. 12, p. 53.
[241] Qur'ān, Nisā: 6.
[242] Al-Sarakhsī (n 67) Vol. 12, p. 53.
[243] Ibn al-Humām (n 63) Vol. 6, p. 239.
[244] Ibid.

that an item is part of the *waqf* only when the property is of less value. The rule does not apply where the property is considered special.[245]

6.8 Types of *Waqf*

A *waqf* can be restricted or open. A restricted *waqf* arises where a person decides to limit the use of the *waqf*. An example of a restricted *waqf* is that which is set up for the use of X and the children of X, or for the purposes of *ḥajj*. It is open when no such restriction exists; for example, a farm *waqf* for use by the public.[246] **12.76**

6.9 Termination of the *Waqf*

A person who has disposed of property to a *waqf* can lawfully withdraw it before it is delivered to the administrator. A trust made in favour of two persons can be withdrawn before either of them accepts it.[247] A *waqf* created by two partners can be revoked before the administrator has accepted assets from both partners.[248] Ibn Yūnus stated that he heard Mālik say that when a person makes a *waqf* of a house but does not vacate the house for an extended period, even if he subsequently vacates the house before his death, the *waqf* is deemed terminated and the property becomes the subject matter of inheritance. Ibn Qāsim, however, stated that so long as the donor has surrendered the property before his death then it is valid even if he returns as a tenant. Muḥammad stated that such *waqf* is valid if the donor has handed over the property to the beneficiary or an agent of the beneficiary so long as the beneficiary is not a child.[249] **12.77**

245 Ibn Anas (n 70) Vol. 4, p. 422.
246 Al-Sarakhsī (n 66) Vol. 12, p. 71.
247 Al-Qarāfī (n 31) Vol. 10, p. 427.
248 Al-Sarakhsī (n 67) Vol. 12, p. 69.
249 Al-Abdarī (n 47) Vol. 10, p. 316.

13

Contracts and Third Parties

1. Introduction

One cardinal feature of valid commercial contracts in Islamic law is the presence of parties to a contract. Without the parties to a contract, there cannot be a valid and legally enforceable agreement. In most cases, except for unilateral contracts already discussed extensively in Chapter 12, the general rule is that there must be a minimum of two parties to a contract. One party makes the offer while the other provides a corresponding acceptance using any of the common forms acceptable in Islamic law. This element of a valid contract is sacrosanct, as contractual obligations are not performed in a vacuum. Obligations under the contract are performed by competent parties who have the requisite legal capacity to negotiate and conclude a contract. 13.01

Beyond the original two parties to a contract, there are however circumstances where contractual rights and obligations have some implications for third parties. There could also be situations where third-party rights can be enforced in a contract concluded between two parties. In essence, third parties can be affected either positively or negatively when two parties conclude a contract. There are contracts that are specifically meant for the benefit of third parties. 13.02

Another important issue is third-party reliance and its effect on the original bilateral contract. Therefore, the principle of privity of contract and its exceptions within the general ambit of Islamic commercial law transcends parties who are directly related to the rights, duties, and obligations under the contract. The discourse extends to any third party who might have an enforceable right or required duty or obligation under the contract. So contracts for the benefit of third parties as well as tripartite contracts generally fall under exceptions to the privity of contract rule. 13.03

Islamic law provides rules which are applicable to tripartite contracts or contracts that confer rights or duties on third parties. These are comprehensively examined in Islamic jurisprudence under some key areas such as *ḥawāla* (contract of debt assignment), *wakāla* (agency contract), and *kafāla* (deed of guarantee). The different legal permutations, types, and variations of these tripartite contracts on one hand, and how bilateral contracts could have legal implications on the rights or obligations of third parties on the other, are the focus of this chapter. However, it is important to emphasize that *wakāla* and *kafāla* have been discussed extensively in Chapters 11 and 12 respectively. Therefore, building on the earlier discussions of these two unique concepts, this 13.04

chapter will focus only on some instances where the contracts have legal implications for third-party rights.

2. Privity of Contract

13.05 Though it is often said that most concepts under the English law of contract do have an equivalent basis in Islamic law,[1] the concept of privity of contract and its exceptions is quite unique and has not been a major focus for Muslim jurists. This may not be unconnected with the recent approach to privity of contract as compared to the traditional common law principle. The whole idea of privity of contract emphasizes the need to limit the class of persons who can enforce contractual rights even though most contracts do have legal implications for third parties.

13.06 Nevertheless, the prevalent use of modern-style Islamic finance contracts has brought to the fore the need to consider the application of some of these English law principles in modern Islamic law contracts. It is generally known that the governing law of most modern Islamic finance contracts remains the English law, so it is pertinent to consider the overlap between classical Islamic jurisprudence of contracts and the modern practice of English contract law, as reflected in both legislation and judicial precedents.

13.07 This section provides a brief overview of some instances where third-party rights and obligations have emerged in contractual relationships that began as bilateral arrangements. Even though the principle of privity of contract was not discussed in Islamic law, Muslim jurists addressed issues that could be considered exceptions to the concept. A few examples are provided below.

13.08 The default rule is that most contracts, particularly bilateral legal arrangements, are between two contracting parties with a valid offer (*'ijāb*) and a corresponding acceptance (*qabūl*).[2] However, there are situations where the effect of such a valid legal arrangement could have legal consequences for a third party or third-party rights; hence, such a contract could give rise to claims by parties who are not directly involved in the original contract. These could be regarded as claims by non-contractual parties.

13.09 A general principle in Islamic contract law is that a person cannot sell property that does not belong to him.[3] In breach of this principle, if a person proceeds to execute

[1] See John A. Makdisi, 'The Islamic Origins of the Common Law' (1999) 77(5) North Carolina Law Review 1635.

[2] Abū Bakr ibn Mas'ūd al-Kāsānī, Badā'i' al-Sanā'i' fi Tartīb al-Sharā'i' (Sharikat al-Maṭbū'āt al-'Ilmīyah, 1910) Vol. 5, p. 133.

[3] This principle is from a *ḥadīth* and its full version is as follows:

> Ja`far ibn Abi Washiyah reported from Yusuf ibn Mahak, from Hakim ibn Hizam (who said): "I asked the Prophet: O Messenger of God. A man comes to me and asks me to sell him what is not with me. I sell him (what he wants) and then buy the goods for him in the market (and deliver them)." The Prophet replied: "Do not sell what you do not possess".

This *ḥadīth* was narrated by Abu Dawud in his Sunan, *Ḥadīth* No. 3503; Al-Tirmidhi in his Sunan, *Ḥadīth* No. 1232; and Al-Nasa'i in his Sunan, *Ḥadīth* No. 4613. See Abu 'Isa Muhammad bin 'Isa Al-Tirmidhi, Al-Jami'

a contract of sale for property which does not belong to him, the real owner, who is a third party, has the right to make a valid claim against the buyer to reclaim his property. In the event that the third-party owner successfully claims the property from the buyer, the seller is liable to the buyer for the price paid. The seller needs to return the price and pay any additional compensation to the buyer.

Furthermore, the sale of a pawned item of property provides a good example of contracts with third-party rights and obligations. This simply shows how contracts in Islamic law go beyond just two parties. **13.10**

After a pawned item of property is sold and it is later discovered that the property belongs to a third party who is different from the pawning debtor, Muslim jurists have considered the rights of third parties after such a sale. In addressing the rights of such a third party who has been discovered to be the legal owner of the pawned property, two situations have been considered by the Hanafi jurists.[4] **13.11**

The first scenario is when the pawned property remains intact at the time it is discovered that a third party is the original owner. In this situation, once the real owner finds out about the sale of the property, he or she is permitted by law to claim and retain it based on the legal right to claim the possession of one's own property. The real owner should not be encumbered in any way. However, another problem arises on the part of the bona fide purchaser for value without notice. In this case, the buyer has a legal remedy to validly request compensation for the price he or she has paid earlier. The buyer's claim is a legal remedy that can be sustained against either the seller or the creditor, depending on which party received the original price paid. The underlying principle here is that a sale was made by a party that had no right to the property, which voids the sale *ab initio*. Since the sales contract is void, the price received must be returned.[5] **13.12**

The second scenario is when the pawned property has been destroyed. In this case, the owner could demand compensation from the pawning debtor, trustee, or buyer, depending on who had custody of the property at the material time. In respect of the pawning debtor who could be considered to be usurping the third party's property and pawning it, such a person is required to pay compensation to the real owner of the destroyed property. The payment of such compensation would have validated the initial sale to the buyer as well as debt repayment to the creditor further to the retroactive ownership conferred on the pawning debtor. So, upon payment of compensation to the real owner, the law then treats the pawned property, which has now been destroyed, as **13.13**

Al-Kabir (Dar al-Gharb al-Islami, 1996) Vol. 4, p. 228; Abu Abdul Rahman Ahmad bin Shuaib Al-Nasa'i, Kitab al-Sunan al-Kubra (Muassasah al-Risalah, 2001) Vol. 7, p. 289; Sulaimān bin Al-Ash'ath Abu Dawud, Sunan Abi Dawud (Al-Maktabah al-Ansāriyyah, 1323AH) Vol. 3, p. 302.

[4] Ibn Al-Humam, Fath Al-Qadir Sharh Al-Hidayah (Matba'ah Mustafa Muhammad) Vol. 8, p. 223.
[5] Wahbah Al-Zuhaili, Financial Transactions in Islamic Jurisprudence, trans. Mahmoud A. El-Gamal (Dār Al-Fikr, 2003) Vol. 2, pp. 176–77 (hereafter Al-Zuhaili, *Financial Transactions*).

if it were the original property of the debtor. This principle also applies to a situation where the true owner suddenly appears and seeks compensation from the seller who is also considered as the trustee of the property in the eyes of the law. Once the seller pays compensation, he is considered retroactively to be the owner of the pawned property; therefore, the seller-trustee has only sold his property to the buyer. In this latter case, the seller-trustee would then have legal recourse against the pawning debtor for compensation.[6]

13.14 Another complex multi-party contractual relationship is seen in a scenario where the real owner of the pawned property which is now destroyed decides to pursue the buyer for compensation. In this case, the buyer is allowed to seek compensation from the seller-trustee who in turn would seek compensation from the debtor. The debtor is required to repay the debt provided the price for the destroyed pawned property was earlier paid to the seller-creditor.[7]

3. Some Contracts with Third-Party Rights

3.1 Guarantees in Contracts (*Kafāla*)

13.15 Although this was already discussed extensively in Chapter 12, it is pertinent to briefly identify how the contract of guarantee inherently has some third-party legal implications. In Islamic jurisprudence, the contract of guarantee is one of the numerous contracts that have third-party implications and legal consequences. This form of contract has its origins in the primary sources of Sharīʿah and has been used by contracting parties since the advent of Islam.[8] In the modern practice of Sharīʿah-compliant commercial and financial transactions, *kafāla* has been utilized in structuring relevant transactions.

13.16 In general terms, *kafāla* is a contract of guarantee where the guarantor joins a principal debtor in jointly assuming a clearly specified debt obligation. The principal debtor is the guaranteed party in this legal relationship. In essence, a back-up debtor steps in if the principal debtor defaults in its payment obligations. This is structured in the form of a backstop for a typical contractual debt arrangement to secure the right of the creditor. Muslim jurists have attributed several meanings to the word *kafāla*. Some of the major definitions are provided below for clarity and comparison.

13.17 According to the Hanbali jurists, *kafāla* is a joint obligation of the principal debtor and the guarantor in the underlying commitment that exists between the debtor and the creditor. In this case, since the right of the creditor to repayment is a joint and several

[6] Ibid, Vol. 2, p. 177.
[7] Ibid.
[8] Wahbah bin Mustafa Al-Zuhaili, al-Fiqh al-Islāmi Wa Adillatuhu (Dār al-Fikr, n.d.) Vol. 6, p. 4142 (hereafter Al-Zuhaili, *al-Fiqh al-Islāmi*).

obligation, the creditor could decide to claim from either of the parties.[9] In essence, once the guarantee kicks in, the obligation becomes a joint responsibility of both the principal debtor and the guarantor, and both become liable jointly and severally.

The Shafi'i jurists define *kafāla* as an undertaking or commitment of a party to a duty or debt that another party is obliged to discharge. It could also mean a commitment or undertaking to produce an asset or even a person at a specified time or place as a legal and enforceable obligation.[10] Therefore, *kafāla* becomes a joint commitment between the guarantor and the guaranteed person, and in such a legal arrangement both parties remain jointly and severally liable until the underlying debt or right is finally settled or fulfilled. **13.18**

In a similar vein, but in a somewhat different manner, the Maliki jurists define *kafāla* as a party's obligation towards the right of another party which is to be fulfilled for the benefit of a third party.[11] While both the principal debtor and the guarantor are still jointly and severally liable for the underlying debt obligation, the latter legally obliges himself or herself to fulfil the right of the creditor in the contractual relationship. In this school of jurisprudence, parties to a deed of guarantee are not allowed to contractually exempt the principal debtor from liability of the underlying obligation. **13.19**

The Hanafi jurists define *kafāla* as a joint obligation of both the principal debtor and the guarantor in respect of the claim to the underlying debt obligation.[12] While the creditor is permitted to claim the debt from either of the parties, he can only request actual payment from the principal debtor and not the guarantor. It thus appears that the obligation of the guarantor is merely meant to secure payment of the debt by the principal debtor (or the guaranteed party).[13] Therefore, the Hanafi jurists only consider the liability to be joint but not several, as the creditor can only claim his or her right from the principal debtor and not the guarantor. The guarantor's obligation is merely to ensure the principal debtor pays the debt he or she guarantees. **13.20**

It is therefore clear that there is difference between the definitions of the majority of Muslim jurists comprising the Hanbali, Shafi'i, and Maliki schools on one hand and the minority opinion of the Hanafi jurists with regard to the nature of *kafāla* as a joint and several obligation. The preferred opinion, which closely resembles the modern practice of *kafāla*, is that of the majority of Muslim jurists, as explained above, where the obligations of the principal debtor and the guarantor are joint and several in nature. The guarantor could be called upon to pay the debt if the debtor defaults. However, these **13.21**

[9] 'Abdullah Ibn Muhammad Ibn Qudāmah, Al-Mughni (Maktaba al-Qāhira, 1969) Vol. 4, p. 410 (hereafter Ibn Qudāmah, *Al-Mughni*); Mansūr bin Yūnus Al-Bahuti, Kashshaf Al-Qinā 'an Matn al-Iqnā' (Dār 'Ālam al-Kutub) pp. 242–43.

[10] Ibn Hajar Al-Haitami, Tuhfah al-Muhtaj fi Sharh al-Minhaj (Dar al-Kutub al-Ilmiyyah, 2001) Vol. 2, p. 294.

[11] Muhammad bin 'Urfah Al-Dasūqi, Hashiyah al-Dasūqi 'ala al-Sharh al-Kabīr (Dar al-Kutub al-'Ilmiyyah, n.d.) Vol. 3, p. 537.

[12] Shams al-Dīn Al-Sarakhsi, Kitab al-Mabsūt (Dār al-Ma'rifah, 1993) Vol. 19, pp. 160–61.

[13] Ibid, Vol. 19, p. 461; Ibn al-Sa'ati, Majma' al-Bahrain Wa Multaqa al-Nirain (Dār al-Kutub al-'Ilmiyyah, 2005) p. 439; 'Abd al-Rahman Al-Kalibuli, Majma' al-Anhar (Dar al-Kutub al-'Ilmiyyah, 1998) Vol. 3, p. 172.

principles are subject to contractual terms and conditions provided they do not contradict any textual evidence of the Qur'ān and Sunnah.

13.22 Another dimension to the definition of *kafāla* is seen in contemporary Muslim jurists' discussion of the subject. In his definition of *kafāla*, al-Zuhaili defines the term as a legal obligation to financially compensate someone for any damage or loss incurred as a result of the act or omission of another person.[14] This definition is quite comprehensive and could be interpreted to include indemnification, which is commonly used in modern contracts. Another modern definition is seen in al-Zarqa's description of *kafāla*, which considers it to be an undertaking to financially compensate a party for any damage that may arise from dealing with another party.[15] Though this definition also mirrors the indemnification clauses in modern bilateral contracts, such as an undertaking to indemnify another party for any loss or damage, there is still a third-party element in the contractual arrangement as the underlying loss or damage could be suffered by such a third party. In this case, the third party is not the guarantor but the beneficiary of the guarantee which is in the form of an indemnification.

13.23 As described above, the nature of *kafāla* is inherent in the contractual arrangement itself as it seeks to secure the performance of a particular obligation. The guarantor gives a binding legal assurance to the creditor for the fulfilment of an obligation which a party has contracted to perform. Effectively, *kafāla* is legally binding and enforceable on the guarantor if the guaranteed party fails in his or her obligations under the contract.[16]

13.24 The textual evidence to support the legitimacy of *kafāla* is found in Qur'ān 12:72: 'They said, "We are missing the measuring-bowl of the king, and whoever brings it back shall deserve a camel-load, and I stand surety (*zā'im*) for it." ' Ibn 'Abbas described the word *za'im* as referring to *kāfil*, which means a guarantor. The act of standing in as a surety for another is a guarantee. This could apply to both current debt obligations as well as future debts. In fact, such a guarantee could also be applied to past debt obligations, as highlighted in the following prophetic precedent narrated by Jabir. The Prophet refused to perform the funeral prayer on a person who died while owing a debt. One day, the corpse of a dead Muslim was brought to him, and he began by asking whether there was any debt due from him. His companions replied in the affirmative and stated that it was two dinars. The Prophet told the companions to pray over the dead Muslim. Abu Qatada al-Ansari immediately came forward and pledged that he would settle the debt on behalf of the dead Muslim. Upon hearing that, the Prophet then proceeded to pray over the dead Muslim. In another narration, the Prophet said: 'The guarantor is liable for the loss and damage of what is guaranteed by him.'[17] In addition to the above

[14] Al-Zuhaili, *al-Fiqh al-Islāmi* (n 8) Vol. 6, p. 4144.

[15] Mustafa Al-Zarqa, Al-Madkhal al-Fiqhi al-'Ām (Dār al-Qalam, 2004) Vol. 1, p. 526.

[16] Al-Tayyār, Al-Fiqh al-Muyassar (Madār al-Watan, 2012) Vol. 6, p. 113.

[17] *Hadīth* No. 2289. See Muhammad bin Isma'il Al-Bukhāri, Al-Jāmi' al-Sahīh (Al-Matba'ah al-Salafiyyah, 1980) Vol. 2, p. 139.

evidence, Ibn Qudama reveals that Muslim jurists unanimously agree on the permissibility of *kafāla* to facilitate commercial activities among people.[18]

3.2 *Wakāla* and Third-Party Rights

The definition, legal validity, elements, and underlying legal issues in an agency contract or *wakāla* have been comprehensively analysed in Chapter 11. However, a brief overview is provided here with emphasis on third-party rights. Even though *wakāla* is considered an ancillary contract, its legal effect involves an element of a contract that has implications on third parties. From the very beginning, an agency contract imposes some rights and obligations on the initial two contractual parties which would have legal consequences for a third party with whom the agent may deal. **13.25**

When the principal delegates authority to the agent to perform certain tasks on his behalf, those tasks would ordinarily involve third parties. While it appears that there are two original parties in a *wakāla* contract (the principal (*muwakkil*) and the agent (*wakīl*)), there is always a third party involved as part of the legal consequences of the agency contract. The dealings to be undertaken by the agent on behalf of the principal could involve dealing with third parties, and any breach or claim that emanates from such sub-contractual engagements could bind the principal. **13.26**

Though the two types of *wakāla* have been described in Chapter 11, it is important to explore how they both involve some third-party legal implications. First, the unrestricted or general *wakāla* involves the full delegation of powers by the principal to the agent to undertake a series of contractual dealings on his behalf without any restriction. If the principal enters into a agency contractual relationship with the agent to help purchase a house, such contract of sale and purchase will involve third parties, such as the seller of the house, and such sale and purchase agreement has its own terms and conditions as well as rights, duties, and obligations which ultimately bind the principal. **13.27**

The second type of *wakāla* contract—the restricted *wakāla*—which includes specific agency instructions, may involve a clear delegation of powers to perform a specific task on behalf of the principal. If in this contractual arrangement the principal specifically requests the agent to sell his real estate property at a particular price, such will still involve third parties and consequential rights and obligations flowing up to the principal. **13.28**

The binding nature of *wakāla* is often emphasized more when it involves third-party rights. In fact, the main objective of a *wakāla* contract is to facilitate the transactions or dealings between a principal and third parties. **13.29**

Muslim jurists have opined on the question of whether the agent can appoint a sub-agent to perform the role delegated to him by the principal. In such a contractual **13.30**

[18] Ibn Qudāmah, *Al-Mughni* (n 9) Vol. 4, p. 402-404

arrangement involving three parties, it is generally agreed that if the principal permits the agent in the agency contract to delegate the authority to another agent, such sub-delegation is valid.[19]

13.31 However, the jurists disagreed on the situation where the agent is not expressly permitted to do so. The Maliki jurists opined that if the original principal has not permitted the agent to delegate the authority to a sub-agent, then the agent cannot proceed with such delegation except in two unique situations. First, if the agent is saddled with the responsibility of a dealing which is not appropriate for him personally to undertake such as in a specialized trade, he is allowed to delegate his authority to a sub-agent, provided the latter is a reputable and well-known expert in the trade. If this condition is not fulfilled, then the agent will be responsible for any financial loss occasioned by the unauthorized delegation of powers. Secondly, if the agent is entrusted with a large number of responsibilities which he cannot undertake personally, he is allowed to seek the assistance of others who will help him in the discharge of the duties. In this second scenario, the agent is not allowed to appoint a sub-agent to independently carry out such responsibilities.[20]

13.32 The Hanafi jurists opined that it is not permissible for the agent to delegate his authority to a sub-agent without the permission of the principal except in the following three situations: first, the distribution of *zakat*; secondly, collection of debts; and thirdly, price estimation.[21] For their part, the Hanbali jurists opined that the agent is not allowed to delegate his authority to a third party if he can undertake the dealing himself. However, if the undertaking is beyond his capability or will burden him unnecessarily, he is allowed to sub-delegate the undertaking. The Shafi'i jurists also agreed that the agent can delegate his undertaking to a sub-agent if he is not able to perform the task or if such task is not appropriate for him without the need for permission of the principal.[22]

13.33 Finally, in modern Islamic financial transactions, the most commonly used *wakāla* is known as the *wakāla bi al-Istithmār* (investment agency). This is one of the easiest ways for Islamic financial institutions and fund managers to make a profit through a pre-agreed fee. In most cases, *wakāla bi al-Istithmār* involves dealing with third parties and it is generally structured in the form of an unrestricted *wakāla* to maximize the return on investment.

[19] 'Abd Al-Rahman Al-Juzairi, Kitab al-Fiqh 'ala al-Madhahib al-Arba'ah (Dār al-Kutub al-'Ilmiyyah, 2003) Vol. 3, p. 179.

[20] Ibid.

[21] Muhammad Amin ibn 'Umar Ibn 'Ābidīn, Radd al-Mul-Mu 'alá al-Durr al-Mukhtār (Maktabah Mustafa al-Bābi, 1966) Vol. 5, p. 527.

[22] Al-Juzairi (n 19) pp. 179–80.

3.3 Third-Party Rights in Contract of Debt Assignment (*Ḥawāla*)

One key exception to the principle of privity of contract and party autonomy is the inherent nature of contract of debt assignment or *ḥawāla*. This means the transfer of debt from the debtor to a third party which emphasizes some rights and obligations in a tripartite contractual arrangement. **13.34**

3.3.1 Definition

In its literal sense, *ḥawāla* simply means an assignment, or transfer from one location or person to another.[23] In the juristic sense of the word, *ḥawāla* means the transfer of a debt or financial liability from an initial debtor to a third party who takes full responsibility to redeem the debt. This transfer of debt arrangement has the effect of relieving the initial debtor of the debt obligation. **13.35**

The Hanafi jurists define *ḥawāla* as a debt assignment legal arrangement where a debt liability is transferred from a debtor to another party who is specifically named in the contract and who then becomes fully liable for the original debt.[24] In essence, the original debtor is replaced by the new debtor. The debt assignment contract has an underlying consideration of a similar debt. **13.36**

In the definition of *ḥawāla*, the Hanafi jurists have expressed two views on the nature of the debt assignment. First, *ḥawāla* could be the assignment of the demand from the debtor to the party who then becomes obliged to fulfil the demand. The second situation is the transfer of both the demand and the debt obligation together to a third party. In such a situation, the original debtor is free from the debt obligation once the debt due to the creditor is assigned to a third party who is obliged to redeem the debt.[25] **13.37**

3.3.2 Legality

The legality of *ḥawāla* is firmly rooted in the *ḥadīth*. Abu Hurairah narrated that the Prophet once said: 'Default on payment by a solvent debtor is unjust, and if anyone of you is transferred to a solvent person, he must accept the transfer.'[26] In a similar narration by Ahmad and Al-Bayhaqi, the Prophet said: 'If one is referred to a solvent person for the recovery of his right, such a person must accept the transfer.'[27] These prophetic instructions for a solvent person to accept a referral for a debt recovery simply point to the fact that *ḥawāla* is permissible under the law. This is further supported by the consensus of opinion among Muslim jurists regarding the permissibility of *ḥawāla*.[28] **13.38**

[23] Hans Wehr, A Dictionary of Modern Written Arabic, ed. J. Milton Cowan (Spoken Language Services, Inc. 1976) p. 218.
[24] Al-Zuhaili, *al-Fiqh al-Islāmi* (n 8) Vol. 6, p. 4187.
[25] Al-Juzairi (n 19) Vol. 3, p. 180.
[26] *Hadīth* No. 2287. See Al-Bukhāri (n 17) Vol. 2, p. 139.
[27] Ibn Qudāmah, *Al-Mughni* (n 9) Vol. 4, p. 335.
[28] Mansur bin Yunus Al-Bahuti, Kashshaf Al-Qina 'an matn al-iqna (Dar 'Alam al-Kutub) Vol. 3, p. 382; Al-Zuhaili, *al-Fiqh al-Islāmi* (n 8) Vol. 6, p. 4189.

3.3.3 Types

13.39 There are two main types of *ḥawāla*: restricted (*muqayyada*) and unrestricted (*mutlaqa*).[29] In a restricted *ḥawāla*, the debt assignment contract permits the third party to fulfil the debt obligation from the assets of the assignor that he has in his possession. In other words, the assignee who is the third party in the tripartite contractual arrangement pays the creditor from the assets of the assignor in his custody to fully redeem the debt obligation.[30] On the other hand, in the general or unrestricted *ḥawāla*, there is no requirement that the assignee pay the debt from the property of the assignor in his custody. The contract of debt assignment in the unrestricted *ḥawāla* does not need to stipulate that the payment to the creditor must be made from the asset of the assignor in the custody of the assignee. It is possible the assignee does not even have any asset of the assignor in his custody but chooses to undertake the payment to the creditor voluntarily to help him.[31]

13.40 It is pertinent to note that the majority of Muslim jurists comprising the Maliki, Shafi'i, and Hanbali scholars only recognize a restricted *ḥawāla* where the assignee owes a similar debt to the assignor which validates the debt transfer and subsequent payment to the creditor. They emphasized that if the assignee does not owe anything to the assignor or have in his custody the property of the assignor, then the contractual arrangement cannot be considered as *ḥawāla*, but rather it is a *kafāla* or guarantee contract.[32]

3.3.4 Elements and Conditions for its Validity

13.41 The majority of Muslim jurists identified the following as the main elements of *ḥawāla*:

1. The transferor or assignor (*al-muḥīl*)
2. The transferee or creditor (*al-muḥal*)
3. The payer or assignee (*al-muḥal ʿalahi*)
4. The debt obligation (*al-muḥal bihi*)
5. The offer and acceptance or *ṣigha*

13.42 The Hanafi jurists opined that *ḥawāla* has just one element, which is the offer and acceptance. The offer emanates from *al-muḥīl* to the *al-muḥal* when the transferor informs the transferee that he has transferred the debt owed to the latter to a third party. The acceptance in this contractual arrangement is seen in the acceptance of the offeror's consent by the creditor (transferor) and the assignee (payer) respectively to the offer made.[33]

13.43 The conditions for the validity of *ḥawāla* have been expressed in different ways by Muslim jurists. For instance, the Hanafi jurists stipulate four conditions, while the

[29] Mufti Muhammad Taqi Usmani, Fiqh al-Buyu ʿala Madhahib al-ʿArbaʿa (Quranic Studies Publishers, 2015) Vol. 1, p. 437.
[30] Ibid.
[31] Ibid, Vol. 1, pp. 437–38.
[32] Ibid, Vol. 1, p. 438.
[33] Al-Juzairi (n 19) Vol. 3, pp. 186–87.

Shafi'i and Maliki jurists identify six different conditions. In contrast, the Hanbali jurists identify five unique conditions. A review of the respective conditions stipulated by the four schools of thought reveals that they all relate to three main issues: legal capacity, consent, and the nature of the debt, as illustrated in Table 13.1.[34]

3.3.5 Legal Consequences

In a *ḥawāla* contractual arrangement, Muslim jurists have opined on the main consequences for the parties involved and the associated debts. The Hanbali jurists considered that once the conditions for the validity of *ḥawāla* have been fulfilled, the transferor is discharged from the debt obligation whether the payer or assignee becomes bankrupt, dies, or denies the debt outright.[35] The Maliki and Shafi'i jurists generally agreed with this view.[36] However, the Hanbali jurists added that if the conditions for *ḥawāla* are not met, then the debt assignment arrangement is not valid, but the contractual arrangement can still take the form of an agency contract.[37] As for the Hanafi jurists, a valid *ḥawāla* discharges the transferor from all debt liabilities and any claim related to such. However, in a situation where the payer becomes bankrupt or dies, the transferee would have a legal recourse against the transferor.[38] **13.44**

4. Third-Party Rights in Contract of Pre-emption (*Shuf'a*)

Pre-emption is one of the key contracts with third-party rights in Islamic law. Even though it relates to underlying interests in land, its modern-day application in Islamic finance and other commercial transactions makes it relevant in any discourse involving third-party rights in contractual relationships. Similarly to *kafāla*, *ḥawāla*, and *wakāla*, *shuf'a* confers immediate and direct rights on a third party in the contractual relationship. **13.45**

4.1 Definition

In literal terms, *shuf'a* means augmentation, fortification, combination, or increase.[39] The word is derived from the verbal noun *shaf'un*, which can literally be interpreted as addition to something, that is, something is being added to another. Applying this literal understanding to the general meaning of pre-emption, one can see that *shuf'a* involves enhancing one's property rights from an adjacent or adjoining property belonging to **13.46**

[34] Ibid, Vol. 3, pp. 186–92.
[35] Ibn Qudamah, Al-Kāfi fi Fiqh al-Imām Ahmad (Dar al-Kutub al-'Ilmiyyah, 1994) Vol. 2, p. 125.
[36] Ibn al-Rif'ah, Kifāyat al-Nabīh Fi Sharh al-Tanbīh (Dar al-Kutub al-'Ilmiyyah, 2009) Vol. 10, p. 163; Ibn Bazīzah, Raudat al-Mustabīn fi Sharh Kitab al-Talqīn (Dar Ibn Hazm, 2010) Vol. 2, p. 1147.
[37] Ibn Qudāmah, *Al-Mughni* (n 9) Vol. 4, p. 392.
[38] Ibid, Vol. 4, pp. 393–94.
[39] See generally Abdullah ibn Abdul Aziz Dar'an, Ahkam al-shuf'a fi fiqh al-Islami (Maktabah al-Taubah, 1994).

Table 13.1 The *Ḥawāla* conditions matrix table

	HANAFI	SHAFI'I	MALIKI	HANBALI
LEGAL CAPACITY	1. The transferor must have requisite full legal capacity. 2. The transferee or creditor must also have the legal capacity. 3. The payer or assignee should have the legal capacity to act independently.			
CONSENT		1. The transferor must consent to the contractual arrangement 2. The transferee or creditor must also consent to the contract.	1. The transferor and the transferee must consent to the *ḥawāla* arrangement.	1. The consent of the transferor is required. The consent of the transferee or the creditor is not required if the payer or assignee is able to discharge the obligation.
NATURE OF DEBT	4. The transferor must owe the debt to the transferee.	3. The debt must be identifiable based on its value or description. 4. The debt must be binding in its nature and its monetary value without time limitation. 5. The transferred debt must be equal to the debt to be discharged by the payer or assignee in its type, quality, and value. 6. Both the original debt of the transferor and the debt of the payer or assignee must be transferable.	2. The transferor must be owed a debt by the transferee while the latter should be owed a debt by the payer or assignee. 3. One of the two debts must be due immediately and not a deferred debt. 4. The debt must be binding. 5. The transferred debt must be equal to the debt to be discharged by the payer or assignee in its type, quality, and value. 6. The two debts must not be realizable from the sale of staple food such as cereals and similar items.	2. The transferred debt must be equal to the debt to be discharged by the payer or assignee in its type, quality, and value. 3. The debt must be identifiable based on its value or description. 4. The debt of the payer must have been firmly established or due at the time of the debt assignment. 5. The debt owed by the payer or assignee must be capable of being realized through ascertainment of its value and amount.

Source: Author.

another person. This conceptual meaning is seen in the Qur'ān 4:85, where a derivative word of *shuf'a* is used: 'Whoever recommends and helps a good cause becomes a partner therein.' In other words, whoever contributes, takes part in, or recommends a good cause will be benefiting from the accruing reward by adding to his own reward.

From the juristic perspective, the word *shuf'a* could either mean the pre-emption property itself or the process of acquiring a property as a result of rights conferred by pre-emption. As an exception to the privity of contract and party autonomy principles, a third party can legally acquire rights in a concluded sale of property even after the offer and acceptance. As a result, the majority of jurists define *shuf'a* as the third-party right in a contract of sale of real estate where the third party is given the right of first refusal in a sale of adjoining property as a result of being a direct neighbour of the seller. The right of pre-emption invalidates a sale from a partner to a buyer by conferring the proprietary rights acquired by the buyer from the sale to another partner who is entitled to such right as a result of being a partner to the original owner of the property. **13.47**

Pre-emption is therefore the right of a third party—the pre-emptor—in acquiring a piece of real estate which was hitherto sold to a buyer by an immediate neighbour with whom the pre-emptor shares a common boundary. The amount to be paid by the pre-emptor to exercise the right of pre-emption is the same amount the buyer paid to purchase the property. Any improvement made by the buyer to the property must be refunded accordingly upon the exercise of the right of pre-emption.[40] **13.48**

4.2 Legal Validity

The affirmative evidence supporting the right of pre-emption is found in numerous sources of Islamic law in a *ḥadīth* narrated by Jabir where the Prophet Muhammad was reported to have decreed that pre-emption rights are legally established for undivided properties. However, in situations where boundaries are clearly delineated (between properties) and road paths are paved and demarcated, there shall be no right of pre-emption.[41] In a similar vein, Jabir narrated that the Prophet once said: 'A neighbour is more worthy of purchasing his neighbour's property. As a result, the decision of such a neighbour should be sought even if he is absent. This is enforced as a legal right since they share a road.'[42] The legal implication of this *ḥadīth* is that the neighbour who shares an undivided property with another must be given the right of first refusal in the sale of such property as a result of pre-emption rights conferred on the neighbour. **13.49**

Some other relevant prophetic precedents include the following: 'The neighbour of a house is more entitled to it in any sale (by the right of pre-emption).'[43] **13.50**

[40] 'Ali Al-Khafīf, Ahkām al-Mu'āmalāt al-Shar'iyyah (Ansar al-Sunnah al-Muhammadiyyah Press, 1947) p. 128.
[41] *Hadīth* No. 2287. See Al-Bukhāri (n 17) Vol. 2, p. 128.
[42] Shaybah al-Hamd, Fiqh al-Islam Sharh Bulugh Al-Maram (Al-Madinah Press, n.d.) Vol. 6, p. 11.
[43] Muhammad ibn Ismail Al-Amir, Subul al-Salam Sharh Bulugh Al-Maram (Dar Ihya Turath al-Arabi, 1960) Vol. 3, p. 74.

> The Messenger of Allah decreed pre-emption in every joint ownership and not divided—it may be dwelling or a garden, it is not lawful for him (for the partner) to sell that until his partner gives his consent. He (the partner) is entitled to buy it when he desires, and he can abandon it if he so likes. And if he (the one partner) sells it without getting the consent of the (other partner), he has the greatest right to it.[44]

13.51 Ibn al-Mundhir emphasized that the people of knowledge unanimously agree that the right of pre-emption is conferred on a partner in the sale of an undivided property such a piece of land, a house, or an orchard.[45] He further added that he is not aware of any scholar that disagreed with this position except Al-Asam, who argues that pre-emption rights could lead to economic harm on the part of property owners since buyers will be discouraged from attempting to purchase a property that could potentially be subject to pre-emption rights.[46] This could ultimately lead to valuation of the underlying property below the market price which would cause unintended harm to property owners.[47] Even though Al-Asam's argument could be considered as having some merits from the logical point of view, it contradicts clear and unambiguous prophetic precedents as well as consensus among the scholars, as highlighted above.

13.52 It is important to identify the objective of the right of pre-emption and appreciate its legality in Islamic jurisprudence. Muslim jurists have explained the wisdom behind such a legal right given to a neighbour in any planned or already executed sale of any property where there is an undivided interest. The objective of conferring such a right on a neighbour is to prevent unnecessary hardship and potential transaction costs when an adjoining property is sold to a stranger. Therefore, such a partner or neighbour is legally conferred with the right of first refusal.

4.3 Elements and Parties to Pre-emption

13.53 Most Muslim jurists opine that the elements or pillars of pre-emption are the pre-emptor or *al-shafi'i*, the party from whom the pre-emption right is claimed or *al-mashfu'u 'alaihi*, and the object of pre-emption or *al-mashfu'u fihi*.

13.54 The pre-emptor or *al-shafi'i*: this is the third party in a contract of sale for a property that is subject to the exercise of the right of pre-emption. The pre-emptor, who can be a partner, co-proprietor, or immediate neighbour, is the party conferred with the right of pre-emption. The majority of Muslim jurists opine that the pre-emptor should only be a partner/co-proprietor based on the legal text that stipulates the sharing of the undivided property.[48] However, the Hanafi jurists emphasize that the pre-emptor could be a

[44] *Hadīth* No. 1208. See Muslim bin al-Hajjāj, Sahīh Muslim (Matba'ah 'Isa al-Bābi, 1955) Vol. 3, p. 1229 (hereafter Muslim, *Sahīh Muslim*).
[45] Ibn Qudāmah, *Al-Mughni* (n 9) Vol. 5, p. 229.
[46] Ibid, Vol. 7, p. 436.
[47] Al-Zuhaili, *Financial Transactions* (n 5) Vol. 2, p. 702.
[48] Al-Zuhaili, *al-Fiqh al-Islāmi* (n 8) Vol. 6, p. 4886.

partner or a neighbour.[49] In order to reconcile both opinions, Ibn al-Qayyim stipulated that the right of pre-emption is established for a neighbour if only he is a partner or co-proprietor in one of the rights of special easement, such as road access or source of drinking water.[50]

There are situations where there are competing interests among multiple pre-emptors who are partners or neighbours of the vendor. The majority of jurists comprising the Maliki, Shafi'i, and Hanbali scholars opined that if all the partners exercise their pre-emption right against the underlying property, the partners are to be granted their pro-rated rights in the property.[51] On the other hand, the Hanafi jurists argued that rather than divide the property according to the proportion of shares of each partner, the right of pre-emption shall be enforced on the property by dividing it equally among the partners without giving any consideration to the quantity of shares of individual partners in the partnership.[52] **13.55**

In the event of the absence of some of the pre-emptors in a situation where they all have competing or concurrent pre-emption claims, the Muslim jurists unanimously agreed that in the presence of some of them at the time of sale, they can validly lay claims of pre-emption which should be granted to them in accordance with their shares in the partnership.[53] The reason for this is that those pre-emptors who are absent may be regarded as having forfeited their pre-emption rights. However, once the pre-emptors who are present have been accorded their pre-emption rights completely, if those that were absent then suddenly emerge, the latter can validly lay claim to their pre-emption rights. This is resolved by dividing the shares of the pre-emptors who have earlier taken their shares to reflect the ownership of the new pre-emptors who have just arrived.[54] **13.56**

The party from whom a pre-emption right is claimed or *al-mashfu'u 'alaihi*: this is the party to whom ownership of the property is being transferred without the consent of the pre-emptor. In order to sustain a valid claim for pre-emption, the underlying property must have been transferred to a buyer with consideration through a valid sale.[55] In the absence of valid consideration through an outright sale, the pre-emptor will not be able to enforce his pre-emption right. That is, no valid pre-emption claim can be sustained against property validly transferred through inheritance, a will, charity, or gift. The justification for this position is found in the relevant *ḥadīths* which all stipulated a sale as a condition for the pre-emption right.[56] **13.57**

[49] Akmal al-Din al-Babarti, al-'Inayah Sharh al-Hidayah (Matba'ah Mustafa al-Halabi, 1970) Vol. 9, p. 369.
[50] Ibn al-Qayyim, I'lam al-Muqi'in 'An Rabb al-'Alamin (Dar al-Kutub al-'Ilmiyyah, 1991) Vol. 2, pp. 95–101.
[51] Muhammad bin Ahmad Ibn Rushd, Bidāyat al-Mujtahid Wa Nihāyat al-Muqtasid (Dār al-Hadīth, 2004) Vol. 4, p. 44; Al-Khatīb Al-Sharbīni, Al-Mughni Al-Muhtaj (Dār al-Ma'rifah, 1997) Vol. 2, pp. 383–84.
[52] Abu Bakar bin Mas'ūd Al-Kasāni, Badāí Al-Sanāi' fi Tartīb al-Sharāi' (Dār al-Kutub al'Ilmiyyah, 1986) Vol. 5, p. 8.
[53] Al-Zuhaili, *al-Fiqh al-Islāmi* (n 8) Vol. 6, p. 903.
[54] Ibid.
[55] Abu 'Umar Dubyān bin Muhammad Al-Dubyān, Al-Mu'āmalāt al-Māliyyah Asālah wa Mu'āsarah (Maktabah al-Malik Fahd Al-Wataniyyah, 1432H) Vol. 10, p. 363.
[56] Muslim, *Sahīh Muslim* (n 44) Vol. 3, p. 1229.

13.58 The object of pre-emption or *al-mashfu'u fihi*: this is the underlying property upon which the pre-emptor seeks to exercise his right to pre-emption. The four Sunni schools of thought in Islamic jurisprudence unanimously agreed that pre-emption can only take place in a sale involving real estate property such as houses, land, orchards, and appurtenances that are attached to them such as buildings or trees.[57] They also agreed that there is no pre-emption in movable property such as animals and merchandise of trade. They rely on the evidence in the *ḥadīth* narrated by Jabir, where it is emphasized that pre-emption is only in a partnership involving land, a home, or a wall.[58]

13.59 It is pertinent to note that the Zahiri jurists allowed pre-emption in movable properties and other types of properties such as animals. They allowed pre-emption in every form of property whether divisible or not.[59]

13.60 Apart from the above three elements of pre-emption, the Maliki jurists add a fourth element to a pre-emption arrangement, which is the form of the contract (*ṣigha*).[60] As the nature of pre-emption is more of an optional claim, it is a right exercisable by the pre-emptor whose legal effect only becomes binding upon its exercise either through a direct and instant request or through litigation. The Hanafi jurists opine that the main element of pre-emption is the ability of the pre-emptor to exercise his right of claim against either of the two contractual parties, that is, the vendor and the vendee, when the reason for such a claim is present and the condition is met.[61] They therefore identify the reason for the claim as the comingling of ownership, while the condition for the claim is that the object should be a real estate.

13.61 The parties to a pre-emption legal arrangement are vendor, vendee, and pre-emptor. First, the vendor is the original owner of the property who has either sold the property or intends to do so. Secondly, the vendee is either the buyer or potential buyer of the property who is considered a stranger to the property without any direct neighbourly relationship to the vendor. Thirdly, the pre-emptor is the third party who is the direct neighbour, co-proprietor, or partner of the vendor.

4.4 Conditions for the Validity of Pre-emption

13.62 For a pre-emption right to be enforced, the following conditions must be met:

1. The extinction of ownership rights on the part of the original owner with no enforceable option available to him. That is, a valid transfer of the property must have been executed.

[57] Abdul Karim Zaydan, Al-Madkhal li dirasah al-Sharī'ah al-Islamiyyah (Al-Quds Press, n.d.) p. 266.
[58] *Hadīth* No. 1608. See Muslim, *Sahīh Muslim* (n 44) Vol. 3, p. 1229.
[59] Ibn Hazm, Al-Mahala (-Amiriyyah Press, 1347 AH) Vol. 9, p. 1594.
[60] Ibn Rushd (n 51) Vol. 4, p. 40.
[61] Muhammad Amin ibn 'Umar Ibn 'Ābidīn, Radd al-Mul-Mu 'alá al-Durr al-Mukhtār (Maktabah Mustafa al-Bābi, 1966) Vol. 6, p. 218.

2. The contract must be commutative by its very nature such as a valid contract of sale or its equivalent.
3. The contract of sale must be valid. A defective sale will negate the right of pre-emption.
4. There must not be direct evidence to prove that the pre-emptor consents to the sale of the property and have failed to exercise his right of pre-emption for a long period of time without a reasonable valid excuse. In such circumstances and in the absence of a valid excuse, the pre-emptor would forfeit his right to claim for pre-emption.
5. The pre-emptor must initiate the claim for pre-emption as soon as possible.[62]

Other conditions stipulated by Muslim jurists as documented in treatises of Islamic jurisprudence include the requirement for the property to be immovable, subject to the dissenting view of the Zahiri jurists.[63] It has also been stipulated that the property should not be owned by the pre-emptor prior to the impugned sale. In addition, there is unanimity among the Muslim jurists on the point that once the right of pre-emption is exercised, it is required that the pre-emptor take the whole property as opposed to mere partitioning which could create greater harm to all the parties involved. In the absence of any of the above conditions, the pre-emption right is rendered nugatory.[64] **13.63**

4.5 Some Specific Rules Conferring Third-Party Pre-emption Rights

The right of pre-emption is merely an exercisable legal right on the part of the pre-emptor whose purpose is to prevent any harm or injury associated with the sale of land to a third party. However, the party upon whom the pre-emption right is conferred has the option to either enforce the right or waive it. If he intends to exercise the right of pre-emption, he is required to do so promptly without further delay as required by the majority of the jurists.[65] On the other hand, the Maliki jurists granted the pre-emptor a maximum of one year from the date of sale of the underlying property to exercise the right.[66] **13.64**

In order to exercise the right of pre-emption, the pre-emptor is required to make his request known within a reasonable time. Reasonableness here is construed as when the pre-emptor becomes aware of the sale contract. This kind of request to exercise a pre-emption right is called instant request or *ṭalab al-muwathaba*.[67] If nothing happens after the first request, the pre-emptor should immediately proceed with a firm request or *ṭalab al-taqrīr* where he is required to expressly disclose his desire to enforce his right **13.65**

[62] See Al-Zuhaili, *al-Fiqh al-Islāmi* (n 8) Vol. 6, pp. 913–22.
[63] Ibid, Vol. 6, p. 389.
[64] Abdul Karim (n 57) p. 272.
[65] Al-Zuhaili, *al-Fiqh al-Islāmi* (n 8) Vol. 6, p. 925.
[66] Mālik bin Anas, Al-Mudawwanah (Dār al-Kutub al-ʿIlmiyyah, 1994) Vol. 4, p. 217.
[67] Ali Al-Khafif, Ahkam al-Muʿamalat al-Shar'iyyah (Dār al-Fikr al-Arabi, 1426 AH) pp. 154–55.

of pre-emption. Such a second request should include some form of action, such as making a formal request at the site of the property. The first and second requests can, however, be made together in a situation where the sale of the property is done, and the pre-emptor goes straight to the vendee to exercise his right of pre-emption.[68] Finally, if the vendee refuses to surrender the underlying property after the first two requests have been made or when the property remains in the possession of the vendor after the sale, the pre-emptor is allowed to institute a lawsuit against either of the parties depending on which of them has possession of the property at the material time. This last request is made through a court action and is called *ṭalab al-khuṣūma*.[69]

13.66 Litigation is considered as a last resort if all prior steps fail to yield the desired result. Usually, the suit is instituted against the vendee since the sale has been concluded and, supposedly, he has taken possession. However, it is advisable to join the vendor as a respondent in the suit. If the vendor is still in possession of the property, then he has to be joined as a party.

13.67 The procedure for indicating one's intention to exercise the pre-emption right is sacrosanct, as failure to follow the established procedure could render the right nugatory. The pre-emptor is required to request the pre-empted property as a whole, whether there is a sole pre-emptor or competing pre-emptors.

13.68 As a third party in the initial sale contract, which is now under scrutiny, the pre-emptor does have some rights and duties in relation to the underlying property with specific reference to the initial sale contract. In respect of the price paid by the vendee, once the pre-emptor has validly exercised his right of pre-emption, he is to pay the exact price paid by the vendee. The Muslim jurists emphasized that there should be similarity or equality between the initial price paid by the vendee and the price to be paid by the pre-emptor. This position is anchored on the understanding that the pre-emptor is only taking the position of the vendee in the ownership of the property, hence the same price should be paid, which ordinarily will be refunded to the vendee.

13.69 The Muslim jurists however disagreed on issues relating to payment for the property on deferred terms and issues relating to discounted sale or increase in the sale price. When a property is sold to a vendee at a discounted price, will the principle of similarity and equality of the price or method of payment subsequently be enforced as part of the pre-emption right? The Hanbali jurists answer this question in the affirmative so that the pre-emptor benefits from both the equivalent price and the manner of payment, that is, on deferred terms. This position is also held by the Maliki jurists and upheld by one of the two views from the Shafi'i jurists. However, the Hanafi jurists argued that the pre-emptor should be given the option of either paying in full instantly or adopting the payment terms on deferred basis.[70]

[68] Ibid, p. 157.
[69] Ibid.
[70] Ibn Rushd (n 51) Vol. 4, p. 43.

In an impugned sale contract where the vendor gave a discount to the vendee and the transaction is later voided on the ground of the exercise of the pre-emption right by a pre-emptor, will the pre-emptor benefit from such a discounted price? There is disagreement among the jurists on this question. While the Hanafi jurists opined that the pre-emptor should benefit from such a price discount since the price paid in reality is connected to the original sale contract, the Hanbali jurists as well as Imam Shafi'i argued that the pre-emptor should not be allowed to benefit from the discount on the ground that the discount is the exclusive right of the vendor which he gave to the vendee, hence it operates outside the right of pre-emption.[71] In addition, another situation could arise where the price paid by the vendee to the vendor is above the market price or what should be paid for a similar transaction, or even when the prevailing market price has increased at the time of enforcement of the pre-emption right. In such situations, the jurists generally argued that the increment should not be extended to the pre-emptor as it will financially harm him.[72] **13.70**

[71] Al-Zuhaili, *al-Fiqh al-Islāmi* (n 8) Vol. 6, pp. 907–08.
[72] Ibn Qudāmah, Al-Mughni (n 9) Vol. 5, p. 322.

14

Performance, Termination, and Rescission of Contracts

1. Introduction

This chapter deals with the demise of a contract under Islamic law. As the reader will come to appreciate, the importance of contracts for the preservation of the Islamic *umma* dictate that termination is perhaps not as straightforward as in the civil law tradition, although even there the parties are subject to at least one, and at times two rounds of pertinent notifications. Muslim scholars, as will become evident, are more concerned with performance, and this dominates the relevant scholarship. Little emphasis is given to factors that vitiate performance, such as *force majeure*, or other extraneous circumstances. The same is true of termination and rescission, but this issue is treated in pragmatic fashion with a view to achieving equitable outcomes both for the contracting parties, as well as any impacted third parties. **14.01**

2. Performance

When a contract becomes binding, the performance of the underlying obligations also becomes obligatory upon the parties.[1] According to the Hanbalis and Shafi'is, a contract becomes binding with the lapse of the contract session (*majlis-al-'aqd*), that is, upon such time as the parties separate from each other.[2] The Hanafis and Malikis, for their part, are of the view that the contract becomes binding the moment the offer is unqualifiedly accepted.[3] This section discusses when a binding contract may be discharged through performance and for that purpose who, among offeror and offeree, must first perform the contract. It should be noted that the performance of a contract either involves *'ayn* (specific property) or *dayn* (debt). The performance of a contract involving each of these is governed by a distinct set of rules. After discussing the **14.02**

[1] Wahba Al-Zuhaylī, Al-Fiqh al-Islāmī wa Adillatuhu (Dār al-Fikr, 2007) Vol. 4, p. 3085.

[2] Abū Zakariyyā Al-Nawawī, Al-Majmū' Sharḥ Al-Muhadhdhab (Dār al-Fikr, n.d.) Vol. 9, p. 169; Ibn Qudāma, Al-Mughnī (Maktabat al-Qāhira, 1968) Vol. 3, p. 482.

[3] Ibn al-Humām, Fat'ḥ al-Qadīr Sharḥ al-Hidāya (Dār al-Fikr, n.d.) Vol. 5, p. 179; Abūbakr Al-Kāsānī, Badā'i' al-Ṣanā'i' fī Tartīb al-Sharā'i' (Dār al-Kutub al-'Ilmiyya, 1986) Vol. 5, p. 228; Muḥammad Al-Ḥaṭṭāb, Mawāhib al-Jalīl fī Sharḥ Mukhtaṣar Khalīl (Dār al-Fikr, 1992) Vol. 4, p. 229; Aḥmad Al-Qarāfī, Anwār al-Burūq fī Anwā' al-Furūq (Dār al-Kutub al-'Ilmiyya, 1998) Vol. 3, p. 444.

delivery of *dayn* and *ʿayn* as a form of contractual performance, this section concludes with non-performance or breach of contract.

2.1 When a Contract is Deemed as Having Been Performed

14.03 There is a specific point in the life of every contract when it is considered performed and the determination of that point of time primarily depends on the nature of the agreed performance. In turn, the nature of performance required to discharge the contract depends on the underlying contract. For instance, the contract of *ijāra* stands performed with the grant of permission from the lessor to enjoy the subject matter of the contract. Where performance necessarily demands the surrender of the subject matter, as in the case of public services (*ajīr mushtarak*), this is successfully discharged by the delivery of the subject matter.[4]

14.04 A sales contract is successfully performed with the transfer of the merchandise or land to the buyer.[5] It may also be said that the contract is performed when the risk in the subject matter is transferred to the buyer which is why the seller is liable if the property is destroyed before its delivery to the buyer. However, according to Ibn Qāsim, where one sells property, such as a house or animals, and stipulates that the seller shall have these in its possession for one year and the house or the animals are destroyed or lost before the year ends, both shall be deemed as being the buyer's own property. This is because upon the conclusion of the contract the liability is transferred to the buyer.[6] The position of the Maliki school is that liability shifts from the moment the contract is concluded and not from the moment possession is transferred.[7] Where the payment of the price is also required alongside delivery of possession, like the sale of merchandise, the contract will be performed upon payment of the price and delivery of possession.[8] There are certain contracts where delivery of possession is not required; instead, performance requires specific work, as in the case of personal services contracts.[9]

2.2 Which Party Must Perform First

14.05 Concerning which party must first perform, namely seller or buyer, Al-Sarakhsī states that the seller should surrender the commodity first and then the buyer must make payment. This is so because the contract usually implies the purchase of a specific item. In contrast, the price of the sold item corresponds to a particular amount, which, unless

[4] Niẓām al-Dīn al-Balkhī, Al-Fatāwā al-Hindiyya (Dār al-Fikr, 1310H) Vol. 4, pp. 413, 437.
[5] See Chapter 9, which discusses when possession is considered to have been transferred to the buyer in sales contracts.
[6] Muḥammad Al-Abdārī, Al-Tāj wa al-Iklīl li Mukhtaṣar al-Khalīl (Dār al-Fikr, 1978) Vol. 4, p. 3.
[7] Ibid, Vol. 6, p. 413.
[8] Al-Kāsānī (n 3) Vol. 5, pp. 243–44.
[9] *Al-Fatāwā al-Hndiyya* (n 4) Vol. 4, pp. 413, 437.

predetermined or associated with the value of a particular commodity, may be discharged with any similar amount or value.[10]

Where the contract concerns the sale of a commodity in exchange for another commodity, transfer from both sides shall be performed simultaneously to ensure equality in the exchange of considerations as none has preference over the other.[11] As to the contract for the sale of currencies (*ṣarf*), Al-Dasūqī states that if one of the parties is forced to surrender the currency first, the contract will be voided. However, the parties can reconcile or take the matter before a judge if the contract is to exchange two fungibles or two different commodities.[12] **14.06**

2.3 Performance of Contract Involving Debt or *Dayn*

Dayn (debt) is any valuable thing presumed to be owned by one person in favour of another and arising from a specific legal cause such as a sale, guarantee, reconciliation, or the redemption of marriage; or as an implication of an agreement such as maintenance or other causes such as usurpation, *zakāt*, and liability for the tort of damage.[13] Contracts involving *dayn* are performed upon delivery, although other alternatives are available. This section discusses the rules governing the performance of a *dayn* contract through its delivery, along with alternatives to the payment of debt and the repercussions for non-payment of the debt. **14.07**

2.3.1 Delivery of Debt

There is consensus among jurists that payment of debt is obligatory. Allah says in the Qur'ān: 'And if one of you entrusts another, then let him who is entrusted discharge his trust [faithfully].'[14] Where a loan has matured, it should be settled immediately as the Prophet stipulated: 'Procrastination (delay) in paying debt by the wealthy person (who has the ability to settle) is unjust.'[15] On the other hand, there is no obligation to settle an unmatured loan. A non-matured debt can also be transformed into maturity by the death or bankruptcy of either party to the contract. Under such circumstances, payment of the debt shall also be immediate.[16] **14.08**

The delivery of debt to the lender is known as *al-adā*. Debts are settled with fungibles, that is, the same commodity as that which is received[17] and also with a better substitute **14.09**

[10] Al-Sarakhsī, Al-Mabsūṭ (Dār al-Ma'rifa, 1993) Vol. 13, p. 193. A similar opinion has also been expressed by al-Dusūqī of the Maliki school. See Al-Dusūqī, Ḥāshiya al-Dusūqī 'alā al-Sharḥ al-Kabīr (Dār al-Fikr, n.d.) Vol. 3, p. 147.
[11] Al-Sarakhsī (n 10) Vol. 13, p. 193.
[12] Al-Dusūqī (n 10) Vol. 3, p. 147.
[13] Al-Kāsānī (n 3) Vol. 7, p. 174; Al-Suyūṭī, Al-Ashbāh wa al-Naẓā'ir (Dār al-Kutub al-'Ilmiyya, 1990) p. 329; *Al-Mughnī* (n 2) Vol. 4, p. 93.
[14] Qur'ān 2:283.
[15] Bukhārī 2287; Muslim 1563.
[16] Muḥammad Al-Qurṭubī, Al-Jāmi' li Aḥkām al-Qur'ān (Dār al-Kutub al-Miṣriyya, 1964) Vol. 3, p. 415.
[17] 'Abd al-'Azīz Al-Bukhārī Al-Ḥanafī, Kashf al-Asrār Sharḥ Uṣūl al-Bazdawī (Dār al-Kitāb al-Islāmī, n.d.) Vol. 1, p. 169.

unless agreed otherwise by the parties. The Prophet took a loan in the form of a young camel and, when he came to settle it, he instructed Abū Rāfī to deliver to the creditor a similar young camel. However, when Abū Rāfī returned, he informed the Prophet that he could only find a better camel, that is one that was seven years of age. The Prophet said to him: 'Give it to him. The best of people are those who are better in settling their debts.'[18] As a result, the commodity agreed to be delivered under the contract of *salam* and *ṣarf* is treated as real property because allowing a substitute in these contracts will effectively amount to an exchange before its delivery. The other party must accept delivery of the commodity if it meets the agreed specification. In the delivery of debts that are fungible, or which have no similitudes, the value of such commodity shall be delivered in the same manner as usurpation and damage to property.[19]

2.3.2 Alternatives to the Payment of Debt

14.10 There are alternatives to settling debts that exonerate debtors from liability. These include situations where the creditor gifts the obligation to the debtor or declares that the transaction was a form of almsgiving. Similarly, other methods of exoneration from liability include *ḥawāla* (transfer of debt), *muqāṣṣa* (transferring the debt towards the creditor to a third party who owes the debtor), or where the parties have agreed to release the debtor from liability.[20]

2.3.3 Failure to Deliver Debt

14.11 As discussed earlier, given that the payment of debt is obligatory, failure to extinguish the debt gives rise to legal action. On that account, if a financially buoyant debtor refuses to settle the debt without any valid justification, a judge can force him to settle it upon the creditor's demand. In such a case, the judge can also order the debtor's detention,[21] in accordance with the Prophet's admonition, whereby 'delay in payment on the part of one who possesses means makes it lawful to dishonour and punish him'.[22] Where the debtor's assets are insufficient to meet his liabilities, the judge can restrict him from disposing of his property in order to mitigate adverse impact on creditors. This line of thinking is consistent with the teachings of the Malikis, Shafi'is, and Hanbalis, as well as Abū Yūsuf and Muḥammad. The judge can also attach and sell the debtor's property so as to divide the sale proceeds among the creditors in proportion to what they are owed,[23] in the same way that the Prophet sold the properties of Mu'ādh and paid his

[18] Muslim 1600; See also *Al-Mughnī* (n 2) Vol. 4, p. 242.
[19] Al-Bukhārī (n 17) Vol. 1, p. 169.
[20] Al-Kāsānī (n 3) Vol. 6, pp. 11, 15; Vol. 7, p. 295; Al-Ṣāwī, Bulghat al-Sālik li Aqrab al-Masālik (Dār al-Ma'ārif, n.d.) Vol. 1, p. 634; Abū Isḥāq Al-Shīrāzī, Al-Muhadhdhab fī Fiqh al-Imām al-*Shafi'ī* (Dār al-Kutub al-'Ilmiyya, n.d.) Vol. 2, p. 388; *Al-Mughnī* (n 2) Vol. 4, pp. 422, 606.
[21] Abū Al-Tarābulsī al-Ḥanafī, Mu'īn al-Ḥukkām fī Mā Yataraddadu bain al-Khaṣmain min al-Aḥkām (Dār al-Fikr, n.d.) Vol. 1, p. 197.
[22] Abū Dā'ūd 3628.
[23] Al-Kāsānī (n 3) Vol. 7, p. 169; Al-Sarakhsī (n 10) Vol. 24, p. 164; Al-Qarāfī, Al-Dhakhīra (Dār al-Gharb, 1994) Vol. 8, p. 168; 'Abdurraḥmān Al-Mālikī, Irshād al-Sālik ilā Ashraf al-Masālik fī Fiqh al-Imāmi Mālik (Muṣtafā al-Bābī al-Ḥalabī, n.d.) Vol. 1, p. 95; Al-Shāfi'ī, Al-Umm (Dār al-Ma'rifa, 1990) Vol. 3, p. 217; Al-Nawawī (n 2) Vol. 13, p. 269.

debt.[24] Similarly, 'Umar sold the property of Usaifī and shared the proceeds among his creditors.[25] Abū Ḥanīfa is of the view that a debtor's disposition shall not be interdicted, as this constitutes a violation of his humanity. Instead, the judge shall order his detention so that if he possesses valuable property, this will be used to settle the debt.[26]

Where the debtor is in dire financial circumstances, the creditor should give him a respite, as Allah stipulates in the Qur'ān: 'And if someone is in hardship, then [let there be] postponement until [a time of] ease. But if you give [from your right as] charity, then it is better for you, if you only knew.'[27] **14.12**

Where a debtor dies before settling his debt, it is obligatory to settle such debt before executing his bequests and sharing his estate amongst his legal heirs as Allah has given preference to such an outcome over sharing one's inheritance. It is stated that 'after any bequest, he [may have] made or debt'.[28] The Prophet has also said that debt is a barrier between a debtor and paradise.[29] **14.13**

2.4 Delivery of *'ayn* (Specific Property)

The party obliged to deliver *'ayn* can perform the contract by effecting its delivery to the other party. In this respect, the time for the delivery of specific property, as the subject matter of the contract's discharge, is of great significance. Therefore, Ibn Rushd maintains that there is unanimity among jurists as to the impressibility of selling merchandise intended for delivery in the future. Jurists contend that the merchandise has to be delivered immediately after the conclusion of the contract.[30] Al-Tasūlī states that the delivery of an identified subject matter of a sales contract is the right of Allah, and delay in its delivery renders the contract defective (*fāsid*).[31] **14.14**

It should be noted that upon surrendering the subject matter, this should be in a state such that the buyer can enjoy it. Otherwise, performance will be deemed incomplete, and the seller will be forced to allow the buyer full access and enjoyment.[32] The subject matter should be free from any encumbrance and be surrendered with all associated accessories.[33] **14.15**

24 Al-Dārquṭnī 2348.
25 Aḥmad bin Ḥajar al-'Asqalānī, Al-Talkhīṣ al-Ḥabīr fī Takhrīj Aḥādīth al-Rāfi'ī al-Kabīr (Dār al-Kutub al-'Ilmiyya, 1419H) Vol. 3, p. 104; see also 'Ali Al-Tasūlī, Al-Bahja fī Sharḥ al-Tuḥfa (Dār al-Kutub al-'Ilmiyya, 1998) Vol. 2, p. 548.
26 Al-Kāsānī (n 3) Vol. 7, p. 169; Al-Sarakhsī (n 10) Vol. 24, p. 164; Al-Qarāfī (n 23) Vol. 8, p. 168; Al-Mālikī(n 23) Vol. 1, p. 95; Al-Shāfi'ī (n 23) Vol. 3, p. 217; Al-Nawawī (n 2) Vol. 13, p. 269.
27 Qur'ān 2:280.
28 Qur'ān 4:11.
29 Al-Mauṣilī, Al-Ikhtiyār li Ta'līl al-Mukhtār (Dār al-Kutub al-'Ilmiyya, 1937) Vol. 5, p. 86.
30 Ibn Rushd Al-Qurṭubī, Bidāyat al-Mujtahid wa Nihāyat al-Muqtaṣid (Muṣṭafā al-Bābī al-Ḥalabī, 1975) Vol. 2, p. 170.
31 Al-Tasūlī (n 25) Vol. 2, p. 19.
32 Majalla, Arts 262, 269, 276.
33 Majalla, Art. 48.

2.5 Breach (Non-performance) of Contract

14.16 Non-performance of a contract without any legal justification is tantamount to its breach, which in turn gives rise to contractual remedies.[34] The *fuqahā* usually discuss breach of contract alongside *ḍamān* (liabilities). *Ḍamān* arises where the Sharīʿah imposes liability on a person due to his non-compliance with the terms of a contract, with a view to protecting the parties' interests. For instance, where a party violates the terms of contract as dictated by the Sharīʿah or as stipulated by the contract, he shall be liable to compensate the injured party in proportion to his loss. Since an instance of imposing liability on a party is primarily a manifestation of breach of contract, making the other party liable in specific contracts, as discussed below, would in fact result in breach of contract.

14.17 In the event of *ijāra* for residential or commercial property, if the property is destroyed in the lessee's possession without negligence, the lessee is not considered liable because this is not attributable to him.[35] This is so even if the lease agreement holds the lessee liable in the absence of negligence, because such stipulation is void.[36] The Hanbalis, however, suggest that such stipulation would create liability by relying on the tradition of the Prophet, according to whom 'Muslims are to fulfil their stipulations', thus implying that a stipulation can create liability even though the law does not.[37]

14.18 In relation to sale contracts, jurists have opined that hiding a defect in the subject matter constitutes a breach that attracts liability equal to the loss suffered.[38] For instance, if the subject matter delivered to the buyer perishes or was destroyed due to the defect which was hidden by the seller, the buyer will receive the whole consideration.[39] If there is an increment in the subject matter of a sold good currently in the possession of the seller following the conclusion of the sale, non-delivery of such increment to the buyer would also amount to a breach of the contract.[40]

14.19 Similarly, jurists have agreed that in gratuitous contracts, the donee is not liable for the damage to goods in its possession without being negligent. The Prophet said that 'there shall be no liability upon a borrower that does not cheat; there is also no liability upon an entrusted who does not cheat'[41] and 'whoever that is entrusted with an entrustment, he shall not be liable'.[42] However, if the donee, without the owner's

[34] Remedies in the event of breach are discussed in Chapter 15.

[35] Al-Kāsānī (n 3) Vol. 4, p. 210; Ibn Juzaī, Al-Qawānīn al-Fiqhiyya (n.p., n.d.) p. 183; Abū Al-ʿAdawī, Ḥāshiyat al-ʿAdawī ʿalā Sharḥ Kifāyat al-Tālib al-Rabbānī (Dār al-Fikr, 1994) Vol. 2, p. 199; Al-Shirbīnī, Mughnī al-Muḥtāj ilā Maʿrifat Alfāẓ al-Minhāj (Dār al-Kutub al-ʿIlmiyya, 1994) Vol. 3, p. 476; Manṣūr Al-Buhūtī, Kashshāf al-Qināʿ ʿan Matn al-Iqnāʿ (Dār al-Kutub al-ʿIlmiyya, n.d.) Vol. 4, p. 19.

[36] Ibn ʿĀbidīn, Radd al-Muḥtār ʿalā al-Durr al-Mukhtār (Dār al-Fikr, 1992) Vol. 5, p. 663, Vol. 6, p. 68.

[37] *Al-Mughnī* (n 2) Vol. 5, p. 397.

[38] Ibn Nujaim, Al-Baḥr al-Rāʾiq Sharḥ Kanz al-Daqāʾiq (Dār al-Kitāb al-Islāmī, n.d.) Vol. 6, p. 57; Al-Dasūqī (n 10) Vol. 3, p. 131.

[39] Dusūqī (n 10) Vol. 3, p. 131.

[40] Al-Kāsānī (n 3) Vol. 5, p. 256.

[41] Al-Dārquṭnī 2961. Al-Darquṭnī states that the *ḥadīth* is weak, even though the chain of narrators stopped with him.

[42] Ibn Māja 2401.

permission, indistinguishably mixes the *wadīʿa* with other property,[43] entrusts it to a third person,[44] or damages it, a breach will have occurred.[45] If the breach is due to the damage or non-delivery of a part of the subject matter which is separable from the remainder, liability would extend only to the non-delivered or damaged part of the subject matter.[46]

The concept of breach in terms of liability has also been discussed in agency contracts. 14.20
If the agent exceeds its mandate imposed by the Sharīʿah or the terms of the contract, this gives rise to a breach, according to Ibn Rushd.[47] For instance, an agent appointed to represent his principal in a suit for recovery of a debt is considered to have breached the agency agreement if he accepts the payment of the debt from the debtor because he was only empowered to represent his principal's interests.[48] In order to avoid breach of the agency agreement, an agent appointed to purchase or sell something will conduct the business of the agency according to the market price of the item.[49] An agent will also be liable for breach of contract if he delays payment for an item purchased on behalf of his principal and the item is lost while in his possession;[50] where he sells something on behalf of his principal and does not surrender the sale proceeds to his principal despite the principal's demand and the money is lost;[51] and where the agent delivers the commodity before receiving the price, he shall be liable to the principal if the buyer is unable to settle it.[52]

3. Termination of Contracts (*Inhā al-ʿAqd*)

Termination of contract absolves the parties from their contractual obligations, al- 14.21
though they may still be liable for damages or restitution. It is important to state that termination and rescission are distinguishable in respect of how the obligations in certain contracts may be extinguished. The effect of rescission is to void the contract *ab initio* (i.e. discharge of obligations retrospectively), whereas termination (or rescission as termination) serves to discharge the parties' obligations prospectively.

43 Al-Kāsānī (n 3) Vol. 6, p. 213; *Al-Fatāwā al-Hindiyya* (n 4) Vol. 4, p. 348; Al-Shīrāzī (n 20) Vol. 2, p. 185; Al-Buhūtī (n 35) Vol. 4, p. 176; *Al-Mughnī* (n 2) Vol. 6, p. 437.

44 Al-Sarakhsī (n 10) Vol. 11, p. 113; Muḥiy al-Dīn Al-Nawawī, Rauḍat al-Ṭālibīn wa ʿUmdat al-Muftīn (Al-Maktab al-Islāmī, 1991) Vol. 6, p. 327; Ibn Juzaī (n 35) p. 246; Al-Buhūtī (n 35) Vol. 4, p. 193.

45 Ibn Juzaī (n 35) p. 379; Al-Kāsānī (n 3) Vol. 6, p. 213; ʿAbd al-Bāqī Al-Zurqānī, Sharḥ al-Zurqānī ʿalā Mukhtaṣar Khalīl (Dār al-Kutub al-ʿIlmiyya, 2002) Vol. 6, p. 204; *Al-Fatāwā al-Hindiyyah* (n 4) Vol. 4, p. 346; *Al-Mughnī* (n 2) Vol. 6, p. 450.

46 Al-Nawawī (n 44) Vol. 6, p. 336; ʿAli Haidar Āfandī, Durar al-Ḥukkām fī Sharḥ Majallat al-Ahkām (Dār al-Jīl, 1991) Vol. 2, p. 253.

47 Ibn Rushd (30) Vol. 4, p. 87.

48 ʿUthmān al-Zailaʿī, Tabyīn al-Ḥaqāʾiq Sharḥ Kanz al-Daqāʾiq (Al-Matbaʿa al-Kubrā al-Amīriyya, 1313H) Vol. 4, p. 278; Al-Nawawī (n 44) Vol. 4, p. 320.

49 Al-Zailaʿī (n 48) Vol. 4, pp. 271–72; Al-Dusūqī (n 10) Vol. 3, p. 382; Al-Buhūtī (n 35) Vol. 3, p. 477.

50 *Al-Mughnī* (n 2) Vol. 5, p. 74; Al-Buhūtī (n 35) Vol. 3, p. 482.

51 *Al-Mughnī* (n 2) Vol. 5, p. 80.

52 Al-Nawawī (n 44) Vol. 4, p. 309; Al-Buhūtī (n 35) Vol. 3, p. 481.

14.22 Termination may be unilateral or bilateral. The parties may decide to put an end to their contract amicably even if there is no breach by one of them. Thus, mutual termination is considered an agreement that is distinct from the contract which the parties seek to terminate. In order for this new agreement (i.e. the termination agreement) to come into force, a fresh offer and acceptance are necessary, as well as fresh subject matter. Indeed, the subject matter of such an agreement is the termination itself. This termination may also have an effect on third parties, for example where any of the contracting parties received a benefit from a third party relating to the contract which the parties are seeking to terminate.

14.23 The parties can always terminate a contract by mutual consent, albeit Islamic law does not allow unilateral termination of contracts. The prohibition of unilateral termination applies even to irregular contracts (*ʿuqūd fāsida*), whereby termination is regulated by the Sharīʿah rather than by the conduct of the parties. Nevertheless, there are certain contracts that can be unilaterally repudiated by a party. This concerns contracts initiated unilaterally, such as *waqf* (endowment) and *waṣiyya* (bequest).

14.24 A party also acquires a right to terminate the contract due to hardship or *force majeure* that has wholly prevented performance of the contract, rendering it impossible. Such hardship must either pertain to the subject matter of the contract (loss or destruction of subject matter) or the contracting parties themselves (insanity or death).

14.25 This section discusses both unilateral and bilateral termination of the contract along with its impact on third parties involved in the subject matter of the contract, as well as the termination of contracts due to impossibility of performance.

3.1 Unilateral Termination

14.26 A party can terminate a binding contract only with the consent of the other party. Nevertheless, some contracts may be unilaterally repudiated. For instance, Abū Ḥanīfa is of the view that a person who declares a *waqf* can rescind it. Even so, his contemporaries contended that a *waqf* is binding and its ownership shifts by declaration. However, Aḥmad bin Ḥanbal suggests that a *waqf* is only binding if its assets are transferred to its intended beneficiaries.[53]

14.27 Since *waṣiyya* (bequest) takes effect after the offeror's death, he can repudiate it at any time before his death, expressly or impliedly.[54] This is based on a narration from Ibn

[53] Al-Sarakhsī (n 10) Vol. 12, p. 27; *Al-Mughnī* (n 2) Vol. 6, p. 5.

[54] Muṣṭafā Al-Suyūṭī Al-Rahaibānī, Maṭālib al-Nuhā fī Sharḥ Ghāyat al-Muntahā (Al-Maktab al-Islāmī, 1994) Vol. 4, p. 460; *Al-Fatāwā al-Hindiyya* (n 4) Vol. 6, p. 92; Al-Kharshī, Sharḥ Mukhtaṣar ʿalā Mukhtaṣar Khalīl (Dār al-Fikr, n.d.) Vol. 8, p. 172; Al-Shirbīnī (n 35) Vol. 3, p. 71; Zakariyya Al-Anṣārī, Asnā al-Maṭālib fī Sharḥ Rauḍ al-Tālib (Dār al-Kitāb al-Islāmī, n.d.) Vol. 3, p. 63.

'Umar, whereby 'a man can change whatever he wants in his bequest'. This is also the opinion of the Hanafis, Malikis, Shafi'is, and Hanbalis.[55]

A suspending contract (*'uqūd mauqūfa*) entered into by a self-appointed agent (*al-fuḍūlī*) can only be validated if the party with the power to make such a contract ratifies it. Such party can, therefore, unilaterally choose to end the contract; as a result, the contract cannot proceed.[56] **14.28**

The majority of jurists, save for the Malikis, maintain that either party to a non-binding contract can repudiate it even without the consent of the other party. The Hanafis, however, opine that such rescission can only become effective if the other party is aware of it. The Shafi'is and Hanbalis did not stipulate such a condition, for example in the case of dismissing an agent where his knowledge of the dismissal is not a requirement.[57] The same applies to other non-binding contracts where either party can unilaterally repudiate, as is the case with partnership, agencies, *qirāḍ* or *muḍāraba* (entrepreneurial partnership), *waṣiyya*, *'āriyya*, *wadī'a*, *qarḍ* (loan), *ju'āla* (placing a reward for a specific task), judgeship, etc.[58] **14.29**

3.2 Negotiated Termination (*Iqāla*)

Iqāla literally means lifting and removing something.[59] Technically, it corresponds to reversing the effects of a contract with the parties' mutual consent with the objective of returning to the parties' pre-contract position.[60] Depending on the nature of the contract, the *iqāla* ranges from recommended (*mandūb*) to obligatory (*wājib*). It will be deemed recommended where one of the parties regrets entering into the contract,[61] as the Prophet said: 'Whoever agrees with a Muslim to cancel a transaction, Allah will forgive his sins on the Day of Resurrection.'[62] The *ḥadīth* in question also indicates the legality of *iqāla*. The *iqāla* is deemed obligatory where the contract is induced through coercion, so that both parties may avoid entering into an agreement that is prohibited.[63] **14.30**

[55] Al-Kāsānī (n 3) Vol. 7, p. 378; Al-Shirbīnī (n 35) Vol. 4, p. 112; Al-Ramlī, Nihāyat al-Muḥtāj ilā Sharḥ al-Minhāj (Dār al-Fikr, Beirut, 1404H/1984) Vol. 6, p. 94; Al-Ḥaṭṭāb (n 3) Vol. 6, p. 369; *Al-Fatāwā al-Hindiyya* (n 4) Vol. 6, p. 92.
[56] Al-Kāsānī (n 3) Vol. 5, p. 151.
[57] *Radd al-Muḥtār* (n 36) Vol. 4, p. 426; Al-Shirbīnī (n 35) Vol. 3, p. 624; Al-Rahaibanī (n 54) Vol. 3, p. 502; Zain al-Dīn Ibn Rajab, Al-Qawā'id (Dār al-Kutub al-'Ilmiyya, n.d.) p. 115.
[58] Al-Suyūṭī (n 13) pp. 275, 276.
[59] Maḥmūd 'Abd al-Mun'im, Mu'jam al-Muṣṭalaḥāt wa al-Alfāẓ al-Fiqhiyya (Dār al-Faḍīla, n.d.) p. 256.
[60] Aḥmad Al-Ḥamawī, Al-Miṣbāḥ al-Munīr fī Gharīb al-Sharḥ al-Kabīr (Al-Maktaba al-'Ilmiyya, n.d.) Vol. 2, p. 421; Al-Shāfi'ī (n 23) Vol. 3, p. 78; *Al-Mughnī* (n 2) Vol. 4, p. 92.
[61] Al-Bābartī, Al-'Ināya Sharḥ al-Hidāya (Dār al-Fikr, n.d.) Vol. 6, p. 486.
[62] Abū Dā'ūd 3460; Ibn Māja 2199; Al-Ḥākim, *al-Mustadrak* 2291.
[63] Ibn Nujaim (n 38) Vol. 6, p. 110.

3.2.1 The Requirements of *Iqāla*

14.31 In order for an *iqāla* to be valid both parties must consent. It should be concluded in the same session, just like other forms of contract.[64] Moreover, the contract to which *iqāla* is being applied should be rescindable, such as sales and leasing agreements, and does not apply to contracts that are not subject to rescission, particularly marriage and divorce.[65] Finally, the subject matter should be existent at the time of *iqāla*.[66]

3.2.2 The Effect of *Iqāla*

14.32 Jurists have differed on whether an *iqāla* culminates in the termination of a contract or the creation of a new contract (of sale). The Hanbalis and Shafi'is, relying on the literal meaning of *iqāla*, have opined that it results in the termination of a contract in relation to its parties and third parties.[67] In this way, *iqāla* differs from the contract of sale which creates or affirms something, while *iqāla* culminates in negation or reversal.

14.33 Mālik opined that *iqāla* is a contract of sales in relation to its parties and others. However, where it is impossible to conclude the sale, it will be considered as having been rescinded.[68] For example, where a commodity is returned back to its previous seller and its value has not changed, it will be deemed a reversal of the sale; but if its value has changed, such as where a skinny animal has become fat, it shall be deemed a new sale.[69] This is due to the fact that a sale is defined as an exchange of a valuable commodity for another and which moreover involves taking something in exchange of, or as a substitute for, another. This meaning is also available in *iqāla*.[70] The rule is that 'in contracts and dispositions, regard is always given to meanings and goals and not to abstract terms and their constructions'.[71]

14.34 Abū Ḥanīfa emphasized that *iqāla* constitutes a rescission in respect of its parties and a sales agreement in respect of third parties.[72] The basis of this opinion is that *iqāla* implies rescission and removal of the effect of sales, and, as a result, a different effect shall not be implied to avoid the parties' shared meaning (*ishtirāk*). The reason why it is transformed into a sales contract in relation to third parties is because there is an element of ownership transfer following an offer and acceptance and consideration. This transformation protects the right of such third party, where it applies, from being left out, as the parties to the contract have no right to disregard the right of others.[73]

64 Muḥammad 'Illīsh, Minaḥ al-Jalīl Sharḥ Mukhtaṣar Khalīl (Dār al-Fikr, 1989) Vol. 5, p. 254.
65 Ibn 'Ābidīn (n 36) Vol. 5, pp. 21, 124.
66 Al-Kāsānī (n 3) Vol. 5, p. 309.
67 *Al-Mughnī* (n 2) Vol. 4, p. 92; Al-Buhūtī (n 35) Vol. 3, p. 248; Al-Nawawī (n 2) Vol. 9, p. 269; Al-Anṣārī (n 54) Vol. 2, p. 74.
68 Al-Kāsānī (n 3) Vol. 5, p. 11.
69 Al-Kharshī (n 54) Vol. 5, p. 166.
70 Al-Kāsānī (n 3) Vol. 5, p. 11; Al-Kharshī (n 54) Vol. 5, p. 166; Mālik ibn Anas, Al-Mudawwana al-Kubrā (Dār al-Kutub al-'Ilmiyya, 1994) Vol. 3, p. 116.
71 Al-Suyūṭī (n 13) pp. 304–09.
72 Al-Mauṣilī (n 29) Vol. 2, p. 11; Al-Sarakhsī (n 10) Vol. 14, p. 66.
73 Al-Kāsānī (n 3) Vol. 5, p. 308.

This disagreement on the legal effect of *iqāla* has an impact on its application. Some of these effects can be seen in the following discussion.

3.2.2.1 Iqāla *with less or more than the original price*

Where the parties to the contract agreed on *iqāla* but did not mention the price, or otherwise suggested a price that is more or less than the original price of sale—or a different consideration whether its value is less or more—the *iqāla* shall be based on the original price or consideration. Identifying a price above the original, suspending the price, or changing its form is void; even so, the *iqāla* shall be valid, based on the rationale considering *iqāla* as rescission (*faskh*). It does not matter whether the *iqāla* was initiated after taking possession of the commodity in the first contract or not, nor whether the commodity is a movable or immovable property, as *faskh* serves to reverse the first contract, and the first contract was concluded with the original price.[74] **14.35**

3.2.2.2 Right of pre-emption (Shufʿa) *over the subject matter of* Iqāla

An often-cited analogy is that a person with the right of pre-emption cannot exercise such right in a sales contract reversed through *iqāla*, especially if such *iqāla* is deemed to constitute rescission (*faskh*). In other words, where the parties have rescinded the contract of sales, the party with the right of pre-emption cannot insist on buying the house unless the owner intends to sell it again. As such, it will be deemed a new contract of sale. This analogy is based on the principle formulated by Muḥammad and Zufr, both Hanafi scholars, because Muḥammad was of the view that *iqāla* is *faskh*, save where it cannot be rescinded, in which case it is transformed into a sales contract. Zufr, on the other hand, maintained that *iqāla* is rescission in relation to all. Other Hanafis, as well as other schools, allow those with the right of *shufʿa* to exercise it in a contract reversed through *iqāla*. Thus, in the view of Abū Ḥanīfa, while *iqāla* is deemed rescission in relation to its parties, it is a sale in relation to a third party who has the right of pre-emption. In the view of Abū Yūsuf, on the other hand, it is a contract of sale in relation to both sides.[75] **14.36**

3.2.2.3 Iqāla *of agents*

The party with power to sell also has the right to exercise *iqāla*. Thus, it is valid for a principal to reverse the sale of his agent through *iqāla* where this was initiated before the agent took possession of the subject matter. If the principal declares the *iqāla* after possession, he shall be liable for the agent's loss as it will be presumed that the agent has purchased it for himself. Abū Ḥanīfa and Muḥammad emphasized that the principal would not incur costs after reversing the sale, whereas Abū Yūsuf was adamant that liability would pass to the principal.[76] Similarly, it is permissible to exercise *iqāla* against **14.37**

[74] Ibid, Vol. 5, p. 307.
[75] Ibid, Vol. 5, p. 308.
[76] *Radd al-Muḥtār* (n 36) Vol. 5, p. 123.

an agent in *salam* contracts according to Abū Ḥanīfa and Muḥammad, contrary to the view expressed by Abū Yūsuf.[77]

3.2.2.4 *Subject matter of* Iqāla

14.38 The subject matter of *iqāla* is a binding contract that may be rescinded through *khiyār*, because such contracts can only be rescinded with the consent of both parties. This is true of sales agreements, *ijāra* (leasing), mortgage (the mortgagor can only set up the *iqāla* subject to the approval of the mortgagee or settlement of his debt), *salam*, reconciliation, *muḍāraba*, as well as partnership (*sharika*). Other agreements that are not subject to *iqāla* are considered non-binding, such as *iʿāra*, *waṣiyya*, and *juʿāla*; the same applies to binding contracts to which the right of rescission (*faskh*) is not applicable, such as *waqf* and marriage, neither of which is rescindable with option.[78]

3.2.3 Effect of Irregular Stipulations on *Iqāla*

14.39 A stipulation that is irregular (*sharṭ fāsid*), normally benefiting one party over the other, cannot be implied because the Sharīʿah has not provided for such stipulation and there is no convention or practice that requires it.[79] Based on the views of Abū Ḥanīfa and Muḥammad, whereby *iqāla* constitutes a form of rescission, it follows that an irregular stipulation in *iqāla* does not invalidate the agreement; rather the stipulation itself is invalid. Thus, where it is stipulated that the price of the commodity to be returned to the seller should be more than its original price, the *iqāla* will be based on the original price only. This is because any addition to the original price resembles usury and bestows benefit upon a single party. Similarly, the condition of making *iqāla* at a lower price than the original is equally of no legal effect because *iqāla* serves to reverse the contract to the parties' original status; this is not possible by offering a lower price. However, a lower price may be accepted where the value of the commodity is decreased because of damage at the hands of the other party. Based on the view according to which *iqāla* is a contract of sale, the stipulation of an irregular condition invalidates the contract.[80]

3.2.4 *Iqālat al-Iqāla* (Reversal of *Iqāla*)

14.40 *Iqālat al-iqāla* refers to the cancellation of *iqāla* and the return to the original contract. This occurs where the parties revoke the original contract.[81] There are several exceptions to this rule, such as the reversal of the *iqāla* in *salam* contracts before possession of the subject matter is invalid because the subject matter of the *salam* is a credit that is shed following the *iqāla*. If the *iqāla* is reversed, the subject matter that was shed will reappear; that which is shed does not reappear.[82]

[77] Ibn Nujaim (n 38) Vol. 6, p. 111.
[78] Al-Sarakhsī (n 10) Vol. 29, p. 55; Malik ibn Anas (n 70) Vol. 2, p. 129; Al-Shirbīnī (n 35) Vol. 2, p. 455; Al-Buhūtī (n 35) Vol. 3, p. 249.
[79] Al-Zuhailī (n 1) Vol. 4, p. 3054.
[80] Al-Kāsānī (n 3) Vol. 5, p. 175; Ibn Nujaim (n 38) Vol. 6, p. 112.
[81] Ibn Nujaim (n 38) Vol. 6, p. 111.
[82] ʿAbd al-Raḥmān Zāda, Majmaʿ al-Anhur fi Sharḥ Multaqā al-Abḥur (Dār al-Kutub al-ʿIlmiyya, 1998) Vol. 2, p. 74.

3.2.5 Invalidator of *Iqāla*

There are several situations that render *iqāla* invalid. First, the *iqāla* becomes void if the subject matter of a sale is lost following *iqāla*, albeit before its surrender to the other party, because *iqāla* constitutes a reversal of the original contract. This is possible only if the sold subject matter is available. However, loss of the price or consideration does not invalidate *iqāla*, neither of which constitutes the subject matter of the contract. This rule does not, however, apply to the *iqāla* of the subject matter of *salam*, as it is valid to reverse this before receipt of the *muslam fīhi* (subject matter of *salam*). It does not matter whether the price promised is a real commodity available at the time of the contract or a credit. Likewise, it does not matter whether it is available at the hands of the offeror of *salam* or whether it is lost. This is because the *muslam fīhi* is a credit that has the legal status of a real commodity that is available on the ground; as a result, it cannot be exchanged for another thing until after its receipt.[83] **14.41**

Any change in the subject matter of a sale invalidates *iqāla*. This change may occur due to an increase in the subject matter of a sale, such as the reproduction of cattle after the *iqāla* or an increment in its value. This is the view of the Malikis, which is contrary to that of the Hanbalis.[84] **14.42**

3.3 *Force Majeure* and Impossibility of Performance

The Sharīʿah recognizes any act of God or unforeseen condition making the performance of contract impossible as a ground for terminating the obligation.[85] Islamic law distinguishes between various types of hardship, yet not all of these allow the debtor to terminate or rescind the contract or its effects. There does not seem to be any restriction for parties willing to agree that the obligor shall be liable for performance or indemnity in the event of *force majeure* or unforeseen incidents. Hence, in the first instance, the regulation of *force majeure* is a matter of agreement. The operation of *force majeure* may be distinguished between executed contracts and executory contracts as well as non-binding contracts. To determine this impact of a *force majeure* event on the various types of executed (sale, gift, and reconciliation) and executory (lease, partnership, and agency) contracts, the death of the parties and the damage/destruction of the subject matter are considered in this section. One should also note that the jurists have used the term *infisākh* to describe contracts that become void due to such impossibility of performance.[86] According to Al-Kāsānī, there are two forms of contractual *infisākh*: *infisākh* by choice and by necessity.[87] This classification shows that *infisākh* can also **14.43**

[83] Ibid, Vol. 2, p. 106; Al-Kharshī (n 54) Vol. 3, p. 106; Ibn Rushd (n 30) Vol. 3, p. 223.

[84] Al-Kharshī (n 54) Vol. 5, p. 88; ʿIllīsh (n 64) Vol. 5, pp. 252–53; Al-Buhūtī, Sharḥ Muntahā al-Irādāt (ʿAlam al-Kutub, 1993) Vol. 2, p. 64.

[85] See Susan E. Rayner, 'A Note on Force Majeure in Islamic Law' (1991) 6 Arab Law Quarterly 86.

[86] Ibn Nujaim, Al-Ashbāh wa al-Naẓāʾir ʿalā Madhahb Abī Hanīfa (Dār al-Kutub al-ʿIlmiya, 1999) p. 292; Al-Suyūṭī (n 13) p. 288; Ibn Rajab (n 57) p. 107; Al-Qarāfī (n 3) Vol. 3, p. 269.

[87] Al-Kāsānī (n 3) Vol. 5, p. 298.

assume the qualities of *faskh*, which corresponds to a unilateral rescission of contract as well as frustration, as elaborated in the works of jurists. The following discussion will however focus on those causes that result from necessity and not by the parties' choice. The necessity or *force majeure* resulting in the frustration of the contract may either pertain to the subject matter, as is the case with its destruction or damage, or has to do with the status of the parties, as is the case with death, insanity, bankruptcy, etc.

3.3.1 Damage to the Subject Matter of the Contract

14.44 Damage to the subject matter of the contract may frustrate the contract. This can be discussed from the perspective of executed contracts (contracts whose effect is executed immediately) and executory contracts (contracts that are not immediately executed).

3.3.1.1 Executed contracts

14.45 Executed contracts are not frustrated by damage to their subject matter, if such subject matter is transferred to the offeree who subsequently assumes ownership and responsibility thereof, while the object is in his possession. Examples include sale, reconciliation, gift, etc.[88] Jurists generally agree that the destruction of the sold commodity by the seller before transfer of possession to the buyer repudiates the contract.[89] The Malikis and Hanbalis have opined that if the merchandise is a fungible property, the contract is annulled, and the loss burdens the seller. On the other hand, where the subject matter is land or identified property (*mu'ayyan*), or is a non-fungible property on which the buyer has no right of delivery, the contract will not be repudiated when damaged; rather, the loss will shift to the buyer.[90] In the Hanafi school, Al-Samarqandī maintains that the loss of, or damage to, the sold commodity before transfer of possession to the buyer burdens the seller and moreover culminates in the decrease of its value, in addition to annulling the contract.[91] Al-Qalyūbī of the Shafi'i school also held the same opinion, further emphasizing that if the damage was due to an act of God, the contract would be annulled and the buyer will not be liable to pay the price.[92] If the destruction is attributable to the buyer, his action shall be deemed a possession that transfers liability to him.[93]

3.3.1.2 Executory contracts

14.46 The execution of certain contracts requires some time, as is the case with *ijāra*, *i'āra*, and *wakāla* agreements. The general rule is that these contracts are invalidated with the destruction of their underlying subject matter, irrespective of the transfer of possession to the buyer.

[88] Al-Ṣāwī (n 20) Vol. 3, p. 195; *Al-Mughnī* (n 2) Vol. 8, p. 209; Al-Samarqandī, Tuḥfat al-Fuqahā' (Dār al-Kutub al-'Ilmiyya, 1994) Vol. 2, p. 41; Al-Nawawī (n 2) Vol. 9, p. 220.

[89] Al-Kāsānī (n 3) Vol. 5, p. 241; Al-Nawawī (n 2) Vol. 9, p. 220; *Al-Mughnī* (n 2) Vol. 4, p. 84.

[90] Al-Ṣāwī (n 20) Vol. 3, p. 196; Al-Mughnī (n 2) Vol. 4, pp. 83, 84.

[91] Al-Samarqandī (n 88) Vol. 2, p. 41.

[92] Al-Qalyūbī, Ḥāshiy al-Qalyūbī wa 'Umaira 'alā Sharḥ al-Maḥallī 'alā al-Minhāj (Dār al-Fikr, 1995) Vol. 2, p. 261.

[93] Al-Kāsānī (n 3) Vol. 5, p. 241; Al-Nawawī (n 2) Vol. 9, p. 220; *Al-Mughnī* (n 2) Vol. 4, p. 84.

3.3.1.2.1 Lease In *ijāra* (lease), whenever the leased property is destroyed the contract shall be rescinded. Where the property is destroyed after its enjoyment, the lease will come to an end for the remainder of the period; as for the period already enjoyed, all fees shall be settled.[94] The lease will also be frustrated if the usufruct for which the contract was entered into is no longer feasible.[95] For instance, if an identified animal was leased for transport and other services, its death or sickness that renders it useless for the purpose of the lease would serve to annul the contract. If the animal was not identified for the lease and an animal among those used dies, the contract cannot be annulled; rather, the lessor can replace it with another and the contract will continue.[96] **14.47**

3.3.1.2.2 Partnership According to Al-Kāsānī, if the subject matter of the partnership, such as its combined capital, is lost as a whole, the partnership shall cease to exist.[97] However, where only part of the capital that is known to belong to one of the parties is lost, this burdens the owner and has no impact on the life of the partnership.[98] **14.48**

3.3.1.2.3 Agency The contract of agency equally becomes annulled where its subject matter is destroyed or ceases to exist. Thus, an agency to purchase a house shall be void if the house is destroyed before its purchase. This is because the agency is not effective as to its subject matter if it is no longer in existence.[99] **14.49**

3.3.2 Death of One or Both Parties to a Binding Contract

Jurists have generally agreed that a contract is not annulled with the death of one of the parties. This is so especially in contracts, such as those relating to sales, that are executed as soon as offer and acceptance are declared, upon which capacity is not needed. As to *ijāra*, the Malikis, Shafi'is, and Hanbalis are of the view that the death of either party does not annul it; rather a lease would be binding on the heirs of the lessor for the contractual period, and the enjoyment of usufruct would be inherited by the lessee.[100] The Hanafis are of the view that if the lessor concludes the lease agreement for another person, for example acting as a guardian or as the appointee of the father of the deceased, or an administrator of *waqf*, the lessor's death will not annul the contract. If the contractor contracts *ijāra* on his own behalf, his death will annul the contract because the contract implies that the usufruct will be attained from his property and as a result of his death, the property no longer belongs to him.[101] The majority of jurists and **14.50**

[94] *Al-Mughnī* (n 2) Vol. 5, p. 330; ʿIllīsh (n 64) Vol. 7, p. 521; *Al-Fatāwā al-Hindiyyah* (n 4) Vol. 4, p. 461; Al-Anṣārī (n 54) Vol. 1, p. 542.

[95] Al-Kāsānī (n 3) Vol. 4, p. 196; Al-Mauṣilī (n 29) Vol. 2, p. 61; Al-Ṣāwī (n 20) Vol. 4, p. 50; Al-Qalyūbī (n 92) Vol. 3, p. 84; *Al-Mughnī* (n 2) Vol. 4, p. 253; Vol. 5, p. 7.

[96] *Al-Fatāwā al-Hindiyya* (n 4) Vol. 4, p. 461; Al-Kāsānī (n 3) Vol. 4, p. 196; Al-Mauṣilī (n 29) Vol. 2, p. 61; Al-Ṣāwī (n 20) Vol. 4, p. 50; Al-Qalyūbī (n 92) Vol. 3, p. 84; *Al-Mughnī* (n 2) Vol. 4, p. 253; Vol. 5, p. 7.

[97] Al-Kāsānī (n 3) Vol. 6, p. 78.

[98] *Radd al-Muḥtār* (n 36) Vol. 4, p. 315.

[99] Al-Buhūtī (n 35) Vol. 3, p. 469.

[100] Al-Shirbīnī, Al-Iqnāʿ fī Ḥalli Alfāẓ Abī Shujāʿ (Dār al-Fikr, n.d.) Vol. 2, p. 350. Al-Ṣāwī (n 20) Vol. 2, p. 496; *Al-Mughnī* (n 2) Vol. 5, p. 384.

[101] Al-Kāsānī (n 3) Vol. 4, p. 222.

Hanafis in particular are of the view that an *ijāra* for personal services comes to end with the death of the person incumbent with performance of the underlying service.[102]

3.3.3 Annulment of Non-binding Contracts because of Death

14.51 Any of the parties at any time can bring to an end a non-binding contract, such as *ʿāriya*, agency, partnership, and entrustment (*wadīʿa*), among others. Jurists are generally agreed that these contracts are annulled when one of the parties dies. In the contract of *iʿāra*, the Hanafis, Shafiʾis, and Hanbalis suggest that whenever the borrower dies the contract is annulled. The Hanafis are of the view that the death of the transferor also invalidates it because *iʿāra* is a contract over a usufruct that is created for a certain period and whenever the transferor dies, the property no longer belongs to him for the contract to be validated.[103] The Shafiʾis share this view and argue that *iʿāra* allows the enjoyment of another's property, which generally requires permission, this becoming annulled upon death.[104] In the Maliki school, however, *ʿāriya* is a binding contract. Where it is concluded for a specific period, it will continue for that period even after the death of any of the parties. Where the *ʿāriya* is for an indefinite period, the preferred opinion in the Maliki school is that it continues until the action for which it was concluded is performed or the time allocated has lapsed.[105]

14.52 Jurists also agree that the death of either agent or principal annuls a *wakāla*, which is a non-binding contract. The death of the principal terminates his power to delegate and the death of the agent eliminates his capacity to act, effectively amounting to his dismissal.[106] Some Malikis[107] and Hanbalis[108] stipulate that the annulment becomes effective from the time the agent is aware of the principal's death.

4. Rescission of Contract (*Faskh*)

14.53 The term *faskh* refers to annulment, repudiation, and separation as well as weakness in mind and body.[109] Technically, the term refers to untying the knot of contract.[110] In other words, it corresponds to lifting the effect of a contract as if it did not happen.[111] It is also described as a situation where the considerations exchanged

[102] Al-Ḥaṭṭāb (n 3) Vol. 5, p. 412; *Al-Mughnī* (n 2) Vol. 5, p. 370; Al-Shīrazī (n 20) Vol. 1, p. 263.
[103] Al-Zailaʿī (n 48) Vol. 5, p. 84; *Radd al-Muḥtār* (n 36) Vol. 5, p. 685.
[104] Nūr al-Dīn Al-Aqʾharī, Ḥāshiyat al-Shubramulsī ʿalā Nihāyat al-Muḥtāj ilā Sharḥ al-Minhāj (Dār al-Fikr, 1984) Vol. 5, p. 131.
[105] Ṣāleh Al-Azharī, Jawāhir al-Iklīl Sharḥ Mukhtaṣar Khalīl (Al-Maktabah al-Thaqāfiyya, n.d.) Vol. 2, p. 146.
[106] Al-Qalyūbī (n 92) Vol. 2, p. 436; *Radd al-Muḥtār* (n 36) Vol. 5, p. 538; Ibn Rushd (n 30) Vol. 2, p. 302; *Al-Mughnī* (n 2) Vol. 5, pp. 88–89; Ibn Juzaī (n 35) p. 216.
[107] Ibn Rushd (n 30) Vol. 2, p. 302; Ibn Juzaī (n 35) p. 216.
[108] *Al-Mughnī* (n 2) Vol. 5, p. 89.
[109] Muḥammad Al-Zubaidī, Tāj al-ʿArūs min Jawāhir alʾArūs (Dār al-Hidāya, n.d.) Vol. 7, p. 319.
[110] Ibn Nujaim (n 86) p. 292; Al-Suyūṭī (n 13) p. 278; Tāj al-Dīn Al-Subkī, Al-Ashbāh wa al-Naẓāʾir (Dār al-Kutub al- ʿIlmiyya, 1991) Vol. 1, p. 234.
[111] Al-Kāsānī (n 3) Vol. 5, p. 182.

return to their original owners.[112] Thus, *faskh* is often used to denote rescission of a contract, such as where one of the parties exercises its right of option (*khiyār*). It also refers to the eventual end of a contract or its performance, as in the case of non-binding contracts (*'uqūd jāiza*).[113]

4.1 Modes of Rescission of Contract

Apart from rescission through judicial intervention, a party may rescind a contract if an acceptable justification is available. This section discusses various modes of rescinding a contract. **14.54**

4.1.1 Rescission by Court Judgment

According to the majority of scholars, a contract can be rescinded through the intervention of the courts at the request of the buyer when the commodity is in the possession of the seller, and also at the request of the seller when the commodity is in the possession of the buyer. According to the Hanafis, where the contract is irregular, it may be annulled by a judge if it is brought to him and the parties to the contract cannot agree on its rescission.[114] **14.55**

4.1.2 Rescission Due to Lawful Justification

Jurists have discussed whether the rescission of certain types of contracts, such as lease, the sale of fruits, and others is allowed by reference to some legally justifiable cause. The Hanafis allow rescission on account of lawful justifications relating to one of the parties or the subject matter of the contract.[115] The Malikis, while allowing rescission in this manner, have also referred to circumstances justifying the rescission of lease agreements. In this regard they stipulate that such agreements may be rescinded where the subject matter of the lease or its usufruct becomes inaccessible on account of usurpation, emergency, or aggression.[116] **14.56**

The Shafi'is do not allow the unilateral rescission of contracts by reference to an excuse. They contend that as the contract is formed with mutual consent, its rescission should also occur through mutual consent. For instance, a guide's inability to travel does not provide justification to rescind the contract nor reduce his obligation.[117] Ibn Qudama has also narrated a similar opinion in the Hanbali school.[118] **14.57**

112 Al-Qarāfī (n 3) Vol. 3, p. 269.
113 Al-Zaila'ī (n 48) Vol. 4, p. 197.
114 Al-Kāsānī (n 3) Vol. 5, pp. 281, 298; Al-Dusūqī (n 10) Vol. 3, p. 121; Al-Shirbīnī (n 35) Vol. 2, pp. 456, 138.
115 Al-Sarakhsī (n 10) Vol. 16, p. 2; Al-Kāsānī (n 3) Vol. 4, p. 197; al-Zaila'ī (n 48) Vol. 5, p. 45.
116 Al-Ṣāwī (n 20) Vol. 4, p. 51.
117 Al-Qalyūbī (n 93) Vol. 3, p. 84; Al-Shīrāzī (n 20) Vol. 1, p. 405, Vol. 2, p. 261.
118 *Al-Mughnī* (n 2) Vol. 5, p. 333.

4.1.3 Rescission Due to Bankruptcy and Insolvency

14.58 The seller has the option of rescinding the contract and keeping the commodity without any obligation to wait for the buyer to pay if it turns out that the buyer is bankrupt. This is consistent with the view of the Malikis, Shafi'is, and Hanbalis.[119] This is based on the saying of the Prophet: '[W]hoever finds his actual property in the possession of a man who became bankrupt he is more entitled to have it back.'[120] This applies equally to a buyer facing financial difficulty or despite having the ability to pay refuses to settle his debt. The Hanafis, however, opine that the seller cannot rescind the contract under such circumstances due to his preference to take property in the possession of his bankrupt debtor.[121]

4.1.4 Rescission by Exercising the Right of Option (*Khiyār*)

14.59 *Khiyār* is the right of a contracting party to either rescind the contract by reference to a lawful justification or implication of contractual agreement.[122] This is generally distinguished into *khiyār* imposed by the Sharīʿah and contractual *khiyār*. Sharīʿah-imposed *khiyār* is implied in every contract and exists regardless of the parties' stipulation. For instance, in *khiyār al-ʿayb* (option in case of defect), a party to a contract has the right to rescind the contract if it finds that the merchandise is defective.[123] Contractual *khiyār*, also termed *khiyār al-sharṭ*,[124] is stipulated by either of the parties aiming to test the merchandise or to consult others regarding their purchase.[125]

4.1.4.1 Purpose of khiyār

14.60 The purpose of Sharīʿah-based *khiyār* is chiefly to avoid the loss likely to be suffered due to the other party's failure to fulfil a condition making the contract binding.[126] Ibn Rushd states that the rationale for permitting *khiyār* is people's need to consult others or even test the commodity.[127] Hence, the seller will have to surrender the commodity to the buyer where the purpose of *khiyār* is to test the commodity. Where the buyer is silent as to whether his purpose is testing or consultation, there is a presumption in favour of consultation, in which case the seller does not have to surrender the commodity to the buyer according to Ibn Rushd.[128]

[119] Al-Ṣāwī (n 20) Vol. 3, p. 351; Al-Shīrāzī (n 20) Vol. 2, pp. 188, 178; Al-Buhūtī (n 35) Vol. 3, p. 240.
[120] Bukhārī 2402; Muslim 1559.
[121] Al-Kāsānī (n 3) Vol. 5, p. 252; Ibn al-Humām (n 3) Vol. 9, p. 279.
[122] *Radd al-Muḥtār* (n 36) Vol. 4, p. 565.
[123] Al-Kāsānī (n 3) Vol. 5, pp. 292–97.
[124] ʿAbd al-Karīm Al-Qazwīnī, Fat'ḥ al-ʿAzīz bi Sharḥ al-Wajīz (Dār al-Fikr, n.d.) Vol. 8, p. 291.
[125] Ibn Rushd Al-Qurṭubī, Al-Muqaddimāt al-Mumahhidāt (Dār al-Gharb al-Islāmī, 1988) Vol. 2, p. 86.
[126] Ibid, Vol. 2, p. 86.
[127] Ibid, Vol. 2, p. 87.
[128] Ibid, Vol. 3, p. 225.

4.1.5 Types of *Khiyār*

The right of option in Islamic law negates the binding nature of otherwise binding contracts. According to Al-Kāsānī, a contract can only be binding if it is not subject to the four types of *khiyār* which are *khiyār al-taʿyīn* (option to identify), *khiyār al-sharṭ* (option of stipulation), *khiyār al-ʿayb* (option in case of defect), and *khiyār al-ru'yā* (option to choose after inspection).[129] In effect, a binding contract will be treated as non-binding as one of its parties shall have the right to rescind the contract as stipulated by its right of option. The following sections discuss *khiyār al-sharṭ* and *khiyār al-ʿayb*. **14.61**

4.1.5.1 Khiyār al-Sharṭ

Khiyār al-sharṭ is a right of option that is created when either party to a contract stipulates a right to affirm or rescind the contract.[130] The right of option can be exercised against the commodity purchased or its price.[131] **14.62**

4.1.5.1.1 Legality of *khiyār al-sharṭ* The majority of jurists agree with the validity of *khiyār al-sharṭ* by reference to the *sunna*, as well as *ijmāʿ*. As far as the *sunna* is concerned, the Prophet is cited saying to a man who complained of being cheated in his purchases: '[W]hen you contract you should say *lā khilāba* (no cheating).'[132] Others have also cited a *ḥadīth* of the Prophet where he said: 'Both the buyer and the seller have the option of cancelling or confirming a bargain unless they separate or the sale is optional.'[133] These scholars have opined that the exception in this *ḥadīth* refers to an option whereby the parties can either confirm or rescind the contract.[134] Imam al-Nawawī and Ibn al- Hummām have both narrated that there is consensus over the validity of *khiyār al-sharṭ*.[135] **14.63**

4.1.5.1.2 Creation of *khiyār al-sharṭ* The right of option to rescind a contract can be created through a simple declaration by the party intending to exercise such option. Ibn Nujaim states that if the seller tells a buyer, 'take it with you for a day; if you accept it, this is the price you are to pay for it', this is enough to create a right of option to rescind.[136] Similarly, the term *lā khilāba* as contained in the *ḥadīth* can be used to create a right of option to rescind the contract if the parties understand its meaning.[137] If they do not know its meaning, there is no option. If it is only the seller who understands its meaning, there are two opinions narrated within the Shafi'i tradition, with the preferred opinion being that no right of option is created.[138] **14.64**

[129] Al-Kāsānī (n 3) Vol. 5, p. 228.
[130] *Radd al-Muḥtār* (n 36) Vol. 4, p. 567.
[131] *Al-Fatāwā al-Hindiyya* (n 4) Vol. 3, p. 39.
[132] Bukhārī 2117.
[133] Bukhārī 2111; Muslim 3930.
[134] Aḥmad Al-Nafrāwī, Al-Fawākih al-Dawānī ʿalā Risālat Ibn Abī Zaid al-Qairawānī (Dār al-Fikr, 1995) Vol. 2, p. 83.
[135] Al-Nawawī (n 2) Vol. 9, pp. 190; 225; Ibn al-Humām (n 3) Vol. 6, p. 300.
[136] Ibn Nujaim (n 38) Vol. 6, p. 6.
[137] *Al-Fatāwā al-Hindiyya* (n 4) Vol. 3, p. 39.
[138] Al-Nawawī (n 2) Vol. 9, p. 192.

14.65 Similarly, where the parties entered the contract on the condition that they would consult the opinion of others within a defined time, this condition will be treated as a valid right of option according to the Hanbalis.[139] They generally contend that the contract may be rescinded even before consultation, while the Shafi'is disagree over the permissibility of rescission before consultation.[140] Where the period of option is not qualified, the Shafi'is and Hanbalis consider it invalid.[141]

14.66 4.1.5.1.3 Requirements of *khiyār al-sharṭ* Certain conditions need to be fulfilled in order for a *khiyār* to be valid and provide an effective right to rescind the contract. These conditions pertain to the time when *khiyār* should be created and its exercise by the right of the option holder. These two conditions are discussed below.

4.1.5.1.3.1 The creation of *khiyār al-sharṭ*

14.67 *Khiyār al-sharṭ* should be created at the moment the contract is formed or immediately thereafter, but certainly before the separation of its parties. In *al-fatāwā al-Hindiyya* it is stated that where one party says 'I stipulate an option on the contract of sales we are going to form', yet upon formation of the contract the option is not stated, there is no option to rescind the contract. This is the view of the Hanafis.[142] It is nonetheless valid where the stipulation of the option is linked to the contract after its formation with the consent of both parties.[143] The Hanafis' view, whereby the stipulated option is the same whether made during or after the contract, is based on the analogy with marriage where the parties can agree to increase or decrease the dowry. This is predicated on the saying of Allah: '[B]ut if, after a dower is prescribed, agree mutually (to vary it), there is no blame on you, and Allah is All-knowing, All-wise.'[144] Thus, if the buyer informs the seller even after the contract: 'I am giving you an option of three days', this option is valid according to Hanafi scholars.[145] The Shafi'is and Hanbalis do not allow the stipulation after the formation of contract, reasoning that the contract becomes binding with the end of its session, arguing further that it cannot become non-binding by a subsequent stipulation.[146] The Malikis allow *khiyār al-sharṭ* after the conclusion of the contract. Their position differs from that of the Hanafis because the Malikis treat such rescission as a new contract of sale wherein the buyer will become the seller, thus implying that the risk will be with the buyer during the subsistence of such option.[147]

[139] *Al-Mughnī* (n 2) Vol. 3, p. 500.
[140] Al-Nawawī (n 2) Vol. 9, pp. 196–97.
[141] *Al-Mughnī* (n 2) Vol. 3, p. 499; Al-Nawawī (n 2) Vol. 9, p. 190.
[142] *Al-Fatāwā al-Hindiyya* (n 4) Vol. 3, p. 40.
[143] *Radd al-Muḥtār* (n 36) Vol. 4, p. 568.
[144] Qur'ān 4:34.
[145] *Al-Fatāwā al-Hindiyyah* (n 4) Vol. 3, p. 39.
[146] *Al-Mughnī* (n 2) Vol. 3, p. 486.
[147] Al-Dusūqī (n 10) Vol. 3, pp. 93–94, 177; Al-Kharshī (n 54) Vol. 4, p. 21.

4.1.5.1.3.2 The period for exercising *khiyār al-sharṭ*

The majority of scholars have suggested that *khiyār al-sharṭ* should be exercised within a defined period of time, because a stipulation for an indefinite period of time constitutes an invalid condition (*sharṭ fāsid*). Moreover, the existence of an indefinite time limit for the rescission of a contract by a party will create ambiguity.[148] **14.68**

Jurists differ on the duration of *khiyār*. According to Aḥmad bin Ḥanbal, Muḥammad bin al-Ḥasan, Abū Yūsuf, Ibn Abī Laila, Ibn Shubruma, Al-Thaurī, Ibn al-Mundhir, Ishāq bin Rahawaihī, Abū Thaur, as well as 'Ubaidullah bin al-Ḥasan al-'Anbari, the parties are free to stipulate whatever time limits they wish.[149] Mālik argues that since the needs of the parties and the subject matter of contracts differ, the length of time depends on the custom prevailing for each transaction.[150] Ibn Rushd contends that the basis of Mālik's opinion is that the right of option serves to test the purchased commodity, hence it is appropriate to allocate such a period that suffices to test and inspect the good in question.[151] Conversely, in the view of Abū Ḥanīfa and his comrade, Zufr, as well as Shafi'i, *khiyār al-sharṭ* cannot last for more than three days.[152] This is based on the *ḥadīth* of the Prophet where he gave a man the right to rescind a contract within three days if he was not satisfied.[153] Where *khiyār* surpasses three days, the contract is *fāsid* (irregular) and can be validated by eliminating additional days according to Abū Ḥanīfa and Zufr, and void according to Imam Shāfi'i.[154] **14.69**

4.1.5.2 Khiyār al-'Ayb *(option of rescinding a defective commodity)*

This is an option granted to a party to return a defective commodity in the event of a defect following possession. There is no dispute among jurists on the availability of this option. This agreement is based on provisions of the Qur'ān and the *sunna*, as well as analogy (*qiyās*). Allah says in the Qur'ān: 'O you who have believed, do not consume one another's wealth unjustly but only [in lawful] business by mutual consent.'[155] The point of inference in the verse is that upon discovery of a defect, the consent needed for a valid contract is negated.[156] **14.70**

Al-Kāsānī has cited the *ḥadīth* of *taṣriya* (the goat whose udder is tied so it should appear as if she produces plenty of milk) as the basis of *khiyār al-'ayb*.[157] The Prophet said that 'it is unlawful for anyone to sell something unless he explains whatever therein. **14.71**

148 Al-Kāsānī (n 3) Vol. 5, p. 174; Al-Nawawī (n 2) Vol. 9, p. 190.
149 Al-Nawawī (n 2) Vol. 9, p. 190; Al-Sarakhsī (n 10) Vol. 13, p. 41; *Al-Mughnī* (n 2) Vol. 3, pp. 498–99.
150 Al-Dusūqī (n 10) Vol. 3, p. 95; Al-Ḥaṭṭāb (n 3) Vol. 4, p. 412.
151 Ibn Rushd (n 30) Vol. 3, p. 225.
152 Al-Kāsānī (n 3) Vol. 5, p. 174; Al-Sarakhsī (n 10) Vol. 13, p. 41; Al-Nawawī (n 2) Vol. 9, p. 190.
153 Al-Darquṭnī 3011.
154 Al-Kāsānī (n 3) Vol. 5, p. 18; Al-Nawawī (n 2) Vol. 9, pp. 190, 194.
155 Qur'ān 4:29.
156 Al-Jaṣṣāṣ, Ahkām al-Qur'ān (Dār al-Kutub al- 'Ilmiyya, 1994) Vol. 2, p. 223.
157 Al-Kāsānī (n 3) Vol. 5, p. 274. The implied *ḥadīth* is transmitted by Muslim (*Ḥadīth* 3908) and therein the Prophet states: 'Whoever purchases a goat whose udder is tied, he has the option of three days to either keep it or return it with a Sā' (measure) of date.'

It is unlawful for anyone who knows that not to explain it.'[158] Once, when the Prophet put his hand into the food item and found it wet from inside, the seller retorted that this was due to the rain. The Prophet then asked him why he had not placed it on top so that people could see its condition, ultimately uttering 'whoever cheats is not of me'.[159] The legal outcome from this *ḥadīth* is that if a seller is aware that a commodity is defective it is mandatory to inform the buyer, lest he commit a sin, according to Ibn Qudama. Al-Subkī[160] and Ibn Rushd call it eating people's properties in vanity, which is prohibited.[161]

14.72 4.1.5.2.1 Contracts on which *khiyār al-'ayb* can be applied The Hanafis have argued that *khiyār al-'ayb* is applicable to the contracts of sale, *ijāra*, *qisma* (division or sharing), reconciliation over money, substitution of reconciliation over intentional murder, dowry, and consideration of redemption in marriage.[162] Ibn Rushd has classified contracts into three categories. First, *khiyār al-'ayb* can be exercised in contracts of exchange made for consideration. Secondly, *khiyār al-'ayb* does not apply to those contracts expressly lacking consideration, such as gifts. Thirdly, there is some disagreement whether this applies to gratuitous contracts.

14.73 4.1.5.2.2 When *khiyār al-'ayb* may be exercised There are three opinions as to the time when the right of option in the purchase of a defective commodity can be exercised. According to the Shafi'i school, as well as a narration from Aḥmad bin Ḥanbal, *khiyār al-'ayb* must be exercised immediately. If the buyer knows of the defect at the time of the contract or immediately thereafter but fails to rescind the contract, the seller shall not compensate him for the defect.[163] The Shafi'is have reasoned that this right must be exercised immediately, and any additional time not implied by *ijmā'* or textual provision permitting *khiyār al-'ayb* is prohibited. Since the nature of a contract is binding, this option should be used immediately so that relevant authorities are not violated. Similarly, the prevention of harm caused by the defective commodity can only be achieved by the immediate exercise of such right. These scholars have also analogized it with the right of *shuf'a* (pre-emption) which is intended to negate *harf*. Thus, *khiyār al-'ayb* must also be exercised immediately just like the right of *shuf'a*.[164]

14.74 According to the Hanafis and the majority of the Hanbalis, the right of option in the sale of a defective commodity can be exercised at a slack phase without time pressure whenever such party intends to exercise it.[165] The Malikis argue that the *khiyār-al-'ayb*

[158] Transmitted by Ahmad in his Musnad ('Ālam al-Kutub, 1998) Vol. 3, p. 491.
[159] Muslim 102.
[160] *Al-Mughnī* (n 2) Vol. 4, p. 109; Taqī al-Dīn Al-Subkī, Takmīlāt al-Majmū' Sharḥ al-Muhadhab li-'Alī ibn 'Abd al-Kāfī al-Subkī (n.p., 1966) Vol. 12, pp. 110, 112.
[161] Ibn Rushd (n 125) Vol. 2, p. 100.
[162] *Radd al-Muḥtār* (n 36) Vol. 4, p. 71.
[163] Al-Subkī (n 160) Vol. 12, p. 13; Ibn Qudāma, Al-Kāfī fī Fiqh al-Imām Aḥmad (Dār al-Kutub al-'Ilmiyya, 1994) Vol. 2, p. 52.
[164] Al-Subkī (n 163) Vol. 12, pp. 135–36.
[165] *Al-Mughnī* (n 2) Vol. 4, p. 109; *Radd al-Muḥtār* (n 36) Vol. 5, p. 32.

should be exercised within a day. If the party with the option delays by two days, he shall be allowed to return it with an oath that he did not consent to what he was given.[166]

4.1.5.2.3 Nature of contract with *khiyār al-ʿayb* *Khiyār al-ʿayb* renders a contract non-binding and is implied in every contract even if the parties have not expressly stipulated that the sold merchandise should be fit and free from any defect.[167] According to the Hanafis and Shafi'is, a buyer of a defective commodity has the right to either affirm the contract as concluded or rescind it and return the defective commodity upon receiving the fee paid.[168] The Hanbalis have argued that the buyer has two options: he can either rescind the contract and return the commodity and take back what he paid or he can keep the commodity and be compensated for the defect, irrespective of whether the seller consents or not. Where compensation may lead to usury, the buyer will either keep the commodity as purchased, or return it as a whole. For example, in the purchase of silver assessed by its value in weight, compensation shall entail buying more silver, which amounts to usury.[169] **14.75**

A third position distinguishes between major and simple defects. A simple defect refers to an insignificant defect from which commodities are not free. Ibn Rushd maintained that such defects do not alter the contract.[170] Ibn Rushd opined that defects costing around 10% of the contract price, or defects equivalent to one-third of the price constitute major defects. These major defects provide an option to the buyer to either affirm the contract without compensation or rescind it.[171] **14.76**

4.2 Rescission of Irregular Contracts (*ʿAqd Fāsid*)

According to the Hanafis, a contract shall be rescinded if it is irregular; that is, where its form is inconsistent with the Sharīʿah. This serves to eliminate the cause of the irregularity in the contract, such as any ambiguity regarding the item's price, period of delivery, or means of security, such as guarantee and mortgage. However, such ambiguity must be serious enough to lead to dispute. The causes of irregularity may involve coercion, uncertainty, ambiguity (*jahāla*), temporary sales, detrimental surrender, or an invalid stipulation which includes the charging of interest.[172] **14.77**

166 Al-Dusūqī (n 10) Vol. 3, p. 121; Al-Ḥaṭṭāb (n 3) Vol. 4, p. 443.
167 Al-Kāsānī (n 3) Vol. 5, p. 274.
168 Al-Shīrāzī (n 20) Vol. 2, p. 50.
169 *Al-Mughnī* (n 2) Vol. 4, pp. 109, 111; Al-Rahaibanī (n 54) Vol. 3, p. 112.
170 Ibn Rushd (n 125) Vol. 2, pp. 101–02.
171 Ibid.
172 Al-Zuhaylī (n 1) Vol. 4, pp. 3165–66.

4.3 Effects of Rescission

14.78 The effect of rescission on a contract can be viewed from the perspective of parties and non-parties alike. Following rescission, the contract is devoid of any legal effect for the parties and restores their pre-contractual position. If the buyer has associated a third party to the subject matter that he received under a rescindable contract, the contract cannot be rescinded so as to protect the third party's right. However, the Shafi'is and Hanbalis hold the right of rescission to be valid and contend that the buyer's transaction with a third party will not be considered executed. The Malikis are of the view that if the subject matter of a sales contract is removed from the second buyer's possession, the repudiation shall be impeded; otherwise, it shall be valid.[173]

14.79 Al-Suyūṭī maintains that in the rescission of a contract based on the option of contract session (*khiyār al-majlis*) or the option of condition (*khiyāral-sharṭ*), or the option of defect or *taṣriya* (udder tying), the effect of the contract is rescinded from the moment it is rescinded.[174] Rescission of contract in the Shafi'i, Hanafi, and Maliki traditions does not produce a retrospective effect. Instead, it takes place at the time it was rescinded. Thus, any proceeds from such subject matter shall belong to the buyer from the moment the contract is formed and the goods come into the possession of the buyer.[175]

[173] Al-Zaylaʿī (n 48) Vol. 4, p. 64; Al-Dusūqī (n 10) Vol. 3, p. 75; Al-Shīrāzī (n 20) Vol. 2, pp. 8, 221; Ibn Qudāma (n 164) Vol. 2, p. 29.

[174] Al-Suyūṭī (n 13) p. 292.

[175] Ibn Nujaim (n 86) p. 292.

15
Damages and Other Remedies

1. Introduction

The subject matter of this chapter concerns the availability of remedies of options (*Khiyār*), damages (*ḍamān*), and specific performance under Islamic law. Options are included as a remedy as they save a party from suffering harm arising from the conduct of another party. As the reader will go on to appreciate, a variety of conditions have been set out to avoid making these remedies applicable in a manner that causes injustice, or which frustrate the ordinary operation of contracts. The secondary sources examined in this chapter are aimed not only at demonstrating the diversity of opinion, but also the current status of the various sub-categories of *ḍamān* and *khiyār*. The reader is directed to other chapters of this book, which examine in the course of their analysis these and other remedies, whether directly or indirectly. 15.01

2. *Khiyārāt* (Options)

This section discusses the Islamic law of options, that is *khiyār al-ru'yā*, *khiyār al-'ayb*, *khiyār al-tadlīs*, and *khiyār al-ta'yīn*, to demonstrate that Islamic contract law ensures the performance of contract and also that the parties are saved from harm. 15.02

2.1 *Khiyār al-ru'yā*

2.1.1 Legality and the Nature of *Khiyār al-ru'yā*

Khiyār al-ru'yā is a more powerful claim as compared to *khiyār al-'a yb* because the former invalidates the sale in its entirety whereas the latter stops the contract from becoming *lāzim* after its conclusion.[1] Where the buyer failed to inspect the subject matter or its *ṣifa* at the time of contract, *Ahnāf* allows this *khiyār*. He opines that this is possible following inspection of the subject matter, after which the buyer can return the subject matter to the seller or retain it for the whole price consideration, irrespective of whether or not the subject matter corresponds to the *ṣifa* stipulated.[2] The same applies even if 15.03

[1] Wahba al-Zuhaylī, Fiqh al Islamī wa Adilatuuh (Dār Al-Fikr, 1989) Vol. 4, p. 576.

[2] 'Abd al-Rḥmān Al-Suyūṭī, Al-Jāmi' al-Ṣaghīr (Dār al-Kutub Al-'Ilmiyya, n.d.) p. 341; Niẓām al-Dīn al-Balkhī, Al-Fatāwā al-Hindiyya (Dār al-Fikr, 1310H) Vol. 3, p. 62; Ibn Nujaim, Al-Ashbāh wa al-Naẓā'ir 'alā Madhahb Abī Ḥanīfa (Dār al Fikr, 2005) p. 247; Ibn al-Humām, Fat'ḥ al-Qadīr Sharḥ al-Hidāya (Dār al-Fikr, n.d.) Vol. 6, p. 309.

the buyer accepts the subject matter before inspecting it, as well as upon ascertaining its characteristics because this *khiyār* is related to the inspection of the subject matter. The *Ahnāf* have relied, *inter alia*, on the *ḥadīth* whereby a person purchases a thing that was not inspected, but in respect of which *khiyār* is present upon inspection.[3] The *Ahnāf* do not allow this *khiyār* for the sale of a subject matter which was not subjected to inspection. For instance, if the seller sells an inherited commodity situated in another city and which he did not inspect, no *khiyār* arises for the seller.[4]

15.04 In addition to Abū Ḥanīfa, the Malikis and Hanbalis also allow *khiyār al-waṣf* for the buyer, that is, the sale of an absent subject matter where the buyer has stipulated *waṣf* for it. However, in situations where the commodity comes with the desired traits, the contract becomes binding. The Hanbalis allow this *khiyār* for the seller if he personally did not inspect the sold goods.[5]

15.05 The Shafi'is disfavour all contracts concerning absent subject matters, whether stipulating their characteristics or not, on the basis of the *ḥadīth* prohibiting *gharar*. The Shafi'is characterize this *ḥadīth* as *ḍa'īf* and *bāṭil*.[6] *Jahāla* (lack of knowledge or ambiguity) is clearly present in the *khiyār al-ru'yā* because the buyer is purchasing without seeing/inspecting, albeit the Hanafis suggest that such *jahāla* does not lead to conflict since the buyer may return the commodity.[7] The Hanafis maintain that the *khiyār al-ru'yā* is available for the benefit of the buyer irrespective of whether the seller describes the characteristics of the subject matter.[8] This is because the ignorance of the buyer pertains to the characteristics of *mabī'*, which does not impede the *ṣiḥa* of the contract.[9] In other words, the absence of inspection (*a'dm al-ru'yā*) renders consent deficient but not extinct. Hence, the contract is concluded, albeit it becomes *ghair lāzim*;[10] to put it another way, this *khiyār* does not hinder the transfer of ownership to the respective parties, rather it only prevents the contract from becoming *lāzim*.[11] Consequently, the seller cannot demand from the buyer the price consideration before *ru'yā* .[12]

[3] Burhān al-Dīn, Al-Muḥīṭ (Dār al Kutub al-'Ilmiyya, 2004) Vol. 6, p. 531.

[4] Al-Sarakhsī, Al-Mabsūṭ (Dār al-Ma'rifa, 1993) Vol. 13, p. 69; Ibn al-Humām (n 2) Vol. 6, pp. 309, 315; Al-Kāsānī, Badā'i' al-Ṣanā'i' fī Tartīb al-Sharā'i' (Dār al-Kutub al-'Ilmiyya, 1986) Vol. 5, p. 292; Ibn 'Ābidīn, Radd al-Muḥtār 'alā al-Durr al-Mukhtār (Dār al-Fikr, 1992) Vol. 4, p. 68; Al-Zuhaylī (n 1) Vol. 4, pp. 577–79.

[5] Ibn Rushd, Bidāyat al-Mujtahid wa Nihāyat al-Muqtaṣid (Muṣṭafā al-Bābī al-Ḥalabī, 1975) Vol. 2, p. 154; Al-Dusūqī, Ḥāshiya al-Dusūqī 'alā al-Sharh al-Kabīr (Dār al-Fikr, n.d.) Vol. 3, p. 25; Al-Kāsānī (n 4) Vol. 5, p. 292; Ibn Nujaim, Al-Nahr Al-Fā'iq Sharḥ Kanz al-Daqā'iq (Dār al-Kutub al-'Ilmiyya, 2002) Vol. 3, p. 381; Ibn Qudāma, Al-Mughnī fī Fiqh al-Imām Aḥmad bin Ḥanbal (Maktabat al-Qāhirah, 1968) Vol. 3, p. 582; Muḥaqqiq al-Ḥillī, Ja'far ibn al-Ḥasan, Al Mukhtasar al Nāfi' fī fiqh al-Imāmīyya (Al-Maktaba al-Ahlīyya, 1964) p. 146.

[6] Ibn al-Humām (n 2) Vol. 6, pp. 309–10; Al-Zuhaylī (n 1) Vol. 4, pp. 576–79.

[7] Ibn Nujaim, Al-Baḥr al-Rā'iq Sharḥ Kanz al-Daqā'iq (Dār al-Kitāb al-Islāmī, n.d.) Vol. 6, p. 43; *Al-Muḥīṭ* (n 3) Vol. 6, p. 531.

[8] *Al-Muḥīṭ* (n 3) Vol. 6, p. 531.

[9] Al-Jṣṣāṣ, Sharh Ṭahāvī (Dār ul Sirāj, 2010) Vol. 3, p. 99.

[10] Zafar Aḥmed Al-'Uthmānī, I'lā al-Sunan (Dār Al-Fikr, n.d.) Vol. 12, p. 371.

[11] *Al-Fatāwā al-Hindiyya* (n 2) Vol. 3, p. 62.

[12] *Al-Baḥr al-Rā'iq* (n 7) Vol. 6, p. 42.

2.1.2 Time when *Khiyār* is Established

The *khiyār* is established only when the buyer inspects the subject matter, not before. Even if the buyer, before inspecting the subject matter, expressly approves it, he would still have the right to return it after inspection under this *khiyār*. There are several reasons for this approach. The Prophet specifically allowed *khiyār* only after inspection. As a result, allowing *khiyār* before inspection would be in violation of a primary source. Moreover, the approval of *mabīʿ* before inspection constitutes an agreement on the subject without any knowledge of it.[13] As to whether the buyer possesses the right to rescind the contract before exercising his *khiyār al-ru'yā*, there are two opinions. The first disallows it, whereas the second does not; albeit, not on the basis of *khiyār al-ru'yā*, but rather on the ground that the contract is *ghair lāzim* and hence may be rescinded.[14] **15.06**

2.1.3 Conditions for the Establishment of *Khiyār al-ru'yā*

This *khiyār* is established in every contract that may be rescinded through the return of the contracted commodity, such as *ijāra*, settlement, sale, and others. Consequently, it does not arise in contracts that are not susceptible to rescission of the sold good, such as *mahr*, *badl al-khulʿ*, and others.[15] In contracts suitable for this *khiyār* the subject matter should be something described with specificity. If both parties exchange specified things/goods, then the *khiyār* will be available to both, as where the price consideration for the seller is *aʿyn* that can be measured or weighed. Similarly, if the buyer has purchased *aʿyn* in return for a loan, the *khiyār* will be for the buyer and not for the seller[16] as there is no *khiyār* in *dayn*.[17] **15.07**

The other condition is that the buyer should not have inspected the subject matter before the conclusion of the contract. A contract concluded while the buyer was inspecting the good under sale is rendered *lāzim*. If the buyer had seen the subject matter some time before the conclusion of the contract and the subject matter remained unvaried at the time of the contract, there would also be no *khiyār*.[18] **15.08**

2.1.4 How to Conduct the Inspection

The *khiyār al-ru'yā* becomes *bāṭil* following the inspection that provides sufficient knowledge to the buyer about the *mabīʿ*.[19] As to the nature of this type of inspection, we are forced to resort to custom, given that the inspection may concern the good(s) as a whole or just part(s) thereof.[20] Moreover, the modalities of the inspection depend **15.09**

[13] Al-Kāsānī (n 4) Vol. 5, p. 295; Al-Zuhaylī (n 1) Vol. 4, p. 580.

[14] Al-Kāsānī (n 4) Vol. 5, pp. 292, 295; *Al-Fatāwā al-Hindiyyah* (n 2) Vol. 3, p. 62; Ibn al-Humām (n 2) Vol. 6, pp. 311, 323.

[15] *Al-Fatāwā al-Hindiyya* (n 2) Vol. 3, p. 62; *Al-Baḥr al-Rā'iq* (n 7) Vol. 6, p. 42.

[16] Al-Kāsānī (n 4) Vol. 5, p. 292; *Al-Baḥr al-Rā'iq* (n 7) Vol. 6, p. 45; Al-Mauṣilī, Al-Ikhtiyār li Taʿlīl al-Mukhtār (Dār al-Kutub al-ʿIlmiyya, 1937) Vol. 3, p. 36.

[17] *Al-Fatāwā al-Hindiyyah* (n 2) Vol. 3, p. 62; *Al-Baḥr al-Rā'iq* (n 7) Vol. 6, p. 42; *Al-Muḥīṭ* (n 3) Vol. 6, p. 532.

[18] Al-Sarakhsī (n 4) Vol. 13, pp. 72–73; Al-Kāsānī (n 4) Vol. 5, pp. 292–93; Ibn al-Humām (n 2) Vol. 6, pp. 323–24; *Al-Muḥīṭ* (n 3) Vol. 6, p. 533; *Al-Fatāwā al-Hindiyya* (n 2) Vol. 3, p. 63; *Al-Baḥr al-Rā'iq* (n 7) Vol. 6, p. 55.

[19] Al-Mauṣilī (n 16) Vol. 2, p. 38. For detailed discussion, see Al-Zuhaylī (n 1) Vol. 4, pp. 582–89.

[20] Al-Kāsānī (n 4) Vol. 5, p. 293; Ibn ʿĀbidīn (n 4) Vol. 4, p. 68.

on the nature of the subject matter. Subject matters may be inspected by smell, taste, touch, and viewing, as is the case with immovable properties.[21] Sometimes the *a'yb* in the subject matter cannot be ascertained by mere inspection and is only revealed through its use. This explains the suggestion of *fuqhahā* that when a person receives land for cultivation the *khiyār* will not be eliminated until that possessor proceeds with the cultivation.[22]

2.1.4.1 When the mabīʿ *is a single object*

15.10 If the *mabīʿ* is of the same kind and the buyer inspects part of it and the uninspected goods are dependent on the inspected goods (i.e. uninspected goods are determined along with the inspection of the inspected goods) there is no option for such uninspected goods, irrespective of whether inspection of the inspected good confers knowledge of the uninspected good. There would be no *khiyār* for the uninspected good because the rule applicable to the *aṣl* (inspected good in this case) applies to the subordinate good (uninspected good in this case). In another instance, if the uninspected good is not subject to the inspected good, and it is only the uninspected good itself that is being considered, then there are certain possibilities. First, if the inspection of a good clearly helps to make a judgment about the situation of the uninspected good, then there is no *khiyār* in the uninspected good. This is so because the uninspected good resembles the inspected good and the objective is the attainment of knowledge about the situation of the (remaining) good, that is, inspecting a part would be tantamount to the inspection of the whole of the good. Secondly, if the inspection of a good does not enlighten the situation of the uninspected good, then there will be *khiyār* about the good not inspected because the objective of knowledge has not been achieved from the inspection and the uninspected (invisible) part has not been inspected at all. According to Abū Yūsuf, it is sufficient to inspect the external surface of the collection of grains, or the face and hindquarters of an animal.[23] In the sale of a goat for its meat, the close inspection must be capable of revealing the quantity of its meat. If it is inspected from a distance, then *khiyār* exists, because the object of the sale is meat and inspection from a distance does not provide sufficient knowledge in this respect. In case of the sale of houses and immovable properties, these should be inspected both internally and externally.[24] In other words, in case of the sale of land only, external inspection is sufficient to conclude *khiyār*. However, if construction is pending inside the property, internal inspection is required to eliminate *khiyār*.[25] In case of the sale of cloth, Abū Ḥanīfa and Muḥammad contended that if the folded cloth is plain, then inspecting the surface is sufficient because that would provide sufficient knowledge about the interior of the

21 Al-Suyūṭī (n 2) p. 342.

22 *Al-Fatāwā al-Hindiyya* (n 2) Vol. 3, p. 65.

23 Al-Sarakhsī (n 4) Vol. 13, pp. 72, 76; Al-Kāsānī (n 4) Vol. 5, p. 293; Ibn al-Humām (n 2) Vol. 6, pp. 314–16; Ibn ʿĀbidīn (n 4) Vol. 4, pp. 69, 70; *Al-Baḥr al-Rāʾiq* (n 7) Vol. 6, p. 47; *Al-Muḥīṭ* (n 3) Vol. 6, p. 537; Al-Zuhaylī (n 1) Vol. 4, p. 583.

24 Al-Kāsānī (n 4) Vol. 5, p. 293; Ibn ʿĀbidīn (n 4) Vol. 4, p. 70; Ibn al-Humām (n 2) Vol. 6, pp. 314–17.

25 *Al-Fatāwā al-Hindiyya* (n 2) Vol. 3, p. 68.

cloth. Where the cloth in question is printed, *khiyār* arises only where the folded cloth is not visible by spreading it. Zufr suggests that the cloth should be spread completely.[26]

2.1.4.2 *Where subject matter comprises more than one object*

If the subject matter consists of more than one item and at the time of the sale the purchaser inspected some without inspecting others, there are two distinct possibilities. First, that subject matter is known in terms of its weight or measurement which is stored in the same utensil. If the purchaser has seen some part of it, there would be no *khiyār*, because the mere inspection of a part of the subject matter does not provide sufficient knowledge about the whole of the subject matter. If such subject matter is stored in two different utensils, then there are two possibilities according to the *Aḥnāf*. First, inspection of a part of the subject matter stored in one utensil gives rise to *khiyār* about the same kind of subject matter stored in the other utensil because the same subject matter stored in two different utensils may be treated as two different subject matters. The second opinion, which is preferred, suggests that both be treated as the same subject matter if the subject matter is of same species or kind, and which does not give rise to *khiyār*. If the commodity stored in both utensils is of the same kind or species, yet both possess different characteristics, then there would be *khiyār*.[27] If oil or ghee is stored in a bottle, then the first Hanafi opinion suggests that inspection from the outside is sufficient to bring the *khiyār al-ru'yā* to an end because the external inspection provides sufficient information about the content stored inside. The second opinion stipulates that *khiyār* in fact exists on the basis that external inspection provides insufficient information about internal content because, for example the colour of the oil inside is tainted by the colour of the bottle in which it is contained.[28] 15.11

2.1.4.3 *When the* mabīʿ *is a collection of dissimilar objects*

The other situation pertains to the subject matter comprising dissimilar objects such as animals, cloth, and others. If a person purchases a collection of dresses, a flock of sheep, a herd of cows, or a heap of watermelons after inspecting only part of these (or not inspecting any) the buyer will possess *khiyār* for the uninspected part because in this case each part is desired by the buyer. In this sense, the objective is the whole of the subject matter and since the subject is not similar in its entirety, inspection of some part only is insufficient as to the qualities of the entire number of objects comprising it.[29] 15.12

2.1.5 Elimination of *Khiyār al-ru'yā*

The buyer cannot surrender its *khiyār al-ru'yā* because this is given to him under the Sharīʿah.[30] Any incident, defect, or *taṣarruf* that transforms *khiyār al-sharṭ* into *bāṭil* 15.13

[26] Al-Kāsānī (n 4) Vol. 5, p. 293.
[27] Al-Kāsānī (n 4) Vol. 5, p. 294; *Al-Muḥīṭ* (n 3) Vol. 6, pp. 537–38.
[28] Al-Kāsānī (n 4) Vol. 5, p. 94; Ibn ʿĀbidīn (n 4) Vol. 4, pp. 70–106.
[29] Al-Kāsānī (n 4) Vol. 5, p. 294; Al-Sarakhsī (n 4) Vol. 13, p. 72; *Al-Baḥr al-Rā'iq* (n 7) Vol. 6, p. 48.
[30] Al-Kāsānī (n 4) Vol. 5, p. 297; *Al-Fatāwā al-Hindiyya* (n 2) Vol. 3, p. 62.

also transforms *khiyār al-ru'yā* into *bāṭil*.[31] This *khiyār* is eliminated in any of the following ways.

15.14 First, with the consent of the buyer after inspection of the subject matter and not before: this acquiescence may be express or implied (through conduct). Hence, following inspection the buyer takes the *mabīʿ* into its possession or undertakes any other conduct that only pertains to owners. A typical example arises where the buyer cuts the cloth or dyes it, consumes the edibles, or constructs a building on the land (if the *mabīʿ* is land). The same is true where the buyer donates the commodity or presents it for sale. These actions with the property of another are prohibited and hence in order to be considered valid, the approval of the buyer for the *mabīʿ* is required.[32] Muḥammad and Al-Sarakhsī contend that *khiyār al-ru'yā* becomes *bāṭil* with the presentation of a good by the buyer for sale. Abū Yūsuf and Qadūrī opine that *khiyār* does not become *bāṭil* on this basis.[33]

15.15 Secondly, the *khiyār al ru'ya* ends with the death of the buyer according to the *Aḥnāf*, which is refuted by the Shafi'is.

15.16 Thirdly, if the subject matter is destroyed[34] or becomes defective while in the possession of the buyer, or the buyer becomes unable to return some part of the subject matter, the *khiyār* ends.[35]

2.1.6 Termination of the Contract

15.17 The buyer should expressly stipulate his rescission of the contract by exercising the *khiyār al-ru'yā*. The buyer's verbal utterance is sufficient before and after taking the *mabīʿ* into his possession, and there is no need for a judicial decision to that effect. However, some conditions must be met. First, the *khiyār al-ru'yā* should be existent at the time of the buyer's declaration to terminate the contract. Secondly, the termination should encompass the entire transaction and not only part of it. Abū Ḥanīfa and Muḥammad emphasize that the seller should possess knowledge of such termination, whereas Abū Yūsuf disagrees.[36]

2.1.7 Inheritance of *Khiyār al-ru'yā*

15.18 *Khiyār al-ru'yā* cannot be inherited according to the Hanafis and Hanbalis. They reason that this *khiyār* is established for the contracting party by the primary sources of Islam

[31] Ibn al-Humām (n 2) Vol. 6, p. 314.
[32] Al-Kāsānī (n 4) Vol. 5, p. 295; Ibn al-Humām (n 2) Vol. 5, p. 141; Al-Sarakhsī (n 4) Vol. 13, p. 76; *Al-Fatāwā al-Hindiyya* (n 2) Vol. 3, p. 64; *Al-Baḥr al-Rā'iq* (n 7) Vol. 6, p. 42.
[33] *Al-Muḥīṭ* (n 3) Vol. 6, p. 534.
[34] Al-Kāsānī (n 4) Vol. 5, pp. 296–97; Ibn al-Humām (n 2) Vol. 5, pp. 141, 149; *Al-Baḥr al-Rā'iq* (n 7) Vol. 6, p. 42.
[35] Al-Mauṣilī (n 16) Vol. 2, p. 39.
[36] Al-Kāsānī (n 4) Vol. 5, p. 294; Ibn al-Humām (n 2) Vol. 6, pp. 312, 323; *Al-Fatāwā al-Hindiyya* (n 2) Vol. 3, p. 64; *Al-Baḥr al-Rā'iq* (n 7) Vol. 6, p. 42; *Al-Muḥīṭ* (n 3) Vol. 6, p. 533. *khiyār al-ru'ya* deters the entire transaction. Therefore, if the buyer purchased clothes and there was some *a'yb*, he would have to either return the whole of the subject matter or retain it. He cannot return some part of the subject matter by retaining the other. See *Al-Muḥīṭ* (n 3) Vol. 6, p. 533.

and that since legal heirs are not contracting parties this is not established for him.[37] Even so, Mālik argues that this can be inherited like *khiyār al-ta'yīn* and *'ayb* on the ground that, just as inheritance may be proved in respect of properties, this may also be established in rights accrued through sale.[38] Wahba Zuḥailī prefers the opinion of the Malikis by suggesting that the heir inherits everything left by the deceased, including the *māl* as well as the rights of *khiyār*.[39]

2.1.8 Time Available to Exercise *Khiyār al-ru'yā*

As to the time available for the exercise of *khiyār al-ru'yā*, the buyer can utilize his *khiyār al-ru'yā* until any event or conduct concluding his right of option of *ru'yā*; in other words, from the buyer's approval of the sale. The factors vitiating the option of *ru'yā* have been discussed above.[40] **15.19**

2.2 *Khiyār al-'ayb*

Anybody aware that a commodity is defective should not sell it unless he reveals the defect to the buyer. For the *ḥadīth* prohibiting this, see *khiyār al-tadlīs*.[41] **15.20**

2.2.1 Establishment of *Khiyār al-'ayb*

When the buyer comes to know of the *'ayb*, he may either retain the good or rescind the contract. If he decides to retain it, he cannot charge for the *'ayb* in the subject matter,[42] irrespective of whether or not the seller knew (and concealed) the defect. This *khiyār* is available regardless of the size of the *'ayb*, so long as this defect occurred while the good was in the possession of the seller and cannot be removed without hardship.[43] This is so because the contract itself requires the subject matter to be free from defect. Where it is not free from defect the *khiyār* is available to the buyer.[44] In this way, there is no need for the incorporation of *sharṭ* in the contract to create *khiyār*.[45] **15.21**

2.2.2 Justification for the *Khiyār al-'ayb*

Al-Kāsānī has reasoned that the *mabī'* should be free from defects because the buyer intends to benefit from it fully, which is not possible with a defective good. Furthermore, it is implicit in all contracts that the buyer will have paid the full price in order to receive the *mabī'* free from *bay'*. If there is no balance between the payment of the entire price **15.22**

[37] Ibn al-Humām (n 2) Vol. 6, p. 323; Ibn 'Ali al-Zayla'ī, *Tabyīn al-ḥaqā'iq Sharḥ Kanz al-Daqā'iq* (DKI, 2000) Vol. 4, p. 30; Vol. 2, p. 33; Al-Sarakhsī (n 4) Vol. 13, p. 72; *Al-Fatāwā al-Hindiyya* (n 2) Vol. 3, p. 63; *Al-Baḥr al-Rā'iq* (n 7) Vol. 6, p. 55.

[38] Al-Kāsānī (n 4) Vol. 5, p. 293.

[39] Al-Zuhaylī (n 1) Vol. 4, p. 595.

[40] Ibn al-Humām (n 2) Vol. 6, pp. 312–13.

[41] Aḥmad Al-Sālūs, Fiqh al-Bay' (Dār al Ṣaqafa, 2008) pp. 649–50.

[42] Ibn al-Humām (n 2) Vol. 6, p. 328.

[43] *Al-Fatāwā al-Hindiyya* (n 2) Vol. 3, p. 71; *Al-Baḥr al-Rā'iq* (n 7) Vol. 6, p. 59; Ibn Nujaim (n 2) Vol. 3, p. 389–90.

[44] Al-Sālūs (n 41) p. 650; Ibn al-Humām (n 2) Vol. 6, p. 328.

[45] *Al-Fatāwā al-Hindiyya* (n 2) Vol. 3, p. 71.

and the delivery of a *mabī'* free from defects, *khiyār* arises. Contracts of sale are based on equality and mutuality, which is ensured only by the fullness and intactness of both considerations. Moreover, the absence of any defect is presumed to have been intended by the buyer. Hence, any defect fails to satisfy the commonality of intention, thus rendering the buyer's consent defective, and creates *khiyār*.[46]

2.2.3 *Ḥukm* of *bay'*

15.23 In the event of defects in the subject matter, the contract is not *lāzim*. In this way, the *milk* (ownership) is also *ghair lāzim* during the term of *khiyār*, until such time as the seller entrusts the subject matter to the buyer free from all defects.[47] If the buyer claims the *'ayb*, the seller cannot compel him to pay the price.[48]

2.2.4 Time to Return the Subject by Exercising *Khiyār al-'ayb*

15.24 Delay in returning the subject matter after realizing the defect does not transform the *khiyār* into *bāṭil*; rather, it becomes *bāṭil* only with acts or words that evince the consent of the buyer. This is the opinion of Abū Khattāb. The Shafi'is on the other hand, argue that the *khiyār al-'ayb* does not come to end at the time *'ayb* becomes known to the buyer. Shafī opines in favour of prompt and immediate extinction of *khiyār*. The buyer comes to know of the *'ayb* but defers the return of the commodity despite having the capacity to do so, in which case the *khiyār* will terminate because of the buyer's implicit approval, which is tantamount to *taṣarruf* in that good.[49]

2.2.5 Conditions for *'Ayb* Establishing *Khiyār al-'ayb*

15.25 Everything that decreases the value of the subject matter (*'ayn* or its *manfa'a*) as per the prevailing commercial custom—or if the subject matter is a manufactured item, then as per the prevailing manufacturing custom—that *'ayb* will establish *khiyār al-'ayb*.[50] This is because the value in this transaction is the objective of the sale and anything that diminishes the value of the subject matter will be counted as *'ayb*.[51] In this way the *'ayb* should fulfil the following conditions to establish *khiyār al-'ayb*:

1. The *'ayb* in the subject matter should exist before its delivery to the buyer. If *'ayb* arose after the delivery of the subject matter into the possession of the buyer, there is no *khiyār*, since granting such *khiyār* would entail the return of a defective subject matter to the seller who in fact supplied a defect-free subject matter. Some scholars suggest that proof of such *'ayb* in the subject matter while in the possession of the seller is not sufficient; rather it is also necessary to prove that such *'ayb* existed in the subject matter while in the possession of the buyer. This is because

[46] Al-Kāsānī (n 4) Vol. 5, p. 274; *Al-Fatāwā al-Hindiyya* (n 2) Vol. 3, p. 71.
[47] Al-Kāsānī (n 4) Vol. 5, p. 274; *Al-Fatāwā al-Hindiyya* (n 2) Vol. 3, p. 71.
[48] Al-Suyūṭī (n 2) p. 349.
[49] Al-Sālūs (n 41) p. 651.
[50] Al-Kāsānī (n 4) Vol. 5, p. 274; Ibn al-Humām (n 2) Vol. 6, p. 330; *Al-Baḥr al-Rā'iq* (n 7) Vol. 6, pp. 63–64. For instances of *'ayb*, see *Al-Fatāwā al-Hindiyya* (n 2) Vol. 3, p. 72.
[51] *Al-Muḥīṭ* (n 3) Vol. 6, p. 542.

such defects may be cured when the subject matter reaches the possession of the buyer.[52]

2. The buyer must be ignorant of the *'ayb* at the time of contract and after assuming possession, because possession completes the *ṣafaqa*. Therefore, knowledge at the time of possession is equivalent to knowledge at the time of contract.[53]
3. There should be no stipulation in the contract absolving the seller from liability in case of any defect in the subject matter.[54] Any agreement that the seller is absolved from all defects in the *mabī'* is valid according to the Hanafis, but is rejected by *Shāfi'ī*. However, Abū Yūsuf contends that such disclaimer by the seller encompasses the defects present at the time of the contract and those defects that may arise in future. Yet, Muḥammad and Zufr maintain that this includes only those defects existent at the time of contract.[55]
4. The removal of *'ayb* is not possible without hardship, otherwise there would be no *khiyār*. There is no *khiyār* if filth is associated with the cloth that can be easily removed. If there are bloodstains on a cloth and the colour of the cloth fades if washed, this would be *'ayb* creating *khiyār*. It is worth noting that if the *'ayb* vanishes before the buyer exercises his right of termination, the *khiyār* would also come to an end.[56]

2.2.6 Proving *'Ayb*

Proof of *'ayb* depends on the type of *'ayb* involved and hence *'ayb* is categorized as either externally visible or hidden. When *'ayb* is visible and can be observed by anyone, such *'ayb* is established by the inspection of the judge or person authorized by him. When *'ayb* is not visible and can be appreciated only by specialized persons such as doctors, this *'ayb* will be established by the statements of such experts, in accordance with the Qur'ān: '[s]o ask of those who know the scripture if you know not.'[57] **15.26**

2.2.7 Return of Subject Matter after *Faskh* of the Contract

After the establishment of *'ayb*, the *faskh* of the contract and the return of the subject matter are determined by whether the subject matter is in the possession of the seller or the buyer. If the subject matter is in the possession of the seller, there is consensus that the *faskh* of the contract occurs with the words of the buyer and in order to terminate the contract there is no need for a judicial verdict or mutual consent of seller and buyer. If the subject matter is in the possession of the buyer, Hanafis suggest that the *faskh* of the contract can be accomplished either with a judicial verdict or mutual consent of the parties. On the contrary, Shafī contends that the words of the buyer are **15.27**

[52] Al-Kāsānī (n 4) Vol. 5, pp. 275–76; *Al-Fatāwā al-Hindiyya* (n 2) Vol. 3, pp. 71–72; *Al-Baḥr al-Rā'iq* (n 7) Vol. 6, pp. 59, 78.

[53] Al-Kāsānī (n 4) Vol. 5, p. 276; *Al-Fatāwā al-Hindiyyah* (n 2) Vol. 3, pp. 71–72; *Al-Baḥr al-Rā'iq* (n 7) Vol. 6, p. 59.

[54] Al-Kāsānī (n 4) Vol. 5, p. 276; *Al-Fatāwā al-Hindiyya* (n 2) Vol. 3, pp. 71–72.

[55] *Al-Muḥīṭ* (n 3) Vol. 6, pp. 596–600; Ibn Nujaim (n 2) Vol. 3, p. 413; Al-Mauṣilī (n 16) Vol. 2, p. 47.

[56] *Al-Baḥr al-Rā'iq* (n 7) Vol. 6, p. 59; Ibn Nujaim (n 2) Vol. 3, p. 389.

[57] Qur'ān, Nahl, 43; Al-Kāsānī (n 4) Vol. 5, p. 278.

sufficient to terminate the contract without the need for mutual consent or a judicial verdict. Shafī reasons that this is a kind of *faskh* for the validity of which there is no need for court intervention or mutual consent, whether before or after delivery of possession. This is the case with *khiyār al-ru'yā* and (as Hanafis also opine) *khiyār al-sharṭ*. Hanafis on the other hand argue that the *ṣafaqa* (*'aqd* or transaction) completes with the transfer of possession, after which no party may unilaterally terminate the *ṣafaqa* as is the case with *iqāla*. In other words, the manner of doing *faskh* of an *'aqd*, which eradicates an *'aqd* from its roots, is similar to the manner of conclusion of an *'aqd*. Therefore, as the contract cannot be concluded unilaterally, it cannot be terminated unilaterally or without judicial intervention. The situation, according to Hanafis, would be different before delivery of possession, because contracts are not completed before delivery of possession.[58] If the seller has an alternative good similar to the defective subject matter in terms of its weight, measurement, or other, then he can give that alternative good to the buyer.[59]

2.2.7.1 Increment in the subject matter to be returned

15.28 If there is some increment in the subject matter (which the buyer intends to return) that cannot be separated, the buyer shall return it to the seller, as in the case of a conceived animal in the womb of its mother and fruit before pollination. So far as the increments that are separate from the subject matter are concerned, they are of two kinds. First, they are accruals not from the good itself, like cash earnings, remunerations, etc. These are for the benefit of the buyer against potential liability arising in case of death or destruction of the subject matter while in his possession. This is based on the *ḥadīth* whereby 'any profit goes to the one who bears the responsibility'.[60] There is no difference of opinion on this issue. Secondly, the increment is generated from the good itself, just as where an animal gives birth or produces milk or where a tree has fruit. This also belongs to the buyer and the *aṣl* (the subject matter) comes to the seller. This is the opinion of Shāfī. Mālik contends that if the increment is fruit, this will belong to the buyer, but if it is a baby animal, this should be returned to the seller along with the mother. Abū Ḥanīfa maintains that where the increment was generated while the original subject matter was in the custody of the buyer, the subject matter and the increment will not be returned to the seller. They reason that the subject matter cannot be returned without the increment because the increment rendered the contract binding and (by exercising the option) the contract cannot be terminated by keeping the increment in the hands of the buyer, which is the *mawjib* of the contract (i.e. which made the contract binding). Similarly, the increment, which corresponds to the *mawjib* of the contract, cannot be returned along with the subject matter because it is not included in the contract. The hanbalis argue that just because the increment was generated while in the possession of the buyer, this does not prevent the return of the subject matter to the seller. This is

[58] Al-Kāsānī (n 4) Vol. 5, p. 281; *Al-Fatāwā al-Hindiyya* (n 2) Vol. 3, p. 71.
[59] *Al-Baḥr al-Rā'iq* (n 7) Vol. 6, p. 59.
[60] Abū Dāwūd 3508; Al Nisā'ī 254/7; Tirmidhī 1285, 1286; Ibn Māja 2442.

similar to the position with cash, which is separate from the subject matter, and allows the return of the subject matter without cash to the seller.[61]

2.2.8 Factors Eliminating *Khiyār al a'yb* and Rendering the Contract *Lāzim*

If the buyer approves the sale after knowing the *'ayb*, his *khiyār* would end because such assent is tantamount to a rejection of any condition that the good is free from defects. The other reason is that this *khiyār* is meant to save the buyer from loss and in such a case he is deemed to be assenting to his own loss. This assent or acquiescence is of two types: express and implied. The express approval or assent is accomplished by the buyer's verbal utterance that he or she approves this *'ayb*. Implied assent arises where the buyer conducts some kind of *taṣarruf* in the defective *mabī'* following his knowledge of the *'ayb*.[62] The silence of the buyer concerning the *'ayb* in the *mabī'* which he knew at the time of contract or delivery of possession amounts to acquiescence.[63] **15.29**

The buyer absolves the seller from responsibility to deliver a defect-free subject matter because the buyer is entitled to surrender his right.[64] **15.30**

The *mabī'* is destroyed and as a result the option to return the *mabī'* becomes impossible. **15.31**

Nuqṣān (reduction, decrease, diminution) occurs in the *mabī'*. The *nuqṣān* may occur either before the delivery of possession to the buyer or afterwards. In each of these two situations, the *nuqṣān* may be an act of God, an act attributable to the buyer, seller, third party, or the subject matter itself. **15.32**

2.2.8.1 Nuqṣān *before transfer of possession to the buyer*

If the *nuqṣān* transpiring before the transfer of possession and attributable to an act of God, or the seller or the subject matter of the sale contract (e.g. animal, vehicle), there would be *khiyār* for the buyer. In this way, if the *nuqṣān* is in the *qadr* (quantity, measurement, number, etc.), the buyer has the option either to reject it or to take the remaining part along with the price of the remaining part. If the *nuqṣān* is in the *waṣf* of the subject matter, the buyer may either leave the good as a whole or take it by paying the entire price. If the *nuqṣān* is attributable to the buyer, he would have no *khiyār* and be liable for the whole price. **15.33**

2.2.8.2 Nuqṣān *after transfer of possession to the buyer*

If *'ayb* occurs in the *mabī'* by an act of God or is otherwise attributable to the *mabī'* or the buyer, according to the majority of scholars, the buyer does not have a right to return the subject matter to the seller. The Malikis, however, contend that the buyer enjoys the right to return the subject matter as well as to receive compensation for the **15.34**

[61] Al-Kāsānī (n 4) Vol. 5, pp. 284–85; *Al-Fatāwā al-Hindiyya* (n 2) Vol. 3, pp. 82–83; *Al-Muḥīṭ* (n 3) Vol. 6, pp. 553–54; Al-'Uthmānī (n 10) Vol. 12, p. 376; Al-Sālūs (n 41) pp. 651–52; *Al-Mughnī* (n 5) Vol. 6, pp. 226–27.
[62] Al-Kāsānī (n 4) Vol. 5, pp. 282–83 *Al-Fatāwā al-Hindiyya* (n 2) Vol. 3, p. 80; Al-Suyūṭī (n 2) p. 351.
[63] Al-Mauṣilī (n 16) Vol. 2, p. 42.
[64] Al-Kāsānī (n 4) Vol. 5, p. 283; Ibn al-Humām (n 2) Vol. 6, p. 363.

resultant *ʿayb*. The Malikis argue that the *khiyār* is given for the benefit of the buyer and failure to provide such right benefits the seller despite the fact that the buyer should be preferred. The majority, on the other hand, stipulate that the good being returned to the seller by the buyer should be on the same *ṣifa* as the seller handed it to the buyer. This is not the case here because when the subject matter left the possession of the seller, it had one *ʿayb* and upon its return to the seller's possession, it has two defects.[65] However, if such defect was created in the subject matter while in the possession of the buyer due to some act of the seller, the buyer would have the right to return it to the seller.[66]

2.3 *Khiyār al-tadlīs*

15.35 *Tadlīs* means to conceal the defect in the subject matter or suggest a quality which does not in fact exist. This is the case where the seller shows an animal un-milked in order to give the impression that it generates large quantities of milk. However, if leaving an animal un-milked is done with the intention of demonstrating that the animal generates large quantities of milk, then this does not amount to concealing a defect. This kind of *khiyār* can be found in the sale of cars, medicines, and fruits.[67] If the buyer decides to retain the subject matter, he would not be entitled to compensation for the concealed defect.[68] The factors governing the underlying *ʿayb*, elimination of *khiyār al-tadlīs* and return of the subject matter, are the same as those applicable in *khiyār al-ʿayb*.

15.36 Islamic scholars have discussed this *khiyār* under *khiyār al-ʿayb* or with a name other than *khiyār al-tadlīs*. Ibn Qudāma discusses this *khiyār* in the chapter on '*masrat*'.[69] Ibn Taymiyya discussed it in the '*khiyār nāqṣiy*'. *Khiyār al-tadlīs* is not found in the Majalla. Al Ḥaskafī discussed seventeen types of *khiyārāt* and mentioned *khiyār ghaban* and *khiyār taghrīr fiʿlī*. Ibn ʿĀbidīn, in the chapter on *khiyār al-ʿayb*, discussed the *ḥadīth* of *masrāt*. Al-Kāsānī also discussed *ḥadīth masrāt* in *khiyār al-ʿayb*.[70]

2.3.1 Prohibition of Sale of Defective Objects

15.37 The person who knows that his good is defective should not sell it unless this is revealed to the buyer. This is based on the *ḥadīth* of the Prophet whereby 'whoever sells defective goods without pointing it out, he will remain subject of the wrath of Allah, and the angels will continue to curse him'.[71] The Prophet happened to pass by a heap of corn. He thrust his hand in that (heap) and his fingers felt wetness. He said to the owner of that heap of corn, 'What is this?' He replied: 'O Messenger of Allah! These have been

65 Al-Kāsānī (n 4) Vol. 5, pp. 282–83; *Al-Baḥr al-Rāʾiq* (n 7) Vol. 6, pp. 78–79.
66 *Al-Baḥr al-Rāʾiq* (n 7) Vol. 6, p. 78.
67 Al-Sālūs (n 41) pp. 681–82.
68 *Al-Mughnī* (n 5) Vol. 6, pp. 223–24.
69 Ibid, Vol. 6, p. 215.
70 Al-Sālūs (n 41) pp. 676–81.
71 Ibn Māja 2256 (Kitāb al-Tijārāt).

drenched by rainfall.' He remarked, 'Why did you not place this (the drenched part of the heap) over the corn so that people might see it? He who deceives is not of us.'[72]

2.3.2 *'Ayb* in *Khiyār al-tadlīs*

There is a difference among jurists as to whether the fact of concealment is a defect entitling the buyer to *khiyār al-tadlīs*. For instance, if the buyer purchases an un-milked animal without knowing that the seller has failed to milk it with the intention of concealing the quantity of milk which that animal can generate, and later the buyer becomes aware, he has the option to either rescind the contract or retain the animal.[73] This is the opinion of Ibn Mas'ūd, Ibn U'mar, Abū Huraira, Anas, Mālik, Ibn Abī Laila, Shaf'ī, and Ishāq Abū Yūsuf. They have based their opinion on the following *ḥadīth* of the Prophet: 'do not tie up the udders of camels and goats. He who buys them after that (has been done) has two choices open to him after milking them: he may keep if he wishes or may return them along with one *ṣā'* of dates.'[74] They also reason that this kind of deceit has an impact on the price of the subject matter. However, some Shafi'is argue that there would be *khiyār* despite such knowledge of the buyer.[75] Abū Ḥanīfa and Muḥammad contend that there is no *khiyār* in this case because they do not count it as a defect, and the concealment of a fact which is not a defect does not provide an option of *khiyār al-tadlīs*. They argue that in case the animal is already milked, the buyer would receive a decreased quantity of milk of the same type; this is clearly not a defect. The same is true where the seller feeds the animal and the stomach of the animal swells, giving the impression to the buyer that it is pregnant.[76] 15.38

2.3.3 Period for *Khiyār al-tadlīs*

There is a difference of opinion concerning the period for this *khiyār*. Aḥmad and Shaf'ī suggest that this is three days, that is, the buyer cannot return the subject matter before the lapse of a three-day period and cannot keep it in his possession after such period. They have relied on the 'three days' as mentioned in a *ḥadīth*. In another opinion, Abū Khattāb says that the *khiyār* is established after the revelation of the deceit, upon which it may be returned before and after the lapse of three days.[77] 15.39

2.3.4 Payment of Compensation in Case of Return of the Subject Matter

If the buyer chooses to return the subject matter to the seller, Shaf'ī, Abū Ḥanīfa, and Abū Yūsuf suggest, based on the above mentioned *ḥadīth*, that the buyer will have to compensate for the benefit (equal to the price of the benefit or the good) he received from such subject matter.[78] However, the Hanbalis argue that he can get the *arsh* 15.40

[72] Muslim, 1579 (Book of Prohibited Actions).
[73] *Al-Mughnī* (n 5) Vol. 6, p. 216.
[74] Bukhārī 2148; Muslim 1524.
[75] Al-Sālūs (n 41) pp. 671, 272.
[76] *Al-Mughnī* (n 5) Vol. 6, p. 216.
[77] Ibid, Vol. 6, p. 221; Sharḥ Ṭaḥāvī (n 9) Vol. 3, p. 64.
[78] Sharḥ Ṭaḥāvī (n 9) Vol. 3, p. 64; *Al-Mughnī* (n 5) Vol. 6, p. 217.

(compensation) for the defect in the good because the defective part of the subject matter is considered absent from that subject matter and the part of the good which is considered absent for the buyer entitles him to take the *arsh*.[79] If the subject matter was defective in its entirety and suffered a new defect while it was in the possession of the buyer, two opinions are attributed to Aḥmad. First, he will not return it to the seller and will get *arsh* for the old defect. This is also the opinion of Thaurī, Shafʿī, and Aṣhāb al Rāi. The reason for this opinion is that the objective of the buyer's right to return the good is to avoid any injury and if the buyer is allowed to return the good to the seller an injury will be inflicted on the seller who will get the good with a new defect, in other words a defect which was not there at the time of delivery to the buyer. This violates the legal maxim 'there should be neither harm (*ḍarar*) nor reciprocating harm (*ḍirār*)'. The second opinion of the Aḥmad suggests that the buyer can return the good by paying the *arsh* for the defect accrued to the good in his possession. If he chooses to keep the good, then he will get the *arsh* for its old defects. This is also the opinion of Mālik, Ishāq, and Nakhʿī.[80]

2.4 *Khiyār al-taʿyīn*

15.41 In *khiyār al-taʿyīn*, the contracting parties agree to defer the specification of the *mabīʿ* to a future date. *Khiyār* is allowed for both buyer and seller. To illustrate the point, a buyer purchases two or three cloths on the condition that in three days he will choose the one he likes. This contract has two dimensions, namely, either the buyer takes one of several things under the price already stipulated for each, or the seller gives one subject matter among several subject matters already specified. In the latter case, the seller has the right to bind the buyer for that good, unless he himself fails to make such good available to the buyer. Hanafis allowed this despite the underlying *jahāla* on the basis of *isteḥsān* arising from public necessity. The Shafi'is and Hanbalis have declared it *bāṭil*.

2.4.1 Conditions for *Khiyār al-taʿyīn*

15.42 Hanafis laid down certain conditions as follows:[81]

1. The choice should be made among two or three goods only, because necessity is in three.
2. The seller should agree in express terms with the buyer on the *khiyār al-taʿyīn* in favor of the buyer, otherwise the sale will become *bāṭil* due to *jahāla*.
3. This *khiyār* should be in *qīmiyāt*, such as different kinds of dresses or linen, as well as satisfy the conditions for *mithliyāt* as there is no point of preference of one over the other.

[79] *Al-Mughnī* (n 5) Vol. 6, p. 229.
[80] Ibid, Vol. 6, pp. 230–31.
[81] Al-Zuhaylī (n 1) Vol. 4, pp. 525–26; *Al-Fatāwā al-Hindiyya* (n 2) Vol. 3, pp. 58–61.

4. The time for this *khiyār* should be equal to the time of *khiyār al-sharṭ*, which is three days according to Abū Ḥanīfa and as per Ṣāḥibain any known period.

2.4.2 *Ḥukm* of *Bay'*

If the seller says 'I have sold you two animals on the condition that you choose one which you like', and the buyer ultimately accepts this offer, ownership in one of these two animals is established for the buyer, in which case the right of *ta'yīn* lies with the buyer and the second animal in the possession of the buyer is considered *amāna* for the seller.[82] The *milk* (ownership) arises for the buyer before exercising his option of *ta'yīn* is *ghair lāzim* and the buyer can even return both goods because *khiyār al-ta'yīn* prevents the contract from becoming *lāzim*, just like *khiyār al-'ayb* and *khiyār al-ru'yā* and hence also prevents the *milk* (ownership) from becoming *lāzim*.[83] 15.43

2.4.3 Circumstances Rendering *Khiyār al-ta'yīn bāṭil* and *Bay' Lāzim*

These circumstances may be categorized into two groups: *ikhtiyārī* (optional) and *ḍarūrī* (mandatory, imperative, unavoidable). 15.44

2.4.3.1 Ikhtiyārī

Ikhtiyār circumstances are either express or implied. Choosing one good, either expressly or impliedly through conduct, renders the choice effective by extinguishing the *khiyār al-ta'yīn* and subsequently transforms the buyer's ownership into *lāzim*. Some *taṣarrufāt* (conduct making transactions) are specific to the contract of sale that make a sale binding, whereas others are particular to *'aqd al-amāna*. It is important to note that the *taṣarruf* which renders a sale binding does not make the *khiyār al ta'yīn bāṭil*. Rather, a *tasaruf* that ends *khiyār al-ta'yīn* should be the one that is made in *amāna* and which will be *nāfidh*, as in this manner it will be demonstrated that the buyer has accomplished the *taṣarruf* on his own property. 15.45

2.4.3.2 Ḍarūrī

Ta'yīn is accomplished through a *ḍarūrī*. For instance, if *mabī'* is destroyed in the buyer's possession, the sale does not become *bāṭil*; rather, the destroyed good is considered specified by the buyer and payment becomes obligatory, and the second good is considered *amāna* in his possession to be returned to the seller. If both goods are destroyed, then the good destroyed first will be the *mabī'* and the second will be *amāna*. If both are destroyed simultaneously, the buyer will pay half the price of each. If the *khiyār* is with the seller and two commodities are in the possession of the buyer, and one of these commodities is destroyed and the other is safe in the possession of the buyer, the seller is entitled to make the sale *lāzim* (binding) for the buyer on the second good that is safe. He cannot make the sale binding concerning the commodity that is destroyed. If possession is not transferred to the buyer and one good is destroyed, the destroyed 15.46

[82] Al-Kāsānī (n 4) Vol. 5, p. 261; *Al-Fatāwā al-Hindiyya* (n 2) Vol. 3, p. 61.
[83] Al-Kāsānī (n 4) Vol. 5: p. 261.

good is considered *amāna* and the seller has the option to either terminate the sale or make the sale *lāzim* on the saved good. In case of destruction of both goods with *khiyār* remaining in the seller, the abovementioned principle will be followed. This *khiyār* does not become *bāṭil* with the death of the buyer but is inherited by his legal heirs. However, the legatee does not have a right to return both goods as this right was only available to its predecessor.[84]

3. Compensation

15.47 Islamic law recognizes three ways in which liability for damages or compensation (*ḍamān*) may arise. The first is by means of contract; secondly through possession that is either acquired by or without transgression; and thirdly on the basis of destruction, whether directly (*mubāshiratan*), or indirectly through a cause (*tasabbaban*).[85]

3.1 Possession

15.48 Possession may give rise to *ḍamān* where a person usurps or steals property that is destroyed while in its possession. However, possession in itself is not always a ground, as is the case with *amāna* contracts, whereby if the subject matter is destroyed or damaged while in the possession of the possessor, there is no *ḍamān* if the goods were destroyed without any negligence; for example a trustee under a *wadī'a* contract, labourer under a *muḍāraba* contract, and a guardian for the orphaned legal heirs.[86]

3.2 Destruction or Damage (*Itlāf*)

15.49 *Ḍamān* also arises due to *itlāf* which means rendering a thing or good devoid of the utility desired in it.[87] *Itlāf* of a property may arise directly without any intermediary or instrumentality between *mutlif* (destructor) and the property, as in cases where the possessor demolishes the property or sets it on fire. Sometimes, *itlāf* occurs through a *ḍamān* instrumentality or an incident, as where the *mutlif* digs a pit in a prohibited place and subsequently vehicles or animals fall in.[88] The existence of *ḍamān* due to *itlāf* has been prescribed by Allah: 'thus, if someone has attacked you, attack him just as he attacked you.'[89] The Prophet said 'there should be neither harm (*ḍarar*) nor reciprocity

[84] Al-Kāsānī (n 4) Vol. 5, pp. 262–63; *Al-Fatāwā al-Hindiyya* (n 2) Vol. 3, pp. 58–61.
[85] Ibn Nujaim (n 2) p. 362; Ibn al-Humām (n 2) Vol. 8, p. 9; Wahba Al-Zuhaylī, *Naẓriat al-Ḍamān* (Dār al-Fikr, 1982) p. 61.
[86] *Al-Mughnī* (n 5) Vol. 9, p. 258; Ibn 'Ābidīn (n 4) Vol. 8, p. 455; Al-Zuhaylī (n 85) pp. 63–64.
[87] Al-Kāsānī (n 4) Vol. 7, pp. 164–65.
[88] Al-Zuhaylī (n 85) pp. 65–67.
[89] Qur'ān, Baqara, 194.

of harm (*ḍirār*)'. *Itlāf* entails rendering a thing devoid of benefit desired or expected from it.[90]

3.3 Contract

Ḍamān arises from the contract against a party that violates the precise conditions thereof as well as of those conditions implied by custom (*'urf*).[91] For instance, a contract may imply the delivery of consideration to the parties and their freedom from any encumbrances. In case of non-delivery of consideration, or the association of the consideration with a third party's rights it is obvious that *ḍamān* arises under such a contract. This is based on the following verse of the Qur'ān: 'O believers! Honour your obligations.'[92] The Prophet also said: 'Muslims are held by their conditions, except those conditions that make the lawful unlawful, or the unlawful lawful.'[93] Hanafis and Malikis contended that the condition would be observed as far as possible and assuming that it was beneficial. Placing a good in a certain place for safekeeping would not be beneficial if the trustee places it in a safer place. Consequently, he would not be liable if it was stolen or destroyed at that safer place. This outcome is grounded on *istiḥsān*, not *qiyās* (analogy), as under *qiyās* the said party is considered *ḍāmin* (liable to compensate) for having disobeyed his instructions. In *istiḥsān*, only the instructions considered beneficial are valid and binding. Another illustration of a non-beneficial condition arises where the bailor says to the bailee: 'protect it with your right hand and not with the left one, or supervise it with your right eye and not with the left one'. These statements are considered non-beneficial.[94] If the trustor stipulates that the trustee should avoid certain actions that are deemed unavoidable in order for the trustee to carry out its mandate, such conditions are *bāṭil* and if destruction arises due to its adherence, no liability arises. If the trustor/principal stipulates that the trustee should not receive assistance from his family in the supervision of the trust property, this condition is considered *bāṭil* if assistance is necessary. In the event the property is destroyed there would be no *ḍamān*.[95] **15.50**

The Shafi'is and Hanbalis suggest that the conditions should be observed where possible, even if not beneficial. Where the bailor has stipulated that the bailee keep a good in a certain place and the latter keeps it elsewhere more securely, the bailee would be liable to compensate for destruction or damage to the property because he disregarded **15.51**

[90] Al-Kāsānī (n 4) Vol. 7, pp. 164–65.
[91] Ibn Nujaim (n 2) pp. 361–62.
[92] Qur'ān, Mā'ida, 1.
[93] Tirmidhī 1352.
[94] Al-Sarakhsī (n 4) Vol. 11, p. 121; Al-Kāsānī (n 4) Vol. 6, p. 210; Ibn al-Humām (n 2) Vol. 7, p. 97; 'Ali Al-Baghdādī, Majma' al Damānāt fi Madh'hab Imām Abu Ḥanifa (Dār al Salām, 1999) Vol. 1, p. 69 ff.
[95] Al-Kāsānī (n 4) Vol. 6, p. 210; Ibn al-Humām (n 2) Vol. 7, p. 518.

the condition without any benefit and *mṣslaḥa*. The Shafi'is and Hanblis allow disregard of such condition only in *ḍarūra* (necessity).[96]

15.52 More specifically, this difference reflects the specification of the place. Kasāni argues that *ta'yīn* (specification) is considered valid where it is beneficial. For instance, if the trustor entrusts his property to the trustee for protection by pointing to one of two rooms of the trustee's house where he should place the property, this is considered unbeneficial if both rooms are equally safe. The Shafi'is suggest that the specification should be adhered to even if this is not beneficial and this rule may be disregarded only in case of necessity.[97] When a property is entrusted for protection generally, without any spatial specification, Hanafis, Malikis and Shafi'is contend that the trustee can take such protective measures as he usually takes for his own property, or which are known in *'urf* for such purpose. For instance, he is free to decide the location for safekeeping, as well as to transfer the property from one place to another, since the owner left this choice to the discretion of the trustee. In such cases there would be no *ḍamān* if the property is destroyed.[98]

15.53 So far, we have considered conditions expressly stipulated in the contract. Conditions implied under the contract through *'urf* are also enforceable on the basis of principles set forth by scholars, in the sense that 'specification (fixation) by *'urf* amounts to specification by express contractual stipulation'; 'conditions specified by custom (*'urf*) are tantamount to mutual agreement'; 'general principles remain unqualified until qualified by evidence from the contract or by connotation'; and 'a custom amongst traders is considered as stipulated amongst them'.[99] Based on the aforementioned scholarship on the role and function of*'urf* it is beyond doubt that *'urf* is as enforceable as the text of a written contract. A person hiring an animal must adhere to prevailing*'urf* with respect to the weight it can carry and its working hours.[100]

3.3.1 Types of Contracts Involving *Ḍamān*

15.54 The contracts giving rise to *ḍamān* are categorized into three groups. The first is *'aqūd ḍamān*, in which *ḍamān* arises with the destruction of a thing while in the possession of the *ḍāmin*. In these contracts, when the possession of a thing is transferred, the possessor becomes liable for *ḍamān*, irrespective of whether the thing is destroyed due to his own acts, those of a third person, or an act of God. These kinds of contracts include sale, loan, compromise on *māl* in return for *māl*, and *iqāla*. However, the nature of *ḍamān* may change with the validity or invalidity of the contract. For instance, a good in the possession of the buyer under a *bāṭil* contract is considered *amāna*, whereas

[96] Abū Isḥāq Al-Shīrāzī, Al-Muhadhdhab fī Fiqh Imām al-Shāfi'ī (Dār al-Kutub al-'Ilmiyya, 1995) Vol. 2, p. 182; Al-Shirbīnī, Mughnī al-Muḥtāj ilā Ma'rifat Alfāẓ al-Minhāj (Dār al-Kutub al-'Ilmiyya, 1994) Vol. 3, p. 111; *Al-Mughnī* (n 5) Vol. 9, p. 259.

[97] Al-Kāsānī (n 4) Vol. 6, p. 210.

[98] Al-Kāsānī (n 4) Vol. 6, p. 208; Ibn al-Humām (n 2) Vol. 7, p. 509; *Al-Mughnī* (n 5) Vol. 9, p. 265; Al-Shīrāzī (n 96) Vol. 2, p. 181.

[99] 'Alī Ḥaidar, Sharḥ Majallat al-Aḥkām (Dār 'Ālam al Kutub, 2003) Vol. 1, p. 51 ff.

[100] Al-Kāsānī (n 4) Vol. 6, p. 215; Ibn al-Humām (n 2) Vol. 8, p. 9; Al-Baghdādī (n 94) Vol. 1, p. 57.

possession under a *fāsid* sales contract gives rise to *ḍamān*. The second category concerns *'aqūd amāna*, in which liability does not arise with mere possession. The person in possession of a good obtained under *'aqd amāna* will become liable only if the destruction of the good occurred due to his negligence or some transgression against the good, as discussed below. These contracts include *i'āra*, *sharika*, *wakāla*, *hiba*, and others. The third category concerns contracts involving the effects of both *ḍamān* and *amāna*, as is the case with *ijāra*, *rehn*, etc. These contracts are generally dominated by the effect of *amāna* and less so, on occasion, the effects of *ḍamān*.[101]

3.3.2 Nature and Amount of Compensation

In compensation for contractual matters, the agreement of the parties as to the nature and amount of compensation is enforceable as far as its implementation is possible. Where there is no such condition, it seems permissible to allow the application of the principle governing the nature of compensation and its quantification resulting from *itlāf*, that is, to give a 'similar thing if it is a thing the like of which can be found in the market (*mithliyāt*), or the value thereof, if it is a thing the like of which cannot be found (*qīmiyāt*)'.[102] If there is no similar commodity available, or if it is available but delivery is not possible, then its price will be paid.[103] The reason for impossibility may be the absence of such a commodity in the market,[104] or, while available, its price is exorbitant.[105] If the compensation is to be ascertained in some specialized field, the *qāḍi* will be assisted by experts. As to the time when the compensation should be quantified, this is the day *itlāf* took place, according to Hanafis, Malikis and Shafi'is.[106] **15.55**

3.3.3 Transformation of *Ma'qūd 'alaih* from *Amāna* to *Damān*

As discussed above, the person entrusted with *wadī'a* is not liable if the commodity is damaged or destroyed in his possession. Non-liability may disappear and *amāna* may turn into *ḍamān* in the following cases:[107] **15.56**

1. If the trustee waives/rejects the protection of the property, the property would come to his *ḍamān* and be liable for compensation in case of its destruction. This may happen by violating the beneficial condition specifying how the good is to be protected, possible deviation from the customary manner of protection, as well as by adopting means of protection that are different from those adopted in respect of its own property. Where the aforementioned arise, the property enters into the trustee's *ḍamān*. If such deviatory actions are taken prior to the destruction of the property and he acts in conformity with the *'aqd al-amāna*, then the majority

[101] For more details on these categories of contracts, see Al-Zuhaylī (n 85) pp. 130–53; Al-Baghdādī (n 94) Vol. 1, p. 479.
[102] Majalla, p. 416; Al-Sarakhsī (n 4) Vol. 11, p. 50; Al-Zuhaylī (n 85) p. 89.
[103] See also Majalla, p. 53.
[104] Al-Sarakhsī (n 4) Vol. 11, p. 50; Ibn 'Ābidīn (n 4) Vol. 9, p. 267; Al-Shawkānī, Nayal al-Awtār (Dār Ibn Jauzī, 2007) Vol. 11, p. 91.
[105] Al-Zuhaylī (n 85) p. 87.
[106] Al-Shirbīnī (n 96) Vol. 2, p. 367; Al-Baghdādī (n 94) Vol. 1, p. 476.
[107] Al-Kāsānī (n 4) Vol. 6, pp. 211–13.

of Hanafi school maintain that he would again be free from the liability to compensate. Others, such as Ẓufr and Shafiʿ, contend that he would not be free from *ḍamān*, but would have to conclude a new contract of *wadīʿa* and the same is true in the event of *iʿāra* and *ijāra*.[108]

2. The trustee does not return the property on the demand of the owner despite being able to do so, in which case the property enters his *ḍamān*. This is so because when the owner demands the property, he removes the trustee from that status and makes him *ḍāmin* for any destruction or damage.[109]
3. The property is actually or constructively destroyed and no benefit from it is possible. This happens, for instance, on the refusal of the trustee to return the property because the owner is stripped of all benefit. The same outcome arises where the trustee mixes the property with his and makes the two inseparable.[110]
4. If the trustee delivers the subject matter to a third person without the owner's permission and without good reason—save if approved by a *qāḍi*.[111]

3.4 Difference between *Ḍamān* Arising from Contract, Possession, or *Itlāf*

15.57 The ramifications of *ḍamān* arising from contract are different from those resulting from possession (*yad*) and *itlāf*. For this reason, the differences between *ḍamān* arising from these sources have been highlighted by *fuqahā*. According to Syūṭī, the contract governs the rules of compensation in *ḍamān al-ʿaqd* whereas in *ḍamān al-yad*, the *mithl*, or *qīma* is paid.[112] Sarakhsī, holding a similar view, reasons that a contract is aimed at profit and in this manner a *ḍamān al-ʿaqd* contract is *mashrūʿ* (allowed by the Sharīʿah). Hence, the difference in loss and compensation that are not avoidable is discarded in the contract. On the other hand, the *itlāf* is forbidden and is not *mashrūʿ*, particularly if the wording of the contract has confined it according to the likeness,[113] meaning that *ḍamān al-itlāf* cannot be more than the value of the thing lost, destroyed, or damaged.[114] Wahba Zuḥailī has compared these more elaborately on the basis of the following points.[115]

[108] Ibn al-Humām (n 2) Vol. 7, p. 519; Al-Shīrāzī (n 96) Vol. 2, p. 186; Al-Shirbīnī (n 96) Vol. 3, p. 117.
[109] Ibn al-Humām (n 2) Vol. 7, pp. 511, 514; Al-Shīrāzī (n 96) Vol. 2, p. 186; Al-Shirbīnī (n 96) Vol. 3, p. 118; *Al-Mughnī* (n 5) Vol. 9, pp. 268–69.
[110] Ibn al-Humām (n 2) Vol. 7, p. 512; Al-Dusūqī (n 5) Vol. 3, p. 420; Al-Shirbīnī (n 96) Vol. 3, p. 117; *Al-Mughnī* (n 5) Vol. 9, pp. 258–59.
[111] Al-Shirbīnī (n 96) Vol. 3, pp. 107–08; *Al-Mughnī* (n 5) Vol. 9, p. 260.
[112] Ibn Nujaim (n 2) p. 362.
[113] This is on the basis of the following verses of the Qur'ān: 'the recompense of evil is evil like it' Ash-Shūrā 40; 'And if you were to harm (them) in retaliation, harm them to the measure you were harmed' Al-Naḥl 126.
[114] Al-Sarakhsī (n 4) Vol. 11, p. 80.
[115] Al-Zuhaylī (n 85) pp. 75–77.

3.4.1 Capacity

In order to hold a person liable for *ḍamān al-ʿaqd*, Hanafis maintain that he should have at least deficient capacity for execution (*ahliyyat al-ʿaqd al-nāqisa*) which is assigned to a person possessing some discretion (*tamyīz*). The majority of *fuqahā* stipulate that the condition for holding a person liable for *ḍamān al-ʿaqd* is that he should be pubescent and possess intellect. For *ḍamān al-yad*, the complete *ahliyyat al-wajūb* (capacity for acquisition) is sufficient and the basis of this kind of capacity is the attribute of being a human, which is established just after birth. In this way, a person is liable for *ḍamān al-yad*, whether a minor with discretion or not. **15.58**

3.4.2 Nature of Compensation

In *ḍamān al-ʿaqd*, the compensation is based on the contract of the parties whereas in *ḍamān al-yad* the likeness, as far as possible, is taken into consideration. **15.59**

3.4.3 Who Can Be Sued

In *ḍamān al-ʿaqd*, there may be more than one person who is responsible. As in *kafāla*, a creditor can sue the principal debtor and claim the surety. The same is true in the case of *sharikat al-mufāwaḍa*, as discussed in the chapter concerning partnership. In *ḍamān al-yad*, every person that has committed some wrong is personally liable and no other person is liable for their actions. **15.60**

3.4.4 *Ijāza* (Approval or Ratification)

Ijāza works effectively in contract. For instance, the owner or the person with authority can ratify the acts of the *faḍūlī*, after which the act of the *faḍūlī* becomes valid. In this way, if the usurper transfers the usurped thing to a third person and the owner approves this transfer, Muḥammad suggests that there would be no *ḍamān*; whereas Abū Ḥanīfa maintains that the usurper will not be absolved from *ḍamān*. In *ḍamān al-itlāf*, Mālik says that if a person wrongfully destroys a thing and the owner absolves him from *ḍamān*, the offender is not absolved.[116] Wahba Zuḥailī notes that the preferred opinion is that the wrongdoer would be absolved from *ḍamān*. **15.61**

3.4.5 Time for the Entitlement of *Damān*

The entitlement to compensation arises when *maḍmūn* (the commodity over which *ḍamān* arises) comes into the possession of the *ḍāmin* (who is liable to pay *ḍamān*). In *ḍamān al-yad*, the liability for *ḍamān* arises at the time the reason (*sabab*) for such entitlement occurred. **15.62**

[116] Ibn Nujaim (n 2) Vol. 2, p. 338; Ibn ʿĀbidīn (n 4) Vol. 9, p. 288.

3.5 Specific Performance

15.63 After the conclusion of the contract of sale, the delivery of subject matter and *thaman* are the *iltezāmāt* (obligations) of the seller. If either refuses to perform his obligation, the other can compel performance through the courts.[117] This position also sits well with the legal maxims set down by scholars as follows: 'conditions must be observed as far as possible';[118] 'there should be neither harm (*ḍarar*) nor reciprocating harm (*ḍirār*)';[119] and 'harm or damage is to be removed'.[120] This is because the fulfilment of a condition would naturally result in the specific performance of the contract and there could be no more effective way to remove the harm or avoid the harm to be inflicted on the parties.

15.64 The remedy of specific performance is also needed for the enforcement of an agreement to sell in which the parties agree to conclude a sale contract over a subject matter at some point in the future. There are two perspectives on the validity of the agreement to sell. First, the agreement to sell is *bāṭil* as the conclusion is associated or dependent on a future event. As per the second perspective, this is valid given that the condition is neither associated with nor dependent on a future event; rather, this is a promise between the parties to conclude and implement a sale in the future. In this way, the promise of one party is not *dayn* on the other. The sale is completed after the *Ijāb* and *qabūl* and the delivery of the considerations to the respective parties. Under the second perspective, which has received recognition in the national laws of several countries, the agreement to sell does not transfer ownership of the property over which the sale contract is to be concluded. If such a sale contract is not concluded, the agreement to sell is enforced through the remedy of specific performance if the quantification of damages is not possible.[121]

[117] Al-Zuhaylī (n 1) Vol. 4, pp. 413–16.
[118] Ḥaidar (n 99) Vol. 1, p. 84.
[119] Ibn Māja 234.
[120] Ḥaidar (n 99) Vol. 1, p. 36.
[121] Taqī 'Usmanī, Fiqh al Buyū' (Maktaba Ma'ārif al Qur'ān, 2015) Vol. 1, pp. 103–13.

16

The Application of Islamic Contract Law in Muslim-Majority Jurisdictions

1. Introduction

16.01 Classical Islamic rules and principles relating to contracts and commercial activity underlie, to a considerable extent, the contractual rules of many Muslim-majority jurisdictions, including those of the United Arab Emirates (UAE). The extent to which the UAE, the case study of this chapter, applies the contractual rules of the Sharīʿah reflects the legal, historical, and religious influences of the region as well as the social desire to modernize and participate in the global economy. The UAE's contract law regime provides a window into the mentality of the Arab people originating is this region, which has been forged through the confluence of history and the dynamic pull of modernity.

16.02 To understand the workings of UAE contract law is to recognize the rapidity with which this country, and, indeed, other states in the region, have emerged from the pre-industrial past, and the UAE has quickly become an advanced commercial, financial, and trading hub with a sophisticated, albeit complex legal system. This complexity, born of the compromises made in the modern global economy, underlies its contract law regime, and showcases the historical, religious, and social factors which have helped to shape its architecture.

16.03 The UAE Civil Code houses most of the country's contract law doctrine. The rules which underlie UAE contract law are indisputably influenced by the Sharīʿah, although the comparative law nature of the Code is equally evident. The UAE Civil Code, along with most Arab Civil Codes in the region, is modelled on the civil law from different European traditions. The original model for these codes is the Egyptian Civil Code, which itself is a comparative law strongly influenced by the French code civil and other European Civil Codes.[1] Civil law gives effect to Islamic rules and principles and complements those areas of Islamic law where modern social and economic developments have no Islamic precursor. Uncertainties have plagued this hybrid experiment, however, as the blending of legal traditions and rules has created a legal apparatus which is alien to the Sharīʿah and challenges its traditional identity. The architects of these codes, the UAE Civil Code amongst them, have sought to fashion a legal framework which prioritizes economic development and growth without relinquishing the region's

[1] William Ballantyne, 'The New Civil Code of the United Arab Emirates: A Further Reassertion of the Shari'a' (1986) 1(3) Arab Law Quarterly 245, p. 247.

Islamic heritage. The result is a complex system of law which harbours many contradictions and exceptions. The UAE system of contractual rules is an insightful example of the legislator's challenge in navigating these tensions.

16.04 The chapter provides a brief overview of the Egyptian Civil Code before considering the UAE Civil Code in which most contract law is located. The analysis focuses on the Sharīʿah's most demanding contractual principle in the context of today's global capitalist economy, namely *ribā* (interest). The chapter takes into consideration the UAE Civil/Commercial Code dichotomy which, like other countries such as Kuwait, assigns commercial activity a primarily secular jurisdiction in which interest and other forbidden transactions are legal. Both the Civil Code and the Commercial Transactions Law are considered in view of *ribā*-related provisions, the way in which the courts have interpreted these, and the applicability of the codes to interest-related provisions. Finally, the Central Bank and Organisations of Financial Institutions and Activities Law is considered with a view to understanding the applicability of Islamic contractual rules to the burgeoning Islamic finance industry.

2. Background of the Egyptian Civil Code

16.05 Prior to the independence and establishment of the UAE in 1971 the peoples of the lower Gulf organized their societies according to tribal and Islamic customs. Tribal customs, which were modified by the introduction of Islam, governed life in both its religious and secular aspects. The tribal chief was bound by the Qur'ān and the principle of consultation (*shūrā*) and coordination with tribal elders, religious leaders, and subchiefs.[2] There was not much written law other than the Majalla, which was the first successful attempt to codify Hanafi civil law.[3] The Majalla was said to be at the right hand of almost every judge in the local and indigenous courts, which operated in parallel with British extraterritorial courts as part of the General Treaty of Peace of 1821. Known henceforth as the Trucial Emirates, these states' reliance on the Majalla was discontinued at the time of independence in favour of the adoption of occidental codes based on the Egyptian model.[4] At the time, most Arab Gulf States had no universities, no law schools, few local legal practitioners, and few judges versed in law other than the Sharīʿah. They were forced to draw on other Arab states for their judges and legal practitioners including Egypt, Jordan, Lebanon, Palestine, Sudan, and Syria. This diverse range of nationalities contributed to a somewhat unpredictable jurisprudence, which is said to have been largely based on practice and the attitudes of the authorities.[5]

[2] Ali Mohammed Khalifa, The United Arab Emirates: Unity in Fragmentation (Westview Press, 1979) p. 8.

[3] The Majalla, Being an English Translation of Al-Majalla Al-Aḥkam Al-ʿAdliyyah and a Complete Code of Islamic Civil Law, trans. C.R. Tyser et al. (Law Publishing Company, 1967).

[4] Ballantyne (n 1) p. 246.

[5] Colin Long, 'Contract Law in the United Arab Emirates' in Robert Nelson (ed.), Corporate Development in the Middle East (Oyez Publishing, 1978) pp. 89–90.

Amongst these nationalities, Egyptian jurists are thought to have had the largest impact on the legislation and jurisprudence of the Arab Gulf States.

16.06 In late nineteenth-century Egypt, European powers had secured the operation of so-called Mixed Courts (*al-Mahākim al-Mukhtaliṭa*) which applied civil codes modelled solely on their French counterparts. Even the judges in these courts were primarily of European origin. In 1883, a National Civil Code established a system of national courts, the so-called *ahliyya* courts, which reproduced the codes of the Mixed Courts. Sharī'ah courts continued to have jurisdiction in personal status matters and some areas of criminal law. Therefore, the civil law was composed largely according to a French format and French understanding of the law.[6] Yet the impression that the Egyptian Codes were a carbon copy of the Code Napoléon may be overstated. While the British Judicial Adviser, Sir Malcolm McIlwaith, referred to Egypt's codes as 'a system of almost pure and unadulterated French law', a US judge of the Mixed Courts, Judge Brinton, wrote that the 'codes were taken as a basis but many changes were made . . . (and) various special provisions drawn from the Muslim law had been inserted'.[7] Although the Majalla had never been formally implemented in Egypt, the distinguished architect of the Egyptian Civil Code 'Abd Al-Razzāq Al-Sanhūrī (d. 1971) claimed, in his preparations for drafting the Civil Code, that many articles in the codes were in conformity with Qadri Pasha's *Murshid al-Ḥayrān* (Guide of the Confused).[8] It seems that there was considerably more borrowing from the *Murshid al-Ḥayrān* in the Egyptian codes than was previously understood.[9] Irrespective of the debate, it is certain that Sanhūrī drew heavily from the case law and jurisprudence produced in the courts from this period which had a massive effect on the subsequent development of Egyptian law, and indirectly, on other Middle Eastern countries.[10]

16.07 The erosion of British extraterritorial jurisdiction in Egypt resulted in the Anglo-Egyptian Treaty of 1936 which instigated the formation of the Committee for the revision of the Egyptian Civil Codes. Al-Sanhūrī and Edouard Lambert, Sanhūrī's Professor of Law in Lyons, eventually produced a 1942 draft Civil Code which, subject to revisions, was promulgated in 1948. Article 1 of the Civil Code of 1948 is seen as an historic reintroduction of Islamic law in secular legislation.[11] Sharī'a principles were to fill the lacunae where law and custom were insufficient sources of law. Article 1 directed judges to issue decisions in accordance with the letter and spirit of the Code itself. Where this was insufficient, custom was to be consulted and in the absence of custom, the principles of the Sharī'ah were to be given effect. The principles of natural law and rules of equity follow in that order in the absence of the Sharī'ah.[12] The explanatory

[6] Enid Hill, 'Al-Sanhuri and Islamic Law: The Place and Significance of Islamic Law in the Life and Work of 'Abd al-Razzaq Ahmad al-Sanhuri' (1988) 3(1) Arab Law Quarterly 33, p. 41.

[7] Ibid, p. 87.

[8] Ibid.

[9] Ibid, p. 61.

[10] Ian Edge, 'Comparative Commercial Law of Egypt and the Arabian Gulf '(1985) 34(1) Cleveland State Law Review 129, p. 132.

[11] Nabil Saleh, 'Civil Codes of Arab Countries: The Sanhuri Codes' (1993) 8(2) Arab Law Quarterly 161, p. 161.

[12] Ibid, pp. 161–62.

memorandum to the Code celebrated the renewed role of the Sharīʿah: 'The circumstances in which a Judge may not be able to find any relevant provision will not be few in number, so the court will in many cases go back to the Sharīʿah and seek inspiration from its principles—a fact which represents an outstanding victory for the Sharīʿah.'[13] Furthermore, the Sharīʿah was to have deeply influenced customary practices so that recourse to custom was indirectly a reference to the Sharīʿah.[14] In practice, the multiplicity of sources from which judges were to draw rules of law resulted in uncertainty, as their delineation and relationship to one another are ambiguous.[15] Such uncertainty has played out in all the Arab jurisdictions that have adopted the Egyptian Code.

16.08 The proportion of Sharīʿah rules and principles blended into the Egyptian Civil Code is open to dispute, however. The claim by some of the draftsmen of the Code that the blending operation succeeded in full is contested.[16] Some observers have assessed the totality of provisions taken from the Sharīʿah as no more than 5–10% of the whole.[17] Anderson, one of the foremost commentators on the role of the Sharīʿah in Egypt's Civil Code, recalled Sanhūrī's testimony before the Committee of Civil Law: '[He] put it on record now that three-quarters, or five-sixths, of the provisions of this Law are based on the decisions of Egyptian courts and on the existing legislation.'[18] Sanhūrī, apparently admitting that little new of the Sharīʿah had been imported into the new code (other than what had been borrowed from Egypt's existing codes which, as to the majority, had been retained), emphasized: 'I assure you that we did not leave a single sound provision of the Sharīʿah which we could have included in this legislation without so doing . . . We adopted from the Sharīʿah all that we could adopt, having regard to sound principles of modern legislation; and we did not fall short in this respect.'[19]

16.09 Sanhūrī's approach to the revision of civil codes was rooted in his understanding of the science of comparative law. He describes his methodology for revising the Iraqi Civil Code of 1953 as comprising two levels:

> I drafted the precepts of sales, selecting them from among many codes, old and new. For example, of the old I used the French code and the Egyptian code, and for the new the German and Swiss codes as well as the Turkish code and the Soviet code, the Franco-Italian proposal, and the Lebanese and Polish codes, and the international project. From all those I chose those that were advanced, and I compared them with each other and made a choice.

[13] J.N.D. Anderson, 'The Shari'a and Civil Law' (1954) 1(1) The Islamic Quarterly 29.
[14] Ibid.
[15] Saleh (n 11) p. 162.
[16] Ibid.
[17] Edge (n 10) p. 133.
[18] Anderson (n 13) p. 31.
[19] Ibid.

Sanhūrī made his choice of rules on account of 'preferred language', and, according to Hill, those texts which had the greatest affinity to his conceptualization of the Sharī'ah. This is where the second level of his methodology came into focus: 16.10

> I compared the selections of these codes with the provisions of the Majalla and the *Murshid al-Ḥayrān*, and those of the Islamic Sharī'a from a general point of view and in all its schools, the doctrines of each school. I got out of these texts a model of precepts of the Sharī'a.[20]

The Egyptian Civil Code introduced French altruistic and moral values which were to be introduced to Egyptian society, reflecting the strong influence which French law had on Sanhūrī from his years of study in France.[21] Although Sanhūrī was proud of and appreciated his Islamic identity and sought to emphasize the values of Eastern civilization vis-à-vis those of the West in his law reform proposals,[22] the committee drafting the proposed law commented that the Code's provisions were enacted after a comparative examination of Western laws, such as the German, Swiss, Italian, French, and Belgian civil laws. Western influence is perhaps most apparent in the individualistic values present in the Code, following the influence of the European laws.[23] 16.11

Sanhūrī let it be known that his ambition was to present a codification founded on the culture and values of Eastern civilization alongside the cosmic theology of the Islamic religion.[24] However, in practice, his proposals, the notes of his lectures, and the work of the committee affirmed that the starting point and the foundation of the proposed Civil Code were all unrelated to his stated ambitions. Sanhūrī explained that the committee had 'always stated that we drew this provision from our case law and statute books and—Praise be to God—it is also consonant with the provisions of the Islamic Sharī'ah'.[25] However, the ideology of the Egyptian Civil Code and the later Arab Codes including the UAE Civil Code were not underpinned by Islamic foundations. Rather, the codes reflected 'the legal and socioeconomic approaches in Europe during the first half of the twentieth century'.[26] Nonetheless, Sanhūrī and the drafting committee claimed that the proposed Civil Code did not contradict Islamic principles.[27] 16.12

[20] 'Abd Al-Razzāq Al-Sanhūrī, 'Al-Kitāb al-Marfū'a illā fakhāmāt rāis layset Taḥdir al-Qānūn al-Madanī al-'Iraqi wal Wathiqatān' (1936) 2(1/2) Majallat al-Qaḍā' 225; cf. Hill (n 6) p. 55.

[21] Guy Bechor, The Sanhuri Code, and the Emergence of Modern Arab Civil Law (1932 to 1949) (Brill, 2007) p. 167.

[22] Ibid, p. 32.

[23] Ibid, p. 148.

[24] Ibid, p. 32.

[25] 'Abd Al-Razzāq Al-Sanhūrī, 'Mashrūa Tanqīḥ Al-Qānūn Al-Madanī' in Aḥmed Al-Jomal (ed) Muṭawwel Al-Jamal fī Sharḥ Al-Qānūn Al-Madanī 89 <https://ahmedazimelgamel.blogspot.com/2018/11/5.html> Accessed 28 June 2021. 2021.

[26] Bechor (n 21) p. 32.

[27] 'Abd Al-Razzāq Al-Sanhūrī (n 25).

3. The *Sanhūrī* Connection: The Civil Codes of Other Arab States

16.13 The Egyptian Civil Code of 1948 strongly influenced the Civil Codes of Arab states including the UAE.[28] The Code was taken as a foundation for other Arab states' Civil Codes, whether in terms of specific rules, linguistic formulation, or its system of classification.[29] Widely respected due to the excellent quality of Egyptian Civil Code's drafting, Sanhūrī had been involved in drafting many Arab states' codes such as the Iraqi Civil Code, the Syrian Civil Code, and Kuwait's 1961 Code of Commerce which deals with the law of obligations. When Arab states gained their independence from British and French colonial rule, they sought to reform their civil and commercial laws by borrowing from other Arab countries. This was viewed as more acceptable than overt borrowing from European civil law.[30] Even those codes with which Sanhūrī was not directly involved often reproduced his earlier work. Qatar's Civil and Commercial Law of 1971 adopted Book Two of the old Kuwaiti Commercial Law.[31] The commission which drafted the Kuwaiti Civil Code was led by an Egyptian jurist, Abdulfattāḥ Abdulbāqī, who stated that the Code was structured along the lines of the Egyptian Civil Code.[32] The Jordanian Civil Code of 1976 on which the UAE Civil Code of 1985 is closely based was not the work of Sanhūrī, but its methodology for interpreting the Code's provisions is similarly based on the Egyptian model. One important distinction is the prioritized role given to the Sharīʿah in the absence of statutory provisions whereas earlier codes referred to the principles of the Sharīʿah as an ancillary source of rules.[33] The Jordanian Civil Code introduced a provision in Article 3 which provided a methodology for interpreting the Code based on the Islamic *fiqh*. The Code is said to have initiated a trend in Arab state legal drafting due to the privileged position the Jordanian legislator gave to the Sharīʿah, which had hitherto been lost with the introduction of secular civil codes.[34] Notably, Jordan and other successor states of the Ottoman Empire had continued to apply the Majalla which Sanhūrī is said to have considered when tailoring codes to these states' local conditions.

16.14 The Jordanian Civil Code's Sharīʿah-related amendments are to be found in the UAE Civil Code as well. Article 1 of UAE Civil Code of 1985 gives pre-eminence to the Sharīʿah as a source of interpretation when the Code is silent on an issue. It states:

> In the absence of a text in this Law, the judge shall adjudicate according to the Islamic Sharīʿah taking into consideration the choice of the most appropriate solutions in the

[28] William Ballantyne, 'The Constitutions of the Gulf States: A Comparative Study' (1986) 1(2) Arab Law Quarterly 158, p. 160.

[29] Moḥammad Al-Qāsim, 'Mulāḥaẓ ḥawel Baḥt Mawad Al-Bab Tamhīdī min Al-Qānūn Al-Madanī' (1982) 6(1) Kuwait University Journal of Law 11, p. 12.

[30] Edge (n 10) p. 130.

[31] Saleh (n 11) p. 165.

[32] Kuwait Civil Law 1980 (Law Commission) Vol. 1, p. 34.

[33] Saleh (n 11) p. 164.

[34] Ibid.

> schools of Imam Mālik and Imam Aḥmad Bin Ḥanbal and, if not found there, then in the schools of Imam al-Shāfiʿī and Imam Abū Ḥanīfa, as the interest so requires.[35]

The specific teachings of the eponyms of the schools of Islamic jurisprudence are to be referred to, in contrast to Islamic *fiqh* or the principles of the Islamic Sharīʿah, which had been referred to in earlier codes. The peculiar role of the Sharīʿah in this hybrid legal system has been described as a material source of law underlying the formal provisions of the Civil Code. The Sharīʿah is a historical source of law for many legal rules in the UAE. The Sharīʿah gains influence through the enactment of Article 7 of the Constitution which states that 'the Islamic Sharīʿah shall be a main source of legislation in the union' but this does not render the Sharīʿah a formal source of law. The UAE and other Arab states introduced constitutions which have as their basic foundations that the Sharīʿah is 'a' or 'the' principal source of legislation.[36] Legislators are directed to consider the Sharīʿah as a material source when making new law, but its injunctions are not mandatory in the absence of formal legislation. This was also the assessment of observers of the Egyptian Constitution which significantly influenced the Kuwaiti and UAE constitutions. In fact, Article 7 is taken verbatim from the Kuwaiti Constitution which was drafted by Sanhūrī. Article 7 is squarely directed at the legislature and its law-making function rather than at the judiciary or citizens.[37] Others argue that the article directs legislators to avoid contradicting the Sharīʿah despite formal provisions which circumscribe its applicability to non-commercial contracts.[38] The argument centres on the question of whether the legislature must have recourse to the Sharīʿah or whether it has discretion to promulgate laws derived from sources other than the Sharīʿah even where these contravene Sharīʿah injunctions.[39] In practice, an analysis of the constitutionality of laws in the UAE shows clearly that many laws violate Sharīʿah injunctions, but are nonetheless upheld by the courts, indicating that the latter argument is stronger in practice. Such is the case, for example, with provisions in the Commercial Code which legalize interest and allow insurance.[40] Both commercial practices are outlawed historically. **16.15**

Article 1 of the UAE Civil Code provides: 'The civil transactions in the United Arab Emirates State shall be subject to the law, whereas the commercial transactions remain subject to the laws and regulations applicable in their regard, pending the issuance of the Federal Commercial Law.'[41] This dichotomy between the law applicable to **16.16**

[35] Federal Law No. 5/1985 Promulgating the Civil Transactions Law of the United Arab Emirates State (Civil Code) as Amended by Federal Law No. 1/1987, section 1, Art. 1.

[36] For an excellent analysis of the lively debate concerning the role of the Sharīʿah in the constitutions of the UAE, see Butti Sultan Butti Ali Al-Muhairi, 'The Position of Shari'a within the UAE Constitution and the Federal Supreme Court's Application of the Constitutional Clause Concerning Shari'a' (1996) 11(3) Arab Law Quarterly 219.

[37] Ibid, p. 225.

[38] Iyad Mohammad Jadalhaq and Mohammed El Hadi El Maknouzi, 'Reading UAE Contract Law through the Lens of Islamic Jurisprudence: A Case Study on the 'Extraneous Cause' Exception in the UAE Civil Code' [2019] Global Jurist 1, 4. See Constitution of the United Arab Emirates, Art. 1.

[39] Butti Sultan Butti Ali Al-Muhairi (n 36) p. 227.

[40] Ibid, p. 226.

[41] Civil Code (n 35) Art. 1.

civil transactions and the law concerning commercial transactions allows for levying interest lawfully in the UAE. It is an approach taken from Kuwait where the Kuwaiti Civil Code (No. 67 of 1980) prohibits the charging of interest whereas its Commercial Code (No. 68 of 1980) permits it.[42] The introduction of modern commercial codes, as in Kuwait in 1961, is said to have constituted a rejection of Sharīʿah principles in modern commercial transactions and to have set in motion a pattern of subsequent legislation that failed to consider the possibilities for modernizing the Sharīʿah.[43] The liberal approach which commercial legislation takes towards the charging of interest may not settle the issue once and for all, however. In the absence of a constitutional clause which provides legal protection for contracts involving interest, it cannot be assumed that contracts tainted with *ribā* will be enforced, particularly in view of the many historical examples of courts' reluctance to circumvent the prohibition.[44]

16.17 Section 4 discusses the general character of the law of obligations in the UAE Civil Code.

4. The Law of Obligations and the Sharīʿah

16.18 The laws relating to obligations are laid out in Book One of the UAE Civil Code. An observer of the Sharīʿah will at once recognize that many articles are borrowed from the classical *fiqh*. These are blended with a much larger body of rules taken from European civilian law and international practices. For example, Article 132 reflects the concern of classical jurists that the offer and acceptance of the contract be discernible and validly expressed in the Arabic language. The article stipulates the following:

> Expression of the will may be verbal or in writing, whether in the past or present tenses or imperative mood, if intended for immediate observation, or by signs customarily followed, even from a non-dumb person, or by effective exchange proving mutual assent or by taking any other attitude indicating beyond any doubt mutual assent.[45]

16.19 Evidently, these rules derive from the Maliki and Hanbali schools as the use of the imperative mood in the formation of contract is seen as future-oriented by the Hanafis and therefore belongs to the category of ambiguous speech, incapable of having a legal effect.[46] Other rules, for example those which distinguish between an offer and an invitation to treat, betray the Code's modern concerns in characteristically modern legal terminology. Article 134 provides that:

1. Display of goods and services showing the consideration thereto is considered an offer.

[42] Ahmed Al-Suwaidi, 'Developments of the Legal Systems of the Gulf Arab States' (1993) 8(4) Arab Law Quarterly 289, p. 291.
[43] Susan E. Rayner, The Theory of Contracts in Islamic Law (Graham & Trotman, 1991) p. 287.
[44] Ibid.
[45] Civil Code (n 35) Art. 132.
[46] Muṣṭafā Aḥmad Al-Zarqā, Al-Madkhal Al-fiqhī (Dār al-Qalam, al-Ṭabʿah 2, 2004) p. 405.

2. Publication, advertising, and lists of current prices as well as any other statement concerning offers or requests addressed to the public or to individuals shall not, in case of doubt, be considered an offer but an invitation to contract.

The extent of borrowing from the classical *fiqh* is extensive, spanning contract formation; nominate and innominate contracts; factors which vitiate consent, for example mistake, misrepresentation, undue influence, and frustration; and remedies including Islamic law's reliance-based approach to damages. For example, Article 274 lays out the Code's principle of compensation for breach of contract. Parties are to be restored to their pre-contractual positions and only if this is impossible may the court see fit to award damages: 'When a contract is or shall be rescinded, the two contracting parties shall be reinstated to their former position, prior to contracting, and in case this is impossible, the Court may award damages.'[47] **16.20**

Expectation interests or the award of damages for lost profits are seen as conjectural and uncertain and hence contrary to the Sharīʿah's exacting requirements. Yet the Code disallows simple classification. The blending of the Sharīʿah with civil law provisions underscores the divergent ideological conceptions embedded within the Code's rules. Article 292, for example, reverses the compensatory principle, permitting damages for lost profits where these are the 'natural consequence' of the breach: 'Damages shall, under all circumstances, be assessed to cover the prejudice sustained and the lost profit provided it is a natural consequence of the prejudicial act.' **16.21**

Damages, which are assessed from an objective perspective, that of the so-called reasonable man, are not limited to reliance expenditures which have been incurred in anticipation of the contract but extend to profits and lost opportunities so long as these are the 'natural consequence' of the breach.[48] **16.22**

It is also notable that the interpretational methodology of the Code has been adopted from the Majalla, reflecting the objective approach to contractual interpretation of the Hanafi school.[49] The same objective tendency had been transplanted into the Egyptian Civil Code.[50] **16.23**

Therefore, the Code has a complex and sometimes contradictory character. Let us turn our attention now to the regulation of *ribā*. Sanhūrī's interpretation of *ribā* was adopted in the Egyptian Civil Code and subsequently implemented in other Arab Civil Codes, including that of the UAE. Section 5 examines the *ribā*-related provisions of the UAE Civil Code. **16.24**

[47] Civil Code (n 35) Art. 274. Article 304 provides for lost profits in the event of extortion, which is both a tortious wrong and a crime.

[48] Mahmoud Fayyad and Ahmad Hayajneh, 'Reconsidering the Special Rules of Mitigation of Damages for Breach of Contract for the Sale of Goods in UAE Law' (2022) 36 Arab Law Quarterly 1, p. 14.

[49] Article 258 deals with the interpretational modus of contract.

[50] Chafik Chehata, 'Les survivances musulmanes dans la codification du droit civil égyptien' (1965) 17(4) Revue internationale de droit compare 839, p. 844. Also remarked upon in Anderson (n 13) p. 5, where he notes that the objective tendency is also used in the German civil law tradition.

5. The UAE Civil Code and *Ribā*

16.25 The Code first addresses *ribā*-related provisions in relation to sales contracts in Articles 575 and 584. Article 575 provides: 'It shall be void that the capital of the sale with future delivery and the object of delivery be two foods or two currencies, it is sufficient for other than food, that they both differ in type and utility.'[51]

16.26 The article relates to classical jurists' concern for the immediate exchange of commodities or currencies with a view to preventing unearned returns. *Ribā al-faḍl* is defined as the prohibition of the unlawful excess from the exchange of countervalues in any transaction relating to two or more species belonging to the same genus and governed according to the same cause (*'illa*).[52] The prohibition applies principally to two precious metals (gold and silver) and four commodities (wheat, barley, dates, and salt) mentioned in a prophetic *ḥadīth*. The tradition of the Prophet Muḥammad stated:

> Gold for gold, same for same, hand to hand, and any difference is *ribā*; silver for silver, same for same, hand to hand, and any difference is *ribā*; wheat for wheat, same for same, hand to hand, and any difference is *ribā*; salt for salt, same for same, hand to hand, and any difference is *ribā*; barley for barley, same for same, hand to hand, and any difference is *ribā*; dates for dates, same for same, hand to hand, and any difference is *ribā*; but if the genera are different, then trade as you wish as long as it is hand to hand.[53]

16.27 The schools of law and even scholars from the same school disagree about the *'illa* underlying the prohibition of dealing in these commodities in trades that are unequal or delayed.[54] Article 575 lays emphasis on the exchange of foodstuffs and their quality of being weighable or measurable, and the property of currency (gold and silver). This is the favoured opinion of the Hanbali jurist, Ibn Qayyim al-Jawziyya (d. 1350) and is similar to the Shafi'i and Maliki interpretations.[55]

16.28 Article 584 is similarly concerned with unearned excess (*ribā*) beyond the original agreement for a deferred payment sale. Essentially, the provision prevents a seller from selling a good on deferred terms at a higher price than the original agreed price.

16.29 In the context of loans *ribā* is addressed in Article 710 which states: 'A loan is the transfer to the borrower of ownership of a sum of money or any fungibles upon condition that the borrower returns, at the end of the loan, a thing equal in amount, kind and quality.'[56]

[51] Civil Code (n 35) Art. 575.
[52] Nabil Saleh, Unlawful Gain and Legitimate Profit in Islamic Law (Graham & Trotman, 1992) p. 17.
[53] Narrated on the authority of Abū Ḥanīfa on the authority of 'Aṭiyya Al-'Awful on the authority of Abū Sa'īd Al-Khuḍrī that the Prophet was to have said; cf. 'Abd Al-Razzāq Al-Sanhūrī, Maṣādir al-Ḥaqq (Dār Iḥyā' al-Turāth al-'arabi, 1st edn, 1953) pp. 159–74.
[54] Saleh (n 52) p. 18.
[55] See Chapter 6 for an in-depth review of the schools' different rulings. Ibid, p. 20.
[56] Civil Code (n 35) Art. 710.

The juristic emphasis upon equivalence and the prevention of an unjustified return is unmistakable. The *fiqh* allows loans (*'aqd al-qarḍ*) to be made with goods which attract the *ribā* prohibition, that is, those measured by weight or volume for the Hanafis and most of the Hanbalis, whereas the Malikis and Shafi'is find the *'illa* (effective cause) in foodstuffs and monies. Because the *ribā*-related rules are relaxed for loans (as opposed to contracts of sale), jurists stipulate that the loan can only be used as a form of charity where the lender passes on the use of the goods for the period of the loan. Loans are forbidden if they do not serve charitable causes or provide some benefit to the lender.[57] 16.30

According to Hanbali *fiqh*, when the thing borrowed is fungible, the borrower may compel the lender to take it back whether the value of the loaned thing has fluctuated or not, so long as a defect has not eroded its value (i.e. a defect caused by the borrower). When the borrowed thing is measurable or weighable, however, the equivalent or equal value should be paid back.[58] When the like (*al-mithl*) is not available, the borrower is indebted to the extent that the value has fluctuated because the borrower is indebted under a personal obligation.[59] Article 710 does not make this distinction, preferring the Hanafi principle that the borrowed value of commodities, both measurable and weighable or accounted for by number, should be returned in like measure, even when the thing, say a borrowed currency, has become obsolete.[60] This renders loans of, for example, agricultural products and articles accounted for by number, which have no like at the place of repayment, impermissible. 16.31

Article 714 invalidates unjustified returns on a loan: 'If the loan contract is conditioned upon paying a benefit that exceeds the contract requirements, other than guaranteeing the borrower's right, the condition is void but the contract is valid.' 16.32

The lender may demand repayment of its equivalent at any time according to the Sharī'ah, whereas Article 718 allows parties to determine the maturity of the loan contract by choice or custom. In the absence of this term, a reasonable period in which the beneficiary will have benefited from the loan is foreseen.[61] Therefore, the loan, in both Islamic and UAE civil law, is ineligible for commercial lending where interest is payable. 16.33

The original Arabic of the article has been described as intentionally obtuse so that the onus of interpretation was left to the courts. The legislator may have sought to test the judiciary's view of the *ribā* prohibition against the backdrop of the social desire to reinvigorate Sharī'ah principles in the commercial statutes of the Gulf States.[62] 16.34

[57] Wahbah al-Zuḥaylī, Financial Transactions in Islamic Jurisprudence, trans. Mahmoud Al. El-Gamal (Dār al-Fikr, 2003) Vol. 1, p. 369. Some distinctions exist between the schools. The Hanafis, for example, allow the lender to gain advantage if the advantage has not been pre-agreed or stipulated in the *qarḍ* contract, whereas the Hanbalis do not allow the lender to gain an advantage or gift unless the gift is deemed part of the payment.

[58] Muwaffaq al-Dīn 'Abd Allāh Ibn Aḥmad Ibn Qudāmah, *al-Mughnī* (Ri'āsat Idārat al-Buḥūth al-'Ilmīyah wa-al-Iftā' wa-l-Da'wah wa-l-Irshād, al-Mamlakah al-'Arabīyah al-Sa'ūdīyah, 1981) Vol. 4, p. 352.

[59] Aḥmad Ibn 'Abd Allah Ba'lī, *Rawl al-Nadī Sharr Kāfī al-Mubtadī* (Dār al-Nawār, 2007) p. 233.

[60] Abū Bakr Ibn Mas'ūd al-Kāsānī, *Badā'i' al-Ṣalā'i' fī Tartīb al-Sharā'i'* (Dār Ihyā' al-Turāith, 1986) p. 395.

[61] Civil Code (n 35) Art. 718.

[62] Rayner (n 43) p. 282.

6. UAE Legislation and the Courts' Interpretation of Sharīʿah-Related Provisions

16.35 Prior to the enactment of the Civil Code, the impact that the Sharīʿah had in the formulation, interpretation, and enforcement of contracts was minimal despite the role of the Sharīʿah in Article 7 of the UAE Constitution. Interest was charged by financial institutions as there was no legislative prohibition in effect.[63] However, the promulgation of federal law changed this calculus as the authority of Sharīʿah become paramount in relation to the very laws which had granted it such authority. It was a period in which Middle Eastern states sought to review their foreign legal borrowings with a view to making them more Islamic.[64] The immediate source of contestation in the UAE, which was tested in the courts, concerned Federal Law No. 10 of 1973 and Federal Law No. 6 of 1978 in relation to Article 7 of the Constitution.

16.36 Article 75 of Federal Law No. 10 of 1973 provided:

> The Supreme Court shall apply the provisions of the Islamic Sharīʿah, federal laws, and other laws in force in the member Emirates of the federation conforming to the Islamic Sharīʿah. Likewise, it shall apply those rules of custom and those principles of natural and comparative law which do not conflict with the principles of the Sharīʿah.

16.37 The article requires the Supreme Court to apply Islamic or other laws in the UAE which are in conformity with the *Sharīʿah*. The order of application resembles the methodology in Article 7 of the Constitution. The *Sharīʿah* is the first source of law, followed by federal laws and then other laws, customs, and principles. Notably, uncertainty ensued regarding the role of the Sharīʿah in Article 7, as there the Sharīʿah is 'a' source of legislation and not the primary source as described in Article 75. Article 75 seemed to question the predominance of the Constitution as it rendered the Sharīʿah a formal source of law as opposed to a material source whose injunctions are essentially religious rules with no legal force unless made compulsory though legislation. The article lent strength to the argument that Article 7 of the Constitution elevated the Sharīʿah above all other sources of law.[65]

16.38 The enactment of Federal Law No. 6 of 1978 magnified this uncertainty and led to litigation, primarily in those areas most sensitive to Sharīʿah injunctions, interest being chief amongst them. Federal Law No. 6 established the federal, first instance, and appeal courts and transferred the local courts of Abu Dhabi, Sharjah, Fujeirah, and Ajman to the federal judiciary. It also granted the Supreme Court the jurisdiction of petition of cassation in relation to federal courts' civil and criminal law decisions.

[63] Long (n 5) pp. 89–90.
[64] Edge (n 10) p. 136.
[65] See Butti Sultan Butti Ali Al-Muhairi (n 36) for an insightful discussion into the opposing arguments of this debate.

The source of confusion centred on Article 8 which states: 16.39

> The Federal Courts shall apply the provisions of the Islamic Sharīʿah, federal laws, and other laws in force, just as they shall apply those rules of custom and general legal principles which do not conflict with the provisions of the Sharīʿah.

Therefore, the federal courts were ordered to apply the Sharīʿah, federal, and other laws 16.40 which do not conflict with the Sharīʿah. The difference in wording whereby the application of other laws need not conform to the Sharīʿah led some observers to argue that federal and other laws were placed on an equal footing with the Sharīʿah.[66] This created a question of conflict as to whether lower courts were bound to conform to the Supreme Court's decision in a petition of cassation regarding a lower court's conformity with Sharīʿah. The validity of local laws in relation to the charging of interest was the principal issue at stake.[67]

The general commercial climate at the time led courts and legal practitioners to expect 16.41 enforcement of commercial interest claims under previous regulation of commercial contracts, namely, Articles 61 and 62 of the Abu Dhabi Code of Civil Procedure, which, although formally applicable only in Abu Dhabi, was, in practice, followed in other Emirates.[68] In 1979, an Abu Dhabi court ruled that Articles 61 and 62, which allowed for the award of pre-judgment interest, were void. The court based its judgment on Article 75 of Federal Law No. 10 of 1973, according to which the award of interest is void *ab initio* per the Sharīʿah. In *Abdullah Rashid Hilal v International Bank of Credit and Commerce,* the Abu Dhabi Court of Appeal struck down a term stipulating interest on a loan which the bank had made to Hilal. The amount of interest or the beneficiary of the interest was irrelevant. The Court of Appeal based its controversial judgment on Article 75 of Law No. 10, and in relation to a prophetic *ḥadīth* which states that 'people shall be bound by the terms of their agreement save where they allow a prohibited thing or prohibit a permissible thing'.[69]

In a petition of cassation brought by *Junatta Bank* against the Abu Dhabi Court of 16.42 Appeal's decision, the Federal Supreme Court upheld the constitutionality of Articles 61 and 62 of Abu Dhabi Law (Local Law No. 3/1970). The Court rejected the Court of Appeal's decision which had ruled the Sharīʿah a higher authority than the Constitution and, as such, its provisions regarding the prohibition of banking interest could not be subject to constitutional review. The Supreme Court ruled that Article 151 of the Constitution was not applicable to the articles due to the protection afforded by Article 148 to laws in force at the time when the Constitution was promulgated.[70] Moreover, Article 7 of the Constitution directs the federal legislature to issue laws and regulations and to have the Sharīʿah as a main source of legislation in the carrying out of that task.

66 Ibid, p. 232.
67 Ibid.
68 Ibid, p. 283.
69 UAE Civ. Appeal No. 5 (Dubai, 21 November 1979); cf. Edge (n 10) pp. 143–44.
70 Butti Sultan Butti Ali Al-Muhairi (n 36) p. 235.

The Supreme Court stated that the charging of simple interest is a necessity in banking operations given its fundamental importance to the economic existence of the state and the well-being of its people. Until such time as this necessity is eliminated, the prohibition should not be considered. Terms providing for interest would be enforced according to parties' contracts but where no agreement exists interest may not be levied or awarded at a rate in excess of 12% per annum in respect of commercial transactions and 9% in respect of non-commercial ones. The total amount awarded may not exceed the amount of the 'Principal Indebtedness', preventing the absolutely forbidden *ribā, the ribā al-jahiliyya* in which the creditor devoured *ribā*, which was doubled and multiplied for an extension of time in which the creditor was allowed to repay the loan. The purpose of these articles is to protect debtors from exploitation. Article 101 of the Constitution rendered this Supreme Court decision final and binding on all.[71]

16.43 In 1981, the Federal Supreme Court, in a landmark case, deemed compound interest illegal.[72] A subsequent decision in 2009 confirmed this ruling.[73] In practice, however, UAE financial institutions continue to deal in compound interest.[74]

16.44 In 1986, an army officer sued a well-known bank in the Court of First Instance in Abu Dhabi. The claimant argued that Article 714 of the recently promulgated Federal Civil Code of 1985 prohibited interest on commercial loans. The Court held that the Civil Code was to be applied exclusively to civil transactions whereas a loan with interest is a commercial transaction and subject to different regulation. The Court's decision anticipated the amendment to the Civil Code in 1987, which stated that civil transactions would be governed by the Civil Code whereas commercial transactions would be subject to the respective laws and regulations until such a code was enacted.[75] The amendment indicated, much as was the case in Kuwait, that interest could be levied in commercial transactions. The amendment was followed by a change of jurisdiction in which all disputes concerning banks or negotiable instruments were to be transferred from the Sharī'ah courts to the civil courts. Moreover, the Abu Dhabi Code of Civil Procedure was amended so that courts were to honour parties' agreements as to the applicable interest rate for the period up to and including the date on which the lawsuit was to be filed. Accordingly, the courts, following the Supreme Court in *Junatta Bank*, were to invoke statutory interest rates only in the absence of specific agreement amongst the parties.[76]

16.45 The interest rate ceilings allowed by the courts were eventually enacted in the UAE Commercial Transactions Law in 1993. Unsurprisingly, the originator of these ceilings was Sanhūrī, whose reflections on classical *fiqh* paved the way for their introduction in

[71] Hind Tamimi, 'Interest under the UAE Law and as Applied by the Courts of Abu Dhabi' (2002) 17 Arab Law Quarterly 50, p. 50 citing Federal Supreme Court, Decision No. 14/9, 28 June 1981 (unpublished).
[72] Rayner (n 43) p. 285.
[73] UAE Federal Supreme Court, No. 85/2009 (18 November 2009).
[74] Tamimi (n 71) p. 51.
[75] Rayner (n 43) pp. 284–85.
[76] Abu Dhabi Law No. 3 of 1987.

the Egyptian Commercial Code and the codes of other Arab states. The following section recounts these arguments.

7. The Egyptian Civil Code and the Regulation of Interest

Interest rates have been regulated since at least the time of the Babylonian Code in 1750 BC, which set interest rate ceilings and other restrictions on the amount of permissible interest. The ancient Greeks under the Athenian reformer Solon (640–560 BC) also set interest rate ceilings and it is well known that Jews and Christians likewise restricted interest-based lending.[77] Therefore, the interest rate ceilings and restrictions established in the Egyptian Civil Code were not without precedent. Yet, the rationale behind the ceilings is intrinsically linked to the *sui generis* interpretations of classical jurisprudence concerning the *ribā* prohibition. This is evident in Sanhūrī's magnum opus, *Maṣādir al-Ḥaqq*, in which he lays out his interpretation of the prohibition. Sanhūrī argues that *ribā* should be prohibited in all ages and all civilizations as a matter of principle. It should be prohibited to prevent monopoly, manipulation of currency prices, and exploitation. However, if the prohibition of *ribā* as a general principle is to be maintained, so should be the distinction between the *ribā* of *jāhiliyya* and that of *nasī'a* (delay) and *faḍl* (inequality). Here Sanhūrī distinguishes his position from that of Ibn Al-Qayyim, who in his *I'alām al-Muwaqqi'īn* distinguishes between manifest and hidden types of *ribā*. Manifest *ribā* is the *ribā* of *jāhiliyya* and *nasī'a* whereas *faḍl* is the hidden variety. Like Ibn Al-Qayyim, Sanhūrī classifies the *ribā* of *jāhiliyya* (the *ribā* of pre-Islamic ignorance) as prohibited in principle where only absolute necessity (*ḍarūra quṣwā*) would allow it. Sanhūrī, however, following the reformist Egyptian jurist Rachīd Riḍā (d. 1935), argues that the *ribā* of *nasī'a* and *faḍl* are only prohibited as a means (*wasā'il, dharī'a*), where a general need (*hājah*) or *maṣlaḥa* would allow it.[78] The *ribā al-jāhiliyya* is where a debtor, unable to repay his loan with interest, is granted an extension of time to repay the loan on condition that he repay a large increase in the principal amount. The debtor is said to have paid the increased principal amount to avoid potential jail time. The monetary effect of the transaction is similar to compound interest. 16.46

Sanhūrī argues that a loan which includes interest is not essentially part of the usurious contracts except by analogy. The traditions of the Prophet mainly deal with sales contracts, not loans, and this is also the case with Islamic jurisprudence (*fiqh*). Therefore, usurious loans, in the modern context, are by analogy (*qiyās*) with sales construed as usurious contracts. This is discussed under the *fiqh* rule, 'every loan that generates benefit is *ribā*'. According to this logic, a loan which includes an explicit excess is interest and 16.47

[77] Saleh Majid and Faris Majid, 'Application of Islamic Law in the Middle East—Interest and Islamic Banking' (n.d.) <www.iraqilawconsultant.com/puplications/majid/article09.html#footnote> accessed 1 March 2022.
[78] 'Abd Al-Razzāq Al-Sanhūrī (n 53) pp. 159–74.

therefore prohibited but not because this excess is *ribā*. Rather, because it is similar to *ribā*. The *ribā* in loans is therefore assimilated to the *ribā al faḍl*.[79]

16.48 All these forms of *ribā* are prohibited, but they are prohibited as a prevention of means rather than prohibited in principle, and therefore the prohibition can be lifted in case a need arises. The worst form of *ribā* is the one that exploits people in need. This is the form which the Qur'ān prohibits and threatens the people who practise it. It takes the form of being offered the alternatives either to repay the loan or to accept a higher debt, which is similar to what we today call compound interest. This type of interest is where the lender receives interest on interest that has accumulated and has been added to the original loan. This form of *ribā* is prohibited absolutely.[80]

16.49 Other forms of *ribā* which include small rates of interest are also prohibited but only to prevent the interest becoming more serious and exploitative. This means that the prohibition can be lifted in the case of public interest. Because we live in a capitalist economy where loans are the primary mechanism to obtain finance, and the borrower is, or can be, the stronger party and the lender is, or can be, the weaker one, interest on capital in the limited amounts discussed is in the public interest. A 'limited amount' means, first, that there should be no interest on accrued interest. Secondly, even the limited interest must be specified in its value and charging methods by the law. Thirdly, even considering all of the above, this formulation of the prohibition may only be necessary in a capitalist system. If this changes and a socialist system is the dominant economic ideology whereby capital is controlled by the state, the need must be reviewed, and the prohibition potentially restored.[81]

16.50 Therefore, Sanhūrī distinguishes between interest and usury inasmuch as usury is the prohibited end product whereas the lesser forms of interest are prohibited to block the means.[82] Khadduri argues that Sanhūrī failed to provide a rationale for the distinction and links this argument to what he terms the 'theoretical question of the harmony between western and Islamic legal standards'.[83] Yet Sanhūrī's primary occupation was to develop Islamic legal concepts according to the variations of circumstances and contexts in modernizing economies and to determine the qualities of each.[84] He did not seek to bring about a harmony between legal families. Perhaps the more relevant question is why we should expect one.[85] On the contrary, Sanhūrī's comparative historical methodology sought the identification of theoretical and practical legal relationships and concepts of law which he gleaned through macro-comparison, a wholly different proposition than a casuistic analysis of individual concepts.[86]

[79] Ibid.
[80] Ibid.
[81] Ibid.
[82] Enid Hill, 'Al-Sanhuri and Islamic Law: The Place and Significance of Islamic Law in the Life and Work of 'Abd al-Razzaq al-Sanhuri, Egyptian Jurist and Scholar' (1988) 3(2) Arab Law Quarterly 182, p. 204.
[83] Majid Khadduri, The Islamic Conception of Justice (Johns Hopkins University Press, 1984) p. 209.
[84] Hill (n 82) p. 204.
[85] Ibid.
[86] Ibid, p. 205.

Sanhūrī's interpretation of *ribā* was adopted in the Egyptian Civil Code in a number of related rules. Article 232 prohibits taking interest on matured interest (compound interest). Therefore, the law forbids the type of *ribā* that was forbidden absolutely, the *ribā al-jāhiliyya*. The earlier Civil Code had allowed compound interest subject to conditions. The Syrian Civil Code (Article 233), the Libyan Civil Code (Article 235), and the Iraqi Civil Code (Article 174) likewise adopted this absolute prohibition. Secondly, interest rate ceilings were stipulated. Interest is allowed at the maximum of 7% so that any interest rate above that level is illegal. Previous legislation allowed for 8%. Article 542 states that the borrower must pay the agreed interest when due. If there is no agreement on interest the loan is interest free. If the loan is due, and the borrower has delayed his repayment, interest on arrears becomes due to the extent of 4% in civil cases and 5% in commercial cases. Thirdly, interest for late payment is not required unless the creditor requests it through the court system. Interest is only calculated from the day the legal demand is filed (Article 226). This article is more restrictive than other Arab Civil Codes, including the UAE, which allow for so-called delay interest (considered below in Section 8.2). **16.51**

Finally, under no circumstances can the total interest charged exceed the principal (Article 232), which according to Sanhūrī 'prevents the creditor from devouring *ribā* doubled and multiplied'. Unusually, this restriction can be eased in cases where a need for long-term productive loans warrants it.[87] **16.52**

The distinction between loans for consumption and those for productive purposes was advanced by Professor M'arūf al-Dwālībī at the conference on Islamic jurisprudence held in Paris in 1951, which Sanhūrī also attended. Al-Dwālībī distinguishes between loans that are intended for consumption and those intended for production. He argued that in the contemporary age the sides are switched; the borrowers are governments and big companies whereas the lenders, including depositors, are the weaker side in need of protection. Therefore, production loans need to have their own rule in Islamic law. This will either be by the state lending to producers or by allowing producers to borrow money with reasonable interest, and it is the latter course which he believes is the advisable one. This can be based on the principle of necessity (*ḍarūra*).[88] **16.53**

Section 8 demonstrates the use of interest rate ceilings in the UAE Commercial Code. **16.54**

8. The UAE Commercial Transactions Law (Commercial Code)

8.1 The Rate of Interest

The Commercial Code of 1993, in Article 76, provides: **16.55**

[87] 'Abd Al-Razzāq Al-Sanhūrī (n 53).
[88] Ibid.

> A creditor shall be entitled to charge interest on a commercial loan according to the rate provided in the contract. If the rate of interest is not specified in the contract, it shall be reckoned according to the market rate prevailing at the time of the transactions, but in this case shall not exceed 12% until payment is made.[89]

16.56 Article 409, paragraph 3 confirms the rule that 'the borrower is bound to repay the loan plus interests to the bank on time and on the agreed terms'.[90]

16.57 Contrary to these articles, until 2000 the courts of Abu Dhabi, in practice, only awarded simple interest at the agreed rate so long as the rate did not exceed 12% per annum. Courts regularly disregarded parties' agreements in which a higher interest rate was agreed.[91] Moreover, there was a view that the Commercial Code's provisions for levying interest applied only to commercial loans, but the Code itself provides for interest to accrue on the late payment of commercial debts. Even in the absence of an agreement, the court will enforce this so-called delay interest.[92] Article 77 states:

> If the contract includes an agreement on the rate of interest and the debtor is late making payment, delay interest shall be calculated on the basis of the agreed rate until full settlement is made.[93]

16.58 The courts confirmed this interpretation in 2000, when the Abu Dhabi Federal Supreme Court in Case No. 254/20 held that simple interest was to be calculated and awarded on the basis of the agreed rate irrespective of whether the interest accrued during the term of the facilities or dealings or whether it concerned delay interest. In the absence of such an agreement interest would be limited to a maximum of 12% per annum until full repayment.[94] The decision marks an important date on which the Commercial Code was finally enforced.[95]

8.2 Delay Interest

16.59 Article 90 further stipulates when interest becomes payable in commercial contracts:

> Interest for delay in settlement of commercial debts shall be payable immediately they fall due unless the law provides otherwise or it is otherwise agreed.

16.60 Yet the commercial debt must have crystallized prior to awarding interest, reflecting the lawmaker's cautious approach. Article 88 provides the following.

[89] Federal Law No. 18/1993 Issuing the Commercial Transactions Law (Commercial Code) Art. 76.
[90] Ibid, Arts 88 and 409 [3].
[91] Tamimi (n 71) p. 52.
[92] Michael Grose, Construction Law in the United Arab Emirates and the Gulf (John Wiley & Sons, 2016) p. 169.
[93] Commercial Code (n 87) Art. 77.
[94] UAE Federal Supreme Court, No. 245/20 (7 May 2000).
[95] Tamimi (n 71) p. 52.

'If the subject of a commercial obligation is a cash sum in an amount known at the time the debt is established and the debtor delays in making settlement, he shall be obliged to pay the creditor the interest specified in Articles 76 and 77 as compensation for the delay unless otherwise agreed.' **16.61**

Thus, in respect of commercial obligations where the sum of money is known, interest accrues at the market rate on the debt from the date on which it falls due, unless the parties have agreed otherwise. Where the amount of debt, on the other hand, is not known at the time it falls due, interest will not have accrued until a judgment has been given.[96] Where a party has breached the contract by delaying payment in a commercial obligation, the courts have been ready to award interest for the 'damage' incurred to the creditor. The award of interest in cases of delayed payment, which in classical *fiqh* is the *ribā al-nasī'a*, is justified on the ground that the interest represents compensation. The creditor has suffered loss because of the delay in payment. This argument relies on the Islamic maxim: 'There shall be no unfair loss nor the causing of such loss.'[97] The argument is a further gloss on Sanhūrī's thinking on the topic. Common to both arguments is the distinction between interest and usury. The former is compensation whereas the latter is exploitative and forbidden. The same rule is found in Article 226 of the Egyptian Civil Code. **16.62**

The Supreme Court has summarized the approach to determining whether a claimed debt has crystallized as follows: **16.63**

> For an amount to be considered as a quantified amount on the date of claim as a requirement for calculating the delay interest from the date of the claim, it should not be subject to the full discretion of the judge to quantify such claimed amount. Moreover, where the claimed amount is based on such firm grounds that the judge has limited discretion to assess the same, the claimed amount shall be considered as quantified at the time of the claim even though such amount is challenged by the debtor.[98]

The Abu Dhabi Federal Supreme Court clarified that delay interest is calculated on the amount of the 'outstanding principal indebtedness' which is the total of the borrowed sums minus any repaid amounts. Repaid amounts are those composed of interest and fees, on one hand, and the principal indebtedness, on the other. The total amount of interest awarded, whether during the transaction or for delay, may not exceed the 'principal indebtedness'. The latter rule is a nod to the absolute prohibition of *ribā al-jāhiliyya*, where the debtor was asked to 'double or multiply' the loan balance for an extension. Compound interest will not be awarded.[99] **16.64**

[96] Federal Supreme Court Nos 435 and 516/21 dated 12 June 2001; Federal Supreme Court No. 417/21 dated 20 June 2001; and Federal Supreme Court No. 371/21 dated 24 June 2001.
[97] Saleh Majid and Faris Majid (n 77).
[98] Federal Supreme Court No. 220/21 dated 31 December 2001; cf. Grose (n 92) p. 171.
[99] Tamimi (n 71) p. 52.

16.65 Industries such as construction, which in recent years has been particularly important for the UAE economy, are strongly affected by the crystallization rule as construction claims typically crystallize upon certification. Crystallization may fall due even later with sub-contractors or sub-suppliers. This constitutes a major constraint on the collection of interest for late payment in the construction industry.[100]

8.3 Financing Charges

16.66 Financing charges are the borrowing costs or loss of investment income which accrue to a creditor as a result of late payment. Although no express provision provides for the compensation of financing charges, they are frequently addressed in parties' terms and conditions and may also be addressed in a claim for damages for breach of contract.[101] Observers argue that such charges are recoverable as damages, in principle. This argument receives some support from the Dubai Court of Cassation which stated:

> In circumstances where neither the law nor the contract provides for the amount of compensation to be paid in respect of contractual liability, the same is left to the discretion of the judge provided that any compensation granted by the judge should include any loss suffered or profit lost and provided also that the above losses are a natural result of the lack of discharge or delay in the discharge of the obligations.[102]

16.67 Compensation for the delay of lost interest is thus recognized as a valid basis for compensation so long as losses suffered or lost profits are the natural result of the delay. The effect is to compensate interest for the time value of money, which is the maxim that the value of money is greater now than the same value of money in the future. The Sharīʿah does not recognize the time value of money as the following example makes clear: the credit sale of one gold coin for ninety-five silver coins is void whereas the spot trade for the same price is valid, according to the Hanafis and Shafi'is. One rationale is that a spot trade does not expose a vulnerable person to exploitation whereas a deferred sale does. One gold coin paid in the future for borrowing ninety-five silver coins represents a time value which is thought to raise a suspicion that a borrower's need is exploited.[103]

16.68 Another argument is that the spot trade is permitted because the difference in values represents compensation. The party, who needs ninety-five silver coins, is willing to compensate the seller with one gold coin. Yet the *fiqh* does not recognize the compensatory basis in delayed transactions because the difference in value reflects the passage of time. To treat the passage of time as capable of compensation would be to treat money as a commodity, whereas a currency per the Sharīʿah is a medium of exchange only. It is of interest then that UAE law recognizes the time value of money as a basis

[100] Grose (n 92) p. 171.
[101] Ibid, p. 173.
[102] Dubai Cassation No. 352/1994 dated 22 April 1995; cf. Grose (n 92) p. 174.
[103] ʿAbd Al-Razzāq Al-Sanhūrī (n 53).

of compensation in a delay interest claim for breach of contract.[104] The compensatory principle on which this reasoning is based leads to the conclusion that a claim for financing charges should also be permitted as the creditor has lost interest due to contractual breach and now seeks to have it recompensed.

The award of interest for breaching a debt obligation can be awarded irrespective of the circumstances of the creditor. The award of interest as compensation for financing charges, however, depends on those circumstances as these are the evidential basis for compensation. The burden of proof lies with the creditor to substantiate the cause and amount of the given loss, and this may present a challenge.[105] 16.69

Therefore, the prohibition of *ribā* has been substantially diluted in the UAE. Western-style commercial and banking practices have become deeply engrained in the structure of Arab commercial life, so much so that it appears unlikely that they will ever be replaced fully by Islamic banking practices.[106] We now turn to consider the jurisdictional issues related to contracts under the civil and commercial codes. 16.70

9. Which Code Governs the Transaction?

Given the Civil/Commercial Code dichotomy, the relevance of which code is superior is an important consideration in relation to issues such as the recoverability of interest or the time limits for commencing legal proceedings, amongst others. We have established that 'commercial' transactions where interest is a contractual term are governed by the Commercial Code, which makes such terms lawful subject to the conditions as set out above. What is the situation, however, when one of the parties to a transaction is a consumer and the other a business? Are such contracts treated as consumer contracts and thus subject to the Civil Code or are they treated as commercial contracts where the Commercial Code is applicable? 16.71

In 1995, the UAE Federal Supreme Court confirmed that if a transaction is personal or civil for one party and commercial for the other, the commercial code is the law applicable to the transaction. The decision turned on a claim brought by a supplier of a mechanical shovel where a part of the purchase price was the subject of the claim. The defendant had argued that the mechanical shovel was not intended for commercial use and hence should be subject to the provisions of the Civil Code. However, because the supplier of the shovel was a business, the Court found in favour of the claimant.[107] The decision confirms the correct application of Article 10 of the Commercial Code.[108] If a 16.72

104 Federal Supreme Court No. 371/18 dated 30 June 1998; 332/21 dated 25 September 2001, and 371/21 dated 24 June 2001.

105 Grose (n 92) p. 174.

106 Rayner (n 43) p. 286.

107 UAE Federal Supreme Court No. 290/17 dated 28 November 1995; confirmed once again in UAE Federal Supreme Court No. 287/18 dated 31 March 1996.

108 Commercial Code (n 89) Art. 10.

contract is concluded in the course of a party's business or is closely connected to that business, the Commercial Code will apply to the transaction irrespective of whether one of the parties is a consumer.

16.73 Are there cases, however, where the contractual rules provided for in the Civil Code are applicable irrespective of whether the Commercial Code is superior? In 2002, the Dubai Court of Cassation held as follows:

> It is settled by this Court as provided by Articles 1 and 2 of the Code of Commercial Practice No. 18 of 1993 that the provisions of the said law are applicable to all commercial transactions even if the person involved is not a trader. Provisions of the Civil Code should be applied to the matters not provided for by the Code of Commercial Practice or commercial custom without being inconsistent with general principles of business activity. The rules of commercial custom are applied if there is no relevant provision in the law; however, if there is no commercial provision, the provisions of civil matters are applicable provided that they are not inconsistent with the general rules of commercial activity.[109]

16.74 Therefore, laws other than the Commercial Code will apply to transactions where these are not covered in the Commercial Code. In practice, the courts regularly apply provisions of the Civil Code to transactions such as those concerning construction contracts where the Civil Code provides detailed rules for these types of transactions. Only in the event of a conflict between the provisions of the codes would the Commercial Code take precedence.[110] This procedural approach whereby a commercial code is superior to a civil code is similar to the juristic methodologies of the *uṣūl al-fiqh*. According to the *uṣūl*, a specific provision should be referred to prior to a general provision. Moreover, a general provision should not be interpreted in such a way that it conflicts with a specific provision, so that the specific rule supersedes a general rule. Finally, general rules are to be interpreted in the broadest manner possible whereas specific rules are to be interpreted narrowly.[111]

16.75 Let us consider the so-called nominate contracts (*'uqūd musammāt*) in the Civil Code, which have been borrowed from the *fiqh*. These include the contracts of sale, employment, hire, partnership, loan, security, guarantee, settlement, and gift. Nominate contracts are highly regulated by the Civil Code and therefore less susceptible to interpretation than are innominate contracts.[112] For example, business partnerships (*sharikāt al-'aqd*) are provided for in the Civil Code.[113] According to the *fiqh*, in contracts of partnership, partners agree to profit ratios which must be stipulated as a term of the partnership. The bases for profit-making are wealth, labour, and liability (*ḍamān*)

[109] Dubai Cassation No. 349/2002 dated 29 December 2002. Confirmed in Federal Supreme Court No. 294/12 dated 28 May 1991.
[110] Grose (n 92) p. 17.
[111] M. Cherif Bassoiuni, 'Islamic Law—The Sharī'ah' (Middle East Institute, 24 January 2012) <.
[112] Grose (n 92) p. 14.
[113] Civil Code (n 35) Arts 683–709.

so that a term providing for a certain amount of profit (as opposed to a ratio of profits) is invalid as it viewed as a guaranteed return (*ribā*).[114]

Article 704 of the UAE Civil Code sets out the terms of the *muḍāraba* partnership in relation to loss:[115] **16.76**

> The owner of the capital shall alone bear any loss, and any provision to the contrary shall be void. If any of the capital in the *muḍāraba* is lost, that shall be accounted for out of the profits, and if the loss exceeds the profits the balance shall be accounted for out of the capital, and the *muḍārib* shall not be liable therefore.

The substance of these provisions has been taken from the *fiqh*, which defines the *muḍāraba* as a silent partnership where the owner of capital (*rabb al-māl*) advances capital to an investment agent (*muḍārib*) to trade on their behalf. Profits are shared according to a pre-agreed formula whereas all financial losses are borne by the provider of capital. The *muḍārib* can only lose his time and effort if profits do not materialize. Any return must result from the performance of the *muḍāraba* and therefore are a ratio of the profit. A fixed amount of profit is an invalid condition because it guarantees a return, which is considered *ribā*.[116] **16.77**

What then is the situation when commercial parties structure their transaction as a partnership but stipulate a term which provides for interest, or guarantees a return? An Islamic finance transaction provides an interesting case study. In 2017, Dana Gas, a UAE energy company, told investors that it could not make payments on its $700 million *sukūk* issuance because the underlying structure was no longer Sharīʿah-compliant 'due to the evolution and continual development of Islamic financial instruments and their interpretation'.[117] The company filed a motion in the UAE courts which sought to declare the *muḍāraba sukūk* unlawful under UAE law. It also obtained injunctions in the UAE court and the English court, prohibiting investors from taking any action under the *muḍāraba* agreement or the purchase undertaking until a final decision was reached in those proceedings.[118] Dana Gas sought to restructure the $700 million issuance so that profit distributions were halved. Structured as *muḍāraba sukūk*, the Dana Gas *sukūk* included periodic distribution amounts at a rate of 7.0% per annum for exchangeable certificates whereas ordinary certificates received a rate of 9.0% per annum irrespective of the performance of the *sukūk*. Moreover, investors would be repaid their investments guaranteeing a return of their funds.[119] The transaction was the equivalent of a conventional bond as is the practice amongst most classes of *sukūk* investment **16.78**

[114] See, for an overview of Islamic partnership laws, Imran Ahsan Khan Nyazee, Islamic Law of Business Organisation: Partnerships (Kitab Bhavan, 1999) p. 137. The apportionment of profits and losses is confirmed Article 692 of the UAE Civil Code.
[115] Ibid, Art. 704.
[116] Wahbah al-Zuḥaylī (n 57) p. 498.
[117] Dana Gas, 'Dana Gas Outlines Broad Terms for Sukūk Discussions' (UAE, 13 June 2017).
[118] *Dana Gas PJSC v Dana Gas Sukūk Ltd* [2017] EWHC 2340 (Comm).
[119] Dana Gas, 'Dana Gas Sukūk Limited' (Offering Circular, 8 May 2013) 6 <www.londonstockexchange.com/specialist-issuers/islamic/danagas-prospectus.pdf> accessed 1 August 2017.

certificates.[120] The case set an odious precedent since other firms could seek to escape their debt obligations by claiming Sharīʿah non-compliance. It threatened to undermine confidence in the Islamic finance industry.

16.79 Dana Gas was able to resolve its dispute with its creditors out of court, so we cannot be sure how the court would have decided. Based on our earlier analysis, however, we may surmise that the interest provisions of the Dana Gas *sukūk*, in view of the commercial nature of the transaction, are lawful under the UAE Commercial Code irrespective of how the transaction was labelled. Terms allowing for the return of investors' principal investments in a *muḍāraba* contract, however, are subject to Article 704, which provides for loss to be passed on to investors (*rabb al-māl*). The purchase undertaking in the Dana Gas *sukūk* guaranteed a return to its investors. Instead, losses were passed on to the debtors of the transaction, Dana Gas, which underlined the transaction's substantive equivalence to a conventional bond. The UAE court, should it have rendered a decision, might have set aside terms related to the guaranteed return of the *sukūk* investment structure, unravelling the transaction with significant financial consequences for investors.[121] The Islamic/secular dichotomy which exists between the Civil and Commercial Codes in relation to the charging of interest poses considerable risks to parties unaware of the contradictions and complexities of this hybrid legal architecture.[122]

16.80 These primarily contractual issues seem to have been the impetus for the recent approval of a Higher Sharīʿa Board for Banking and Finance in the UAE.[123] The board, which is an organ of the central bank, will be responsible for rule-setting, standards, and general principles for the Islamic finance industry.[124] The Board subsequently adopted the Accounting and Auditing Organization for Islamic Financial Institutions (AAOIFI) Sharīʿah standards which represents an important step by UAE authorities to shore up confidence in the Islamic finance industry. Notably, however, such standards

[120] In 2007, Sheikh Taqi Usmani (then chairman of the AAOIFI Sharīʿah board) declared that 85% of the *sukūk* market was not compliant with the Sharīʿah. Subsequently, AAOIFI issued a statement in relation to *sukūk* based on the *mushāraka* contract, which provided that the purchase undertaking 'should not be based on an exercise price which is calculated by reference to the face value of the *sukūk* at the maturity date or upon the earlier dissolution of a *sukūk*'. Instead, the purchase undertaking should be based on the 'net asset value, market value, cash equivalent value or any price agree upon at the time of purchase'; cf. Farmida Bi, 'AAOIFI Statement on Sukūk and its Implications' (Norton Rose Fulbright, September 2008).

[121] The pertinent issue in relation to the Dana Gas *Sukūk* structure is the scheduled redemption or purchase undertaking in which the *Muḍārib* liquidates the *muḍāraba* assets and repays *sukūk* holders their capital investments. As noted, a purchase undertaking to buy back the underlying assets from the originator at face value on the 'scheduled redemption date' or in the event of a default indicates that the investors have not assumed the risks of ownership associated with the underlying *sukūk* assets. The originator has retained true ownership of the assets and thus the credit rating of the *sukūk* issuance is at the same level as the originator's senior unsecured rating for long-term *sukūk*. See Standard & Poor's Ratings Services, 'Methodology for Rating Sukūk' (Standard & Poor's, 19 January 2015) <www.econostrum.info/attachment/545518> accessed 17 October 2018.

[122] Jonathan Ercanbrack, 'Islamic Financial Law and the Law of the United Arab Emirates: Disjuncture and the Necessity for Reform' (2019) 33 Arab Law Quarterly 152.

[123] Federal Law No. (14) of 2018 Regarding the Central Bank & Organization of Financial Institutions and Activities, Art. 17.

[124] Emirates News Agency, 'UAE Cabinet Approves Establishment of Both UAE Council for Fatwa and Sharīʿa Board for Banking and Finance', 30 May 2017.

affect fully-fledged Islamic banks, Islamic windows of conventional banks, and finance companies offering Sharīʿah-compliant products and services in the UAE.[125] The law does not apply to non-financial companies such as Dana Gas. *Prima facie*, the mandate will prevent financial institutions from dealing in interest although consideration of the risk profile of transactions is necessary before one can come to that conclusion definitively. The AAOIFI mandate will also require acquiescence from the judiciary which will be charged with enforcing AAOIFI standards. As the 2018 Central Bank Law is a specialized law applicable to financial institutions, presumably it will be given effect to in cases involving financial institutions. However, a recent appeal before the Dubai Court of Cassation, involving the Sharīʿah compliance of *murābaḥa* facilities, throws this conclusion into doubt.[126] The Court of Cassation set out its own definition of the *murābaḥa* contract and invoked the Maliki school of jurisprudence as the standard. Although the Court did not definitively state whether the transaction was Sharīʿah-compliant and therefore whether it should be enforced, the decision underscores the importance of Sharīʿah compliance.[127] The Court expressly stated that there are no rules or guidelines under UAE law which specify the relevant criteria for Sharīʿah compliance. Therefore, the decision indicates that the Court will determine the Sharīʿah compliance of transactions which hold themselves out as Islamic irrespective of the AAOIFI mandate or even the civil law/commercial law dichotomy with respect to the charging of interest. Notably, commodity *murābaḥa* transactions are a form of sales contract under UAE law, and sales contracts are governed by the Civil Code.

It is important to keep in mind that UAE law does not operate according to a system of judicial precedent, so that the case is not capable of conclusive interpretation. The decisions of one court will have no binding authority on another court in another case. **16.81**

[125] Accounting and Auditing Organization for Islamic Financial Institutions, 'AAOIFI Welcomes UAE's Adoption of its Standards' (AAOIFI, n.d.) <https://aaoifi.com/announcement/aaoifi-welcomes-uaes-adoption-of-its-standards/?lang=en> accessed 15 March 2022.

[126] Dubai Court of Cassation Appeals Nos 898 and 927 of 2019.

[127] Clifford Chance, 'Dubai Court of Cassation Decision on Validity of Murābaḥa Contracts' (Clifford Chance, n.d.).

Index

Tables are indicated by *t* following the para number

acceptance *see* offer and acceptance
agents and agency contracts (*wakāla*) 9.56, 9.61, 11.01–11.34
  acceptance, and 11.09
  agency in sale 11.22
  agency in litigation 11.28–11.29
  agency to purchase property 11.27
  agency with consideration 11.30–11.32
  agent's absolute power to sell 11.23–11.24
  agent's qualified power to sell 11.25–11.26
  agent, nature of 11.06
  annulment of agency contracts because of death 14.51–14.52
  bodily acts of worship 11.18
  consent, and 11.07
  death, and 10.42
  delegation of certain tasks and functions 11.12–11.13
  essential elements of *wakāla* 11.03–11.09
  fees/compensation (*'ujr*) for work or services 9.64
  Hajj and *'Umrah* 11.19
  impossibility of performance 14.49
  insanity, termination of agency agreements and 10.42, 11.34
  intoxication, termination of agency, and 11.34
  ju'āla contracts, and 11.38
  legal effects of agency 11.21–11.11.29
  matters delegated upon which jurists disagree 11.19–11.20
  matters which agents cannot undertake 11.15–11.18
  muḍāraba agreements, and 10.77
  nature of agency 11.02
  negotiated termination of contracts (*iqāla*) 14.37
  non-binding nature of agency contracts 11.32, 11.33, 14.29, 14.52
  object of agency 11.11
  offers, and 11.08
  parties to *wakāla* contract 11.04
  partnerships 10.29–10.30, 10.49, 10.77
  pecuniary acts of worship 11.14
  permissibility 11.13, 11.28
  principal, nature of 11.05
  sinful actions and crimes 11.17
  termination of agency: death 11.34
  termination of agency: dismissal or resignation 11.33
  testimony, oaths, and vows 11.16
  third party rights 13.25–13.33
  when agency takes effect 11.10
  woman marrying through agent 11.20
agricultural partnership contracts *see under* partnership contracts
al-takhliya, possession obtained by 5.56
ambiguity and uncertainty (*gharar*) 5.05, 5.65, 6.38–6.47
  Civil Codes, prohibition of *gharar* in 6.46–6.47
  consent, and 7.07
  contingent contracts 6.45
  definitions of *gharar* 6.38
  fāsid contracts 7.38
  formation of valid contract, and 7.10
  gharar red flags in contracts 6.42–6.45
  Information symmetry, importance of 6.44
  legal basis for prohibition of *gharar* 6.39
  major *gharar* 6.40, 6.41
  major *gharar*, examples of 6.41
  nominal *gharar* 6.40
  price, and 7.15
  valid contracts, and 7.15
analogical deduction (*qiyās*) 1.39, 1.43–1.46, 8.50, 8.52, 14.70, 15.50
ancillary contracts 11.01–11.99
  agency *see* agents and agency contracts (*wakāla*)
  ijāra see *ijāra* contracts
  istiṣna' see *istiṣna'* contracts
  ju'āla see *ju'āla* contracts
  salam see *salam* contracts
  ṣarf see *ṣarf* contracts
anwā' al-ahlīyya see legal capacity
'āqidān see parties (*'āqidān*)
auction sales (*bay' al-muzāyada*) 9.18–9.19
  reverse auctions 9.19

Austin, John 1.17, 6.96
autonomy *see* party autonomy

bankruptcy and insolvency 14.58
barter trade/commodity exchange (*bay' al-muqāyaḍa*) 9.15
  barter trade involving dried and fresh fruits (*bay' al-muzābana*) 9.87
  prohibited contracts of sale 9.87
Bentham, Jeremy 1.17
bilateral contracts 9.01–9.103
  classification of 9.06–9.07
  general contract of sale *see* general contract of sale
  nature of 9.02–9.05
  partnership contracts *see* partnership contracts
  prohibited contracts of sale *see* prohibited contracts of sale
  security or guarantee contracts *see* security or guarantee contracts
  types of *see* types of contracts of sale and applicable legal principles
  usufruct-based contracts *see* usufruct-based contracts
bilateral promises (*muwā'ada*) 9.03, 9.05
  contract, and 1.11–1.12
  meaning of 1.11–1.12
binding promises (*wa'ad*) 12.04–12.20
  binding nature of promise 12.12–12.14
  condition precedent 12.15–12.16
  conditions applicable to binding promise 12.19
  lawfulness of actions invoking promises 12.06–12.07
  nature of 12.04
  non-obligatory nature of promise 12.10–12.11
  permissibility of *wa'ad* 12.05
  promise becoming binding 12.15–12.18
  promisee's reliance on promise 12.17–12.18
  revocation of promise 12.20
  whether promise binding on promisor 12.08–12.19
bonds, Islamic (*ṣukūk*) 1.05

capacity *see* legal capacity (*ahlīyya*)
commutative contracts 7.44, 7.68, 9.04, 9.07, 9.08, 9.21
conceptual theory of contractual obligation 1.09–1.13
  promise, concept of 1.11
  reciprocity between parties 1.10
  rules of contract derived from original sources of Islamic law 1.13
  sanctity of contract 1.09
  unilateral promise 1.11
conditional stipulations 8.03, 8.41–8.62
  Hanafi and *Shafi'i* Schools 8.49–8.53
  Hanbali and *Maliki* Schools 8.54–8.62
  role of the will 8.41–8.48
conditions (*shurūṭ*) 7.57–7.71
  bāṭil conditions 7.69–7.71
  conditional stipulations *see* conditional stipulations
  conditions beneficial to contract and parties 7.59
  conditions conflicting with essence of contract 7.60
  conditions conflicting with essence of contract: no adverse effects 7.61
  conditions linked to *muqtaḍā* of the contract 7.58
  fāsid conditions 7.66, 7.68
  valid conditions: based on 'urf 7.66–7.67
  valid conditions: emphasizing contract's objectives 7.64
  valid conditions: in conformity with contract 7.63
  valid conditions: validated by the *shar'* 7.65
conduct
  consent inferred from conduct of parties 7.07
  contract by see *ījāb* and *qabūl* through conduct and *mu'āṭāt*
coercion 6.66–6.71
  consent of coerced party 2.34
  constraining/complete coercion 6.67, 6.68, 6.69
  core elements 6.66
  definition of 6.66
  effect of 6.66, 6.67, 6.69, 6.71, 7.22, 12.40, 14.30
  justified coercion/legal compulsion 2.34, 6.70, 12.40
  moral coercion 6.67
  nature of 6.66
  non-constraining/incomplete coercion 6.67, 6.68, 6.69
  prohibited elements in contract, as 6.48
  separation of parties after contract session 2.53
  third party, by 6.66
  unjust coercion 6.67–6.69
  vitiating legal capacity 6.66
  words uttered under 4.27, 4.30
commodity exchange *see* barter trade/commodity exchange (*bay' al-muqāyaḍa*)
compensation *see* damages/compensation (*ḍamān*)

consensus (*ijmā*) 1.39, 1.40–1.42, 1.47, 8.28, 11.63, 14.63
consent
agency 11.07
bilateral contracts 9.03
coercion, consent through 2.34
contracts, and 4.26, 7.07
express consent 7.07
factors vitiating consent 3.17
foundation of contract, as 2.32
freely provided 2.34, 7.06
inferred from conduct of parties 7.07
intention to contract, and *see* mutual assent (*tarāḍī*) and intention to contract
intoxicated person, consent of 2.36
jest, given in 2.35
means of implying consent 4.20
mistake vitiating 3.17, 3.19, 16.21
mutual consent *see* mutual consent
paramount in contractual relations 6.68
ratification of past offer or acceptance, as 7.08
consideration *see* subject matter
contract (*aqd*)
agency *see* agents and agency contracts
ancillary contracts *see* ancillary contracts
bilateral contracts *see* bilateral contracts
commutative contracts 7.44, 7.68, 9.04, 9.07, 9.08, 9.21
consent *see* consent
contingent contracts 6.45
contractual terms *see* contractual terms
contractual uncertainty/ambiguity *see* ambiguity and uncertainty (*gharar*)
debt assignment *see* debt assignment contracts (*ḥawāla*)
definition of 1.07–1.08, 4.25, 4.31
essential elements *see* essential elements of a valid contract
express and implied contracts 1.19–1.20
form of *see* form of contract (*ṣīgha*)
formation of *see* formation of contract
general principles *see* general principles and sources of Islamic contract law
general theory of *see* general theory of contract
gratuitous *see* unilateral/gratuitous contracts
guarantees *see* guarantee contracts (*kafāla*)
intention to contract *see* mutual assent (*tarāḍī*) and intention to contract
invalid contracts *see* invalid contracts
leases *see* lease contracts
legal capacity *see* legal capacity (*ahlīyya*)
non-binding *see* non-binding contracts
non-commutative contracts 1.11, 7.44
offer and acceptance *see* offer and acceptance
origins 1.08
partnership *see* partnership contracts
performance *see* performance
pre-emption *see* pre-emption contracts (*shuf ʿa*)
prohibited *see* prohibited contracts of sale; prohibited elements in contract
rescission *see* rescission of contracts (*faskh*)
subject matter of *see* subject matter of contract (*maḥal al ʿaqd/maʿqud ʿalaihi*)
termination *see* termination of contracts (*inhā-al-ʿaqd*)
third parties *see* third parties and contracts
types of contract 7.01
unilateral *see* unilateral/gratuitous contracts
valid contracts *see* valid contracts
see also Muslim majority jurisdictions, Islamic contract law in
contractual terms 8.01–8.62
conditional stipulations *see* conditional stipulations
governed by detailed rules, prohibitions and exceptions 8.01
rights of option *see* rights of option
co-ownership *see* partnership contracts, equity-based
currency exchange (*bay ʿ al-ṣarf*) 9.14
custody of subject matter *see* possession/custody of subject matter of contract
custom (*ʿurf*) 1.32, 1.39, 1.52–1.54, 2.21, 2.28, 2.30, 2.49, 2.53, 7.08, 7.69
conditions based on 7.62, 7.66–7.67
customary trade practices 6.12
offer and acceptance, and 7.08
subject matter of contract, and 5.03–5.04, 5.08, 5.20, 5.25, 5.62

damages/compensation (*ḍamān*) 15.47–15.62
approval or ratification (*ijāza*) 15.61
capacity 15.58
contract 15.50–15.56
destruction or damage (*itlāf*) 15.49
difference between *ḍamān* arising from contract, possession, or *itlāf* 15.57–15.62
liability 15.60
nature and amount of compensation 15.55, 15.59
possession 15.48
time for the entitlement of 15.62
transformation of *maqūd aʿlaih* from *amāna* to *damān* 15.56
types of contracts involving *ḍamān* 15.54
when arising 15.50–15.53

death
  acquired attribute, as 3.18, 3.19
  agency contracts, and 10.42
  annulment of non-binding contracts because of 14.51–14.52
  dissolution of the *muḍāraba*, and 10.86
  offer, ending of 2.65
  partnerships 10.86
  party, death of 2.65, 14.24, 14.50
  terminal illness *see* terminal illness
  termination of contract, and 11.45, 14.24, 14.43
  termination of *ju'āla* contract 11.45
  vitiating consent 3.17
debt assignment contracts (*ḥawāla*) 9.56, 9.60
  definition 13.35–13.37
  elements and conditions for its validity 13.41–13.43, 13.43*t*
  legal consequences 13.44
  legality 13.38
  restricted *ḥawāla* (*muqayyada*) 13.39, 13.40
  third party rights 13.34–13.44
  unrestricted *ḥawāla* (*mutlaqa*) 13.39
debt, contracts involving
  alternatives to payment of debt 14.10
  delivery of debt 14.08–14.09
  failure to deliver debt 14.11–14.13
  performance of 14.07–14.13
debt for a debt sale (*bay' al-kālī bi al-kālī*) 9.90
deception *see* fraud, deception, and misrepresentation
defective goods and commodities
  concealment of defect see *khiyār al tadlīs* (option for concealment of defect)
  inspection option see *khiyār al-ru'ya* (option of inspection)
  knowledge of defect see *khiyār-al-a'yb* (option for defect)
  sale with defective conditions 7.44
  see also rights of option (*khiyārāt*)
delivery of subject matter of contract 5.29–5.36
  juridical (*shar'ī*) capacity to deliver 5.30, 5.31–5.32
  obstacles to physical possession of subject matter 5.33–5.34
  physical (*ḥissī*) capacity to deliver 5.30, 5.33–5.36
  subject matter deliverable after contract conclusion 5.35
  subject matter owned by others 5.31–5.32
  subject matter should be deliverable at time of contract 5.29
  usurped property 5.36
disabled persons, *sīgha* by 2.09–2.10
Egyptian Civil Code 16.03
  background 16.05–16.12
  influencing civil codes of Arab states 16.13
  regulation of interest and 16.47–16.5
electronic communication 2.41
electronic contracts 1.20, 1.52, 2.52
endowment (*waqf*) 12.61–12.77
  administration of *waqf* property 12.74
  beneficiary 12.70–12.71
  capacity and authority of the parties 12.69–12.71
  conditions for valid *waqf* 12.63–12.71
  creation of 12.62
  delivery 12.67–12.68
  life of 12.72
  meaning and nature of 12.61
  purpose of 12.73
  subject matter, conditions for 12.64
  subject matter, nature of 12.65–12.66
  termination of 12.77
  things associated with *waqf* property 12.75
  types of 12.76
  waqf associated with conditions 12.63
equitable rulings (*istiḥsān*) 1.39, 1.47–1.51, 8.22, 8.25, 8.50, 10.46, 10.60, 10.73, 11.25, 11.84
essential elements of a valid contract 1.55–1.61
  form of contract (*ṣigha*) 1.57
  parties (*'āqidān*) 1.59
  subject matter of contract (*ma'qud 'alaihi*) 1.60–1.61
evidence
  criminal cases 3.103
  duty to testify 3.101
  non-property matters 3.103
  reluctance to accept written documents 3.102
  requisites of testimony 3.104
  types of 3.102
  women's testimony see women's testimony (*shahādāt*)

faskh see rescission of contracts (*faskh*)
financing through *sharika and muḍāraba* 10.89–10.93
  diminishing *mushāraka* 10.90–10.93
  muḍāraba and *sharika* as modes of financing 10.89
fāsid contracts 7.34–7.45
  bay' al-īnah 7.39–7.44
  bay' al-majhūl 7.38
  bay' al-wafā 7.45
  causes 7.35–7.36
  conditions *see under* conditions (*shurūṭ*)
  effects of *fāsid* contract and its revocation 7.37
  instances of 7.38–7.45

nature of 7.34
sale with defective conditions 7.44
two sales in one and conditions in sale 7.40–7.43
fictitious contracts of sale (*bay' al-talji'a*) 9.91–9.92
force majeure and impossibility of performance 14.24, 14.43–52
agency 14.49
annulment of non-binding contracts because of death 14.51–14.52
contractual *infisākh* by choice or necessity 14.43
damage to subject matter of contract 14.44–14.49
death of one or both parties to binding contract 14.50
executed contracts 14.45
executory contracts 14.46
leases 14.47
partnerships 14.48
regulation of *force majeure* as matter of agreement 14.43
form of contract (*ṣīgha*) 1.57
characteristics of *ṣīgha* 2.11
disabled persons, *sīgha* by 2.09–2.10
form and substance, debate of 1.21–1.30
sign language, *ṣīgha* in 2.09–2.10
see also offer and acceptance
formation of contract
choice and contentment 4.24.27, 4.30
conditions for 7.05–7.10
consent, and *see* consent; mutual assent (*tarāḍī*) and intention to contract
individual's will 4.26–4.27
non-revocable contracts 4.29
objective approach to intent 4.28–4.29
revocable contracts 4.28
role of intent in 4.22–4.34
theological background of contract law 4.22–4.24
theory of cause 4.32–4.33
verbal utterances in *see* formation of contract, verbal utterances in 4.20, 4.35–4.49
formation of contract, verbal utterances in 4.20, 4.35–4.49
apparent and hidden intent 4.35
basic sincerity 4.39
clear and explicit language, requirement for 4.40, 4.42
clear words but no discernible intention 4.38
command form 4.41
complex actions and intent 4.39, 4.50–4.65
explicit and allusive speech 4.36
implication 4.45–4.46
manifest correspondence between words and intentions 4.37
no correspondence between the words and intentions 4.37
no formalism in 4.47
real and metaphorical meanings 4.42–4.44
signs and customs 4.47
silence, and 4.48
forward sales (*bay' al-salam*) 9.13
fraud, deception, and misrepresentation 6.55–6.65
consent, and 7.06
effects on contract 6.64–6.65
elements 6.60–6.63
nature and meaning 6.56–6.59
freedom of contract, principle of 1.19, 1.36, 6.66
future contracts 1.11, 1.12

games of chance (*maysir*) and gambling (*qimār*) 6.45, 6.50–6.54
derivatives 6.54
features of gambling 6.53
meaning of gambling 6.51–6.52
general contract of sale 9.08–9.21
auction sales (*bay' al-muzāyada*) 9.18–9.19
bargaining or negotiable sales (*bay' al-musāwama*) 9.17
barter trade/commodity exchange (*bay' al-muqāyaḍa*) 9.15
classification on price stipulation 9.16–9.21
classification on subject matter of contract 9.12–9.15
currency exchange (*bay ' al-ṣarf*) 9.14
elements 9.09–9.10
forward sales (*bay' al-salam*) 9.13
general sales (*bay' al-muṭlaq*) 9.12
nature of 9.08
spot payments and deferred payments 9.21
trust sales (*bay' al-'amāna*) 9.19
general principles and sources of Islamic contract law 1.01–1.61
debate of form and substance 1.21–1.30
essential elements of a valid contract *see* essential elements of a valid contract
general theory of contract *see* general theory of contract
sources of Islamic contract law *see* sources of Islamic contract law
general theory of contract 1.06, 1.07–1.20
basic elements of contract 1.08
conceptual theory of contractual obligation 1.09–1.13
express and implied contract 1.19–1.20
Islamic law, in 1.14–1.1.18

gharar see ambiguity and uncertainty (*gharar*)
ghasb see usurpation (*ghasb*)
gifts (*hiba*) 4.59, 5.01
  agents, and 11.12, 11.13
  co-ownership, and 10.04, 10.39
  damage to subject matter, and 14.45
  differing from other transactions 12.23
  father to his children, gifts by 12.33
  financial leases 9.30
  gift deeds 1.24, 1.59
  gratuitous contracts, as *see* gratuitous contracts
  irrevocable nature of 4.28
  khiyār-al-a'yb, and 14.72
  married women 3.94
  minors 7.25
  nature and validity 12.21–12.22
  nominate contracts, and 16.76
  offer and acceptance, and 2.10, 7.07, 12.25–12.26
  option to withdraw, and 8.21
  parties 12.27
  possession (*hauzi*) in a gift 12.29–12.31
  pre-emption claims, and 13.57
  prior ownership, condition of 5.37
  requirements of valid gift 12.24–12.31
  revocation of 12.34–12.36
  several donees, gift to 5.75
  subject matter 12.28
  terminally ill persons 3.81
  unilateral contracts, as 5.25, 8.21, 9.02, 12.03, 12.21–12.36
  wills, and 12.53
  witnessing a gift 12.32
gratuitous contracts *see* unilateral/gratuitous contracts
guarantee contracts (*kafāla*) 9.56, 9.58, 13.40
  definitions of 13.16–13.22
  legitimacy of 13.24
  nature of 13.16–13.17, 13.23
  third party rights, and 13.04, 13.15–13.24

Hajj 11.19
ḥajr see interdiction (*ḥajr*)
harmonization of laws 1.54
ḥawāla see debt assignment contracts (*ḥawāla*)
ḥissī capacity to deliver 5.30, 5.33–5.36
hoarding, illegal profiteering, and price fixing 6.72–6.80
  cartels 6.72, 6.76
  definition of hoarding 6.72
  effect of profiteering on contracts 6.77–6.78
  market monopoly, prohibition of 6.72
  permissible price control 6.76
  price fixing, prohibition of 6.73–6.75
  profit rate or limit not stipulated 6.79–6.80

ījāb and *qabūl,* communication of 2.37–2.42
  electronic communication 2.41
  ījāb and *qabūl* from/to concerned parties 2.38
  instantaneous methods of communication 2.40–2.41
  postal communication 2.42
ījāb and *qabūl,* completion of contract with 2.43–2.45
  direct communication 2.43
  postal communication 2.44–2.45
ījāb and *qabūl,* express 2.04–2.21
  concept of *ījāb* and *qabūl* 2.05
  conditional offers 2.13
  conformity of *qabūl with ījāb* 2.12
  counter offers 2.14
  disabled persons, *sīgha* by 2.09–2.10
  form of *ījāb* and *qabūl* 2.06–2.08
  fresh offers 2.15
  safaqa wāḥida and *ṣafaqa mutafarraqa* 2.16–2.19
  ṣīgha, characteristics of 2.11
  ṣīgha in sign language 2.09–2.10
  words to be used 2.20–2.21
ījāb and *qabūl* through conduct and *mu'āṭāt* 1.19, 2.22–2.31
  mu'āṭāt, opinions on permissibility of 2.26–2.31
  mu'āṭāt, sale by 2.24
  offer and acceptance implied from conduct 2.22–2.23
  silence as acceptance 2.23
ijāra contracts 11.48–11.62
  effect of 11.55
  elements of 11.51–11.54
  guaranteeing usurped property from usurpation 11.57
  Islamic banks, application by 11.61
  meaning of 11.48
  nature of 11.50
  object matter of 11.54
  obligations of lessor 11.56
  parties to 11.53
  personal financing, and 11.62
  ṣīgha 11.52
  surrender of possession of leased property 11.56
  termination of 11.59–11.60
ijmā
  source of Islamic contract law, as 1.40–1.42
  see also consensus (*ijmā*)
illness, terminal *see* terminal illness

imbecility (*al-ma'tūh*) 3.55–3.57, 3.70
  definitions 3.55
  divine attribute, as 3.18
  interdiction (*hajr*) of the imbecile 3.22, 3.45, 3.48, 3.56–3.57
  legal capacity, and 3.17, 3.18, 3.19, 3.71, 7.09
  principal, inability to be 11.05
impermissible subject matter 5.02–5.03, 5.08, 5.17–5.24
  examples of 6.49
  formation of valid contract, and 7.10
  invalid contracts 7.47, 7.56
  impure and non-beneficial things 5.17–5.19, 7.56
  mixing of wine or other impurities with a pure subject matter 5.24
  permissible property becoming impermissible 5.15–5.16
  permitting impermissible subject matter 5.20–5.24
  permitting impermissible subject matter: benefit 5.21
  permitting impermissible subject matter: necessity 5.22–5.23
  prohibited element in contracts, as 6.49
  see also invalid contracts
implied contracts 1.19–1.20
impossibility of performance see *force majeure* and impossibility of performance
inan sharikat-al-amwāl (partnership) 10.24–10.44
  agency between partners 10.29 –10.30
  basics of 10.28
  destruction or loss of capital 10.44
  dissolution 10.40–10.44
  equality in contribution of capital and distribution of profits 10.31 –10.33
  expiration of period of 10.43
  formation of 10.25
  general *'inān* 10.27
  loss of capacity of either party 10.42
  recission of contract by either party 10.41
  rights of partners 10.34–10.39
  surety agreements 10.25, 10.27
influence of Islamic law 1.02–1.03
inhā-al-'aqd see termination of contracts (*inhā-al-'aqd*)
injunctions
  divine injunctions 1.17
  moral injunctions 1.16
  Sharī'ah injunctions 16.15, 16.38, 16.39
insanity (*junūn*) or mental incompetence 3.70
  acquired attribute, as 3.18, 3.19
  agency contracts, termination of 10.42, 11.34
  defective capacity 7.24
  definitions 3.43–3.44
  dissolution of the *muḍāraba, and* 10.86
  divine attribute, as 3.18
  ijāra contracts, and 1.53
  insanity from birth and 'intermittent insanity' 3.47
  interdiction (*ḥajr*) of the insane 3.22, 3.45–3.54
  legal capacity, and 3.17, 3.18, 3.19, 3.71, 7.09
  offer, ending of 2.65
  partnerships 10.86
  principal, inability to be 11.05
  termination of contract, and 14.24, 14.43
  termination of *ju'āla* contract 11.45
inspection of object of sale 8.28–8.29
intent (*nīyya*) 4.01–4.65
  contract formation, role in *see* formation of contract 4.22–4.34
  contract law, intent in 4.16–4.21
  fiqh of worship (*al-'ibādāt*), role of intent in 4.08–4.15
  fundamental concept, as 4.03
  legal commands, (*mu'amalāt*), role of intent in 4.05–4.06
  nature of 4.01–4.02
  ritual acts and law 4.04, 4.09
intention to contract *see* mutual assent (*tarāḍī*) and intention to contract
interdiction (*ḥajr*)
  imbecility 3.22, 3.45, 3.48, 3.56–3.57
  insanity 3.22, 3.45–3.54
  legal capacity 3.22
  minority 3.22, 3.41, 3.42, 3.45, 3.48, 3.50
  prodigality 3.48, 3.65–3.69
  terminally illness 3.80–3.85
interest and usury (*ribā*) 6.15–6.37, 8.41, 8.43
  broad classification of *ribā* 6.20–6.22
  conventional interest rates as a benchmark, use of 6.25, 6.99
  discount and early payment 7.16
  Global Financial Crisis, and 6.19
  interest and late payment compensation 6.30–6.35
  loan extension and increase 7.16
  loan moratorium 6.26–6.29
  loans 12.51
  meaning of *ribā* 6.16, 6.18
  profit and interest, differences between 6.23–6.25
  prohibition of *ribā* 6.17
  rules of *ribā,* 7.16
  UAE, and *see* United Arab Emirates (UAE)
  valid contracts, and 7.16
  waiver of interest clause 6.36–6.37

intoxication
  acquired attribute, as 3.19
  consent of intoxicated person 2.36
  intoxicating drinks, forbidding of 5.23, 5.24
  legal capacity, as impediment to 3.19, 3.20
  no correspondence between the words and intentions 4.37
  termination of agency, and 11.34
invalid contracts 7.01–7.46, 7.71
  capacity of parties, causes of invalidity and 7.47
  causes of invalidity 7.47–7.49
  conditions *see under* conditions (*shurūṭ*)
  effect of 7.50
  fāsid contracts see *fāsid* contracts
  illegality of object of contract 7.49
  instances of 7.51–7.56
  sale of impure objects 7.56
  sale of liabilities, including debts 7.52–7.55
  subject matter, causes of invalidity and 7.48
  see also prohibited elements in contract; valid contracts
istiḥsān
  source of Islamic contract law, as 1.47–1.51
  see also equitable rulings (*istiḥsān*)
istiṣna' contracts 11.83–11.95
  defining the rule of *istiṣna'* 11.84
  difference between *istiṣna'* and *salam* 11.93
  effect of 11.89
  essential elements of 11.85–11.88
  nature of 11.83
  object of 11.88
  parallel or investment *istiṣna'* 11.91–11.92
  parties to 11.87
  ṣīgha 11.86
  termination of 11.95
  traditional or normal *istiṣna'* 11.90
  types of 11.90–11.92
iqāla see negotiated termination of contracts (*iqāla*)

jesting 4.27, 4.30, 7.06
  acquired attribute, as 3.19
  choice, and 4.30
  consent given in jest 2.35
  contract made in jest 7.06
  divorce 4.29
  impediment to legal capacity, as 3.17
  legal effects 4.27, 4.37, 7.06, 7.35
  vitiating consent 3.17
ju'āla contracts 11.35–11.47
  consideration 11.42
  contemporary applications of 11.47
  difference between *ju'āla* and *ijāra* 11.46
  effects of 11.43–11.44
  elements of 11.36–11.42
  nature of 11.35, 11.43
  parties to 11.38
  ṣīgha 11.37
  subject matter of 11.39–11.41
  termination of 11.45

khiyār see offer and acceptance; rights of option
khiyār-al-a'yb (option in case of defect) 8.30–8.40, 14.61, 14.70–14.76, 15.20–15.34
  conditions for *a'yb* establishing 15.25
  contracts applied to 14.72
  effects of 14.75–14.76
  establishment of 15.21
  exercise of 14.73–14.74
  factors eliminating *khiyār al a'yb* and rendering contract *lāzim* 15.29–15.32
  ḥukm of *bay'* 15.23
  increment in subject matter to be returned 15.28
  justification for 15.22
  nature of 14.70–14.71
  nature of contracts with *khiyār-al-a'yb* 14.75
  nuqṣān after transfer of possession to buyer 15.34
  nuqṣān before transfer of possession to buyer 15.33
  proving *a'yb* 15.26
  return of subject matter after *faskh* of contract 15.27
  time to return subject by exercising 15.24
khiyār al-ru'ya (option to choose after inspection) 8.28–8.29, 14.61, 15.02–15.19
  conditions for establishment of 15.06–15.08
  elimination of 15.13–15.16
  inheritance of 15.18
  legality and the nature of 15.02–15.04
  mabī' as collection of dissimilar objects 15.12
  mabī' as single object 15.10
  nature of inspection 15.09–15.13
  subject matter comprising more than one object 15.11
  termination of contract 15.17
  time available to exercise 15.19
  time when *khiyār* is established 15.05
khiyār-al-sharṭ (option of stipulation) 14.61, 14.62–14.69
  creation of 14.64–14.65, 14.67
  legality of 14.63
  nature of 14.62
  period for exercising 14.68–14.69
  requirements of 14.66–14.69

khiyār al tadlīs (concealment of defect) 6.64, 8.40, 15.35–15.40
  a'yb in *khiyār al tadlīs* 15.38
  meaning of *tadlīs* 15.35
  payment of compensation for return of subject matter 15.40
  period for 15.39
  prohibition of sale of defective objects 15.37
Khiyār al ta'yīn 15.41–15.46
  circumstances rendering *khiyār al ta'yīn bāṭil* and *bay' lāzim* 15.44–15.46
  conditions for 15.42
  ḍarūrī (mandatory or unavoidable) 15.46
  ḥukm of *bay* 15.43
  ikhtiyārī (optional) 15.45
  nature of 15.41
khiyārāt see rights of option (*khiyārāt*)
knowledge of subject matter of contract
  acquiring knowledge of subject matter 5.67–5.75
  contractual uncertainty/ambiguity 5.05, 5.65
  description, knowledge by 5.69
  description of packaged goods, sale by 5.71
  description, sale by 5.70
  extent of knowledge of subject matter 5.66
  gifts to several donees 5.75
  immovable property 5.74
  inspection or examination, knowledge through 5.68
  specification, need for 5.72–5.73
  subject matter should be *ma'lūm* 5.65

lease contracts 1.24–1.25, 9.22–9.32
  consideration 9.22–9.23, 9.26
  death of one or both parties to binding contract 14.50
  financial leases 9.30
  forward leases 9.31–9.32
  ijāra contracts see *ijāra* contracts
  impossibility of performance 14.47, 14.50
  operating leases 9.29
  pillars of 9.26–9.27
  purpose 9.25
  subject matter 9.24, 9.26
legal capacity (*ahlīyya*) 3.01–3.106
  age of majority 3.34–3.42
  damages/compensation 15.58
  definition of 3.04–3.08, 3.16–3.17
  formation of valid contract, and 7.09
  forms of (*anwā' al-ahlīyya*) 3.09
  gharar, and 6.44
  impediments to *see* legal capacity, impediments to (*'awāriḍ al-ahlīyya*)
  invalid contracts 7.47
  legal bases/foundations of (*nuṣūṣ shari'iyyah*) 3.10–3.15
  loss of 10.42
  nature of 3.01
  partnerships 10.42, 10.77
  terminal illness 3.14
  theological foundations of 3.05–3.08
  women *see* women's legal capacity; women's testimony (*shahādāt*)
legal capacity, impediments to (*'awāriḍ al-ahlīyya*) 3.16–3.21
  definitions 3.16–3.17
  acquired attributes 3.18, 3.19–3.20
  divine attributes 3.18, 3.21
  imbecility *see* imbecility (*al-ma'tūh*)
  insanity *see* insanity (*junūn*) or mental incompetence
  interdiction (*ḥajr*) 3.22
  minors *see* minority (*ṣighar*)
  prodigals *see* prodigality (*sufahā'*)
  terminal illness *see* terminal illness
  women's capacity *see* women's legal capacity
  women's testimony *see* women's testimony
legal compulsion *see* coercion
legal positivism 6.96
legal realism 6.97
legal ruse (*hila*) 1.22, 4.55
loan contracts (*qarḍ*) 12.37–12.52
  being 'known, requirement of 12.49
  concept of 12.37
  contracting parties 12.42
  essential elements and requirements of 12.39–12.42
  extension and increase of loans 7.16
  fungibles and non-fungibles 12.46–12.47
  interest 6.26–6.29, 7.16, 12.51
  legal nature of 12.38
  loan moratorium 6.26–6.29
  matured and non-matured loans 12.50
  offer and acceptance 12.40–12.41
  real property 12.48
  subject matter of loan 12.45–12.49
  terminal illness, and 12.50
  termination of 12.52
  types of loans 12.50
  whether *Bait-ul-Māl* (Public Treasury) can take loan 12.43–12.44

ma'qud 'alaihi see subject matter of contract (*maḥal al 'aqd/ma'qud 'alaihi*)
maysir see games of chance (*maysir*) and gambling (*qimār*)
meeting of minds *see* mutual consent

minority (*ṣighar*)
acts of ritual and worship (*al-'ibādāt*) 3.33
age of majority 3.34–3.42
agency 11.05
beneficial transactions 7.24
capacity of the minor (*ṣabī*) 3.23–3.33, 3.71, 7.09, 7.24–7.26
contract validity 3.28–3.31, 7.24–7.26
criminal liability 3.32
defective capacity 7.24–7.26
definition of 3.23
discerning child 3.23, 3.27–3.33
divine attribute, as 3.18
financial transactions 3.27
gifts 7.25
ijāra contracts, and 11.53
injurious transactions 7.25
interdiction (*ḥajr*) 3.22, 3.41, 3.42, 3.45, 3.48, 3.50
non-discerning child 3.23, 3.24–3.26
principal, children's inability to be 11.05
transactions oscillating between harm and benefit 7.26
misdescription 8.22–8.23
misrepresentation *see* fraud, deception, and misrepresentation
mistake
acquired attribute, as 3.19
choice, and 4.30
impediment to legal capacity, as 3.17
option to rescind or affirm, and 8.10
prohibited contracts, and 9.76
vitiating consent 3.17, 3.19, 16.21
monetization (*tawarruq*) 9.101–9.103
mu'āṭāt see offer and acceptance
muḍāraba (partnership) 10.70–10.88
absolute *muḍāraba* 10.82
capacity of parties for 10.77
capital 10.78
death or insanity of partners 10.86
destruction of capital 10.88
dissolution 10.83
elements of 10.74
expiration of period of 10.85
justification of 10.71–10.73
nature of 10.70
profit sharing 10.79–10.80
relations between the parties 10.75
types of 10.81
unilateral termination 10.84
violation of agreement or directions of *rab-ul-māl* 10.87
mufāwaḍa aharikat-al-amwāl (partnership) 10.45–10.10.56
agreements of agency and surety 10.49
conditions of 10.48
dissolution 10.56
equality in capital, profit and loss 10.50
formation of 10.47
generality of trade 10.52
incorporation of term '*mufāwaḍa*' in agreement 10.51
legitimacy of 10.46
nature of 10.45
rights and duties of partners 10.53–10.55
surety agreements 10.13, 10.30, 10.45, 10.47, 10.49, 10.53, 10.56, 10.65, 10.69
Muslim majority jurisdictions, Islamic contract law in 1.02, 1.03, 1.08, 16.01–16.82
Egyptian Civil Code *see* Egyptian Civil Code
Sanḥurī connection: civil codes of other Arab States 16.13–16.16
United Arab Emirates (UAE) *see* United Arab Emirates (UAE)
mutual assent (*tarāḍī*) and intention to contract 2.32–2.36
consent as foundation of contract 2.32
consent of coerced party 2.34
consent of *hāzil* 2.35
consent of intoxicated person 2.36
intention to contract 2.33
mutual consent
contract validity, and 9.08, 9.80, 9.92
intention to contract, and *see* mutual assent (*tarāḍī*) and intention to contract
options 8.06, 8.25
prices 6.73
profit distribution 9.47
Qur'ān 1.35, 2.27, 2.30, 2.32, 4.24, 6.39, 14.70
termination of contracts 14.23, 14.30, 14.57, 15.27

negotiated termination of contracts (*iqāla*) 14.22, 14.30–14.42
agents 14.37
effects of 14.32–14.34
effects of irregular stipulations 14.39
invalidation of 14.41–14.42
less or more than original price, *iqālah* with 14.35
meaning of 14.30
requirements of 14.31
reversal of *iqāla* (*iqālat al-iqāla*) 14.40
right of pre-emption over subject matter 14.36
subject matter of 14.38
non-binding contracts
agency contracts 11.32, 11.33, 14.29, 14.52

annulment of non-binding contracts because of death 14.51–14.52
examples of 4.28, 14.29
istiṣna' 11.89
ju'āla, 11.43, 11.46
khiyār-al-a'yb rendering contract non-binding 14.75
nature of 4.28
non-binding sale contracts 9.75
non-binding promises 12.10–12.12
rights of option, and 8.02, 8.12
unilateral revocation/rescission 4.28, 9.75, 14.29, 14.53, 14.61
noncommutative contracts *see* unilateral/ gratuitous contracts

offer and acceptance 2.01–2.65
change of subject matter, effect of 2.64
clear and explicit language, requirement for 4.40
communication of *ījāb* and *qabūl* see *ījāb* and *qabūl,* communication of
completion of contract see *ījāb* and *qabūl,* completion of contract with
conditional offers 2.13
contracts with *khiyār al majlis* 2.56–2.65
counter-offers 2.14
death of party 2.65
electronic contracts 1.20
express and implied contracts 1.19
express *ījāb* and *qabūl* see *ījāb* and *qabūl,* express
formation of valid contract, and 7.06–7.08
fresh offers 2.15, 2.60, 14.22
ījāb and *qabūl,* conduct and see *ījāb* and *qabūl* through conduct and *mu'āṭāt*
insanity of party 2.65
lapse of time, effect of 2.65
mutual assent *see* mutual assent (*tarāḍī*) and intention to contract
non-fulfilment of condition precedent, effect of 2.65
option to withdraw offer or acceptance 8.21
part acceptance of offer 2.16–2.19
preceding each other 7.08
ratification of past offer or acceptance 7.08
rejection of offer 2.58
revocation of offer *see* revocation of offer
session, and *see* session (*majlis*) and its expiration
termination of offer 2.57
types of *ijāb* and *qabūl* 2.02–2.21
see also formation of contract
options *see* rights of option (*khiyārāt*)
ownership of subject matter 5.37–5.5.47
absence of title 5.43
encumbrance on owner's title 5.45
establishment of ownership 5.47
gharar, and 6.42–6.43
jointly owned property 5.46
ownership and title 5.37, 5.42–5.47
pasture 5.39
perfect and imperfect title 5.42–5.46
sale by a *wakil* 5.44
sale of permissible things 5.38–5.41
water 5.40
wild animals and birds 5.41

parties (*'āqidān*)
autonomy *see* party autonomy
consent inferred from conduct of parties 7.07
death of party 2.65, 14.24, 14.50
essential elements of a valid contract 1.59
legal capacity 1.19
party autonomy *see* party autonomy
reciprocity between parties (*mīthāq*) 1.10
third parties *see* third parties and contracts
partnership contracts 9.37–9.55
annulment because of death of a party 14.51
contractual/business partnership (*shirka al-'uqūd*) 9.38
equity-based *see* partnership contracts, equity-based
impossibility of performance 14.48
irrigation contracts (*musāqa*) 9.39, 9.48–9.50
joint enterprise/business partnership contracts (*shirka al-'uqūd*) 9.41
joint ownership partnership contracts (*shirka 'amlāk*) 9.38, 9.41
plantation partnership contracts (*mughārasa*) 9.39, 9.54–9.55
share-cropping contracts (*muzāra'a*) 9.39, 9.51–9.53
trust partnership contracts (*muḍāraba*) 9.39, 9.40, 9.45–9.47
venture partnership contracts (*mushāraka*) 9.39, 9.40, 9.42–9.44
partnership contracts, equity-based 10.01–10.93
co-owners, rights of 10.05–10.07
co-ownership, definition of 10.03
co-ownership, types of 10.04
financing *see* financing through *sharika and muḍāraba*
general public's common rights 10.02
muḍāraba see *muḍāraba* (partnership)
nature of 10.01
sharikat-al-'al-see *sharikat-al-'al*-(partnership)

party autonomy
coercion, and 6.66
contract law, in 1.19, 1.36, 6.01–6.99, 8.01, 8.62
debt assignment, and 13.34
Islamic law, in 4.26
permissibility rule, and 6.97
prices, and 6.73
relationships governed by principles in Qur'ān and Sunnah 6.01
restrictions on 8.41–8.43, 8.53
sale of property, and 13.47
pawnbroking contracts (*rahn*) 9.56, 9.59
sale of pawned property, third party rights and 13.10–13.14
payment *see* price
performance 14.02–14.02
breach (non-performance) of contract 14.16–14.20
contracts involving debt (*dayn*) 14.07–14.13
delivery of *'ayn* (specific property) 14.14–14.15
force majeure see *force majeure* and impossibility of performance
nature of 14.02
party to perform first 14.05–14.06
when contract is deemed to have been performed 14.03–14.04
permissibility
agency 11.13, 11.28
commercial law 1.18, 1.20
default rule in every transaction, as 6.95
general principle of 1.20, 6.04, 6.07, 6.11, 6.94–6.99, 8.42, 8.44–8.45
ḥawāla, permissibility of 13.38
kafāla, permissibility of 13.24
mu'āṭāt, permissibility of 2.26–2.31
subject matter of contract *see* permissible subject matter
wa'ad, permissibility of 12.05
permissible subject matter 5.02–5.03, 5.08, 5.10–5.16
formation of valid contract, and 7.10
illegality of object of contract 7.49
immoveable property and associated rights 5.12, 5.14
intellectual property 5.13
moveable property 5.14
nature of 5.10
permissible property becoming impermissible 5.15–5.16
purification of impure things 5.11
sale of permissible things, ownership and 5.38–5.41
sale of rights permissible by custom 5.12
see also valid contracts
possession/custody of subject matter of contract 5.48–5.64
gharar, and 6.42–6.43
immoveable property, possession of 5.57–5.59
moveable property, possession of 5.60–5.64
possession obtained by *al-takhliya* 5.56
transfer of possession 5.55–5.56
subject matter should be in seller's possession or custody 5.48–5.54
postal communication 2.42, 2.44–2.45, 2.46
pre-emption contracts (*shuf'a*)
conditions for the validity of pre-emption 13.62–13.63
definition 13.46–13.48
elements of 13.53
gifts, and 13.57
legal validity 13.49–13.52
parties to pre-emption 13.54–13.61
right of pre-emption over subject matter of *iqāla* 14.36
specific rules conferring third-party pre-emption rights 13.64–13.70
subject matter of sale, and 5.12
third party rights 13.45–13.70
price
buyers capitalizing on farmers' ignorance of prices (*bay' talaqy al-rukbān*) 9.85–9.86
classification of contracts on basis of price stipulation 9.16–9.21
deferred payment 9.21
fair market prices 6.80
fāsid contracts 7.39–7.43
fraudulent sale or manipulative overpricing (*bay' al-najsh*) 9.96–9.97
gharar, and 7.15
mutual consent, and 6.73
party autonomy, and 6.73
payment of 8.24, 9.21
price control 6.76
price fixing *see* hoarding, illegal profiteering, and price fixing
spot payment 9.21
valid contracts, and 7.15
privity of contract 13.05–13.14
prodigality (*sufahā'*) 3.31, 3.58–3.3.78
acquired attribute, as 3.19, 3.60
contracts, effect on 3.70–3.78
definitions 3.58–3.64
interdiction of the prodigal (*safīh*) 3.48, 3.65–3.69
legal capacity, and 3.17, 3.48

profit
earned through proactive entrepreneurial effort 6.24
excessive profit 6.80
external benchmarks/indicators to determine profit rates 6.24–6.25
factors determining 6.80
interest, and 6.23–6.25
loan moratoriums, and 6.26–6.29
illegal profiteering *see* hoarding, illegal profiteering, and price fixing
partnerships *see* partnership contracts
profit rate or limit not stipulated 6.80
profiteering *see* hoarding, illegal profiteering, and price fixing
profiteering, illegal *see* hoarding, illegal profiteering, and price fixing
prohibited contracts of sale 9.76–9.103
barter trade involving dried and fresh fruits (*bayʿ al-muzābana*) 9.87 9.87
buyers capitalizing on farmers' ignorance of prices (*bayʿ talaqy al-rukbān*) 9.85–9.86
fictitious contracts of sale (*bayʿ al-talji'a*) 9.91–9.92
fraudulent sale or manipulative overpricing (*bayʿ al-najsh*) 9.96–9.97
monetization (*tawarruq*) 9.101–9.103
reasons for prohibition 9.76, 9.79–9.81
sale and buy-back agreement (*bayʿ al-ʿina*) 9.98–9.100, 9.101, 9.102
sale by urbanite on behalf of nomad (*bayʿ al-ḥāḍir li bād*) 9.83–9.84
sale of debt for a debt (*bayʿ al-kālī bi al-kālī*) 9.90
sale of grains in exchange for dry or processed grains (*bayʿ al-muḥāqala*) 9.88
sale with right of redemption (*bayʿ al-wafā*) 9.93–9.95
toss sales (*bayʿ al-munābadha*) 9.89
types of 9.82–9.103
prohibited elements in contract 6.01–6.99
ambiguity and uncertainty *see* ambiguity and uncertainty (*gharar*)
coercion 6.66–6.71 *see also* coercion
fraud, deception, and misrepresentation *see* fraud, deception, and misrepresentation
games of chance (*maysir*) and gambling (*qimār*) 6.45, 6.50–6.54
impermissible subject matter 6.49
interest and usury *see* interest and usury (*ribā*)
positive dimension of prohibited elements 6.94–6.99
reasons for prohibition 9.76, 9.79–9.81
theory of prohibition in contractual dealings 6.05–6.14
usurpation *see* usurpation (*ghasb*)
see also invalid contracts; valid contracts
promises
bilateral promises 1.11–1.12, 9.03, 9.05
binding promises *see* binding promises (*waʿad*)
concept of 1.11
public interest 1.39, 1.51, 6.70, 12.43
e-commerce 1.20
interest rates 16.50
price control 6.76

qabūl see offer and acceptance
qimār see games of chance (*maysir*) and gambling (*qimār*)
qiyās
analogical deduction 1.39, 1.43–1.46, 8.50, 8.52, 14.70, 15.50
source of Islamic contract law, as 1.43–1.46
qarḍ see loans (*qarḍ*)

reciprocity between parties (*mīthāq*) 1.10
redemption right, sale with (*bayʿ al-wafā*) 9.93–9.95
remedies
damages *see* damages/compensation (*damān*)
options (*khiyārāt*) see *khiyār al aʿyb*; *khiyār al ruʿya*; *khiyār al tadlīs*; *khiyār al taʿyīn*
specific performance *see* specific performance
rescission of contracts (*faskh*) 14.53–14.79
bankruptcy and insolvency, rescission due to 14.58
court judgment, rescission by 14.55
effects of 14.21, 14.78–14.79
irregular contracts (*ʿaqd fāsid*), rescission of 14.77
lawful justification, rescission due to 14.56–14.57
meaning of *faskh* 14.53
modes of rescission 14.54–14.76
non-binding contracts *see* non-binding contracts
options *see* rescission of contracts (*faskh*): exercising right of option (*khiyār*)
partnerships 10.41, 14.29
rescission of contracts (*faskh*): exercising right of option (*khiyār*) 14.59–14.76
khiyār-al-aʿyb see *khiyār-al-aʿyb b* (option in case of defect)
khiyār-al-sharṭ see *khiyār-al-sharṭ* (option of stipulation)
nature of *khiyār* 14.59
purpose of *khiyār* 14.60
types of *khiyār* 14.61–14.76

revocation of offer 2.59–2.63, 7.08
communication of revocation 2.63
fixed duration of offer 2.59
fresh offer, effect of 2.60
revocation of part of *ījāb* 2.59
when the offer can be revoked 2.61–2.62
ribā see interest and usury (*ribā*)
rights of option (*khiyārāt*) 8.06–8.40
concealment of defect, for see *khiyār al tadlīs* (option for concealment of defect)
default condition: *khiyār al-sharṭ* 8.09–8.19
defect, for see *khiyār-al-a'yb* (option for defect)
extinguishing options 8.12
identify, to (*khiyār-al-ta'yīn*) 14.61
inspection option see *khiyār al-ru'ya* (option of choice after inspection)
loss or damage to object of sale 8.13–8.19
misdescription, option for (*khiyār al-waṣf*) 8.22–8.23
nature of 8.02
options implied by operation of law 8.07, 8.20–8.40
options requiring mutual consent 8.06, 8.08–8.19
payment option (*khiyār al-naqd*) 8.24
selection option (*khiyār al-ta'yīn*) 8.25–8.27
stipulation option see *khiyār-al-sharṭ* (option of stipulation)
withdrawal of offer or acceptance (*khiyār al-majlis*) 8.21
see also rescission of contracts (*faskh*): exercising right of option (*khiyār*)

safaqa wāḥida and *ṣafaqa mutafarraqa* 2.16–2.19
salam contracts 11.63–11.82
conditions applicable to both commodity and consideration 11.67
delivery of subject matter (commodity) 11.70–11.72, 11.75, 11.76
difference between *salam* and *istiṣna'* 11.93
essential elements of 11.64–11.68
modern applications of 11.78–11.82
nature of 11.63
object of *salam* 11.67–11.68, 12.47
ownership of exchanged commodities 11.74
parties to 11.66
requirements of *salam* payment 11.68
requirements/conditions of the commodity 11.69–11.73
security as to the obligation 11.77
seller's inability to make delivery 11.76
sīgha 11.65
sale and buy-back agreement (*bay' al-'īna*) 9.98–9.100, 9.101, 9.102
sanctity of contract 1.09, 1.34, 6.68, 8.44
sanctity of property 6.84
ṣarf contracts 11.96–11.99
conditions for validity of 11.98
legal effects of 11.99
legality of 11.97
nature of 11.96
Searle, John 4.39, 4.49, 4.50–4.52
secondary sources of Islamic contract law 1.32, 1.38–1.53
ijmā 1.40–1.42
qiyās 1.43–1.46
istiḥsān 1.47–1.51
'urf 1.52–1.53
security or guarantee contracts 9.56–9.61
agency contracts (*wakāla*) 9.56, 9.61
debt assignment contracts (*ḥawāla*) 9.56, 9.60
guarantee contracts (*kafāla*) *see* guarantee contracts (*kafāla*)
inherent nature as accessory or subordinate contracts 9.57
pawnbroking contracts (*rahn*) 9.56, 9.59
see also surety contracts
services and supply contracts 9.62–9.65
commission contracts (*ju'āla*) 9.62, 9.63
fees/compensation (*'ujr*) for work or services 9.62, 9.64
ijāra contracts see *ijāra* contracts
supply contracts (*bay' al-'istijrār*) 9.62, 9.65
session (*majlis*) and its expiration 2.46–2.47
basic concept of *khiyār* 2.49–2.51
contracting out of *khiyār al majlis* 2.54–2.55
justification 2.51–2.52
offer and acceptance, completion of 7.08
option to withdraw offer or acceptance 8.21
separation of parties after contract session, effect of 2.49, 2.53, 2.59
termination of *khiyār al qabūl* and *khiyār al majlis* 2.53
shar'ī capacity to deliver 5.30, 5.31–5.32
sharikat-al-'al-(partnership) 10.08–10.69
definition of 10.08–10.09
entitlement to profit 10.14
formation of 10.12–10.13
legal nature of partnership 10.15
sharikat-al-abdān see *sharikat-al-abdān* (partnership)
sharikat-al-amwāl see *sharikat-al-amwāl* (partnership)
Sharikat-al-wujūh see *sharikat-al-wujūh* (partnership)
types of 10.10–10.11

sharikat-al-abdān (partnership) 10.57–10.65
acceptance of work and liability 10.62–10.63
distribution of profit 10.64
distribution of profit: *mufāwaḍa sharikat-al-abdān* 10.65
inan sharikat-al-abdān and its conditions 10.58–10.64
nature of 10.57
nature of subject matter 10.59–10.60
similarity of profession 10.61
sharikat-al-amwāl (partnership) 10.16–10.56
conditions for 10.17–10.22
form of capital to establish partnership 10.21–10.22
inan sharikat-al-amwāl *see* inan sharikat-al-amwāl (partnership)
kinds of see *inan sharikat-al-amwāl* (partnership); *mufāwaḍa aharikat-al-amwāl* (partnership)
mixing of capital 10.19–10.20
nature of 10.16
presence of capital 10.18
sharikat-al-wujūh (partnership) 10.66–10.70
inan sharikat-al-wujūh 10.67
mufāwaḍa sharikat-al-wujūh 10.69
shuf'a see pre-emption contracts (*shuf'a*)
shurūṭ see conditions (*shurūṭ*)
ṣīgha
form of contract *see* form of contract (*ṣīgha*)
sign language, in 2.09–2.10
sign language 2.09–2.10
silence
acceptance, as 2.23, 4.46
acquiescence, as 15.29
deliberate silence 6.63
inconsequential unless supported by the facts 4.48
rejection, as 2.45
tacit approval, as 11.08
title to property, and 5.42
sources of Islamic contract law 1.31–1.61
positive law 1.54
primary sources 1.20, 1.33–1.37
Qur'ān 1.33–1.35
secondary sources *see* secondary sources of Islamic contract law
Sunnah 1.33, 1.36–1.37
specific performance 15.63–15.64
subject matter of contract (*maḥal al 'aqd/ma'qud 'alaihi*) 1.60–1.61, 5.01–5.75
advance payment of consideration see *salam* contracts
delivery *see* delivery of subject matter of contract
change of subject matter, effect of 2.64, 14.45
conditions for validity of 1.60–1.61
contractual uncertainty/ambiguity 5.05, 5.65
see also ambiguity and uncertainty (*gharar*)
custom, and 5.03–5.04, 5.08, 5.20, 5.25, 5.62
defective subject matter *see* defective goods and commodities
essential elements of a valid contract, and 1.60–1.61
existence of subject matter 5.25–5.28
formation of valid contract, and 7.10
gifts 12.28
gifts, damage to subject matter, and 14.45
immovable property 5.07, 5.09, 5.10, 5.12, 5.14, 5.49–5.51, 5.54, 5.55, 5.57–5.59, 5.74
impermissible *see* impermissible subject matter
impossibility of performance 14.44–14.49
invalid contracts 7.47
knowledge of *see* knowledge of subject matter of contract
legality of subject matter 5.06–5.24
loss or destruction of 8.13–8.19, 14.24
movable property 5.04, 5.07, 5.09, 5.10, 5.14, 5.49–5.50, 5.54, 5.60–5.64
nature of 5.01, 5.06–5.09
ownership *see* ownership of subject matter
permissible *see* permissible subject matter
possession of *see* possession/custody of subject matter of contract
property, concept of 5.06–5.09
unilateral/gratuitous contracts 5.25, 5.65, 14.72
value and benefit 5.06–5.07
surety contracts 8.50
claiming the surety 15.60
guarantee, as 13.24
'inān partnerships 10.25, 10.27
mufāwaḍa partnerships 10.13, 10.30, 10.45, 10.47, 10.49, 10.53, 10.56, 10.65, 10.69
see also security or guarantee contracts
suspended contracts 7.22–7.33
causes of suspension 7.23–7.33
contracts binding on both parties 7.33
contracts binding on one party but not on other 7.32
contracts likely to become binding 7.31
contracts not binding on the parties 7.30
defective capacity 7.24–7.26
nature of 7.22
suspension due to lack of proper authority 7.27
suspension due to rights of third parties 7.28

terminal illness 3.79–3.85
  acknowledgements of debt 3.83, 3.84
  definition 3.79
  interdiction of the terminally ill individual 3.80–3.85
  legal capacity 3.16
  loans 12.50
  marriage 3.82
  protecting creditors' rights 3.81
  protecting heirs' rights 3.80, 3.82, 3.83
  salam contracts 11.66
termination of contracts (*inhā-al-'aqd*) 14.21–14.52
  bilateral termination *see* negotiated termination of contracts (*iqāla*)
  effect of 14.21
  force majeure see *force majeure* and impossibility of performance
  hardship 14.24
  impossibility of performance see *force majeure* and impossibility of performance
  mutual consent, by 14.23, 14.30, 14.57, 15.27
  suspending contracts 14.28
  unilateral termination 14.22, 14.23, 14.26–14.29
theory of contract *see* general theory of contract
third parties and contracts 13.01–13.70
  agency contracts (*wakāla*) 13.25–13.33
  contractual rights and obligations, third parties and 13.01–13.04
  debt assignment contracts *see* debt assignment contracts (*ḥawāla*)
  guarantee in contracts (*kafāla*) 13.04, 13.15–13.24
  pre-emption *see* pre-emption contracts (*shuf'a*)
  privity of contract 13.05–13.14
toss sales (*bay' al-munābadha*) 9.89
trust sales (*bay' al-'amāna*) 9.16, 9.20
types of contracts of sale and applicable legal principles 9.66–9.75
  binding sale (*bay' lāzim*) 9.66, 9.75
  contingent or withheld sale (*bay' mawqūf*) 9.66, 9.72, 9.73
  defective or voidable (*bay' fāsid*) 9.66, 9.70, 9.71
  enforceable (*bay' mun'aqid*) 9.66, 9.68
  immediately effective (*bay' nāfidh*) 9.66, 9.72
  non-binding sale (*bay ghayr lāzim*) 9.66, 9.75
  unauthorized acts 9.74
  valid (*bay' ṣaḥīḥ*) 9.66, 9.70
  void (*bay' bāṭil*) 9.66, 9.68–9.69

'Umrah 11.19
unilateral/gratuitous contracts 1.59, 5.65, 12.01–12.77, 13.01
  acts of charity, as 5.29
  concept of promise, and 1.11
  donee, liability of 14.19
  endowment *see* endowment (*waqf*)
  existence of subject matter 5.25
  gifts *see* gifts (*hiba*)
  gratuitous contracts as unilateral contracts 12.02
  identified/known subject matter 5.65
  khiyār-al-a'yb, and 14.72
  lending for gratuitous use 9.33–9.36
  loans *see* loans (*qarḍ*)
  nature of 12.02
  option to withdraw, and 8.21
  promise *see* binding promises (*wa'ad*)
  undeliverable subject matter 5.29
  unilateral contracts, as 12.02
  wakāla contracts 11.30
  wills *see* wills (*waṣiyya*)
United Arab Emirates (UAE) 16.01–16.04, 16.14–16.46
  Civil Code and *ribā* 16.26–16.35
  Commercial Transactions Law (Commercial Code) 16.56–16.71
  delay interest 16.60–16.66
  Egyptian Civil Code, and 16.03, 16.13
  financing charges 16.67–16.71
  interest rate 16.56–16.59
  law of obligations and the Sharī'ah 16.18–16.25
  legislation and courts' interpretation of Sharī'ah-related provisions 16.36–16.46
  nature of code governing transactions 16.72–16.82
  Sharī'ah, and 16.14–16.16, 16.18–16–16.25, 16.36–16.46
'urf
  source of Islamic contract law, as 1.52–1.53
  see also custom (*'urf*)
usufruct-based contracts 9.22–9.36
  ijāra contracts see *ijāra* contracts
  impossibility of performance 14.47
  lease contracts *see* lease contracts
  lending for gratuitous use 9.33–9.36
usurpation (*ghasb*) 6.81–6.6.93
  definition of usurpation 6.81
  effect on contract 6.91–6.93
  effect on usurped property 6.85–6.90
  guaranteeing usurped property from usurpation 11.57
  prohibition of *ghasb* 6.82–6.84
usury *see* interest and usury (*ribā*)

valid contracts 7.02–7.33
  enforcement (*nifādh*) of contract, conditions for 7.11

external attributes of contract, conditions for 7.14
formation of contract, conditions for 7.05–7.10
conditions for binding (*luzūm*) contract 7.13
conditions for validity (*siḥa*) of contract 7.12
fāsid contracts see *fāsid* contracts
gharar, and 7.15
nature of valid (*ṣaḥīḥ*) contracts 7.02–7.03, 7.18–7.19
ribā, and 7.16
types of *see* valid contracts, types of
valid conditions *see under* conditions (*shurūṭ*)
see also invalid contracts
valid contracts, types of 7.18–7.33
ja'iz or *ghayr lāzim* contracts 7.21
mawquf contracts *see* suspended contracts
nāfidh lāzim contracts 7.20

wa'ad see binding promises (*wa'ad*)
waqf see endowment (*waqf*)
wakāla see agents and agency contracts (*wakāla*)
wills (*waṣiyya*) 12.53–12.60
conditional will 12.56
conditions of valid will 12.54–12.55
invalid wills 12.59–12.60
meaning and nature of 12.53
parties 12.54
quantum of will 12.55
revocation of 12.57–12.58
women's legal capacity 3.86–3.100
cultural constraints 3.86
property rights 3.86, 3.87, 3.90, 3.94–3.97
spiritual equality between men and women 3.88, 3.90
woman marrying through agent 11.20
women's different legal capacity 3.89–3.100
women's testimony (*shahādāt*) 3.101–3.106
criminal cases, testimony not allowed in 3.103
lone woman's testimony 3.105
non-property matters closed to women 3.103
reasoning behind law of women's testimony 3.103–3.104, 3.106